Taking Sides: Clashing Views in
Science, Technology, and Society, 13/e
Thomas A. Easton

http://create.mheducation.com

ISBN-10: 1259665941   ISBN-13: 9781259665943

Contents

Detailed Table of Contents

Unit 1: The Place of Science and Technology in Society

Issue: Is the Distinction between Basic and Applied Research Useful?
Yes: Nils Roll-Hansen, from "Why the Distinction between Basic (Theoretical) and Applied (Practical) Research Is Important to the Politics of Science," Original Work (2010)
No: Venkatesh Narayanamurti, Tolu Odumosu, and Lee Vinsel, from "RIP: The Basic/Applied Research Dichotomy," *Issues in Science and Technology* (2013)

Nils Roll-Hansen argues that the difference between basic and applied research is important to studies of the history of science and to science policy. The two differ profoundly in their criteria for success or failure, their effects on social processes, and in their degree of autonomy from political and economic interests. The distinction must not be blurred over in the interest of promoting innovation and economic growth. Venkatesh Narayanamurti, Tolu Odumosu, and Lee Vinsel argue that the distinction between basic and applied research fails to reflect what actually happens in scientific research. They urge an "invention/discovery" model and hence a more holistic, long-term view of the research process in order to enhance innovation that has public utility and identify ways to intervene with public policy.

Issue: Should the Public Have to Pay to See the Results of Federally Funded Research?
Yes: Ralph Oman, from "Testimony before the U.S. House of Representatives Committee on the Judiciary, Subcommittee on Courts, The Internet, and Intellectual Property, Hearing on 'The Fair Copyright in Research Works Act,' " U.S. House of Representatives (2008)
No: Stuart M. Shieber, from "Testimony before the U.S. House of Representatives Committee on Science, Space and Technology, Subcommittee on Investigations and Oversight, Hearing on 'Examining Public Access and Scholarly Publication Interests,' " U.S. House of Representatives (2012)

Attorney and past register of copyrights Ralph Oman contends that "If the NIH [National Institutes of Health] succeeds in putting all of the NIH-related peer-reviewed articles on its online database for free within one year of publication, the private publishers will be hard-pressed to survive." Allowing private publishers to continue to profit by publishing the results of publically funded research is the best way to ensure public benefit. Stuart M. Shieber argues that the concerns of traditional journal publishers that open access publishing will endanger their survival are not justified. The data show that publisher profitability has increased despite the recent economic downturn. Providing open access to the publicly funded research literature amplifies the diffusion of knowledge and benefits researchers, taxpayers, and everyone who gains from new medicines, new technologies, new jobs, and new solutions to long-standing problems of every kind.

Issue: Can Science Be Trusted Without Government Regulation?
Yes: David R. Franz, from "The Dual Use Dilemma: Crying Out for Leadership," *Saint Louis University Journal of Health Law & Policy* (2013)
No: Robert Gatter, from "Regulating Dual Use Research to Promote Public Trust: A Reply to Dr. Franz," *Saint Louis University Journal of Health Law & Policy* (2013)

David R. Franz argues that "when rules for the few become too disruptive to the work of the many, communities of trust can break down." Exceptional research leaders create a culture of responsibility in which safety rulebooks can be thin and their laboratories will be safer, more secure, and more productive. Government regulation leads to thicker rulebooks and more wasted effort without increasing safety and security. Robert Gatter argues that the research enterprise must be trustworthy to the public at large. Because scientists share a bias in favor of discovery rather than public safety, they cannot be trusted to regulate themselves. Government regulation is essential.

Unit 2: Energy and the Environment

Issue: Can We Reduce Carbon Emissions Enough to Limit Global Warming?
Yes: Lisa Jacobson, from "Testimony before the U.S. Senate Committee on Environment and Public Works, Hearing on 'Examining the International Climate Change Negotiations,' " U.S. Senate (2015)

No: Stephen D. Eule, from "Testimony before the U.S. Senate Committee on Environment and Public Works, Hearing on 'Examining the International Climate Change Negotiations,' " U.S. Senate (2015)

Lisa Jacobson argues that an international agreement to limit carbon emissions will spur investment in clean energy technologies. Success is achievable, and the U.S. business community is already considering climate change impacts in its energy and corporate strategies. "The private sector is going to be a key partner in delivering the innovation, investment and technologies that will help... meet... mitigation targets." Stephen D. Eule argues that the COP21 agreement is unlikely to succeed. In the United States, promised emissions reductions will be inadequate, they will probably not be achieved, and if they were they would threaten the competitive position of American businesses. It would also destroy history's most successful economic system. "Affordable, available, and scalable energy is not the problem, it is the solution."

Issue: Would a Carbon Tax Help Slow Global Warming?
Yes: James Rydge, from "Implementing Effective Carbon Pricing," *The New Climate Economy* (2015)
No: Robert P. Murphy, Patrick J. Michaels, and Paul C. Knappenberger, from "The Case Against a Carbon Tax," Cato Institute (2015)

James Rydge argues that the case for using carbon pricing (via a carbon tax or a cap-and-trade system) as an important component of efforts to bring carbon emissions and their effects on global climate change under control is strong, momentum is growing, and effects on competitiveness can be dealt with via international cooperation. Therefore all developed and emerging economies, and others where possible, should commit to introducing or strengthening carbon pricing by 2020, and should phase out fossil fuel subsidies. Robert P. Murphy, Patrick J. Michaels, and Paul C. Knappenberger argue that the economics of climate change reveal that the case for a U.S. carbon tax is very weak, partly because reining in global warming cannot be justified in cost/benefit terms. Even a well-designed carbon tax would probably cause more harm than good.

Issue: Is Home Solar the Wave of the Future?
Yes: Peter Bronski et al., from "The Economics of Grid Defection," Rocky Mountain Institute (2014)
No: Peter Kind, from "Disruptive Challenges: Financial Implications and Strategic Responses to a Changing Retail Electric Business," Edison Electric Institute (2013)

Peter Bronski et al., of the Rocky Mountain Institute (RMI) argue that the combination of home solar power with storage technologies such as batteries offer to make the electricity grid optional for many consumers, perhaps as early as the 2020s. Utilities have an opportunity to exploit the spread of "distributed electricity generation" to provide a robust, reliable electricity supply. Peter Kind, executive director of Energy Infrastructure Advocates, argues that increased interest in "distributed energy resources" such as home solar power and energy efficiency, among other factors, is threatening to reduce revenue and increase costs for electrical utilities. In order to protect investors and capital availability, electrical utilities must consider new charges for customers who reduce their electricity usage, decreased payments to homeowners using net metering, and even new charges to users of "distributed energy resources" to offset "stranded costs" (such as no longer needed power plants).

Unit 3: Human Health and Welfare

Issue: Do We Have a Population Problem?
Yes: Dennis Dimick, from "As World's Population Booms, Will Its Resources Be Enough for Us?" *National Geographic* (2014)
No: Tom Bethell, from "Population, Economy, and God," *The American Spectator* (2009)

Dennis Dimick argues that new projections of higher population growth through the twenty-first century are reason for concern, largely because of the conflict between population size and resource use. The environmental impact of population also depends on technology, affluence, and waste, but educated women have smaller families and technology (electric lights, for instance) aids education. Controlling population appears to be essential. Tom Bethell argues that population alarmists project their fears onto popular concerns, currently the environment, and every time their scare-mongering turns out to be based on faulty premises. Blaming environmental problems will be no different. Societies are sustained not by population control but by belief in God.

Issue: Can Vaccines Cause Autism?
Yes: Arjun Walia, from "Scientific Evidence Suggests the Vaccine-Autism Link Can No Longer Be Ignored," *Collective Evolution* (2013)
No: Harriet Hall, from "Vaccines and Autism: A Deadly Manufactroversy," *Skeptic* (2009)

Arjun Walia argues that the scientific consensus on the safety of vaccines may be suspect because "the corporate media is owned by the major vaccine manufacturers." He describes 22 studies that suggest that the connection between childhood vaccines and autism is real or that suggest possible mechanisms for the connection. Harriet Hall argues that the controversy over whether vaccines cause autism has been manufactured by dishonest, self-serving researchers and physicians, ignorant celebrities, conspiracy theorists, and the media. The result is a resurgence of preventable diseases and childhood deaths. Vaccines save lives. Autism's causes are probably genetic.

Issue: Is the Fracking Industry Adequately Regulated for Public Safety?
Yes: Arthur Herman, from "The Liberal War on American Energy Independence," *Commentary* (2015)
No: Paul Solotaroff, from "What's Killing the Babies of Vernal, Utah?" *Rolling Stone* (2015)

Arthur Herman argues that there is no proof that the fracking industry is causing environmental and health problems. Anyone who says there is is attacking American prosperity and the well-being of the working class. Paul Solotaroff argues that we cannot trust local and state health and environmental officials to do anything about obvious health issues. There is too much money involved.

Issue: Is the Process for Decommissioning Nuclear Reactors Sound?
Yes: Marvin S. Fertel, from "Testimony before the U.S. Senate Committee on Environment and Public Works, Hearing on 'Nuclear Reactor Decommissioning: Stakeholder Views,' " U.S. Senate (2014)
No: Geoffrey H. Fettus, from "Testimony before the U.S. Senate Committee on Environment and Public Works, Hearing on 'Nuclear Reactor Decommissioning: Stakeholder Views,' " U.S. Senate (2014)

Marvin S. Fertel argues that existing procedures for decommissioning nuclear power plants are proven, appropriate, and adequate for protecting public health and the environment. Geoffrey H. Fettus argues that decommissioning nuclear power plants is a long-term process that requires long-term monitoring and regulation, currently not provided for in decommissioning procedures. In addition, current funding approaches leave a "plausible risk" that taxpayers could be left to bear large portions of the costs involved.

Issue: Should Genetically Modified Foods Be Labeled?
Yes: Todd Daloz, from "Testimony before the U.S. House of Representatives Committee on Energy and Commerce, Subcommittee on Health, Hearing on 'A National Framework for the Review and Labeling of Biotechnology in Food,' " U.S. House of Representatives (2015)
No: L. Val Giddings, from "Testimony before the U.S. House of Representatives Committee on Energy and Commerce, Subcommittee on Health, Hearing on 'A National Framework for the Review and Labeling of Biotechnology in Food,' " U.S. House of Representatives (2015)

Todd Daloz argues that Vermont's legislation requiring labeling of genetically modified crops (GMOs) is amply justified by the public's need for factual information about the food they eat, and that federal preemption of state labeling laws, without providing a suitable substitute, is unreasonable. L. Val Giddings argues that there is no scientific doubt that GMO crops are safe to eat, the federal government already has sufficient authority to regulate the sale and labeling of GMO foods, and the push for labeling laws is a thinly disguised effort to ban GMOs in favor of less safe and more expensive alternatives, such as organic foods.

Unit 4: Space

Issue: Can We Stop an Asteroid or Comet Impact?
Yes: Michael F. A'Hearn, from "Testimony before the U.S. House of Representatives Committee on Science, Space, and Technology, Hearing on 'Threats from Space: A Review of Private and International Efforts to Track and Mitigate Asteroids and Meteors, Part II,' " U.S. House of Representatives (2013)
No: Clark R. Chapman, from "What Will Happen When the Next Asteroid Strikes?" *Astronomy Magazine* (2011)

Michael F. A'Hearn argues that even impacts by small (less than 140 meters in diameter) near-Earth objects (NEOs) can be damaging and that present detection programs focus only on larger NEOs and will take many years to complete their inventory. The probability that even a small NEO will strike Earth in the near future is small, but the potential damage is so great that investing in identifying and tracking NEOs, and researching ways of preventing impact, is worthwhile. Clark R. Chapman argues that though the consequences of an asteroid or comet impact would be catastrophic, efforts to prevent the impact would be futile. It is far more appropriate to incorporate such impact disasters into more conventional disaster planning.

Amie Stepanovich argues that the increased use of unmanned aerial systems (or "drones") to conduct surveillance in the United States must be accompanied by increased privacy protections. The current state of the law is insufficient to address the drone surveillance threat to the interests of the general public, who clearly have a stake (are stakeholders) in the issue. The U.S. Department of Homeland Security, Office of Inspector General, argues that planning is inadequate for the use of resources devoted to serving the purposes of the U.S. Customs and Border Protection (CBP) unmanned aircraft systems program, to provide reconnaissance, surveillance, targeting, and acquisition capabilities to serve the needs of stakeholders. The list of stakeholders does not include the general public, and privacy concerns are not mentioned.

Unit 6: Ethics

Issue: Is "Animal Rights" Just Another Excuse for Terrorism?
Yes: John J. Miller, from "In the Name of the Animals: America Faces a New Kind of Terrorism," *National Review* (2006)
No: Steven Best, from "Dispatches from a Police State: Animal Rights in the Crosshairs of State Repression," *International Journal of Inclusive Democracy* (2007)

Journalist John Miller argues that animal rights extremists have adopted terrorist tactics in their effort to stop the use of animals in scientific research. Because of the benefits of such research, if the terrorists win, everyone loses. Professor Steven Best argues that the new Animal Enterprise Protection Act is excessively broad and vague, imposes disproportionate penalties, endangers free speech, and detracts from prosecution of real terrorism. The animal liberation movement, on the other hand, is both a necessary effort to emancipate animals from human exploitation, and part of a larger resistance movement opposed to exploitation and hierarchies of any and all kinds.

Issue: Should Genetically Engineered Mosquitoes Be Released into the Environment to Fight Disease?
Yes: Hadyn Parry, from "Testimony before the U.S. House of Representatives Committee on Science, Space, and Technology, Hearing on 'Science of Zika: The DNA of an Epidemic,' " U.S. House of Representatives (2016)
No: Eric Hoffman, from "Genetically Engineered Mosquitoes in the U.S.," Friends of the Earth (2012)

Hadyn Parry argues that genetically engineered mosquitoes hold the potential to reduce mosquito populations and control the spread of diseases such as Zika and dengue. Eric Hoffman, a biotechnology campaigner with Friends of the Earth, argues that a great deal of research remains to be done to prove the safety to both the environment and public health of releasing genetically engineered mosquitoes. In addition, medical ethics require that participants in a medical trial must be able to opt out at any time, which means that a single resident of a release area must be able to call a halt to the release program.

Issue: Is Gene-Editing of Human Embryos Coming Soon?
Yes: Antonio Regalado, from "Engineering the Perfect Baby," *MIT Technology Review* (2015)
No: Elizabeth McNally, from "Testimony before the U.S. House of Representatives Committee on Science, Space, and Technology, Subcommittee on Research and Technology, Hearing on 'The Science and Ethics of Genetically Engineered Human DNA,' " U.S. House of Representatives (2015)

Antonio Regalado describes recent progress in using the new CRISPR technology to edit the genes of mammalian cells, including embryos. He argues that although many people involved in the research are cautious, what was until recently only a theoretical possibility is now a very real possibility. We are very close to being able to engineer the genes of human embryos (for a variety of reasons) and most people have no idea of what is coming. Elizabeth McNally agrees that the technology is developing rapidly and has much to offer but is more reserved in her evaluation. She argues that it is necessary to regulate the technology and its uses, including limiting or prohibiting uses where changes would be passed to the next generation. However, "the justified use of this approach is certainly conceivable and may one day be appropriate."

Preface

Those who must deal with scientific and technological issues—scientists, politicians, sociologists, business managers, and anyone who is concerned about energy policy, genetically modified foods, government intrusiveness, expensive space programs, or the morality of medical research, among many other issues—must be able to consider, evaluate, and choose among alternatives. Making choices is an essential aspect of the scientific method. It is also an inescapable feature of every public debate over a scientific or technological issue, for there can be no debate if there are no alternatives.

The ability to evaluate and to select among alternatives—as well as to know when the data do not permit selection—is called critical thinking. It is essential not only in science and technology but in every other aspect of life as well. *Taking Sides: Clashing Views in Science, Technology, and Society* is designed to stimulate and cultivate this ability by holding up for consideration issues that have provoked substantial debate. Each of these issues has at least two sides, usually more. However, each issue is expressed in terms of a single question in order to draw the lines of debate more clearly. The ideas and answers that emerge from the clash of opposing points of view should be more complex than those offered by the students before the reading assignment.

The issues in this book were chosen because they are currently of particular concern to both science and society. They touch on the nature of science and research, the relationship between science and society, the uses of technology, and the potential threats that technological advances can pose to human survival. And they come from a variety of fields, including computer and space science, biology, environmentalism, law enforcement, and public health.

Organization of the book For each issue, I have provided an *Issue Introduction*, which provides some historical background and discusses why the issue is important. Each issue concludes with an *Exploring the Issue* section that offers thought questions, hints to where the debaters share common ground, and additional material both on- and off-line, including relevant Internet site addresses (URLs).

Which answer to the issue question—yes or no—is the correct answer? Perhaps neither. Perhaps both.

Students should read, think about, and discuss the readings and then come to their own conclusions without letting my or their instructor's opinions (which sometimes show!) dictate theirs. The additional readings should prove helpful. It is worth stressing that the issues covered in this book are all *live* issues; that is, the debates they represent are active and ongoing.

Taking Sides: Clashing Views in Science, Technology, and Society is only one title in the Taking Sides series. If you are interested in seeing other titles, please visit http://create .mheducation.com.

Thomas A. Easton
Mount Ida College

Editor of This Volume

THOMAS A. EASTON recently retired as professor of science at Thomas College in Waterville, Maine, where he had taught environmental science; science, technology, and society; physical anthropology; and computer science since 1983. He continues to teach part-time and is currently the acting chair of the Department of Natural & Applied Sciences at Mount Ida College in Newton, MA. He received a BA in biology from Colby College in 1966 and a PhD in theoretical biology from the University of Chicago in 1971. He writes and speaks frequently on scientific and futuristic issues. His books include *Focus on Human Biology,* 2nd ed., coauthored with Carl E. Rischer (HarperCollins, 1995), *Careers in Science,* 4th ed. (VGM Career Horizons, 2004), *Classic Edition Sources: Environmental Studies,* 5th ed. (McGraw-Hill, 2014), *Taking Sides: Clashing Views on Controversial Issues in Science, Technology, and Society* (McGraw-Hill, 13th ed., 2017), and *Taking Sides: Clashing Views on Controversial Environmental Issues* (McGraw-Hill, 17th ed., 2017). Dr. Easton is also a well-known writer and critic of science fiction.

Academic Advisory Board Members

Members of the Academic Advisory Board are instrumental in the final selection of articles for each edition of Taking Sides. Their review of articles for content, level, and appropriateness provides critical direction to the editors and staff. We think that you will find their careful consideration well reflected in this volume.

Grace Auyang
University of Cincinnati

Claudius A. Carnegie
Florida International University

Robert Cole
Saint Louis University

Paul DiBara
Curry College

Michael Efthimiades
Vaughn College of Aeronautics

Sarah Greenwald
Appalachian State University

James Hollenbeck
Indiana University Southeast

John A. Kromkowski
The Catholic University of America

Michael Martel
Ohio University

Timothy McGettigan
Colorado State University, Pueblo

Robert Moody
Fort Hays State University

Joseph B. Mosca
Monmouth University

Mike Theiss
University of Wisconsin–Marathon

Introduction

In his 2008 inaugural address, President Barack Obama said, "We will build the roads and bridges, the electric grids, and digital lines that feed our commerce and bind us together. We will restore science to its rightful place and wield technology's wonders to raise health care's quality and lower its costs." At the 2010 meeting of the American Association for the Advancement of Science, Eric Lander, cochair of the President's Council of Advisors on Science and Technology, asked, "What is the rightful place of science?" and answered that it belongs "in the president's cabinet and policy-making, in the nation's classrooms; as an engine to propel the American economy; as a critical investment in the federal budget, even in times of austerity; as a tool for diplomacy and international understanding and as an organizing principle for space exploration." (See Eric S. Lander, "Obama Advisor Weighs 'The Rightful Place of Science,'" *Science News* [June 5, 2010]; the question is also discussed in Daniel Sarewitz, "The Rightful Place of Science," *Issues in Science and Technology* [Summer 2009].) However, John Marburger, science advisor to President George W. Bush, notes in "Science's Uncertain Authority in Policy," *Issues in Science and Technology* (Summer 2010), that policymakers often ignore science in favor of preference, prejudice, and expedience.

The discussion of "the rightful place of science" is important for several reasons. One is simply that previous administrations have often made decisions based less on evidence than on politics and ideology. Today, the conservative or right-wing side of American society is waging what has been called a "war on science," refusing to accept scientific truths that threaten religious beliefs (e.g., evolution), desperate wishes (e.g., vaccine safety and alternative medicine), profit (e.g., global warming), and more; see Shawn Lawrence Otto, *Fool Me Twice: Fighting the Assault on Science in America* (Rodale, 2011); John Grant, *Denying Science: Conspiracy Theories, Media Distortions, and the War against Reality* (Prometheus, 2011); and Shawn Lawrence Otto, "America's Science Problem," *Scientific American* (November 2012).

The other—closely related—reason for discussing "the rightful place of science" is that a great many of the issues that the United States and the world face today cannot be properly understood without a solid grounding in climatology, ecology, physics, and engineering (among other areas). This is not going to change. In the twenty-first century, we cannot escape science and technology. Their fruits—the clothes we wear, the foods we eat, the tools we use—surround us. They also fill us with both hope and dread for the future, for although new discoveries promise us cures for diseases and other problems, new insights into the wonders of nature, new gadgets, new industries, and new jobs (among other things), the past has taught us that technological developments can have unforeseen and terrible consequences.

Those consequences do *not* belong to science, for science is nothing more (or less) than a systematic approach to gaining knowledge about the world. Technology is the application of knowledge (including scientific knowledge) to accomplish things we otherwise could not. It is not just devices such as hammers and computers and jet aircraft, but also management systems and institutions and even political philosophies. And it is of course such *uses* of knowledge that affect our lives for good and ill.

We cannot say, "for good *or* ill." Technology is neither an unalloyed blessing nor an unmitigated curse. Every new technology offers both new benefits and new problems, and the two sorts of consequences cannot be separated from each other. Automobiles provide rapid, convenient personal transportation, but precisely because of that benefit, they also create suburbs, urban sprawl, crowded highways, and air pollution, and even contribute to global climate change.

Optimists vs. Pessimists

The inescapable pairing of good and bad consequences helps to account for why so many issues of science and technology stir debate in our society. Optimists focus on the benefits of technology and are confident that we will be able to cope with any problems that arise. Pessimists fear the problems and are sure their costs will outweigh any possible benefits.

Sometimes the costs of new technologies are immediate and tangible. When new devices—steamship boilers or space shuttles—fail or new drugs prove to have unforeseen side effects, people die. Sometimes the costs are less obvious.

The proponents of technology answer that if a machine fails, it needs to be fixed, not banned. If a drug has side effects, it may need to be refined or its permitted recipients may have to be better defined (the banned tranquilizer thalidomide is famous for causing birth defects when taken early in pregnancy; it is apparently quite safe for men and nonpregnant women).

Certainty vs. Uncertainty

Another root for the debates over science and technology is uncertainty. Science is by its very nature uncertain. Its truths are provisional, open to revision.

Unfortunately, most people are told by politicians, religious leaders, and newspaper columnists that truth is certain. They therefore believe that if someone admits uncertainty, their position is weak and they need not be heeded. This is, of course, an open invitation for demagogues to prey upon fears of disaster or side effects or upon the wish to be told that the omens of greenhouse warming and ozone holes (etc.) are mere figments of the scientific imagination. Businesses may try to emphasize uncertainty to forestall government regulations; see David Michaels, *Doubt Is Their Product: How Industry's Assault on Science Threatens Your Health* (Oxford University Press, 2008).

Is Science Just Another Religion?

Science and technology have come to play a huge role in human culture, largely because they have led to vast improvements in nutrition, health care, comfort, communication, transportation, and humanity's ability to affect the world. However, science has also enhanced understanding of human behavior and of how the universe works, and in this it frequently contradicts what people have long thought they knew. Furthermore, it actively rejects any role of God in scientific explanation.

Many people therefore reject what science tells us. They see science as just another way of explaining how the world and humanity came to be; in this view, science is no truer than religious accounts. Indeed, some say science is just another religion, with less claim on followers' allegiance than other religions that have been divinely sanctioned and hallowed by longer traditions. Certainly, they see little significant difference between the scientist's faith in reason, evidence, and skepticism as the best way to achieve truth about the world and the religious believer's faith in revelation and scripture. This becomes very explicit in connection with the debates between creationists and evolutionists. Even religious people who do not favor creationism may reject science because they see it as denying both the existence of God and the importance of "human values" (meaning behaviors that are affirmed by traditional religion). This leads

to a basic antipathy between science and religion, especially conservative religion, and especially in areas—such as human origins—where science and scripture seem to be talking about the same things but are contradicting each other. This point can be illustrated by mentioning the Italian physicist Galileo Galilei (1564–1642), who in 1616 was attacked by the Roman Catholic Church for teaching Copernican astronomy and thus contradicting the teachings of the Church. Another example arose when evolutionary theorist Charles Darwin first published *On the Origin of Species by Means of Natural Selection* in 1859. Mano Singham notes in "The Science and Religion Wars," *Phi Delta Kappan* (February 2000), that "In the triangle formed by science, mainstream religion, and fringe beliefs, it is the conflict between science and fringe beliefs that is usually the source of the most heated, acrimonious, and public debate." Michael Ruse takes a more measured tone when he asks "Is Evolution a Secular Religion?" *Science* (March 7, 2003); his answer is that "Today's professional evolutionism is no more a secular religion than is industrial chemistry" but there is also a "popular evolutionism" that treads on religious ground and must be carefully distinguished. In recent years, efforts to counter "evolutionism" by mandating the teaching of creationism or "intelligent design" (ID) in public schools have made frequent appearances in the news, but so have the defeats of those efforts. One of the most recent defeats was in Dover, Pennsylvania, where the judge declared that "ID is not science." See Jeffrey Mervis, "Judge Jones Defines Science—And Why Intelligent Design Isn't," *Science* (January 6, 2006), and Sid Perkins, "Evolution in Action," *Science News* (February 25, 2006).

Even if religion does not enter the debate, some people reject new developments in science and technology (and in other areas) because they seem "unnatural." For most people, "natural" seems to mean any device or procedure to which they have become accustomed. Very few realize how "unnatural" are such ordinary things as circumcision and horseshoes and baseball.

Yet new ideas are inevitable. The search for and the application of knowledge is perhaps the human species' single most defining characteristic. Other creatures also use tools, communicate, love, play, and reason. Only humans have embraced change. We are forever creating variations on our religions, languages, politics, and tools. Innovation is as natural to us as building dams is to a beaver.

Efforts to encourage innovation are a perennial topic in discussions of how nations can deal with problems and stimulate their economies (see David H. Guston,

"Innovation Policy: Not Just a Jumbo Shrimp," *Nature* [August 21, 2008]). India has a National Innovation Foundation, and a similar government agency has been suggested for the United States (see Robert Atkinson and Howard Wial, "Creating a National Innovation Foundation," *Issues in Science and Technology* [Fall 2008]; see also Robert Atkinson and Howard Wial, *Boosting Productivity, Innovation, and Growth through a National Innovation Foundation* [Washington, DC: Brookings Institution and Information Technology and Innovation Foundation, 2008], available online at www.brookings.edu/~/media/Files /rc/reports/2008/04_federal_role_atkinson_wial/NIF%20Report .pdf or www.itif.org/files/NIF.pdf). The closest we have come so far is the Defense Advanced Research Projects Agency (DARPA; www.darpa.mil/), famous for its initiation of Internet technology, and ARPA-Energy (http://arpa-e.energy .gov/), launched in 2007 with hopes for equally impressive results in the field of energy.

Voodoo Science

Public confusion over science and technology is increased by several factors. One is the failure of public education. In 2002, the Committee on Technological Literacy of the National Academy of Engineering and the National Research Council published a report (*Technically Speaking: Why All Americans Need to Know More about Technology*) that said that although the United States is defined by and dependent on science and technology, "its citizens are not equipped to make well-considered decisions or to think critically about technology. As a society, we are not even fully aware of or conversant with the technologies we use every day."

A second factor is the willingness of some to mislead. Alarmists stress awful possible consequences of new technology without paying attention to actual evidence, they demand certainty when it is impossible, and they reject the new because it is untraditional or even "unthinkable." And then there are the marketers, hypesters, fraudsters, activists, and even legitimate scientists and critics who oversell their claims. Robert L. Park, author of *Voodoo Science: The Road from Foolishness to Fraud* (Oxford University Press, 2002), lists seven warning signs "that a scientific claim lies well outside the bounds of rational scientific discourse" and should be viewed warily:

- The discoverer pitches his claim directly to the media, without permitting peer review.
- The discoverer says that a powerful establishment is trying to suppress his or her work.

- The scientific effect involved is always at the very limit of detection.
- Evidence for a discovery is only anecdotal.
- The discoverer says a belief is credible because it has endured for centuries.
- The discoverer has worked in isolation.
- The discoverer must propose new laws of nature to explain an observation.

The Soul of Science

The standard picture of science—a world of observations and hypotheses, experiments and theories, a world of sterile white coats and laboratories and cold, unfeeling logic—is a myth of our times. It has more to do with the way science is presented by both scientists and the media than with the way scientists actually do their work. In practice, scientists are often less orderly, less logical, and more prone to very human conflicts of personality than most people suspect.

The myth remains because it helps to organize science. It provides labels and a framework for what a scientist does; it may thus be especially valuable to student scientists who are still learning the ropes. In addition, it embodies certain important ideals of scientific thought. It is these ideals that make the scientific approach the most powerful and reliable guide to truth about the world that human beings have yet devised.

The Ideals of Science: Skepticism, Communication, and Reproducibility

The soul of science is a very simple idea: *Check it out.* Scholars used to think that all they had to do to do their duty by the truth was to say "According to . . ." some ancient authority such as Aristotle or the Bible. If someone with a suitably illustrious reputation had once said something was so, it was so. Arguing with authority or holy writ could get you charged with heresy and imprisoned or burned at the stake.

This attitude is the opposite of everything that modern science stands for. As Carl Sagan says in *The Demon-Haunted World: Science as a Candle in the Dark* (Random House, 1995, p. 28), "One of the great commandments of science is, 'Mistrust arguments from authority.'" Scientific knowledge is based not on authority but on reality itself. Scientists take nothing on faith. They are *skeptical*. When they want to know something, they do not look it up in the library or take others' word for it. They go into the laboratory, the forest, the desert—wherever they can find the phenomena they wish to know about—and they ask those phenomena directly. They look for answers in the book of nature. And if they think they know the answer already, it is not of books that they ask, "Are we right?" but of nature. This is the point of "scientific experiments"—they are how scientists ask nature whether their ideas check out.

This "check it out" ideal is, however, an ideal. No one can possibly check everything out for himself or herself. Even scientists, in practice, look things up in books. They too rely on authorities. But the authorities they rely on are other scientists who have studied nature and reported what they learned. In principle, everything those authorities report can be checked. Observations in the lab or in the field can be repeated. New theoretical or computer models can be designed. What is in the books can be confirmed.

In fact, a good part of the official "scientific method" is designed to make it possible for any scientist's findings or conclusions to be confirmed. Scientists do not say, "Vitamin D is essential for strong bones. Believe me. I know." They say, "I know that vitamin D is essential for proper bone formation because I raised rats without vitamin D in their diet, and their bones turned out soft and crooked. When I gave them vitamin D, their bones hardened and straightened. Here is the kind of rat I used, the kind of food I fed them, the amount of vitamin D I gave them. Go thou and do likewise, and you will see what I saw."

Communication is therefore an essential part of modern science. That is, in order to function as a scientist, you must not keep secrets. You must tell others not just what you have learned by studying nature, but how you learned it. You must spell out your methods in enough detail to let others repeat your work.

Scientific knowledge is thus *reproducible* knowledge. Strictly speaking, if a person says "I can see it, but you can't," that person is not a scientist. Scientific knowledge exists for everyone. Anyone who takes the time to learn the proper techniques can confirm it. They don't have to believe in it first.

As an exercise, devise a way to convince a red-green colorblind person, who sees no difference between red and green, that such a difference really exists. That is, show that a knowledge of colors is reproducible, and therefore scientific knowledge, rather than something more like belief in ghosts or telepathy.

Here's a hint: Photographic light meters respond to light hitting a sensor. Photographic filters permit light of only a single color to pass through. And yes, there is an app for this!

The Standard Model of the Scientific Method

As it is usually presented, the scientific method has five major components. They include *observation, generalization* (identifying a pattern), stating a *hypothesis* (a tentative extension of the pattern or explanation for why the pattern exists), and *experimentation* (testing that explanation). The results of the tests are then *communicated* to other members of the scientific community, usually by publishing the findings. How each of these components contributes to the scientific method is discussed briefly below.

Observation

The basic units of science—and the only real facts the scientist knows—are the individual *observations*. Using them, we look for patterns, suggest explanations, and devise tests for our ideas. Our observations can be casual, as when we notice a black van parked in front of the fire hydrant on our block. They may also be more deliberate, as what a police detective notices when he or she sets out to find clues to who has been burglarizing apartments in our neighborhood.

Generalization

After we have made many observations, we try to discern a pattern among them. A statement of such a pattern is a *generalization*. We might form a generalization if we realized that every time there was a burglary on the block, that black van was parked by the hydrant.

Cautious experimenters do not jump to conclusions. When they think they see a pattern, they often make a few more observations just to be sure the pattern holds up. This practice of strengthening or confirming findings by *replicating* them is a very important part of the scientific process. In our example, the police would wait for the van to show up again and for another burglary to happen. Only then might they descend on the alleged villains. Is there loot in the van? Burglary tools?

The Hypothesis

A tentative explanation suggesting why a particular pattern exists is called a *hypothesis*. In our example, the hypothesis that comes to mind is obvious: The burglars drive to work in that black van.

The mark of a good hypothesis is that it is *testable*. The best hypotheses are *predictive*. Can you devise a predictive test for the "burglars use the black van" hypothesis?

Unfortunately, tests can fail even when the hypothesis is perfectly correct. How might that happen with our example?

Many philosophers of science insist on *falsification* as a crucial aspect of the scientific method. That is, when a test of a hypothesis shows the hypothesis to be false, the hypothesis must be rejected and replaced with another.

The Experiment

The *experiment* is the most formal part of the scientific process. The concept, however, is very simple: An experiment is nothing more than a test of a hypothesis. It is what a scientist—or a detective—does to check an idea out.

If the experiment does not falsify the hypothesis, that does not mean the hypothesis is true. It simply means that the scientist has not yet come up with the test that falsifies it. The more times and the more different ways that falsification fails, the more probable it is that the hypothesis is true. Unfortunately, because it is impossible to do all the possible tests of a hypothesis, the scientist can never *prove* it is true.

Consider the hypothesis that all cats are black. If you see a black cat, you don't really know anything at all about all cats. If you see a white cat, though, you certainly know that not all cats are black. You would have to look at every cat on Earth to prove the hypothesis. It takes just one to disprove it.

This is why philosophers of science say that *science is the art of disproving*, not proving. If a hypothesis withstands many attempts to disprove it, then it may be a good explanation of what is going on. If it fails just one test, it is clearly wrong and must be replaced with a new hypothesis.

However, researchers who study what scientists actually do point out that the truth is a little different. Almost all scientists, when they come up with what strikes them as a good explanation of a phenomenon or pattern, do *not* try to disprove their hypothesis. Instead, they design experiments to *confirm* it. If an experiment fails to confirm the hypothesis, the researcher tries another experiment, not another hypothesis.

Police detectives may do the same thing. Think of the one who found no evidence of wrongdoing in the black van but arrested the suspects anyway. Armed with a search warrant, he later searched their apartments. He was saying, in effect, "I *know* they're guilty. I just have to find the evidence to prove it."

The logical weakness in this approach is obvious, but that does not keep researchers (or detectives) from falling in love with their ideas and holding onto them

as long as possible. Sometimes they hold on so long, even without confirmation of their hypothesis, that they wind up looking ridiculous. Sometimes the confirmations add up over the years and whatever attempts are made to disprove the hypothesis fail to do so. The hypothesis may then be elevated to the rank of a *theory, principle,* or *law.* Theories are explanations of how things work (the theory of evolution *by means of* natural selection). Principles and laws tend to be statements of things that happen, such as the law of gravity (masses attract each other, or what goes up must come down) or the gas law (if you increase the pressure on an enclosed gas, the volume will decrease and the temperature will increase).

Communication

Each scientist is obligated to share her or his hypotheses, methods, and findings with the rest of the scientific community. This sharing serves two purposes. First, it supports the basic ideal of skepticism by making it possible for others to say, "Oh, yeah? Let me check that." It tells those others where to see what the scientist saw, what techniques to use, and what tools to use.

Second, it gets the word out so that others can use what has been discovered. This is essential because science is a cooperative endeavor. People who work thousands of miles apart build with and upon each other's discoveries, and some of the most exciting discoveries have involved bringing together information from very different fields, as when geochemistry, paleontology, and astronomy came together to reveal that what killed off the dinosaurs 65 million years ago was apparently the impact of a massive comet or asteroid with the Earth.

Scientific cooperation stretches across time as well. Every generation of scientists both uses and adds to what previous generations have discovered. As Isaac Newton said, "If I have seen further than [other men], it is by standing upon the shoulders of Giants" (Letter to Robert Hooke, February 5, 1675/6).

The communication of science begins with a process called "peer review," which typically has three stages. The first occurs when a scientist seeks funding—from government agencies, foundations, or other sources—to carry out a research program. He or she must prepare a report describing the intended work, laying out background, hypotheses, planned experiments, expected results, and even the broader impacts on other fields. Committees of other scientists then go over the report to see whether the scientist knows his or her area, has the necessary abilities, and is realistic in his or her plans.

Once the scientist has the needed funding, has done the work, and has written a report of the results, that report will go to a scientific journal. Before publishing the report, the journal's editors will show it to other workers in the same or related fields and ask whether the work was done adequately, the conclusions are justified, and the report should be published.

The third stage of peer review happens after publication, when the broader scientific community gets to see and judge the work.

This three-stage quality-control filter can, of course, be short-circuited. Any scientist with independent wealth can avoid the first stage quite easily, but such scientists are much, much rarer today than they were a century or so ago. Those who remain are the object of envy. Surely it is fair to say that they are not frowned upon as are those who avoid the later two stages of the "peer review" mechanism by using vanity presses and press conferences.

On the other hand, it is certainly possible for the standard peer review mechanisms to fail. By their nature, these mechanisms are more likely to approve ideas that do not contradict what the reviewers think they already know. Yet unconventional ideas are not necessarily wrong, as Alfred Wegener proved when he tried to gain acceptance for the idea of continental drift in the early twentieth century. At the time, geologists believed the crust of the Earth—which was solid rock, after all—did not behave like liquid. Yet Wegener was proposing that the continents floated about like icebergs in the sea, bumping into each other, tearing apart (to produce matching profiles like those of South America and Africa), and bumping again. It was not until the 1960s that most geologists accepted his ideas as genuine insights instead of hare-brained delusions.

The Need for Controls

Many years ago, I read a description of a wish machine. It consisted of an ordinary stereo amplifier with two unusual attachments. The wires that would normally be connected to a microphone were connected instead to a pair of copper plates. The wires that would normally be connected to a speaker were connected instead to a whip antenna of the sort we usually see on cars.

To use this device, one put a picture of some desired item between the copper plates. It could be a photo of a person with whom one wanted a date, a lottery ticket, a college, anything. One test case used a photo of a pest-infested cornfield. One then wished fervently for the date, a winning ticket, a college acceptance, or whatever else one craved. In the test case, that meant wishing that all the cornfield pests should drop dead.

Supposedly the wish would be picked up by the copper plates, amplified by the stereo amplifier, and then sent via the whip antenna wherever wish-orders have to go. Whoever or whatever fills those orders would get the message, and then. . . . Well, in the test case, the result was that when the testers checked the cornfield, there was no longer any sign of pests.

What's more, the process worked equally well whether the amplifier was plugged in or not.

I'm willing to bet that you are now feeling very much like a scientist—skeptical. The true, dedicated scientist, however, does not stop with saying, "Oh, yeah? Tell me another one!" Instead, he or she says something like, "Mmm. I wonder. Let's check this out." (Must we, really? After all, we can be quite sure that the wish machine does not work because if it did, it would be on the market. Casinos would then be unable to make a profit for their backers. Deadly diseases would not be deadly. And so on.)

Where must the scientist begin? The standard model of the scientific method says the first step is observation. Here, our observations (as well as our necessary generalization) are simply the description of the wish machine and the claims for its effectiveness. Perhaps we even have an example of the physical device itself.

What is our hypothesis? We have two choices, one consistent with the claims for the device, one denying those claims: The wish machine always works, or the wish machine never works. Both are equally testable, but perhaps one is more easily falsifiable. (Which one?)

How do we test the hypothesis? Set up the wish machine, and perform the experiment of making a wish. If the wish comes true, the device works. If it does not, it doesn't.

Can it really be that simple? In essence, yes. But in fact, no.

Even if you don't believe that wishing can make something happen, sometimes wishes do come true by sheer coincidence. Therefore, if the wish machine is as nonsensical as most people think it is, sometimes it will *seem* to work. We therefore need a way to shield against the misleading effects of coincidence. We need a way to *control* the possibilities of error.

Coincidence is not, of course, the only source of error we need to watch out for. For instance, there is a very human tendency to interpret events in such a way as to agree with our preexisting beliefs, our prejudices. If we believe in wishes, we therefore need a way to guard against our willingness to interpret near misses as not quite misses at all. There is also a human tendency not to look for mistakes when the results agree with our prejudices. That cornfield, for instance, might not have been as badly infested as the testers said it was, or a farmer might have sprayed it with pesticide whether the testers had wished or not, or the field they checked might have been the wrong one.

We would also like to check whether the wish machine does indeed work equally well plugged in or not, and then we must guard against the tendency to wish harder when we know it's plugged in. We would like to know whether the photo between the copper plates makes any difference, and then we must guard against the tendency to wish harder when we know the wish matches the photo.

Coincidence is easy to protect against. All that is necessary is to repeat the experiment enough times to be sure we are not seeing flukes. This is one major purpose of replication.

Our willingness to shade the results in our favor can be defeated by having someone else judge the results of our wishing experiments. Our eagerness to overlook "favorable" errors can be defeated by taking great care to avoid any errors at all; peer reviewers also help by pointing out such problems.

The other sources of error are harder to avoid, but scientists have developed a number of helpful *control* techniques. One is "blinding." In essence, it means setting things up so the scientist does not know what he or she is doing.

In the pharmaceutical industry, this technique is used whenever a new drug must be tested. A group of patients are selected. Half of them—chosen randomly to avoid any unconscious bias that might put sicker, taller, shorter, male, female, homosexual, black, or white patients in one group instead of the other—are given the drug. The others are given a dummy pill, or a sugar pill, also known as a placebo. In all other respects, the two groups are treated exactly the same. Drug (and other) researchers take great pains to be sure groups of experimental subjects are alike in every way but the one way being tested. Here that means the only difference between the groups should be which one gets the drug and which one gets the placebo.

Unfortunately, placebos can have real medical effects, apparently because we *believe* our doctors when they tell us that a pill will cure what ails us. We have faith in them, and our minds do their best to bring our bodies into line. This mind-over-body "placebo effect" seems to be akin to faith healing.

Single Blind. The researchers therefore do not tell the patients what pill they are getting. The patients are "blinded" to what is going on. Both placebo and drug then gain equal advantage from the placebo effect. If the drug seems to work better or worse than the placebo, then the researchers can be sure of a real difference between the two.

Double Blind. Or can they? Unfortunately, if the researchers know what pill they are handing out, they can give subtle, unconscious cues. Or they may interpret any changes in symptoms in favor of the drug. It is therefore best to keep the researchers in the dark too; since both researchers and patients are now blind to the truth, the experiment is said to be "double blind." Drug trials often use pills that differ only in color or in the number on the bottle, and the code is not broken until all the results are in. This way nobody knows who gets what until the knowledge can no longer make a difference.

Obviously, the double-blind approach can work only when there are human beings on both sides of the experiment, as experimenter and as experimental subject. When the object of the experiment is an inanimate object such as a wish machine, only the single-blind approach is possible.

With suitable precautions against coincidence, self-delusion, wishful thinking, bias, and other sources of error, the wish machine could be convincingly tested. Yet it cannot be perfectly tested, for perhaps it works only sometimes, when the aurora glows green over Copenhagen, in months without an "r," or when certain people use it. It is impossible to rule out all the possibilities, although we can rule out enough to be pretty confident as we call the gadget nonsense.

Very similar precautions are essential in every scientific field, for the same sources of error lie in wait wherever experiments are done, and they serve very much the same function. However, we must stress that no controls and no peer review system, no matter how elaborate, can completely protect a scientist—or science—from error.

Here, as well as in the logical impossibility of proof (experiments only fail to disprove) and science's dependence on the progressive growth of knowledge (its requirement that each scientist make his or her discoveries while standing on the shoulders of the giants who went before, if you will) lies the uncertainty that is the hallmark of science. Yet it is also a hallmark of science that its methods guarantee that uncertainty will be reduced (not eliminated). Frauds and errors will be detected and corrected. Limited understandings of truth will be extended.

Those who bear this in mind will be better equipped to deal with issues of certainty and risk.

Something else to bear in mind is that argument is an inevitable part of science. The combination of communication and skepticism very frequently leads scientists into debates with each other. The scientist's willingness to be skeptical about and hence to challenge received wisdom leads to debates with everyone else. A book like this one is an unrealistic portrayal of science only because it covers such a small fraction of all the arguments available.

Is Science Worth It?

What scientists do as they apply their methods is called *research*. Scientists who perform *basic or fundamental research* seek no specific result. Basic research is motivated essentially by curiosity. It is the study of some intriguing aspect of nature for its own sake. Basic researchers have revealed vast amounts of detail about the chemistry and function of genes, explored the behavior of electrons in semiconductors, revealed the structure of the atom, discovered radioactivity, and opened our minds to the immensity in both time and space of the universe in which we live.

Applied or strategic research is more mission-oriented. Applied scientists turn basic discoveries into devices and processes, such as transistors, computers, antibiotics, vaccines, nuclear weapons and power plants, and communications and weather satellites. There are thousands of such examples, all of which are answers to specific problems or needs, and many of which were quite surprising to the basic researchers who first gained the raw knowledge that led to these developments.

It is easy to see what drives the effort to put science to work. Society has a host of problems that cry out for immediate solutions. Yet there is also a need for research that is not tied to explicit need because such research undeniably supplies a great many of the ideas, facts, and techniques that problem-solving researchers then use in solving society's problems. Basic researchers, of course, use the same ideas, facts, and techniques as they continue their probings into the way nature works.

In 1945—after the scientific and technological successes of World War II—Vannevar Bush argued in *Science, the Endless Frontier* (National Science Foundation, 1990) that science would continue to benefit society best if it were supported with generous funding but not controlled by society. On the record, he was quite right, for the next half-century saw an unprecedented degree of progress in medicine, transportation, computers, communications, weapons, and a great deal more.

There have been and will continue to be problems that emerge from science and its applications in technology. Some people respond like Bill Joy, who argues in "Why the Future Doesn't Need Us," *Wired* (April 2000), that some technologies—notably robotics, genetic engineering, and nanotechnology—are so hazardous that we should refrain

from developing them. On the whole, however, argue those like George Conrades ("Basic Research: Long-Term Problems Facing a Long-Term Investment," *Vital Speeches of the Day* [May 15, 1999]), the value of the opportunities greatly outweighs the hazards of the problems. Others are less sanguine. David H. Guston and Kenneth Keniston ("Updating the Social Contract for Science," *Technology Review* [November/December 1994]) argue that despite the obvious successes of science and technology, public attitudes toward scientific research also depend on the vast expense of the scientific enterprise and the perceived risks. As a result, the public should not be "excluded from decision making about science." That is, decisions should not be left to the experts alone.

Conflict also arises over the function of science in our society. Traditionally, scientists have seen themselves as engaged in the disinterested pursuit of knowledge, solving the puzzles set before them by nature with little concern for whether the solutions to these puzzles might prove helpful to human enterprises such as war, health care, and commerce, among many more. Yet again and again the solutions found by scientists have proved useful. They have founded industries. And scientists love to quote Michael Faraday, who, when asked by politicians what good the new electricity might be, replied: "Someday, sir, you will tax it."

Not surprisingly, society has come to expect science to be useful. When asked to fund research, it feels it has the right to target research on issues of social concern, to demand results of immediate value, to forbid research it deems dangerous or disruptive, and to control access to research results that might be misused by terrorists or others.

Private interests such as corporations often feel that they have similar rights in regard to research they have funded. For instance, tobacco companies have displayed a strong tendency to fund research that shows tobacco to be safe and to cancel funding for studies that come up with other results, which might interfere with profits.

One argument for public funding is that it avoids such conflict-of-interest issues. Yet politicians have their own interests, and their control of the purse strings—just like a corporation's—can give their demands a certain undeniable persuasiveness.

Public Policy

The question of targeting research is only one way in which science and technology intersect the broader realm of public policy. Here the question becomes how society should allocate its resources in general: toward education or prisons; health care or welfare; research or trade; and encouraging new technologies or cleaning up after old ones?

The problem is that money is finite. Faced with competing worthy goals, we must make choices. We must also run the risk that our choices will turn out, in hindsight, to have been wrong.

The Purpose of This Book

Is there any prospect that the debates over the proper function of science, the acceptability of new technologies, or the truth of forecasts of disaster will soon fall quiet? Surely not, for some of the old issues will forever refuse to die (think of evolution versus creationism), and there will always be new issues to debate afresh. Some of the new issues will strut upon the stage of history only briefly, but they will in their existence reflect something significant about the way human beings view science and technology. Some will remain controversial as long as has evolution or the population explosion (which has been debated ever since Thomas Malthus' 1798 "Essay on the Principle of Population"). Some will flourish and fade and return to prominence; early editions of this book included the debate over whether the last stocks of smallpox virus should

be destroyed; they were not, and the war on terrorism has brought awareness of the virus and the need for smallpox vaccine back onto the public stage. The loss of the space shuttle *Columbia* reawakened the debate over whether space should be explored by people or machines. Some issues will remain live but change their form, as has the debate over government interception of electronic communications. And there will always be more issues than can be squeezed into a book like this one—think, for instance, of the debate over whether elections should use electronic voting machines (discussed by Steve Ditlea, "Hack the Vote," *Popular Mechanics* [November 2004]).

Since almost all of these science and technology issues can or will affect the conditions of our daily lives, we should know something about them. We can begin by examining the nature of science and a few of the current controversies over issues in science and technology. After all, if one does not know what science, the scientific mode of thought, and their strengths and limitations are, one cannot think critically and constructively about any issue with a scientific or technological component. Nor can one hope to make informed choices among competing scientific, technological, or political and social priorities.

Unit 1

The Place of Science and Technology in Society

*T*he partnership between human society and science and technology is an uneasy one. Science and technology offer undoubted benefits, in both the short and long term, but they also challenge received wisdom and political ideology. The issues in this section deal with whether public access to publicly funded research should take precedence over the right of private interests to make money, whether the full results of scientific research should be available to all, and whether commerce or freedom is a better foundation for regulation.

Selected, Edited, and with Issue Framing Material by:
Thomas A. Easton, *Mount Ida College*

ISSUE

Is the Distinction between Basic and Applied Research Useful?

YES: **Nils Roll-Hansen**, from "Why the Distinction between Basic (Theoretical) and Applied (Practical) Research Is Important to the Politics of Science," Original Work (2010)

NO: **Venkatesh Narayanamurti, Tolu Odumosu, and Lee Vinsel**, from "RIP: The Basic/Applied Research Dichotomy," *Issues in Science and Technology* (2013)

Learning Outcomes

After reading this issue, you will be able to:

- Explain the different roles of basic and applied research.
- Describe the different criteria for success of basic and applied research.
- Explain why government policymakers seem to prefer applied research.
- Describe how basic research reflects liberal democratic values.

ISSUE SUMMARY

YES: Nils Roll-Hansen argues that the difference between basic and applied research is important to studies of the history of science and to science policy. The two differ profoundly in their criteria for success or failure, their effects on social processes, and in their degree of autonomy from political and economic interests. The distinction must not be blurred over in the interest of promoting innovation and economic growth.

NO: Venkatesh Narayanamurti, Tolu Odumosu, and Lee Vinsel argue that the distinction between basic and applied research fails to reflect what actually happens in scientific research. They urge an "invention/discovery" model and hence a more holistic, long-term view of the research process in order to enhance innovation that has public utility and identify ways to intervene with public policy.

One of the major activities of scientists is scientific research. Traditionally, research is divided into two types. *Basic research* (also known as pure or fundamental research) seeks no specific result. It is motivated essentially by curiosity. It is the study of some intriguing aspect of nature for its own sake. It has revealed vast amounts of detail about the chemistry and function of genes, discovered ways to cut and splice genes at will, and learned how to insert into one organism genes from other organisms. It has revealed the structure of the atom and discovered radioactivity. It has opened our minds to the immensity in both time and space of the universe in which we live.

It has yielded photos of the surface of Mars. And a great deal more.

Applied research is more mission oriented. A great many of the scientists who work for government and industry are applied researchers. They seek answers to specific problems. They want cures for diseases, methods for analyzing problems, and ways to control various phenomena. They develop means for realizing the dreams of basic researchers (such as the spacecraft that have yielded photos of other planets). They have taken the knowledge and techniques developed by basic research in genetics, molecular biology, quantum physics, electronics, and other areas and created wondrous technologies (genetic engineering, computers, communications). In the process, they have created new industries with immense potentials for growth and impact on human welfare.

The unexpected fruits or "spinoffs" of basic research have been used to justify steady growth in funding for this side of science ever since Vannevar Bush's 1945 report, *Science, the Endless Frontier* (Washington, DC: National Science Foundation, reprinted 1990). Yet the debate over the value of basic research has been going on for decades. As early as 1953, Warren Weaver ("Fundamental Questions in Science," *Scientific American,* September 1953) was concerned that the successes of applied science meant neglect of basic science. By the 1990s, there was a movement to focus on "national goals" and "science in the national interest" and to emphasize applied research over basic research. The thrust was toward commercial success, international competitiveness, more jobs, and increased prosperity. See Eliot Marshall, "R&D Policy that Emphasizes the 'D,'" *Science* (March 26, 1993).

A similar message has come from the Carnegie Commission on Science, Technology, and Government, which in September 1992 issued a report (*Enabling the Future: Linking Science and Technology to Societal Needs*) calling for a "National Forum on Science and Technology Goals" to help define, debate, focus, and articulate science and technology goals and to monitor the development and implementation of policies to achieve them. For a good discussion of this topic, see Gary Chapman, "The National Forum on Science and Technology Goals," *Communications of the ACM* (January 1994). "A coordinator of the 21st Century Project, a national campaign to reorient U.S. science and technology policy in the post–Cold War era," Chapman strongly favors "new . . . models that incorporate public participation, diversity, equity, and attention to national needs."

Today, the rhetoric involves the need to foster innovation and improve the nation's competitive position *vis-a-vis* other nations. As President Obama said in his January 2011 State of the Union address, "The first step to winning the future is encouraging American innovation." We need new industries, new products, and new processes, and the world's fastest growing economies are encouraging specific industries and development projects with government policy and funding. See Fareed Zakaria, "Innovate Better," *Time* (June 13, 2011). China is already one of the world's economic powerhouses. With its eye on maintaining and improving that status, it is rapidly building a national innovation system; see Tang Yuankai, "Growth Through Innovation," *Beijing Review* (July 19, 2012). At a February 6, 2013, hearing of the United States House Committee on Science, Space, and Technology,

Richard K. Templeton, Chairman, President, and CEO of Texas Instruments, testified that "federal funding of fundamental scientific research is critical to our nation's continued competitiveness, economic growth and workforce development. It will shape our future" and the interaction of industry, universities, and government is a key element of "the U.S. innovation ecosystem." At the same hearing, Charles M. Vest, President of the National Academy of Engineering, said that "if we invest well in basic research and in education, we undoubtedly will be surprised by what new innovations arise."

It is easy to see what drives this rhetoric. Society has a host of problems that cry out for solutions as soon as possible. They involve health care, global warming, energy supply, weather forecasting, and of course keeping the economy booming in order to provide jobs and wealth. The answers lie in the relatively short-term fruits of applied research, though commentators such as Chapman recognize that there is a great deal of interplay between basic and applied research and argue that even basic research (though they may avoid the term in favor of research and development, or R&D) should be directed toward societal needs.

There is also resistance by conservative politicians to basic research that reveals truths that run counter to their beliefs. We thus see attempts to ignore the fruits of evolutionary biology and climate science research, as well as demands that the National Science Foundation fund only political science research that the NSF director "certifies as promoting national security or the economic interests of the United States"; see Jeffrey Mervis, "Bill Would Set New Rules for Choosing NSF Grants," *Science* (May 3, 2013), and Dante D'Orazio, "National Science Foundation Dodges Congressional Politics by Canceling New Political Science Research," *The Verge* (August 3, 2013) (http://www.theverge.com/2013/8/3/4585464/nsf-dodges-congressional-politics-by-canceling-2013-political-science-research-funding). Applied research is politically safer.

Looking back at our initial definitions, we see that research that is directed toward society's problems cannot be basic research. Yet basic research undeniably supplies a great many of the ideas, facts, and techniques which applied researchers then use in their search for answers to society's problems. Basic researchers, of course, use the same ideas, facts, and techniques (as well as the fruits of applied research) as they continue their probing into the way nature works. And basic research also creates applied researchers. When the late Howard E. Simmons (1929–1997), received the American Chemical Society's Priestley Medal, he spoke strongly in favor of basic research, emphasizing its value to long-term progress (see *Chemical*

& Engineering News, March 14, 1994). He also encouraged more attention to science education and stressed that from industry's perspective, basic research at the university level plays a crucial role in producing "bright young scientists, broadly trained, but solid in the fundamentals, whose curiosity about the world has been piqued."

In "Endangered Support of Basic Science," a short essay in the May 1994 *Scientific American*, the late Victor F. Weisskopf (1908–2002), an MIT emeritus professor of physics and a Manhattan Project leader, wrote that "Today we cannot afford the kind of lavish funding that basic science enjoyed during the decades following World War II." However, we cannot afford to abandon basic research. "Basic science . . . creates important educational, ethical and political values. It fosters a critical, antidogmatic spirit, a readiness to say, 'I was wrong,' and an idealistic inclination to do work where there is little financial gain. Basic science establishes a bond between humans and nature; it does not recognize industrial, national, racial and ideological barriers. . . . Science cannot flourish unless it is pursued for the sake of pure knowledge and insight."

Unfortunately, because of its lack of specific direction, many government decision makers see basic research as a luxury society cannot afford. The payoff is not immediate, society has other needs that require funding, and the money is limited. Indeed, policymakers argue over whether even applied research should receive government funding, on the grounds that the private sector, guided by markets, should handle this task. In July 2012, *The Economist* ran an online debate on "Research Funding: Should Public Money Finance Applied Research?" (http://www.economist.com/debate/days/view/863). Andrew Miller,

Labour MP and Chair of the House of Commons Science and Technology Select Committee, argued that the private sector would only rarely invest in the long-term, low-return applied research that was crucial to the early development of space technology or future energy potential such as advanced battery technology. There is thus a need for public funding. If he seems to be talking about basic research rather than applied, he also questioned the validity of distinguishing the one from the other. He said, "I do not believe these labels can be used precisely enough to justify funding decisions." His opponent, Terence Kealey, Vice Chancellor of the University of Buckingham, argued against public funding of basic research on the grounds that private firms will choose not to invest in the same research. Indeed, it does seem rational to wait to reap the fruits of the public funding.

In the YES selection, Nils Roll-Hansen argues that the difference between basic and applied research is important to studies of the history of science and to science policy. The two differ profoundly in their criteria for success or failure, their effects on social processes, and in their degree of autonomy from political and economic interests. The distinction must not be blurred over in the interest of promoting innovation and economic growth. In the NO selection, Venkatesh Narayanamurti, Tolu Odumosu, and Lee Vinsel argue that the distinction between basic and applied research fails to reflect what actually happens in scientific research. They urge an "invention/discovery" model and hence a more holistic, long-term view of the research process in order to enhance innovation that has public utility and identify ways to intervene with public policy.

YES

Nils Roll-Hansen

Why the Distinction between Basic (Theoretical) and Applied (Practical) Research Is Important to the Politics of Science

Introduction

The distinction between "basic" and "applied" research or science was taken for granted half a century ago, in the aftermath of World War II. Basic science was often called "pure science" or simply "science." It had a double social role. On the one hand it was a crucial ingredient in the ideology of liberal democracy, and on the other it was a knowledge base that served practical tasks through applied science. According to this ideal of science, truthfulness is the root value. And scientific research, perceived as search for generally valid knowledge, ought to be as free as possible from the interference of special economic, political, ideological and religious interests. This Weberian ideal type "science" was championed by defenders of classical liberal and enlightenment political ideals, like Karl Popper and Michael Polanyi. It was most famously codified by the sociologist Robert Merton in his "ethos of science." His set of norms for scientific behaviour described an international scientific community committed to produce knowledge, valid and accessible for all, in a critical spirit free from discrimination on grounds of race, sex, religion, ethnic group, etc.

In the 1960s this classical liberal ideal of science came under double pressure, from above and below, so to speak. From above it was eroded by growing political and administrative steering of science in order to serve economic growth. From below political radicalism, inspired by Marxist theory of science and symbolized by the "student revolution," reacted against ideas of "objectivity" and "truth" that served capitalism. Thus government planning and grass roots radicalism alike perceived the academic "ivory tower" as an obstacle to progressive science and technology. Elsewhere I have argued that present politics of science is still reluctant to squarely face this ambiguous ideological legacy. The present paper will focus on the economic framing that has tended to dominate science studies and science policy since after 1960.

My distinction between basic and applied research reflects the different social functions of science and politics as social institutions. Basic science is dedicated to increasing and managing knowledge of general validity, and research is its dynamic element. The role of politics is to produce agreement, decisions, and collective action. Applied science can roughly be understood as the area of overlap between science and politics. The superior goal is solution of practical economic, social, and political problems, but success depends on properly taking into account the most advanced scientific knowledge and methods.

The purpose of distinctions between basic research, applied research, and technological development is not to separate these activities, but to grasp the differences in order to better coordinate and combine their activities. The concepts are ideal types and not sharply defined and exclusive categories. In spite of overlap and intertwining they carry different expectations and have different societal effects, which the politics of science needs to address. My paper focuses on the difference between basic research on the one hand and applied research and technological development on the other. Where nothing else is stated, the term "applied research" will stand for "applied research and technological development."

1. A Traditional Conception of Applied and Basic Research

During the second half of the 19th century, applied research expanded rapidly. In universities it was growing to a volume that demanded clearer rules of responsibility and public accountability. This led to the establishment of new special institutions for applied research, "practical-scientific" work, in fisheries, agriculture, geological surveying, statistics, etc., in many countries.

The present paper discusses primarily three kinds of difference between applied and basic research:

1. Different criteria for success or failure.
2. Different effects on social processes.
3. Institutional differences, e.g., in degree of autonomy from political and economic interests.

It is the way these differences are combined that gives the distinction between applied and basic research substance and political importance.

In applied research the dominant criterion is solution of specific practical problems. Practical technical success is the superior yardstick of evaluation both in advance, of projects, and retrospectively, of results. Adequate scientific competence is a necessary condition, but the choice of problem as well as the success of the result is decided politically rather than scientifically. Applied research is funded by government agencies, private firms, non-governmental interest organizations, etc., to further their respective goals—improvement in social and medical services, technical efficiency and economic profitability, ideological and political acclaim, etc.

Basic research, on the other hand, is successful when it discovers new phenomena or invents new ideas of general interest. The importance is judged in the first instance by the discipline in question. But interdisciplinary relevance is characteristic of much significant basic research. And the ultimate criterion is contributions to our general world picture. The aim of basic research is theoretical, to improve general understanding. It has no specific aim outside of this. But it is, of course, not by accident that improved understanding of the world increases our ability to act rationally and efficiently, to develop new, efficient, and beneficial technologies. Briefly, the result of successful basic research is what we find in the textbooks.

Applied research is an instrument in the service of its patron, helping to solve practical problems as recognized by politicians, government bureaucrats, commercial entrepreneurs, etc. It helps to interpret and refine the problems of the patron, to make them researchable, and then investigate and develop solutions. The missions of applied research are framed by the problems set by the patron. In this sense it is subordinate to social, economic and political aims external to science.

Basic research is not subject to the same kind of external steering. It has in principle no obligations of loyalty to specific patrons, and its ideal is autonomy from particular political and economic interests. It is responsible only

to common human and societal interests—the "common good." This concept of basic science has been understood as a crucial principle of the enlightenment tradition of the West. The autonomy from politics, religion and economic interests builds on a belief that knowledge and understanding is in general a good thing, and that increasing such knowledge and understanding will mostly lead to a better life. However, it is part of the tradition that such beliefs are subjected to critical scrutiny.

In accordance with the enlightenment tradition, a main role of basic scientific research is to improve our understanding of the world. Science is a major source of the concepts and ideas needed for a precise formulation of political and other practical problems. In this sense it is prior to politics. Sometimes basic research has a direct and dramatic effect by discovering new threatening problems and thus immediately setting a new political agenda. The present grave concern over climate change is a striking example of how politics depends on science to assess and respond to a threatening problem.

Thus science does not only provide means (instruments) for solving problems set by politics, it also shapes political values and goals. Applied research is set up to serve the first task while basic research also serves the second. From the point of view of liberal democratic decision-making, there is an important difference between solving recognized problems and introducing new problems. In the first case, science has an *instrumental* role subordinate to politics. In the second case, the role is political *enlightenment*, which is highly dependent on autonomy and independence from political authorities. When science is asked for advice on a threat like climate change, which is still mainly a prediction about future events, the importance of autonomy becomes particularly acute and correspondingly hard to maintain against political pressure.

2. The OECD Classification of Research

In the early 1960s the OECD set up an international comparative system for research statistics. The purpose was to help economic growth and development, and it therefore took a broad view of scientific research, including not only "basic research" but also "applied research" and "experimental development." The OECD classification in this way followed the contemporary trend to expand the concept of scientific research to cover all of "research and development" ("R&D"). Within a few decades this broad concept of "research" had largely replaced the traditional concept of "science" in public discourse.

Nevertheless, the OECD classification of the early 1960s with its distinctions between basic research, applied research and experimental development is still used in international research statistics:

> R&D is a term covering three activities: basic research, applied research and experimental development. . . . Basic research is experimental or theoretical work undertaken primarily to acquire new knowledge of the underlying foundation of phenomena and observable facts, without any particular application or use in view. Applied research is also original investigation undertaken in order to acquire new knowledge. It is, however, directed primarily towards a practical aim or objective. Experimental development is systematic work, drawing on existing knowledge gained from research and/or practical experience that is directed to producing new materials, products or devices, to installing new processes, systems and services, or to improving substantially those already produced or installed.

These OECD categories and definitions have been much criticized for not being sufficiently clear and objective as the basis for a dependable and stable statistics. For instance critics have argued that the distinction between basic and applied appears highly dependent on the subjective attitude of the researcher. And individual projects will often include so much both of basic and applied aspects that they do not comfortably fit either category. This balance may also shift as a project develops. Over time a statistics built on such subjective and flexible categories seems liable to reflect changes in fashions and attitudes rather than register changes in substance of research, critics have argued. But as noted above the OECD classification was based on a traditional conception of science developed from historical experience. This gave substance to the distinction between basic and applied research in terms of intellectual content as well as social effects, institutional differentiation, and criteria for success.

The primary interest of OECD was natural science and its applications in industry, agriculture and medicine. However, the system also included social science and the humanities. These latter fields do not easily fit the British-American concept of "science," though they are well covered by the continental European term "Wissenschaft." The ideal of scientific knowledge as knowledge of universal laws was foreign, especially to the humanities. Their knowledge, often defined as "understanding," was typically embodied in accounts of individual phenomena and events. It was "idiographic" (individually descriptive) and radically different from the "nomothetic" (lawlike) knowledge of natural science. The feeling of being pressed into alien and unsuitable categories has motivated criticism

and rejection of the OECD distinction between basic and applied research in the humanities.

By the early 21st century this criticism has less force. As biology has displaced physics as the leading natural science the ideal of scientific knowledge as a knowledge of universal laws has given way to more limited generalizations and explanation in terms of mechanisms. Apt and accurate general terms for description and classification have emerged as an essential basis in natural science much like in the humanities and social science, and the philosophical tension is likely to ease.

In recent decades both scholarly studies and practical politics of science have tended to concentrate on the inclusive category of "research" (R&D) and not take much interest in the differences between basic and applied. There is concern that this will undermine the autonomy of science. Basic research consumes only a small fraction of the total resources for R&D and can easily be overshadowed by applied research and technological development backed by strong external political and economic interests.

There is also concern that preoccupation with the broad category of "research" also makes comparison between countries less meaningful because it obscures critical differences in their needs for research of different kinds. For instance, keeping up an independent and strong military capability demands large investments in development of defence technology. Similarly, a large high-tech industry, producing pharmaceuticals, advanced electronics, etc., goes with high investment in appropriate applied research and technological development. On the other hand, countries mostly exporting semi-fabricated or raw materials have smaller needs for this type of research.

But in spite of scholarly neglect and political-administrative doubts the expression "basic research," and implicitly a distinction between "basic" and "applied," seems to be indispensable in debates over science policy. There is a widespread feeling that "basic research" designates a valuable social activity in need of defence against commercialization and bureaucratic control. In a survey interview with scientists and policy-makers Jan Calvert has shown how ambiguous the term "basic research" is and how the meaning shifts with user and context. However, she thinks this vigorous flora of different meanings and definitions also indicates how "resilient and necessary the term must be."

However imperfect, the OECD statistics over basic research, applied research and experimental development do in a useful way monitor changes over time as well as differences between countries. And as long as participants in science policy debates are aware of the ambiguities, and clearly understand the differences, communication need not suffer.

3. The Economic Approach to Science Policy

After World War II, in the early years of the cold war, intellectual freedom was a main topic in political debates about science. Left wing enthusiasm for a socially useful science on the Soviet model had subsided and scientific freedom became the leading idea. The European scientific tradition was seen as a crucial support for liberal democracy against totalitarian regimes of the left as well as the right. By the early 1960s the focus of science policy had shifted to economic growth and social development. Science was recognized as a fundamental motor in economic growth and supported by public money on a scale unknown before the war. How to distribute resources between different kinds and areas of research now became the main issue. In this economic perspective the justification of applied research and experimental development was easy to see, but basic research became a problem.

The nuclear physicist and science administrator Alvin M. Weinberg considered two possible justifications of basic research: Either as a "Branch of High Culture" or as "An Overhead Charge on Applied Science and Technology." The philosopher and historian of science Stephen Toulmin did not find a simple high culture doctrine reassuring. It was unlikely to impress governments geared to economic growth. He opted instead for basic science as a "tertiary industry." This new branch of "industry" would soak up the work force otherwise doomed to unemployment by the rapid progress of technological efficiency in production of all the goods needed for a comfortable life. Liberating people from trivial production tasks and giving them the opportunity to pursue science for its own sake would be an important contribution to a superior quality of life in the new society that was emerging. Down to earth economists were hesitant to acclaim Toulmin's utopian dream and insisted that basic science had to be considered either as investment or consumption. Resources for basic research could be justified either because of "positive output consequences" or "because it is a pleasurable consumption activity."

In other words: On closer economic scrutiny Toulmin's argument did not get beyond science as "high culture." This implied that public spending on basic research had to be justified politically in competition with other cultural activities like art and literature, or even sport—if it was not simply seen as a necessary overhead on applied research and technological development. It is striking how the science policy debate in the 1960s had narrowed down to an economic perspective. The idea of (basic) science as a pillar of liberal democracy had receded to the background.

Recent analysis and discussion in the "economics of science" still largely follows the 1960s tradition in framing basic research in economic categories. For instance, [Mirowski's and Sent's] *Science Bought and Sold* (2002) is a collection of papers ranging from classic contributions by Charles Sanders Peirce, Richard R. Nelson, Kenneth Arrow, and Michael Polanyi, to recent contributions by historians, philosophers, economists and sociologists of science like Paul Foreman, Philip Kitcher, Michel Callon, Paul David and Steve Fuller.

Kenneth Arrow in a paper on "Economics of Welfare and the Allocation of Resources for Innovation" starts by defining "invention" as roughly synonymous to "the production of knowledge." He cited a paper by Richard Nelson, "The Simple Economics of Basic Science," where the economic and technological perspective on scientific research had been more explicitly presented. Nelson argued that the US should spend more on "basic science" in order to be internationally competitive economically and technologically. The paper, first published in 1959, starts by referring to the Sputnik-shock, still fresh in the public mind. Nelson's epistemology has an instrumentalist flavour which makes good sense in economics but is more problematic for theories of natural science. . . .

Nelson stressed that basic research is not a "homogeneous commodity." But his concerns hardly went beyond an economic perspective. He argued that a free-enterprise economy will under-invest in common welfare commodities like education and public health, which are important economic factors, because such investment is not profitable for private firms. Nelson's worry is that this problem of "external economies" also applies to "basic science." He still uses the term "science" rather than "research." . . .

From the 1960s on the OECD has promoted radical reform of the research system. Traditional basic research has been seen as locked up in the academic "ivory tower," bound in a straight-jacket of old-fashioned scientific disciplines and lacking contact with the practical problems of society. To make science socially useful, governments must intervene more actively by increased funding of applied research, by directing basic research toward national goals, and by supporting interdisciplinary research suitable to illuminate and solve pressing social problems. Science and scholarship, according to OECD policy, have to become much more integrated with public administration, social services, business and industry, was the repeated message to OECD member countries.

By the mid-1990s there was a growing feeling that a radical change had taken place both in the size of the research system and in its organization and social functions. The differences and the distance between basic and applied research seemed to shrink and disappear. The academic ivory tower was finally crumbling, and the OECD economic approach to science policy appeared to have been fruitful. But there was also a notable uneasiness about the effects. *The New Production of Knowledge*, sponsored by the Swedish research policy establishment and published in 1994, distinguishes two different ways of doing scientific research, Mode 1 and Mode 2, corresponding roughly to two different kinds of knowledge, theoretical and practical. Mode 1 stands for the traditional academic and discipline-oriented research and knowledge. Mode 2 is "different in nearly every respect." It "operates within a context of application" and is "transdisciplinary rather than mono- or multidisciplinary." Though Mode 2 has a number of characteristics typical of applied research the inclusive and open character suggests that "research and development" (R&D) is the appropriate statistical category. However, Gibbons et al. do not discuss the OECD statistical classification. They are apparently groping for a new approach which is inspired by humanities and social science and demands radically new categories: "The problem of language is particularly difficult when trying to describe the nature of Mode 2 in areas where natural science is involved."

The thesis of the *The New Production of Knowledge* is that Mode 2 is expanding in economic as well as epistemic importance and threatens to marginalize or swallow up the traditional academic and disciplinary Mode 1 way of doing science. Mode 2 implies political and economic steering, which the old institutions of Mode 1 will have to adapt to. Interpreted as a unification of theoretical and practical science under the governance of politics and economics, Mode 2 comes into conflict with the traditional liberal ideal of scientific autonomy. Basic science as an autonomous institution responsible for true knowledge, cultural enlightenment, education, etc., but not for direct economic social usefulness, becomes more difficult to discern and harder to legitimate. . . .

The Mode 2 picture of science has dominated science policy discourse in recent years, supported by the influential broad trends of social constructivism. Historical and sociological studies of science have concentrated on the social and individual conditions of knowledge production rather than the way in which science achieves progress in dependable (true) knowledge about the objects under study. In this "subjectivist" perspective the legitimacy for external control and governing of the scientific enterprise looms large and the arguments for scientific autonomy become hard to discern.

But there have also been persistent critics arguing that there are important differences between basic and applied research and that it undermines sound science policy if these differences are rejected or neglected. Illka Niiniluoto, for instance, characterizes basic and applied by two fundamentally different goals, epistemic and practical. The primary task of basic research is "cognitive" to help us "*explain* and *understand* reality" and develop a "*world view.*" Applied research and technological development on the other hand are also subject to practical technical goals. They are governed by "technological utility" and should be assessed according to this. . . .

4. "Pasteur's Quadrant"

In spite of theories that see basic and applied research as a seamless whole, practical science policy perceives a persistent dilemma in dividing resources between the two. "Basic research" and [the] more or less equivalent wordings "curiosity drive research," "blue skies research," "bottom up research," and "pure science," keep cropping up as expressions of Mode 1 ideals. Science administrators and politicians have given much attention to an attempt to overcome this dilemma by Donald Stokes, [a] political scientist with extensive practical experience in American science policy. In *Pasteur's Quadrant. Basic Science and Technological Innovation* (1997), he argues that the difficulties can be overcome by concentrating on the most outstanding research because here the theoretical and practical come together. The paradigm example is Louis Pasteur. His contributions are truly outstanding both with respect to basic theoretical and applied technological results.

To explain his solution to the perceived dilemma Stokes drew a four box diagram where Pasteur [occupies] the box for research that aims simultaneously for theoretical as well as practical results:

"Quadrant Model of Scientific Research"

Research is inspired by:

		Considerations of use?	
		No	Yes
Quest for fundamental understanding	Yes	Pure basic research (Bohr)	Use-inspired basic research (Pasteur)
	No		Pure applied research (Edison)

Stokes holds that since World War II it has been widely believed that "the categories of basic and applied research are radically separate" and that their "goals are inevitably in tension." The solution, he argues, lies in taking note of an historical insight: The annals of science are "rich with cases of research that is guided both by understanding and by use, confounding the view of basic and applied science as inherently separate realms." This historical experience points to a research policy that gives priority to the upper left hand corner of his diagram, 'Pasteur's quadrant.' Here belongs the "major work of John Maynard Keynes, the fundamental research of the Manhattan project, and Irving Langmuir's surface physics" as well as Pasteur's biomedical contributions, according to Stokes.

But how well does this solution stand up to the concepts of basic and applied research sketched in this paper? First: The Manhattan project appears misplaced. It was primarily applied research and experimental development, aiming to produce a fission bomb. Second: The troublesome dilemmas are not between the lifelong contributions of prominent scientists. Individual scientists can, of course, participate in basic as well as in applied projects. Some of the best draw inspiration from such rotation. At the ground level, however, the choice is between individual projects with a well specified goal. When the problem or theme is clearly defined and thus made accessible to effective research the individual projects usually emerge with either a theoretical or a practical purpose. The lifelong careers of Pasteur, Keynes, and Langmuir are probably best understood as a series of interacting individual projects. Some were derived of their theoretical interests; some were commissions to help solve practical social or economic problems.

Some "research projects" are large and can more properly be called "research programmes." On a closer look they usually contain many individual projects focused on different problems some of basic scientific character some practical. The pioneering Norwegian acid rain project of the 1970s is a characteristic example. It investigated the effects of acid rain on fresh water fish and on forests and contributed important new understanding of the basic natural processes involved as well [as] answers on the extent and character of damage done.

Other large scale projects have a clearly defined primary purpose that classifies them primarily as applied or basic. But this does not prevent there being parts which qualify as clearly belonging in the other category. The Apollo "project" of the 1960s successfully put a human being on the Moon, but also gave important basic results, like geological knowledge about the Moon. On the other hand, the Large Hadron Collider at CERN . . . is a very large and complicated specialized machine built to investigate basic phenomena in high energy particle physics. Its main purpose is basic research. But in building and operating the machine numerous problems of technological development had to be solved. It is all the applied sub-projects that make this CERN project in basic research so costly.

These two examples, Apollo and the CERN experiment, illustrate the difference in criteria for success. In the first case, research was primarily the necessary instrument for putting a man on the Moon. In the second, new understanding of the nature of the smallest components of matter is the goal. In large projects interesting spin-off in terms of unexpected theoretical discoveries or new technology is likely. But this was not the reason for funding them.

The important and valid point in Stokes' promotion of "Pasteur's quadrant" is that interaction between the most challenging theoretical and practical problems can be highly productive. Theory provides practice with new concepts and theories, and practice presents theory with unexpected facts. Some of the most important achievements, both in basic and applied research, have their origin in settings which include both. This indicates that interaction between basic and applied research is most effectively secured by institutions and individuals that are in some way concerned with both.

Pasteur, for instance, started his career in crystallography investigating the difference of organic from inorganic chemistry. He found asymmetry in crystals of organic compounds to be explained by asymmetry in molecular structure, and speculated that the asymmetry of organic molecules was the secret of life. This "organismic" view inspired his refutation of spontaneous generation in micro-organisms and development of a germ theory. Together these theories remained a continuing hard core in his later researches in applied microbiology, on brewing, diseases of animals and plants, vaccination, etc. This conceptual and theoretical framework was not a result of his involvement in practical technological problems, as has been assumed by economists referring to Stokes' ideas about "Pasteur's quadrant." Rather it was a precondition for his ability to formulate soluble and fruitful questions in applied research.

On this background a general research policy that gives priority to Pasteur's quadrant appears problematic. Increasing scientific specialization makes decision-makers more and more dependent on formal criteria deriving from experts' schematic reports. If individual research projects are rated by adding their score in the basic and applied dimension the result may be to favour projects with an average score in both over those which excel in one. When competition is tough and only a small fraction are funded there is increasing risk that the most innovative projects are squeezed out because they are so clearly either theoretical or practical. It is hardly a good idea to cut support for Edison and Bohr because Pasteur apparently solves the dilemma of choosing between basic and applied research. . . .

5. Subordinating Science to Politics?

One of the "hardest, most neglected problems in contemporary philosophy of science" is "the question of how we balance epistemic values against other kinds of concern." In his *Science, Truth, and Democracy* Kitcher develops the idea of a "well-ordered science" to solve this problem. On one central point there is apparently a direct contradiction to the present paper. Kitcher rejects the distinction between science and technology: Not only does it lack a sound empirical basis; it is directly harmful by blocking important criticism of science and technology. However, his concept of basic research is quite different from mine.

In Kitcher's view the traditional conception of basic research is built on the myth of "pure science." This myth holds that the aim of scientific "inquiry is *merely* to discover truth" (my emphasis). With the cloning of Dolly as his example Kitcher argues convincingly that all science aims not only at any truth but at truths that are socially *significant*, i.e., not isolated and independent of social and moral values. Thus traditional "basic science" does not exist in the real world, and Kitcher draws the general conclusion that "moral and social values" are "intrinsic to the practice of the sciences," i.e., to all kinds of scientific activity.

It is not difficult to agree that all science, including basic research, must in the last instance be judged on its contribution to human well-being. The question is whether this principle leads to the view that there are no politically significant differences between basic and applied research. Perhaps it is the other way around that this distinction is necessary in order to organize a science that will effectively contribute to the desired goal? . . .

[T]he third edition of [Hackett's] *The Handbook of Science and Technology Studies* (2008) appears dismissive of the distinction between basic ("pure") and applied science or research, in line with Kitcher's view. The papers in the section on "Institutions and Economics" suggest that it is "no longer possible to focus on science's institutional autonomy as it was understood in the time of Merton or Polanyi." A weakness in the approach that dominates this *Handbook* is its preoccupation with the period after World War II and the impact of the Cold War on the organization

and funding of American science and technology. Ideas of "pure science," "academic freedom," etc., are narrowly related to this context. Their roots in the political and ideological conflicts of the inter-war period are neglected, and there are repeated references to a "Mertonian" view which is quite different from the ethos of science described by Robert Merton. He did not "treat science as subsisting beyond and outside of politics."

Contrary to the conception of science as separated from politics, Merton was concerned about science as an essential component of modern liberal democracy. His worry was that totalitarian ideologies like German Nazism and Soviet Communism were destroying the institution of science. Merton's ethos of science was formulated well before the advent of the Cold War. . . . When Merton used the term "science" he had in mind basic science as something different from technology. Throughout the *Handbook*, however, the primary interest is in science and technology as a whole, "technoscience" as it is often called. When the term science is used it usually refers to science and technology, not to science in Merton's sense.

Conclusion

This paper aims to delineate and make plausible a distinction between basic research on the one hand and applied research and technological development on the other. It is argued that this distinction, even if poorly understood, lies at the core of present controversies in science policy. Basic research differs from applied by its internal scientific criteria for success, its enlightenment social effects, and the relative autonomy of its institutions.

This distinction has long been central to the politics of scientific research and scientific institutions. It was instrumental in the institutional differentiation of scientific research between universities, technical colleges, industrial laboratories and government institutions of applied research in the late 19th century. It was a main issue in the ideologically charged debates over democracy and freedom in society and science around the Second World War. It was recognized as a fundamental premise in the 1960s seminal debates on criteria of scientific choice. It became marginalized and sometimes explicitly rejected as meaningless and harmful by the new wave of science studies starting around 1970. But there are now signs that a new recognition of the political and cultural importance of this distinction is emerging.

I argue that the distinction makes good philosophical sense when not interpreted in terms of rigid and exclusive metaphysical categories, and that the interaction between science and politics in politically sensitive areas like genetics is more adequately understood with this distinction than without. . . .

The problem with external political and economic steering of scientific research is not that it in general is misguided. On the contrary, strong external steering is good for some kinds of research and bad for others. Typical applied research belongs to the first kind and typical basic research to the second. Applied research is appropriately subject to practical economic and political interests, while basic research needs autonomy in its service of human welfare. I do not claim to have given a convincing argument for this view, but I hope to have shown that there are good reasons to take it more seriously than has been done in science studies during recent decades.

NILS ROLL-HANSEN is a professor emeritus of history and philosophy at the University of Oslo.

Venkatesh Narayanamurti,
Tolu Odumosu, and Lee Vinsel

 **NO**

RIP: The Basic/Applied Research Dichotomy

U.S. science policy since World War II has in large measure been driven by Vannevar Bush's famous paper *Science—The Endless Frontier*. Bush's separation of research into "basic" and "applied" domains has been enshrined in much of U.S. science and technology policy over the past seven decades, and this false dichotomy has become a barrier to the development of a coherent national innovation policy. Much of the debate centers on the appropriate federal role in innovation. Bush argued successfully that funding basic research was a necessary role for government, with the implication that applied research should be left to the auspices of markets. However, the original distinction does not reflect what actually happens in research, and its narrow focus on the stated goals of an individual research project prevents us from taking a more productive holistic view of the research enterprise.

By examining the evolution of the famous linear model of innovation, which holds that scientific research precedes technological innovation, and the problematic description of engineering as "applied science," we seek to challenge the existing dichotomies between basic and applied research and between science and engineering. To illustrate our alternative view of the research enterprise, we will follow the path of knowledge development through a series of Nobel Prizes in Physics over several decades.

This mini-history reveals how knowledge grows through a richly interwoven system of scientific and technological research in which there is no clear hierarchy of importance and no straightforward linear trajectory. Accepting this reality has profound implications for the design of research institutions, the allocation of resources, and the national policies that guide research. This in turn can open the door to game-changing discoveries and inventions and put the nation on the path to a more sustainable science and technology ecosystem.

History of an Idea

Although some observers cite Vannevar Bush as the source of the linear model of innovation, the concept actually has deep roots in long-held cultural assumptions that give priority to the work of the head over the work of the hand and thus to the creation of scientific knowledge over technical expertise. If one puts this assumption aside, it opens up a new way of understanding the entire innovation process. We will focus our attention on how it affects our understanding of research.

The question of whether understanding always precedes invention has long been a troubling one. For example, it is widely accepted that many technologies reached relatively advanced stages of development before detailed scientific explanations about how the technologies worked emerged. In one of the most famous examples, James Watt invented his steam engine before the laws of thermodynamics were postulated. In fact, the science of thermodynamics owes a great deal to the steam engine. This and other examples should make it clear that assumptions about what has been called basic and applied research do not accurately describe what actually happens in research.

In 1997, Donald Stokes's book *Pasteur's Quadrant: Basic Science and Technological Innovation* was published posthumously. In this work, Stokes argued that scientific efforts were best carried out in what he termed "Pasteur's Quadrant," where researchers are motivated simultaneously by expanding understanding and increasing our abilities (technological, including medicine) to improve the world. Stokes's primary contribution was in expanding the linear model into a two-dimensional plane that sought to integrate the idea of the unsullied quest for knowledge with the desire to solve a practical problem.

Stokes's model comprises three quadrants, each exemplified by a historical figure in science and technology. The pure basic research quadrant exemplified by Niels Bohr represents the traditional view of scientific research as being inspired primarily by a desire to extend fundamental understanding. The pure applied research quadrant is exemplified in Edison, who represents the classical inventor, driven to solve a practical problem. Louis Pasteur's quadrant is a perfect mix of the two, inventor and scientist in one, expanding knowledge in the pursuit of practical problems. Stokes described this final quadrant as "use-inspired basic research." The fourth quadrant is not fully described in Stokes' framework.

The publication of Stokes's book excited many in the science policy and academic communities, who believed it would free us from the blinders of the linear model. A blurb on the back of the book quotes U.S. Congressman George E. Brown Jr.: "Stokes's analysis will, one hopes, finally lay to rest the unhelpful separation between 'basic' and 'applied' research that has misinformed science policy for decades." However, it has become clear that although Stokes's analysis cleared the ground for future research, it did not go far enough, nor did his work result in sufficient change in how policymakers discuss and structure research. Whereas Stokes notes how "often technology is the inspiration of science rather than the other way around," his revised dynamic model does not recognize the full complexity of innovation, preferring to keep science and technology in separate worlds that mix only in the shared agora of "use-inspired basic research." It is also significant that Stokes's framework preserves the language of the linear model in the continued use of the terms basic and applied as descriptors of research.

We see a need to jettison this conception of research in order to understand the complex interplay among the forces of innovation. We propose a more dynamic model in which radical innovation often arises only through the integration of science and technology.

Invention and Discovery

A critical liability of the basic/applied categorization is that it is based on the motivation of the individual researcher at the time of the work. The efficacy and effectiveness of the research endeavor cannot be fully appreciated in the limited time frame captured by a singular attention to the motivations of the researchers in question. Admittedly, motivations are important. Aiming to find a cure for cancer or advance the frontiers of communications can be a powerful incentive, stimulating groundbreaking research. However, motivations are only one aspect of the research process. To more completely capture the full arc of research, it is important to consider a broader time scale than that implied by just considering the initial research motivations. Expanding the focus

from research motivations to also include questions of how the research is taken up in the world and how it is connected to other science and technology allows us to escape the basic/applied dichotomy. The future-oriented aspects of research are as important as the initial motivation. Considering the implications of research in the long term requires an emphasis on visionary future technologies, taking into account the well-being of society, and not being content with a porous dichotomy between basic and applied research.

We propose using the terms "invention" and "discovery" to describe the twin channels of research practice. For us, invention is the "accumulation and creation of knowledge that results in a new tool, device, or process that accomplishes a specific purpose." Discovery is the "creation of new knowledge and facts about the world." Considering the phases of invention and discovery along with research motivations and institutional settings enables a much more holistic and long-term view of the research process. This allows us to examine the ways in which research generates innovation and leads to further research in a virtuous cycle.

Innovation is a complex, nonlinear process. Still, straightforward and sufficiently realized representations such as Stokes's Pasteur's quadrant are useful as analytical aids. We propose the model of the discovery-invention cycle, which will serve to illustrate the interconnectedness of the processes of invention and discovery, and the need for consideration of research effectiveness over longer time frames than is currently the case. Such a model allows for a more reliable consideration of innovation through time. The model could also aid in discerning possible bottlenecks in the functioning of the cycle of innovation, indicating possible avenues for policy intervention.

A Family of Nobel Prizes

To illustrate this idea, [let us] trace the evolution of the current information and communication age. What can be said about the research that has enabled the recent explosion of information and communication technologies? How does our model enable a deeper understanding of the multiplicity of research directions that have shaped the current information era? To fully answer this question, it is necessary to examine research snapshots over time, paying attention to the development of knowledge and the twin processes of invention and discovery, tracing their interconnections through time. To our mind, the clearest place for selecting snapshots that illustrate the evolution of invention and discovery that enables the information age is the Nobel Prize awards.

We have thus examined the Nobel Prizes in Physics from 1956, 1964, 1985, 1998, 2000, and 2009, which were all related to information technologies. We describe these kinds of clearly intersecting Nobels as a family of prizes in that they are all closely related. Similar families can be found in areas such as nuclear magnetic resonance and imaging.

The birth of the current information age can be traced to the invention of the transistor. This work was recognized with the 1956 Physics Nobel Prize awarded jointly to William Shockley, John Bardeen, and Walter Brattain "for their researches on semiconductors and their discovery of the transistor effect." Building on early work on the effect of electric fields on metal semiconductor junctions, the interdisciplinary Bell Labs team built a working bipolar-contact transistor and clearly demonstrated (discovered) the transistor effect. This work and successive refinements enabled a class of devices that successfully replaced electromechanical switches, allowing for successive generations of smaller, more efficient, and more intricate circuits. Although the Nobel was awarded for the discovery of the transistor effect, the team of Shockley, Bardeen, and Brattain had to invent the bipolar-contact transistor to demonstrate it. Their work was thus of a dual nature, encompassing both discovery and invention. The discovery of the transistor effect catalyzed a whole body of further research into semiconductor physics, increasing knowledge about this extremely important phenomenon. The invention of the bipolar contact transistor led to a new class of devices that effectively replaced vacuum tubes and catalyzed further research into new kinds of semiconductor devices. The 1956 Nobel is therefore exemplary of a particular kind of knowledge-making that affects both later discoveries and later inventions. We call this kind of research radical innovation. The 1956 prize is situated at the intersection of invention and discovery, and it is from this prize that we begin to trace the innovation cycle for the prize family that describes critical moments in the information age.

The second prize in this family is the 1964 Nobel Prize, which was awarded jointly to Charles Townes and the other half to both Nicolay Basov and Aleksandr Prokhorov. Most global communications traffic is carried by transcontinental fiber optic networks, which use light as the signal carrier. Townes's work on the stimulated emission of microwave radiation earned him his half of the Nobel. This experimental work showed that it was possible to build amplifier oscillators with low noise characteristics capable of the spontaneous emission of microwaves with almost perfect amplification. The maser (microwave amplification by the stimulated emission of radiation effect) was observed in his experiments. Later, Basov and Prokhorov, along with Townes, extended the maser effect to consideration of its application in the visible spectrum, and thus the laser was invented. Laser light allows for the transmission of very high-energy pulses of light at very high frequencies and is crucial for modern high-speed communication systems. This Nobel acknowledges critical work that was also simultaneously discovery (the maser effect) and invention (the maser and the laser), both central to the rise of the information and communication age. Thus, the 1964 Nobel is also situated at the intersection of invention and discovery. The work on lasers built directly on previous work by Einstein, but practical and operational masers and lasers were enabled by advancements in electronic amplifiers made possible by the solid-state electronics revolution, which began with the invention of the transistor.

Although scientists and engineers conducted a great deal of foundational work on the science of information technology in the 1960s, the next wave of Nobel recognition for this research did not come until the 1980s. Advancements in the semiconductor industry led to the development of new kinds of devices such as the metal oxide silicon field effect transistor (MOSFET). The two-dimensional nature of the conducting layer of the MOSFET provided a convenient avenue to study electrical conduction in reduced dimensions. Klaus von Klitzing discovered that under certain conditions, voltage across a current-carrying wire increased in uniform steps. Von Klitzing received the 1985 Nobel Prize for what is known as the quantized Hall effect. This work belongs in the discovery category, although it did have important useful applications.

The 2000 Nobel Prize was awarded jointly to Zhores Alferov and Herbert Kroemer for "developing semiconductor heterostructures" and to Jack Kilby for "his part in the invention of the integrated circuit." Both of these achievements can be classified primarily as inventions, and both built on work done by Shockley et al. This research enabled a new class of semiconductor device that could be used in high-speed circuits and optoelectronics. Alferov and Kroemer showed that creating a double junction with a thin layer of semiconductors would allow for much higher concentrations of holes and electrons, enabling faster switching speeds and allowing for laser operation at practical temperatures. Their invention produced tangible improvements in lasers and light-emitting diodes. It was the work on heterostructures that enabled the modern room-temperature lasers used in fiber optic communication systems. Alferov and Kroemer's work on heterostructures also led to the discovery of a new form of matter, as discussed below.

Jack Kilby's work on integrated circuits at Texas Instruments earned him his half of the Nobel for showing that entire circuits could be realized with semiconductor substrates. Shockley, Bardeen, and Brattain had invented semiconductor-based transistors, but these were discrete components and were used in circuits with components made from other materials. The genius of Kilby's work was in realizing that semiconductors could be arranged in such a way that the entire circuit, not just the transistor, could be realized on a chip. This invention of a process of building entire circuits out of semiconductors allowed for economies of scale, bringing down the cost of circuits. Further research into process technologies allowed escalating progress on the shrinking of these circuits, so that in a few short years, chips containing billions of transistors were possible.

Alferov and Kroemer's work was also valuable to Horst Stormer and his collaborators, who combined it with advancements in crystal growth techniques to produce two-dimensional electron layers with mobility orders of magnitude greater than in silicon MOSFETs. Stormer and Daniel Tsui then began exploring some observed unusual behavior that occurred in two-dimensional electrical conduction. They discovered a new kind of particle that appeared to have only one-third the charge of the previously thought-indivisible electron. Robert Laughlin then showed through calculations that what they had observed was a new form of quantum liquid where interactions between billions of electrons in the quantum liquid led to swirls in the liquid behaving like particles with a fractional electron charge. This phenomenon is clearly a new discovery, but it was enabled by previous inventions and resulted in important practical applications such as the high-frequency transistors used in cell phones. For their work, Laughlin, Stormer, and Tsui were awarded the 1998 Nobel Prize in Physics, an achievement situated firmly in the discovery category.

The 2009 Nobel was awarded to Charles Kao for "groundbreaking achievements concerning the transmission of light in fibers for optical communication" and to Willard Boyle and George Smith for "the invention of the imaging semiconductor circuit—the CCD." Both of these achievements were directly influenced by previous inventions and discoveries in this area. Kao was primarily concerned [with] building a workable waveguide for light for use in communications systems. His inquiries led to astonishing process improvements in glass production, as he predicted that glass fibers of a certain purity would allow long-distance laser light communication. Of course, the work on heterostructures that allowed for room-temperature lasers was critical to assembling the technologies of fiber communication. Kao, however, not only created new processes for measuring the purity of glass but also actively encouraged various manufacturers to improve their processes in this respect. Working directly in industry, Kao's work built on the work by Alferov and Kromer, enabling the physical infrastructure of the information age. Boyle and Smith continued the tradition of Bell Labs inquiry. Adding a brilliant twist to the work that Shockley et al. had done on the transistor, they designed and invented the charge-coupled device (CCD), a semiconductor circuit that enabled digital imagery and video. Kao's work was clearly aimed at discovering the ideal conditions for the propagation of light in fibers of glass, but he also went further in shepherding the invention and development of the new fiber optic devices.

These six Nobel Prizes highlight the multiple kinds of knowledge that play into the innovations that have enabled the current information and communications age. From the discovery of the transistor effect, which relied on the invention of the bipolar junction transistor and led to all the marvelous processors and chips in everything from computers to cars, to the invention of the integrated circuit, which made the power of modern computers possible while shrinking their cost and increasing accessibility. The invention of fiber optics built on previous work on heterostructures and made the physical infrastructure and speed of the global communications networks possible. In fact, the desire to improve the electrical conductivity of heterostructures led to the unexpected discovery of fractional quantization in two-dimensional systems and a new form of quantum fluid. Each of these could probably be classified as "basic" or "applied" research, but that classification obscures the complexity and multiple nature of the research described above and does not help remove the prejudices of many against what is now labeled as "applied research." Thinking in terms of invention and discovery through time helps reconstruct the many pathways that research travels along in the creation of radical innovations.

In our model, the discovery-invention cycle can be traversed in both directions, and research knowledge is seen as an integrated whole that mutates over time (as it traverses the cycle). The bidirectionality of the cycle reflects the reality that inventions are not always the product of discovery but can also be the product of other inventions. Simultaneously, important discoveries can arise from new inventions. Observing the cycle of research over time is essential to understanding how progress occurs.

Seeing with Fresh Eyes

The switch from a basic/applied nomenclature to discovery-invention is not a mere semantic refinement. It enables us to see the entire research enterprise in a new way.

First, it eliminates the tendency to see research proceeding on two fundamentally different and separate tracks. All types of research interact in complex and often surprising ways. To capitalize on these opportunities, we must be willing to see research holistically. Also, by introducing new language, we hope to escape the cognitive trap of thinking about research solely in terms of the researcher's initial motivations. All results must be understood in their larger context.

Second, adopting a long time frame is essential to attaining a full understanding of the path of research. The network of interactions traced in the Nobel Prizes discussed above becomes clear only when one takes into account a 50-year history. This extended view is important to understanding the development of both novel science and novel technologies.

Third, the discovery-invention cycle could be useful in identifying problematic bottlenecks in research. Once we recognize the complex interrelationship of discovery and invention, we are more likely to see that problems can occur in many parts of the cycle and that we need to heed the interactions among a variety of institutions and types of research.

Bringing together the notions of research time horizons and bottlenecks, we argue that successful radical innovation arises from knowledge traveling the innovation cycle. If, as argued above, all parts of the innovation process must be adequately encouraged for the cycle to function effectively, then the notion of traveling also emphasizes that we should have deep and sustained communication between scientists and engineers, between theorists and practitioners. Rather than separating researchers according to their motivation, we must strive to bring all forms of research into deeper congress.

This fresh view of the research enterprise can lead us to rethinking the design of research institutions to align with the principles of long time frames, a premium on futuristic ideas, and the encouragement of interaction among different elements of the research ecosystem. This is especially pertinent in the case of the mission-oriented agencies such as the Department of Energy and the National Institutes of Health.

Implications for Research Policy

The pertinent question is how these insights play out in the messy world of policymaking. First, there is an obvious need to complicate the simple and unhelpful distinction between basic and applied research. The notion of the innovation cycle is a very useful aid in thinking about research holistically. It draws attention to the entirety of research practice and allows one to pose the question of public utility to an entire range of activities.

Second, the nature of the public good, and thus the appropriate role for the federal government, changes. The simple and clear notions of basic and applied were useful in one way: They provided a clear litmus test for limits to federal involvement in the research process. The idea that government funding is necessary to pursue research opportunities that aren't able to attract private funding is a useful one that has contributed to the long-term well-being and productivity of the nation. But through the lens of the discovery-invention cycle, we can see that it would deny federal funding to some types of research that are essential to long-term progress. We suggest that federal support is most appropriate for research that focuses on long-term projects with clear public utility. The difference here is that such research could have its near-term focus on either new knowledge or new technology.

The public good must be understood over the long term, and the best way to ensure that the research enterprise contributes as much as possible to meeting our national goals is to make funding decisions about discovery and invention research in a long-term holistic context.

Venkatesh Narayanamurti is the Benjamin Peirce Professor of technology and public policy and professor of physics at Harvard University and the director of the Science, Technology, and Public Policy Program at the Harvard Kennedy School.

Tolu Odumosu is a postdoctoral research fellow in the Science, Technology, and Public Policy Program at the Harvard Kennedy School and at Harvard's School of Engineering and Applied Sciences.

Lee Vinsel is a postdoctoral research fellow in the Science, Technology, and Society Program at the Harvard Kennedy School and at Harvard's School of Engineering and Applied Sciences.

EXPLORING THE ISSUE

Is the Distinction Between Basic and Applied Research Useful?

Critical Thinking and Reflection

1. Many scientific research projects have both basic and applied elements. Is it always possible to separate these elements?
2. In the invention/discovery model, invention corresponds at least roughly to applied research and discovery to basic. Is there a reason why invention comes first in the name of the model?
3. Should scientific research aim primarily at benefiting national security and the economy or at discovering truths about nature?
4. Is it possible to choose basic research that has "clear public utility" for funding?
5. In what ways does basic research influence politics and policymaking? In what ways does applied research influence politics and policymaking?

Is There Common Ground?

There is little disagreement that scientific research has both basic and applied (or discovery and invention) elements. Policymakers argue over which deserves government funding (and why), as well as over the nature of the eventual benefits.

1. Construct an argument that the increased understanding of the world that comes from basic research is more important than the economic benefits of applied research.
2. Construct an argument that the economic benefits of applied research are more important than the increased understanding of the world that comes from basic research.
3. Can one actually separate increased understanding from economic benefits?

Additional Resources

Vannevar Bush, *Science, the Endless Frontier: A Report to the President* (Washington, DC: U.S. GovernmentPrinting Office, 1945).

Royal Society of Great Britain, *The Scientific Century: Securing Our Future Prosperity* (London: Royal Society, 2010).

Nils Roll-Hansen, "Why the Distinction Between Basic (Theoretical) and Applied (Practical) Research Is Important in the Politics of Science," *Centre for Philosophy of Natural and Social Science. Technical report No. 04/09* (London School of Economics, 2009).

Internet References . . .

Basic versus Applied Research

http://psych.csufresno.edu/psy144/Content/Design/Types/appliedvsbasic.html

Federation of American Scientists

https://www.fas.org/

Research and Development: Essential Foundation for U.S. Competitiveness in a Global Economy

http://www.nsf.gov/statistics/nsb0803/start.htm

Selected, Edited, and with Issue Framing Material by:
Thomas A. Easton, *Mount Ida College*

ISSUE

Should the Public Have to Pay to See the Results of Federally Funded Research?

YES: Ralph Oman, from "Testimony before the U.S. House of Representatives Committee on the Judiciary, Subcommittee on Courts, The Internet, and Intellectual Property, Hearing on 'The Fair Copyright in Research Works Act,'" U.S. House of Representatives (2008)

NO: Stuart M. Shieber, from "Testimony before the U.S. House of Representatives Committee on Science, Space and Technology, Subcommittee on Investigations and Oversight, Hearing on 'Examining Public Access and Scholarly Publication Interests,'" U.S. House of Representatives (2012)

Learning Outcomes
After studying this issue, students will be able to:
• Explain how peer review helps to assure the quality of scientific publications.
• Explain why peer review and open access can coexist.
• Explain why university and college libraries favor open access publishing.
• Explain the role of profit in academic publishing.

ISSUE SUMMARY

YES: Attorney and past register of copyrights Ralph Oman contends that "If the NIH [National Institutes of Health] succeeds in putting all of the NIH-related peer-reviewed articles on its online database for free within one year of publication, the private publishers will be hard-pressed to survive." Allowing private publishers to continue to profit by publishing the results of publically funded research is the best way to ensure public benefit.

NO: Stuart M. Shieber argues that the concerns of traditional journal publishers that open access publishing will endanger their survival are not justified. The data show that publisher profitability has increased despite the recent economic downturn. Providing open access to the publicly funded research literature amplifies the diffusion of knowledge and benefits researchers, taxpayers, and everyone who gains from new medicines, new technologies, new jobs, and new solutions to long-standing problems of every kind.

According to Peter Suber's "Open Access Overview" (www.earlham.edu/~peters/fos/overview.htm), "open access" refers to the broad-based movement to put peer-reviewed research articles online, free of charge, and without most copyright and licensing restrictions. According to his "Timeline of the Open Access Movement" (www.earlham .edu/~peters/fos/timeline.htm), the movement has roots in the 1960s, well before the Internet came to exist as we know it today. Project Gutenberg (www.gutenberg.org/wiki/ Main_Page), which makes public-domain novels and other books freely available, was launched in 1971. For many years, the open access movement was no threat to the standard modes of scientific publishing, but by 2004 it was clear that scientific (and other) journals were becoming so expensive that university and college libraries were being forced to cut back on the number of journals they could subscribe to; on April 17, 2012, Harvard's Faculty

Advisory Council sent a memo to faculty saying "Major Periodical Subscriptions Cannot Be Sustained" (http://isites .harvard.edu/icb/icb.do?keyword=k77982&tabgroupid=icb .tabgroup143448).

In response to a report from the House Appropriations Committee urging the National Institutes of Health to require NIH-funded research reports to be deposited in NIH's Internet archive, PubMed Central, NIH director Elias Zerhouni convened meetings with representatives of academic publishers, and others. Publishers expressed concern that making reports freely available would threaten their continued existence. See Jocelyn Kaiser, "House Weighs Proposal to Block Mandatory 'Open Access'," *Science* (September 19, 2008).

Pressure was rising to do something about the problem, and open access looked like a possible solution, as exemplified by the Public Library of Science (PLoS) (see Theodora Bloom, et al., "PLoS Biology at 5: The Future Is Open Access," *PLoS Biology* (October 2008). Leah Hoffman, "Open for Business," *Communications of the ACM* (April 2012), notes that "Open access is growing fast in both recognition and popularity, making it a force to be reckoned with in the future of academic publishing."

According to Walt Crawford, "Open Access: It's Never Simple," *Online* (July/August 2008), one major objection to the traditional mode of scholarly publication—meaning that university and college libraries pay to subscribe to a journal—is that subscriptions have become remarkably expensive. Springer-Verlag's journal prices for 2010 can be seen at www.springer.com/librarians/price+lists? SGWID=0-40585-0-0-0; sixteen of those journals are priced at over $10,000 a year. The prices of Elsevier's titles are listed at www.elsevier.com/wps/find/journalpricing.cws_home /subscrippricelistlibr/description; *Life Sciences* cost a library $7,399 for 2012 compared to $4,031 a year in 2000 and $2,325 in 1995. Subscription prices for print journals have grown about 10 percent per year, with electronic access and mixed access being priced even higher. Aggregated (multi-journal) electronic-access packages appeared in 2001 to help stabilize prices; see Frances L. Chen, Paul Wrynn, and Judith L. Rieke, "Electronic Journal Access: How Does It Affect the Print Subscription Price?" *Bulletin of the Medical Library Association* (October 2001). Michael P. Taylor, "Opinion: Academic Publishing Is Broken: The Current System by Which Academics Publish Their Scientific Discoveries Is a Massive Waste of Money," *The Scientist* (March 19, 2012), reinforces these points.

Today aggregated packages (such as Ebsco) are commonplace, with many academic libraries using them to replace paper subscriptions. But even these can be expensive. It is no surprise that libraries are among the strongest backers of the open access movement in the United States and elsewhere (for a Canadian view, see Heather Morrison and Andrew Waller, "Open Access and Evolving Scholarly Communication," *C&RL News*, September 2008). Some researchers are addressing the concern that open access journals are somehow inferior to subscription journals in terms of quality control by studying their "impact factor" (how often papers are cited); K. A. Clauson, et al., "Open-Access Publishing for Pharmacy-Focused Journals," *American Journal of Health-System Pharmacists* (August 15, 2008), find that impact factors are actually greater for journals with some form of open access. Yet as open access journals proliferate, it is clear that some are of much less quality than others; see Martin Enserink, "As Open Access Explodes, How to Tell the Good from the Bad and the Ugly?" *Science* (November 23, 2012).

The pressure for open access does not come only from government agencies such as NIH. Some see open access as a movement to democratize what has until recently been an elite resource; see Ron Miller, "Open Access Battles to Democratize Academic Publishing," *EContent* (April 2009). Leslie Chan, Subbiah Arunachalam, and Barbara Kirsop, "Open Access: A Giant Leap Towards Bridging Health Inequities," *Bulletin of the World Health Organization* (August 2009), argue that only through open access publishing can the latest research results reach those who need them. Harvard University's arts and sciences faculty "has directly challenged the authority of academic journals to control access to research results" by voting to put faculty work in a free online repository, following similar moves by the Howard Hughes Medical Institute and the Wellcome Trust in London. A comment by Patricia Schroeder of the Association of American Publishers that "Publishers may not be as quite as excited to take articles from Harvard" seems more than a little wishful, considering Harvard's reputation. See Andrew Lawler, "Harvard Faculty Votes to Make Open Access Its Default Mode," *Science* (February 22, 2008). In December 2009, Robin Peek, "OAW [Open Access Week] 2009 Exceeds Expectations," *Information Today*, noted that 100 universities had already announced plans to require researchers to deposit research information in open access repositories. The Obama administration has opened discussions over whether to broaden open access beyond the NIH program; see Jocelyn Kaiser, "White House Mulls Plan to Broaden Access to Published Papers," *Science* (January 15, 2010). In July 2010, the Information Policy, Census, and National Archives Subcommittee of the House Committee on Oversight and Government Reform held a hearing to discuss the open access debate, touching on two bills, one that would extend the NIH policy to eleven other research agencies and shorten the 12-month delay before depositing papers in an open archive to just 6 months, and one that would revise copyright law to forbid the practice entirely. Testimony recapitulated many of the points mentioned here; see Jocelyn Kaiser, "House Hearing Explores Debate over Free Access to Journal Articles," *ScienceInsider* (July 30, 2010).

Are print journals actually threatened by the open access movement? Many commentators remark that journals offer much more than just research reports. However, they may not prove able to sustain high subscription prices. They will be obliged to adapt, as many are already doing, according to Jennifer Howard, "Scholarly Presses Discuss How They're Adapting to a Brave New E-World," *Chronicle of Higher Education* (July 11, 2008). One such adaptation is publishing books that can be freely downloaded in hope that actual book sales will follow; see John Murphy, "New Entry Tries New Publishing Model," *Research Information* (December 2008). Charles Oppenheim, "Electronic Scholarly Publishing and Open Access," *Journal of Information Science* (vol. 34, no. 4, 2008), expects pressure for open access publishing to continue, and not just in the United States. In 2012 the United Kingdom announced a requirement to require open access publishing of publicly funded research. Still, no one really expects open access publishing to completely displace the traditional mode; see Jocelyn Kaiser, "Free Journals Grow Amid Ongoing Debate," *Science* (August 20, 2010).

In 2007, legislation mandated that federally funded research reports be given to PubMed Central. The resulting Public Access Policy is described in Robin Peek, "Coming to Grips with the NIH Policy," *Information Today* (September 2008); see also Robin Peek, "The Battle over PubMed Central Continues," *Information Today* (November 2008). The debate continued into 2012, but when journal publisher Elsevier pulled its support from the latest bill, it appeared dead, at least for now; see Jennifer Howard, "Legislation to Bar Public-Access Requirement on Federal Research Is Dead," *The Chronicle of Higher Education*

(February 27, 2012). On February 22, 2013, the White House's Office of Science and Technology Policy issued a "policy memorandum" directing all Federal agencies with more than $100 million in R&D spending to develop plans to make publically accessible within one year of publication the results of all their research; see Jocelyn Kaiser, "U.S. Agencies Directed to Make Research Papers Available," *Science* (March 1, 2013).

A hearing on an earlier bill was held on September 11, 2008. Publisher representatives such as Martin Frank, executive director of the American Physiological Society, supported the bill, arguing that "By protecting copyright for research works, [it] will continue to provide incentives for private-sector investment in the peer review process which helps to ensure the quality and integrity of scientific research." In the YES selection, attorney and past register of copyrights Ralph Oman contends in his testimony that "If the NIH [National Institutes of Health] succeeds in putting all of the NIH-related peer-reviewed articles on its online database for free within one year of publication, the private publishers will be hard-pressed to survive." Allowing private publishers to continue to profit by publishing the results of publically funded research is the best way to ensure public benefit. In the NO selection, from a 2012 hearing of the House Committee on Science, Space and Technology, Subcommittee on Investigations and Oversight, on Examining Public Access and Scholarly Publication, Stuart M. Shieber argues that the concerns of traditional journal publishers that open access publishing will endanger their survival are not justified. The data show that publisher profitability has increased despite the recent economic downturn. Providing open access to the publicly funded research literature amplifies the diffusion of knowledge and benefits researchers, taxpayers, and everyone who gains from new medicines, new technologies, new jobs, and new solutions to long-standing problems of every kind.

YES ↵

Ralph Oman

Testimony before the U.S. House of Representatives Committee on the Judiciary, Subcommittee on Courts, The Internet, and Intellectual Property, Hearing on "The Fair Copyright in Research Works Act"

Mr. Chairman and members of the Subcommittee. It is a great honor to appear again before this distinguished panel. It has been a few years since my last appearance.

Thank you for the opportunity to testify on this matter of importance to copyright generally, and to the public, to the research community, to the authors of scientific, technical, and medical articles, and to the publishers of STM journals. I would like to focus on the larger policy issues that undergird the American copyright system and discuss the proposal of the National Institutes of Health that requires recipients of NIH research grants to effectively renounce copyright in their peer-reviewed article manuscripts just 12 months after publication. I will also briefly mention the bill introduced by Chairman Conyers that seeks to moderate the impact of the NIH proposal in a way that will encourage the broadest possible dissemination of high quality, peer-reviewed articles without running roughshod over the rights of authors and copyright owners.

This hearing is important on another level. The language in the appropriations bill that has given rise to this controversy was never vetted by the Judiciary Committee—the committee with intellectual property expertise. With your scrutiny today, the Subcommittee puts this narrow dispute in the larger context of the constitutional mandate—to promote the progress of science for the public interest. Other than celebrating the Judiciary Committee's involvement, I will not comment on the wisdom of legislating on appropriations bills. Into that Serbonian Bog I will not wade.

Instead, I simply applaud your decision, Mr. Chairman, to give a full airing of these issues before your expert Subcommittee. They bear directly on the copyright policies of our government and the incentives to authorship and publication under U.S. copyright law. For reasons I will discuss, the NIH proposal seems short-sighted, counterproductive, damaging to U.S. creativity, which this subcommittee fosters and safeguards, and contrary to the NIH's own interests in encouraging broad public dissemination of peer-reviewed learned articles. The Appropriations Committee, to its credit, sensed that the NIH proposal ventured into sensitive territory and added a very important proviso. That proviso directed the NIH to "implement the public access policy in a manner consistent with copyright law." In my opinion, the NIH has fallen short of that dictate in several respects, and, with this committee's expert guidance, they should refine their proposal in ways that are true to both the letter and spirit of the copyright law, and the essential policies behind it.

In this debate, three key questions must be answered. First, what policy will result in the broadest dissemination of high quality, peer-reviewed scholarly articles? Second, is it fair for the U.S. government to appropriate the value-added contributions of the private STM publishers? And, third, is the NIH correct in its assumption that the STM publishers will continue to publish their journals even if they lose 50 percent of their paid subscriptions?

Many of my colleagues in academia recognize that the STM publishers perform many vital functions in bringing these articles into the public forum. For one thing, they make substantial investments in the

Oman, Ralph. The U.S. House of Representatives, September 11, 2008.

peer-review process. While they do not as a general rule pay the reviewers, the publishers hire in-house teams to support outside specialists. These teams arrange and coordinate effective distribution, stay close to the academic experts in the discipline personally and professionally, follow the literature, and engage in on-going communications with the authors about the reviewers' comments and the incorporation of those comments into the manuscript.

In addition to the peer-review process, the publishers make judgments about which of the manuscripts to publish, depending on their quality and the level of interest in the research itself. They also edit the manuscripts and make them presentable for publication.

My basic concern about the NIH proposal is that it will, sooner rather than later, destroy the commercial market for these scientific, technical, and medical journals. If this dark prophesy comes to pass, who, I wonder, will handle all of these expensive and sensitive administrative details? Some of my academic colleagues are confident that this change in the mechanics of scientific publishing will have little or no impact on the private sector, and that it will remain as robust as ever, even if the NIH freely publishes all of the NIH peer-reviewed article manuscripts shortly after private publication. Some claim that they have "evidence" that STM publishing will continue to flourish. I have not seen that evidence. To me, it suggests an element of wishful thinking. In my experience, Congress is normally reluctant to hang major legislative change in copyright policy on the thin reed of wishful thinking. With the prospect of free copies available in the near term, who in the face of experience and reality can reasonably expect that subscribers to STM journals, faced with their own budgetary constraints and needs, will not look with real favor on alternative free sources? I can't. It is belied by common sense. Certainly, many university and industry librarians will cancel their subscriptions to these learned journals, with some estimates of a cancellation rate approaching 50 percent. With plummeting sales, how could the STM publishers stay in business? This is a critical point, and one that this committee has a special sensitivity to. It really goes to the heart of the matter, in terms of public policy.

It is a basic premise of copyright that the law is designed to benefit the public, not reward authors or publishers. But, as James Madison wrote in the Federalist Papers, "the public good fully coincides" with the rights of authors and copyright owners. With that admonition, we consider the NIH proposal. It seems clear that Congress would not want the NIH free access policy to

cause many or all of the private STM publishers to fade away. Of course, if fair market competition, or a change in the culture of academic publishing, or costly overhead were eventually to drive the private publishers out of business, so be it. It is one thing that they should suffer demise because of changes in the marketplace, and it is another to be brought down by an ill-considered governmental fiat. The NIH does not intend to perform any of the vetting, selection, and editing functions now performed by the learned societies, by the professional organizations, and by the STM publishers, and I doubt if Congress wants to increase their budget so they can take on these additional responsibilities. So the question occurs: who is going to do it? I do not see replacements for the publishers raising their hands to volunteer. For this reason alone, I question the wisdom of the NIH provision. And there are larger issues as well. Experience teaches that as a general rule Congress prefers to keep the hairy snout of the federal government out of the peer-review and manuscript selection process. We live in an open society, and, with a weather eye on the First Amendment, we try to keep the government at arms length from these delicate publication decisions, so as not to skew the process.

That being said, the NIH provision brings back vivid memories of the debate we had in 1980 with the Small Business and University Patent Procedure Act. In that debate, Senator Russell Long, Chairman of the Senate Finance Committee, following the script written by Admiral Rickover, the father of the nuclear submarine, argued in favor of existing government policy—that patents developed with government research money belong to the taxpayers who subsidize the research. Senator Bayh and Senator Dole reasoned that the taxpayers would get a far greater return on their investment if we instead facilitated private sector ownership and commercialization of the inventions, putting these inventions to work for the people. We are about to celebrate the 30th anniversary of Bayh/Dole, and no one is arguing for its repeal.

The same policy arguments apply in the NIH case. If the NIH succeeds in putting all of the NIH-related peer-reviewed articles on its online database for free within one year of publication, the private publishers will be hard-pressed to survive. To me, it seems far more likely that the U.S. taxpayer will achieve the desired objective— the broadest possible dissemination of the peer-reviewed article manuscripts—under the current system. With the private STM publishers running the peer-review process, selecting the articles, and aggressively marketing their journals to libraries and other research institutions, both foreign and domestic, the current system lets the publishers bring their professional judgment and expertise into the process and ensures high quality scholarship. Paid subscriptions keep the current system perking along, without intrusive government involvement, and without an infusion of funds from the government fisc. If the NIH provision is fully implemented, it will almost certainly end this self-policing and self-financing system and get the federal government deeply into the STM publishing business.

Finally, Mr. Chairman, I would like to mention a few related issues. First, I wonder if any of the manuscript articles that the NIH will publish contain preexisting materials that the NIH researcher did not create and therefore does not own. Here, I am thinking of charts, diagrams, photographs, and illustrations. Will the NIH commandeer the rights of those creators as well, or will it require the NIH researcher to clear all of those ancillary rights as part of the "contract." Today, of course, the publishers often help the author clear these rights, including electronic distribution rights. Will the NIH undertake this task if the publishers drop out of the picture?

Second, I wonder if the NIH proposal really serves our international interests. Our trade negotiators are constantly fighting for strong intellectual property protection, which is under siege in many countries around the world. I assume that some of the authors (or at least co-authors) are foreign nationals, and would fall under the protection of the Berne Convention. And I assume some of the impacted publisher/copyright owners are foreign as well. As I will note in a moment, the NIH policy will seriously threaten the protection of American authored and published works in foreign countries. This government edict from the NIH, not promulgated "in a manner consistent with copyright law," has a crippling effect on the value of the copyright in these works. Some of my academic colleagues argue that the Berne Convention has no relevance to the NIH policy. They see it as a simple contract matter, and they note that the researchers get very valuable consideration for their assignment of copyright to the NIH under the contract. Granted, the researchers do receive a generous stipend, averaging $400,000, but that fact also makes the whole arrangement suspect. To a serious researcher, an NIH grant is a matter of life and death professionally. To claim that the assignment of the reproduction right is "voluntary"— the product of a free market negotiation—strikes me as disingenuous.

In fact, the government involvement puts the NIH "contract" in a suspect category in the Berne and TRIPs context. It is not a private contract between commercial interests. Let me draw a hypothetical. The U.S. motion picture industry is now permitted to exhibit theatrically only 10 or so films per year in China. Suppose the government of China were to offer the American film producers a deal: "If you sign a contract waiving your reproduction right, we will allow you to exhibit 100 films a year." The producers would crunch the numbers and calculate the bottom line, even while complaining bitterly that the deal is outrageous and clearly a violation of the spirit of copyright and the Berne Convention. Nonetheless, they might conclude that on balance they would make more money with the proffered deal than they now make with limited access to the huge Chinese market. So, in the end, they might sign on the dotted line. Could the United States take that "contract" to the WTO and press a claim under TRIPs that China is not complying with its treaty obligations? I think so. The ensuing mass piracy of American films in China would be a direct result of this unwaivering government action that diminishes copyright, disguised as a "contract." In any case, the NIH free access policy is an unfortunate international precedent for a country like the United States, whose great strength is intellectual property.

The NIH should reconsider the long term consequences of its proposal. The dedicated researchers who benefit from the NIH grants take great professional pride in being published in prestigious learned journals, all of which constitute a valuable and reliable resource for future research. The NIH itself recognizes that "publication in peer-reviewed journals is a major factor in determining the professional standing of scientists; institutions use publication in peer-reviewed journals in making hiring, promotion, and tenure decisions."

Despite some grumbling about high subscription prices, very few researchers, academics, or librarians are suggesting that the journals have outlived their usefulness. The STM publishers should be given the right to compete fairly in a changing marketplace, in which they will innovate and have the opportunity to flourish on their own merits, as long as their copyrights are protected. Congress should require the NIH to demonstrate convincingly that their free access policy will not jeopardize the existence of the STM publishers and the indispensable role they play in vetting and selecting peer-reviewed articles. Absent that proof, the NIH should rethink their current policy of involuntary assignment. Current law gives the NIH some discretion in implementing their open access policy in a manner consistent with copyright. If the NIH do not amend their policy, Congress should direct them to do so. The Chairman's bill will allow the publishers to continue publishing. It will preserve the STM journals as valuable professional tools for scientific research, thereby promoting the progress of science. By restoring the status quo ante, the Chairman's bill will give the evolving free market a chance to come to grips with the new online technologies without undercutting the incentives that publishers have relied on for two hundred years. I would urge its enactment.

Ralph Oman is Pravel Professorial Lecturer in Intellectual Property Law and fellow of the Creative and Innovative Economy Center, The George Washington University Law School. He is a counsel for the intellectual property practice group of the firm Dechert, LLP, and has served as register of copyrights of the United States and as chief counsel of the Senate Subcommittee on Patents, Copyrights, and Trademarks.

Stuart M. Shieber    **NO**

Testimony before the U.S. House of Representatives Committee on Science, Space and Technology, Subcommittee on Investigations and Oversight, Hearing on "Examining Public Access and Scholarly Publication Interests"

The Potential for Open Access

The mission of the university is to create, preserve, and disseminate knowledge to the benefit of all. In Harvard's Faculty of Arts and Sciences (FAS), where I hold my faculty post, we codify this in the FAS Grey Book, which states that research policy "should encourage the notion that ideas or creative works produced at the University should be used for the greatest possible public benefit. This would normally mean the widest possible dissemination and use of such ideas or materials."

At one time, the widest possible dissemination was achieved by distributing the scholarly articles describing the fruits of research in the form of printed issues of peer-reviewed journals, sent to the research libraries of the world for reading by their patrons, and paid for by subscription fees. These fees covered the various services provided to the authors of the articles—management of the peer review process, copy-editing, typesetting, and other production processes—as well as the printing, binding, and shipping of the physical objects.

Thanks to the forward thinking of federal science funding agencies, including NSF, DARPA, NASA, and DOE, we now have available computing and networking technologies that hold the promise of transforming the mechanisms for disseminating and using knowledge in ways not imaginable even a few decades ago. The internet allows nearly instantaneous distribution of content for essentially zero marginal cost to a large and rapidly increasing proportion of humanity. Ideally, this would ramify in a universality of access to research results, thereby truly achieving the widest possible dissemination.

The benefits of such so-called *open access* are manifold. The signatories of the 2002 Budapest Open Access Initiative state that

> The public good [open access] make[s] possible is the world-wide electronic distribution of the peer-reviewed journal literature and completely free and unrestricted access to it by all scientists, scholars, teachers, students, and other curious minds. Removing access barriers to this literature will accelerate research, enrich education, share the learning of the rich with the poor and the poor with the rich, make this literature as useful as it can be, and lay the foundation for uniting humanity in a common intellectual conversation and quest for knowledge.

From a more pragmatic point of view, a large body of research has shown that public research has a large positive impact on economic growth, and that access to the scholarly literature is central to that impact. Martin and Tang's recent review of the literature concludes that "there have been numerous attempts to measure the economic impact of publicly funded research and development (R&D), all of which show a large positive contribution to economic growth." It is therefore not surprising that Houghton's modeling of the effect of broader public access to federally funded research shows that the benefits to the US economy come to the billions of dollars and are eight times the costs.

Opening access to the literature makes it available not only to human readers, but to computer processing as well. There are some million and a half scholarly

Shieber, Stuart M. From statement before U.S. House of Representatives, March 29, 2012.

articles published each year. No human can read them all or even the tiny fraction in a particular subfield, but computers can, and computer analysis of the text, known as *text mining,* has the potential not only to extract high-quality structured data from article databases but even to generate new research hypotheses. My own field of research, computational linguistics, includes text mining. I have collaborated with colleagues in the East Asian Languages and Civilization department on text mining of tens of thousands of classical Chinese biographies and with colleagues in the History department on computational analysis of pre-modern Latin texts. Performing similar analyses on the current research literature, however, is encumbered by proscriptions of copyright and contract because the dominant publishing mechanisms are not open.

In Harvard's response to the Office of Science and Technology Policy's request for information on public access, Provost Alan Garber highlighted the economic potential for the kinds of reuse enabled by open access.

> Public access not only facilitates innovation in research-driven industries such as medicine and manufacturing. It stimulates the growth of a new industry adding value to the newly accessible research itself. This new industry includes search, current awareness, impact measurement, data integration, citation linking, text and data mining, translation, indexing, organizing, recommending, and summarizing. These new services not only create new jobs and pay taxes, but they make the underlying research itself more useful. Research funding agencies needn't take on the job of provide all these services themselves. As long as they ensure that the funded research is digital, online, free of charge, and free for reuse, they can rely on an after-market of motivated developers and entrepreneurs to bring it to users in the forms in which it will be most useful. Indeed, scholarly publishers are themselves in a good position to provide many of these value-added services, which could provide an additional revenue source for the industry.

Finally, free and open access to the scholarly literature is an intrinsic good. It is in the interest of the researchers generating the research and those who might build upon it, the public who take interest in the research, the press who help interpret the results, and the government who funds these efforts. All things being equal, open access to the research literature ought to be the standard.

Systemic Problems in the Journal Publishing System

Unfortunately, over the last several years, it has become increasingly clear to many that this goal of the "widest possible dissemination" was in jeopardy because of systemic problems in the current mechanisms of scholarly communication, which are not able to take full advantage of the new technologies to maximize the access to research and therefore its potential for social good.

By way of background, I should review the standard process for disseminating research results. Scholars and researchers—often with government funding—perform research and write up their results in the form of articles, which are submitted to journals that are under the editorial control of the editor-in-chief and editorial boards made up of other scholars. These editors find appropriate reviewers, also scholars, to read and provide detailed reviews of the articles, which authors use to improve the quality of the articles. Reviewers also provide advice to the editors on whether the articles are appropriate for publication in the journal, the final decisions being made by the editors. Participants in these aspects of the publishing process are overwhelmingly volunteers, scholars who provide their time freely as a necessary part of their engagement in the research enterprise. The management of this process, handling the logistics, is typically performed by the journal's publisher, who receives the copyright in the article from the author for its services. The publisher also handles any further production process such as copy-editing and typesetting of accepted articles and their distribution to subscribers through print issue or more commonly these days through online access. This access is provided to researchers by their institutional libraries, which pay for annual subscriptions to the journals.

Libraries have observed with alarm a long-term dramatic rise in subscription costs of journals. The Association of Research Libraries, whose members represent the leading research libraries of the United States and Canada, have tracked serials expenditures for over three decades. From 1986 through 2010 (the most recent year with available data), expenditures in ARL libraries have increased by a factor of almost 5. Even discounting for inflation, the increase is almost 2.5 times. These increases correspond to an annualized rate of almost 7% per year, during a period in which inflation has averaged less than 3%.

Another diagnostic of the market dysfunction in the journal publishing system is the huge disparity in subscription costs between different journals. Bergstrom and Bergstrom showed that even within a single field of research, commercial journals are *on average* five times more expensive per page than non-profit journals. When compared by cost per citation, which controls better for journal quality, the disparity becomes even greater, a factor of 10 times. Odylzko notes that "The great disparity in costs among journals is a sign of an industry that has not had to worry about efficiency." Finally, the extraordinary profit margins, increasing even over the last few years while research libraries' budgets were under tremendous pressure, provide yet another signal of the absence of a functioning competitive market.

The Harvard library system is the largest academic library in the world, and the fifth largest library of any sort. In attempting to provide access to research results to our faculty and students, the university subscribes to tens of thousands of serials at a cost of about 9 million dollars per year. Nonetheless, we too have been buffeted by the tremendous growth in journal costs over the last decades, with Harvard's serials expenditures growing by a factor of 3 between 1986 and 2004. Such geometric increases in expenditures could not be sustained indefinitely. Over the years since 2004 our journal expenditure increases have been curtailed through an aggressive effort at deduplication, elimination of print subscriptions, and a painful series of journal cancellations. As a researcher, I know that Harvard does not subscribe to all of the journals that I would like access to for my own research, and if Harvard, with its scale, cannot provide optimal subscription access, other universities without our resources are in an even more restricted position.

Correspondingly, the articles that we ourselves generate as authors are not able to be accessed as broadly as we would like. We write articles not for direct financial gain—we are not paid for the articles and receive no royalties—but rather so that others can read them and make use of the discoveries they describe. To the extent that access is limited, those goals are thwarted.

The economic causes of these observed phenomena are quite understandable. Journal access is a monopolistic good. Libraries can buy access to a journal's articles only from the publisher of that journal, by virtue of the monopoly character of copyright. In addition, the high prices of journals are hidden from the "consumers" of the journals, the researchers reading the articles, because an intermediary, the library, pays the subscriptions on their behalf. The market therefore embeds a moral hazard. Under such conditions, market failure is not surprising; one would expect inelasticity of demand, hyperinflation, and inefficiency in the market, and that is what we observe. Prices inflate, leading to some libraries canceling journals, leading to further price increases to recoup revenue—a spiral that

ends in higher and higher prices paid by fewer and fewer libraries. The market is structured to provide institutions a Hobson's choice between unsustainable expenditures or reduced access.

The unfortunate side effect of this market dysfunction has been that as fewer libraries can afford the journals, access to the research results they contain is diminished. In 2005, then Provost of Harvard Steven Hyman appointed an ad hoc committee, which I chaired, to examine these issues and make recommendations as to what measures Harvard might pursue to mitigate this problem of access to our writings. Since then, we have been pursuing a variety of approaches to maximize access to the writings of Harvard researchers.

Addressing Insufficient Access Through an Open Access Policy

One of these approaches involves the self-imposition by faculty of an open-access policy according to which faculty grant a license to the university to distribute our scholarly articles and commit to providing copies of our manuscript articles for such distribution. By virtue of this kind of policy, the problem of access limitation is mitigated by providing a supplemental venue for access to the articles. Four years ago, in February of 2008, the members of the Faculty of Arts and Sciences at Harvard became the first school to enact such a policy, by unanimous vote as it turned out.

In order to guarantee the freedom of faculty authors to choose the rights situation for their articles, the license is waivable at the sole discretion of the author, so faculty retain control over whether the university is granted this license. But the policy has the effect that by default, the university holds a license to our articles, which can therefore be distributed from a repository that we have set up for that purpose. Since the FAS vote, six other schools at Harvard—Harvard Law School, Harvard Kennedy School of Government, Harvard Graduate School of Education, Harvard Business School, Harvard Divinity School, and Harvard Graduate School of Design—have passed this same kind of policy, and similar policies have been voted by faculty bodies at many other universities as well, including Massachusetts Institute of Technology, Stanford, Princeton, Columbia, and Duke. Notably, the policies have seen broad faculty support, with faculty imposing these policies on themselves typically by unanimous or near unanimous votes.

Because of these policies in the seven Harvard schools, Harvard's article repository, called DASH (for Digital

Access to Scholarship at Harvard), now provides access to over 7,000 articles representing 4,000 Harvard-affiliated authors. Articles in DASH have been downloaded almost three-quarters of a million times. The number of waivers of the license has been very small; we estimate the waiver rate at about 5%. Because of the policy, as faculty authors we are retaining rights to openly distribute the vast majority of the articles that we write.

The process of consultation in preparation for the faculty vote was a long one. I started speaking with faculty committees, departments, and individuals about two years before the actual vote. During that time and since, I have not met a single faculty member or researcher who objected to the principle underlying the open-access policies at Harvard, to obtain the widest possible dissemination for our scholarly results, and have been struck by the broad support for the kind of open dissemination of articles that the policy and the repository allow.

This approach to the access limitation problem, the provision of supplemental access venues, is also seen in the extraordinarily successful public access policy of the National Institutes of Health (NIH), which Congress mandated effective April, 2008. By virtue of that policy, researchers funded by NIH provide copies of their articles for distribution from NIH's PubMed Central (PMC) repository. Today, PMC provides free online access to 2.4 million articles downloaded a million times per day by half a million users. NIH's own analysis has shown that a quarter of the users are researchers. The hundreds of thousands of articles they are accessing per day demonstrates the large latent demand for articles not being satisfied by the journals' subscription base. Companies account for another 17%, showing that the policy benefits small businesses and corporations, who need access to scientific advances to spur innovation. Finally, the general public accounts for 40% of the users, some quarter of a million people per day, demonstrating that these articles are of tremendous interest to the taxpayers who fund the research in the first place and who deserve access to the results that they have underwritten.

The Standard Objection to Open Access Policies

The standard objection to these open-access policies is that supplemental access to scholarly articles, such as that provided by institutional repositories like Harvard's DASH or subject-based repositories like NIH's PubMed Central, could supplant subscription access to such an extent that subscriptions would come under substantial price pressure. Sufficient price pressure, in this scenario, could harm the

publishing industry, the viability of journals, and the peer review and journal production processes.

There is no question that the services provided by journals are valuable to the research enterprise, so such concerns must be taken seriously. By now, however, these arguments have been aired and addressed in great detail. I recommend the report "The Future of Taxpayer-Funded Research: Who Will Control Access to the Results?" by my co-panelist Elliott Maxwell, which provides detailed support for the report's conclusion that "There is no persuasive evidence that increased access threatens the sustainability of traditional subscription-supported journals, or their ability to fund rigorous peer review." The reasons are manifold, including the fact that supplemental access covers only a fraction of the articles in any given journal, is often delayed relative to publication, and typically provides a manuscript version of the article rather than the version of record. Consistent with this reasoning, the empirical evidence shows no such discernible effect. After four years of the NIH policy, for instance, subscription prices have continued to increase, as have publisher margins. The NIH states that "while the U.S. economy has suffered a downturn during the time period 2007 to 2011, scientific publishing has grown: The number of journals dedicated to publishing biological sciences/agriculture articles and medicine/health articles increased 15% and 19%, respectively. The average subscription prices of biology journals and health sciences journals increased 26% and 23%, respectively. Publishers forecast increases to the rate of growth of the medical journal market, from 4.5% in 2011 to 6.3% in 2014."

Open Access Journal Publishing as an Alternative to Subscription Journal Publishing

Nonetheless, it does not violate the laws of economics that increased supplemental access (even if delayed) to a sufficiently high proportion of articles (even if to a deprecated version) could put price pressure on subscription journals, perhaps even so much so that journals would not be able to recoup their costs. In this hypothetical case, would that be the end of journals? No, because even if publishers (again, merely by hypothesis and counterfactually) add no value for the readers (beyond what the readers are already getting in the [again hypothetical] universal open access), the author and the author's institution gain much value: vetting, copyediting, typesetting, and most importantly, imprimatur of the journal. This is value that authors and their institutions should be, would be, and are willing to pay for. The upshot is that journals will merely switch to a different business model, in which the journal charges a one-time *publication fee* to cover the costs of publishing the article.

I state this as though this publication-fee revenue model is itself hypothetical, but it is not. Open-access journals already exist in the thousands. They operate in exactly the same way as traditional subscription journals—providing management of peer review, production services, and distribution—with the sole exception that they do not charge for online access, so that access is free and open to anyone. The publication-fee revenue model for open-access journals is a proven mechanism. The prestigious non-profit open-access publisher Public Library of Science is generating surplus revenue and is on track to publish some 3% of the world biomedical literature through its journal *PLoS ONE* alone. The BioMed Central division of the commercial publisher Springer is generating profits for its parent company using the same revenue model. Indeed, the growth of open-access journals over the past few years has been meteoric. There are now over 7,000 open-access journals, many using the publication-fee model, and many of the largest, most established commercial journal publishers—Elsevier, Springer, Wiley-Blackwell, SAGE—now operate open-access journals using the publication-fee revenue model. Were supplemental access to cause sufficient price pressure to put the subscription model in danger, the result would merely be further uptake of this already burgeoning alternative revenue model.

In this scenario, the cost of journal publishing would be borne not by the libraries on behalf of their readers, but by funding agencies and research institutions on behalf of their authors. Already, funding agencies such as Wellcome Trust and Howard Hughes Medical Institute underwrite open access author charges, and in fact mandate open access. Federal granting agencies such as NSF and NIH allow grant funds to be used for open-access publication fees as well (though grantees must prebudget for these unpredictable charges). Not all fields have the sort of grant funding opportunities that could underwrite these fees. For those fields, the researcher's employing institution, as de facto funder of the research, should underwrite charges for publication in open-access journals. Here again, Harvard has taken an early stand as one of the initial signatories—along with Cornell, Dartmouth, MIT, and University of California, Berkeley—of the Compact for Open-Access Publishing Equity, which commits these universities and the dozen or so additional signatories to establishing mechanisms for underwriting reasonable open-access publication fees. The Compact acknowledges the fact that the services that journal publishers provide are important, cost money, and deserve to be funded, and commits the universities to doing so, albeit with a revenue model that avoids the market dysfunction of the subscription journal system.

Advantages of the Open Access Publishing System

The primary advantage of the open-access journal publishing system is the open access that it provides. Since revenue does not depend on limiting access to those willing to pay, journals have no incentive to limit access, and in fact have incentive to provide as broad access as possible to increase the value of their brand. In fact, open-access journals can provide access not only in the traditional sense, allowing anyone to access the articles for the purpose of reading them, but can provide the articles unencumbered by any use restrictions, thereby allowing the articles to be used, re-used, analyzed, and data-mined in ways we are not even able to predict.

A perhaps less obvious advantage of the publication-fee revenue model for open-access journals is that the factors leading to the subscription market failure do not inhere in the publication-fee model. Bergstrom and Bergstrom explain why:

> Journal articles differ [from conventional goods such as cars] in that they are not substitutes for each other in the same way as cars are. Rather, they are complements. Scientists are not satisfied with seeing only the top articles in their field. They want access to articles of the second and third rank as well. Thus for a library, a second copy of a top academic journal is not a good substitute for a journal of the second rank. Because of this lack of substitutability, commercial publishers of established second-rank journals have substantial monopoly power and are able to sell their product at prices that are much higher than their average costs and several times higher than the price of higher quality, non-profit journals.
>
> By contrast, the market for authors' inputs appears to be much more competitive. If journals supported themselves by author fees, it is not likely that one Open Access journal could charge author fees several times higher than those charged by another of similar quality. An author, deciding where to publish, is likely to consider different journals of similar quality as close substitutes. Unlike a reader, who would much prefer access to two journals rather than to two copies of one, an author with two papers has no strong

reason to prefer publishing once in each journal rather than twice in the cheaper one.

If the entire market were to switch from Reader Pays to Author Pays, competing journals would be closer substitutes in the view of authors than they are in the view of subscribers. As publishers shift from selling complements to selling substitutes, the greater competition would be likely to force commercial publishers to reduce their profit margins dramatically.

Again, the empirical evidence supports this view. Even the most expensive open-access publication fees, such as those of the prestigious Public Library of Science journals, are less than $3,000 per article, with a more typical value in the $1,000–1,500 range. By contrast, the average revenue per article for subscription journal articles is about $5,000. Thus, the open-access model better leverages free market principles: Despite providing unencumbered access to the literature, it costs no more overall per article, and may end up costing much less, than the current system. The savings to universities and funding agencies could be substantial.

Conclusion

I began my comments by quoting the mission of academics such as myself to provide the widest possible dissemination—open access—to the ideas and knowledge resulting from our research. Government, too, has an underlying goal of promoting the dissemination of knowledge, expressed in Thomas Jefferson's view that "by far the most important bill in our whole code is that for the diffusion of knowledge among the people." The federal agencies and science policies that this committee oversees have led to knowledge breakthroughs of the most fundamental sort—in our understanding of the physical universe, in our ability to comprehend fundamental biological processes, and, in my own field, in the revolutionary abilities to transform and transmit information.

Open access policies build on these information technology breakthroughs to maximize the return on the taxpayers' enormous investment in that research, and magnify the usefulness of that research. They bring economic benefits that far exceed the costs. The NIH has shown one successful model, which could be replicated at other funding agencies, as envisioned in the recently re-introduced bipartisan Federal Research Public Access Act (FRPAA).

Providing open access to the publicly-funded research literature—amplifying the "diffusion of knowledge"—will benefit researchers, taxpayers, and every person who gains from new medicines, new technologies, new jobs, and new solutions to longstanding problems of every kind.

STUART M. SHIEBER is the James O. Welch, Jr., and Virginia B. Welch Professor of computer science at Harvard University. As a faculty member, he led the development and enactment of Harvard's open access policies. He also serves as the faculty director of Harvard's Office for Scholarly Communication.

EXPLORING THE ISSUE

Should the Public Have to Pay to See the Results of Federally Funded Research?

Critical Thinking and Reflection

1. How does peer review help to ensure the quality of scientific publications?
2. Are "open access" and "peer review" mutually contradictory concepts?
3. Why can university libraries not subscribe to all available high-quality academic journals?
4. Should academic publishing be profit oriented?

Is There Common Ground?

At the core of the debate lie two points: the right of academic publishers to make a profit and the right of the public to have access to the fruits of scientific research. High journal prices favor the former while impeding the latter. In one form, open access publishing says the academic publishers can make a profit for a limited time before articles get put into open access archives. On the other hand, no one really expects open access publishing to completely displace the traditional mode; see Jocelyn Kaiser, "Free Journals Grow Amid Ongoing Debate," *Science* (August 20, 2010).

1. Is this form of open access publishing a viable compromise?
2. Some areas of science have long circulated preprints of articles to give other scientists and even the public a first look at reports. Journals later publish edited, peer-reviewed versions of the reports. Is this a viable compromise?

3. What services do journal publishers provide to researchers? Do these services justify high journal prices?
4. If we reject the idea that academic publishing should be profit oriented, how can the publishers remain in business? Should academic publishing be run by the government?

Additional Resources

Theodora Bloom, et al., "PLoS Biology at 5: The Future Is Open Access," *PLoS Biology* (October 2008).

Jennifer Howard, "Legislation to Bar Public-Access Requirement on Federal Research Is Dead," *The Chronicle of Higher Education* (February 27, 2012).

Jocelyn Kaiser, "Free Journals Grow Amid Ongoing Debate," *Science* (August 20, 2010).

Michael P. Taylor, "Opinion: Academic Publishing Is Broken: The Current System by Which Academics Publish Their Scientific Discoveries Is a Massive Waste of Money," *The Scientist* (March 19, 2012).

Internet References . . .

Directory of Open Access Journals

The Directory of Open Access Journals lists over 8,000 free, full-text, quality-controlled scientific and scholarly journals, many of which can be searched at the article level.

www.doaj.org/

BioMed Central Open Access Charter

BioMed Central calls itself the "open access publisher." It defines open access publishing as making materials "universally and freely accessible via the Internet, in an easily readable format . . . immediately upon publication" and commits itself to maintaining an open access policy.

www.biomedcentral.com

Selected, Edited, and with Issue Framing Material by:
Thomas A. Easton, *Mount Ida College*

ISSUE

Can Science Be Trusted Without Government Regulation?

YES: David R. Franz, from "The Dual Use Dilemma: Crying Out for Leadership," *Saint Louis University Journal of Health Law & Policy* (2013)

NO: Robert Gatter, from "Regulating Dual Use Research to Promote Public Trust: A Reply to Dr. Franz," *Saint Louis University Journal of Health Law & Policy* (2013)

Learning Outcomes

After reading this issue, you will be able to:

- Explain what "dual-use" research is.
- Explain why a government agency would ask researchers and journal editors to leave details out of a scientific paper.
- Describe the role of responsible laboratory leadership in preventing breaches of biosecurity.
- Discuss the role of government regulation in preventing breaches of biosecurity.

ISSUE SUMMARY

YES: David R. Franz argues that "when rules for the few become too disruptive to the work of the many, communities of trust can break down." Exceptional research leaders create a culture of responsibility in which safety rulebooks can be thin and their laboratories will be safer, more secure, and more productive. Government regulation leads to thicker rulebooks and more wasted effort without increasing safety and security.

NO: Robert Gatter argues that the research enterprise must be trustworthy to the public at large. Because scientists share a bias in favor of discovery rather than public safety, they cannot be trusted to regulate themselves. Government regulation is essential.

"**D**ual Use Research of Concern," or DURC, is now a widespread concern. According to the National Science Advisory Board for Biosecurity (NSABB), it means "research that, based on current understanding, can be reasonably anticipated to provide knowledge, products, or technologies that could be directly misapplied by others to pose a threat to public health and safety, agricultural crops and other plants, animals, the environment or materiel." A major question being debated among scientists, bureaucrats, and legislators, among others, is how to enjoy the benefits of DURC without having to face the risks.

The topic came to prominence with research on the H5N1 bird flu. H5N1 is deadly to domestic poultry. Occasionally it infects people, and the death rate among those who are taken to hospitals is about 60 percent (no one knows how many cases are not taken to hospitals; the actual death rate may be much less). Fortunately, the virus does not spread easily from human to human. In an effort to understand why, research teams led by Ron Fouchier of Erasmus MC in Rotterdam, the Netherlands, and Yoshihiro Kawaoka of the University of Wisconsin, Madison, modified the virus so that it could move more easily through the air between ferrets (which respond to flu similarly to humans), and potentially from human to human. In the fall of 2011, the two teams submitted papers to *Nature* and *Science* explaining how they had modified the virus. The journals accepted the papers but delayed publication while the United States' National Science Advisory Board for Biosecurity (NSABB) deliberated over whether key details should be removed or "redacted" from the papers (and made available only to researchers with a clear need to know) in order to prevent terrorists from learning how to create a flu pandemic (widespread epidemic). Critics called the modified virus an "Armageddon virus," and the media—*CNN*, the *New York Times*, *Time*, and many other magazines and blogs—gave the story major attention. There was even a call on Facebook to suppress the research. The potentials for bioterrorism and accidental releases from labs were major concerns; see Laurie Garrett, "The Bioterrorist Next Door," *Foreign Policy* (December 15, 2011), Fred Guterl, "Waiting to Explode," *Scientific American* (June 2012), and Tina Hesman Saey, "Designer Flu," *Science News* (June 2, 2012).

Those who oppose redaction argue that the details may be crucial to identifying a dangerous pandemic in its early stages and mounting an appropriate response; see Jon Cohen, "Does Forewarned = Forearmed with Lab-Made Avian Influenza Strains?" *Science* (February 17, 2012). In December 2011 the NSABB recommended redaction, and soon thereafter the researchers announced a 60-day moratorium on further research (the moratorium has since then been extended); see Josh Fischman, "Science and Security Clash on Bird-Flu Papers," *Chronicle of Higher Education* (January 6, 2012), and Alice Park, "Scientists Agree to Halt Work on Dangerous Bird Flu Strain," *Time* (January 20, 2012).

Some scientists cautioned that the modified flu virus may not actually be a serious threat and urged the NSABB to reconsider its decision. In February 2012, the World Health Organization (WHO) convened a group of flu researchers, public health officials, and journal editors from eleven countries to discuss the issue. The group recommended that the papers be published with all their details. On March 29, 2012, the U.S. government issued a "Policy for Oversight of Life Sciences Dual Use Research of Concern" (http://oba.od.nih.gov/oba/biosecurity /pdf/united_states_government_policy_for_oversight_of_durc _final_version_032812.pdf). Very shortly afterwards, the NSABB re-reviewed the H5N1 papers and recommended publication in full. See Jon Cohen and David Malakoff, "On Second Thought, Flu Papers Get Go-Ahead," *Science* (April 6, 2012). The *Nature* paper, Masaki Imai, et al., "Experimental Adaptation of an Influenza H5 HA Confers Respiratory Droplet Transmission to a Reassortant H5

HA/H1N1 Virus in Ferrets" (http://www.nature.com/nature /journal/vaop/ncurrent/full/nature10831.html), appeared online May 2, 2012, and on paper June 21, 2012. The *Science* paper, Sander Herfst, et al., "Airborne Transmission of Influenza A/H5N1 Virus Between Ferrets" (http://www .sciencemag.org/content/336/6088/1534.full), was published on June 22, 2012, along with several essays reviewing the situation and an attempt to assess the likelihood that the virus could actually jump to humans and cause problems. Critics remain concerned that, as Thomas Ingleby of the Center for Biosecurity of the University of Pittsburgh Medical Center said, "We are playing with fire"; see Libby Lewis, "Science Journal Could Give Recipe for Deadly Avian Flu Virus," CNN (May 12, 2012) (http://www.cnn.com/2012/05/12/us/journal-avian-flu/index .html). By late 2012, a National Institutes of Health (NIH) plan that would call for stringent reviews of whether similar research should receive government funding, or even be classified, was being discussed by the NSABB; see David Malakoff, "Proposed H5N1 Research Reviews Raise Concerns," *Science* (December 7, 2012), and David Malakoff and Martin Enserink, "New U.S. Rules Increase Oversight of H5N1 Studies, Other Risky Science," *Science* (March 1, 2013).

The debate over whether publication of the details of the bird-flu papers should be redacted or not has been intense. Concern that they may lead to new and more onerous controls on research and publication seem to have been justified; see David Malakoff, "U.S. Agencies to Start Screening Biomedical Proposals for Dual Use," *Science* (April 6, 2012). Despite new controls, however, researchers are eager to resume research in this area; see David Malakoff, "H5N1 Researchers Ready as Moratorium Nears End," *Science* (January 4, 2013).

The basic question of control over scientific and technical knowledge is not new. In 2001, the destruction of New York's World Trade Towers and the unrelated mailing of anthrax spores to several public figures created a climate of fear and mistrust that led to heightened concern about security. Part of that fear and mistrust was aimed at science and technology, for the al Qaeda terrorists had used computers and the Internet for communicating with each other and the person responsible for the anthrax scare (currently thought to be anthrax researcher Bruce Ivins; see David Willman, *The Mirage Man: Bruce Ivins, the Anthrax Attacks, and America's Rush to War* [Bantam, 2011]) obviously knew too much about anthrax.

"Even before . . . 2001, White House directives and agencies used the label SBU [sensitive but unclassified] to safeguard from public disclosure information that does not meet the standards for classification"; see Genevieve J. Knezo, "'Sensitive but Unclassified' and Other Federal Security Controls on Scientific and Technical Information: History and Current Controversy" (Congressional Research Service Report for Congress, April 2, 2003). See also John D. Kraemer and Lawrence O. Gostin, "The Limits of Government Regulation of Science," *Science* (March 2, 2012). In March 2002, the Bush Administration declared that some information—notably the results of scientific research, especially in the life sciences—might not be classified in the ways long familiar to researchers in nuclear physics (for instance), but it could still be considered "sensitive" and thus worthy of restrictions on publication and dissemination. The Defense Department announced—and promptly dropped—plans to restrict the use and spread of unclassified DoD-funded research. However, a National Academy of Sciences report on agricultural bioterrorism that contained no classified information was censored on the insistence of the Department of Agriculture "to keep potentially dangerous information away from enemies of the United States." National security experts warned "that the current system of openness in science could lead to dire consequences." See Richard Monastersky, "Publish and Perish?" *Chronicle of Higher Education* (October 11, 2002). However, many have objected to inventing and attempting to restrict the new "sensitive but unclassified" category of information. Steven Teitelbaum, president of the Federation of American Societies for Experimental Biology, said, "information should be either classified or not classified." Charles M. Vest, in "Response and Responsibility: Balancing Security and Openness in Research and Education," *Report of the President for the Academic Year 2001–2002* (Cambridge, MA: Massachusetts Institute of Technology, 2002), argued that openness in science must preempt fears of the consequences of scientific knowledge falling into the wrong hands.

In July 2002, researchers announced that they had successfully assembled a polio virus from biochemicals and the virus's gene map. Members of Congress called for more care in releasing such information, and the American Society for Microbiology (ASM) began to debate voluntary restrictions on publication. By August 2002, the ASM had policy guidelines dictating that journal submissions that contain "information . . . that could be put to inappropriate use" be carefully reviewed and even rejected; see David Malakoff, "Researchers See Progress in Finding the Right Balance," *Science* (October 18, 2002). Soon thereafter, the federal government took its own steps in the same direction with the formation of the NSABB; see Jennifer

Couzin, "U.S. Agencies Unveil Plan for Biosecurity Peer Review," *Science* (March 12, 2004).

In October 2005, scientists reassembled the deadly 1918 flu from synthesized subunits (see Phillip A. Sharp, "1918 Flu and Responsible Science" [Editorial], *Science,* October 7, 2005). In 2006, there were calls for authors, journal editors, and reviewers to do risk-benefit analysis before publishing "dual-use" work (see Yudhijit Bhattacharjee, "U.S. Panel Calls for Extra Review of Dual-Use Research," *Science,* July 21, 2006, and Robert F. Service, "Synthetic Biologists Debate Policing Themselves," *Science,* May 26, 2006). The relevance of the debate outside biology became clear when researchers omitted important details from a study of how a dirty-bomb attack could affect Los Angeles harbor (see Yudhijit Bhattacharjee, "Should Academics Self-Censor Their Findings on Terrorism?" *Science,* May 19, 2006).

A paper by Lawrence M. Wein and Yifan Liu, "Analyzing a Bioterror Attack on the Food Supply: The Case of Botulinum Toxin in Milk," on how terrorists might attack the U.S. milk supply and on how to safeguard it, was scheduled for the May 30, 2005, issue of the *Proceedings of the National Academy of Sciences.* However, Stewart Simonson, Assistant Secretary of the Department of Health and Human Services, asked the NAS not to publish the paper on the grounds that it provides "a road map for terrorists and publication is not in the interests of the United States." The journal put the paper on hold while it studied the issue; it appeared online (http://www.pnas.org /cgi/content/abstract/0408526102v1) on June 28, 2005, and in print in the July 12, 2005, issue of *PNAS.* The Department of Health and Human Services continues to believe publication is a mistake, for the "consequences could be dire." It should come as no surprise that Frida Kuhlau, Anna T. Hoglund, Kathinka Evers, and Stefan Eriksson, "A Precautionary Principle for Dual Use Research in the Life Sciences," *Bioethics* (January 2011), note that the precautionary principle—more familiar in environmental and public health contexts—may reasonably be applied to dual-use biological research.

When in March/April 2006, *Technology Review* published Mark Williams' "The Knowledge," which stressed the ominous implications of current knowledge and the ready availability of materials and equipment (DNA synthesizers can be bought on eBay!), it also published a rebuttal. Allison M. Macfarlane, "Assessing the Threat," *Technology Review* (March/April 2006), noted that turning biological agents of destruction into useful weapons is much harder than it seems and the real hazards are impossible to estimate without more research. For now, she thinks, it makes more sense to focus on more imminent threats, such as those involving nuclear weapons.

Are there other possible answers besides restricting—voluntarily or otherwise—publication of potentially hazardous work? In an editorial, "Dual-Use Research of Concern: Publish *and* Perish?" *Indian Journal of Medical Research* (January 2011), K. Satyanarayana finds that "the real challenges would continue to be governance and enforcement as scientists are clearly averse to any external intervention." John D. Steinbruner and Elisa D. Harris, "Controlling Dangerous Pathogens," *Issues in Science and Technology* (Spring 2003), call for a global body that could oversee and regulate potentially dangerous disease research. Robert H. Sprinkle proposes "The Biosecurity Trust," *Bioscience* (March 2003). Ruth R. Faden and Ruth A. Karron, "The Obligation to Prevent the Next Dual-Use Controversy," *Science* (February 11, 2012), argue that the need for some such oversight mechanism is urgent. No such organization yet exists, although the new screening rules are a step in that direction.

On February 22, 2013, the *Saint Louis University Journal of Health Law & Policy* and the Center for Health Law Studies at that school held a symposium on "Regulating Dual-Use Research in Life Sciences." At the same time, the U.S. government released proposed rules for regulating DURC, which led to lively discussions during the symposium. Two participants in those discussions were David R. Franz and Robert Gatter. In the YES selection, Dr. Franz argues that "when rules for the few become too disruptive to the work of the many, communities of trust can break down." Exceptional research leaders create a culture of responsibility in which safety rulebooks can be thin and their laboratories will be safer, more secure, and more productive. Government regulation leads to thicker rulebooks and more wasted effort without increasing safety and security. In the NO selection, Dr. Gatter argues that the research enterprise must be trustworthy to the public at large. Because scientists share a bias in favor of discovery rather than public safety, they cannot be trusted to regulate themselves. Government regulation is essential.

David R. Franz

The Dual Use Dilemma: Crying Out for Leadership

I. Introduction

Between October 2011 and March 2012, a controversy regarding the publication of results of H5N1 influenza virus research by two scientists led to additional oversight of a relatively broad segment of the infectious disease research enterprise in the U.S. The episode has been described as an example of the "dual use dilemma," legitimate and open research that could be exploited for harm by others. Why is *leadership* important in the context of the dual use dilemma? Is not dual use about technology and knowledge being misused for harm? Can we not just control the knowledge and technologies? How is the dual use dilemma related to the *insider threat* in research and clinical laboratories? What is our interest in these low likelihood events in twenty-first century America? The recent concern regarding Dual Use Research (DUR) is focused on the traditional agents of biological warfare and the influenza viruses. Yet, these *Select Agents* are but a small part of the spectrum of biological threats and risks we humans, our animals, and plants face today. Therefore, Dual Use Research of Concern (DURC) cannot be understood in isolation. What follows is a short history of the misuse—and use—of biology in what will always be a dangerous world. We cannot reduce risk to zero, but we can increase safety, security, and productivity in our laboratories without layering another set of regulations over the enterprise each time an individual scientist does something thoughtless or even malevolent.

II. DURC Background

A. A Short History of Laboratory Biosafety—1940s Onward

The U.S. conducted offensive biological warfare research, development, and field-testing from mid-1942 until late 1969, when President Nixon traveled to Fort Detrick,

Maryland, to announce that the U.S. would end its biological weapons program two National Security memoranda, the first dated November 25, 1969, and the second February 20, 1970, the U.S. Government renounced development, production, and stockpiling of biological weapons. Further, the U.S. declared its intent to maintain only quantities of agents necessary for the development of vaccines, drugs, and diagnostics. While I am convinced the weapons testing during the more than 25 years of the offensive program demonstrated *nuclear equivalence* of biological weapons, the real legacy of this program is the development and implementation of the foundational principles of modern laboratory biological *safety*.

During the 1960s, Dr. Arnold G. Wedum, M.D., Ph.D, Director of Industrial Health and Safety at Fort Detrick, was the principal proponent and leader of a system of containment facilities, equipment, and procedures developed to greatly enhance the safety of the employees of the offensive program and the rural community in which the core laboratories were operated. Many of Dr. Wedum's principles of biological safety served as the basis for the U.S. Centers for Disease Control and Prevention's (CDC) publication called *Biosafety in Microbiological and Biomedical Laboratories* (BMBL). The BMBL is now updated regularly and has become the biosafety *bible* in laboratories around the globe. Thus, in what we might today call a reverse dual use model, some very important good has ultimately come from a program that was designed to do harm.

By the end of the twentieth century, the principles of biosafety—facilities, equipment, and procedures—were codified, enhanced, respected, and followed by the scientists in the relatively few high containment labs in the U.S. The original U.S. high-containment labs were commissioned from 1971 to 1972 at Fort Detrick within the U.S. Army Medical Research Institute of Infectious Diseases (USAMRIID), and in Atlanta at the CDC just a few years later.

I served as Deputy Commander (1993–1995) and Commander (1995–1998) of USAMRIID. My command briefings during the mid-90s often listed three top priorities—"biosafety, biosafety, and biosafety." We had good people in harm's way during peacetime and in war in Biosafety Level-4 (BSL-4) labs where one needle stick, one bone fragment through a surgical glove, or even the bite of an infected laboratory animal could mean almost certain death to a scientist or technician. While the institute was located on a fenced and guarded military installation with twenty-four hour unarmed guards, as well as redundant locking systems with personal identification number codes for laboratory suite entry, my focus was on the safety of the employees and the community, as well as the productivity of our laboratory. I learned in those six years that the same leadership approach that makes people safe, makes an organization productive, and gives a community a sense of well being, is based on nurturing a culture of responsibility and trust.

B. Laboratory Biosecurity—Mid-90s and Beyond

In 1995, Mr. Larry Wayne Harris mailed a letter requesting an isolate of *Yersinia pestis (Y. pestis)*, the plague bacillus, from the American Type Culture Collection (ATCC) in Manassas, Virginia. It was eventually discovered that the letterhead he used—"Small Animal Microbiology Laboratory, 266 Cleveland Avenue, Lancaster, Ohio" and the "Ohio Environmental Protection Agency approval number 890"—were fraudulent. While the ATCC ultimately shipped the vials of *Y. pestis*, Mr. Harris became impatient and called to follow up on his order. In doing so, he alerted authorities and the Federal Bureau of Investigation (FBI) became involved. While other incidents—Aum Shinrikyo sarin attack in Tokyo on March 20, 1995 and the B'nai B'rith incident in Washington D.C. involving a petri dish of *B. cereus* in 1997—contributed to our increased concern about both the illicit acquisition and malevolent use of biological agents, it was the Harris incident that most greatly influenced our thinking regarding laboratory biological *security* in the U.S.

The Select Agent Rule became law and was implemented in 1997. This new rule made the transfer between laboratories illegal for designated bacteria, viruses, or toxins without CDC approval. Intially, the rule only affected agent transfers, which meant that many academic and clinical labs with select agent pathogens could maintain them without breaking the law. Only after an inspection by the CDC (or, for some pathogens, the U.S. Department of Agriculture) could a laboratory be certified to transfer pathogens on the list, and then once certified, transfer only to a similarly certified laboratory. The era of laboratory biosecurity had begun. As a result of his actions, Harris, the individual most directly responsible for the Select Agent Rule, was required to complete 200 hours of community service. Legitimate research with the listed agents would forever be more costly and probably less productive in government, academic, and industrial labs where the new rules were promulgated.

C. DURC—2003 and Beyond

The World Trade Center attacks on September 11, 2001 (9/11), and the first case of inhalational anthrax concerning the anthrax letters discovered on October 4, 2001 (1 0/4), changed everything. The U.S. biosecurity budget went from $137 million in 1997, to $14.5 billion spent on biodefense from 2001 to 2004. Soon many more laboratories sought and received Select Agent certification.

Today, it is almost impossible to put one's mind back into the state of infectious disease research before 2002, when thousands of new scientists began working with this short list of threat agents. After 9/11, 10/4, and the increased funding for new high-containment labs and Select Agent research, the next layer of DURC regulation in the life sciences was beginning to unfold. It would take another legitimate, even respected scientist, this time not trying to do harm, but possibly for personal or professional gain, to drive the U.S. Government to further regulate the traditional select agents and influenza viruses.

About ten years before the 2012 controversy regarding the publication of information on the intentional development of a recombinant H5N1 influenza virus transmissible between mammals, there was the reasonable observation by the U.S. biological sciences community that it should "think about policing itself" before the government intervened with undue regulation. The now well-known Fink Report by the National Academies of Science, *Biotechnology Research in an Age of Terrorism: The Dual-Use Dilemma*, was a direct result. At that time, factors that triggered the perceived need for the study and subsequent report included: (1) a surprise result of Australian attempts to design a rodent sterilization virus, (2) the second *de novo* synthesis of poliovirus from a "web recipe," and (3) a new understanding of the implications of the Smallpox Inhibitor of Complement Enzymes "SPICE gene" in orthopox viruses.

The nation was now working in a backdrop of 9/ll and 10/4, so misuse of biology was on our minds. Although the term "dual use" had been used in other settings, it was the Fink Report that really codified the term in this context. The Fink Report also suggested that a national-level committee be formed and composed of equal numbers of biology and security experts to help the government cope with the dual use dilemma. The eventual response from the U.S. Government was the formation of the National Science Advisory Board for Biosecurity (NSABB) in 2004. Initially, the NSABB described DUR as "research yielding new technologies or information with the potential for both benevolent and malevolent applications. . . ." Later, after realizing that a significant percentage of the technology and knowledge in the life sciences enterprise could be used for good or harm, the NSABB chose the term DURC to define a subset of dual use knowledge and technologies. The NSABB described DURC as "research that, based on current understanding, can be reasonably anticipated to provide knowledge, products, or technologies that could be directly misapplied by others to pose a threat to public health and safety, agricultural crops and other plants, animals, the environment or materiel." . . .

III. Regulatory Approaches: Value and Cost

. . . Actions to protect us have taken place in the name of public safety and security. The Antiterrorism and Effective Death Penalty Act of 1996, the Select Agent Rule, Army Regulation 50-1, and the new DURC policies are all domestic U.S. Government actions. These regulations are wide nets cast, rather than leadership-based approaches, to deal with troubled or frustrated personnel more broadly. Due to the nature of the dual use dilemma (technical surprise or ethical lapse) and insider threat (individual or small group sociopathic behavior), these wide cast, but superficial regulatory nets are, at best, very blunt instruments. Very few studies have looked at the productivity of the enterprise before and after 2001, but the subject deserves our attention. At least anecdotally, compliance with these regulatory approaches has forced laboratories to hire additional contractors to manage the programs, which has diverted funds from legitimate research, subsequently slowing progress. Even with these regulations in place, the U.S. Government cannot assure increased security.

Possibly the greatest value in the international laws and resolutions is in their role as norms, tools of education, and awareness. Further, dialogues around international laws and resolutions have led to some increased understanding by bringing experts from many nations together to discuss them, as well as the visible boundary lines which they paint on the life sciences court. In other cases, the international laws have been barriers to communication and understanding. Regulations may do harm when they overburden the life sciences community or build walls internationally, instead of simply painting the boundary lines. Internationally, there have been more focused actions for nations who crossed the line: the Trilateral Agreements (because of Former Soviet Union behavior) and UNSCR 687 (in response to Iraqi behavior). Domestically, . . . individual acts . . . have increased oversight, and broad regulatory management has become the norm within the life sciences community.

IV. Why So Little Emphasis on Leadership?

A. Leadership Models

During the past 20 years, the role of leaders, particularly in U.S. Government laboratories where insider threats seem to be of greater concern than DURC, have changed dramatically. In this regard, the period before 9/11 can be clearly differentiated from the period after. In the past, laboratory leaders grew up within their organizations, took personal responsibility for their organizations, and molded laboratory cultures in a way that resulted in productivity and safety. Security was viewed differently before 9/11, but was appropriate for that day and time. Patriotism and teamwork were underlying principles, and the mission and focus on scientific ethics was the norm.

Leaders who knew their organizations well also knew their people well enough to practice preventive intervention in the rare case of outlier behavior. The troubled scientist would seek out the leader for help if trust was there or the leader would observe and intervene in time if the leader was enlightened and appropriately engaged. Outlier employees were counseled and helped or weeded from the organization. A self-centered, arrogant, or insensitive manager would miss the warning signs, and thus, be unable to avert disaster. Such poor leaders did not last in those days. Today, there is much less thought given to these issues. Rather, much more time is spent trying to assure compliance with regulations. The challenge of heavy-handed regulation is also facing academic researchers in this country today.

B. Really Hard, but Rare Problems with No Perfect Solution

We are dealing with two very hard problems in a very complex, even messy, world today. The spectrum of natural disease kills millions of people globally each year. Our government has focused enormous energy and treasure on hopefully rare, but potentially high-impact intentional events. Much of this is related to the *terror* factor and the vast unknowns. Most Americans do not notice the deaths of 50,000 humans from seasonal influenza complications, 30,000 from auto accidents, or even the 10,000 deaths associated with gun homicides annually, unless they involve one of our loved ones. Yet, the unknowns frighten us. As we face fiscal constraints nationally, the challenge is to balance our preparations and resolve regarding those vast unknowns.

Dr. Lederberg told us "there is no technical solution." He proposed ethical or moral solutions, but acknowledged that such personal controls would not appeal to an individual set on doing harm. Just as epidemiologists tell us that protecting a percentage of a population with a vaccine will indirectly protect unvaccinated individuals within a population, so too, establishing a corporate culture of responsibility will help reduce the likelihood that an individual within that culture will go astray.

Secretary of the Navy, Richard Danzig, Ph.D., has told us that "we are driving in the dark" with regard to understanding the risk in national security. We cannot know what lies ahead. We have spent time and hundreds of millions of dollars trying to predict what is coming and for what to prepare. The insider threat is a very hard case while the DURC challenge is also difficult, but more easily dealt with. Interestingly, both respond to a very similar set of behavioral tools. We are much more likely to divert, dissuade, deter, or just discover individuals prone to either course in a healthy corporate culture than in an unhealthy one. So we get two-for-one—DURC and the insider threat—protection in a healthy life sciences laboratory culture.

C. Rethinking DURC: Did the Science Community Do the Right Thing?

It's not surprising that we have focused our energies on the technologies, the science, and the microbiological agents rather than on the behavior of the scientists. At the national level, our elected officials seek to do something to make the public feel safer, so they regulate what they cannot directly control. For DUR, it started with the beloved Fink Report, so we must bear part of the responsibility. When we called it DUR and listed the seven examples of research that might be misused, we forced ourselves to look at the technologies, the knowledge, and the science. If we had instead called for "Responsible Life Science Research," the term now preferred by many of our international colleagues, we would have had to focus on human behavior. I believe more effective outcomes would have resulted if we had focused more on individual and corporate responsibility than on regulation to control technologies and knowledge. No matter if the individual scientist is armed with an oligonucleotide synthesizer or the organization with a freezer full of Select Agents, they are less likely to do harm with them in a healthy laboratory culture than in an unhealthy one.

D. Leadership and DURC or Actually "Responsible Life Sciences Research"

Leadership is related only indirectly to DUR, but it is very much related to responsibility, which is the real problem. Leaders, by definition, demonstrate personal responsibility and they, by definition, develop cultures of responsibility in the organizations that they lead. Responsible organizations contribute, again with enormous influence by their leaders, to networks of responsibility. Responsible leaders, groups of responsible individuals, and networks of responsible groups provide *herd immunity* that protects the whole. It's simple, but it requires smart, caring, humble, and strong leaders throughout the organization. . . .

Humility is not the first word that comes to mind when the average person thinks about leadership; it is probably power, authority, or even arrogance. But humility is absolutely essential to great leadership and what is sometimes perceived as arrogance is often simply confidence. Humility facilitates another characteristic of a great leader—appreciating employees who are smarter than you. Bo Peabody, in his book, *Lucky or Smart? Secrets to an Entrepreneurial Life,* tells would-be entrepreneurs to create an environment where smart people gather and then be smart enough to stay out of the way. He goes on to say that managers are A-students and entrepreneurs are B-students. Likewise, it is not unusual to find that the best leaders are very comfortable when surrounded by people who are smarter than they.

In industry and even in academia today, the great leaders rise to the top on merit. As the moral underpinnings of the electorate weaken, elected officials in a democracy can become more interested in their own position of authority than the good of their electorate or even their nation. When they do, their inclination is to try to *control* when the issues are too complex for them to resolve quickly and easily. As in the case with DURC and the insider threat, they often choose to regulate and in doing so, upset the balance between appropriate regulation and freedom. An over-regulated individual, organization, or nation will not attain its full potential.

V. Conclusion

A. Our Place in the World

Exceptional leaders and thinkers drafted the intellectual and legal foundation of the U.S. We were made a free and powerful nation by great leaders. Leaders in our most productive laboratories demonstrate personal responsibility and inculcate corporate responsibility. With the global proliferation of biological technologies and knowledge, we now face well-qualified and serious competition in the life sciences. Patrick Lencioni, in his book, *Healthy Organizations,* states "because of this global competition, it will become ever more difficult to have a competitive advantage based on knowledge and technologies," but a healthy organization can compete on this new, more level playing field. DURC issues and insider threat are rare, but potentially harmful outcomes of the life sciences enterprise. Both are outlier risks that are more likely to occur in an unhealthy or poorly led organization.

Personal and corporate responsibility provide herd immunity, which can protect, rehabilitate, or ferret out the outliers in an organization. Communities of trust characterize the kind of corporate responsibility typically orchestrated by enlightened leadership. Every organization needs regulation; we must know the boundaries of the playing field and the rules of the game. The greater the potential for injury in the game, the thicker the rulebook. The safety rulebook in a high-containment infectious disease laboratory is *thick* and applies to everyone. The DURC and the insider threat rulebooks are there for the outliers, but they impact all of us. When rules for the few become too disruptive to the work of the many, communities of trust can break down. Laboratories with exceptional leaders armed with well thought-out and *thin* DURC and insider threat rulebooks will always be safer, more secure, and far more productive than laboratories where the many are overregulated because of the few. It takes courage to do the right thing—to mentor, grow leaders, and then give them the responsibility, authority, and the freedom to succeed. Will we find leaders with the wisdom and the moral courage to rebalance our approach to DURC and the insider threat?

DAVID R. FRANZ is former Commander of the U.S. Army Medical Research Institute of Infectious Diseases (AMRIID) and a founding member of the National Science Advisory Board for Biosecurity. His current focus is responsible life sciences research and the role of international engagement as a component of global biosecurity policy.

Robert Gatter

 **NO**

Regulating Dual Use Research to Promote Public Trust: A Reply to Dr. Franz

. . . **D**r. David Franz makes a persuasive argument that protecting the public against risks posed by dual use research of concern (DURC) requires strong leadership among scientists who manage the laboratories in which such research takes place. Among other things, he calls on scientists, regulators, and others interested in DURC oversight to devote as much attention to developing stronger laboratory leadership as has been spent on creating rules and regulations.

Importantly, Dr. Franz is skeptical of the government's regulating scientists and research institutions, including the newly proposed federal rules concerning DURC. He writes that regulations cannot make us safe in the face of dual use risks and that, instead, they create compliance tasks that distract scientists and divert resources from research.

More fundamentally, Dr. Franz depicts life science research as "over-regulated" and argues that such regulation is antithetical to maintaining laboratories as "communities of trust" in which safe and productive research can take place. Indeed, this is the closing message of his article. After acknowledging that regulations are necessary to establish "the boundaries of the playing field and the rules of the game," he observes that, in the context of DURC, "[t]he safety rulebook in a high-containment infectious disease laboratory is *thick*. . . ." Moreover, he explains that many of the rules respond to the conduct of very few bad actors, and yet those rules apply to every scientist and lab worker. From this, Dr. Franz warns that, "[w]hen rules for the few become too disruptive to the work of the many, communities of trust can break down." Meanwhile, "[l]aboratories with exceptional leaders armed with well thought-out, and *thin* . . . rulebooks," he says, "will always be safer, more secure, and far more productive than labs where the many are overregulated. . . ."

Dr. Franz's observations bring into play a complicated relationship between regulation and trust, which has significant implications for how the law should be used to steer conduct with respect to DURC in life science research. Both trust and regulation are necessary components to the research enterprise. I defer to Dr. Franz's view that trust among laboratory workers and scientists is vital to safety and productivity. Equally vital, however, is *public* trust in researchers and research institutions. Put another way, it is not enough for scientists to trust each other and the leadership of their research institutions; the research enterprise generally must also be trustworthy to the public at large.

Controversy over the publication of two studies in which scientists manipulated the genes of a certain strain of highly pathogenic avian influenza (H5N1) to create new pathogens that are easily transmissible among ferrets (a model for human influenza transmission) draws into question the trustworthiness of researchers and research institutions. This research involved significant risks to public safety by creating new and potentially virulent pathogens that could be accidentally released or misused, and demonstrated methods for creating other potentially dangerous pathogens, which could be misused in war or bioterrorism. Yet, it does not appear that those risks were acknowledged or discussed by the scientists or research institutions involved until just before the studies were to be published, and then only when outsiders raised questions.

Under these circumstances, regulators, legislators, news media, and voters are more than justified to question whether research oversight is sufficient to assure public safety. The public may fairly interpret the story of the ferret flu studies as an example of how a single-minded drive toward discovery can blind scientists to the full measure of the risks their work imposes on the public.

The ferret studies were designed to create new influenza strains that were not only highly pathogenic, but also easily transmissible between mammals. It was no surprise, then, that each of the studies resulted in new strains of

H5N1 that were transmitted between ferrets. Given the risks inherent in the objectives and design of these experiments, why were the public safety risks not discussed and compared to the benefits of the research until the eleventh hour prior to publication, well after the studies were completed? Why did the lead researchers not present a risk-benefit analysis as part of their research proposals? Why did their research institutions not require such a risk-benefit analysis as a condition for allowing the studies to be conducted on their premises? Why did the National Institutes of Health (NIH) approve government funding for each of the studies without first conducting a risk-benefit analysis and without first questioning whether the value of two studies was worth doubling the safety risks to the public?

The thesis of this essay is that a discovery imperative lies at the core of science, that this drive to discover causes scientists to undervalue research risks, and that public trust in life sciences research requires a regulatory check on that bias. Despite Dr. Franz's observation that research regulation diminishes trust within laboratories, I argue that the right kind of regulation will create a foundation for public trust in researchers and their institutions. Moreover, I claim that the newly proposed DURC regulations are the right kind of regulation.

A. The Ferret Studies, Their Approval, and Their Publication

In 2012, two different research teams completed similar experiments proving that H5N1 is susceptible to genetic modifications that will make it easily transmissible among humans. As an avian influenza, H5N1 most commonly infects a variety of domestic and wild birds. Yet, it is capable of leaping the species barrier to infect humans. To date, more than 600 human infections have been recorded worldwide with a mortality rate of close to 60%. Despite these infections, there has not been an outbreak of H5N1 among humans because the strains of H5N1 involved in these infections were not easily transmitted from human-to-human through, for example, sneezing. This led some scientists to question whether H5N1 poses much of a pandemic threat. These scientists hypothesized that the genetic alterations necessary to permit an avian H5N1 to both infect a human and to become easily transmissible among humans are so numerous as to be highly unlikely to ever occur in nature. To address this hypothesis, the two research teams designed experiments to identify what, if any, genetic modifications to H5N1 would make it easily transmissible among humans.

Both of the studies were funded in part by the National Institute of Allergy and Infectious Diseases (NIAID), which is the division of NIH responsible for influenza research. Yet, the funding review at NIH and NIAID was purely scientific and was unlikely to have included any assessment of the dual use risks posed by either project. Federal regulations provide that NIH assess "the scientific merit and significance of the project, the competency of the proposed staff . . . the feasibility of the project, the likelihood of its producing meaningful results, the proposed project period, and the adequacy of the applicant's resources available for the project. . . ." Likewise, grant application guidelines under the NIAID state that reviewers should judge an application solely on "its ability to make a strong impact on its field," which "is a function of . . . the importance of the topic," defined as "the significance and innovation of the research problem—its ability to move the frontier of knowledge forward."

One of the two studies—the one designed by Yoshihiro Kawaoka, Ph.D.—was conducted at the University of Wisconsin-Madison, and involved recombinant DNA (rDNA) methods. The research team clipped a gene from a H5N1 cell and "stitched" it together with genes from a human H1N1 virus cell. Research, like Dr. Kawaoka's that uses rDNA techniques, is subject to NIH Guidelines which instruct the research institution not to permit any such research unless it has first been reviewed and approved by an Institutional Biosafety Committee (IBC). An IBC consists of at least five members, including two community members, who collectively have "experience and expertise in recombinant [DNA] technology and the capability to assess the safety of recombinant [DNA] research and to identify any potential risk to public health or the environment." The University of Wisconsin-Madison's IBC that reviewed and approved Dr. Kawaoka's study had 17 members, 15 of whom were employed by the University as faculty or staff.

An IBC's review determines the level of biosafety laboratory standards that should be applied to proposed research pursuant to NIH's rDNA Guidelines (Guidelines). These Guidelines specify for IBCs the level of biosafety standards to be employed based on the biological material on which the research is being conducted. When the research involves H5N1 and when it could result in creating a more virulent and less treatable form of influenza, then more stringent biosafety standards might apply than provided for in the Guidelines. In this case, an IBC is instructed to refer the matter as a "major action" to NIH and its Recombinant DNA Advisory Committee (RAC). The University of Wisconsin-Madison's IBC reviewed Dr. Kawaoka's study proposal, but the IBC did not refer the proposal to NIH and RAC for federal review, even though the research team proposed creating a new strain of H5N1 that was virulent and much more transmissible among humans than what otherwise occurred in nature. Instead, the University of Wisconsin's IBC approved the study locally and, with that approval, the research began.

In both of the studies, researchers created a new pathogen through genetic manipulation of a naturally occurring H5N1 virus. They then infected laboratory ferrets with the new pathogen. Ferrets are considered to be a good model for human influenza infection because, like humans, ferrets can spread seasonal influenza. The researchers next observed that the genetically modified H5N1 was transmitted to uninfected ferrets. It was through this observation that the researchers concluded it was possible for an avian H5N1 strain that infected a mammal to undergo genetic changes so as to also become easily transmissible among those mammals.

The researchers also discovered that very few genetic changes may be necessary to convert an H5N1 strain capable of leaping the species barrier to infect a human into a strain that is also capable of airborne transmission between humans. Each of the two research teams found only four or five genetic changes between the H5N1 strain with which they started and the modified H5N1 that was easily transmitted between the ferrets. This led the researchers to their final conclusions that avian H5N1 is not incapable of making the genetic changes necessary to become easily transmissible among humans, and that those genetic changes may be so few as to justify the view that an H5N1 pandemic is a real public health threat.

Each of the research teams drafted their experiments, results, and conclusions and submitted their articles for publication. One of the articles was accepted for publication in *Science* and the other in *Nature*. Just before publication, however, the journals' editors became concerned that publication of these studies posed a bioterror risk. The editors sought input from NIH and its National Science Advisory Board for Biosecurity (NSABB) as to whether the publication of the studies created an unacceptable biosecurity risk. The concern was that the publications could provide a blueprint for creating a lethal and transmissible pathogen that could be misused for terrorism. NSABB reviewed the studies and recommended that both journals publish only redacted versions to eliminate the description of how the research teams created the new pathogens they studied.

NSABB's recommendation started a firestorm of controversy. At issue was the value of these research findings to influenza scientists and public health officials who sought to prepare for an influenza pandemic, as compared to the risk that the research posed to national security.

Once it became clear that the new pathogens had not been lethal among the ferrets in either experiment, and that the methods of the experiments were available as a result of earlier published papers and presentations at scientific conferences, NSABB reversed itself. It recommended that both journals publish each of the articles without redaction. The articles were published later in 2012.

B. The Discovery Imperative and Bias in Science

To the scientist, "discovery is *everything*." That is how Harvard biologist Edward O. Wilson, Ph.D., describes it. Scientists, he says, "know the first rule of the professional game book: Make an important discovery, and you are a successful scientist. . . . You go into the textbooks." It goes deeper than success and fame, however. Discovery drives the scientist at an emotional level. It is "thrilling," Dr. Wilson says. "There is no feeling more pleasant, no drug more addictive, than setting foot on virgin soil." Meanwhile, if, as a scientist, you "[f]ail to discover . . . you are little or nothing in the culture of science, no matter how much you learn and write about science."

If Dr. Wilson is to be believed, then discovery is an imperative in the professional ethos of science. As such, it demands of researchers a single-minded zeal to add to the body of scientific knowledge. To punctuate his point, Dr. Wilson borrows a quote: "The scientific method is doing your damnedest, no holds barred."

Such "investigative zeal" leads, in turn, to a professional bias toward conducting research and blinding scientists to the risks that an experiment can pose to the public. It is a close kin to what others refer to as a "White Hat Bias" in science; a "bias leading to distortion of information," which, in the case of DURC, is a protocol's risks and benefits "in the service of what may be perceived to be righteous ends." Because it arises from the *profession's* imperative to discover, this bias affects not only the scientist who designs and conducts an experiment, but also every other scientist who might have a role in reviewing the experiment for funding or for institutional approval. In short, this bias of the profession travels from one degree to another with each and every scientist no matter the role he or she plays, if any, with respect to a particular experiment.

In particular, the discovery imperative creates a bias among scientists to overvalue the benefits of an experiment and to undervalue its risks, even among scientists whose roles are limited to participating in the institutional review of an experiment proposed by a colleague. The bias is so pervasive that one experienced chair of an Institutional Review Board (IRB) wrote about it. He observed that researchers on IRBs "share a constantly reinforced bias for experimentation per se," which, he said, "normally follow[ed] the socialization of scientists." This professional bias, the author opined, created a real "potential for inappropriate overvaluation of benefits over risks. . . ." Other commentators have found additional anecdotal evidence of such a bias. For example, Professor Richard Saver describes instances in which investigators conducting human subjects research and the IRBs that approved the research have been criticized for allowing the researchers' "investigative zeal" to result in subjects being exposed to potentially unjustifiable research risks, even in the absence of financial conflicts of interest.

All of the above suggests that the ever-present bias associated with the discovery imperative could have been at work during the design, funding, and institutional approval of the ferret studies. It certainly would explain why there were several lost opportunities prior to the onset of the research to account for the dual use risks of each study and to assure that they were more than offset by research benefits. For example, the discovery imperative can explain why the lead scientists on each of the studies designed their research protocols without expressly completing a dual use risk-benefit analysis. Likewise, it also can explain why the IBC that reviewed and approved Dr. Kawaoka's study failed to account for the full measure of the biosafety risks of the experiment.

The discovery imperative and its associated biases also explain, at least in part, why a public policy that relies completely on scientists to identify and manage dual use risks is unsustainable. There must be some external check on that bias before we can expect the public to trust researchers and research institutions to manage DURC effectively. This provides one way that regulation generally, and the proposed federal rules for oversight of DURC in particular, play a vital role.

C. Bounded Self-Regulation as a Means for Promoting Public Trust in Scientists

As I have written elsewhere, regulating for trust is tricky. The law is a powerful vehicle for expressing and enforcing important social norms. It can signal to researchers and research institutions that they are obligated to protect the

public from dual use risks that are not clearly justified by the benefits of that research which give rise to those risks. By creating a means to hold science accountable when its practitioners breach that obligation, the law can also provide a basis for the public to trust that science has a strong incentive to live up to its obligation.

For this to work, however, the law must tread somewhat lightly. If, in the hope of gaining greater compliance, the law takes primary control of DURC oversight, the entire effort to promote public trust in the research enterprise could backfire. By taking primary control of DURC oversight, the law would signal that scientists and research institutions cannot be trusted to sufficiently protect public safety. Why else would it be necessary to regulate them so completely?

In the end, promoting public trust in researchers and research institutions to manage dual use risks requires the law to hit a regulatory sweet spot—enough regulation to provide a foundation for the public to believe that scientists have a strong incentive to abide by the norm of protecting public safety, but not so much regulation as to signal that scientists are not sufficiently trustworthy to be given substantial authority to oversee DURC. A model for hitting that sweet spot is bounded self-regulation. Under this model, regulators set boundary procedures and standards by which a target of regulation must abide or suffer some form of legally mandated penalty. Within these boundaries, however, those who are subject to the regulations are permitted to exercise their own judgment about how to apply the boundary standards, and regulators defer to those judgments.

This regulatory technique is particularly useful where the goal of regulation is to signal the trustworthiness of the targets of regulation so as to increase public trust. Accordingly, it has a unique application in health law where trust is viewed as exceptionally important.

The value of promoting trust in the context of scientific research is clear. Society needs the expertise of scientists to advance our collective knowledge about our world, which, of course, requires experimentation. Society might want to assess the risks and benefits of scientists' experiments on a case-by-case basis. Even then, however, it requires the expertise of scientists to identify those risks and benefits; to assess the probability that the risks and benefits actually materialize; and to place those risks, benefits, and probabilities into context for lay people. In short, there is no way to escape our reliance on scientists to conduct experiments, as well as to help us determine whether the risks of research are worth the benefits. Given the reality of our reliance on the expertise of scientists, society needs a basis for trusting not only in the technical expertise of scientists, but also in their fidelity to our collective interests, which, at times, may mean halting the pursuit of discovery in the name of public safety.

Given the importance of public trust in scientific research, it is not surprising to find the regulatory model of bounded self-regulation already in use. Medical researchers and their institutions have been deputized by federal law to review proposed research involving human research subjects to assure that the benefits of research outweigh the risks, and that human subjects participate on an informed and voluntary basis. Likewise, federal policy deputizes scientists and their institutions to review proposed research involving rDNA techniques to assure that the research will comply with applicable biosafety standards under federal guidelines. In each instance, procedures and standards are set by federal law and the task of administering those standards is delegated to researchers at the research institutions in which proposed research will take place if approved. Research institutions that fail to abide by the boundary procedures and standards are subject to losing their eligibility for federal research funds, which is a powerful incentive for compliance. In this way, these laws fall within the realm of bounded self-regulation because the law signals, through its delegation of authority, that researchers and research institutions are trustworthy, while also providing boundaries for the exercise of discretion and a substantial penalty for violating those boundaries.

Using this model of bounded self-regulation does not guarantee success. Despite employing this model, the regulations both for protecting human subjects and for overseeing rDNA research are rife with flaws. Where the government regulates as a tool to promote public trust, the model of bounded self-regulation gives the government an opportunity to succeed where a command and control model does not.

D. New Federal Policies for DURC Oversight

In response to the ferret studies, the federal government developed two new policies for the oversight of DURC. The first policy was released on March 29, 2012 (2012 Policy), and it requested that all federal agencies conducting or funding life sciences research review their projects to determine if any involve DURC and to report their findings to the Assistant to the President for Homeland Security and Counterterrorism. Additionally, if an agency finds that it is funding or conducting any DURC, the 2012 Policy provides that the agency should work with the

researcher and research institution to develop a plan to mitigate the dual use risks. If those risks cannot be mitigated adequately, then agencies may take more extreme measures, such as classifying the research or terminating its federal funding.

The second policy is a policy in name only. From an administrative law perspective, it is proposed rule-making for which notice was provided and comments requested on February 22, 2013 (2013 Proposed Rules). The 2013 Proposed Rules describe the DURC oversight responsibilities of researchers, research institutions, and federal agencies. Researchers would be obligated to assess whether their proposed research meets the definition of DURC and, if so, to work with the research institution's review board to develop a dual use risk mitigation plan. If finalized, the 2013 Proposed Rules would require research institutions that receive federal funding to establish a board to review research proposals for the purpose of determining if they involve DURC and, if so, develop and enforce dual use risk mitigation plans for the research. The board may be internal or external to the research institution, and it may be a unique committee or an existing committee (such as an IBC) whose charge is expanded to include DURC oversight. The 2013 Proposed Rules do not require a particular make-up of the committee's membership, so long as it has "sufficient breadth of expertise to assess the dual use potential of the range of relevant life sciences research conducted at a given research facility" and has knowledge of dual use issues, federal law, and available risk mitigation alternatives. Additionally, a research institution must notify the agency funding the research, if and when, the institution's review board identifies the funded research as DURC, and it must provide that agency with a copy of the dual use risk mitigation plan developed by the institution. As for funding agencies, the 2013 Proposed Rules incorporate the powers and responsibilities described in the 2012 Policy. Any institution subject to the 2013 Proposed Rules would risk losing its eligibility for federal research funding if it failed to comply.

The 2012 Policy and the 2013 Proposed Rules are positive steps to promoting public trust in scientists and research institutions conducting DURC, because they employ the bounded self-regulation model. Together they set boundary standards and procedures that will add to the accountability of researchers and research institutions with respect to the dual use risks that their research imposes on the public. First, they require researchers and research institutions to be deliberate in assessing whether their proposed research meets the definition of DURC and, if so, to identify the precise dual use risks at issue and then develop a plan of mitigation. This diminishes the likelihood that proposed research will proceed on the assumption that the research does not pose any dual use risks or that dual use risks are simply a price of pursuing discovery. Second, they provide for the funding agency to make a fresh assessment of dual use risks and mitigation plans for DURC that they fund. Moreover, they empower the funding agency to classify research or even refuse to fund research that the agency perceives to have dual use risks that cannot be sufficiently mitigated. In this way, the agency's review is a potentially powerful check on the ability of the researcher and research institution to identify and manage dual use risks effectively. It forces scientists and their institutions either to stand in the shoes of the funding agency when managing DURC, or risk that the funding agency will step in to manage or withhold funding for the research.

At the same time, the 2012 Policy and the 2013 Proposed Rules rely on researchers and research institutions to take the lead in the oversight of DURC. They defer to the researcher and his or her institution to identify DURC and to develop plans for mitigation. Federal regulators override the institutional plan to manage DURC only where they find it significantly lacking. This leaves plenty of opportunity and an incentive for science to develop its own norms for protecting the public in the case of DURC.

This is not to say that the 2012 Policy and the 2013 Proposed Rules are perfect. They are not. In particular, the 2013 Proposed Rules should instruct scientists and their institutions to not only assess and mitigate dual use risks, but to articulate why those risks, once mitigated, are justified by the likely benefits of the research. The rules should also identify whether research benefits must merely, clearly, or substantially outweigh dual use risks, and they should require that the institutional review process apply that standard. Finally, the 2013 Proposed Rules should do more than demand life sciences expertise on the institutional committees that review DURC. Those committees should be required to have a sufficient number of institutionally unaffiliated members to act as an additional check on the bias created by the discovery imperative.

In the end, Dr. Franz and I agree that life scientists and their research institutions should not be over-regulated because doing so undermines trust. Yet, fear of over-regulation should not result in closing the door on all regulation. Instead, the answer is finding the right regulatory technique that allows scientists to regulate themselves within legal boundaries that help assure the public that the profession of science has a strong incentive to protect society while pursuing the next discovery.

Robert Gatter is a Distinguished Scholar at the University of Pittsburgh Medical Center's Center for Biosecurity and a professor of public health and medicine at the University of Pittsburgh. During the 1960s, he headed the international effort to eliminate smallpox.

EXPLORING THE ISSUE

Can Science Be Trusted Without Government Regulation?

Critical Thinking and Reflection

1. What is "discovery bias"? Is there anything similar in other fields (such as "treatment bias" in medicine or "driving bias" in errand-running)?
2. Is there anything similar to "discovery bias" in other fields (such as "treatment bias" in medicine or "driving bias" in errand-running)?
3. Do such biases limit our ability to see alternatives?
4. Does publishing the full methods and results of the Fouchier and Kawaoka H5N1 studies seem likely to increase our ability to protect public health from a future H5N1 pandemic?

Is There Common Ground?

David R. Franz sees a role for regulation in setting the boundaries of the field of play and defining the rules of the game. Robert Gatter thinks that much more is necessary if life scientists are to warrant the public's trust, but he does say at the end of his paper, "life scientists and their research institutions should not be over-regulated because doing so undermines trust." They thus agree that over-regulation can be a problem. They differ in how much regulation is over-regulation.

1. Is more-regulated research more trustworthy than less-regulated research?
2. Does "discovery bias" blind a researcher to the ethical and moral dimensions of research?
3. If exceptional laboratory leadership makes regulation less necessary, is it reasonable to try to rely on such leadership?

Additional Resources

Jon Cohen, "Does Forewarned = Forearmed with Lab-Made Avian Influenza Strains?" *Science* (February 17, 2012).

Fred Guterl, "Waiting to Explode," *Scientific American* (June 2012).

Sander Herfst, et al., "Airborne Transmission of Influenza A/H5N1 Virus Between Ferrets," *Science* (June 22, 2012) (http://www.sciencemag.org/content/336/6088/1534.full).

Masaki Imai, et al., "Experimental Adaptation of an Influenza H5 HA Confers Respiratory Droplet Transmission to a Reassortant H5 HA/H1N1 Virus in Ferrets," *Nature* (June 21, 2012) (http://www.nature.com/nature/journal/vaop/ncurrent/full/nature10831.html).

Carl Zimmer, "Could Information about a Lab-Made Virus Really Help Evildoers Create a Biological Weapon?" *Slate* (December 22, 2011) (http://www.slate.com/articles/technology/future_tense/2011/12/h5n1_the_lab_made_virus_the_u_s_fears_could_be_made_into_a_biological_weapon_.html).

Internet References . . .

National Science Advisory Board for Biosecurity (NSABB)

http://oba.od.nih.gov/biosecurity/about_nsabb.html

Office of Declassification: History of Classification and Declassification

http://fas.org/irp/doddir/doe/history.htm

United States Senate Committee on Homeland Security & Government Affairs Hearing on "Biological Security: The Risk of Dual-Use Research"

http://www.hsgac.senate.gov/hearings/biological -security-the-risk-of-dual-use-research

Unit 2

UNIT

Energy and the Environment

*A*s the damage that human beings do to their environment in the course of obtaining food, water, wood, ore, energy, and other resources has become clear, many people have grown concerned. Some of that concern is for the environment—the landscapes and living things with which humanity shares its world. Some of that concern is more for human welfare; it focuses on the ways in which environmental damage threatens human health, prosperity, or even survival.

Among the major environmental issues are those related to energy. By releasing vast amounts of carbon dioxide, fossil fuels threaten to change the world's climate. Potential solutions include warding off excess solar heating, greatly expanding the use of hydroelectric power, and replacing fossil fuels with hydrogen.

Selected, Edited, and with Issue Framing Material by:
Thomas A. Easton, *Mount Ida College*

ISSUE

Can We Reduce Carbon Emissions Enough to Limit Global Warming?

YES: Lisa Jacobson, from "Testimony before the U.S. Senate Committee on Environment and Public Works, Hearing on 'Examining the International Climate Change Negotiations,'" U.S. Senate (2015)

NO: Stephen D. Eule, from "Testimony before the U.S. Senate Committee on Environment and Public Works, Hearing on 'Examining the International Climate Change Negotiations,'" U.S. Senate (2015)

Learning Outcomes
After reading this issue, you will be able to: • Explain why limiting carbon emissions is thought to be necessary to control global warming.   • Explain how businesses can help to limit carbon emissions.   • Describe how limiting carbon emissions threatens businesses.   • Describe why an international agreement to limit carbon emissions may not work.

ISSUE SUMMARY

YES: Lisa Jacobson argues that an international agreement to limit carbon emissions will spur investment in clean energy technologies. Success is achievable, and the U.S. business community is already considering climate change impacts in its energy and corporate strategies. "The private sector is going to be a key partner in delivering the innovation, investment and technologies that will help . . . meet . . . mitigation targets."

NO: Stephen D. Eule argues that the COP21 agreement is unlikely to succeed. In the United States, promised emissions reductions will be inadequate, they will probably not be achieved, and if it happens it would threaten the competitive position of American businesses. It would also destroy history's most successful economic system. "Affordable, available, and scalable energy is not the problem, it is the solution."

$\mathbf{T}$he idea that the heat-trapping ability of infrared-absorbing gases in the atmosphere is similar to that of the glass panes in a greenhouse (hence the "greenhouse effect") was first proposed by the French mathematical physicist Jean-Baptiste-Joseph Fourier in 1827. In 1896, the Swedish chemist Svante Arrhenius, who later won the 1903 Nobel Prize in chemistry, predicted that if atmospheric carbon dioxide (CO_2) levels doubled due to the burning of fossil fuels, the resulting increase in the average temperature at the Earth's surface would amount to four to six degrees Celsius (seven to ten degrees Fahrenheit).

The Arrhenius prediction about global warming was all but forgotten for more than half a century until direct observations and historical data demonstrated that by 1960, atmospheric CO_2 levels had risen to 315 ppm from the preindustrial level of 280 ppm. Careful measurements since then have shown that the CO_2 level is now above 400 ppm, and rising (http://www.esrl.noaa.gov/gmd/ccgg/trends/). The Arrhenius prediction that the average temperature on Earth will rise more than four degrees Celsius may well come true before the end of the twenty-first century if present fossil fuel use and forest destruction trends continue. Most atmospheric scientists agree that such a warming will be accompanied by changes in the world's weather patterns and a significant increase in sea levels. The data on which these conclusions are based, as well as the conclusions themselves, have been vigorously debated for years.

In 1988, due to concern about the potentially serious disruptive effects that would result from significant, short-term changes in world climate, the United Nations Environment Programme joined with the World Meteorological Organization to establish the Intergovernmental Panel on Climate Change (IPCC) to assess the available scientific, technical, and socioeconomic information regarding greenhouse gas-induced climate change. Thousands of meteorologists and other atmospheric and climate scientists have participated in periodic reviews of the data. The Fifth Assessment Report of the IPCC, which appeared in 2013–2014, is very clear that global climate change is real, it is caused by human activities, and its impacts on ecosystems and human well-being (especially in developing nations) will be serious. It also outlined the steps that must be taken to prevent, ease, or cope with these impacts. Other reports (see Nicholas Stern, *Stern Review: The Economics of Climate Change*, Executive Summary, October 30, 2006 [http://webarchive.nationalarchives.gov.uk /20080910140413/http://www.hm-treasury.gov.uk/independent _reviews/stern_review_economics_climate_change/sternreview _index.cfm]) make it clear that although taking steps now to limit future impacts of global warming would be very expensive, "the benefits of strong, early action considerably outweigh the costs. . . . Ignoring climate change will eventually damage economic growth. . . . Tackling climate change is the pro-growth strategy for the longer term, and it can be done in a way that does not cap the aspirations for growth of rich or poor countries. The earlier effective action is taken, the less costly it will be."

Exactly what will global warming do to the world and its people? Richard B. Primack, *Walden Warming* (University of Chicago Press, 2014), has compared wildflower blooming times, as recorded in Henry David Thoreau's mid-1800s notebooks, and found that warming has already shifted those times as much as six weeks earlier in the year. This does not sound very catastrophic, but our future is much more than a matter of wildflower blooming times. Projections have grown steadily worse; see Eli Kintisch, "Projections of Climate Change Go from Bad to Worse, Scientists Report," *Science* (March 20, 2009). Effects include rising sea level, more extreme weather events, reduced global harvests, reduced nutrient levels of crops (Mary Macvean, "Rising Carbon Dioxide Levels Affect Nutrients in Crops, Study Says," *Los Angeles Times*, May 7, 2014; http:// www.latimes.com/science/sciencenow/la-sci-sn-carbon-dioxide -crops-20140507-story.html), and threats to the economies and

security of nations (see the report of the U.S. Department of Defense to Congress, "National Security Implications of Climate-Related Risks and a Changing Climate," July 23, 2015 [http://www.defense.gov/pubs/150724-Congressional-Report -on-National-Implications-of-Climate-Change.pdf?source =GovDelivery]). As rainfall patterns change and the seas rise, millions of people will flee their homelands; see Alex de Sherbinin, Koko Warner, and Charles Erhart, "Casualties of Climate Change," *Scientific American* (January 2011). The potential for conflict is emphasized in the IPCC's Fifth Assessment Report.

It seems clear that something must be done, but what? How urgently? And with what aim? Should we be trying to reduce or prevent human suffering? Or to avoid political conflicts? Or to protect the global economy—meaning standards of living, jobs, and businesses? The humanitarian and economic approaches are obviously connected, for protecting jobs certainly has much to do with easing or preventing suffering. However, these approaches can also conflict. In October 2009, the Government Accountability Office (GAO) released "Climate Change Adaptation: Strategic Federal Planning Could Help Government Officials Make More Informed Decisions" (GAO-10-113; http://www .gao.gov/products/GAO-10-113), which notes the need for multi-agency coordination and strategic (long-term) planning, both of which are often resisted by bureaucrats and politicians. Robert Engelman, *Population, Climate Change, and Women's Lives* (Worldwatch Institute, 2010), notes that addressing population size and growth would help, but "Despite its key contribution to climate change, population plays little role in current discussions on how to address this serious challenge."

According to David Rotman, "Climate Change: The Moral Choices," *Technology Review* (April 11, 2013) (http://www .technologyreview.com/review/513526/climate-change-the -moral-choices/), ethicists are only now addressing the question of what ethical behavior means in the global warming context. Is it right to value present benefits (such as cheap, convenient energy) more than benefits to future generations (such as freedom from the consequences of global warming)?

In June 2015, Pope Francis repeated this point more strongly; you can find his encyclical, "Laudato Si," at http://w2.vatican.va/content/francesco/en/encyclicals/documents /papa-francesco_20150524_enciclica-laudato-si.html. For a summary, see Emma Green, "The Pope's Moral Case for Taking on Climate Change," *The Atlantic* (June 18, 2015) (http:// w2.vatican.va/content/francesco/en/encyclicals/documents /papa-francesco_20150524_enciclica-laudato-si.html). Christopher J. Hale lists "The 5 Most Important Points of Pope Francis's Climate Change Encyclical," *Time.com* (July 2015) (http://time.com/3925520/pope-francis-climate-change-encyclical/), as:

1. Climate change is real, and it's getting worse.
2. Human beings are a major contributor to climate change.
3. Climate change disproportionately affects the poor.
4. We can and must make things better.
5. Individuals can help, but politicians must lead the charge.

Conservative politicians and anti–global warming forces have been vigorous in their reactions against this message. See Antonia Blumberg, "Fox News Pundit Calls Pope Francis 'The Most Dangerous Person on the Planet' for Suggesting Climate Change Is Real," *Huffington Post* (June 18, 2015) (http://www.huffingtonpost.com/2015/06/18/greg-gutfeld-pope-francis_n_7616156.html). Yet the sense that the problem is real and we have a responsibility to do something about it is growing; in fact, when the environmental group Urgenda (Urgent Agenda) sued the Dutch government, saying that failing to do enough was a human rights violation, a Dutch court said the Dutch government must do more to reduce carbon dioxide emissions ("Dutch Court Orders Government to Cut More CO_2," *Science*, July 3, 2015).

In May 2010, the National Research Council released three books, *Advancing the Science of Climate Change* (http://www.nap.edu/catalog.php?record_id=12782), *Limiting the Magnitude of Future Climate Change* (http://www.nap.edu/catalog.php?record_id=12785), and *Adapting to the Impacts of Climate Change* (http://www.nap.edu/catalog.php?record_id=12783). Together, they stress the reality of the problem, the need for immediate action to keep the problem from getting worse, and the need for advance planning and preparation to deal with the impacts. Computer simulations suggest that since 1980, climate changes have reduced maize and wheat harvests by 3.8–5.5 percent; see D. B. Lobell, W. Schlenker, and J. Costa-Roberts, "Climate Trends and Global Crop Production since 1980," *Science* (published online May 5, 2011). At a meeting of the International Emissions Trading Association, Christiana Figueres, executive secretary of the United Nations framework convention on climate change, said that the situation is urgent and the world must immediately agree to change its goal from limiting global warming to 2.0°C to limiting it to 1.5°C, or "we are in big trouble"; see Fiona Harvey, "UN Chief Challenges World to Agree to Tougher Target for Climate Change," *The Guardian* (June 1, 2011). In May 2014, the U.S. Global Change Research Program released the National Climate Assessment (http://nca2014.globalchange.gov/), which stresses

that global warming is real, serious (with effects varying by region), and primarily due to human activities, chiefly the burning of fossil fuels. In 2014, the Climate Science Panel of the American Association for the Advancement of Science (AAAS) released "What We Know: The Reality, Risks and Response to Climate Change," stressed in no uncertain terms that global warming and climate change are real, that they are caused by human activities, and that we face serious consequences if we do nothing.

However, there remains resistance to the idea that global climate change is real, is caused by human activities, or poses any threat to the environment or human well-being. Most of the remaining critics of the reality of global warming are either employed by or funded by industries and nations that have a financial stake in resisting proposals for significant reductions in the release of greenhouse gases. See, e.g., Suzanne Goldenberg, "Work of Prominent Climate Change Denier Was Funded by Energy Industry," *The Guardian* (February 21, 2015) (http://www.theguardian.com/environment/2015/feb/21/climate-change-denier-willie-soon-funded-energy-industry). Some fossil-fuel-industry funding is funneled through conservative organizations such as the Heartland Institute (http://heartland.org/), which in 2013 made news by spreading disinformation about scientific acceptance of global warming; see Phil Plait, "The Heartland Institute and the American Meteorological Society," *Slate* (December 10, 2013) (http://www.slate.com/blogs/bad_astronomy/2013/12/10/heartland_institute_sowing_global_warming_doubt.html?wpisrc=burger_bar).

U.S. President Barack Obama indicated that his administration would take global warming more seriously than did his predecessors. In June 2009, the U.S. House of Representatives passed an energy and climate bill that promised to cap carbon emissions and stimulate use of renewable energy. The Senate version of the bill failed to pass; see Daniel Stone, "Who Killed the Climate and Energy Bill?" *Newsweek* (September 15, 2010). The Obama administration also said it was committed to negotiating seriously at the Copenhagen Climate Change Conference in December 2009. Unfortunately, the Copenhagen meeting ended with little accomplished except agreements to limit global temperature increases to two degrees Celsius by 2100, but only through voluntary cuts in carbon emissions; to have developed nations report their cuts; to have developed nations fund mitigation and adaptation in developing nations; and to continue talking about the problem (see Elizabeth Finkel, "Senate Looms as Bigger Hurdle after Copenhagen," *Science*, January 1, 2010). There were few signs that the world is ready to take the extensive actions deemed necessary by many; see, e.g., Janet L. Sawin and William R. Moomaw, "Renewing the Future and Protecting the Climate," *World Watch* (July/August 2010).

When the UN Framework Convention on Climate Change met in Lima, Peru, in December 2014, it was able to report agreement among 190 nations, both developed and developing, that they would develop action plans immediately; see David Talbot, "Lima Climate Accord Might Boost Renewables," *Technology Review* (December 16, 2014) (http://www.technologyreview.com/news/533581/lima-climate-accord-might-boost-renewables/). When the Convention met in Paris in December 2015, the world's nations brought with them those plans, in the form of promises to cut carbon emissions by specific amounts (Intended Nationally Determined Contributions, or INDCs). When the meeting was over, 195 countries had agreed to implement those plans. "For the agreement to have legal force, it must be ratified by at least 55 of the 195 countries that adopted it without objection Saturday. Those 55 countries must represent at least 55% of all global-warming emissions." After that, it will be essential to eliminate subsidies for the fossil fuel industries, impose carbon taxes, seek broader political consensus, and invest in renewable energy technologies such as solar power; see John D. Sutter, "Hooray for the Paris Agreement! Now What?" CNN.com (December 14, 2015) (http://www.cnn.com/2015/12/14/opinions/sutter-cop21-climate-5-things/). According to the UN News Centre (http://www.un.org/apps/news/story.asp?NewsID=52802#.VoKOQ1m7BnA), UN Secretary-General Ban Ki-Moon commented: "When historians look back on this day, they will say that global cooperation to secure a future safe from climate change took a dramatic new turn here in Paris. Today, we can look into the eyes of our children and grandchildren, and we can finally say, tell them that we have joined hands to bequeath a more habitable world to them and to future generations."

Can it be done? Will it be done? These are the important questions, and they have been under discussion since before the COP21 meeting actually convened in Paris. On November 18, 2015, the United States Senate Committee on Environment and Public Works held a hearing on "Examining the International Climate Negotiations." The following readings are drawn from testimony before that hearing. In the YES selection, Lisa Jacobson argues that an international agreement to limit carbon emissions will spur investment in clean energy technologies. Success is achievable, and the U.S. business community is already considering climate change impacts in its energy and corporate strategies. "The private sector is going to be a key partner in delivering the innovation, investment and technologies that will help . . . meet . . . mitigation targets." In the NO selection, Stephen D. Eule argues that the COP21 agreement is unlikely to succeed. In the United States, promised emissions reductions will be inadequate, they will probably not be achieved, and if it happens it would threaten the competitive position of American businesses. It would also destroy history's most successful economic system. "Affordable, available, and scalable energy is not the problem, it is the solution."

YES ⤶

Lisa Jacobson

Testimony before the U.S. Senate Committee on Environment and Public Works, Hearing on "Examining the International Climate Change Negotiations"

... Through my testimony, I will address the Council's engagement in the international climate change process, the contributions that clean energy technologies are making to reduce US greenhouse gas emissions and what the coalition seeks out of a Paris climate change agreement in December.

As an important backdrop to my testimony at this hearing, the Council would also like to share some of the findings from the 2015 edition of the *Sustainable Energy in America Factbook*. The *Factbook* was researched and produced by Bloomberg New Energy Finance and commissioned by the Business Council for Sustainable Energy. It is a quantitative and objective report, intended to be a resource for policymakers with up to date, accurate market information. Its goal is to offer important benchmarks on the contributions that sustainable energy technologies are making in the US energy system today. It also provides information on finance and investment trends in clean energy resources.

The 2015 edition of *Sustainable Energy in America Factbook* points to the dramatic changes underway in the US energy sector over the past several years. Traditional energy sources are declining, while natural gas, renewable energy and energy efficiency are playing a larger role.

These changes are increasing the diversity of the country's energy mix, improving our energy security, cutting energy waste, increasing our energy productivity and reducing air pollution and greenhouse gas emissions.

BCSE and Its Engagement with the International Climate Change Negotiations

BCSE members in the energy efficiency, natural gas and renewable energy sectors offer readily-available low-carbon and zero-carbon energy solutions. This portfolio of technologies can be used today to provide reliable, affordable and clean energy options for public and private sector customers. In 2014, US investment in clean energy technologies reached $51.8 billion and these sectors are providing hundreds of thousands of well-paying jobs.

The Council will bring a delegation of its members to attend as business observers to the 21st Conference of the Parties (COP 21) of the United Nations Framework Convention on Climate Change (UNFCCC) in Paris, France this December. The organization has consistently engaged in the international climate change process since the early 1990s. The BCSE participates in this process to offer clean energy business expertise to the negotiators and stakeholders, providing information on deployment trends, technology costs as well as policy best practices.

BCSE members view the climate change negotiations as a valuable forum to share knowledge on policy frameworks and to help to inform the policy choices of countries looking to reduce greenhouse gas emissions and deploy clean energy options.

Further, BCSE members view the outcomes of the international climate change negotiations as important signals to the market that countries are serious about investing in low-carbon solutions. These signals will serve to reduce the uncertainty that can stall private sector investment. The scope and scale of the intended nationally-determined commitments of 161 countries under consideration at COP 21, will also spur investment and advance low-carbon investments trends that are already occurring.

US government leadership and engagement in the international climate change process supports US clean energy business interests and expands clean energy business opportunities outside our borders. US leadership increases the ambition of other nations and helps showcase

Testimony before the U.S. Senate Committee on Environment and Public Works, Hearing on "Examining the International Climate Negotiations," U.S. Senate, November 2015.

US technology innovations and policy frameworks. BCSE is especially pleased that the upcoming negotiations in Paris will create new forums for sub-national actors, including state and local government officials as well as the private sector to showcase their efforts to reduce emissions and adapt to climate change.

Unlocking Investment, Innovation and Clean Energy Deployment—A Road Map to a Meaningful Paris Climate Change Agreement

The coalition of clean energy industries represented by the Business Council for Sustainable Energy calls for governments to deliver a clear, concise and durable climate change agreement at the 21st Conference of the Parties (COP 21) of the United Nations Framework Convention on Climate Change (UNFCCC) in Paris, France in December 2015.

With over 91% of global emissions and 90% of the global population covered by the intended nationally-determined contributions (INDCs) of 161 countries, nations are showing a collective commitment to spur investment, innovation and deployment of clean energy technologies in countries around the world. While the unconditional INDCs are estimated to deliver only 42% of the emissions reductions needed to reach the 2°C pathway, the Council believes that a well-structured Paris agreement can facilitate higher levels of ambition over time.

Of note, in 2014, global investment in clean energy topped $310 billion, proving that the low-carbon transformation of the energy sector is well underway. This transformation is driven by falling technology costs, business innovations and supportive policy frameworks. But as we look toward the next several decades, even higher levels of investment will be needed. The International Energy Agency estimates that $500 billion annually by 2020 and $1 trillion annually by 2030 will need to be invested in low-carbon energy in order to keep global warming below 2°C and avoid the worst effects of climate change. The world energy markets cannot afford any backtracking at this critical time.

The key elements of a Paris agreement and supporting decisions include:

- **Participation by all countries** to address climate change.
- **A clear and durable structure** that provides transparent and predictable schedules for the monitoring, review and evaluation of emissions mitigation target and timetables, with a built-in mechanism to adjust country goals and actions as needed over a longer time horizon.
- **Continued international climate finance** support by donor countries, both to meet existing commitments and to expand public-private finance mechanisms in a post-2020 environment.
- **Protection of innovation systems** that enable the deployment of existing clean-energy solutions and creation of next generation low-carbon technology solutions. When the private sector makes investment decisions in a country, it assesses a potential market based on the existence of stable policies, sound infrastructure, and effective legal frameworks that encourage competition and innovation and that protect intellectual property rights (IPRs).
- **Recognition of the role of market-based mechanisms** as cost-effective cooperative tools for countries to meet mitigation and development objectives, accompanied by an accounting system to protect environmental integrity and to avoid double-counting of emissions reductions.
- **Recognition of the role of the private sector** and the need for public-private partnerships to deliver the technology solutions and investment capital needed to transform the energy sector and help close the ambition gap between national targets and a 2°C pathway. The preparations for COP 21 in Paris have made new inroads toward recognizing the necessity and importance of the contributions of the private sector, cities, states and other non-state actors in addressing climate change. These actors and their contributions should be recognized in the new global framework that governs climate action into the future.

The Changing US Energy Landscape

The 2015 edition of *Sustainable Energy in America Factbook* points to the dramatic changes underway in the US energy sector over the past several years. Traditional energy sources are declining, while natural gas, renewable energy and energy efficiency are playing a larger role.

These changes are increasing the diversity of the country's energy mix, improving our energy security, cutting energy waste, increasing our energy productivity and reducing air pollution and greenhouse gas emissions.

Behind this change are a portfolio of new energy innovations, technologies, and applications. These include: newly applied techniques for extracting natural gas from shale rock formations; lower-cost and higher-efficiency photovoltaic panels for converting sunlight to electrons; highly efficient, natural gas end-use applications; natural gas vehicles and battery and fuel cell electric vehicles; and 'smart meters' that allow consumers to monitor, modulate, and cut electricity consumption, among others.

The *Factbook* looks at a broad spectrum of sustainable energy technologies and provides data on a wide range of clean energy industries including natural gas, renewable energy sources (including solar, wind, hydropower, geothermal, biomass, biogas and waste to energy—but excluding liquid biofuels), stationary fuel cells and other distributed technologies, as well as energy efficiency.

The *Factbook* shows that the US economy is becoming more energy productive and less energy intensive. By one measure—United States gross domestic product (GDP) per unit of energy consumed—productivity has increased by 54% since 1990. Between 2007 and 2014, total energy use fell 2.4%, while GDP grew 8%. This was driven largely by advances in energy efficiency in the transportation, power generation and buildings sectors.

Between 2007 and 2014:

- Total energy use fell 2.4%, while GDP grew 8%.
- Energy productivity of the US economy has increased 11%, and 1.4% from 2013 to 2014.
- Annualized electricity demand growth has been zero.
- Energy-related carbon dioxide emissions have decreased by 9.2%.

While energy demand has fallen more steeply than it has in at least 50 years, the use of natural gas and renewable energy has increased. Natural gas provided the US with 28% of its total energy supply in 2014 of which 27% was used to produce electricity via natural gas-fired power plants. This was up from just 22% of electricity from gas-fired power plants in 2007. Renewable energy in 2014 was 9.7% of total US energy mix whereas electrical generation from renewable resources increased from 8.3% to 12.9% between 2007 and 2014.

The Role of Domestic Electricity Sector Policy in Deploying Clean Energy Technologies

The US power sector is undergoing rapid changes and clean energy technologies in the energy efficiency, natural gas and renewable energy sectors are playing a larger role in the electricity mix.

These changes have been happening due to a range of factors, including cost reductions in certain sectors, technology and business innovations and supportive policy frameworks.

The final Clean Power Plan that regulates carbon emissions from existing power plants was released in August 2015. The structure of the regulation reflects the direction that US power markets are taking and, as it is implemented, will provide investment certainty to inform future decisions.

While the BCSE favors a legislative approach to addressing greenhouse gas emissions, the release of the Clean Power Plan was a historic development and demonstrates federal leadership to address global climate change.

It is important to note that the Clean Power Plan provides flexibility to states to implement the standard. This flexibility will allow states to meet their targets with a broad portfolio of affordable and reliable technologies, including an array of energy efficiency, natural gas and renewable energy solutions. In addition, states can consider the use of carbon capture utilization and storage (CCUS) and well as carbon capture and sequestration (CCS) technologies for compliance if they have carbon utilization and sequestration capacity.

The Clean Power Plan also offers an opportunity for constructive partnership and dialogue between state policymakers and the private sector, with clear opportunities to explore state-specific or multi-state options for compliance.

The Business Council for Sustainable Energy and its members are engaging in state plan development stakeholder processes and understand that state plans must match clean energy solutions to each state's unique requirements. To assist the development of state plans, the Council, in partnership with Bloomberg New Energy Finance (BNEF), released state specific factsheets that discuss the energy landscape in Minnesota, Nevada, Pennsylvania and Virginia. The factsheets also consider deployment trends and technology costs of various technology and resource options. In all of these states, BNEF finds a foundation that positions these states well to meet the Clean Power Plan targets, based on the policy and market conditions already in place.

BCSE will continue to engage with EPA and states as plan development continues. We will also work with state and federal policymakers to adopt policies that provide certainty for low and zero carbon investments in the US.

Clean Energy Businesses Take Action to Address Climate Change

The US business community is increasingly considering climate change impacts in its energy and corporate strategies. Clean energy companies, including several Council members, have recently announced new pledges to reduce greenhouse gas emissions as well as other climate-friendly sustainability initiatives.

BCSE members making recent pledges include: Calpine, ENER-G Rudox, Ingersoll Rand, Johnson Controls, Kingspan Insulated Panels—North America, PG&E, Qualcomm Incorporated, and Schneider Electric.

Council member efforts as well as other US company actions show that addressing climate change is becoming a mainstream business issue.

The private sector is going to be a key partner in delivering the innovation, investment and technologies that will help the US and other countries meet their mitigation targets. By leading by example and showing what is possible, these American companies are adding to the global momentum for a positive outcome at the Paris negotiations for a new international climate change agreement.

Lisa Jacobson is the president of the Business Council for Sustainable Energy, an industry group representing businesses in the energy efficiency, natural gas, and renewable energy industries.

Stephen D. Eule

 **NO**

Testimony before the U.S. Senate Committee on Environment and Public Works, Hearing on "Examining the International Climate Change Negotiations"

. . . **C**limate change is among the most complex issues facing the international community. Negotiations are currently taking place under the United Nations Framework Convention on Climate Change (UNFCCC). The Framework Convention was adopted in 1992 and entered into force in 1994. The U.S. Senate gave its advice and consent to ratification of the agreement in 1992 by voice vote. This consent, however, came with the understanding that any future agreement pursuant to the UNFCCC that included emissions target and timetables would be subject to the Senate's advice and consent.

The ultimate goal of the UNFCCC is the "stabilization of greenhouse gas concentrations in the atmosphere at a level [undefined] that would prevent dangerous anthropogenic interference with the climate system." This goal should be "achieved within a time frame that would allow ecosystems to adapt naturally top climate change, to ensure that food production is not threatened and to enable economic development to proceed in a sustainable manner." More than 190 governments are Parties to the UNFCCC.

Since 1995, the Conference of the Parties (COP) to the UNFCCC have met annually, and in December of this year, the 21st meeting of the COP will take place in Paris, France in December with a goal of completing a new agreement.

From the very beginning, the structure of the UNFCCC has virtually guaranteed gridlock. Consider the notion of historical responsibility, which plays an oversized role in the dynamics between and among developed, emerging, and developing country Parties. Developing countries assert that as developed countries bear "historical responsibility" for most of the build-up of atmospheric carbon dioxide, they bear a greater responsibility to reduce emissions and to provide finance for reductions in developing countries.

Historical responsibility buttresses the UNFCCC principle of "common but differentiated responsibilities and respective capabilities" under which, ". . . developed country Parties should take the lead in combating climate change and the adverse effects thereof." In other words, developing countries are not expected to do as much as developed countries, which have greater economic and technological capabilities to curb emissions. This principle of common but differentiated responsibilities is on full display in the 1997 Kyoto Protocol, which only saddles developed countries only with binding obligations to reduce emissions.

Over the years, however, it has become readily apparent that developed countries alone cannot reduce global emissions by themselves—all countries have to participate. Developing countries, however, have been reticent to take on any substantial obligations for the reasons cited above and because economic development remains their priority. Paris is supposed to be the first agreement that would bring developing countries into the fold as full partners.

The first cracks in this UNFCCC wall separating developed from developing countries appeared in the Bali Roadmap that emerged from the UNFCCC talks in Indonesia in 2007, where developing countries agreed to consider "nationally appropriate mitigation actions" that are "measurable, reportable, and verifiable."

The Durban Platform for Enhanced Action, which was adopted at COP-17 in 2011, charged the Parties to

Testimony before the U.S. Senate Committee on Environment and Public Works, Hearing on "Examining the International Climate Negotiations," U.S. Senate, November 2015.

adopt a "protocol, another legal instrument or an agreed outcome with legal force" at COP-21 and for it to "come into effect and be implemented from 2020."

Unlike the Kyoto Protocol, which was a top-down treaty, the Paris agreement is anticipated to be a bottom-up treaty, with each country setting goals based on their unique national circumstances. These Intended Nationally Determined Contributions, or INDCs, will form the basis of the country-specific commitments under the new UN climate treaty. It is also expected that periodic review of these commitments will be instituted along with measuring, reporting, and verification to ensure the integrity and ambition of the commitments.

Despite many negotiating sessions this year, there are still many issues that need to be ironed out before an agreement is reached, including financial assistance under the UNFCCC's Green Climate Fund, loss and damages, intellectual property and technology transfer, and a long-term global goal. These and other issues of particular interest to the business community are outlined below.

A Technology Challenge

As a practical matter, any long-range numeric goal makes assumptions about the pace of technology development and diffusion, an inherently unpredictable process. At its most fundamental level, reducing carbon dioxide emissions from energy is a technology challenge that, as a 2002 article in *Science* famously noted, "cannot be simply regulated away." Neither can it be negotiated away.

The development of technology and its commercial adoption are among the most important factors determining how quickly and at what cost greenhouse gas emissions can be reduced. In many developing countries, providing citizens with energy services is a much more pressing need than addressing climate change. It is a simple fact that much of the energy needed to power economic growth will likely be supplied by fossil fuels. Many developing countries have large resources of coal, natural gas, and oil, and it would be unrealistic to expect them not to use it. However, the increased use of existing and advanced technologies can limit the environmental impact of using these fuels, reduce demand for them through efficiency, and provide alternate sources of energy.

Existing technologies can make a start, but they are not capable of significantly reducing greenhouse gas emissions on a global scale and at an acceptable cost. New, and in some cases revolutionary, energy technologies, many still years if not decades over the horizon, will have to be developed and adopted commercially along with the infrastructure to support them. But there is a great deal of uncertainty about how fast, or even if, these technologies will progress.

The Chamber puts a heavy emphasis on developing new technologies because it recognizes that unless and until alternate technologies can compete with traditional fuels on cost, performance, and scalability, they will not be used commercially to a great degree. That is why the Chamber will continue to support policies designed to lower the cost of alternative energy rather than raising the cost of traditional energy. Unfortunately, the Obama Administration has adopted an approach to raise the cost of affordable energy at home and in the international negotiations. As we will see, not only does this approach jeopardize U.S. competitiveness and growth going forward, it also will have a small impact on global GHG emission trends.

The U.S. INDC Lacks Basic Information to Allow a Rigorous Assessment of the Goal

The Obama Administration has set a goal to cut its net greenhouse gas emissions 26% to 28% from the 2005 level by 2025, with a "best effort" to achieve 28%. Its submission to the UNFCC is supposed to provide "information to facilitate the clarity, transparency, and understanding of the contribution." But rather than providing a clear roadmap to 2025, the INDC leads us instead into terra incognita.

This lack of transparency is all the more disappointing because the U.S. INDC claims that, "The target reflects a *planning process* that examine opportunities under existing regulatory authorities to reduce emissions in 2025 of all greenhouse gases from all sources in every economic sector" [emphasis added]. While regulatory proposals used to support the INDC are developed in a public process, the planning process the administration undertook to develop its international commitment did not allow for any opportunity to get input from the public, the business community, other stakeholders, and the Congress. This is despite the fact that the outcome of this process is sure to have far-reaching effects on the economy and employment.

A close examination of the INDC raises more questions than it answers. Nowhere does it explain how the administration intends to achieve the unrealistic goals it has set out. In the absence of a detailed explanation of how the administration intends to meet the goal, the Congress, foreign governments, and stakeholders here and abroad have no basis on which to assess its cost or achievability.

So how does the U.S. commitment add up? It does not. According to the Environmental Protection Agency's (EPA) most recent GHG inventory, net GHG emissions—which include sinks (e.g., removals of carbon dioxide from the atmosphere by forest growth)—were about 6.4 billion metric tons of carbon dioxide equivalent (TCO_2 eq.) in 2005 and about 5.8 billion TCO_2 eq. in 2013. To achieve a 28% reduction in 2025, emissions would have to drop to 4.6 billion TCO_2 eq. That represents a total reduction of about 1.8 billion TCO_2 eq. from the 2005 level, or 1.2 billion TCO_2 from the 2013 level.

Reducing economy-wide GHG emission by such a large amount will be no easy task. Based on our analysis of the existing programs and programs announced by the administration—including programs covering existing and new fossil-fuel power plants, automobile efficiency standards and new standards for heavy trucks, methane emissions from oil and gas operations, appliance efficiency standards, hydrofluorocarbons, land use management, and other areas—we estimate that in 2025 total net GHG emissions would still be about 800 million TCO_2 eq., or 45%, short of the needed 1.8 billion TCO_2 in reductions needed to meet the President's 28% emissions target. Other analysts have come to similar conclusions.

Conspicuous by its absence in the INDC is any reference to emissions from industry. It is hard to imagine that the administration does not intend to get at least some reductions from energy-intensive industrial sectors. Indeed, EPA's fiscal year 2015 budget proposal notes the agency intends to begin considering new GHG regulations on the refining, pulp and paper, iron and steel, livestock, and cement sectors. None of this is detailed in the INDC.

As if these flaws are not enough, the centerpiece of the INDC, EPA's Clean Power Plan, has serious legal vulnerabilities (at a minimum). In its *Utility Air Regulatory Group v. EPA* ruling, the Supreme Court warned the EPA that, "When an agency claims to discover in a long-extant statute an unheralded power to regulate 'a significant portion of the American economy,' we typically greet its announcement with a measure of skepticism. We expect Congress to speak clearly if it wishes to assign to an agency decisions of vast 'economic and political significance'" [citations omitted].

In using a little-used 300-word provision of the Clean Air Act to redesign fundamentally the nation's electricity markets, EPA goes far beyond the bounds of the regulatory authority granted to it by Congress. It is no wonder, then, that the Clean Power Plan is facing substantial legal opposition, with lawsuits filed by 27 states, 24 national trade associations (including a coalition of 16 trade groups led by the U.S. Chamber), 37 rural electric cooperatives, 10 major companies, and three labor unions.

Under these circumstances, it is difficult to see how the administration proposes to sell such an unrealistic, bare-bones plan to the international community, much less to constituencies here at home. Further, because the Obama Administration has decided to defy Congress and implement its climate plan through executive action, nothing it commits to at Paris, including the promise of billions of dollars in financial assistance, will be legally binding on any future administration. The legal limbo the administration's actions have created will have real consequences for business as it tries to plan for the future.

The Paris Commitments Are Extremely Unequal

A new international agreement should take into account changing trends in global emissions and economic development. Developing countries will account for the vast majority of future GHG emissions globally. The International Energy Agency's (IEA) most recent midrange forecast for energy-related carbon dioxide emissions, for example, suggests developing countries will account for 70% of global carbon dioxide emissions from energy in 2030 and 170% of the increase in those emissions between 2013 and 2030.

If the world truly is serious about reducing GHG emissions appreciably, developing countries will have to take on meaningful commitments, something that, based on current evidence, they are not prepared to do. Not only are they not prepared to make meaningful commitments, but under the principle of "common but differentiated responsibilities and respective capabilities" enshrined in the UNFCCC, they are not obligated to do anything without financial and other support from developed countries. Moreover, the inescapable fact is developing countries have a much greater interest in pursuing economic growth and poverty eradication than they do in reducing GHG emissions. These mutually-reinforcing dynamics have led to large disparities in the level of commitments being offered between Annex I and Non-Annex I countries. . . .

The Paris Commitments Will Not Result in a Carbon-Constrained World

In light of the wide disparity in ambition between developed and developing countries noted in the preceding section, it is not surprising that the commitments proffered by developed and developing countries thus far will not curt global GHG emissions and may not even slow their growth appreciably.

Earlier this month, the UNFCCC released a *Synthesis report on the aggregate effect of the intended nationally determined contributions,* its stab at analyzing the impact country pledges will have on global GHG emissions. The analysis evaluated the 119 Intended Nationally Determined Contributions (INDCs), covering about 80% of global net GHG emissions, the UNFCCC received as of 1 October 2015.

The report found that even in the extraordinarily unlikely occurrence that each country fulfills its INDC to the letter—including unconditional as well as conditional elements—emissions in 2030 will be considerably higher (a median of about 8.6 billion TCO_2 eq.) than they were in 2010.

Based on the UNFCCC study and the INDCs submitted by developed countries, it is clear that all of the actual burden of reducing emissions would fall on Australia, Canada, Europe, Japan, New Zealand, and the United States, countries that accounted for just about 27% of total global GHG emissions in 2010. We estimate that if these countries met the goals laid out in their INDCs, their emissions would drop a combined 4.1 billion TCO_2 eq. from 2010 to 2030. If the U.S. INDC goal is reached, it would account for more than half of the 4.1 million TCO_2 reduction for this group of advanced economies.

In the meantime, emissions from the rest of the world would jump anywhere from 8.6 to 12.1 billion TCO_2 eq. from 2010 to 2030, a range equivalent to about 1.5 to 2.1 times total U.S. emissions in 2010. Again, this assumes the INDCs are fulfilled to the letter. If not, the emission increases from the rest of the world will be even larger.

Moreover, it is questionable whether the INDCs would even slow global emissions growth appreciably. . . . When taking into account the broad range of possible outcomes, it is likely that even if countries fulfill their commitments, the resulting trajectory of global GHG emissions will not be all that much different from business as usual. . . .

China and India alone account for 70% of the total coal capacity under construction or planned, and Asia about 89%. The capacity of natural gas- and oil-fired power stations also is expected to grow considerably over the next few years, by about 565 billion and 50 billion watts, respectively. This building spree is not the kind of activity one would expect to see in a carbon constrained world—even green Europe is building coal plants (and is a growing market for U.S. coal exports).

Under Administration's INDC, U.S. Will Leak GHG Emissions—and Jobs and Industries—to Other Countries

It is important to note that despite these costs, EPA admits that its Clean Power Plan, the heart of the U.S. INDC, will have no discernible impact on the climate, and that all of the benefits will come from reductions in other pollutants EPA already regulates within a margin of safety.

The administration's plan will be ineffective largely because any emissions reductions achieved will be more than offset by increases in emissions from other countries, in particular developing countries. Addressing climate change will be of considerably less interest to these countries, where the main priority of governments is poverty eradication.

Another reason GHG emissions in these other countries would continue to grow is because of "carbon leakage" from the U.S. as energy intensive industries flee to more countries with less regulation and lower energy costs. It is well understood that America's abundance of affordable, reliable energy provides businesses a critical operating advantage in today's intensely competitive global economy. . . . Affordable and reliable fuel and electricity, supplied by a diverse mix of coal, nuclear, and increasingly natural gas, give American industry an enormous economic edge, and they are driving a manufacturing revival in areas of the country desperately in need of jobs and investment.

Unfortunately, EPA's Clean Power Plan and other burdensome EPA regulations threaten to throw away this national energy advantage. Instead of attracting foreign investment to the United States, EPA rules could repel this investment into the United States and perhaps even force U.S. companies to shift their investment focus overseas.

Because U.S. businesses compete on a global scale, the electricity and related price increases resulting from EPA's rule will severely disadvantage energy intensive, trade-exposed industries such as chemicals, manufacturing, steel, and pulp and paper. As a result, GHG emissions would not be reduced in the global sense, but simply *moved* to other countries that have not implemented similar restrictions.

Europe provides a cautionary tale. According to the Energy Information Administration, Europe's residential electricity prices have increased at a much faster rate than in the United States. Regulatory structures—including the Emissions Trading System, taxes, user fees, large (and unsustainable) subsidies and mandates for renewable energy technologies, and the mix and cost of fuels—all conspire to make Europe's electricity prices among the highest in the world.

That continent's exorbitant energy prices, largely policy-driven, are ruining its competitiveness and turning energy-intensive industries into endangered species. More and more, we are seeing European companies fleeing sky-high energy costs and shifting production to the United States and other countries.

This is consistent with the conclusion of the Inter-governmental Panel on Climate Change (IPCC) Fourth Assessment report, which found that actions governments took to implement the Kyoto Protocol resulted in economy-wide leakage on the order of 5% to 20%, not insignificant amounts. Similar results could be expected in the United States as a result of implementation of the U.S. in general, and EPA regulations in particular.

Trust but Measure, Report, and Verify [MRV] Activities

An issue that does not receive the attention it deserves is measuring, reporting, and verification of climate policies. As things stand now, the system of MRV that is likely to come out of Paris will focus not on whether a country meets its emissions goal, but on whether it implements the policies and measures designed to meet its goal. In other words, MRV is more about process than results.

Most of the burden of MRV will, as it should, fall on governments. Like other developed countries, the United States has a long history of reporting on its climate change-related activities through its national communications to the UNFCCC. Where MRV is expected to impose or lead to obligations on companies, the UNFCCC should consult with business to design reliable MRV procedures. In particular, business would like to be able to count on existing experience and reporting procedures and to avoid redundant, overlapping, ambiguous, or needlessly expensive or burdensome requirements.

MRV will be especially challenging in developing countries. Transparency is a key to open markets and planning, and businesses will be reticent to invest in developing economies without assurances that its investments in emission reduction and offset projects are real and that government activities in support of INDCs have integrity.

As the recent revelation that the Chinese have been low-balling its coal usage demonstrates, however, that there is still a lot we take for granted. If a sophisticated country like China cannot keep track of something as rudimentary as coal consumption, what can we expect from other governments with fewer resources and capacity? And even the best MRV system will fall short if it is applied to countries

whose social systems and economies that do not function under the rule of law and other legal and social norms that exist in advanced democracies.

Intellectual Property Rights under Assault

The Convention also states that Annex II Parties, a sub-set of Annex I Parties that includes the United States, "shall take all practicable steps to promote, facilitate and finance, as appropriate, the transfer of, or access to, environmentally sound technologies and know-how to other Parties, particularly developing country Parties, to enable them to implement the provisions of the Convention."

Developing countries have used this provision deftly to justify their attempts to weaken intellectual property rights (IPR) protections, ostensibly to remove the supposed "barriers" to technology transfer raised by IPR. Compulsory licensing and a fund supported by developed countries to buy down IP are two of many proposals being bruited.

For example, one option in the most recent (11 November) draft text of the Paris agreement says that ". . . developed country Parties shall provide financial resources . . . to meet the full costs of IPRs of environmentally sound technologies, know-how and such technologies will be provided to developing country Parties *free of cost* in order to enhance their actions to address the adverse effects of climate change." Similar optional language appears in other sections of the text, as well.

IPR serves as a fundamental catalyst of innovation, and study after study has shown that it is not a barrier to technology transfer. A weakened IPR regime such as that being proposed above would provide precious little incentive for companies to invest in advanced technologies if after years of research and development and millions or even billions of dollars invested, their inventions could be expropriated outright by companies in developing countries and manufactured and sold around the world at reduced cost. Under such a circumstance, some of the most innovative companies in the developed world would simply abandon the development of advanced energy technologies.

The United States should continue to encourage the proper environment for technology commerce, cooperation, and investment in developing countries—*e.g.*, transparent markets, the rule of law, property rights, *etc.* Developing countries must be convinced that intellectual property rights protections are in their interests as well as ours, and that technology commerce is technology transfer. The Chamber and other businesses and business groups have in the past urged U.S. negotiators to join with their colleagues from Europe, Japan, and other developed countries in declaring that any weakening of intellectual property would be unacceptable.

Climate Finance—Show Us the Money

Financing issues are among the most controversial in the UNFCCC, and they could derail a Paris agreement. Many developing country INDCs, either in whole or in part, are conditioned on financial support and technology transfer (India's INDC, for example, carries a price tag of $2.5 trillion).

The Green Climate Fund (GCF) was proposed at COP-15 in Copenhagen in 2009, refined in subsequent meetings, and became operational in 2014. GCF aims to provide support to developing country efforts to reduce their GHG emissions and to adapt climate change. To date, about $10.2 billion has been pledged to GCF, with about $5.9 billion has been "announced and signed." The President affirmed a pledge of $3 billion over four years ago during the G-20 meeting in Australia in 2014, and his administration requested $500 million for the GCF in its fiscal year 2016 budget.

Developed countries in Copenhagen also committed to "mobilizing jointly USD 100 billion a year by 2020 to address the needs of developing countries." This is supposed to be "new and additional" money, not money moved from other funds. While many developing countries see most of this as government-to-government funding, developed countries have implied that most funding will come from private sector sources leveraged by government money.

Moreover, developing countries view this $100 billion figure for 2020 as "only the starting point for the post-2020 period and not the ending point." Draft negotiating text suggests this sum should be scaled up predictably after 2020. How much? The text is silent on this, but submissions to the UNFCCC suggest some Parties are seeking quite a bit more than $100 billion. For example, the African Group supports ramping funding up to $600 billion by 2030. China has proposed that, "Commitments by developed country Parties on providing finance, technology and capacity-building support to developing country Parties shall be of the same legal bindingness as their mitigation commitments," and it has called for developed countries to provide the GCF "at least 1% of their GDP per year from 2020." For the U.S., 1% of GDP in 2014 works out to around $170 billion.

There is also the question of how this money will be spent. For example, should U.S. funds be used to support projects that increase the efficiency, and therefore the competitiveness, of state-run foreign firms that compete against U.S. companies? These sorts of concerns may become more pronounced as the GCF increases its activities over time.

However these issues and other finance are worked out in Paris, it is clear that a significant portion of the expected funds—certainly tens if not hundreds of billions of dollars over many years—would be coming from public sources and would have to be appropriated by Congress.

The Long-Term Global Emissions Goals Being Proposed Are Unrealistic

Although every expectation is that the Paris agreement will be a bottom-up treaty, a collective long-term goal is under discussion, too. Most of the proposals are in the range of a 40% to 70% reduction in global GHG emissions from the 2010 level by 2050, with net zero emissions being achieved within a decade or two after that. Characteristic of these is the European Union's proposal calling for a 60% cut in global GHG emissions below their 2010 level by 2050.

A global goal of such a magnitude is completely unrealistic. It would require cuts in emissions in developing countries that they are unwilling to make and developing countries would be would be unwilling to pay for. Even if, for example, all developed countries cut their emissions to "0" by 2050—which will not happen—total emissions from developing countries, which are expected to their combined populations grow by more than 2 billion people, would still have to be about one-third lower than they were in 2010, and so would emissions per capita. But even that would not be enough. They also would have to avoid future emissions of around 30 billion TCO_2 eq. (more than five times current U.S. GHG emissions). Put another way, to reach a 60-by-50 goal even if developed countries emissions collapse to zero in 2050, all of the additional economic activity in developing countries in 2050 compared to 2010—all the energy use, industrial processes, agricultural activity, etc.—would have to be zero-emitting or have their emissions offset in some way.

Large developing countries understand that accepting such emissions limits would have devastating impacts on their economic progress. Despite many opportunities, large developing countries have never agreed to a binding global emissions goal of this magnitude, and they are almost certain not to do so in Paris. That is unless developed countries pledge they are prepared to foot the bill, something that, given the trillions of dollars in costs involved, developed countries simply cannot do.

Developing countries, therefore, will carry on using affordable fossil fuels to boost economic growth and lift their people out of poverty. For them, cutting GHG emissions will always take a backseat to these goals. . . .

Conclusion

Business needs a predictable environment in which to operate and plan. Unfortunately, the administration's INDC adds to the already large uncertainty surrounding a new international agreement and would result in higher energy prices for American businesses and consumers. Its INDC does not provide any guidance in how it intends to meet its goal of a 26% to 28% reduction in net GHG emissions by 2025 from the 2005 level. By our estimates, emissions reductions due to existing and proposed regulations would fall short of the administration's goal by 800 million TCO_2 eq., or 45% of the total goal. Clearly, the administration anticipates that the industrial sector will have to make up for a big chunk, but by no means all, of this shortfall. But without any detail, neither domestic stakeholders nor Parties to the UNFCCC know how this gap might be filled.

Moreover, based on what we have seen so far, large emerging economies have shown very little interest in reducing emissions in any meaningful way, certainly nothing coming close to what the administration is proposing for the United States. An agreement locking such disparities in emissions pledges into place would jeopardize America's energy advantage and leak U.S. industries, their jobs, and their emissions overseas. As a result, the U.S. will see no environmental gain for a great deal of economic pain.

And to what purpose? Christiana Figueres, Executive Secretary of UNFCCC, recently had this to say about the goal of the UNFCCC: "This is the first time in the history of mankind that we are setting ourselves the task of intentionally, within a defined period of time, to change the economic development model that has been reigning for at least 150 years, since the Industrial Revolution."

The same economic system the UNFCCC Secretary wants to discard is the same model that produced the largest flourishing of human health and welfare in all of human history. In the past two to three decades, in particular, there has been tremendous improvement in the lot of people throughout the world owing in large part to greater economic freedom and access to modern energy services. The rest of the world understands that affordable, available, and scalable energy is the not the problem, it is the solution.

Finally, the administration's insistence on not consulting with the Congress or with stakeholders ensures that U.S. political backing for the Paris agreement will remain weak. Back in 1997, the Clinton Administration disregarded clear guidance from the Senate, the Byrd-Hagel Resolution, and signed the Kyoto Protocol, a treaty it knew was political poison and that it never bothered to submit to the Senate for ratification.

Judging from this latest episode in U.S. climate diplomacy, the Obama Administration looks set to repeat the mistake of signing onto a lopsided deal and making promises future presidents and Congresses may be neither willing nor able to keep. As the late, great Yogi Berra might have said, "It's déjà vu all over again."

Stephen D. Eule is the vice president of the U.S. Chamber of Commerce's Institute for 21st Century Energy. Previously he served under President Bush as the director of the Office of Climate Change Policy & Technology at the Department of Energy.

EXPLORING THE ISSUE

Can We Reduce Carbon Emissions Enough to Limit Global Warming?

Critical Thinking and Reflection

1. What seems likely to happen if we do not manage to limit carbon emissions?
2. Helping developing nations limit their carbon emissions as they grow their economies will be expensive. Will it be worth it?
3. The U.S. Chamber of Commerce sees efforts to limit carbon emissions as an attack on history's most successful economic system. What is that economic system? Does it need to be changed?

Is There Common Ground?

Both sides in this issue agree that the COP21 climate conference in Paris is likely to produce an international agreement to limit carbon emissions (as it did). They differ on whether such an agreement can or will successfully limit global warming or climate change over the next century or so. They also differ on whether such an agreement will be good or bad for business.

1. Why would the Business Council for Sustainable Energy have a more positive opinion on whether limiting carbon emissions would be good for business?
2. Why would the U.S. Chamber of Commerce have a more negative opinion on whether limiting carbon emissions would be good for business?
3. It is entirely possible that there might be other ways, besides an international agreement, to limit carbon emissions and hold back global warming. There are even hints to such alternative approaches in the readings. Describe at least one such alternative.

Additional Resources

National Research Council, *Advancing the Science of Climate Change* (http://www.nap.edu/catalog.php?record_id=12782) (May 2010).

National Research Council, *Limiting the Magnitude of Future Climate Change* (http://www.nap.edu/catalog.php?record_id=12785) (May 2010).

National Research Council, *Adapting to the Impacts of Climate Change* (http://www.nap.edu/catalog.php?record_id=12783) (May 2010).

Pope Francis, "Laudato Si," June 2015, at http://w2.vatican.va/content/francesco/en/encyclicals-/documents/papa-francesco_20150524_enciclica-laudato-si.html.

Naomi Klein, *This Changes Everything: Capitalism vs. The Climate* (Simon & Schuster, 2014).

Richard B. Primack, *Walden Warming* (University of Chicago Press, 2014).

Internet References . . .

350.org

http://www.350.org/

Greenpeace: Fighting Global Warming

http://www.greenpeace.org/usa/global-warming/

Intergovernmental Panel on Climate Change: Climate Change 2014: Fifth Assessment Report

http://ar5-syr.ipcc.ch/

The National Renewable Energy Laboratory

http://www.nrel.gov/

United Nations Framework Convention on Climate Change

http://unfccc.int/2860.php

Selected, Edited, and with Issue Framing Material by:
Thomas A. Easton, *Mount Ida College*

ISSUE

Would a Carbon Tax Help
Slow Global Warming?

YES: James Rydge, from "Implementing Effective Carbon Pricing," *The New Climate Economy* (2015)

NO: Robert P. Murphy, Patrick J. Michaels, and Paul C. Knappenberger, from "The Case Against a Carbon Tax," Cato Institute (2015)

Learning Outcomes

After reading this issue, you will be able to:

- Explain what carbon pricing is.
- Explain how carbon pricing could help reduce emissions of greenhouse gases.
- Explain why international cooperation is essential to a working carbon pricing scheme.
- Explain what is meant by the "social cost of carbon."
- Discuss whether or not it is fair for Americans to pay for a "social cost of carbon" that affects other nations.

ISSUE SUMMARY

YES: James Rydge argues that the case for using carbon pricing (via a carbon tax or a cap-and-trade system) as an important component of efforts to bring carbon emissions and their effects on global climate change under control is strong, momentum is growing, and effects on competitiveness can be dealt with via international cooperation. Therefore, all developed and emerging economies, and others where possible, should commit to introducing or strengthening carbon pricing by 2020, and should phase out fossil fuel subsidies.

NO: Robert P. Murphy, Patrick J. Michaels, and Paul C. Knappenberger argue that the economics of climate change reveal that the case for a U.S. carbon tax is very weak, partly because reining in global warming cannot be justified in cost/benefit terms. Even a well-designed carbon tax would probably cause more harm than good.

The Environmental Protection Agency (EPA) was established in 1970 in response to concerns about air and water pollution. During the next two decades an unprecedented series of legislative acts and administrative rules were promulgated, placing numerous restrictions on industrial and commercial activities that might result in the pollution, degradation, or contamination of land, air, water, food, and the workplace.

Such forms of regulatory control have always been opposed by the affected industrial corporations and developers as well as by advocates of a free-market policy. More moderate critics of the government's regulatory program recognize that adequate environmental protection will not result from completely voluntary policies. They suggest that a new set of strategies is needed. Arguing that "top down, federal, command and control legislation" is not an appropriate or effective means of preventing environmental degradation, they propose a wide range of alternative tactics, many of which are designed to operate through the economic marketplace. The first significant congressional response to these proposals was the incorporation of tradable pollution emission rights into the 1990 Clean Air Act amendments as a means for reducing acid rain–causing sulfur dioxide emissions. More recently, the 1997 international negotiations on controlling global warming, held in Kyoto, Japan, resulted in a protocol that includes emissions trading as one of the key elements in the plan to limit the atmospheric buildup of greenhouse gases.

Charles W. Schmidt, "The Market for Pollution," *Environmental Health Perspectives* (August 2001), argues that emissions trading schemes represent "the most significant developments" in the use of economic incentives to motivate corporations to reduce pollution. However, many environmentalists oppose the idea of allowing anyone to pay to pollute, either on moral grounds or because they doubt that these tactics will actually achieve the goal of controlling pollution. Diminishment of the acid rain problem is often cited as an example of how well emission rights trading can work, but in "Dispelling the Myths of the Acid Rain Story," *Environment* (July–August 1998), Don Munton argues that other control measures, such as switching to low-sulfur fuels, deserve much more of the credit for reducing sulfur dioxide emissions. Recent assessments of the acid rain program by the EPA and such organizations as the Environmental Defense Fund are more positive. So is the corporate world: In September 2001, *The Economist* ("Economic Man, Cleaner Planet") reported that economic incentives have proved very useful and "market forces are only just beginning to make inroads into green policymaking." In March 2002, *Pipeline and Gas Journal* reported that "Despite uncertainty surrounding U.S. and international environmental policies, companies in a wide range of industries—especially those in the energy field—are increasingly using emission reduction credits as a way to meet the challenges of cutting greenhouse gas emissions."

In "A Low-Cost Way to Control Climate Change," *Issues in Science and Technology* (Spring 1998), Byron Swift argues that the "cap-and-trade" feature of the U.S. Acid Rain Program has been so successful that a similar system for implementing the Kyoto Protocol's emissions trading mandate as a cost-effective means of controlling greenhouse gases should work. In March 2001, the U.S. Senate Committee on Agriculture, Nutrition, and Forestry held a "Hearing on Biomass and Environmental Trading Opportunities for Agriculture and Forestry," in which witnesses urged Congress to encourage trading for both its economic and its environmental benefits. Richard L. Sandor, chairman and chief executive officer of Environmental Financial Products LLC, said that "200 million tons of CO_2 could be sequestered through soils and forestry in the United States per year. At the most conservative prices of $20–$30 per ton, this could potentially generate $4–$6 billion in additional agricultural income."

A number of carbon trading schemes have been implemented, though with limited success. Europe's attempt to implement a cap-and-trade system to control carbon emissions did not work. According to Marianne Lavelle, "The Carbon Market Has a Dirty Little Secret," *U.S. News and World Report* (May 14, 2007), in Europe the value of tradable emissions allowances fell so low, partly because too many allowances were issued, that it became cheaper to burn more fossil fuel and emit more carbon than to burn and emit less. Clearly, future trading schemes would need to be designed to avoid this and related problems. Other approaches might also be needed, such as "carbon offsets," meaning that corporations, governments, and even individuals compensate for carbon dioxide emissions by investing in activities that remove carbon dioxide from the air or reduce emissions from a different source. See Anja Kollmuss, "Carbon Offsets 101," *World Watch* (July/August 2007). Unfortunately, present carbon-offset schemes contain loopholes that mean they may do little to reduce overall emissions; see Madhusree Mukerjee, "A Mechanism of Hot Air," *Scientific American* (June 2009).

On May 21, 2009, the House Energy and Commerce Committee approved H.R. 2454, the American Clean Energy and Security Act. The goal of the Act, said Committee Chair Henry A. Waxman (D-CA), was to "break our dependence on foreign oil, make our nation the world leader in clean energy jobs and technology, and cut global warming pollution. I am grateful to my colleagues who supported this legislation and to President Obama for his outstanding leadership on these critical issues." Among other things, the Act established Title VII of the Clean Air Act to provide a declining limit on global warming pollution (a "cap" as in "cap-and-trade") and to hold industries accountable for pollution reduction under the limit. The aim was to cut global warming pollution by 17 percent compared to 2005 levels in 2020, by 42 percent in 2030, and by 83 percent in 2050. In June 2009, the House of Representatives passed a version of the bill that also called for utilities to use more renewable energy sources. However, the Senate refused to pass any version of the bill at all.

According to the 2014 *Fifth Assessment Report* from the Intergovernmental Panel on Climate Change (ipcc.ch), the threat of global warming appears worse than ever, and it is clearer than ever that human-caused carbon emissions are responsible. And even in 2009, the Global Humanitarian Forum's "Human Impact Report: Climate Change—The Anatomy of a Silent Crisis" (May 29, 2009) said that global warming was already affecting over 300 million people and was already responsible for 300,000 deaths per year. Unfortunately, it is inevitable that the deadly impact of global warming must grow worse for many years before it can be stopped.

Yet the debate over the proper actions to take is by no means over. Some analysts argue that a carbon tax would be more effective; see Bettina B. F. Wittneben, "Exxon Is Right: Let Us Re-Examine Our Choice for a Cap-and-Trade System over a Carbon Tax," *Energy Policy* (June 2009). But that alternative has also failed to gain traction in Congress.

Cap-and-trade, carbon tax, and carbon offset schemes are all variations on the basic idea of putting a price on carbon (a "carbon price"), and all are variations on the idea that those who pollute should be obliged to make up in some way for the costs they impose on society and which are borne by institutions (taxpayers, insurance companies, etc.) outside the polluting corporations. Such costs are known as "negativeexternalities" (seehttp://economics.fundamentalfinance.com/negative-externality.php). Unfortunately, our society does not deal well with negative externalities, preferring instead to give polluters (such as the fossil fuel industry) subsidies (such as tax breaks) which encourage them to pollute more, instead of less. The International Monetary Fund recently made it clear that it considers climate change a threat to the world's economies and it is time to implement carbon pricing and end fossil fuel subsidies (Samantha Page, "Now Is the Time for a Carbon Tax, IMF Chief Says," *Climate Progress*, October 8, 2015; http://thinkprogress.org/climate/2015/10/08/3710467/imf-says-to-tax-carbon/). In the YES selection, James Rydge argues that the case for using carbon pricing (via a carbon tax or a cap-and-trade system) as an important component of efforts to bring carbon emissions and their effects on global climate change under control is strong, momentum is growing, and effects on competitiveness can be dealt with via international cooperation. Therefore, all developed and emerging economies, and others where possible, should commit to introducing or strengthening carbon pricing by 2020, and should phase out fossil fuel subsidies. In the NO selection, Robert P. Murphy, Patrick J. Michaels, and Paul C. Knappenberger argue that the economics of climate change reveal that the case for a U.S. carbon tax is very weak, partly because reining in global warming cannot be justified in cost/benefit terms. Even a well-designed carbon tax would probably cause more harm than good.

YES

James Rydge

Implementing Effective Carbon Pricing

Overview

Support for carbon pricing is growing around the world. Governments, businesses and investors are recognising that nationally-appropriate taxes and trading schemes, as part of a well-aligned package of policies for low-carbon change, can reduce greenhouse gas (GHG) emissions without harming the economy. Strong, predictable and rising carbon prices send an important signal to markets, helping to align expectations on the direction of change, thereby steering consumption choices and the type of investments made in infrastructure and innovation. They also raise fiscal revenues that can be put to productive uses. Around 40 national jurisdictions and over 20 cities, states and regions, have adopted or are planning explicit carbon prices, covering about 12% of global GHG emissions. The number of carbon pricing instruments implemented or scheduled has almost doubled from 20 to 38 since 2012. Over 1000 major companies and investors have endorsed carbon pricing, and around 450 now use an internal carbon price (US$40/t CO_2 or higher for some major oil companies) to guide investment decisions, up from 150 companies in 2014.

While this momentum is encouraging, current price levels and coverage of emissions are still very low. Carbon prices vary significantly, from less than US$1 to US$130 per tonne of CO_2e, with around 85% of emissions priced at less than US$10 per tonne. This is considerably lower than the price that economic models suggest is needed to meet the 2°C global warming goal adopted by the international community.

International cooperation on carbon pricing and subsidy reform, in particular between countries of the G20, and with the support of the World Bank, the Organisation for Economic Co-operation and Development (OECD) and the International Monetary Fund (IMF), can help mitigate concerns holding back faster progress. Cooperation can help to overcome concerns about competitiveness impacts from unilateral policy action, improve knowledge-sharing and transparency, provide opportunities to link emission trading schemes, and reduce the costs of action.

Introduction

It is now widely acknowledged that one of the most important steps that governments in advanced and emerging economies can take to build a more robust economy and a safer climate is to put an explicit price on carbon. A strong, predictable and rising explicit carbon price—applied through policies appropriate to the national context, including carbon taxes or cap-and-trade systems—can send important signals across the economy, helping to guide consumption choices and investments towards low-carbon activities and away from carbon-intensive ones. It can also be a better way to raise revenue for productive uses than many existing taxes, such as on employment. Phasing out fossil fuel subsidies—effectively, negative carbon prices—is also crucial, as they distort markets and encourage wasteful use, contributing to air pollution and increasing importing countries' vulnerability to volatile prices.

Around 40 national jurisdictions and over 20 cities, states and regions, have implemented or scheduled an explicit price on carbon, covering an estimated 7 Gt CO_2e, or about 12% of annual global greenhouse gas (GHG) emissions. This is triple the coverage of a decade ago. The number of carbon pricing instruments (implemented or scheduled) has almost doubled from 20 to 38 since 2012. Concerns persist that pricing carbon will hurt industrial competitiveness, so most explicit prices are still quite low, less than US$10 per tonne of CO_2, and there is often no mechanism or plan to increase them. Several countries have also provided exemptions or special treatment to their most polluting energy-intensive industries, thus limiting the effectiveness of the carbon price.

International cooperation can help to overcome this barrier. Trading partners can coordinate the introduction of carbon prices of roughly comparable levels, and thus overcome competitiveness concerns. By working together, countries can also benefit from knowledge-sharing on best practice, along with greater transparency and the opportunity to link trading schemes.

Conditions are now particularly favourable for both carbon pricing and reform of fossil fuel consumption subsidies, due to the fall in global oil prices over the last year, combined with lower gas and coal prices. G20 countries have already agreed to phase out inefficient fossil fuel subsidies, and several are now acting with support of international institutions such as the International Monetary Fund (IMF), the International Energy Agency (IEA), the Organisation for Economic Co-operation and Development (OECD) and The World Bank. The Asia-Pacific Economic Cooperation (APEC) economies have made a similar commitment.

There is a strong case for countries to build on these commitments and introduce meaningful explicit carbon prices across countries at the same time. This working paper begins by looking at the strong momentum for carbon pricing around the world, including growing support from the private sector. It then examines the benefits of carbon pricing, and explains what is needed for successful implementation, drawing on lessons from different countries. Finally, it discusses how to advance international cooperation on carbon pricing, with particular attention to members of the G20.

Growing Momentum for Carbon Pricing

The use of explicit carbon pricing is increasing. In 2014, China launched two pilot regional emissions trading schemes (ETSs), bringing the total to seven, and announced plans to transition to a national carbon pricing system from 2017. The scheme will be the world's largest, twice the size of the European Union Emissions Trading System (EU ETS), covering around 3–4 billion tonnes of CO_2—equivalent to the total annual emissions of the European Union (EU), or India, Brazil and Japan combined. In January 2015, South Korea launched its ETS, the second largest cap-and-trade system in the world, covering more than 500 business entities from 23 sectors. Permits have traded in the range of US$7–8 per tonne. The European Union approved important reforms in 2014 to strengthen and revitalise its carbon market, and it has provisionally agreed that implementation of these reforms will be brought forward from 2021 to 2019. California and Quebec linked their carbon trading schemes in 2014, enabling trade in allowances and many other benefits, and in April 2015, Ontario announced that it will launch an ETS linked to the California and Quebec schemes.

As part of wider fiscal reforms, Chile approved a carbon tax in September 2014, to start in 2018; the rate is

US$5 per tonne of CO_2e and applies to the power sector and large industries, covering around 55% of emissions. South Africa plans to introduce a carbon tax in 2016. . . .

Support for carbon pricing is also building in the private sector. Many major businesses, including in high-emitting sectors such as oil and gas, are now endorsing carbon pricing—an important shift after many years of business opposition. They see it as a way to drive efficiency and profitable new business opportunities. More than 1,000 businesses and investors expressed support for carbon pricing at the UN Climate Summit in September 2014, including BP, British Airways, Cemex, Braskem, Royal Dutch Shell, Statkraft, Unilever, Statoil and DONG Energy. At the time of writing 437 businesses are reported to be already using an internal carbon price in assessing investments, up from 150 in 2014. Shell, for example, uses a price of US$40 per tonne of CO_2e, Statoil ASA US$50, and ExxonMobil US$80. In May 2015, at the Business & Climate Summit 2015 in Paris, 25 global business networks representing more than 6.5 million companies called for "robust and effective carbon pricing mechanisms as a key component to gear investment and orient consumer behaviour towards low-carbon solutions and achieve global net emissions reduction at the least economic costs."

These developments reflect an increasing understanding of how to design successful carbon pricing policies and unlock their benefits at the national and corporate level; countries and businesses are recognising the wide range of economic benefits that are possible. They are also learning how to manage many of the challenges that can arise around these reforms, which may make it easier for others in the future.

Conditions are now particularly favourable for both carbon pricing and fossil fuel consumption subsidy reform due to the fall in global oil prices over the last year, combined with lower gas and coal prices. While it is not yet clear whether these lower fossil fuel prices will last, in the short term they can help to offset any energy price increases resulting from these measures, making it easier for consumers and businesses to adjust, and reducing political resistance. It is notable that a number of countries, including Mexico, India and Indonesia, have seized the opportunity to advance reform of fossil fuel subsidies over the last year. Many of these reforms are expected to be permanent—i.e., they are unlikely to be reversed if energy prices rise. This stronger momentum is supported by the G20 commitment to rationalise or phase out fossil fuel subsidies from 2009, which was reaffirmed again most recently in 2014, as well as a similar commitment from APEC countries.

The Economic and Climate Case for Carbon Pricing

. . . Experience with carbon prices to date suggests that they have four key benefits: they are an efficient way to reduce GHG emissions; they are a useful way to raise revenue to support public priorities; they provide wider environmental and energy security benefits; and they provide a clear and credible price signal to guide business expectations. Below we address each of these in turn, and examine key factors for successful implementation.

Carbon Prices Are an Efficient Way to Reduce GHG Emissions

Carbon prices set through broad-based taxes or cap-and-trade systems are an economically efficient way to tackle the greenhouse gas market failure. Recent evidence from the electricity sector indicates that these have been the cheapest policies to reduce emissions. Carbon prices come in many forms, and even non-price-based regulatory measures to reduce GHG emissions impose an "implicit" price on the release of carbon and thus can be considered "implicit carbon taxes." Here we focus on explicit carbon prices.

Governments have learned much about the design of explicit carbon pricing policy instruments over recent years. Key lessons and examples are summarised in the recent World Bank report, *FASTER Principles for Successful Carbon Pricing.*

One of the key lessons, for example, is that cap-and-trade systems need to be responsive to market shocks to maintain robust prices. Europe's economic downturn after the financial crash in 2008 called for downward adjustments to the caps in the EU ETS, but policy design did not allow this, leading to substantial surpluses and a sharp drop in prices. The EU ETS has been through a difficult time, but is now on a path to reform based on lessons learned. The European Commission has agreed to "backload" some permits, i.e. set aside until a later date, to reduce those surpluses, and has proposed a "market stability reserve" to help keep prices higher and less volatile.

In addition to good design, the broader policy context is important. A range of policies are needed to tackle different market failures and barriers—including structural, political and behavioural barriers—that can limit the effectiveness of the economic incentives created by carbon pricing. For example, additional policy instruments are needed to tackle barriers that are commonly faced by industry, such as short investment payback periods and capital constraints, prescriptive standards, entrenched customer preferences and other factors.

Carbon prices and complementary policies must also be well aligned and integrated, both within the policy package itself and across the wider economy. The OECD, together with the IEA, the International Transport Forum (ITF) and the Nuclear Energy Agency (NEA), recently published a landmark study on aligning and integrating policies for the transition to a low-carbon economy. They conclude that much can be done in non-climate policy portfolios to facilitate the implementation of core climate policy instruments, such as carbon pricing, and improve their effectiveness. "Misalignments" that unintentionally hinder the climate policy signal exist in finance, taxation, innovation and trade, as well as in sector-specific regulatory frameworks in electricity, mobility and land use. In such cases, policy reform can often have broader benefits for society and the climate, such as reduced costs, improved effectiveness, clearer market signals, and a generally lower risk of policy failure.

Fossil fuel subsidies are one of many examples of misalignment. They are often justified on the grounds of helping the poor or increasing the competitiveness of business and industry. However, energy and fossil fuel subsidies are inefficient ways of achieving these objectives, and there are much more effective approaches. For example, it is estimated that on average only 7% of the benefits from fossil fuel subsidies reach the poorest 20% of the population. Governments apply consumption subsidies in many ways, such as by keeping local energy prices below international market prices, or through grants or vouchers to make energy more affordable. Subsidies and tax breaks are also used to support the production of fossil fuels. These are essentially negative carbon prices. Together, these subsidies to fossil fuels add up to about US$600 billion per year. This includes consumption subsidies in emerging and developing economies of around US$548 billion in 2013, and fossil fuel exploration, production and consumption support in OECD countries of around US$55–90 billion a year.

Phasing out subsidies to the production and consumption of fossil fuels, as part of wider fiscal and energy sector reform, has many benefits. It can reduce the burden on national budgets; for example, support to fossil fuel consumption in 40 developing countries represents around 5% of GDP and 25–30% of government revenues. Reducing this economic distortion allows for a more productive and efficient allocation of resources, which can lead to gains in real incomes and GDP. Angola's spending on fossil fuel subsidies in 2014, for example, was higher than its spending on health and education combined, and represented 3.7% of GDP. In its 2015 budget, the Angolan government cut fossil fuel subsidies by 60%.

Reforms also lead to higher energy prices. This can provide additional revenues for utilities to invest in upgrading or expanding supply infrastructure, in particular renewable energy, which becomes more competitive as fossil fuel prices rise. Pricing reforms are considered important for expanding energy access in sub-Saharan Africa, for example. At the same time, they encourage investment in energy efficiency and conservation, and reduce CO_2 emissions and air pollution from fossil fuel combustion, among other benefits.

There is growing momentum to reform fossil fuel consumption subsidies, helped in part by lower oil prices (which reduce the impact on energy price rises) and motivated by growing fiscal pressures, including in oil-exporting nations where consumption subsidies are often high. In addition to the reasons outlined earlier, reforms have also been motivated by fuel smuggling from countries with subsidised fuels to those without. (It is estimated, for example, that around 10% of fuel consumption is smuggled from Angola to the Republic of Congo and the Democratic Republic of Congo.) But it remains true that subsidy reform is very challenging institutionally and politically. . . .

There has been mixed success on reform of fossil fuel production subsidies. Lower oil prices have led to some increased calls from industry to increase production subsidies, and some governments have acted on such requests, in part due to the royalties they receive from these industries. In the UK, for example, the government already provides generous tax breaks to the oil and gas industry, but agreed to increase support for North Sea oil producers in 2015. In Alberta, Canada, however, a newly elected government has pledged to review the Province's royalties on fossil fuel production.

Carbon Pricing Instruments Can Be Useful for Raising Revenue to Support Public Priorities

The emerging evidence shows that carbon pricing is an effective way to reduce emissions without harming the economy. Sweden introduced its carbon tax in 1991; its economy grew by nearly 60% in 1990–2013 while emissions fell by 23%. In the Canadian province of British Columbia, there was no evidence that the carbon tax adversely affected GDP growth over the five-year period following its introduction in 2008. It did, however, lead to a large and unexpected drop in oil product consumption (reflecting the fact that more substitution options were available in practice than were predicted prior to the introduction of the carbon tax) and GHG emissions fell by about 10% in 2008–2011, compared with a 1% reduction in the rest of Canada. The nine US states in the Regional Greenhouse Gas Initiative (RGGI) grew their economies by 9.2% in 2009–2013—better than the other 41 states' 8.8%—while reducing their combined emissions by 18% (vs. 4% in the other states). A recent study found that in 2012–2014 alone, RGGI had a net economic benefit of US$1.3 billion on the nine member states' economies.

Economies are always changing, and those that embrace change do better. Governments need to undertake regular reforms to ensure their economies can respond to opportunities to maintain and enhance their efficiency, productivity and competitiveness. Fiscal reform is central to this task. Fiscal reform involving broad-based carbon prices provides an opportunity to lower the burden of existing taxes on work effort and capital accumulation. This can provide incentives for increasing employment and investment, thus boosting growth. For example, British Columbia has used its carbon tax revenues, around 3% of the total budget, to lower income and corporate taxes.

Multiple other benefits of this type of fiscal reform are becoming more widely acknowledged. For example, reducing taxes on work and capital reduces the incentive for people and businesses to stay in the informal sector (fully or partially) as a way to evade taxes. Carbon prices are also a higher-quality tax base over the short to medium term, as they are usually collected from a relatively small number of firms (e.g. electricity producers, fuel suppliers). This could be particularly valuable in counties with large informal sectors and/or tax evasion problems, as ensuring compliance could be easier and less costly compared with other broader-based taxes.

Governments can use carbon tax revenues in a number of ways. The use of revenues should be guided by good principles of public finance, including efficiency, and consideration of distribution and incidence, i.e. where the burden of the tax falls. Some potential productive uses include: reducing existing distortionary taxes, as discussed above; reducing public sector debt/GDP ratios (e.g. the introduction of a carbon tax in Ireland in 2010 raised much-needed revenues and avoided even harsher fiscal tightening measures); spending on public priorities such as health and education; funding innovation (e.g. Quebec and California use revenues from their ETS auctions to fund low-carbon technology advancement); financing international climate action and other climate policies (e.g. the EU distributes EU ETS auction revenues to EU Member States, which use them to fund innovation and climate- and energy-related activities, among other things); and public financing support for infrastructure investment, for example by capitalising green investment banks. The most productive uses will differ by country, based on their existing social and economic structures, including tax.

Governments often also use a share of the carbon tax revenues to compensate those who are disadvantaged by reform, including consumers facing higher energy prices. Although carbon pricing will increase the efficiency of resource use, with net economic benefits overall, some people and economic sectors may be adversely affected. Neglecting them, or failing to clearly communicate the policies that are put in place to help smooth the transition, has been a major factor in strong resistance to carbon pricing. In most cases, clear and well-communicated policies will be needed to alleviate any distributional impacts on affected groups, in particular on poorer households. . . . This needs to be well targeted and may be in the form of cash transfers or social security payments, reductions in marginal income tax rates, or financial help to invest in energy efficiency measures that can offset higher energy bills. International institutions such as the World Bank are helping countries to develop such complementary compensation policies. The more revenue is spent on compensation, of course, the less is available for other productive uses.

Wider Environmental and Economic Security Benefits from Carbon Prices

These include local environmental benefits from reduced local air pollution, reduced traffic congestion, and better-functioning ecosystems. The human health and avoided mortality benefits of reducing health pollution are particularly large. The World Health Organization (WHO) has estimated that, in 2012, outdoor air pollution—much of it linked to fossil fuel use—caused 3.7 million premature deaths. . . . [T]he value of premature deaths from PM2.5 air pollution averaged the equivalent of over 4% of GDP in the 15 largest CO_2 emitters in 2010. Measures that reduce greenhouse gases and air pollution together in these countries would yield health benefits valued at US$73 per tonne of CO_2 abated. Carbon pricing can also drive enhanced energy security in energy-importing nations by reducing their reliance on fossil fuels. Moreover, by driving investment in energy efficiency and renewable energy, a carbon price can reduce exposure to increasingly volatile fossil fuel prices and less risk of disruption to energy supplies.

Clear and Credible Price Signals to Guide Expectations

Clear and credible price signals across the economy can align expectations and help provide the private sector with the certainty needed to invest in the three key drivers of growth, resource efficiency, infrastructure and innovation. This can help to accelerate and scale up investments in more efficient products, new business models, new markets, new skills and jobs, and more productive ways of working and operating.

Where carbon prices have long-term credibility, and are aligned with complementary policies, they can provide the incentive to invest in low-carbon infrastructure. Even though such investments will often lead to significant returns over time, clear long-term policy signals can help to ensure upfront financing is available given that the low-carbon investments often have high upfront costs and different risk-return profiles from high-carbon investments. Weak, absent or unclear carbon price signals will slow investment and change and increase the economic and social costs of a low-carbon economic transition.

Experience shows that many existing carbon prices have failed to send a clear and strong signal, limiting their effectiveness. This was the case initially with the EU ETS, for example, which has been hampered by a surplus of permits and resulting low prices, a lack of credibility around the future of the policy, and unclear signals as key energy-intensive industries were given overly generous compensation. As of April 2015, allowances in the EU ETS were trading at around US$8 per tonne of CO_2e, and in California, at around US$13 per tonne.

Weak carbon prices, including fossil fuel subsidies, also fail to send clear low-carbon signals to investors. This is reflected in the continued high levels of investment in fossil fuel-based energy, around US$950 billion in 2013. Price floors, as used in the UK, California and in the seven Chinese pilot schemes, can ensure a minimum price level in emissions trading, providing greater certainty and more consistent policy signals. This ensures that industries covered by the carbon price, investors and technology providers can make decisions knowing what the minimum price in the system will be at any time in the future.

However, with or without price floors, current prices are likely to be too low to send clear and sufficient signals to investors, consumers and technology providers. As of April 2015, prices in China's emissions trading pilot schemes were in the range of US$4–8 per tonne. South Korea and Switzerland's ETS prices were around US$9 per tonne. South Africa's carbon tax is planned to start in early 2016 at about US$10 per tonne of CO_2, and rise by 10% per year, but with substantial tax exemptions in some sectors. Ireland, Denmark and British Columbia have carbon taxes in the US$22–24 range. France, which in its 2014 budget adopted a carbon tax of €7 per tonne of CO_2, raised it to €14.50 for 2015. It will increase to €22 for 2016 and legislation approved in July 2015 will raise the tax to €56 in 2020 and to €100 in 2030. Sweden has a price of US$130 per tonne of CO_2e in some sectors. This has sent clear signals that have led to a strong economy and large emissions reductions at the same time.

Many estimates of the costs of projected climate change, including from modelling exercises, also suggest higher carbon prices would be appropriate. For example, analysis for the US government has recommended a "social cost of carbon" (an estimate of the economic damage associated with a one tonne increase in carbon dioxide emissions in a given year) of around US$36 per tonne of CO_2 (the average of US$11–56, with the low end based on a higher discount rate), rising to around US$50 (US$16–73) in 2030. Prices today are also at the lower end of the spectrum of internal carbon prices that businesses are already applying to guide their own internal investment decisions. In 2015 the Carbon Disclosure Project (CDP) found 437 worldwide were using internal carbon prices as a tool to drive investments in GHG emission reductions and mitigate risks from future climate policies. Nearly 600 other companies said they are considering carbon pricing in the next two years. The prices reported ranged from under US$1 to over US$150 per tonne of CO_2e. Several of the companies are in the oil and gas sector, such as Shell (US$40), ConocoPhillips (US$6–51) and ExxonMobil (US$80), but the list also includes companies in a wide range of other sectors, such as Google (US$14), Microsoft (US$4.4), Disney (US$10–20), and Nestlé (US$15.47). . . .

International Cooperation

A Better Way to Overcome Competitiveness Concerns

We have learned a great deal from experiences to date with carbon pricing at the national and regional levels, and there is growing evidence that carbon pricing is good for both the economy and the climate. But there are still major impediments to scaling up the use of carbon pricing across sectors and countries because of anxieties around competitiveness impacts. Greater international coordination on pricing carbon and reforming fossil fuel subsidies can help to minimise the real or perceived impacts on competitiveness of unilateral action.

Recent evidence from carbon pricing shows that these concerns around competitiveness have not materialised on a significant scale in practice. . . . [T]he direct competitiveness impacts of a carbon price are small for countries that moved early, and there is little evidence of "carbon leakage" (the movement of production and emissions to locations with less stringent climate policy). This is partly due to the lack of stringency of carbon prices to date. And the latest research suggests that even at higher carbon prices, the impacts on industrial competitiveness in Europe are likely to be low.

Nevertheless, there are often concerns about the potential competitiveness impacts and carbon leakage from high carbon prices for a small group of carbon-intensive and trade-exposed industries, such as cement, paper, metals and chemicals, which compete largely on cost. These risks are real where carbon price signals are strong and the stringency of climate policies differ significantly across jurisdictions. However, the actual impact from higher carbon prices on competitiveness and location decisions is complex and hard to ascertain, and must be examined in the context of the wider business environment. In practice, investment and production location decisions are determined by a range of factors, such as proximity to product markets, transport costs, construction costs of new facilities, labour costs, access to materials, business risk, other taxes, local institutions and local infrastructure, with climate policy generally a less significant issue. Other factors may also come into play, including the intensity of competition, opportunities for abatement in a sector, profitability, and price sensitivity of customers. Different policies have been used or proposed to tackle these concerns, including free allocation of allowances and border carbon adjustments (BCAs). Both of these approaches are problematic, however.

Many emissions trading systems have allocated permits for free to industry. Methods of free allocation (e.g. grandfathering, output-based allocation and fixed sector benchmarking) differ in terms of administrative complexity and effectiveness in preventing leakage, and need to be revised over time, but they all reduce the potential benefits of carbon pricing, since the revenues that could have been put to productive use are forgone. Today, this practice is increasingly confined to shielding trade-exposed and emissions-intensive industries from perceived adverse effects on their international competitiveness, as in the EU ETS. In the power sector, free permits are mostly limited to situations where producers cannot pass on carbon costs (as in China), but in Eastern Europe, for example, they still support large and politically influential coal-fired generators. Governments have also kept effective tax rates on the carbon content of different types of energy use low, on average, with taxes on high-emitting types of energy, such as coal, low or non-existent in many countries.

Other forms of compensation can include lump-sum rebates; administrative exemptions; support for energy efficiency improvements; payments to reskill workers or restructure operations (to increase efficiency and competitiveness in the medium to long term); or funding for low-carbon research and development. Experience suggests that the level of compensation required to ensure an initial profit-neutral impact from carbon pricing is likely to be relatively small, perhaps around 15% of total carbon tax revenues, according to some analyses. Where compensation is provided, there are good grounds for making it temporary, with clear phase-out plans as the industry and firms adjust and the competitiveness concerns subside, and governments should avoid applying total exemptions from carbon prices.

Some have called for the introduction of BCAs, measures that would apply a tax on the carbon embedded in traded products and services. Some commentators have argued that they would "level the playing field" with countries with weak or no climate policies. BCAs have also been suggested as a "threat" to spur countries towards more comprehensive global climate action. . . . [H]owever, they are controversial, especially where they are seen as discriminating against developing countries, and significant technical and administrative challenges exist around their implementation.

Compensation, including free allowances, and BCAs are second-best instruments. A better approach is to coordinate policies internationally to overcome these competitiveness and leakage concerns, by reducing the differences in pricing and subsidy policies between trading partners. We now have the experience and momentum to move to the first-best option. Sharing knowledge and experience among countries on the factors that have enabled successful reforms, as well as the challenges, is the first step to international cooperation.

How to Foster Greater International Cooperation on Carbon Pricing

As noted earlier, carbon pricing is already spreading around the world. Several initiatives are helping to accelerate action. The World Bank is working with the We Mean Business Coalition of major corporate associations and other partners to increase knowledge on how to design and implement successful carbon pricing systems through the Carbon Pricing Leadership Coalition (CPLC).

They are developing forward-looking carbon pricing pathways that look at how business and government can define the business and economic case for carbon pricing. As mentioned above, the World Bank Group and the OECD, with inputs from the IMF, have also developed a set of principles for successful carbon pricing, based on the lessons learned from carbon pricing experience in jurisdictions around the world. Their report contains many rich examples that complement the work in this paper. The aim of this work is to enlarge the number of countries and businesses adopting and supporting carbon pricing prior to the UN Climate Change Conference (COP21) in Paris and beyond.

The World Bank Partnership for Market Readiness (PMR) has also helped to accelerate action. The PMR provides support to countries to prepare and implement carbon pricing instruments, and other climate policies, with the aim of scaling up emissions reductions. It serves as a platform to share lessons between countries and organisations. The International Carbon Action Partnership (ICAP) also runs summer schools and training for officials of governments considering introducing carbon pricing.

These initiatives should not be taken to mean that a common carbon pricing policy instrument will be implemented across countries. The actual policies and prices adopted will vary widely, with each country or region in most cases choosing its own "bottom-up" policies. Instruments are chosen and designed, and prices set, to reflect each country's climate ambition, increasingly as expressed in its INDC, the existing economic structure and policy landscape, including other climate and energy policies; and a range of other political, social and economic factors, as alluded to above.

Nevertheless, analyses have shown that there are potential benefits from linking carbon pricing schemes across countries or sub-national regions, to minimise price differences. This can send a more consistent and credible global price signal that aligns expectations worldwide on the direction of change. Linking cap-and-trade schemes can also lower the cost of a given level of emission reductions—for example, by ensuring the lowest-cost emissions reductions are realised across the linked countries, reducing price volatility and increasing market liquidity. It also helps to reduce competitiveness concerns and potential for emissions "leakage" from having multiple unconnected carbon markets with different prices and levels of effort.

In practice, the benefits of linking are greatest when markets have a similar size, similar levels of ambition, and other common features, such as the types of price controls and allocation methods used. The extent of existing tax and externality distortions is also relevant. Most of the roughly 20 cap-and-trade schemes in operation have established or proposed at least one international linkage with another cap-and-trade or credit system. California and Quebec linked their carbon pricing schemes in 2014, and Ontario will soon join them. Quebec faces the biggest impact from its linking with California. As Quebec has a far smaller market, just over one-sixth the size of California's, lower emissions intensity and fewer cheap abatement opportunities, the carbon price in Quebec will fall substantially and largely be determined by California. The Californian price will rise slightly from linking. These differentials mean that Quebec will purchase excess allowances from California resulting in a net flow of revenue to California. The EU ETS already links 31 countries, with potential to be extended to other neighbouring countries. RGGI links nine US states in a relatively compact area, whose economies and energy systems are fairly interconnected.

There are three key ways for countries to increase their cooperation on carbon pricing:

1. *Commit to carbon pricing:* The G20 has a unique opportunity to lead on carbon pricing. It made a commitment on the phase-out of inefficient fossil fuel subsidies in 2009 and reaffirmed this repeatedly, most recently in 2014. This is an important piece of signalling, and it has marshalled institutional support from the OECD, the World Bank, the IEA and the IMF, which are providing research and helping countries to implement reform.

   There is a clear opportunity now for the countries of the G20 to build on these initial efforts. Prior to the Paris Climate Change Conference, it would send a strong signal if G20 countries committed at the G20 Leaders Summit in Turkey this November to establishing clear, credible and rising explicit carbon prices across their economies, as part of a well-aligned and integrated multiple policy framework for low-carbon growth and development. This would help to progress the international climate agreement in Paris and support stronger domestic action. The exact approach for G20 countries to implement the commitment could be agreed in Beijing in 2016. A coalition of "countries of the willing" could also form to start early action and demonstrate leadership in the G20.

   Countries beyond the G20 could also commit to introducing carbon pricing policies, including the phasing out of fossil fuel subsidies, in a way that is consistent with this commitment, subject to their own institutional capacity and support from international organisations to implement such policies. A sensible first step in many countries is to mandate monitoring, reporting and verification (MRV) of emissions for businesses and industry.

   In addition, strategies to link between different carbon pricing schemes to maximise the benefits from linking could be explored, and the existing linkages could be strengthened.

2. *Commit to annual reporting on action and progress:* A coordinated group of international institutions, such as the OECD, the IEA and the IMF, could work together to promote transparency and create clear and aligned expectations among businesses and investors on the level and direction of subsidy phase-out and carbon pricing in the G20 and other countries. This could also be reflected, for example, in the World Bank's annual *State and Trends of Carbon Pricing* report, where plans are already underway to begin assessing the effectiveness of existing and planned carbon pricing systems, which will add an important qualitative element to the international debate and assessment of progress.

3. *Commit to knowledge-sharing that builds on existing peer review processes:* Achieving these commitments will require sharing knowledge of best practices across G20 countries and with other countries. Mutual learning and review, in particular with neighbouring countries, can help to build trust, and accelerate and scale up action. The G20 and APEC are undertaking voluntary peer review processes on fossil fuel subsidies, and this could be extended to carbon pricing. And international institutions are already providing support for fossil fuel subsidy reform and now also for carbon pricing; their role could be strengthened to better support country efforts to make progress.

Conclusion and Recommendation

The case for carbon pricing is strong, and there is growing momentum. The use of carbon pricing is increasing as awareness of its multiple benefits grows and countries understand how to manage the costs of change better, such as by ensuring a just transition for affected workers and alleviating impacts on low-income households. Learning from recent experiences of carbon pricing around the world can help countries and businesses implement carbon pricing successfully. Governments are also realising that carbon pricing is central to structural reforms for managing economic change and the climate risk that they will face over the coming decades.

Cooperation across G20 or other willing governments is essential if the world is to accelerate action on carbon pricing. It can promote learning and reduce many of the perceived risks of carbon pricing, such as competitiveness concerns, and thereby reduce political resistance. Countries of the G20 are well placed to take the lead and 2015 provides a good opportunity to cooperate around the establishment or strengthening of carbon prices.

The global mitigation potential in 2030 from implementing this commitment is significant. Mitigation analysis conducted for this report, based on IEA modelling scenarios, examined the impact on global GHG emissions if carbon prices increased to an average of US$75 per tonne of CO_2e in developed countries and US$35 per tonne in developing countries. (Fossil fuel subsidy phase-out was excluded due to uncertainty around the estimates.) The potential global annual emissions savings from this level of carbon pricing in 2030 are estimated to be in the order of 2.8–5.6 Gt of CO_2e. In the light of this analysis, **the Global Commission on the Economy and Climate recommends that all developed and emerging economies, and others where possible, commit to introducing or strengthening carbon pricing by 2020, and should phase out fossil fuel subsidies.**

Governments should integrate these measures into broader fiscal reform strategies, prioritising the use of resulting revenues to offset impacts on low-income households and for other productive uses such as financing reductions in existing distortionary taxes. Coalitions of willing governments should work together to enhance efficiency and minimise impacts on competitiveness, building on existing peer-review processes to share knowledge, and reporting annually on progress. All major businesses should adopt internal carbon prices in their business strategies, and actively support carbon pricing policy.

JAMES RYDGE is the lead economist for the Global Commission on the Economy and Climate. He has a PhD in economics and a master's in finance from the University of Sydney.

Robert P. Murphy, Patrick J. Michaels,
and Paul C. Knappenberger

 **NO**

The Case Against a Carbon Tax

Executive Summary

A vigorous campaign aimed at American policymakers and the general public has tried to create the perception that a federal carbon tax (or similar type of "carbon price") is a crucial element in the urgently needed response to climate change. Within conservative and libertarian circles, a small but vocal group of academics, analysts, and political officials are claiming that a revenue-neutral carbon tax swap could even deliver a "double dividend"—meaning that the conventional economy would be spurred in addition to any climate benefits. The present study details several serious problems with these claims. The actual *economics* of climate change—as summarized in the peer-reviewed literature as well as the U.N. and Obama Administration reports—reveal that the case for a U.S. carbon tax is weaker than the public has been told.

In the policy debate over carbon taxes, a key concept is the "social cost of carbon," which is defined as the (present value of) future damages caused by emitting an additional ton of carbon dioxide. Estimates of the SCC are already being used to evaluate federal regulations, and will serve as the basis for any U.S. carbon tax. Yet the computer simulations used to generate SCC estimates are largely arbitrary, with plausible adjustments in parameters—such as the discount rate—causing the estimate to shift by at least an order of magnitude. Indeed, MIT economist Robert Pindyck considers the whole process so fraught with unwarranted precision that he has called such computer simulations "close to useless" for guiding policy.

Future economic damages from carbon dioxide emissions can only be estimated in conjunction with forecasts of climate change. But recent history shows those forecasts are in flux, with an increasing number of forecasts of less warming appearing in the scientific literature in the last four years. Additionally, we show some rather stark evidence that the family of models used by the U.N.'s Intergovernmental Panel on Climate Change (IPCC) are experiencing a profound failure that greatly reduces their forecast utility.

Ironically, the latest U.N. Intergovernmental Panel on Climate Change (IPCC) report indicated that a popular climate target cannot be justified in cost/benefit terms. Specifically, in the middle-of-the-road scenarios, the economic compliance costs of limiting global warming to 2 degrees Celsius would likely be higher than the climate change damages that such a cap would avoid. In other words, the U.N.'s own report shows that aggressive emission cutbacks—even if achieved through an "efficient" carbon tax—would probably cause more harm than good.

If the case for emission cutbacks is weaker than the public has been led to believe, the claim of a "double dividend" is on even shakier ground. There really is a "consensus" in this literature, and it is that carbon taxes cause more economic damage than generic taxes on labor or capital, so that in general even a revenue-neutral carbon tax swap will probably reduce conventional GDP growth. (The driver of this result is that carbon taxes fall on narrower segments of the economy, and thus to raise a given amount of revenue require a higher tax rate.) Furthermore, in the real world at least *some* of the new carbon tax receipts would probably be devoted to higher spending (on "green investments") and lump-sum transfers to poorer citizens to help offset the impact of higher energy prices. Thus in practice the economic drag of a new carbon tax could be far worse than the idealized revenue-neutral simulations depict.

When moving from academic theory to historical experience, we see that carbon taxes have not lived up to the promises of their supporters. In Australia, the carbon tax was quickly removed after the public recoiled against electricity price hikes and a faltering economy. Even in British Columbia—touted as the world's finest example of a carbon tax—the experience has been underwhelming. After an initial (but temporary) drop, the B.C. carbon tax has not yielded significant reductions in gasoline purchases, and it has arguably reduced the B.C. economy's performance relative to the rest of Canada.

Both in theory and practice, economic analysis shows that the case for a U.S. carbon tax is weaker than its most vocal supporters have led the public to believe. At the same time, there is mounting evidence in the *physical* science of climate change to suggest that human emissions of carbon dioxide do not cause as much warming as is assumed in the current suite of official models. Policymakers and the general public must not confuse the confidence of carbon tax proponents with the actual strength of their case.

Introduction

Over the years, Americans have been subject to a growing drumbeat of the (ostensibly) urgent need for aggressive government action on climate change. After two failed attempts at a U.S. federal cap-and-trade program, those wishing to curb emissions have switched their focus to a *carbon tax*.

Although environmental regulation and taxes are traditionally associated with progressive Democrats, in recent years several vocal intellectuals and political officials from the right have begun pitching a carbon tax to libertarians and conservatives. They argue that climate science respects no ideology and that a carbon tax is a "market solution" far preferable to the top-down regulations that liberal Democrats will otherwise implement. In particular, advocates of a carbon tax claim that if it is *revenue neutral* then a "tax swap" deal involving reductions in corporate and personal income tax rates might deliver stronger economic growth *and* reduce the harms from climate change, whatever they might be.

Although they often claim to be merely repeating the findings of "consensus science," advocates of aggressive government intervention stand on very shaky ground. Using standard results from the economics of climate change—as codified in the peer-reviewed literature and published reports from the U.N. and Obama Administration—we can show that the case for a carbon tax is weaker than the public has been led to believe. Furthermore, the real-world experiences of carbon taxes in Australia and British Columbia cast serious doubt on the promises of a "market-friendly" carbon tax in the United States.

The present study will summarize some of the key issues in the climate policy debate, showing that a U.S. carbon tax is a dubious proposal in both theory and practice.

The "Social Cost of Carbon"

The "social cost of carbon" (often abbreviated SCC) is a key concept in the economics of climate change and related policy discussions of a carbon tax. The SCC is defined as the present-discounted value of the net future external damages from an additional unit of carbon dioxide emissions. In terms of economic theory, the SCC measures the "negative externalities" from emitting CO_2 (and other greenhouse gases expressed in CO_2-equivalents), and helps quantify the "market failure" where consumers and firms do not fully take into account the true costs of their carbon-intensive activities. To a first approximation, the "optimal" carbon tax would reflect the SCC (along the emission trajectory that would obtain with the carbon tax regime), and in practice the Obama Administration has issued estimates of the SCC that are being used in the cost/benefit evaluation of federal regulations (such as minimum energy efficiency standards) that aim to reduce emissions relative to the baseline.

It is important to note that the SCC reflects the estimated damages of climate change on the *entire world*. This means that if the SCC (calculated in this fashion) is used in federal cost/benefit analyses, the analyst is contrasting benefits accruing mostly to non-Americans with costs borne mostly by Americans. Whether the reader thinks this is valid or not, it is clearly an important issue that has not been made clear in the U.S. debate on climate change policy. In any event, the Office of Management and Budget (OMB), in its Circular A-4, clearly states that federal regulatory analyses should focus on domestic impacts:

> Your analysis should focus on benefits and costs that accrue to citizens and residents of the United States. Where you choose to evaluate a regulation that is likely to have effects beyond the borders of the United States, these effects should be reported separately.

However, when the Obama Administration's Interagency Working Group calculated the SCC, it ignored this clear OMB guideline, and only reported a *global* value of the SCC. Thus, if a regulation (or carbon tax) is thought to reduce carbon dioxide emissions, then the estimated benefits (calculated with use of the SCC) will vastly overstate the benefits *to Americans*.

As an affluent nation, the U.S. economy is much less vulnerable to the vagaries of weather and climate. Using two different approaches, the Working Group in 2010 "determined that a range of values from 7 to 23 percent should be used to adjust the global SCC to calculate domestic effects. Reported domestic values should use this range." Therefore, following OMB's clear guideline on reporting the *domestic* impacts of proposed regulations, the SCC value would need to be reduced anywhere from 77 to 93 percent, in order to show the benefit to Americans from stipulated reductions in carbon dioxide emissions. To repeat, these figures all derive from the Obama Administration's own Working Group report.

In addition to such procedural problems with the use of the SCC in federal policy, there are deeper, conceptual problems. The average layperson may have the belief that the "social cost of carbon" is an empirical fact of nature that scientists in white lab coats measure with their equipment. However, in reality the SCC is a malleable concept that is entirely driven by the analyst's (largely arbitrary) initial assumptions. The estimated SCC can be quite large, modest, or even *negative*—this latter meaning that greenhouse gas emissions should arguably be subsidized to benefit humanity—depending on defensible adjustments of the inputs to the analysis.

The most popular current approach used by U.S. policymakers to estimate the SCC involves the use of computer-based Integrated Assessment Models (IAMs), which are complex simulations of the entire global economy and climate system for hundreds of years. Officially, the IAMs are supposed to rely on the latest results in the *physical* science of climate change, as well as *economic* analyses of the impacts of climate change on human welfare, where these impacts are measured in monetary units but include a wide range of non-market categories (such as flooding and loss of ecosystem services). With particular assumptions about the path of emissions, the physical sensitivity of the climate system to atmospheric CO_2 concentrations, and the impact on humans from changing climate conditions, the IAMs estimate the flow of *incremental* damages occurring centuries into the future as a result of an additional unit of CO_2 emissions in some particular year. Then this flow of additional dollar damages (over the centuries) can be turned into an equivalent present value expressed in the dollars at the date of the emission, using a discount rate chosen by the analyst, where this rate is typically *not* derived from observations of market rates of interest but is instead picked (quite openly) according to the analyst's ethical views on how future generations should be treated.

In May 2013, the Interagency Working Group produced an updated SCC value by incorporating revisions to the underlying three Integrated Assessment Models (IAMs) used by the IWG in its initial 2010 SCC determination. But, at that time, the IWG did *not* update the equilibrium climate sensitivity (ECS) employed in the IAMs. The ECS is a critical concept in the physical science of climate change. Loosely speaking, it refers to the long-run (after taking into account certain feedbacks) warming in response to a doubling of carbon dioxide concentrations. Thus, it is incredibly significant that the published

estimates of the ECS were trending downward, and yet the Obama Administration Working Group did not adjust this key input into the Integrated Assessment computer models. Specifically, they made no downward adjustment in this key parameter in their May 2013 update despite there having been, since January 1, 2011, at least 15 new studies and 21 experiments (involving more than 45 researchers) examining the ECS, each lowering the best estimate and tightening the error distribution about that estimate. . . .

The abundance of literature supporting a lower climate sensitivity was at least partially reflected in the latest (2013) assessment of the Intergovernmental Panel on Climate Change (IPCC):

> Equilibrium climate sensitivity is *likely* in the range 1.5°C to 4.5°C (*high confidence*), *extremely unlikely* less than 1°C (*high confidence*), and *very unlikely* greater than 6°C (*medium confidence*). The lower temperature limit of the assessed *likely* range is thus less than the 2°C in the AR4 [Fourth Assessment Report] . . .

Clearly, the IWG's assessment of the low end of the probability density function that best describes the current level of scientific understanding of the climate sensitivity is indefensible.

The 2013 study of Otto et al., which was available at the time of the IWG's 2013 revision, is particularly noteworthy in that 15 of the paper's 17 authors were also lead authors of the 2013 IPCC report. Otto has a mean sensitivity of 2.0°C and a 5–95% confidence interval of 1.1 to 3.9°C. If the IPCC truly defined the consensus, that consensus has now changed. Instead of a 95th percentile value of 7.14°C, as used by the IWG, a survey of the recent scientific literature suggests a value of 3.5°C—more than 50% lower. This is very significant and important difference because the high end of the ECS distribution has a large impact on the SCC determination—a fact frequently commented on by the IWG.

Yet to repeat, the problem with the SCC as a tool in policy analysis goes beyond quibbles over the proper parameter values. At least the equilibrium climate sensitivity (ECS) is an *objectively defined* (in principle) feature of nature. In contrast, there are other parameters needed to calculate the SCC that by their very essence are subjective, such as the analyst's view on the proper weight to be given to the welfare of future generations. Needless to say, this approach to "measuring" the SCC 10 is hardly the way physicists estimate the mass of the moon or the charge on an electron. To quote MIT economist Robert

Pindyck (who *favors* a U.S. carbon tax) in his scathing *Journal of Economic Literature* article:

> And here we see a major problem with IAM-based climate policy analysis: The modeler has a great deal of freedom in choosing functional forms, parameter values, and other inputs, and different choices can give wildly different estimates of the SCC and the optimal amount of abatement. You might think that some input choices are more reasonable or defensible than others, but no, "reasonable" is very much in the eye of the modeler. **Thus these models can be used to obtain almost any result one desires.** [bold added.]

To see just how significant some of the apparently innocuous assumptions can be, consider the latest estimates of the SCC put out by the Obama Administration's Working Group. For an additional ton of emissions in the year 2015, using a 3% discount rate the SCC is $36. However, if we use a 2.5% discount rate, the SCC rises to $56/ton, while a 5% discount rate yields a SCC of only $11/ton. Note that this huge swing in the estimated "social cost" of carbon relies on the same underlying models of climate change and economic growth; the only change is in adjustments of the discount rate which are quite plausible. Indeed, the Administration's Working Group came under harsh criticism because it ignored explicit OMB guidance to include a *7 percent* discount rate in all federal cost/benefit analyses, presumably because the SCC at such a discount rate would be close to $0/ton or even negative.

The reason the Obama Administration estimates of the SCC are so heavily dependent on the discount rate is that the three underlying computer models all show relatively modest damages from climate change in the early decades. Indeed, one model (Richard Tol's FUND model) actually exhibits *net benefits* from global warming through about 3°C of warming relative to preindustrial temperatures. The higher the discount rate, the more weight is placed on earlier time periods (when global warming is not as destructive or is even beneficial) and the less important are the large damages that will not occur in the computer simulations until future 11 centuries. Economists do not agree on the appropriate discount rate to use in such settings, because the usual arguments in favor of market-based measures (which would yield a very low SCC) are not as compelling when we cannot bind future policymakers. Such are the difficulties in making public policy on the basis of threats that will not fully manifest themselves for another two generations.

If the economic models were updated to more accurately reflect the latest developments from the physical and biological sciences, the estimated "social cost of carbon" would likewise decline between one-third and two thirds, because lower temperature increases would translate into reduced climate-change damages. This is a sizeable and significant reduction.

Then there are problems with the climate models themselves. There is clearly a large and growing discrepancy between their predictions and what is being observed.

. . . John Christy of University of Alabama-Huntsville, dramatically shows the climate modelling problem in a nutshell. . . . [M]odel-predicted and observed temperatures, not at the surface, but in the lower troposphere, roughly from 5,000 to 30,000 feet, are less compromised by earth's complicated surface and man's role in altering it. More important, though, is that it is the vertical profile of temperature that determines atmospheric stability. When the "lapse rate," or the difference between the lowest layers and higher levels is large, the atmosphere is unstable. Instability is the principal source for global precipitation. While models can be (and are) "tuned" to mimic surface temperatures, the same can't be done as easily in the vertical.

. . . [T]he air above the surface is warming far more slowly than had been predicted, so that the difference between the surface and the upper air has changed very little. This means that observed global precipitation should be the same as it was. The forecast warming of the upper layers . . . would reduce the surface-to-upper air temperature difference, which would tend to reduce precipitation.

That means that the models themselves are making systematic errors in their precipitation projections. This has a dramatic effect on the resultant climate. When the surface is wet, which is what occurs after it rains, the sun's energy is directed towards the evaporation of that moisture rather than the direct heating of the surface. In other words, much of what we call "sensible weather" (the kind of weather you can sense) is determined by the vertical distribution of temperature. If the popular climate models get that wrong (which is what's happening) then all the subsidiary weather caused by it is also incorrectly specified.

Therefore there are problems and arbitrariness not just with the economic assumptions, but with the physical models that are used as input to the SCC calculations. The situation is even worse than described above by Pindyck.

So, even though the modelled sensitivities are dropping, there are still indications that the models themselves are too hot. None of the current batch of "official" SCC calculations accounts for this.

Besides the arbitrariness and/or dubious choices for the major input parameters, another problem with use of the SCC as a guide to setting carbon taxes is the problem of *leakage*. Strictly speaking, it would make sense (even in textbook theory) to calibrate only a *worldwide and uniformly enforced* carbon tax to the SCC. If a carbon tax is applied only to certain jurisdictions, then emission cutbacks in the affected region are partially offset by increased emissions (relative to the baseline) in the non-regulated regions. Depending on the specifics, leakage can greatly increase the economic costs of achieving a desired climate goal, and thus the "optimal" carbon tax is lower if applied unilaterally in limited jurisdictions.

To get a sense of the magnitude of the problems of leakage, consider the results from William Nordhaus, a pioneer in the economics of climate change, and creator of the DICE model (one of the three used by the Obama Administration). After studying his 2007 model runs, Nordhaus reported that relative to the case of the entire globe enforcing the carbon tax, to achieve a given environmental objective (such as a temperature ceiling or atmospheric concentration) with only 50 percent of planetary emissions covered would involve an economic abatement cost penalty of *250 percent*. Even if the top 15 countries (by emissions) participated in the carbon tax program, covering three-quarters of the globe's emissions, Nordhaus still estimated that compliance costs for a given objective would be 70 percent higher than for the full-coverage baseline case.

To see the tremendous problem of limited participation from a different perspective, one can use the same model that EPA uses to calculate the effect of various policy proposals. The Model for the Assessment of Greenhouse-Gas Induced Climate Change (MAGICC) is available and easy-to-use on the Cato Institute website. MAGICC shows that even if the U.S. linearly reduced its emissions to *zero* by the year 2050, the average global temperature in the year 2100 would be 0.1°C—that's one-tenth of a degree—lower than would otherwise be the case. Note that this calculation does not even take into account "leakage," the fact that complete cessation of U.S. emissions would induce other nations to increase their economic activities and hence emissions. Our point in using these results from the MAGICC modeling is not to christen them as confident projections, but rather to show that *even on their own terms, using an EPA-endorsed model*, American policymakers have much less control over global climate change than they often imply.

U.N. Reports Can't Justify Popular Climate Goal

Although the goal's selection was never formally explained, advocates of government intervention to mitigate climate change have broadly settled on a *minimum* goal of limiting global warming (relative to preindustrial times) to 2°C, with many pushing for much more stringent objectives (such as limiting atmospheric greenhouse gas concentrations to 350 ppm of CO_2). Given the confidence with which carbon tax advocates refer to the "consensus" among scientists on the key issues in the climate change debate, the innocent American public would surely conclude that the periodic reports from the United Nations Intergovernmental Panel on Climate Change (IPCC) would *easily* justify implementation of government policies to hit the 2°C target.

Ironically, this is not the case. According to 2013 IPCC report [often referred to as "AR5" for "Fifth Assessment Report"], to "likely" limit global warming to 2°C would require stabilizing atmospheric concentrations between 430–480 ppm by the year 2100. The same AR5 report shows that achieving this climate goal would entail reductions in consumption in the year 2100 of 4.8 percent (which is the central estimate, and relative to the baseline). These are the *costs* of achieving the popular 2°C goal, according to the latest U.N. report.

In contrast, to compute the *benefits* of the 2°C goal we would need to know the *reduction* in climate change damages that would result under business-as-usual versus the mitigation scenario (with the temperature ceiling). Even under the most pessimistic emission scenario with no government controls (RCP8.5), by 2100 the AR5's central estimate of global warming is about 4.5°C, and a more realistic business-as-usual scenario (between RPC6 and RPC8.5) would involve warming by 2100 of less than 4°C. Therefore the *gross* benefits of the stipulated mitigation policy are the climate change damages from 4°C warming minus the climate change damages from 2°C warming.

Unfortunately, the AR5 report does not allow us to compute such figures, because just about all of the comprehensive analyses of the impacts of global warming consider ranges of 2.5°C–3°C. The AR5 *does* contain a table summarizing some of the estimates in the literature, out of which the most promising (for our task) are two results from Roson and van der Mensbrugghe's 2012 study. They estimated that 2.3°C warming would reduce GDP by 1.8 percent, while 4.9°C warming would reduce GDP by 4.6 percent. (Note that this particular estimate was the *only* one in the AR5 table that estimated the impact of warming higher than 3.2°C.)

Therefore, using ballpark figures, one could conclude from the AR5 summary of impacts that limiting climate change to 2°C rather than an unrestricted 4°C of warming, would mean that the Earth in the year 2100 would be spared about (4.6 − 1.8) = 2.8 percent of GDP loss in climate change damages. In contrast, the same IPCC AR5 report told us that the *economic compliance* costs of the mitigation goal would be 4.8 percent of consumption in the year 2100.

As this demonstration has shown, even if we take the IPCC's numbers at face value, and even assuming away the practical problems that would prevent mitigation policies from reaching the theoretical ideal, the popular climate goal of limiting global warming to 2°C would most likely entail greater economic damages than it would deliver in benefits (in the form of reduced climate change damages). The pursuit of more aggressive goals, and/or the use of imperfectly designed policy tools to achieve them, would, of course, only make the mismatch between costs and benefits even worse.

"Fat Tails" and Carbon Tax as Insurance?

As a postscript to these observations, we note that the leaders in the pro-carbon tax camp are abandoning traditional cost/benefit analysis as (allegedly) inappropriate in the context of climate change. For example, Harvard economist Martin Weitzman has warned that climate scenarios involve "fat tails" that (mathematically) make the conventionally-calculated social cost of carbon tend to infinity. Weitzman and others have moved away from treating a carbon tax as a policy response to a given (and known) negative externality, and instead liken it to a form of insurance pertaining to a catastrophe that *might* happen but with unknown likelihood. But the utility of such "insurance" is being compromised, given the strong emerging evidence very large warming is unlikely.

This approach, which is growing in popularity among the advocates of aggressive government intervention, has several problems. In the first place, the whole *purpose* of the periodic IPCC reports was to produce a compilation of the "consensus" research in order to guide policymakers. But when the models and methods contained in the IPCC reports do not yield aggressive enough action, critics such as Weitzman point out their (admitted) shortcomings and propose that policymakers take actions based on what we *don't* know. Yet as economist David R. Henderson points out, broad-based uncertainty cuts *both* ways in the climate change policy debate. For example, it is *possible* that the Earth is headed into a period of prolonged cooling, in which case offsetting anthropogenic warming would be beneficial—meaning that a carbon tax would be undesirable.

Another problem with Weitzman's approach—as Nordhaus, among other critics, has pointed out—is that it could be used to justify aggressive actions against *several* catastrophic risks, including asteroids, rogue artificial intelligence developments, and bio-weapons. After all, we can't *rule out* humanity's destruction from a genetically engineered virus in the year 2100, and what's worse we are not even sure how to construct the probability distribution on such events. Does that mean we should be willing to forfeit 5 percent of global consumption to merely reduce the likelihood of this catastrophe?

This question leads into the final problem with the insurance analogy: With actual insurance, the risks are well-known and quantifiable, and competition among insurers provides rates that are reasonable for the damages involved. Furthermore, for all practical purposes buying the insurance policy *eliminates* the (financial) risk. Yet to be analogous to the type of "insurance" that Weitzman et al. are advocating, a homeowner would be told that there was a roving gang of arsonists who might, decades from now, set his home on fire, that a fire policy would cost 5 percent of income every year until then, and that even if the house were struck by the arsonists, the company would indemnify the owner for only *some* of the damages. Who would buy such an "insurance" policy?

Carbon Tax Reform "Win-Wins"? The Elusive "Double Dividend"

Some proponents of a carbon tax have tried to decouple it entirely from the climate change debate. They argue that if the receipts from a carbon tax were devoted to reductions in taxes on labor or capital, then the economic cost of the carbon tax 18 would be reduced and might even be *negative*. In other words, they claim that by "taxing bads, not goods," the U.S. might experience a "double dividend" in which we tackle climate change *and* boost conventional economic growth.

Such claims of a double dividend are emphasized in appeals to libertarians and conservatives to embrace a carbon "tax swap" deal. For example, in a 2008 *NYT* oped calling for a revenue-neutral carbon tax swap, Arthur Laffer and Bob Inglis wrote, "Conservatives do not have to agree that humans are causing climate change to recognize a sensible energy solution." For another example, in his 2015 study titled, "The Conservative Case for a Carbon Tax," Niskanen Center president Jerry Taylor writes, "Even if conservative narratives about climate change science and public policy are to some extent correct, conservatives should say 'yes' to a revenue-neutral carbon tax."

The idea of revenue-neutral "pro-growth" carbon tax reform for the U.S. is arguably a red herring, as it is very unlikely that any national politically feasible deal will respect revenue neutrality. On lower jurisdictions, note that Governor Jerry Brown wanted to use California's cap-and-trade revenue for high-speed rail, while the website for the Regional Greenhouse Gas Initiative (RGGI)—which is the cap-and-trade program for power plants in participating Northeast and Mid-Atlantic states—proudly explains how its revenues have been spent on renewables, energy efficiency projects, and other "green" investments. And far from insisting on revenue neutrality, Washington State Governor Jay Inslee wants to install a new state level cap-and-trade levy on carbon emissions to fund his $12.2 billion transportation plan.

Ironically enough, even Taylor *in his very study appealing to conservatives* touts a *non*-revenue-neutral carbon tax (which would impose a net tax hike of at least $695 billion in its first 20 years). It is possible that this was a mere oversight (i.e. that in his study Taylor genuinely believed he was pushing a revenue neutral plan but was simply ignorant of its details), but all doubts were removed a month later in a Niskanen Center post in which Taylor wrote: "But what if a tax-for-regulation swap were to come up in an attempt to address budget deficits and the looming fiscal imbalance? . . . But even were those fears realized, conservatives should take heart: using carbon tax revenues to reduce the deficit makes good economic sense."

With progressives enumerating the various "green" investments that could be funded by a carbon tax, and with even one of the leaders in the conservative pro-carbon tax camp laying the intellectual foundation for a net tax hike, it should be clear that a revenue-neutral deal at the federal level is very unlikely. . . .

Robert P. Murphy is a senior economist with the Institute for Energy Research (IER) specializing in climate change and a research fellow with the Independent Institute. Among his recent books is *Choice: Cooperation, Enterprise, and Human Action* (Independent Institute, 2015). He also has written in support of Intelligent Design theory and expressed skepticism about biological evolution.

Patrick J. Michaels is the director of the Center for the Study of Science at the Cato Institute. Michaels is a past president of the American Association of State Climatologists and was program chair for the Committee on Applied Climatology of the American Meteorological Society. He was a research professor of environmental sciences at the University of Virginia for 30 years. Michaels was a contributing author and is a reviewer of the United Nations Intergovernmental Panel on Climate Change, which was awarded the Nobel Peace Prize in 2007. He is well known as a skeptic on the issue of global warming.

Paul C. Knappenberger is the assistant director of the Center for the Study of Science at the Cato Institute, and coordinates the scientific and outreach activities for the Center. He has over 20 years of experience in climate research and public outreach, including 10 years with the Virginia State Climatology Office and 15 years as the Research Coordinator for New Hope Environmental Services, Inc.

EXPLORING THE ISSUE

Would a Carbon Tax Help Slow Global Warming?

Critical Thinking and Reflection

1. Murphy et al. define the "social cost of carbon" in strictly financial terms. Are there nonfinancial costs of carbon emissions? What are some?
2. Murphy et al. object that the future effects of global warming have been overestimated, in part because the atmosphere has warmed less than expected in recent years. Look up "global warming hiatus" (start here: http://news.stanford.edu/news/2015/september/global-warming-hiatus-091715.html) and discuss whether their objection has merit.
3. In what ways do fossil fuel subsidies encourage continued emissions of greenhouse gases?

Is There Common Ground?

Both sides of this issue agree on at least one of the obstacles that stand in the way of a global carbon pricing effort. This is "leakage," which occurs when one country imposes carbon pricing on businesses that then move carbon-intensive operations such as manufacturing to other countries where they need not pay a carbon price. They differ on how straightforward it may be to overcome this problem. Searching on "carbon leakage" will find a great deal of information on the topic.

1. Which industries are likely to be affected by leakage? (See, e.g., http://www.carbontrust.com/media/84908/ctc767-tackling-carbon-leakage.pdf.)
2. Describe some of the methods that have been proposed for dealing with leakage.

3. Rydge suggests that international cooperation would be able to prevent or minimize leakage. What form would that international cooperation be likely to take?

Additional Resources

A. Denny Hillerman et al., *Pricing Carbon: The European Union Emissions Trading Scheme* (Cambridge University Press, 2010).

Larry Kreiser, Mikael Skou Andersen, Birgitte Egelund Olsen, Stefan Speck, Janet E. Milne, and Hope Ashiabor (eds.), *Carbon Pricing: Design, Experiences and Issues* (Elgar, 2015).

Karsten Neuhoff, *Climate Policy after Copenhagen: The Role of Carbon Pricing* (Cambridge University Press, 2011).

Internet References . . .

Carbon-Price.com

http://carbon-price.com/experts/

Global Subsidies Initiative

https://www.iisd.org/GSI/fossil-fuel-subsidies

The Carbon Trust

http://www.carbontrust.com/home/

The World Bank on Pricing Carbon

http://www.worldbank.org/en/programs/pricing-carbon

Selected, Edited, and with Issue Framing Material by:
Thomas A. Easton, *Mount Ida College*

ISSUE

Is Home Solar the Wave of the Future?

YES: Peter Bronski et al., from "The Economics of Grid Defection," Rocky Mountain Institute (2014)

NO: Peter Kind, from "Disruptive Challenges: Financial Implications and Strategic Responses to a Changing Retail Electric Business," Edison Electric Institute (2013)

Learning Outcomes

After reading this issue, you will be able to:

- Explain the benefits of home solar power.
- Explain why electric utilities see home solar as a threat.
- Explain why home solar power users still need the electric utility's infrastructure (or grid).
- Discuss ways utilities can raise the money to maintain the infrastructure (or grid).

ISSUE SUMMARY

YES: Peter Bronski et al., of the Rocky Mountain Institute (RMI) argue that the combination of home solar power with storage technologies such as batteries offer to make the electricity grid optional for many consumers, perhaps as early as the 2020s. Utilities have an opportunity to exploit the spread of "distributed electricity generation" to provide a robust, reliable electricity supply.

NO: Peter Kind, executive director of Energy Infrastructure Advocates, argues that increased interest in "distributed energy resources" such as home solar power and energy efficiency, among other factors, is threatening to reduce revenue and increase costs for electrical utilities. In order to protect investors and capital availability, electrical utilities must consider new charges for customers who reduce their electricity usage, decreased payments to homeowners using net metering, and even new charges to users of "distributed energy resources" to offset "stranded costs" (such as no longer needed power plants).

We have known how to generate electricity from the sun for many years. One technique that has actually been put to use by electric utilities uses mirrors to concentrate sunlight on a boiler, generate steam, and spin the turbines of electrical generators. The largest and most recent example is the Ivanpah solar farm in California's Mojave Desert; it was designed to produce over a million megawatt-hours of electricity per year, but weather and start-up issues have affected its performance (see Pete Danko, "At Ivanpah Solar Power Plant, Energy Production Falling Well Short of Expectations," *Breaking Energy*, October 29, 2014; http://breakingenergy.com/2014/10/29/at-ivanpah-solar-power-plant-energy-production-falling-well-short-of-expectations/).

A more direct use of sunlight to generate electricity relies on solar cells. They can be deployed anywhere a flat surface faces the sun—on rooves, on free-standing frameworks, and even on roads (the first example is a portion of a bike path in the Netherlands—see http://www.npr.org/blogs/thetwo-way/2014/11/10/363023227/solar-bike-path-opens-this-week-in-the-netherlands. Of course, no solar power system can generate electricity when the sun isn't shining, as at night or in cloudy weather.

An effective solar power system therefore needs backup electricity sources or storage mechanisms such as batteries. It could also be an interconnected system spread out across multiple time zones. One solution is the "smart grid" that has been under discussion for the last few years. Russell Kay, "The Smart Grid," *Computerworld* (May 11, 2009), describes it as a more advanced and efficient version of the current grid (the network of power plants, power lines, substations, and computerized control stations that controls the distribution of electricity even when disrupted by storms, power plant failures, and other problems), with digital controls to coordinate a host of small and intermittent electricity sources, such as home solar and wind power. See also Mike Martin, "The Great Green Grid," *E Magazine* (July–August 2010).

As the price of solar cells has come down, their popularity has been increasing, aided by federal corporate investment credits and federal and state tax breaks, and even local subsidies, for homeowners. It now seems entirely possible that the technology could become very widely used. James M. Higgins, "Your Solar-Powered Future: It's Closer than You Thought," *The Futurist* (May–June 2009), tells us that "Ten years from now, power generation will be much more widely distributed. Homes and businesses alike will install solar-energy conversion systems for most—if not all—of their electrical needs." Ken Zweibel, James Mason, and Vasilis Fthenakis, "A Solar Grand Plan," *Scientific American* (January 2008), believe that with appropriate investment, solar can replace most or all conventional electricity generation; Mark Z. Jacobson and Mark A. Delucchi, "A Path to Sustainable Energy by 2030," *Scientific American* (November 2009), think it will take longer. But the process is already under way. At present, businesses such as SolarCity (http://www.solarcity.com/), Sungevity (http://www.sungevity.com/), Sunrun (http://www.sunrun.com/), and Vivint (http://www.vivintsolar.com/) offer consumers the chance to let the company install solar cells on home rooftops, use some of the electricity generated, and sell the rest to utilities. People can also buy solar systems outright, with or without battery backup.

In November 2014, Deutsche Bank released a report on Vivint which predicted that the cost of rooftop solar electricity, already equal to or less than the cost of coal and oil-fueled electricity in ten states of the United States, would match or beat those costs in all 50 states by 2016. And the technology is expected to get even cheaper. See Lucas Mearian, "Rooftop Solar Electricity on Pace to Beat Coal, Oil," *Computerworld* (November 18, 2014) (http://www.computerworld.com/article/2848875/rooftop-solar-electricity-on-pace-to-beat-coal-oil.html).

It is not surprising that consumers find rooftop solar appealing. It's already cheaper than utility electricity in some places, some states have implemented "net metering" (meaning that a homeowner who generates more electricity than needed can sell it to the local power company, and the power company has to buy it), in operation it does not emit greenhouse gases and thus contribute to global warming, and it offers independence from external systems. It also offers advantages to utilities, for if rooftop solar spreads, there will be less need to build huge new power plants. If homeowners opt to combine rooftop solar with battery storage systems, the need for poles and wires declines as well. However, that need does not seem likely to go away entirely; solar power depends on a steady supply of sunshine, and battery systems have finite capacity. Given a long spell of cloudy weather, people would still need the power company.

But, according to David Biello, "Solar Wars," *Scientific American* (November 2014), the trend is already worrying electrical utilities. As more and more states mandate that utilities buy surplus electricity from home providers and as home providers proliferate, the utilities see a day coming when their profits will be seriously affected. Worse yet, regulators require them to maintain the electrical grid—poles, wires, transformers, and power plants—that currently supplies everyone with a dependable supply of electricity and to recoup the costs by charging their customers. If they lose customers, they must either charge the remaining customers more or find a way to bill noncustomers. In Florida, local government seems prepared to help by preventing people from disconnecting from the grid (http://www.nbc-2.com/story/24790572/cape-woman-living-of-the-grid-challenged-by-city#.VGjCsMltgpE). In Hawaii, utilities restrict or block rooftop solar. In other states, they are pushing hard to do the same.

Is home solar power really a threat to utilities? If you take the stance that utilities have a right to keep making money and attracting investors the same way they have for the last century, perhaps it is. But if you think that home solar power offers ways to retool their business model, perhaps not. In the YES selection, Peter Bronski et al. of the Rocky Mountain Institute argue that the combination of home solar power with storage technologies such as batteries offers to make the electricity grid optional for many consumers, perhaps as early as the 2020s. Utilities have opportunities to exploit the spread of "distributed electricity generation" to provide a robust, reliable electricity supply. The authors are working on a second report about the implications of these "disruptive opportunities" for utility business models. In the NO selection, Peter Kind, executive director of Energy Infrastructure Advocates, argues that increased interest in "distributed energy resources" such as home solar power and energy efficiency, among other factors, is threatening to reduce revenue and increase costs for electrical utilities. In order to protect investors and capital availability, electrical utilities must consider new charges for customers who reduce their electricity usage, decreased payments to homeowners using net metering, and even new charges to users of "distributed energy resources" to offset "stranded costs" (such as no longer needed power plants).

YES ↵

Peter Bronski et al.

The Economics of Grid Defection

Introduction

Utilities in the United States today face a variety of challenges to their traditional business models. An aging grid makes substantial investment in maintaining and modernizing system infrastructure a looming need. Meanwhile, myriad factors are making kWh sales decay a real concern, threatening the traditional mechanism by which regulated utilities recover costs and earn allowed market returns associated with infrastructure investment, as well as threatening the business model for all other types of utilities. These factors include:

- The falling costs and growing adoption of distributed generation (DG) and the prevalence of net-metering policies for integrating that DG
- Flat or even declining electricity demand, driven in part by increasing energy efficiency efforts as well as expanding demand-side strategies to manage electricity consumption

In addition, the electricity sector faces increasing social and regulatory pressures to reduce the carbon intensity and other environmental and health impacts of power generation.

Together, these forces undermine the "old" model of central power generation, transmission, and distribution. In particular, the combination of increasing costs and declining revenues creates upward price pressure. Yet higher retail electricity prices further prompt customers to invest in efficiency and distributed generation, creating a self-reinforcing cycle sometimes known as the utility death spiral.

The idea of a utility death spiral, while not new, is increasingly relevant in its potential reality. Once upon a time, the utility death spiral was considered a potential outcome of efficiency. The growth of grid-connected distributed generation later added to death spiral concern. And while some customers have more choice than others, the trend of increasing options for electricity supply is likely here to stay. Now, there's also a fundamentally different growing threat and emerging opportunity wrapped up into one: combined distributed generation and energy storage. Other challenges, such as DG alone and energy efficiency, still maintain customers' grid dependence. Combined DG and storage, and in particular, solar-plus-battery systems, give a customer the option to go from grid connected to grid defected—customers could secede from the macro grid entirely.

Utilities have recently acknowledged this day could come. The Edison Electric Institute's January 2013 report, *Disruptive Challenges*, noted:

> Due to the variable nature of renewables, there is a perception that customers will always need to remain on the grid. While we would expect customers to remain on the grid until a fully viable and economic distributed non-variable resource is available, one can imagine a day when battery storage technology or micro turbines could allow customers to be electric grid independent.

Two mutually reinforcing accelerants—declining costs for distributed energy technologies and increasing adoption of those technologies—are rapidly transforming the electricity market in ways that suggest grid parity (i.e., economic and technical service equality with the electrical grid) for solar-plus-battery systems is coming sooner than many had anticipated.

Declining Costs for Distributed Energy Technologies

Trends for Solar PV

The distributed U.S. solar industry has experienced robust growth in recent years, delivering an average annual installed capacity increase of 62% from 2010 to 2012. Lower hardware costs (largely thanks to the collapse in PV module prices) and the rapid expansion of third-party financing for residential and commercial customers have fueled this growth.

We expect solar PV's levelized cost of energy (LCOE) to continue to decline through 2020 and beyond, despite both the likely end of the residential renewable energy tax credit and the reduction (from 30% to 10%) of the business energy investment tax credit in 2016. Further drops in upfront costs per installed Watt and additional improvements in solar PV finance (i.e., reduced cost of capital) will help drive the continued declines in solar PV's LCOE.

Trends for Battery Technology

Electric vehicle (EV) market growth has driven the lithium-ion (Li-ion) battery industry's recent expansion. Though it lags behind the growth of the solar PV market, it has still been significant in recent years. Coupled with greater opportunities for on-grid energy storage, including those enabled by regulations such as the Federal Energy Regulatory Commission's (FERC) Order 755 and California's AB 2514, battery demand is surging. Opportunities in both the vehicle and grid markets will continue to drive the energy storage industry for the foreseeable future, yielding lower costs for batteries for mobile and stationary applications.

Support Technologies Unlock More Value

The evolution of support systems—including improved energy systems controls—is progressing apace. Synergistically, these controls have improved the value proposition of solar PV and batteries, thus creating further demand. In addition, smart inverters have seen price reductions and continue to offer new capabilities, unlocking new opportunities for their application and the increased integration of distributed energy resources.

Given the fast-moving technology landscape, we took a conservative view that represents steady progress and is aligned with published projections. However, with high innovation rates in solar, storage, and support technologies, it is conceivable that we underestimate progress in our base case.

Forces Driving Adoption of Off-Grid Systems

Based on our research and interviews with subject matter experts, we identified at least five forces driving the increased adoption of off-grid hybrid distributed generation and storage systems:

- Interest in reliability and resilience
- Demand for cleaner energy
- Pursuit of better economics
- Utility and grid frustration
- Regulatory changes

Interest in Reliability and Resilience

From severe weather events such as Superstorm Sandy, to direct physical attacks on grid infrastructure in Arkansas and Silicon Valley, to reports on the potential for major system damage from geomagnetic storms, the fragility of the U.S. electric grid is now a nearly constant media topic. As a byproduct of the U.S.'s early advance into the electrical age, our systems are among the oldest on the planet and experience triple the frequency disruptions and ten times the duration of system outages compared to some OECD peer nations such as Germany and Denmark. In fact, in little over a decade, the U.S. has witnessed some of the most severe power outages in its history.

An increasingly popular solution to these reliability challenges is islandable microgrids, which produce and consume power locally in small, self-balancing networks capable of separating from and rejoining the larger grid on demand. They have a point of common coupling to the grid, and include both generation and loads that can be managed in a coordinated manner. Navigant Research forecasts the microgrid market to reach as high as $40 billion in the U.S. by 2020.

A more extreme example of this trend, yet similarly connected to reliability and resilience interests, is permanently off-grid buildings. Prior to 2000 off-grid solar installations made up over 50% of solar PV projects. While currently a minute portion of total solar PV sales, such off-grid solar has actually continued its growth in absolute sales. Though the majority of solar PV was off grid prior to 2000 primarily because it was used in remote locations where grid connection was a more difficult and expensive proposition, we're likely in the midst of a new era of off-grid solar PV (with batteries) within grid-accessible locations. The conversation has shifted from being off grid out of necessity to being off grid out of choice.

Demand for Cleaner Energy

Demand for cleaner energy with a lower carbon intensity and softer environmental footprint is on the rise.

On the commercial side, major corporations such as Walmart, Costco, IKEA, and Apple are increasingly "going solar." According to the World Wildlife Fund's *Power Forward* report, nearly 60% of Fortune 100 and Global 100 companies have renewable energy targets, greenhouse gas emissions goals, or both. These commitments are driving increased investment in renewable energy, including distributed solar PV. As of mid-2013, cumulative U.S. commercial solar installations totaled 3,380 MW, a 40% increase over the previous year.

On the residential side, a 2012 survey of nearly 200 solar homeowners found that even if solar's economics weren't favorable, 1 in 4 would *still* have chosen to install a solar PV system because of their passion for the environment. An earlier survey of more than 640 solar installs—primarily residential—found that reducing one's carbon footprint ranked nearly equal with reducing one's energy bill among the top reasons customers chose to go solar. Small residential applications for completely off-grid homes have existed within the United States for many years. These homes and businesses were usually owned by the environmentally-driven consumer, as these buildings had to be energy sippers, because of the then-high cost of renewable energy technologies such as solar, wind, and storage.

Pursuit of Better Economics

Most remote locations without substantial energy infrastructure—like many islands—have been largely dependent on diesel fuel and diesel gensets to meet their electrical needs. In places such as Hawaii, Puerto Rico, Alaskan villages, and the U.S. Virgin Islands, expensive imported petroleum (e.g., diesel, fuel oil) provides 68%–99% of electricity generation, resulting in retail electricity prices of $0.36–$0.50 per kWh or more.

Thus on islands and anywhere with high retail electricity prices, there is a strong economic case for reducing the use of diesel fuel as a primary fuel source for electrical power, especially considering that the retail price of diesel in the U.S. has increased 233%-real in the past 15 years.

Yet in 2013, liquid fuels were used for nearly 5% of global electricity production, accounting for 948 billion kilowatt-hours of generation, 387 GW of installed capacity, and nearly 5 million barrels/day of fuel consumption. Further, projections from a new Navigant Research report suggest that annual installations of standby diesel generators will reach 82 GW per year by 2018, signifying a growing opportunity for solar-plus-battery systems.

Utility and Grid Frustration

While in the past the grid barely warranted a second thought for most people, sentiment is changing. This change will only get worse as interconnection delays and red tape, arguments over net metering, and potentially rising prices continue to affect consumers. This reputational erosion poses additional challenges to utilities, above and beyond the increasingly competitive economics of off-grid solutions.

For example, in Hawaii, where utility interconnection limitations are making it impossible for many customers to take on grid-connected solar, off-grid development is increasing. Similar desires from individuals for some semblance of energy independence—particularly the right to garner external financing for systems on their private property—led to an unlikely political alliance between conservatives and liberals in Georgia in 2012, as well as current, similarly across-the-aisle political activities in Arizona.

Regulatory Changes

Rapid scaling of solar PV, and now grid-connected solar-plus-battery systems, are requiring federal, utility, state, and local regulators to explore new regulatory frameworks. Distributed generation and storage don't fit neatly into the traditional utility model of generation, distribution, and load or existing pricing structures that recover utilities' fixed costs through energy sales.

In California, where battery storage targets and incentives have made solar-plus-battery systems more attractive, utilities including Southern California Edison, PG&E, and Sempra Energy have made it challenging for system owners with storage to net meter their power. The utilities expressed concern that customers could store grid electricity on their batteries and then sell it back to the grid at higher prices. This upset current customers who have had battery storage for some time and were surprised by the utilities' decisions. The matter impacts both California Public Utility Commission regulation as well as the state's Renewable Portfolio Standard.

Perceived negative outcomes from regulation can drive customers, who desire solar PV and batteries for other factors, to pursue off-grid solutions.

In addition, incentives to promote storage could accelerate battery price declines, thereby increasing uptake of off-grid solutions. Several pro-storage regulations have recently been enacted. While they were primarily created with grid connectivity in mind, the overall development of the storage market and accompanying controls and other integration systems likely will lead to more robust and affordable off-grid storage applications. . . .

Conclusion

Rising retail electricity prices (driven in part by rising utility costs), increasing energy efficiency, falling costs for distributed energy technologies such as solar-plus-battery systems, and increasing adoption of distributed energy options are fundamentally shifting the landscape of the electricity system. Our analysis shows that solar-plus-battery systems will reach grid parity—for growing numbers of customers in certain geographies, especially those with high retail electricity prices—well within the 30-year period by which utilities capitalize major power assets. Millions of customers, commercial earlier than residential, representing billions of dollars in utility revenues will find themselves in a position to cost effectively defect from the grid if they so choose.

The so-called utility death spiral is proving not just a hypothetical threat, but a real, near, and present one. The coming grid parity of solar-plus-battery systems in the foreseeable future, among other factors, signals the eventual demise of traditional utility business models. Furthermore, early adopters and kWh sales decay will make utilities feel the pinch even before the rapidly approaching day of grid parity is here, while more aggressive technology improvements and investments in demand-side improvements beyond our base case would accelerate grid parity. Though utilities could and should see this as a threat, especially if they cling to increasingly challenged legacy business models, they can also see solar-plus-battery systems as an opportunity to add value to the grid and their business. When solar-plus-battery systems are integrated into a network, new opportunities open up that generate even greater value for customers and the network (e.g., potentially better customer-side economics, additional sizing options, ability of distributed systems to share excess generation or storage). The United States' electric grid is in the midst of transformation, but that shift need not be an either/or between central and distributed generation. Both forms of generation, connected by an evolving grid, have a role to play.

Having conducted an analysis of when and where grid parity will happen in this report, the important next question is how utilities, regulators, technology providers, and customers might work together to reshape the market—either within existing regulatory frameworks or under an evolved regulatory landscape—to tap into and maximize new sources of value offered by these disruptive opportunities to build the best electricity system of the future that delivers value and affordability to customers and society. The implications of these disruptive opportunities on business model design are the subject of ongoing work by the authors and their institutions, covered in a forthcoming report to follow soon.

PETER BRONSKI is the editorial director at the Rocky Mountain Institute, a nonprofit "think-and-do" tank that promotes the cost-effective shift from fossil fuels to efficiency and renewables.

JON CREYTS is a managing director at the Rocky Mountain Institute, a nonprofit "think-and-do" tank that promotes the cost-effective shift from fossil fuels to efficiency and renewables.

LEIA GUCCIONE is a manager with the Rocky Mountain Institute's electricity and industrial practices, where she specializes in microgrids, campus energy systems, industrial ecosystems, distributed generation and storage, and renewable energy procurement strategies.

MAITE MADRAZO is currently a research assistant in the Institute for Sustainable Enterprise, University of Michigan.

JAMES MANDEL is a principal at the Rocky Mountain Institute, working in industrial and electricity practices.

BODHI RADER is an associate with RMI's electricity practice, where he specializes in microgrids, distributed renewable generation, energy storage, vehicle-to-grid technology, and smart grids.

DAN SEIF is a former principal with RMI's electricity and industrial practices, and is focusing on industrial efficiency and solar PV thrusts.

PETER LILIENTHAL is the original developer of the HOMER® software at the National Renewable Energy Laboratory and founded HOMER Energy in 2009 to enhance and commercialize the software.

JOHN GLASSMIRE is a globally-minded engineer at HOMER Energy who has worked across a wide-range of infrastructure projects. He has interests in sustainable design, renewable energy, project management, and international development.

JEFFREY ABROMOWITZ worked with HOMER Energy, which provides software and consulting services for distributed power systems.

MARK CROWDIS is president of Reznick Think Energy, which he founded in 2000.

JOHN RICHARDSON is an investment banking analyst with Reznick Capital Markets Securities.

EVAN SCHMITT is currently a financial analyst at Infigen Energy.

HELEN TOCCO is a civil engineer with CohnReznick Think Energy.

Peter Kind

Disruptive Challenges: Financial Implications and Strategic Responses to a Changing Retail Electric Business

Executive Summary

Recent technological and economic changes are expected to challenge and transform the electric utility industry. These changes (or "disruptive challenges") arise due to a convergence of factors, including: falling costs of distributed generation and other distributed energy resources (DER); an enhanced focus on development of new DER technologies; increasing customer, regulatory, and political interest in demand-side management technologies (DSM); government programs to incentivize selected technologies; the declining price of natural gas; slowing economic growth trends; and rising electricity prices in certain areas of the country. Taken together, these factors are potential "game changers" to the U.S. electric utility industry, and are likely to dramatically impact customers, employees, investors, and the availability of capital to fund future investment. The timing of such transformative changes is unclear, but with the potential for technological innovation (e.g., solar photovoltaic or PV) becoming economically viable due to this confluence of forces, the industry and its stakeholders must proactively assess the impacts and alternatives available to address disruptive challenges in a timely manner.

This paper considers the financial risks and investor implications related to disruptive challenges, the potential strategic responses to these challenges, and the likely investor expectations to utility plans going forward. There are valuable lessons to be learned from other industries, as well as prior utility sector paradigm shifts, that can assist us in exploring risks and potential strategic responses.

The financial risks created by disruptive challenges include declining utility revenues, increasing costs, and lower profitability potential, particularly over the long-term. As DER and DSM programs continue to capture "market share," for example, utility revenues will be reduced.

Adding the higher costs to integrate DER, increasing subsidies for DSM and direct metering of DER will result in the potential for a squeeze on profitability and, thus, credit metrics. While the regulatory process is expected to allow for recovery of lost revenues in future rate cases, tariff structures in most states call for non-DER customers to pay for (or absorb) lost revenues. As DER penetration increases, this is a cost-recovery structure that will lead to political pressure to undo these cross subsidies and may result in utility stranded cost exposure.

While the various disruptive challenges facing the electric utility industry may have different implications, they all create adverse impacts on revenues, as well as on investor returns, and require individual solutions as part of a comprehensive program to address these disruptive trends. Left unaddressed, these financial pressures could have a major impact on realized equity returns, required investor returns, and credit quality. As a result, the future cost and availability of capital for the electric utility industry would be adversely impacted. This would lead to increasing customer rate pressures.

The regulatory paradigm that has supported recovery of utility investment has been in place since the electric utility industry reached a mature state in the first half of the 20th century. Until there is a significant, clear, and present threat to this recovery paradigm, it is likely that the financial markets will not focus on these disruptive challenges, despite the fact that electric utility capital investment is recovered over a period of 30 or more years (i.e., which exposes the industry to stranded cost risks). However, with the current level of lost load nationwide from DER being less than 1 percent, investors are not taking notice of this phenomenon, despite the fact that the pace of change is increasing and will likely increase further as costs of disruptive technologies benefit further from scale efficiencies.

Investors, particularly equity investors, have developed confidence throughout time in a durable industry financial recovery model and, thus, tend to focus on earnings growth potential over a 12- to 24-month period.

So, despite the risks that a rapidly growing level of DER penetration and other disruptive challenges may impose, they are not currently being discussed by the investment community and factored into the valuation calculus reflected in the capital markets. In fact, electric utility valuations and access to capital today are as strong as we have seen in decades, reflecting the relative safety of utilities in this uncertain economic environment.

In the late 1970s, deregulation started to take hold in two industries that share similar characteristics with the electric utility industry—the airline industry and the telecommunications industry (or "the telephone utility business"). Both industries were price- and franchise-regulated, with large barriers to entry due to regulation and the capital-intensive nature of these businesses. Airline industry changes were driven by regulatory actions (a move to competition), and the telecommunications industry experienced technology changes that encouraged regulators to allow competition. Both industries have experienced significant shifts in the landscape of industry players as a result.

In the airline sector, each of the major U.S. carriers that were in existence prior to deregulation in 1978 faced bankruptcy. The telecommunication businesses of 1978, meanwhile, are not recognizable today, nor are the names of many of the players and the service they once provided ("the plain old telephone service"). Both industries experienced poor financial market results by many of the former incumbent players for their investors (equity and fixed-income) and have sought mergers of necessity to achieve scale economies to respond to competitive dynamics.

The combination of new technologies, increasing costs, and changing customer-usage trends allow us to consider alternative scenarios for how the future of the electric sector may develop. Without fundamental changes to regulatory rules and recovery paradigms, one can speculate as to the adverse impact of disruptive challenges on electric utilities, investors, and access to capital, as well as the resulting impact on customers from a price and service perspective. We have the benefit of lessons learned from other industries to shift the story and move the industry in a direction that will allow for customers, investors, and the U.S. economy to benefit and prosper.

Revising utility tariff structures, particularly in states with potential for high DER adoption, to mitigate (or eliminate) cross subsidies and provide proper customer price signals will support economic implementation of DER while limiting stress on non-DER participants and utility finances. This is a near-term, must-consider action by all policy setting industry stakeholders.

The electric utility sector will benefit from proactive assessment and planning to address disruptive challenges. Thirty year investments need to be made on the basis that they will be recoverable in the future in a timely manner. To the extent that increased risk is incurred, capital deployment and recovery mechanisms need to be adapted accordingly. The paper addresses possible strategic responses to competitive threats in order to protect investors and capital availability. While the paper does not propose new business models for the industry to pursue to address disruptive challenges in order to protect investors and retain access to capital, it does highlight several of the expectations and objectives of investors, which may lead to business model transformation alternatives.

Background

As a result of a confluence of factors (i.e., technological innovation, public policy support for sustainability and efficiency, declining trends in electricity demand growth, rising price pressures to maintain and upgrade the U.S. distribution grid, and enhancement of the generation fleet), the threat of disruptive forces (i.e., new products/markets that replace existing products/markets) impacting the utility industry is increasing and is adding to the effects of other types of disruptive forces like declining sales and end-use efficiency. While we cannot lay out an exact roadmap or timeline for the impact of potential disruptive forces, given the current shift in competitive dynamics, the utility industry and its stakeholders must be prepared to address these challenges in a way that will benefit customers, long-term economic growth, and investors. Recent business history has provided many examples of companies and whole industries that either failed or were slow to respond to disruptive forces and suffered as a result.

Today, a variety of disruptive technologies are emerging that may compete with utility-provided services. Such technologies include solar photovoltaics (PV), battery storage, fuel cells, geothermal energy systems, wind, micro turbines, and electric vehicle (EV) enhanced storage. As the cost curve for these technologies improves, they could directly threaten the centralized utility model. To promote the growth of these technologies in the near-term, policymakers have sought to encourage disruptive competing energy sources through various subsidy programs, such as tax incentives, renewable portfolio standards, and net metering where the pricing structure of utility services allows customers to engage in the use of new technologies, while shifting costs/lost revenues to remaining non-participating customers.

In addition, energy efficiency and DSM programs also promote reduced utility revenues while causing the utility to incur implementation costs. While decoupling recovery mechanisms, for example, may support recovery of lost revenues and costs, under/over recovery charges are typically imposed based on energy usage and, therefore, adversely impact non-participants of these programs. While the financial community is generally quite supportive of decoupling to capture lost revenues, investors have not delved into the long-term business and financial impact of cross subsidization on future customer rates inherent in most decoupling models and the effective recovery thereof. In other words, will non-DER participants continue to subsidize participants or will there be political pressure to not allow cost pass thru over time?

The threat to the centralized utility service model is likely to come from new technologies or customer behavioral changes that reduce load. Any recovery paradigms that force cost of service to be spread over fewer units of sales (i.e., kilowatt-hours or kWh) enhance the ongoing competitive threat of disruptive alternatives. While the cost—recovery challenges of lost load can be partially addressed by revising tariff structures (such as a fixed charge or demand charge service component), there is often significant opposition to these recovery structures in order to encourage the utilization of new technologies and to promote customer behavior change.

But, even if cross-subsidies are removed from rate structures, customers are not precluded from leaving the system entirely if a more cost-competitive alternative is available (e.g., a scenario where efficient energy storage combined with distributed generation could create the ultimate risk to grid viability). While tariff restructuring can be used to mitigate lost revenues, the longer-term threat of fully exiting from the grid (or customers solely using the electric grid for backup purposes) raises the potential for irreparable damages to revenues and growth prospects. This suggests that an old-line industry with 30-year cost recovery of investment is vulnerable to cost-recovery threats from disruptive forces.

Generators in organized, competitive markets are more directly exposed to threats from new technologies and enhanced efficiency programs, both of which reduce electricity use and demand. Reduced energy use and demand translate into lower prices for wholesale power and reduced profitability. With reduced profitability

comes less cash flow to invest and to support the needs of generation customers. While every market-driven business is subject to competitive forces, public policy programs that provide for subsidized growth of competing technologies and/or participant economic incentives do not provide a level playing field upon which generators can compete fairly against new entrants. As an example, subsidized demand response programs or state contracted generation additions create threats to the generation owner (who competes based upon free market supply and demand forces).

According to the Solar Electric Power Association (SEPA), there were 200,000 distributed solar customers (aggregating 2,400 megawatts or MW) in the United States as of 2011. Thus, the largest near-term threat to the utility model represents less than 1 percent of the U.S. retail electricity market. Therefore, the current level of activity can be "covered over" without noticeable impact on utilities or their customers. However, at the present time, 70 percent of the distributed activity is concentrated within 10 utilities, which obviously speaks to the increased risk allocated to a small set of companies. As previously stated, due to a confluence of recent factors, the threat to the utility model from disruptive forces is now increasingly viable. One prominent example is in the area of distributed solar PV, where the threats to the centralized utility business model have accelerated due to:

- The decline in the price of PV panels from $3.80/watt in 2008 to $0.86/watt in mid-2012. While some will question the sustainability of cost-curve trends experienced, it is expected that PV panel costs will not increase (or not increase meaningfully) even as the current supply glut is resolved. As a result, the all-in cost of PV solar installation approximates $5/watt, with expectations of the cost declining further as scale is realized;
- An increase in utility rates such that the competitive price opportunity for PV solar is now "in the market" for approximately 16 percent of the U.S. retail electricity market where rates are at or above $0.15/kWh. In addition, projections by PV industry participants suggest that the "in the money" market size will double the share of contestable revenue by 2017 (to 33 percent, or $170 billion of annual utility revenue);
- Tax incentives that promote specific renewable resources, including the 30-percent Investment Tax Credit (ITC) that is effective through 2016 and five-year accelerated depreciation recovery of net asset costs;

- Public policies to encourage renewable resource development through Renewable Portfolio Standards (RPS), which are in place in 29 states and the District of Columbia and which call for renewable generation goals within a state's energy mix;
- Public policies to encourage net metering, which are in effect in 43 states and the District of Columbia (3 additional states have utilities with voluntary net metering programs) and which typically allow customers to sell excess energy generated back to the utility at a price greater than the avoided variable cost;
- Time-of-use rates, structured for higher electric rates during daylight hours, that create incentives for installing distributed solar PV, thereby taking advantage of solar benefit (vs. time-of-use peak rates) and net metering subsidies; and
- The evolution of capital markets' access to businesses that leverage the dynamics outlined above to support a for-profit business model. Examples include tax equity financing, project finance lending, residential PV leasing models (i.e., "no money down" for customers), and public equity markets for pure play renewable resource providers and owners. As an illustration, U.S. tax equity investment is running at $7.5 billion annualized for 2012. Add other sources of capital, including traditional equity, and this suggests the potential to fund a large and growing industry.

Bloomberg New Energy Finance (BNEF) projects that distributed solar capacity will grow rapidly as a result of the competitive dynamics highlighted. BNEF projects 22-percent compound annual growth in PV installations through 2020, resulting in 30 gigawatts (GW) of capacity overall (and approximately 4.5 GW coming from distributed PV). This would account for 10 percent of capacity in key markets coming from distributed resources and even a larger share of year-round energy generated.

Assuming a decline in load, and possibly customers served, of 10 percent due to DER with full subsidization of DER participants, the average impact on base electricity prices for non-DER participants will be a 20 percent or more increase in rates, and the ongoing rate of growth in electricity prices will double for non-DER participants (before accounting for the impact of the increased cost of serving distributed resources). The fundamental drivers previously highlighted could suggest even further erosion of utility market share if public policy is not addressed to normalize this competitive threat.

While the immediate threat from solar PV is location dependent, if the cost curve of PV continues to bend

and electricity rates continue to increase, it will open up the opportunity for PV to viably expand into more regions of the country. According to ThinkEquity, a boutique investment bank, as the installed cost of PV declines from $5/watt to $3.5/watt (a 30-percent decline), the targeted addressable market increases by 500 percent, including 18 states and 20 million homes, and customer demand for PV increases by 14 times. If PV system costs decline even further, the market opportunity grows exponentially. In addition, other DER technologies being developed may also pose additional viable alternatives to the centralized utility model.

Due to the variable nature of renewable DER, there is a perception that customers will always need to remain on the grid. While we would expect customers to remain on the grid until a fully viable and economic distributed non-variable resource is available, one can imagine a day when battery storage technology or micro turbines could allow customers to be electric grid independent. To put this into perspective, who would have believed 10 years ago that traditional wire line telephone customers could economically "cut the cord?"

The cost of providing interconnection and back-up supply for variable resources will add to the utility cost burden. If not properly addressed in the tariff structure, the provision of these services will create additional lost revenues and will further challenge non-DER participants in terms of being allocated costs incurred to serve others.

Another outcome of the trend of rising electricity prices is the potential growth in the market for energy efficiency solutions. Combining electricity price trends, customer sustainability objectives, and ratemaking incentives via cross-subsidies, it is estimated that spending on energy efficiency programs will increase by as much as 300 percent from 2010 to 2025, within a projected range of $6 to $16 billion per year. This level of spending on energy efficiency services will have a meaningful impact on utility load and, thus, will create significant additional lost revenue exposure.

The financial implications of these threats are fairly evident. Start with the increased cost of supporting a network capable of managing and integrating distributed generation sources. Next, under most rate structures, add the decline in revenues attributed to revenues lost from sales foregone. These forces lead to increased revenues required from remaining customers (unless fixed costs are recovered through a service charge tariff structure) and sought through rate increases. The result of higher electricity prices and competitive threats will encourage a higher rate of DER additions, or will promote greater use of efficiency or demand-side solutions.

Increased uncertainty and risk will not be welcomed by investors, who will seek a higher return on investment and force defensive-minded investors to reduce exposure to the sector. These competitive and financial risks would likely erode credit quality. The decline in credit quality will lead to a higher cost of capital, putting further pressure on customer rates. Ultimately, capital availability will be reduced, and this will affect future investment plans. The cycle of decline has been previously witnessed in technology-disrupted sectors (such as telecommunications) and other deregulated industries (airlines).

Disruptive Threats—Strategic Considerations

A disruptive innovation is defined as "an innovation that helps create a new market and value network, and eventually goes on to disrupt an existing market and value network (over a few years or decades), displacing an earlier technology. The term is used in business and technology literature to describe innovations that improve a product or service in ways that the market does not expect, typically first by designing for a different set of consumers in the new market and later by lowering prices in the existing market."

Disruptive forces, if not actively addressed, threaten the viability of old-line exposed industries. Examples of once-dominant, blue chip companies/entities being threatened or succumbing to new entrants due to innovation include Kodak and the U.S. Postal Service (USPS). For years, Kodak owned the film and related supplies market. The company watched as the photo business was transformed by digital technology and finally filed for bankruptcy in 2012.

Meanwhile, the USPS is a monopoly, government-run agency with a mission of delivering mail and providing an essential service to keep the economy moving. The USPS has been threatened for decades by private package delivery services (e.g., UPS and FedEx) that compete to offer more efficient and flexible service. Today, the primary threat to USPS' viability is the delivery of information by email, including commercial correspondence such as bills and bill payments, bank and brokerage statements, etc. Many experts believe that the USPS must dramatically restructure its operations and costs to have a chance to protect its viability as an independent agency.

Participants in all industries must prepare for and develop plans to address disruptive threats, including plans to replace their own technology with more innovative, more valuable customer services offered at competitive prices. The traditional wire line telephone players, including AT&T and Verizon, for example, became leaders in U.S. wireless telephone services, which over time could make the old line telephone product extinct. But these innovative, former old-line telephone providers had the vision to get in front of the trend to wireless and lead the development of non-regulated infrastructure networks and consumer marketing skills. As a result, they now hold large domestic market shares. In fact, they have now further leveraged technology innovation to create new products that expand their customer offerings.

The electric utility sector has not previously experienced a viable disruptive threat to its service offering due to customer reliance and the solid economic value of its product. However, a combination of technological innovation, public/regulatory policy, and changes in consumer objectives and preferences has resulted in distributed generation and other DER being on a path to becoming a viable alternative to the electric utility model. While investors are eager to support innovation and economic progress, they do not support the use of subsidies to attack the financial viability of their invested capital. Utility investors may not be opposed to DER technologies, but, in order for utilities to maintain their access to capital, it is essential that the financial implications of DER technologies be addressed so that non-DER participants and investors are not left to pay for revenues lost (and costs unrecovered) from DER participants. . . .

Strategic Implications of Distribution 2020 Disruptive Forces

The threats posed to the electric utility industry from disruptive forces, particularly distributed resources, have serious long-term implications for the traditional electric utility business model and investor opportunities. While the potential for significant immediate business impact is currently low (due to low DER participation to date), the industry and its stakeholders must begin to seriously address these challenges in order to mitigate the potential impact of disruptive forces, given the prospects for significant DER participation in the future.

One example of a significant potential adverse impact to utility investors stems from net metering. Utilities have witnessed the implementation of net metering rules in all but a handful of states. Lost revenues from DER are being recovered from non-DER customers in order to encourage distributed generation implementation. This type of lost revenue recovery drives up the prices of those non-participating customers and creates the environment for ongoing loss of additional customers as the system cost is transferred to a smaller and smaller base of remaining customers.

Utility investors are not being compensated for the risks associated with customer losses resulting from increasing DER. It is difficult to identify a rate case in which the cost-of-capital implications of net metering were considered. At the point when utility investors become focused on these new risks and start to witness significant customer and earnings erosion trends, they will respond to these challenges. But, by then, it may be too late to repair the utility business model.

DER is not the only disruptive risk the industry faces. Energy efficiency and DSM programs that promote lower electricity sales pressure earnings required to support capital investment. Without a tariff structure that properly allocates fixed vs. variable costs, any structure for lost revenues would come at a cost to non-participating customers, who will then be more motivated to find alternatives to reduce their consumption. While it is not the objective of this paper to outline new business model alternatives to address disruptive challenges, there are a number of actions that utilities and stakeholders should consider on a timely basis to align the interests of all stakeholders, while avoiding additional subsidies for non-participating customers.

These actions include:
Immediate Actions:

- Institute a monthly customer service charge to all tariffs in all states in order to recover fixed costs and eliminate the cross-subsidy biases that are created by distributed resources and net metering, energy efficiency, and demand-side resources;
- Develop a tariff structure to reflect the cost of service and value provided to DER customers, being off-peak service, back-up interruptible service, and the pathway to sell DER resources to the utility or other energy supply providers; and
- Analyze revision of net metering programs in all states so that self-generated DER sales to utilities are treated as supply-side purchases at a market-derived price. From a load provider's perspective, this would support the adoption of distributed resources on economically driven bases, as opposed to being incentivized by cross subsidies.

Longer-term Actions:

- Assess appropriateness of depreciation recovery lives based on the economic useful life of the investment, factoring the potential for disruptive loss of customers;
- Consider a stranded cost charge in all states to be paid by DER and fully departing customers to recognize the portion of investment deemed stranded as customers depart;
- Consider a customer advance in aid of construction in all states to recover upfront the cost of adding new customers and, thus, mitigate future stranded cost risk;
- Apply more stringent capital expenditure evaluation tools to factor-in potential investment that may be subject to stranded cost risk, including the potential to recover such investment through a customer hook-up charge or over a shorter depreciable life;
- Identify new business models and services that can be provided by electric utilities in all states to customers in order to recover lost margin while providing a valuable customer service—this was a key factor in the survival of the incumbent telephone players post deregulation; and
- Factor the threat of disruptive forces in the requested cost of capital being sought.

Investors have no desire to sit by and watch as disruptive forces slice away at the value and financial prospects of their investment. While the utility sector provides an important public good for customers, utilities and financial managers of investments have a fiduciary responsibility to protect the value of invested capital. Prompt action to mitigate lost revenue, while protecting customers from cross-subsidization better aligns the interests of customers and investors.

As growth in earnings and value is a major component of equity investment returns, what will investors expect to see as a strategic response from the industry to disruptive forces? The way to realize growth in earnings is to develop profit streams to counterbalance the impact of disruptive forces. Examples of new profit sources would include ownership of distributed resources with the receipt of an ongoing service fee or rate basing the investment and financial incentives for utilities to encourage demand side/energy efficiency benefits for customers. From an investor perspective, this may be easier said than done because the history of the electric utility industry in achieving non-regulated profits/value creation streams has not been a pleasant experience. So, investors will want to see very clear cut programs to capture value that are consistent with the core strengths of utilities: ability to execute construction projects, to provide dependable service with high reliability, and to access relatively low-cost capital.

Summary

While the threat of disruptive forces on the utility industry has been limited to date, economic fundamentals and public policies in place are likely to encourage significant future disruption to the utility business model. Technology innovation and rate structures that encourage cross subsidization of DER and/or behavioral modification by customers must be addressed quickly to mitigate further damage to the utility franchise and to better align interests of all stakeholders.

Utility investors seek a return on investment that depends on the increase in the value of their investment through growth in earnings and dividends. When customers have the opportunity to reduce their use of a product or find another provider of such service, utility earnings growth is threatened. As this threat to growth becomes more evident, investors will become less attracted to investments in the utility sector. This will be manifested via a higher cost of capital and less capital available to be allocated to the sector. Investors today appear confident in the utility regulatory model since the threat of disruptive forces has been modest to date. However, the competitive economics of distributed energy resources, such as PV solar, have improved significantly based on technology innovation and government incentives and subsidies, including tax and tariff-shifting incentives. But with policies in place that encourage cross subsidization of proactive customers, those not able or willing to respond to change will not be able to bear the responsibility left behind by proactive DER participating customers. It should not be left to the utility investor to bear the cost of these subsidies and the threat to their investment value.

This paper encourages an immediate focus on revising state and federal policies that do not align the interests of customers and investors, particularly revising utility tariff structures in order to eliminate cross subsidies (by non-DER participants) and utility investor cost-recovery uncertainties. In addition, utilities and stakeholders must develop policies and strategies to reduce the risk of ongoing customer disruption, including assessing business models where utilities can add value to customers and investors by providing new services.

While the pace of disruption cannot be predicted, the mere fact that we are seeing the beginning of customer disruption and that there is a large universe of companies pursuing this opportunity highlight the importance of proactive and timely planning to address these challenges early on so that uneconomic disruption does not proceed further. Ultimately, all stakeholders must embrace change in technology and business models in order to maintain a viable utility industry. . . .

PETER KIND is the executive director of Energy Infrastructure Advocates.

120 Taking Sides: Clashing Views in Science, Technology, and Society, 13/e

EXPLORING THE ISSUE

Is Home Solar the Wave of the Future?

Critical Thinking and Reflection

1. What do people mean when they call a technology "disruptive"?
2. What other industries might feel threatened by the growth in home solar power?
3. In what ways do early adopters of home solar power hasten the utility "death spiral"?

Is There Common Ground?

Both of our selections agree that the growing use of home solar power is likely to mean changes in the way that homeowners gain their electricity supply. To the Rocky Mountain Institute's team, these changes are desirable, for they promise lower prices, less dependence on fossil fuels, less contribution to global warming, and opportunities for utilities to retool their business models. To the electric utilities, these changes are not desirable, for they threaten loss of revenue, loss of investor confidence, and pressure to change traditional ways of doing business.

1. Both the Rocky Mountain Institute's team and Peter Kind agree that there is a need to identify new business models and services. What else can an electric utility do besides sell electricity?

2. Why do electric utilities need income even if they aren't selling electricity?
3. How can electric utilities take advantage of the trend toward home solar power?

Additional Resources

David Biello, "Solar Wars," *Scientific American* (November 2014).

Michael Boxwell, *Solar Electricity Handbook, 2014 Edition: A Simple Practical Guide to Solar Energy— Designing and Installing Photovoltaic Solar Electric Systems* (Greenstream, 2013).

John Schaeffer, *Real Goods Solar Living Sourcebook: Your Complete Guide to Living beyond the Grid with Renewable Energy Technologies and Sustainable Living* (New Society, 2014).

Internet References . . .

Rocky Mountain Institute

http://www.rmi.org/

The Edison Electric Institute

http://www.eei.org/Pages/default.aspx

Vivint Solar

http://www.vivintsolar.com/

Unit 3

UNIT

Human Health and Welfare

*M*any people are concerned about new technological and scientific discoveries because they fear their potential impacts on human health and welfare. In the past, fears have been expressed concerning nuclear bombs and power plants, irradiated food, the internal combustion engine, medications such as thalidomide and diethylstilbestrol, pesticides and other chemicals, and more. Because human birth rates have declined, at least in developed nations, the hazards of excess population have fallen out of the headlines, but a few people do still struggle to remind us that a smaller population makes many problems less worrisome. On the public-health front, people worry about whether hydraulic fracturing (fracking) for oil and gas pollutes the environment and threatens public health. There are similar concerns about the hazards of decommissioning nuclear reactors that have outlived their usefulness. And some people are so worried about the supposed dangers of genetically modified (GM) foods that they want anything containing GM crops to be labeled so they can avoid them. It is worth stressing that risks may be real (as they are with toxic chemicals) or not (as with vaccines), but either way there may be a trade-off for genuine health benefits.

Selected, Edited, and with Issue Framing Material by:
Thomas A. Easton, *Mount Ida College*

ISSUE

Do We Have a Population Problem?

YES: Dennis Dimick, from "As World's Population Booms, Will Its Resources Be Enough for Us?" *National Geographic* (2014)

NO: Tom Bethell, from "Population, Economy, and God," *The American Spectator* (2009)

Learning Outcomes
After reading this issue, you will be able to:
• Explain why unrestrained population growth is not sustainable. • Explain why past predictions of population disaster have not come true. • Explain the potential benefits of stabilizing or reducing population. • Explain the potential drawbacks of stabilizing or reducing population.

ISSUE SUMMARY

YES: Dennis Dimick argues that new projections of higher population growth through the twenty-first century are reason for concern, largely because of the conflict between population size and resource use. The environmental impact of population also depends on technology, affluence, and waste, but educated women have smaller families and technology (electric lights, for instance) aids education. Controlling population appears to be essential.

NO: Tom Bethell argues that population alarmists project their fears onto popular concerns, currently the environment, and every time their scare-mongering turns out to be based on faulty premises. Blaming environmental problems will be no different. Societies are sustained not by population control but by belief in God.

In 1798 the British economist Thomas Malthus published his *Essay on the Principle of Population.* In it, he pointed with alarm at the way the human population grew geometrically (a hockey-stick-shaped curve of increase) and at how agricultural productivity grew only arithmetically (a straight-line increase). It was obvious, he said, that the population must inevitably outstrip its food supply and experience famine. Contrary to the conventional wisdom of the time, population growth was not necessarily a good thing. Indeed, it led inexorably to catastrophe. For many years, Malthus was something of a laughing stock. The doom he forecast kept receding into the future as new lands were opened to agriculture, new agricultural technologies appeared, new ways of preserving food limited the waste of spoilage, and the birth rate dropped in

the industrialized nations (the "demographic transition"). The food supply kept ahead of population growth and seemed likely—to most observers—to continue to do so. Malthus's ideas were dismissed as irrelevant fantasies.

Yet overall population kept growing. In Malthus's time, there were about 1 billion human beings on Earth. By 1950—when Warren S. Thompson worried that civilization would be endangered by the rapid growth of Asian and Latin American populations during the next five decades (see "Population," *Scientific American*, February 1950)— there were a little over 2.5 billion. In 1999 the tally passed 6 billion. It passed 7 billion in 2011. By 2025 it will be over 8 billion. Until fairly recently, most experts thought that population would peak at about 9 billion around 2050 and then begin to level off and even decline. Some projected a 2100 world population of about 10 billion; see

Jocelyn Keiser, "10 Billion Plus: Why World Population Projections Were Too Low," *Science Insider* (May 4, 2011) (http://scim.ag/_worldpop). However, in 2014 the United Nations released estimates indicating that population would not level off before 2100. Indeed, it could reach 12 billion, or even a bit more, largely due to continuing high growth rates in Africa; see Patrick Gerland, et al., "World Population Stabilization Unlikely This Century," *Science* (October 10, 2014).

While global agricultural production has also increased, it has not kept up with rising demand, and—because of the loss of topsoil to erosion, the exhaustion of aquifers for irrigation water, and the high price of energy for making fertilizer (among other things)—the prospect of improvement seems exceedingly slim to many observers. Two centuries never saw Malthus's forecasts of doom come to pass. Population continued to grow, and environmentalists pointed with alarm at a great many problems that resulted from human use of the world's resources (air and water pollution, erosion, loss of soil fertility and groundwater, loss of species, and a great deal more). "Cornucopian" economists such as the late Julian Simon insisted that the more people there are on Earth, the more people there are to solve problems and that humans can find ways around all possible resource shortages. See Simon's essay, "Life on Earth Is Getting Better, Not Worse," *The Futurist* (August 1983). See also David Malakoff, "Are More People Necessarily a Problem?" *Science* (July 29, 2011) (a special issue on population).

Was Malthus wrong? Both environmental scientists and many economists now say that if population continues to grow, problems are inevitable. But some experts still project that population will level off and then decline. Fred Pearce, *The Coming Population Crash: and Our Planet's Surprising Future* (Beacon, 2010), is optimistic about the effects on human well-being of the coming decline in population. Do we still need to work on controlling population? Historian Matthew Connolly, *Fatal Misconception: The Struggle to Control World Population* (Belknap Press, 2010), argues that the twentieth-century movement to control population was an oppressive movement that failed to deliver on its promises. Now that population growth is slowing, the age of population control is over. Yet there remains the issue of "carrying capacity," defined very simply as the size of the population that the environment can support, or "carry," indefinitely, through both good years and bad. It is not the size of the population that can prosper in good times alone, for such a large population must suffer catastrophically when droughts, floods, or blights arrive or the climate warms or cools. It is a long-

term concept, where "long-term" means not decades or generations, nor even centuries, but millennia or more. See Mark Nathan Cohen, "Carrying Capacity," *Free Inquiry* (August/September 2004); T. C. R. White, "The Role of Food, Weather, and Climate in Limiting the Abundance of Animals," *Biological Reviews* (August 2008); and David Pimentel, et al., "Will Limited Land, Water, and Energy Control Human Population Numbers in the Future?" *Human Ecology* (August 2010).

What is Earth's carrying capacity for human beings? It is surely impossible to set a precise figure on the number of human beings the world can support for the long run. As Joel E. Cohen discusses in *How Many People Can the Earth Support?* (W. W. Norton, 1996), estimates of Earth's carrying capacity range from under a billion to over a trillion. The precise number depends on our choices of diet, standard of living, level of technology, willingness to share with others at home and abroad, and desire for an intact physical, chemical, and biological environment (including wildlife and natural environments), as well as on whether or not our morality permits restraint in reproduction and our political or religious ideology permits educating and empowering women. The key, Cohen stresses, is human choice, and the choices are ones we must make within the next 50 years. Phoebe Hall, "Carrying Capacity," *E—The Environmental Magazine* (March/April 2003), notes that even countries with large land areas and small populations, such as Australia and Canada, can be overpopulated in terms of resource availability. The critical resource appears to be food supply; see Russell Hopfenberg, "Human Carrying Capacity Is Determined by Food Availability," *Population & Environment* (November 2003).

Andrew R. B. Ferguson, in "Perceiving the Population Bomb," *World Watch* (July/August 2001), sets the maximum sustainable human population at about 2 billion. Sandra Postel, in the Worldwatch Institute's *State of the World 1994* (W.W. Norton, 1994), says, "As a result of our population size, consumption patterns, and technology choices, we have surpassed the planet's carrying capacity. This is plainly evident by the extent to which we are damaging and depleting natural capital" (including land and water). The point is reiterated by Robert Kunzig, "By 2045 Global Population Is Projected to Reach Nine Billion. Can the Planet Take the Strain?" *National Geographic* (January 2011) (*National Geographic* ran numerous articles on population-related issues during 2011). Thomas L. Friedman, "The Earth Is Full," *New York Times* (June 7, 2011), thinks a crisis is imminent but we will learn and move on; see also Paul Gilding, *The Great Disruption: Why the Climate Crisis Will*

Bring On the End of Shopping and the Birth of a New World (Bloomsbury Press, 2011).

Or is the crisis less urgent? Many people, relying on pre-2014 estimates of future population, think population growth is now declining and world population will actually begin to decline during this century. See Jeff Wise, "About that Overpopulation Problem," *Slate* (January 9, 2013) (http://www.slate.com/articles/technology/future_tense/2013/01/world_population_may_actually_start_declining_not_exploding.html. If they are right, there is clearly hope. But most estimates of carrying capacity put it at well below the current world population size, and it will take a long time for global population to fall far enough to reach such levels. Perhaps we are moving in the right direction, but it remains an open question whether our numbers will decline far enough soon enough (i.e., before environmental problems become critical). On the other hand, Jeroen Van den Bergh and Piet Rietveld, "Reconsidering the Limits to World Population: Meta-Analysis and Meta-Prediction," *Bioscience* (March 2004), set their best estimate of human global carrying capacity at 7.7 billion, which is distinctly reassuring. J. T. Trevors, "Total Abuse of the Earth: Human Overpopulation and Climate Change," *Water, Air, and Soil Pollution* (January 2010, Suppl. 1), is less optimistic, noting that we are in unsustainable territory and "The party [of endless growth and consumption] is over. . . . Humans cannot bribe nor buy nature."

How high a level will population actually reach? Fertility levels are definitely declining in many developed nations; see Alan Booth and Ann C. Crouter (eds.), *The New population problem: Why Families in Developed Countries Are Shrinking and What It Means* (Lawrence Erlbaum Associates, 2005). The visibility of this fertility decline is among the reasons mentioned by Martha Campbell, "Why the Silence on Population?" *Population and Environment* (May 2007). Yet Doug Moss, "What Birth Dearth?" *E—The Environmental Magazine* (November–December 2006), reminds us that there is still a large surplus of births—and therefore a growing population—in the less developed world. If we think globally, there is no shortage of people. However, many countries are so concerned about changing age distributions that they are trying to encourage larger—not smaller—families. See Robert Engelman, "Unnatural Increase? A Short History of Population Trends and Influences," *World Watch* (September/October 2008—a special issue on population issues), "Population and Sustainability," *Scientific American Earth 3.0* (Summer 2009), and his book *More: Population, Nature, and What Women Want* (Island Press,

2008). On the other hand, David E. Bloom, "7 Billion and Counting," *Science* (July 29, 2011), notes that "Despite alarmist predictions, historical increases in population have not been economically catastrophic. Moreover, changes in population age structure [providing for more workers] have opened the door to increased prosperity." Jonathan A. Foley, "Can We Feed the World & Sustain the Planet?" *Scientific American* (November 2011), thinks that with revisions to the world's agricultural systems, a growing population's demand for food can be met, at least through 2050.

Some people worry that a decline in population will not be good for human welfare. Michael Meyer, "Birth Dearth," *Newsweek* (September 27, 2004), argues that a shrinking population will mean that the economic growth that has meant constantly increasing standards of living must come to an end, government programs (from war to benefits for the poor and elderly) will no longer be affordable, a shrinking number of young people will have to support a growing elderly population, and despite some environmental benefits, quality of life will suffer. China is already feeling some of these effects; see Wang Feng, "China's Population Destiny: The Looming Crisis," *Current History* (September 2010), and Mara Hvistendahl, "Has China Outgrown the One-Child Policy?" *Science* (September 17, 2010). Julia Whitty, "The Last Taboo," *Mother Jones* (May–June 2010), argues that even though the topic of overpopulation has become unpopular, it is clear that we are already using the Earth's resources faster than they can be replenished and the only answer is to slow and eventually reverse population growth. Scott Victor Valentine, "Disarming the Population Bomb," *International Journal of Sustainable Development and World Ecology* (April 2010), calls for "a renewed international focus on managed population reduction as a key enabler of sustainable development." As things stand, the current size and continued growth of population threaten the United Nations' Millennium Development Goals (including alleviating global poverty, improving health, and protecting the environment; see http://www.un.org/millenniumgoals/); see Willard Cates, Jr., et al., "Family Planning and the Millennium Development Goals," *Science* (September 24, 2010). Paul R. Ehrlich and Anne H. Ehrlich, "Solving the Human Predicament," *International Journal of Environmental Studies* (August 2012), stress the contribution of population to environmental problems and see hope in a wide variety of grassroots movements.

In the YES selection, Dennis Dimick argues that new projections of higher population growth through the twenty-first century are reason for concern, largely because of the conflict between population size and resource use. The environmental impact of population also depends on technology, affluence, and waste, but educated women have smaller families and technology (electric lights, for instance) aids education. Controlling population appears to be essential. In the NO selection, Tom Bethell argues that population alarmists project their fears onto popular concerns, currently the environment, and every time their scaremongering turns out to be based on faulty premises. Blaming environmental problems will be no different. Societies are sustained not by population control but by belief in God.

YES ↵

Dennis Dimick

As World's Population Booms, Will Its Resources Be Enough for Us?

This week, two conflicting projections of the world's future population were released. . . . [A] new United Nations and University of Washington study in the journal *Science* says it's highly likely we'll see 9.6 billion Earthlings by 2050, and up to 11 billion or more by 2100. These researchers used a new "probabilistic" statistical method that establishes a specific range of uncertainty around their results. Another study in the journal *Global Environmental Change* projects that the global population will peak at 9.4 billion later this century and fall below 9 billion by 2100, based on a survey of population experts. Who is right? We'll know in a hundred years.

Population debates like this are why, in 2011, *National Geographic* published a series called "7 Billion" on world population, its trends, implications, and future. After years of examining global environmental issues such as climate change, energy, food supply, and freshwater, we thought the time was ripe for a deep discussion of people and how we are connected to all these other issues—issues that are getting increased attention today, amid the new population projections.

After all, how many of us there are, how many children we have, how long we live, and where and how we live affect virtually every aspect of the planet upon which we rely to survive: the land, oceans, fisheries, forests, wildlife, grasslands, rivers and lakes, groundwater, air quality, atmosphere, weather, and climate.

World population passed 7 billion on October 31, 2011, according to the United Nations. Just who the 7 billionth person was and where he or she was born remain a mystery; there is no actual cadre of census takers who go house to house in every country, counting people. Instead, population estimates are made by most national governments and international organizations such as the UN. These estimates are based on assumptions about existing population size and expectations of fertility, mortality, and migration in a geographic area.

We've been on a big growth spurt during the past century or so. In 1900, demographers had the world's population at 1.6 billion, in 1950 it was about 2.5 billion, by 2000 it was more than 6 billion. Now, there are about 7.2 billion of us.

In recent years we've been adding about a billion people every 12 or 13 years or so. Precisely how many of us are here right now is also a matter of debate, depending on whom you consult: The United Nations offers a range of current population figures and trends, the U.S. Census Bureau has its own estimate, and the Population Reference Bureau also tracks us.

The new UN study out this week projects that the world's population growth may not stop any time soon. That is a reversal from estimates done five years ago, when demographers—people who study population trends—were projecting that by 2045, world population likely would reach about 9 billion and begin to level off soon after.

But now, the UN researchers who published these new projections in the journal *Science* say that a flattening of population growth is not going to happen soon without rapid fertility declines—or a reduction in the number of children per mother—in most parts of sub-Saharan Africa that are still experiencing rapid population growth. As Rob Kunzig wrote for *National Geographic*, the new study estimates that "there's an 80 percent chance . . . that the actual number of people in 2100 will be somewhere between 9.6 and 12.3 billion."

A History of Debates Over Population

In a famous 1798 essay, the Reverend Thomas Malthus proposed that human population would grow more rapidly than our ability to grow food, and that eventually we would starve.

He asserted that the population would grow geometrically—1, 2, 4, 8, 16, 32—and that food production would increase only arithmetically—1, 2, 3, 4, 5, 6. So food production would not keep up with our expanding appetites. You might imagine Malthus' scenario on geometric population growth as being like compound interest: A couple have two children and those children each produce two children. Those four children produce two children each to make eight, and those eight children each have their own two kids, leaving 16 kids in that generation. But worldwide, the current median fertility rate is about 2.5, (or five children between two couples), so, like compound interest, the population numbers can rise even faster.

Even though more than 800 million people worldwide don't have enough to eat now, the mass starvation Mathus envisioned hasn't happened. This is primarily because advances in agriculture—including improved plant breeding and the use of chemical fertilizers—have kept global harvests increasing fast enough to mostly keep up with demand. Still, researchers such as Jeffrey Sachs and Paul Ehrlich continue to worry that Malthus eventually might be right.

Ehrlich, a Stanford University population biologist, wrote a 1968 bestseller called *The Population Bomb*, which warned of mass starvation in the 1970s and 1980s because of overpopulation. Even though he drastically missed that forecast, he continues to argue that humanity is heading for calamity. Ehrlich says the key issue now is not just the number of people on Earth, but a dramatic rise in our recent consumption of natural resources, which Elizabeth Kolbert explored in 2011 in an article called "The Anthropocene—The Age of Man."

As part of this human-dominated era, the past half century also has been referred to as a period of "Great Acceleration" by Will Steffen at The International Geosphere-Biosphere Program. Besides a near tripling of human population since the end of World War II, our presence has been marked by a dramatic increase in human activity—the damming of rivers, soaring water use, expansion of cropland, increased use of irrigation and fertilizers, a loss of forests, and more motor vehicles. There also has been a sharp rise in the use of coal, oil, and gas, and a rapid increase in the atmosphere of methane and carbon dioxide, greenhouse gases that result from changes in land use and the burning of such fuels.

Measuring Our Rising Impact

As a result of this massive expansion of our presence on Earth, scientists Ehrlich, John Holdren, and Barry Commoner in the early 1970s devised a formula to measure our rising impact, called IPAT, in which (I)mpact

equals (P)opulation multiplied by (A)ffluence multiplied by (T)echnology.

The IPAT formula, they said, can help us realize that our cumulative impact on the planet is not just in population numbers, but also in the increasing amount of natural resources each person uses. . . . [T]rise in our cumulative impact since 1950—rising population combined with our expanding demand for resources—has been profound.

IPAT is a useful reminder that population, consumption, and technology all help shape our environmental impact, but it shouldn't be taken too literally. University of California ecologist John Harte has said that IPAT ". . . conveys the notion that population is a linear multiplier. . . . In reality, population plays a much more dynamic and complex role in shaping environmental quality."

One of our biggest impacts is agriculture. Whether we can grow enough food sustainably for an expanding world population also presents an urgent challenge, and this becomes only more so in light of these new population projections. Where will food for an additional 2 to 3 billion people come from when we are already barely keeping up with 7 billion? Such questions underpin a 2014 *National Geographic* series on the future of food.

As climate change damages crop yields and extreme weather disrupts harvests, growing enough food for our expanding population has become what The 2014 World Food Prize Symposium calls "the greatest challenge in human history."

Population's Structure: Fertility, Mortality, and Migration

Population is not just about numbers of people. Demographers typically focus on three dimensions—fertility, mortality, and migration—when examining population trends. Fertility examines how many children a woman bears in her lifetime, mortality looks at how long we live, and migration focuses on where we live and move. Each of these population qualities influences the nature of our presence and impact across the planet.

The newly reported higher world population projections result from continuing high fertility in sub-Saharan Africa. The median number of children per woman in the region remains at 4.6, well above both the global mean of 2.5 and the replacement level of 2.1. Since 1970, a global decline in fertility—from about 5 children per woman to about 2.5—has occurred across most of the world: Fewer babies have been born, family size has shrunk, and population growth has slowed. In the United States, fertility is now slightly below replacement level.

Reducing fertility is essential if future population growth is to be reined in. Cynthia Gorney wrote about the dramatic story of declining Brazilian fertility as part of *National Geographic's* 7 Billion series. Average family size dropped from 6.3 children to 1.9 children per woman over two generations in Brazil, the result of improving education for girls, more career opportunities, and the increased availability of contraception.

Mortality—or birth rates versus death rates—and migration (where we live and move) also affect the structure of population. Living longer can cause a region's population to increase even if birth rates remain constant. Youthful nations in the Middle East and Africa, where there are more young people than old, struggle to provide sufficient land, food, water, housing, education, and employment for young people. Besides the search for a life with more opportunity elsewhere, migration also is driven by the need to escape political disruption or declining environmental conditions such as chronic drought and food shortages.

A paradox of lower fertility and reduced population growth rates is that as education and affluence improves, consumption of natural resources increases per person. In other words, . . . as we get richer, each of us consumes more natural resources and energy, typically carbon-based fuels such as coal, oil, and gas. This can be seen in consumption patterns that include higher protein foods such as meat and dairy, more consumer goods, bigger houses, more vehicles, and more air travel.

When it comes to natural resources, studies indicate we are living beyond our means. An ongoing Global Footprint Network study says we now use the equivalent of 1.5 planets to provide the resources we use, and to absorb our waste. A study by the Stockholm Resilience Institute has identified a set of "nine planetary boundaries" for conditions in which we could live and thrive for generations, but it shows that we already have exceeded the institute's boundaries for biodiversity loss, nitrogen pollution, and climate change.

Those of us reading this article are among an elite crowd of Earthlings. We have reliable electricity, access to Internet-connected computers and phones, and time available to contemplate these issues.

About one-fifth of those on Earth still don't have access to reliable electricity. So as we debate population, things we take for granted—reliable lighting and cooking facilities, for example—remain beyond the reach of about 1.3 billion or more people. Lifting people from the darkness of energy poverty could help improve lives.

Improved education, especially for girls, is cited as a key driver of declining family size. Having light at night can become a gateway to better education for millions of young people and the realization that opportunities and choices besides bearing many children can await.

So when we debate population, it's important to also discuss the impact—the how we live—of the population equation. While new projections of even higher world population in the decades ahead are cause for concern, we should be equally concerned about—and be willing to address—the increasing effects of resource consumption and its waste.

DENNIS DIMICK is *National Geographic's* executive editor for the Environment.

Tom Bethell    **NO**

Population, Economy, and God

World population, once "exploding," is still increasing, and "momentum" ensures that it will do so for decades to come. But fertility rates have tumbled. In Europe every country has fallen below replacement level. Some governments, especially France's, are beginning to use financial incentives to restore fertility rates but the effort, if generous enough to work—by paying women to have a third child—could bankrupt the welfare state.

In rich countries, a total fertility rate of 2.1 babies per woman is needed if population is to remain stable. But in the European Union as a whole the rate is down to 1.5. Germany is at 1.4, and Italy, Spain, and Greece are at 1.3. The fertility rate in France is now 2.0, or close to replacement. But the uneasy question is whether this is due to subsidies or to the growing Muslim population.

All over the world, with a few anomalies, there is a strong inverse correlation between GDP per capita and babies per family. It's a paradox, because wealthier people can obviously afford lots of children. But very predictably they have fewer. Hong Kong (1.02), Singapore, and Taiwan are three of the richest countries in the world, and three of the four lowest in total fertility. The countries with the highest fertility rates are Mali (7.4), Niger, and Uganda. Guess how low they are on the wealth chart.

Here's a news item. Carl Djerassi, one of the inventors of the birth control pill, recently deplored the sharp decline of total fertility in Austria (1.4), the country of his birth. A Catholic news story seized on that and reported that one of the pill's inventors had said the pill had caused a "demographic catastrophe." Austria's leading Catholic, Cardinal Schönborn, said the Vatican had predicted 40 years ago that the pill would promote a dramatic fall in birth rates.

Djerassi, 85, an emeritus professor of chemistry at Stanford, did warn of a catastrophe and he said that Austria should admit more immigrants. But he denied that people have smaller families "because of the availability of birth control." They do so "for personal, economic, cultural, and other reasons," of which "changes in the status of women" was the most important. Japan has an even worse

demographic problem, he said, "yet the pill was only legalized there in 1999 and is still not used widely." (Japan's fertility rate is 1.22.) (In fact, if the pill and abortion really were illegal more children surely would be born, if only because unintentional pregnancies would come to term.)

Austrian families who had decided against children wanted "to enjoy their schnitzels while leaving the rest of the world to get on with it," Djerassi also said. That may have rankled because the country had just put his face on a postage stamp.

So what is causing these dramatic declines? It's under way in many countries outside Europe too. In Mexico, fertility has moved down close to replacement level—having been as high as six babies per woman in the 1970s.

Obviously economic growth has been the dominant factor but there are other considerations.

Young couples hardly read Paul Ehrlich before deciding whether to have children, but scaremongering authors have played a key role in creating our anti-natalist mood. Books warning of a (then) newfangled emergency, the "population explosion," began appearing soon after World War II. Consider *Road to Survival* (1948), by William Vogt, or *People! Challenge to Survival*, by the same author. An anti-people fanatic before his time, Vogt was hypnotized by the Malthusian doctrine that population growth would overtake the food supply. That would lead to a war of all against all. Paul Ehrlich projected that the 1980s would see massive die-offs from starvation. (Obesity turned out to be the greater health threat.)

In that earlier period, the population controllers didn't feel they had to mince words. Vogt wrote in 1960 that "tens of thousands of children born every year in the United States should, solely for their own sakes, never have seen the light of day. . . . There are hundreds of thousands of others, technically legitimate since their parents have engaged in some sort of marriage ritual, but whose birth is as much of a crime against them as it is against the bastards."

At a time when the world population still had not reached 3 billion—today it is 6.7 billion—Vogt thought "drastic measures are inescapable." He warned of "mounting population pressures in the Soviet Union," where, by the century's end, "there may be 300 million Russians." It was time for them "to begin control of one of the most powerful causes of war—overpopulation."

Note: the population of Russia by 2000 was 145 million; today it is 141 million. (Fertility rate: 1.4.)

Population alarmists have long enjoyed the freedom to project their fears onto whatever cause is uppermost in the progressive mind. Then it was war. Today it is the environment, which, we are told, human beings are ruining. This will be shown to have been as false as the earlier warnings, but not before our environmental scares have done much harm to a fragile economy (at the rate things are going with Obama). All previous scares were based on faulty premises, and the latest one, based on "science," will be no different.

I believe that two interacting factors shape population growth or decline: economic prosperity and belief in God. As to the first, there is no doubt that rising material prosperity discourages additional children. Fewer infants die; large families are no longer needed to support older parents. The welfare state—which only rich countries can afford—has greatly compounded this effect. When people believe that the government will take care of them, pay their pensions and treat their maladies, children do seem less essential.

A rise in prosperity also encourages people to think that they can dispense with God. Religion diminishes when wealth increases—that's my theory. But with a twist that I shall come to. Wealth generates independence, including independence from God, or (if you will) Providence. God is gradually forgotten, then assumed not to exist. This will tend to drive childbearing down even further. Hedonism will become predominant. Remember, Jesus warned that it's the rich, not the poor, who are at spiritual hazard.

The legalization of abortion reflected the decline of religious faith in America, but it must also have led others to conclude that God was no longer to be feared. That's why I don't quite believe Djerassi when he tries to disassociate the pill from fertility. The ready availability of the pill told society at large that sex without consequences was perfectly acceptable. Then, by degrees, that self-indulgent view became an anti-natalist worldview.

It became so ingrained that many people now think it obvious. Sex became a "free" pastime as long as it was restricted to consenting adults. Furthermore, anyone who questioned that premise risked denunciation as a bigot.

The U.S. has been seen as the great stumbling block to any theory linking prosperity, lack of faith, and low fertility. Prosperity here has been high, and overall fertility is at replacement. But I am wary of this version of American exceptionalism. How much lower would U.S. fertility fall without the influx of Latino immigrants and their many offspring? Nicholas Eberstadt, a demographer at AEI, tells me that Mexican immigrants now actually have a higher fertility rate in the U.S. than they do in Mexico. (Maybe because they come to American hospitals for free medical care?)

I wonder also if religious vitality here is what it's cracked up to be. Surely it has weakened considerably. A recent survey by Trinity College in Hartford, funded by the Lilly Endowment, showed that the percentage of Americans identifying themselves as Christian dropped to 76 percent from 86 percent in 1990; those with "no" religion, 8.2 percent of the population in 1990, are now 15 percent.

As a social force, the U.S. Catholic bishops have withered away to a shocking extent. Hollywood once respected and feared their opinion. Today, the most highly placed of these bishops are unwilling to publicly rebuke proabortion politicians who call themselves Catholic, even when they give scandal by receiving Communion in public. How the mitered have fallen. They daren't challenge the rich and powerful.

But there is another factor. Calling yourself a Christian when the pollster phones imposes no cost and selfreported piety may well be inflated. We have to distinguish between mere self-labelers and actual churchgoers. And beyond that there are groups with intense religious belief who retain the morale to ignore the surrounding materialism and keep on having children.

The ultra-Orthodox in Israel are the best example. Other Jewish congregations may go to synagogue, but they have children at perhaps one-third the ultra-Orthodox rate. At about seven or eight children per family, theirs is one of the highest fertility rates in the world. And they don't permit birth control—Carl Djerassi, please note. In the U.S. Orthodox Jews again far outbreed their more secular sisters.

The Mormons are also distinctive. Utah, about twothirds Mormon, has the highest fertility rate (2.63 in 2006) among the 50 states; Vermont has the lowest (1.69). In the recent Trinity Survey, Northern New England is now "the least religious section of the country." Vermont is the least religious state; 34 percent of residents say they have "no religion." So minimal faith and low fertility are demonstrably linked. Mormon fertility is declining, to be sure, and I recognize that I am flirting with a circular argument: deciding which groups are the most fervent by looking at their birth rates.

Then there's the Muslim concern. It's hard to avoid concluding that the lost Christian zeal has been appropriated by Islam. In the U.S., Muslims have doubled since 1990 (from a low base, to 0.6% of the population). The rise of Islam suggests that the meager European fertility rates would be even lower if Muslims had not contributed disproportionately to European childbearing.

It's hard to pin down the numbers, though. Fertility in France has risen, but Nick Eberstadt tells me that the French government won't reveal how many of these babies are born to Muslim parents. "They treat it as a state secret," he said. In other countries such as Switzerland, where lots of guest workers are employed, the fertility rate would be much lower than it already is (1.44) were it not for the numerous offspring of those guest workers.

When a population is not replacing itself, the welfare state creates its own hazard. Lots of new workers are needed to support the retirees. Germany's low fertility will require an annual immigration of 200,000 just to maintain the current population. Where will they come from? Many arrive from Turkey, where the fertility rate has also declined (to about 2.0). But not as far as it has declined among native Germans. So the concern is that in the welfare states of Europe, believing Muslims are slowly replacing the low-morale, low-fertility, materialistic non-believers who once formed a Christian majority.

I could summarize the argument with this overstatement: The intelligentsia stopped believing in God in the 19th century. In the 20th it tried to build a new society, man without God. It failed. Then came a new twist. Man stopped believing in himself. He saw himself as a mere polluter—a blot on the landscape. Theologians tell us that creatures cannot exist without the support of God. A corollary may be that societies cannot long endure without being sustained by a *belief* in God.

TOM BETHELL is a senior editor of *The American Spectator*.

EXPLORING THE ISSUE

Do We Have a Population Problem?

Critical Thinking and Reflection

1. Is it possible to have too many people on Earth?
2. What is wrong with the statement that there is no population problem because all of Earth's human population could fit inside the state of Texas?
3. What does population have to do with sustainability?
4. What is more important for long-term survival of the human species—population control or belief in God?

Is There Common Ground?

The essayists for this issue agree that human population continues to grow and that long-term human survival (or sustainability) matters. They disagree on the best way to achieve long-term human survival.

1. Does quality of life seem likely to suffer more with a declining population or a growing population?
2. What are the key features of "quality of life"? (One good place to start your research is www.foe.co.uk/community/tools/isew/)
3. How might we determine what the Earth's carrying capacity for human beings really is?
4. What is the influence (if any) of religious faith on carrying capacity?

Additional Resources

Matthew Connolly, *Fatal Misconception: The Struggle to Control World Population* (Belknap Press, 2010).

Jonathan A. Foley, "Can We Feed the World & Sustain the Planet?" *Scientific American* (November 2011).

David Malakoff, "Are More People Necessarily a Problem?" *Science* (July 29, 2011).

Fred Pearce, *The Coming Population Crash: And Our Planet's Surprising Future* (Beacon, 2010).

Julia Whitty, "The Last Taboo," *Mother Jones* (May–June 2010).

Internet References . . .

Facing the Future: People and the Planet

www.facingthefuture.org/

Population Reference Bureau

www.prb.org/

United States & World Population Clocks

www.census.gov/main/www/popclock.html

Selected, Edited, and with Issue Framing Material by:
Thomas A. Easton, *Mount Ida College*

ISSUE

Can Vaccines Cause Autism?

YES: Arjun Walia, from "Scientific Evidence Suggests the Vaccine-Autism Link Can No Longer Be Ignored," *Collective Evolution* (2013)

NO: Harriet Hall, from "Vaccines and Autism: A Deadly Manufactroversy," *Skeptic* (2009)

Learning Outcomes

After reading this issue, you will be able to:

- Explain why many people have thought childhood vaccines can cause autism.
- Explain how scientific evidence fails to support the idea that vaccines can cause autism.
- Explain why many people continue to believe that childhood vaccines can cause autism.
- Discuss where research into the causes of autism should focus.

ISSUE SUMMARY

YES: Arjun Walia argues that the scientific consensus on the safety of vaccines may be suspect because "the corporate media is owned by the major vaccine manufacturers." He describes 22 studies that suggest that the connection between childhood vaccines and autism is real or that suggest possible mechanisms for the connection.

NO: Harriet Hall argues that the controversy over whether vaccines cause autism has been manufactured by dishonest, self-serving researchers and physicians, ignorant celebrities, conspiracy theorists, and the media. The result is a resurgence of preventable diseases and childhood deaths. Vaccines save lives. Autism's causes are probably genetic.

Not so long ago, childhood infectious diseases claimed an astonishing number of young lives:

- Between 1940 and 1948, whooping cough (pertussis) killed 64 of every 100,000 children less than one year old. By 1974, extensive use of vaccines had reduced that toll to less than 1 per 100,000 (James D. Cherry, "Historical Perspective on Pertussis and Use of Vaccines to Prevent It: 100 Years of Pertussis [the Cough of 100 Days]," *Microbe*, March 2007).
- Before the measles vaccine came into wide use in the 1960s, "nearly all children got measles by the time they were 15 years of age. Each year in the United States about 450–500 people died because of measles, 48,000 were hospitalized, 7,000 had seizures, and about 1,000 suffered

permanent brain damage or deafness. Today there are only about 60 cases a year reported in the United States, and most of these originate outside the country" (http://www.cdc.gov/measles/about/overview.html).
- Before the polio vaccine became available, the United States saw about 50,000 polio cases per year, with thousands of victims, mostly children, needing braces, crutches, wheelchairs, or iron lungs. Today polio is rare in the United States.
- Before the mumps vaccine became available, about 200,000 cases of mumps and 20–30 deaths occurred each year in the United States. Mumps outbreaks still occur but are much smaller; in 2009–2010 an outbreak consisted of 1,521 cases.
- In 1921, the United States saw 206,000 cases of diphtheria, with 15,520 deaths. The diphtheria vaccine came into use in the 1920s, and since then the incidence of this disease has declined

tremendously. There were no cases at all in the 2004–2008 period.

- Hib (*Haemophilus influenzae* type b) meningitis kills up to 1 in 20 of infected children and leaves 1 in 5 with brain damage or deafness. "Before the Hib vaccine was available, Hib caused serious infections in 20,000 children and killed about 1,000 children each year. Since the vaccine's introduction in 1987, the incidence of severe Hib disease has declined by 99 percent in the United States" (http://www.vaccinateyourbaby.org/why/history /hib.cfm).

It is perhaps unfortunate that the Bad Old Days those numbers describe were so long ago. Whole generations have grown up with no memory of what vaccines have saved us from. Today a baby gets stuck with a needle and cries, and a parent feels that this is horrible, that the baby is being hurt for no good reason. At the same time, vaccines have always had side effects (including occasionally causing the disease they are intended to ward off), and when one of these side effects shows up, there is again a sense that children are being endangered without good reason. As a result, some parents today choose not to vaccinate their children. When enough parents make that choice, the old diseases can and do crop up again, and children die.

In addition, there is a fear that childhood vaccines can cause autism, which is rooted in a 1998 study by Andrew Wakefield, a British gastroenterologist. The study proved to have major ethical and procedural lapses and was retracted; Wakefield himself lost his position and his medical license. However, he considers himself a victim of the medical establishment and insists that his results were sound and he will be vindicated; see Andrew J. Wakefield, *Callous Disregard: Autism and Vaccines—The Truth Behind a Tragedy* (Skyhorse, 2011). An enormous number of parents of autistic children have come to view him as a hero, for only he (they think) has an answer to why their children suffer and to how that suffering might have been prevented—by refusing vaccinations. This view has been promoted by uncritical media and celebrities such as Jenny McCarthy (who wrote the foreword to Wakefield's book; see also Michael Specter, "Jenny McCarthy's Dangerous Views," *The New Yorker*, July 16, 2013, http://www.newyorker.com/tech /elements/jenny-mccarthys-dangerous-views). One claim is that the government has admitted that vaccines cause autism because the federal Vaccine Court (National Vaccine Injury Compensation Program [NVICP; http://www.hrsa .gov/vaccinecompensation/index.html]) has awarded damages

to autism cases. It is worth stressing that the Vaccine Court awards damages for "table injuries." A "table injury" is an injury listed as known to follow vaccines at least occasionally; if medical records show a child has such an injury soon after vaccination, the correlation is enough to justify awarding damages. Autism is not a table injury, but possibly related conditions such as encephalopathy are. Many parents now use the purported connection between childhood vaccines and autism to justify refusing to have their children vaccinated.

As evidence against the vaccines-autism link has accumulated, the idea that parents have the right to choose whether to have their children vaccinated has gained momentum; the "essential handbook for the vaccination choice movement" is Louise Kuo Habakus, Mary Holland, and Kim Mack Rosenberg, eds., *Vaccine Epidemic: How Corporate Greed, Biased Science, and Coercive Government Threaten Our Human Rights, Our Health, and Our Children* (Skyhorse, 2011, 2012). The opposing view is that vaccinations protect public health by preventing not just infection by deadly diseases but also the spread of these diseases through a population, and indeed in numerous cases the declining popularity of vaccinations has resulted in outbreaks of disease and the deaths of both children and adults. One strong supporter of the view that vaccines do not cause autism is Alison Singer, who left Autism Speaks, an organization that promotes the need for more research into the vaccines-autism link, to found the Autism Science Foundation, which promotes the need for more research into the causes of autism; see Meredith Wadman, "A Voice for Science," *Nature* (November 3, 2011). Since that time, Autism Speaks has also recognized that research does not support claims of a link between vaccines and autism (https://www.autismspeaks.org/science /science-news/no-mmr-autism-link-large-study-vaccinated-vs -unvaccinated-kids).

Seth Mnookin, *The Panic Virus: The True Story Behind the Vaccine-Autism Controversy* (Simon and Schuster, 2011), reviews the history of vaccines and earlier anti-vaccine movements, the Wakefield story, and the exploitation of families with autistic children by quacks who use the supposed vaccine connection to encourage distrust of the medical establishment and peddle expensive, useless, and even damaging treatments. Jeffrey S. Gerber and Paul A. Offit, "Vaccines and Autism: A Tale of Shifting Hypotheses," *Clinical Infectious Diseases* (February 15, 2009), argue that the scientific evidence neither shows a link between vaccines and autism nor supports any of the popular suggested mechanisms. Research on the causes of autism should focus on more promising leads.

Those who believe there is a connection between childhood vaccines and autism are only rarely convinced by evidence that there is no connection. It does not help that no one has a good idea of how the connection might work. Is it the mercury-based preservative, thimerosal, in the vaccines? When thimerosal was removed from vaccines the upward trend of autism diagnoses did not change. Is it the sheer number of vaccinations children undergo? Is it the age at which vaccines are administered? Do vaccines damage the intestinal lining and allow nerve-damaging proteins to enter the blood? There are a number of studies that suggest possible mechanisms, but none can say anything stronger than "maybe." It has even been suggested (controversially) that an imbalance of bacterial types in the mix that inhabits the intestine maybe involved; see http://theconversation.com/can-a-gut-bacteria-imbalance-really-cause-autism-9128. In the YES selection, Arjun Walia argues that the scientific consensus on the safety of vaccines may be suspect because "the corporate media is [*sic*] owned by the major vaccine manufacturers." He describes 22 studies that suggest that the connection between childhood vaccines and autism is real or that suggest possible mechanisms for the connection. In the NO selection, Harriet Hall argues that the controversy over whether vaccines cause autism has been manufactured by dishonest, self-serving researchers and physicians, ignorant celebrities, conspiracy theorists, and the media. The result is a resurgence of preventable diseases and childhood deaths. Vaccines save lives. Autism's causes are probably genetic.

YES

Arjun Walia

Scientific Evidence Suggests the Vaccine-Autism Link Can No Longer Be Ignored

Concerns regarding vaccinations continue to increase exponentially in light of all of the information and documentation that has surfaced over the past few years. As a result, corporate media has responded to alternative media, stating that the increase of persons who are choosing to opt out of vaccines and the recommended vaccine schedule is a result of 'fear mongering.' This may not be too surprising as the corporate media is owned by the major vaccine manufacturers, and the major vaccine manufacturers are owned by corporate media. Given this fact, it's easy to fathom the possibility that these institutions are desperately trying to protect the reputation of their product.

For example, if we take a look at GlaxoSmithKline and Pfizer, they are owned by the same financial institutions and groups that own Time Warner (CNN, HBO etc.) and General Electric (NBC, Comcast, Universal Pictures etc.). This is seen throughout all of the major vaccine manufacturers and all of the 6 corporations that control our mainstream media. Keep in mind that these are the major funders of all 'medical research' that's used to administer drugs and vaccinations. Despite these connections, medical research and documentation exists to show that vaccines might indeed be a cause for concern.

Vaccines and Autism, Both Sides of the Coin

Here we will simply present information from both sides of the coin because many are not even aware that two sides exist. We've presented multiple studies, citing multiple research papers and published research conducted by doctors and universities from all across the world. . . . We'd also like to present medical research that indicates the many dangers associated with vaccines, and have done this on multiple occasions. We do this because the safety of vaccinations is commonly pushed by the mainstream

media, without ever mentioning or citing the abundant medical research that should also be taken into consideration when discussing vaccinations. **Please keep in mind that there is evidence on both sides.** At the same time, some of the evidence on the side that negates a positive outlook on vaccination has been labelled fraudulent, but then again many haven't.

The vaccine-autism debate has been going on for years. It has been a tale of shifting beliefs as child vaccination rates remain high. On February 1998, Andrew Wakefield, a British gastroenterologist and his colleagues published a paper that supposedly linked Autism to Vaccines. More specifically, he claimed that the MMR vaccine was responsible for intestinal inflammation that led to translocation of usually non-permeable peptides to the bloodstream and, subsequently, to the brain, where they affected development. His work was unpublished, and he lost his medical license despite the fact multiple studies seem to support Andrew Wakefield's work (here (http://vran.org/wp-content/documents/VRAN-Abnormal%20 Measles-Mumps-Rubella-Antibodies-CNS-Autoimmunity -Children-Autism-Singh-Lin-Newell-Nelson.pdf) is one example, and here (http://www.mdpi.com/1099-4300/14/11/2227) is another.) He has been labelled a fraud by the mainstream medical world, some experts claim that his research and methods are weak and based on very little evidence. **Dr. Wakefield's research will NOT be used in this article.**

At the same time I must mention that multiple studies from around the world have concluded that there is no link between autism and the MMR vaccine. It can become quite a confusing subject given that we have multiple medical studies contradicting each other. Was Dr. Wakefield exposing something that the medical industry did not want you to know? It is known that vaccine manufacturers suppress harmful data regarding their product, as mentioned and illustrated earlier in the article. Regardless of the MMR vaccine and autism debate, there are still a number of studies that link vaccines to a possible autism connection. Please keep in mind that multiple courts worldwide have ruled in favour of vaccines causing autism, brain damage and other complications, that include the MMR vaccine.

Here (http://www.collective-evolution.com/2012/09/07/rob-schneider-speaks-out-against-vaccines) is a great video narrated by Rob Schneider outlining the vaccine-autism link. Below that you will find a list of 22 medical studies that show possible connections to vaccines and autism. Please keep in mind that we've only presented 22 studies here, there are many more published papers that document the link. Hopefully this inspires you to further your research on the subject. Also keep in mind that autism is only one of the multiple shown consequences of vaccine administration, as they have been linked to a number of other ailments.

1. A study published in the journal *Annals of Epidemiology* (http://www.ncbi.nlm.nih.gov/pubmed/21058170) has shown that giving the Hepatitis B vaccine to newborn baby boys could triple the risk of developing an autism spectrum disorder compared to boys who were not vaccinated as neonates. The research was conducted at Stony Brook University Medical Centre, NY.

2. A study published in the *Journal of Inorganic Biochemistry* (http://omsj.org/reports/tomljenovic%202011.pdf) by researchers at the Neural Dynamics Group, Department of Ophthalmology and Visual Sciences at the University of British Columbia determined that aluminum, a highly neurotoxic metal and the most commonly used vaccine adjuvant may be a significant contributing factor to the rising prevalence of ASD in the Western World. They showed that the correlation between ASD prevalence and the aluminum adjuvant exposure appears to be the highest at 3–4 months of age. The studies also show that children from countries with the highest ASD appear to have a much higher exposure to aluminum from vaccines. The study points out that several prominent milestones of brain development coincide with major vaccination periods for infants. These include the onset of synaptogenesis (birth), maximal growth velocity of the hippocampus and the onset of amygdala maturation. Furthermore, major developmental transition in many bio-behavioural symptoms such as sleep, temperature regulation, respiration and brain wave patterns, all of which are regulated by the neuroendocrine network. Many of these aspects of brain function are known to be impaired in autism, such as sleeping and brain wave patterns.

According to the FDA, vaccines represent a special category of drugs as they are generally given to healthy individuals. Further according to the FDA, "this places significant emphasis on their vaccine safety." While the FDA does set an upper limit for aluminum in vaccines at no more than 850/mg/dose, it is important to note that this amount was selected empirically from data showing that aluminum in such amounts enhanced the antigenicity of the vaccine, rather than from existing safety. Given that the scientific evidence appears to indicate that vaccine safety is not as firmly established as often believed, it would seem ill advised to exclude paediatric vaccinations as a possible cause of adverse long-term neurodevelopment outcomes, including those associated with autism.

3. A study published in the *Journal of Toxicology and Environmental Health, Part A: Current Issues* (http://www.ncbi.nlm.nih.gov/pubmed/21623535) by the Department of Economics and Finance at the University of New York shows how researchers suspect one or more environmental triggers are needed to develop autism, regardless of whether individuals have a genetic predisposition or not. They determined that one of those triggers might be the "battery of vaccinations that young children receive." Researchers found a positive and statistically significant relationship between autism and vaccinations. They determined that the higher the proportion of children receiving recommended vaccinations, the higher the prevalence of autism. A [1%] increase in vaccination was associated with an additional 680 children having autism. The results suggest that vaccines may be linked to autism and encourages more in depth study before continually administering these vaccines.

4. A study published in the *Journal of Toxicology* (http://www.hindawi.com/journals/jt/2013/801517/) by the Department of Neurosurgery at The Methodist Neurological Institute in Houston has shown that ASD is a disorder caused by a problem in brain development. They looked at B-cells and their sensitivity levels to thimerosal, a commonly used additive in many vaccines. They determined that ASD patients have a heightened sensitivity to thimerosal which would restrict cell proliferation that is typically found after vaccination. The research shows that individuals who have this hypersensitivity to thimerosal could make them highly susceptible to toxins like thimerosal, and that individuals with a mild mitochondrial defect may be affected by

thimerosal. The fact that ASD patients' B cells exhibit hypersensitivity to thimerosal tells us something.

5. A study published in the *Journal of Biomedical Sciences* (http://www.ncbi.nlm.nih.gov/pubmed/12145534) determined that the autoimmunity to the central nervous system may play a causal role in autism. Researchers discovered that because many autistic children harbour elevated levels of measles antibodies, they should conduct a serological study of measles-mumps-rubella (MMR) and myelin basic protein (MBP) autoantibodies. They used serum samples of 125 autistic children and 92 controlled children. Their analysis showed a significant increase in the level of MMR antibodies in autistic children. The study concludes that the autistic children had an inappropriate or abnormal antibody response to MMR. The study determined that autism could be a result from an atypical measles infection that produces neurological symptoms in some children. The source of this virus could be a variant of MV, or it could be the MMR vaccine.

6. Study published in the *Annals of Clinical Psychiatry* (http://www.collective-evolution.com/2013/09/12/22-medical-studies-that-show-vaccines-can-cause-autism/Study%20published%20in%20the%20Annals%20of%20Clinical%20Psychiatry) suggests that autism is likely triggered by a virus, and that measles virus (MV and/or MMR vaccine) might be a very good candidate. It supports the hypothesis that a virus-dincued autoimmune response may play a causal role in autism.

7. A study published in the *American Journal of Clinical Nutrition* (http://ajcn.nutrition.org/content/80/6/1611.full) determined that an increased vulnerability to oxidative stress and decreased capacity for methylation may contribute to the development and clinical manifestation of autism. It's well known that viral infections cause increased oxidative stress. Research suggests (http://www.ncbi.nlm.nih.gov/pubmed/11895129) that metals, including those found in many vaccines are directly involved in increasing oxidative stress.

8. A study published by the Department of Pharmaceutical Sciences (http://www.ncbi.nlm.nih.gov/pubmed/14745455) at Northeastern University, Boston determined that a novel growth factor signalling pathway that regulates methionine synthase (MS) activity and thereby modulates methylation reactions. The potent inhibition of this pathway by ethanol, lead, mercury, aluminum and thimerosal suggests that it may be an important target of neurodevelopmental toxins. . . .

9. A study published in the *Journal of Child Neurology* (http://jcn.sagepub.com/content/22/11/1308.abstract) examined the question of what is leading to the apparent increase in autism. They expressed that if there is any link between autism and mercury, it is crucial that the first reports of the question are not falsely stating that no link occurs. Researchers determined that a significant relation does exist between the blood levels of mercury and the diagnosis of an autism spectrum disorder.

10. A study published in the *Journal of Child Neurology* (http://jcn.sagepub.com/content/21/2/170.abstract) noted that autistic spectrum disorders can be associated with mitochondrial dysfunction. Researchers determined that children who have mitochondrial-related dysfunctional cellular energy metabolism might be more prone to undergo autistic regression between 18 and 30 months of age if they also have infections or immunizations at the same time.

11. A study conducted by Massachusetts General Hospital (http://www.ncbi.nlm.nih.gov/pubmed/16151044) at the Centre for Morphometric Analysis by the Department of Paediatric Neurology illustrates how autistic brains have a growth spurt shortly after birth and then slow in growth a few short years later. Researchers have determined that neuroinflammation appears to be present in autistic brain tissue from childhood through adulthood. The study excerpt reads:

> Oxidative stress, brain inflammation and microgliosis have been much documented in association with toxic exposures including various heavy metals. The awareness that the brain as well as medical conditions of children with autism may be conditioned by chronic biomedical abnormalities such as inflammation opens the possibility that meaningful biomedical interventions may be possible well past the window of maximal neuroplasticity in early childhood because the basis for assuming that all deficits can be attributed to fixed early developmental alterations in net . . .

12. A study conducted by the Department of Paediatrics at the University of Arkansas (http://www.ncbi.nlm.nih.gov/pubmed/15527868) determined that thimerosal-induced cytotoxicity was associated with the depletion of intracellular glutathione (GSH) in both cell lines. The study

outlines how many vaccines have been neuro-toxic, especially to the developing brain. Depletion of GSH is commonly associated with autism. Although thimerosal has been removed from most children's vaccines, it is still present in flu vaccines given to pregnant women, the elderly and to children in developing countries.

13. A study published in the *Public Library of Science (PLOS)* (http://www.plosone.org/article /info%3Adoi%2F10.1371%2Fjournal.pone.0068444) determined that elevation in peripheral oxidative stress is consistent with, and may contribute to more severe functional impairments in the ASD group. We know that oxidative stress is triggered by heavy metals, like the ones contained in multiple vaccines.

14. A study conducted by the University of Texas Health Science Centre (http://www.ncbi.nlm.nih.gov /pubmed/16338635) by the Department of Family and Community Medicine determined that for each 1,000 Ib of environmentally released mercury, there was a 43% increase in the rate of special education services and a 61% increase in the rate of autism. Researchers emphasized that further research was needed regarding the association between environmentally released mercury and developmental disorders such as autism.

15. A study published in the *International Journal of Toxicology* (http://www.ncbi.nlm.nih.gov/pubmed /12933322) determined that in light of the biological plausibility of mercury's role in neurodevelopment disorders, the present study provides further insight into one possible mechanism by which early mercury exposures could increase the risk of autism.

16. A study published in the *Journal of Toxicology and Environmental Health* (http://www.ncbi.nlm.nih .gov/pubmed/17454560) determined that mercury exposure can induce immune, sensory, neurological, motor and behavioural dysfunctions similar to traits defining or associated with ASDs. Based upon differential diagnoses, 8 of 9 patients examined were exposed to significant mercury from thimerosal-containing vaccine preparations during their fetal/infant developmental periods. These previously normal developing children suffered mercury encephalopathies that manifested with clinical symptoms consistent with regressive ASDs. Evidence for mercury intoxication should be considered in the differential diagnosis as contributing to some regressive ASDs.

17. A study published by the US National Library of Medicine (http://civileats.com/wp-content/uploads /2009/01/palmer2008.pdf) conducted by the University of Texas Health Science Centre suspected that persistent low-dose exposures to various environmental toxicants including mercury, that occur during critical windows of neural development among genetically susceptible children, may increase the risk for developmental disorders such as autism.

18. A study conducted by the Department of Obstetrics and Gynaecology (http://www.ane.pl/pdf /7020.pdf) at University of Pittsburgh's School of Medicine showed that macaques are commonly used in pre-clinical vaccine safety testing. *Collective Evolution* does not support animals testing, we feel there is a large amount of evidence and research that already indicated the links to vaccines in which some animals have been used to illustrate. The objective of this study was to compare early infant cognition and behaviour with amygdala size and opioid binding in rhesus macaques receiving the recommended childhood vaccines. The animal model, which examines for the first time, behavioural, functional and neuromorphometric consequences of the childhood vaccine regimen, mimics certain neurological abnormalities of autism. These findings raise important safety issues while providing a potential model for examining aspects of causation and disease pathogenesis in acquired disorders of behaviour and development.

19. A study conducted by The George Washington University School of Public Health (http:// www.ncbi.nlm.nih.gov/pubmed/18482737) from the Department of Epidemiology and Biostatistics determined that significantly increased rate ratios were observed for autism and autism spectrum disorders as a result of exposure to mercury from thimerosal-containing vaccines.

20. A study published in the journal *Cell Biology and Toxicology* (http://www.ncbi.nlm.nih.gov/pubmed /19357975) by Kinki University in Osaka, Japan determined that in combination with the brain pathology observed in patients diagnosed with autism, the present study helps to support the possible biological plausability for how low-dose exposure to mercury from thimerosal-containing vaccines may be associated with autism.

21. A study published by the journal *Lab Medicine* (http://labmed.ascpjournals.org/content/33/9/708 .full.pdf) determined that vaccinations may be one of the triggers for autism. Researchers discovered that substantial data demonstrates immune abnormality in many autistic children consistent with impaired resistance to infection, activation of inflammatory responses and autoimmunity.

Impaired resistance may predispose to vaccine injury in autism.

22. A study published in the journal *Neurochemical Research* (http://www.ncbi.nlm.nih.gov/pmc/articles/PMC3264864/?tool=pubmed) determined that since excessive accumulation of extracellular glutamate is linked with excitotoxicity, data implies that neonatal exposure to thimerosal-containing vaccines might induce excitotoxic brain injuries, leading to neurodevelopmental disorders.

Arjun Walia writes for *Collective Evolution*, a website and magazine that is "about creating change and talking about how we can get there."

Harriet Hall    **NO**

Vaccines and Autism: A Deadly Manufactroversy

During a question and answer session after a talk I recently gave, I was asked for my opinion about the vaccine/autism controversy. That was easy: my opinion is that there is no controversy. The evidence is in. The scientific community has reached a clear consensus that vaccines don't cause autism. There is no controversy.

There is, however, a manufactroversy—a manufactured controversy—created by junk science, dishonest researchers, professional misconduct, outright fraud, lies, misrepresentations, irresponsible reporting, unfortunate media publicity, poor judgment, celebrities who think they are wiser than the whole of medical science, and a few maverick doctors who ought to know better. Thousands of parents have been frightened into rejecting or delaying immunizations for their children. The immunization rate has dropped, resulting in the return of endemic measles in the U.K. and various outbreaks of vaccine-preventable diseases in the U.S. Children have died. Herd immunity has been lost. The public health consequences are serious and are likely to get worse before they get better—a load of unscientific nonsense has put us all at risk.

The story is appalling. It involves high drama, charismatic personalities, conspiracy theories, accusations, intimidation, and even death threats. It would make a good movie. It does make a good book: Dr. Paul Offit has explained what happened in *Autism's False Prophets: Bad Science, Risky Medicine, and the Search for a Cure*. I can't tell the whole story here, but I'll try to cover the highlights as I understand them. I'll include some new revelations that were not available to Offit when his book went to press. As I see it, there were 3 main stages to this fiasco:

1. the MMR scare,
2. the mercury/thimerosal scare, and
3. the vaccines-in-general scare.

The MMR Scare

In 1998 a British doctor named Andrew Wakefield published an article in the respected medical journal *The Lancet*. He did intestinal biopsies via colonoscopy on 12 children with intestinal symptoms and developmental disorders, 10 of whom were autistic, and found a pattern of intestinal inflammation. The parents of 8 of the autistic children thought they had developed their autistic symptoms right after they got the MMR vaccine. The published paper stated clearly: "We did not prove an association between measles, mumps, and rubella vaccine and the syndrome described. Virological studies are underway that may help to resolve this issue."

"Falsehood flies,
and the truth comes limping after."
— Jonathan Swift

Despite this disclaimer, Wakefield immediately held a press conference to say the MMR vaccine probably caused autism and to recommend stopping MMR injections. Instead, he recommended giving the 3 individual components separately at intervals of a year or more. The media exploded with warnings like "Ban Three-in-One Jab, Urge Doctors." The components were not available as individual vaccines, so people simply stopped immunizing. The immunization rate in the U.K. dropped from 93% to 75% (and to 50% in the London area). Confirmed cases of measles in England and Wales rose from 56 in 1998 to 1348 in 2008; two children died. In one small hospital in Ireland, 100 children were admitted for pneumonia and brain swelling caused by measles and three of them died. So, 14 years after measles had been declared under control in the U.K. it was declared endemic again in 2008.

Wakefield's data was later discredited (more about that later) but even if it had been right, it wouldn't have been good science. To show that intestinal inflammation is linked to autism, you would have to compare the rate in autistic children to the rate in non-autistic children. Wakefield used no controls. To implicate the MMR vaccine, you would have to show that the rate of autism was greater in children who got the vaccine and verify that autism developed after the shot. Wakefield made no attempt to do that.

His thinking was fanciful and full of assumptions. He hypothesized that measles virus damaged the intestinal wall, that the bowel then leaked some unidentified protein, and that said protein went to the brain and somehow caused autism. There was no good rationale for separating and delaying the components, because if measles was the culprit, wouldn't one expect it to cause the same harm when given individually? As one of his critics pointed out: "Single vaccines, spaced a year apart, clearly expose children to greater risk of infection, as well as additional distress and expense, and no evidence had been produced upon which to adopt such a policy."

Wakefield had been involved in questionable research before. He published a study in 1993 where he allegedly found measles RNA in intestinal biopsies from patients with Crohn's disease (an inflammatory bowel disease). He claimed that natural measles infections and measles vaccines were the cause of that disease. Others tried to replicate his findings and couldn't. No one else could find measles RNA in Crohn's patients; they determined that Crohn's patients were no more likely to have had measles than other patients, and people who had had MMR vaccines were no more likely to develop Crohn's. Wakefield had to admit he was wrong, and in 1998 he published another paper entitled "Measles RNA Is Not Detected in Inflammatory Bowel Disease." In a related incident, at a national meeting he stated that Crohn's patients had higher levels of measles *antibody* in their *blood*. An audience member said that was not true—he knew because he was the one who had personally done the blood tests Wakefield was referring to. Wakefield was forced to back down.

In 2002, Wakefield published another paper showing that measles RNA had been detected in intestinal biopsies of patients with bowel disease and developmental disorders. The tests were done at Unigenetics lab. Actually, Wakefield's own lab had looked for measles RNA in the patients in the 1998 study. His research assistant, Nicholas Chadwick, later testified that he had been present in the operating room when intestinal biopsies and spinal fluid samples were obtained and had personally tested all the samples for RNA with a polymerase chain reaction (PCR) test. The results were all negative, and he testified that Wakefield knew the results were negative when he submitted his paper to The Lancet. Chadwick had asked that his name be taken off the paper. So the statement in the paper that "virologic studies were underway" was misleading. Virologic studies had already been done in Wakefield's own lab and were negative. Wakefield was dissatisfied with those results and went to Unigenetics hoping for a different answer.

Soon Wakefield's credibility started to dissolve. The Lancet retracted his paper. Richard Horton, editor of The

Lancet, described the original paper as "fatally flawed" and apologized for publishing it. Of Wakefield's 12 co-authors, 10 issued a retraction:

We wish to make it clear that in this paper no causal link was established between [the] vaccine and autism, as the data were insufficient. However the possibility of such a link was raised, and consequent events have had major implications for public health. In view of this, we consider now is the appropriate time that we should together formally retract the interpretation placed upon these findings in the paper, according to precedent.

Attempts to replicate Wakefield's study all failed. Other studies showed that the detection of measles virus was no greater in autistics, that the rate of intestinal disease was no greater in autistics, that there was no correlation between MMR and autism onset, and that there was no correlation between MMR and autism, period.

In 2001 the Royal Free Hospital asked Wakefield to resign. In 2003, Brian Deer began an extensive investigation leading to an exposé in the The Sunday Times and on British television. In 2005 the General Medical Council (the British equivalent of state medical licensing boards in the U.S.) charged Wakefield with several counts of professional misconduct.

One disturbing revelation followed another. They discovered that two years before his study was published, Wakefield had been approached by a lawyer representing several families with autistic children. The lawyer specifically hired Wakefield to do research to find justification for a class action suit against MMR manufacturers. The children of the lawyer's clients were referred to Wakefield for the study, and 11 of his 12 subjects were eventually litigants. Wakefield failed to disclose this conflict of interest. He also failed to disclose how the subjects were recruited for his study.

Wakefield was paid a total of nearly half a million pounds plus expenses by the lawyer. The payments were billed through a company of Wakefield's wife. He never declared his source of funding until it was revealed by Brian Deer. Originally he had denied being paid at all. Even after he admitted it, he lied about the amount he was paid. Before the study was published, Wakefield had filed patents for his own separate measles vaccine, as well as other autism-related products. He failed to disclose this significant conflict of interest. Human research must be approved by the hospital's ethics committee. Wakefield's study was not approved. When confronted, Wakefield first claimed that it was approved, then claimed he didn't need approval. Wakefield *bought* blood samples for his research from children (as young as 4) attending his son's birthday party. He callously joked in public about them crying, fainting and vomiting. He paid the kids £5 each.

The General Medical Council accused him of ordering invasive and potentially harmful studies (colonoscopies and spinal taps) without proper approval and contrary to the children's clinical interests, when these diagnostic tests were not indicated by the children's symptoms or medical history. One child suffered multiple bowel perforations during the colonoscopy. Several had problems with the anesthetic. Children were subjected to sedation for other non-indicated tests like MRIs. Brian Deer was able to access the medical records of Wakefield's subjects. He found that several of them had evidence of autistic symptoms documented in their medical records *before* they got the MMR vaccine. The intestinal biopsies were originally reported as normal by hospital pathologists. They were reviewed, re-interpreted, and reported as abnormal in Wakefield's paper.

All the reports of measles RNA in intestinal biopsies came from one lab, Unigenetics. Other labs tried to replicate their results and failed. An investigation revealed that:

- Unigenetics found measles RNA with a test that should only detect DNA.
- They failed to use proper controls.
- The lab was contaminated with DNA from an adjoining Plasmid Room.
- Duplicate samples that disagreed were reported as positive.
- Positive controls were occasionally negative and negative ones positive.
- The lab was never accredited.
- It refused to take part in a quality control program.
- When tested by an outside investigator, it failed to identify which coded samples contained measles virus.
- The investigator said "I do not believe that there is any measles virus in any of the cases they have looked at."
- The lab is no longer in business.

So both Wakefield and his study have been completely discredited. He moved to the U.S. and is now working in an autism clinic. He has many followers who still believe he was right.

The Mercury/Thimerosal Scare

In 1998, U.S. legislation mandated measuring mercury in foods and drugs. The data came in slowly, and by 1999 the FDA had learned that infants could get as much as 187.5 mcg of mercury from the thimerosal in all their

vaccines. They were concerned because mercury is toxic. Mercury poisoning caused the Minamata disaster in Japan; however, that was methylmercury and the mercury in vaccines was ethylmercury. The amount of mercury in vaccines was within recommended guidelines. EPA guidelines for permissible mercury exposure were based on methylmercury and were conservative—they were keyed to protect the most vulnerable patients, fetuses. There were no EPA guidelines for ethylmercury, but it was considered to be far less dangerous because it is eliminated more rapidly from the body.

Two mothers of autistic children published their own "research" saying that the symptoms of autism were identical to those of mercury poisoning. I don't agree. You can look up the descriptions of mercury poisoning and autism and draw your own conclusions. I don't see how anyone could confuse the two—their presentations are entirely different, with only a few symptoms that could be interpreted as similar.

Thimerosal is a preservative that allows vaccines to be sold in multi-dose vials. It contains ethylmercury. It was tested and found to be safe before it was added to vaccines. Animal studies showed no adverse effects. In 1929 in Indiana it was tested as a treatment in a meningitis outbreak—adults injected with 2 million mcg (10,000 times the total amount in all children's vaccines) didn't develop symptoms of mercury poisoning.

A study from the Seychelles showed that children getting high doses of methylmercury from fish did not develop neurologic symptoms. A study of children in the Faroes who were exposed in utero to whale meat highly contaminated with methylmercury showed subtle neurologic abnormalities (not autism), but a causal connection was not clear because the fish there were also contaminated with PCBs. The World Health Organization concluded:

> The theoretical risk from exposure to thimerosal has to be balanced against the known high risk of having no preservative in vaccines. Therefore, WHO, UNICEF, the European Agency for Evaluation of Medicinal Products (EMEA), and other key agencies continue to recommend the use of vaccines containing this preservative because of the proven benefit of vaccines in preventing death and disease and the lack of data indicating harm.

In 1999 the U.S. removed thimerosal from vaccines. Why? The decision was not based on evidence but on one person's opinion. Neal Halsey railroaded the committee and threatened to hold his own press conference if they didn't do what he wanted. He meant well. His passion convinced the other committee members to invoke the precautionary principle—essentially bending over backwards to prevent any possible harm from a high total body burden of mercury from a combination of diet, environmental and vaccine sources. He didn't even consider autism: he was only concerned about possible subtle neurologic damage.

They announced their decision in words guaranteed to confuse the public and create suspicion: "current levels of thimerosal will not hurt children, but reducing those levels will make safe vaccines even safer." A 2007 editorial in *The New England Journal of Medicine* stated:

> Although the precautionary principle assumes that there is no harm in exercising caution, the alarm caused by the removal of thimerosal from vaccines has been quite harmful. For instance, after the July 1999 announcement by the CDC and AAP, about 10 percent of hospitals suspended use of the hepatitis B vaccine for all newborns, regardless of their level of risk. [Because a thimerosal-free hepatitis B vaccine was not available.] One 3-month-old child born to a Michigan mother infected with hepatitis B virus died of overwhelming infection.

It went on to point out:

> The notion that thimerosal caused autism has given rise to a cottage industry of charlatans offering false hope, partly in the form of mercury-chelating agents. In August 2005, a 5-year-old autistic boy in suburban Pittsburgh died from an arrhythmia caused by the injection of the chelating agent EDTA. Although the notion that thimerosal causes autism has now been disproved by several excellent epidemiologic studies, about 10,000 autistic children in the United States receive mercury-chelating agents every year.

A further insanity has been perpetrated by the father-and-son team of Mark and David Geier. They claimed that autistics have premature puberty and high testosterone levels (there is no evidence that this is true). They hypothesized that testosterone forms sheet-like complexes with mercury in the brain (there is no evidence that this is true), preventing mercury's removal by chelation. Their solution? They administered the drug Lupron to lower testosterone levels to supposedly facilitate mercury excretion. The treatment amounts to chemical castration.

Lupron is sometimes ordered by the courts to chemically castrate sex offenders, and it is used to treat precocious puberty and certain other medical conditions. It is not a benign drug. It can interfere with normal development and puberty and can put children's heart and bones and their future fertility at risk. The treatment involves painful daily injections and costs $5000 to $6000 a month. The Geiers use 10 times the recommended dose. The company that makes Lupron does not support its use for this purpose.

Like Wakefield, the Geiers have been accused of professional misconduct. They built their own lab in their basement and formed their own institute to conduct Lupron studies. Then they formed their own Institutional Review Board (IRB) to approve studies. IRBs are required by law and must follow strict guidelines to ensure that studies are ethical and to protect the rights of subjects. The IRB they formed was illegal. They packed the board with friends and relatives: every single member of this IRB was either one of the Geiers, an anti-thimerosal activist, a Geier associate, or a lawyer suing on behalf of "vaccine-injured" clients. One was the mother of a child who was a subject in the research. Even worse, they let the principal investigator sit as the chair of the IRB overseeing his own research protocols. Oh, and the IRB wasn't even registered until 2 years *after* the research was done.

Mark Geier has made a career of testifying as an expert witness in autism cases. He has not impressed the judges. Here are a few of the judge's comments:

- "Seriously intellectually dishonest"
- ". . . not reliable or grounded in scientific methodology and procedure . . . his testimony is subjective belief and unsupported speculation."
- "I cannot give his opinion any credence."
- ". . . a professional witness in areas for which he has no training, expertise, and experience."

When thimerosal was removed from vaccines, there were no studies showing that it was harmful. After its removal, study after study showed that it was *not* harmful. But activist groups didn't let the new evidence interfere with their beliefs.

Anti-vaccine groups have viciously attacked medical doctors and researchers for simply stating what the current scientific evidence shows. They accuse them of being shills for "Big Pharma" or covering up for government agencies, and they call them offensive names; but they don't stop there. They threaten people who write about the scientific evidence, and they threaten their children. Dr. Offit, the author of *Autism's False Prophets*, received a direct death threat that got the FBI involved. He had to use a bodyguard and cancel a book tour. One threatening phone call ominously demonstrated that the caller knew Offit's children's names, ages, and where they went to school. Another scientist who received threats was so afraid for her children's safety that she vowed never to write anything about autism again. One anti-vaccine activist had the bad grace to accuse science blogger Orac of lying when he said he was mourning his mother-in-law's death from cancer. She refused to believe he could be sorry his mother-in-law died because he's not sorry about supporting vaccines that kill children.

There was no thimerosal in any vaccine except the flu vaccine after 2002. The "mercury militia" expected autism rates to drop, thereby proving the mercury connection. Autism rates rose. Instead of relinquishing their belief, they made implausible attempts to implicate new sources of atmospheric mercury, from cremations of bodies with mercury amalgam fillings or from pollution wafted across the Pacific from China.

The Vaccines-in-General Scare

If the MMR scare can be attributed to Andrew Wakefield and the mercury scare to Neal Halsey, the next stage of hysteria is epitomized by Jenny McCarthy, actress and anti-vaccine activist extraordinaire.

Jenny's son Evan is autistic. At first she subscribed to the fanciful notion that she was an Indigo mother and Evan was a Crystal child. Indigos are "difficult" children who are alleged to possess special traits or abilities such as telepathy, empathy, and creativity, and are said to represent the next stage in human evolution. Many of them fit the diagnosis of attention-deficit/hyperactivity disorder (ADHD). Crystal children represent an even more advanced evolutionary step. They are "so sensitive, so vulnerable to the world around them, that they go inward, disconnect as best they can from even humans and do their best to survive in a world where they really don't yet fit." They are often diagnosed as autistic.

After a while McCarthy gave up on that fantasy and accepted that Evan was autistic. She became convinced that vaccines had caused his autism. She treated him with unproven dietary restrictions, anti-yeast treatments, and supplements, and claims to have cured him. She thinks her "Mommy instincts" are more valid than science. She says "My science is Evan, and he's at home. That's my science." She realizes that withholding vaccines will lead to the deaths of children. As quoted by *Time* magazine:

> I do believe sadly it's going to take some diseases coming back to realize that we need to change and develop vaccines that are safe. If the vaccine companies are not listening to us, it's their f___ing fault that the diseases are coming back. They're making a product that's s___. If you give us a safe vaccine, we'll use it. It shouldn't be polio versus autism.

She and her partner Jim Carrey have spoken out at every opportunity on talk shows, on the Internet, and through books and public appearances. When someone questions Jenny's beliefs her usual tactic is to try to shout them down. She is supported by maverick doctor Jay Gordon, who values listening to parents over science and who supports a delayed vaccine schedule not because of any evidence but just because he thinks it's a good idea. On one talk show, a pregnant mother with several autistic children tried to tell Gordon that her child who had the worst autism was the one who had *not* been vaccinated. He not only refused to listen to what she was saying but tried to drown her out, loudly insisting she mustn't vaccinate the new baby.

A member of Quackwatch's "Healthfraud" online discussion list reported sitting next to Evan's paternal grandmother at a dinner. Grandma said Evan's symptoms of autism were evident *before* he was vaccinated, and he is not doing as well as Jenny says. Grandma is writing her own book—I look forward to its revelations.

Jenny and her cohorts claim they are not anti-vaccine, but they are certainly a good facsimile thereof. The goalposts keep moving. First it was the MMR vaccine, then it was thimerosal, then it was mercury from all sources, then it was other vaccine ingredients, then it was too many vaccines, then it was giving vaccines too early. They will not be satisfied until science can offer a 100% safe and a 100% effective vaccine proven to have no side effects of any kind even in a rare susceptible individual. That's not going to happen in this universe.

The other vaccine ingredients that have been questioned include formaldehyde, aluminum, ether, anti-freeze, and human aborted fetal tissue. Scientists have explained over and over that these ingredients are either not present in vaccines or are harmless, but activists ignore the facts and keep making the same false claims. Formaldehyde is harmless in small amounts and is even produced naturally in the human body. Aluminum is an adjuvant used to increase the efficacy of vaccines, and is not harmful. Ether might be used in the manufacturing process but is not present in the vaccines. There is no ethylene glycol or even diethylene glycol in vaccines. (Anti-freeze is ethylene glycol.) And to obtain enough virus to make a vaccine, the virus must be grown in tissue cultures that were originally derived from monkey, chicken, or sometimes human fetal cells; but there is no human or animal tissue of any kind present in the vaccine itself. Apple trees grow in soil, but there is no soil in applesauce.

Some anti-vaccine websites perpetuate the myth that infectious diseases were already disappearing and that the vaccines had nothing to do with it. Those myths are easily dispelled by historical data. Vaccine critics ignore the large body of evidence from incidents around the world where as the vaccination rate dropped, the rate of disease rose; and when the vaccination rate rose again, the disease rate dropped. No one can seriously deny the effectiveness of vaccines. They are the most impressive accomplishment of modern medicine.

Giving up the known benefits of vaccines because of a vague hypothetical possibility of risk is a poor trade-off. We were able to eradicate smallpox, and we ought to be able to eradicate all the diseases that are spread solely by human-to-human contact. Once enough people have been vaccinated to eradicate the disease, no one will ever have to be vaccinated for that disease again. Smallpox is long gone; polio and measles are next on the list. Polio had been reduced to only 3 countries a few years ago. Then Nigeria stopped vaccinating due to rumors that the vaccines were an American plot to sterilize their children or give them AIDS. The polio rate soared and the disease broke out to several other countries, as far away as Malaysia.

When the rate of immunization reaches a certain level, the population is protected by what we call herd immunity. It means there are not enough susceptible people for the disease to keep spreading through a community. In many places the herd immunity has already been lost. It is only a matter of time before diseases break out again. One traveler from a country with polio could reintroduce the disease into the U.S. Lowered vaccination rates endanger even those who have been vaccinated, because the protection is not 100%. People who are immunosuppressed, chronically ill, or too young to have been vaccinated are also put at risk. Parents who choose to delay vaccination are prolonging their children's period of risk. And they are endangering everyone else's public health.

Scientists had been urged to "listen to the parents." They *did* listen to the parents and then conducted research to test the parents' hypotheses. There were various kinds of studies in different countries by different research groups. The results were consistent:

- 10 studies showed MMR doesn't cause autism
- 6 studies showed thimerosal doesn't cause autism
- 3 studies showed thimerosal doesn't cause subtle neurological problems

Now it's the parents who won't listen to the scientists.

Autistic children and their parents are being misled and victimized with useless, untested, disproven, expensive, time-consuming, and even dangerous treatments. Despite the evidence that mercury doesn't cause autism, children are still being treated with IV chelation to remove mercury—at least one child has died as a result. Along with Lupron injections for chemical castration, children are being treated with secretin, restricted diets, supplements of all kinds, intravenous hydrogen peroxide, DAN (Defeat Autism Now) protocols, cranial manipulation, facilitated communication, and other nonsense. One family was strongly urged to take out a second mortgage on their home so they could buy a home hyperbaric oxygen chamber.

The real tragedy is that all this hoopla is diverting attention from research into effective treatments (usually behavioral) and into the real causes of autism (almost certainly genetic, with environmental triggers not ruled out).

An anti-anti-vaccine backlash is now afoot. Outbreaks of vaccine-preventable diseases are being reported. Scientists are speaking out. Blogs like Respectful Insolence and Science-Based Medicine have covered the subject in depth. The *Chicago Tribune* published an exposé of the Geiers. Even *Reader's Digest* has contradicted Jenny. They said that vaccines save lives and do not cause autism and they stressed that the science is not on Jenny's side. Let us hope that sanity will prevail before too many more children die from vaccine-preventable diseases. They are dying now. The Jenny McCarthy Body Count webpage is keeping track of the numbers.

HARRIET HALL is a retired family physician and former Air Force flight surgeon who writes about medicine, complementary and alternative medicine, science, quackery, and critical thinking.

EXPLORING THE ISSUE

Can Vaccines Cause Autism?

Critical Thinking and Reflection

1. Vaccines work by stimulating the body's immune system to attack bacteria and viruses that are composed of proteins and other chemicals not native to the body. How then can they stimulate immune systems into attacking things that belong to the body? (Hint: think of "mistaken identity.")
2. With so much evidence that vaccines do not cause autism, why do people continue to believe they do?
3. Vaccines have side effects. Sometimes those side effects kill. Are vaccines worth the risk?
4. Many of the diseases we vaccinate against, such as whooping cough, are caused by bacteria. Why don't we just use antibiotics?

Is There Common Ground?

No one argues that we should not do everything we can to keep our children healthy. Vaccines have side effects, but if we stop using them, we risk returning to the days when childhood diseases killed children in large numbers. Antibiotics don't work against viruses such as those that cause measles and mumps, and they have side effects too. One of the most notable, thanks to natural selection, is antibiotic-resistant bacteria.

1. Must we just accept the risks?
2. How many children must die or develop autism as a result of disease-prevention efforts before we give up trying to prevent disease?
3. If we look to history for guidance in answering that last question, how far back should we look?

Additional Resources

Jeffrey S. Gerber and Paul A. Offit, "Vaccines and Autism: A Tale of Shifting Hypotheses," *Clinical Infectious Diseases* (February 15, 2009).

Louise Kuo Habakus, Mary Holland, and Kim Mack Rosenberg, eds., *Vaccine Epidemic: How Corporate Greed, Biased Science, and Coercive Government Threaten Our Human Rights, Our Health, and Our Children* (Skyhorse, 2011, 2012).

Seth Mnookin, *The Panic Virus: The True Story Behind the Vaccine-Autism Controversy* (Simon and Schuster, 2011).

Paul A. Offit, *Autism's False Prophets: Bad Science, Risky Medicine, and the Search for a Cure* (Columbia University Press, 2008).

Andrew J. Wakefield, *Callous Disregard: Autism and Vaccines—The Truth Behind a Tragedy* (Skyhorse, 2011).

Internet References . . .

Autism Speaks

http://www.autismspeaks.org/

The Autism Science Foundation

http://www.autismsciencefoundation.org/

Vaccinate Your Baby

http://www.vaccinateyourbaby.org/

Selected, Edited, and with Issue Framing Material by:
Thomas A. Easton, *Mount Ida College*

ISSUE

Is the Fracking Industry Adequately Regulated for Public Safety?

YES: Arthur Herman, from "The Liberal War on American Energy Independence," *Commentary* (2015)

NO: Paul Solotaroff, from "What's Killing the Babies of Vernal, Utah?" *Rolling Stone* (2015)

Learning Outcomes

After reading this issue, you will be able to:

- Explain how hydraulic fracturing (fracking) for shale gas may threaten human health.
- Describe the economic benefits of fracking.
- Discuss whether the economic benefits of an industrial process such as fracking should outweigh other considerations, such as public health.
- Discuss whether increasing prices through regulation of an industry, in order to protect public health, is justifiable.

ISSUE SUMMARY

YES: Arthur Herman argues that there is no proof that the fracking industry is causing environmental and health problems. Anyone who says there is is attacking American prosperity and the well-being of the working class.

NO: Paul Solotaroff argues that we cannot trust local and state health and environmental officials to do anything about obvious health issues. There is too much money involved.

Fossil fuels have undeniable advantages. They are compact and easy to transport. In the form of petroleum and natural gas and their derivatives, they are well suited to powering automobiles, trucks, and airplanes. They are also abundant and relatively inexpensive, although the end of the era of oil abundance is in sight. However, fossil fuels also have disadvantages, for their use puts carbon dioxide in the air, which threatens us with global warming. Oil is associated with disastrous oil spills such as the one that resulted from the failure of the British Petroleum Deepwater Horizon drilling rig in the Gulf of Mexico in 2010. Coal mining leaves enormous scars on the landscape, and coal burning emits pollutants that must be controlled. Natural gas alone seems relatively benign, for though it emits carbon dioxide when burned, it emits less than oil or coal; on the other hand, the amount of methane released when drilling for natural gas may mean the overall impact of natural gas on global warming is greater than that of coal; see Robert W. Howarth, Rence Santoro, and Anthony Ingraffea, "Methane and the Greenhouse-Gas Footprint of Natural Gas from Shale Formations," *Climatic Change Letters* (June 2011). It produces fewer air pollutants, it cannot be spilled (if released, it can cause explosions and fires, but outdoors it mixes with air and blows away), and obtaining it has not meant huge damage to the environment. Indeed, some see it as a valuable partner for renewable energy; see Saya Kitasei, "Powering the Low-Carbon Economy: The Once and Future Roles of Renewable Energy and Natural Gas," *Worldwatch Report 184* (Worldwatch Institute, 2010). Much of the United States' demand for natural gas is met by domestic production, but demand is rising. Lacking new sources of natural gas or a shift to coal, nuclear power, or alternatives such as wind and solar power, the nation must inevitably become more dependent on foreign energy suppliers.

It has long been known that large amounts of "unconventional" natural gas reside in deep layers of sedimentary rock such as shale. However, this gas could not be extracted with existing technology, at least not at a price that would permit a profit once the gas was sold. In recent years, this has changed, for drilling technology now allows drillers to bend drill holes horizontally to follow rock layers. Injecting millions of gallons of water and chemicals at extraordinarily high pressure can fracture (or "frack") the rock surrounding a drill hole and permit trapped gas to escape. See Richard A. Kerr, "Natural Gas from Shale Bursts onto the Scene," *Science* (June 25, 2010). Mark Fischetti, "The Drillers Are Coming," *Scientific American* (July 2010), notes that the Marcellus shale formation, which stretches from upstate New York through Pennsylvania to Tennessee, may contain enough gas to meet U.S. needs for 40 years. There are other shale formations in the United States, Canada, Europe, and China. The total U.S. supply may be enough to meet needs for a century; see Steve Levine, "Kaboom!" *New Republic* (May 13, 2010). See also Peter Heywood, "Fracking: Safer and Greener?" *The Chemical Engineer* (April 2012), and Tom Wilber, *Under the Surface: Fracking, Fortunes and the Fate of the Marcellus Shale* (Cornell University Press, 2012). The same technology is being applied to extracting oil from shale formations; see Edwin Dobb, "America Strikes Oil: The Promise and Risk of Fracking," *National Geographic* (March 2013), and supply projections are rising; much more carbon will thus be added to the atmosphere when we need to be adding less. Reinforcing his point are new projections that say we have more reserves of oil and gas, largely due to fracking of oil shale, and can continue burning fossil fuels even longer before we run out; see "Supply Shock from North American Oil Rippling through Global Markets," International Energy Agency press release (May 14, 2013) (http://iea.org/newsroomandevents/pressreleases/2013/may-/name,38080,en.html).

Not surprisingly, many people are concerned about the environmental impacts of "fracking" and disposing of used water, chemicals, and drilling wastes. Richard A. Kerr describes threats to groundwater in "Not Under My Backyard, Thank You," *Science* (June 25, 2010); see also Sharon Kelly, "The Trouble with Fracking," *National Wildlife* (World Edition) (October/November 2011). But the industry insists that it will deal responsibly with its wastes and hastens to reassure people living near drilling sites. Alex Halperin, "Drill, Maybe Drill?" *American Prospect* (May 2010), describes the debate over shale-gas drilling in upstate New York. The area has suffered large job losses, something the shale-gas industry could remedy. Many landowners—including farmers—see the potential for huge boosts to their income. But the industry has reportedly persuaded people to lease drilling rights on their property by making promises that cannot be kept. Environmental impacts are a huge concern. Indeed, one recent study found amounts of methane in drinking water supplies near natural gas wells so high as to pose "a potential explosion hazard"; see Stephen G. Osborn, Avner Vengosh, Nathaniel R. Warner, and Robert B. Jackson, "Methane Contamination of Drinking Water Accompanying Gas-Well Drilling and Hydraulic Fracturing," *Proceedings of the National Academy of Science (PNAS)* (http://www.nicholas.duke.edu/hydrofracking/Osborn%20et%20al%20%20Hydrofracking%202011.pdf) (May 17, 2011). See also Joyce Nelson, "A 'Big Fracking Problem': Natural Gas Industry's 'Fracking' Risks Causing Earthquakes," *CCPA Monitor* (February 2011), and Francois H. Cornet, "Earthquakes Induced by Fluid Injections," *Science* (June 12, 2015). Linda Marsa, "Fracking Nation," *Discover* (May 2011), is concerned that fracking may release radioactive and other toxic materials from shale in the process of gas extraction. Chris Mooney, "The Truth about Fracking," *Scientific American* (November 2011), notes that a great deal of research into the safety and side effects of fracking has not yet been done, but the problems may lie less in the technology itself than in carelessness in well drilling and waste disposal.

Fracking has been banned in New York and Vermont, as well as in many smaller venues; for a complete list of bans, see http://keeptapwatersafe.org/global-bans-on-fracking/. Several states require that fracking companies reveal the makeup of the chemicals they use. And regulations for fracking wastewater treatment and disposal are proliferating. The potential problems are discussed in Brian Colleran, "The Drill's About to Drop," *E—The Environmental Magazine* (March/April 2010). James C. Morriss, III, and Christopher D. Smith, "The Shales and Shale-Nots: Environmental Regulation of Natural Gas Development," *Energy Litigation Journal* (Summer 2010), contend that if companies in the industry act to prevent problems before regulators require such action, this both demands a better understanding of the technology and prevents future litigation. Andrew A. Rosenberg, Pallavi Phartiyal, Gretchen Goldman, and Lewis M. Branscomb, "Exposing Fracking to Sunlight," *Issues in Science and Technology* (Fall 2014), note "the importance of communities developing trust in both industry and government. . . . To overcome the gridlock and suspicions in public conversations on fracking, decision makers should immediately enact federal policies that would require states to implement comprehensive baseline analysis and monitoring programs for air and water at all well sites. The collected information must be made publicly available and accessible to provide communities with trustworthy information about environmental quality and potential impacts on public health."

In 2004 an Environmental Protection Agency (EPA) study said that fracking was little or no threat to drinking water and Congress exempted fracking from federal regulation. Now, however, the EPA is conducting a $1.9 million study to reevaluate fracking technology. To see the draft report, released in 2015, go to http://www2 .epa.gov/hfstudy/executive-summary-hydraulic-fracturing-study -draft-assessment-2015. It finds that there are numerous ways in which fracking can affect groundwater, but, perhaps partly because of limited data, there is no evidence of "widespread, systemic impacts on drinking water resources in the United States." (Local effects seem to be another matter.) Erik Stokstad, "Will Fracking Put Too Much Fizz in Your Water?" *Science* (June 27, 2014) (part of a special section on fracking), reports similar results from a Pennsylvania study, with many or most problems due to faulty well construction. At a May 5, 2011, hearing of the House Science, Space, and Technology Committee on whether additional studies are needed to determine whether fracking is safe, chairman Ralph Hall (R-TX) called the EPA study "yet another example of this administration's desire to stop domestic energy development through regulation." Scientists are more concerned about potential side effects of the technology; see Rachel Ehrenberg, "The Facts Behind the Frack," *Science News* (September 8, 2012). Among the side effects of fracking—indeed, of just using methane as a fuel—is accelerated

global warming; see Marianne Lavelle, "Good Gas, Bad Gas," *National Geographic* (December 2012). Perhaps it is time for a different approach: Clay Farris Naff, "Can Fracking Lead the Way to Clean Energy?" *The Humanist* (April 2014), suggests using the deep-drilling technology of fracking to combine carbon dioxide–generating power plants with geothermal power plants.

So far, the only new fracking regulations from the EPA address air pollution; see, e.g., Jeff Johnson, "EPA Issues Fracking Rules," *Chemical & Engineering News* (April 23, 2012). President Barack Obama has set up an interagency oversight committee to streamline regulation and ensure the industry's "safe and responsible development"; see Ben Wolfgang, "Obama Issues Order to Coordinate Fracking Oversight," *Washington Times* (April 13, 2012). Regulations are not nearly as restrictive as Hall feared. Nor does it seem quite fair when Kevin D. Williamson, "The Truth about Fracking," *National Review* (February 20, 2012), says that "the opposition to fracking isn't at its heart environmental or economic or scientific. It's ideological, and that ideology is *nihilism*." Environmentalists, he says, are opposed to modern technological civilization and would like nothing better than to phase out the human species.

In the YES selection, Arthur Herman argues that there is no proof that the fracking industry is causing environmental and health problems. Anyone who says there is is attacking American prosperity and the well-being of the working class. In the NO selection, Paul Solotaroff argues that we cannot trust local and state health and environmental officials to do anything about obvious health issues. There is too much money involved.

YES

Arthur Herman

The Liberal War on American Energy Independence: Social Snobbery Masquerading as Environmentalism

Fracking gasholes
We know you know
For a million reasons
We must say no no no
No no no no no.

—*'Fracking Gasholes' by XOEarth*

WILLIAMSPORT is a town of 29,000 in Pennsylvania's upper Susquehanna Valley. When I decided to stop there in the spring of 2012 on the way to upstate New York, I figured it for a place lost in time—a sleepy burg still guided by small-town values (Williamsport hosts the Little League World Series every summer) but with the sad and deserted appearance you'd expect in an area where the main industry, steelmaking, receded from sight in the 1970s.

That is why I was surprised to find a new mall on its outskirts, as well as construction sites for banks and office buildings. Instead of a boarded-up downtown, there were new restaurants opening. The hotel was also bustling—and expensive. I had had trouble finding parking in a lot jammed with pickup trucks and SUVs. In the hotel elevator were two men in green jumpsuits, both carrying tool bags of a kind I recognized from crews working on offshore oil rigs in the North Sea. They were natural-gas drillers coming back for some sleep after a long night working in the gas field.

They were frackers.

Williamsport sits on the edge of the Marcellus Shale area, the second-largest natural-gas find in the world. It stretches across most of Pennsylvania and into New York, West Virginia, Ohio, and Maryland. Most of it was inaccessible until a decade ago, when a combination of new extraction technologies—including hydraulic fracturing, or "fracking," and horizontal drilling—opened up the shale to energy development.

Since 2002, fracking has generated in Pennsylvania more than 24,000 drilling jobs and some 200,000 other support jobs in trucking, construction, and infrastructure, according to the state's Department of Labor and Industry. Wages in the gas field average $62,000 a year—$20,000 higher than the state average.

To Pennsylvania, fracking has brought in $4 billion in investment, including a steady flow of income to local landowners and local governments leasing mineral rights to their land. According to National Resources Economics, Inc., full development of the Marcellus Shale could bring another 211,000 jobs to this one state alone, not to mention other states on the formation, including New York.

But there will be no such jobs in the state of New York. In December, Governor Andrew Cuomo announced a complete ban on the use of hydraulic fracturing. The cost of that move was already foreshadowed three years ago when I drove across the border from Pennsylvania into New York. The busy modern highway coming out of Williamsport, U.S. Route 15, shrinks down into a meandering, largely empty two-lane road. On the way to Ithaca, I passed through miles of a deserted rural landscape dotted with collapsing barns and tumble-down houses reminiscent of Appalachia.

The one thing that broke the dismal monotony were the signs, many painted by hand, that had sprouted up along the road and in the fields, all saying the same thing: Ron Paul for President. The state was then in its fifth year of a moratorium on fracking, and that moratorium had turned upstate New York's rural residents into libertarians. Bitter ones, at that. They didn't particularly care about Ron Paul's views on Israel or the Federal Reserve. All they wanted was a chance to collect the lucrative fees a gas company would pay them to drill on their land; they would have voted for anyone who would help them make their land generate an income again for themselves and their families.

This sort of gain is precisely what the left's war on fracking (which has scored its most significant victory so far with Cuomo's permanent ban) aims to prevent. It is nothing less than a policy of selective immiseration.

FRACKING—a technique that uses a mixture of chemicals, sand, and water to break apart deep formations of oil- and gas-rich shale rock and draw the oil and gas to the surface—is the most important American industrial enterprise of the 21st century. It joins the automobile industry, aircraft and aerospace, the computer and the digital revolution, as one of America's great successes in technological innovation, productivity, and entrepreneurial flair. Like other industrial revolutions, including the first in 18th-century Britain, the fracking revolution is bringing about enormous changes in how we live—and sharply altering the nation's income-distribution curve.

The fracking revolution has also brought America's oil and gas industry back to life. In 2000, fracking accounted for less than 3 percent of all oil and natural-gas production in the United States, which was then importing more than 60 percent of its oil. Today, fracking accounts for more than 40 percent, and that percentage is going steadily upward, as the U.S. replaces one country after another on the list of the world's biggest oil and gas producers. Our oil imports from OPEC countries have shrunk by half.

Indeed, the production gushing from America's shale oil and gas deposits—from Eagle Ford in Texas to the Marcellus Formation in Pennsylvania and the Bakken oil field in North Dakota—doesn't just promise the long-elusive goal of energy independence. It points to an energy *dominance* and economic power that the United States hasn't seen for 100 years, since the heyday of John D. Rockefeller and Standard Oil.

The difference is that instead of that power being lodged in a single megacorporation or the Seven Sisters of the 1950s (Mobil, Shell, Esso, etc.), the fracking revolution is being created by hundreds of smaller, more agile independents who are transforming the technology as fast as they are pumping the oil and natural gas out of the ground.

They are also pumping out jobs by the tens of thousands. It is no longer the case that good-paying blue-collar employment in America is on the verge of extinction. Fracking employs thousands of people in physically demanding jobs that require no college degree and pay, in many cases, six figures.

In North Dakota, where fracking has turned the Bakken Shale formation into the most productive oil patch in the country, an entry-level job hauling water and helping to move rigs and machinery averages $67,000 a year. A well specialist with a couple of years experience will be looking at a $100,000 salary, while a directional driller—the highest job a fracking employee can hold without a B.A.—earns close to $200,000.

Overall, the fracking boom has driven up North Dakota's per capita income to $57,367 in 2012—the highest in the nation save for Washington D.C. The per capita figure has jumped 31 percent since 2008, the year after the fracking boom got under way, compared with 10 percent for frackless South Dakota.

The other beneficiaries are private landowners, many of them farmers. They have been able to lease out the mineral rights to their land for large sums; and if a well opens up, it quickly becomes a gusher of cash. In North Dakota, that has produced a series of so-called High Plains millionaires; for other landowners, leasing fees have become a lifeline for their farm or property.

Private-property rights, often of middle-income people, are the real drivers behind the fracking revolution, with county and state governments leasing rights on their lands not far behind. It's one reason so many state capitals have been amenable to the fracking revolution: They've been prime beneficiaries.

Under the Obama administration, the number of oil- and gas-drilling leases on federal lands has fallen, and oil production on federal lands is at levels lower than in 2007. Nevertheless, America's oil production jumped by 1 million barrels a day last year thanks to fracking—even as we're bringing up more natural gas than at any time in our history.

In less than a decade, the boom has already changed the energy map, with the rise of states such as Pennsylvania, Ohio, and North Dakota joining Texas, Oklahoma, and Alaska as major energy producers, and with many others poised to join the club, from Illinois and Wisconsin to Alabama and California.

Indeed, the fracking revolution is the one sector of the Obama economy that's been steadily booming, creating more than 625,000 jobs in the shale-gas sector alone—a number estimated to grow to 870,000 in 2015. Its benefits also flow in trickle-down savings by lowering the cost of energy, particularly natural gas. Mercator Energy, a Colorado-based energy broker, has calculated it's saving American families more than $32.5 billion in lower natural-gas bills for home heating and electricity.

It has also had a positive impact on U.S. manufacturing, especially petrochemical and plastics firms that have cashed in on lower natural-gas and oil prices and the increasingly abundant supply. From 2010 to 2012, energy-intensive manufacturers added 196,000 jobs as Rust Belt cities such as Lansing, Michigan, and Gary, Indiana, have been revived by cheaper, more abundant energy.

Wallace Tyner, an economist at Purdue University, estimates that between 2008 and 2035 the fracking revolution (oil and gas combined) will add an average of $473 billion per year to the U.S. economy. That's roughly 3 percent of today's GDP.

The most striking change, however, has been at the gas pump. Falling U.S. demand for imported oil (a drop of 40 percent since 2005) has lowered global prices overall, and has been a huge factor in oil's 25 percent price plunge in 2014. Filling up the family car at $2.80 a gallon versus $3.80 a gallon is a great benefit to Americans, especially in low-income households. A strong case can be made that the shale revolution's impact on natural-gas prices has been the equivalent of a poverty-relief program, since the nation's poor on average spend four times more of their incomes on home energy than do the more affluent. On average, the drop in natural-gas prices has given low-income families an effective tax rebate of some $10 billion a year.

This is one of the most notable aspects of the fracking revolution. Unlike the computer and digital revolution, for example, which created an industry dominated by Ph.D.'s and college-trained engineers, this is an economic bonanza of particular meaning to those in the middle- and low-income brackets, with the potential to benefit many more.

Yet today's liberal left is, virtually without exception, implacably opposed to fracking, from the national to the state to the local level. In the forefront have been environmental lobbying interests. In localities such as Ithaca, New York—the hub of the anti-fracking movement in New York State—liberal elites have banded together to prevent an economic transformation that would pad the wallets of their neighbors and upset the socioeconomic status quo.

OF ALL THE NATIONAL environmental groups, the Sierra Club probably has the mildest official position: that further fracking in the United States must stop until its overall impact on the environment has been studied more carefully. More typical is Greenpeace's April 2012 joint statement on fracking (co-signed by the Water and Environment Alliance and Friends of the Earth Europe) that makes a fracking well seem not entirely different from a nuclear-waste dump.

That document asserts that "fracking is a high-risk activity that impacts human health and the wider environment." It warns that natural-gas development through fracking "could cause contamination of surface and groundwater (including drinking water)" and pollutes both soil and air while it "disrupts the landscape and impacts upon rural and conservation areas." Greenpeace also claims that fracking and its related activities produce smog, particulates, and toxic methane gas; cause

workers to expose themselves to toxic chemicals used in the fracking process; increase "risks of earthquakes"; and lock local communities such as Lycoming County into a "boom and bust economy" that will run out when the oil and gas run out. Greenpeace and its allies insist that these places look to "tourism and agriculture instead."

The document creates a dire picture, yet nearly every one of these claims is false. Since fracking operates thousands of feet below the aquifer, the risk to drinking water is nil; and there are no proven cases of water supplies becoming contaminated from fracking, despite the thousands of fracking wells drilled both in the United States and Canada. Yet the charge is repeated ad nauseam in anti-fracking ads, films, and pamphlets.

Such is the charge that fracking exposes people, including workers, to dangerous chemicals. More than 99 percent of the fluid used to fracture rock in the operation is nothing more than water and sand mixed together. In fact, most of the statistical risks associated with fracking in terms of contact with dangerous chemicals (benzene is a favorite example, radioactive isotopes another, methane yet another) are no higher, and sometimes lower, than those associated with any other industrial job or outdoor activity, including driving a big-rig truck.

The charge that fracking can leak methane into drinking water stems from a Duke University study that examined a mere 68 water wells in a region of Pennsylvania and New York in which 20,000 water wells are drilled each year—and those who conducted the study never bothered to ask whether any methane concentrations existed before the fracking began (which turned out to be the case).

That fracking might cause earthquakes is another oft-repeated alarmist charge with no facts or evidence behind it. In certain conditions, deep underground injections of water and sand used in fracking can lead to detectable seismic activities, but so can favored green projects such as geothermal-energy exploration or sequestering carbon dioxide underground. None of these adds up to seismic rumblings any human being will notice, let alone an Irving Allen movie-style catastrophe. And given the fact that for years there have been thousands of fracking wells around the country that operate without any detectable seismic activity, the argument seems clearly driven more by the need to generate emotion than the imperative to weigh actual evidence.

But perhaps the oddest claim from groups such as Greenpeace is that increasing the use of natural gas will not reduce greenhouse-gas emissions. The evidence is overwhelmingly the opposite. As natural gas continues to squeeze out coal as a cheap supply of energy, especially for power plants, the greenhouse-gas-emission index will inevitably head downward. In fact, since the shale boom, those emissions in the United States have been cut by almost 20 percent, a number that one would expect to make any environmental activist smile.

All of which suggests that the war on fracking is waged in defiance of facts. And that, in turn, suggests a particular agenda is at work in the anti-fracking camp. A hint of it appears in Greenpeace's claim that local communities would be better off sticking to "sustainable agriculture and tourism," meaning organic farming and microbreweries that cater to the tastes of affluent and sophisticated out-of-towners. The war on fracking is a war on economic growth, which the shale revolution has managed to sustain in the middle of the Obama recession, and a war on the upward mobility any industrial revolution like fracking triggers.

It is part of what the Manhattan Institute's Fred Siegel has called the "liberal revolt against the masses," and a good place to see it in action is in New York State.

IN 2006, then-gubernatorial candidate Eliot Spitzer made a campaign swing through the so-called Southern Tier of upstate New York. The Manhattanite expressed shock at a landscape that was "devastated," as he put it, and was steadily being abandoned for lack of jobs and economic opportunity. "This is not the New York we dream of," he said.

Much the same had been true of large portions of rural Pennsylvania. Fracking reversed the downward course there. But the moratorium Spitzer's successor, Andrew Cuomo, placed on fracking in 2008 before locking it in permanently late last year has frozen those portions of the state in their relative poverty.

Local farmers have been furious over the de facto ban. They are frustrated that the valuable source of income that fracking would generate has been denied them—and that Albany and its liberal enablers are content to crush them under the twin burden of some of the highest property taxes in the country and a regulatory regime that, in Fred Siegel's words, "makes it hard to eke out a living from small dairy herds."

Locals are furious, too, that the ban is denying blue-collar jobs that could help young people find work in a fracking site and could transform local standards of living. In 2012, the state's health department determined that hydro-fracking could be done safely in the state and concluded that "significant adverse impacts on human health are not expected from routine HVHF (hydro-fracking) operations." This was not what state officials wanted to hear, and the report was buried. When someone leaked it to the *New York Times*, the Department of Environmental Conservation's

spokesperson quickly disavowed it. Meanwhile, Cuomo's acting health commissioner, Howard Zucker, served as front man for his boss's permanent ban.

Ithaca is the center of New York's anti-fracking hard-liners. Their leader is Helen Slottje, who organized the Community Environmental Defense Fund to use local zoning regulations to keep fracking out of the surrounding county. She admits that many local people down the hill from Ithaca resent their efforts and think that she and her environmentalist militia are little more than thieves stealing money from their pockets.

But Slottje dismisses their worries, just as she angrily dismisses the charge that she's a classic example of someone who opposes salutary change because she doesn't want it in her own back yard. "If a serial killer knocks on your door," she says, "it's not NIMBYism to fight back." She doesn't bother to wonder whether her comparison of frackers to serial killers might be slightly exaggerated. She simply adds, "We're not NIMBY, we're NIABY. Not In Anyone's Back Yard."

She is joined in her activism by the Duncan Hines heiress Adelaide Gomer, whose anti-fracking Park Foundation is based in Ithaca and bankrolls much of the activism. "Hydro-fracking will turn our area into an industrial site," she has proclaimed. After citing the usual charges about poisoning the aquifer, she also adds, "It will ruin the ambience, the beauty of the region." The beauty of falling-down barns, rusted cars and farm equipment, and abandoned farmhouses may be lost on the locals, but it's united the rich and influential in New York City. They want to keep things that way—and keep the "creepy advances of environment-trashing frackers" out of the state.

Gomer was able to mobilize demonstrations around the state to maintain the ban despite lobbying in Albany to overturn it, while celebrities such as Alec Baldwin, Robert de Niro, Yoko Ono, Debra Winger, Carrie Fisher, David Byrne, Jimmy Fallon, Martha Stewart, Lady Gaga, and the Beastie Boys signed an Artists Against Fracking petition. Like other Manhattanites, they have no reason to worry much about low land prices in the Southern Tier—but they do worry about development that would benefit the locals while possibly spoiling the view.

By cloaking their social snobbery in the clothes of the environmentalist movement, New York's well-heeled have managed to forestall the kind of wealth transfer that fracking has brought to Pennsylvania. Indeed, some like Slottje are hoping to spread the same anti-fracking gospel back across the state line and stop Pennsylvania's economic boom dead in its tracks.

A similar class divide is a feature of the debate in California. The Golden State has always been a mainstay of American energy production, going back to the 1920s and even as late as the 1960s, when the state ranked second in oil production after Texas. Not coincidentally, that was also the heyday of California's economic boom and the vast expansion of its state resources, including its university system—the same system that now provides the dubious environmental-impact studies and willing young demonstrators and foot soldiers for the war on fracking.

California is now fourth in oil production in the United States. Its large shale-oil reserves may top 15 billion barrels. The Monterey Shale field runs for 200 miles from Bakersfield to central California and is largely untapped. Opening up the Monterey field could mean as much as $25 billion in revenues for strapped state coffers, according to a study by University of Wyoming's Tim Considine and Edward Manderson. California's natural-gas reserves may be four times those in North Dakota's Bakken range.

There are also studies suggesting that the economic ripple effect of fracking in California could spread $30 billion to $80 billion of additional wealth across the state for every 1 billion barrels of oil production. (California currently produces around 200 million barrels a year.)

Yet the state's governor, Jerry Brown, and its political establishment have chosen not to listen to the industry or the analysts or the advocates for the unemployed who point to California's dismal jobless rate, which, at 7.2 percent, is higher than those of Texas (4.9 percent) and North Dakota (2.7 percent). Instead, green activists and Hollywood, not to mention Silicon Valley, are clearly in command.

In April 2013, after considerable political controversy and debate, a federal judge blocked fracking throughout the state. Plaintiffs in the case were the Sierra Club and the Center for Biological Diversity, the organization made famous for protecting the spotted owl in New Mexico and the Upper Northwest. "We're very excited," said the Sierra Club's spokeswoman when the ruling came down. "I'm sure the Champagne is flowing in San Francisco," she added, since many of the anti-fracking campaign's wealthy contributors are Silicon Valley millionaires.

The same is true of Hollywood royalty such as David Geffen and Robert Redford, and younger stars like Matt Damon. Damon was the top-billed name in Hollywood's first anti-fracking movie, 2012's *Promised Land*. The movie's own standing as a fearless piece of populist muckraking was compromised when it turned out that part of *Promised Land*'s financing had come from OPEC member and natural-gas exporter Qatar. *Promised Land*'s fictional depiction of fracking's evil is ballasted by the documentaries *Gaslands* and *Gaslands Two*, which repeat many of the same myths and misrepresentations about fracking while introducing several more (such as

the claim that the evil genius behind fracking is Dick Cheney).

Yet for all their clout, the Hollywood left and environmental activists have been steadily losing ground in Washington, even under Barack Obama. While the Obama EPA has been happy to impose draconian rules on coal carbon emissions for power plants, it has been curiously reluctant to push federal regulation of fracking. It has left the job to the states instead—an almost unique example of the administration's respect for states rights. Ron Binz, Obama's nominee to head the Federal Energy Regulatory Commission (FERC) in 2013, dismissed natural gas and fracking as "dead-end technology," touted a federal push to halt the switch from coal to natural gas for power generation, and insisted on conversion to wind and solar power instead.

But Binz changed his tune when he showed up at his confirmation hearing in front of the Senate Energy Committee, declaring natural gas "a very great fuel" and "the near-perfect fuel for the next couple of decades"—and swearing off any effort by FERC to use its regulatory powers to hamper the free flow of gas from pipelines to trading markets, let alone from the fracking wellhead. (Binz won committee approval by one vote.)

Binz is not alone. To the fury of environmentalist groups, the president himself has touted the success of fracking in producing jobs and growth. "America is closer to energy independence than we've been in decades," he announced in his 2014 State of the Union Address. "One of the reasons why is natural gas. If extracted safely, it's the bridge fuel that can power our economy with less of the carbon pollution that causes climate change."

The Sierra Club's executive director Michael Brune had a swift riposte: "Make no mistake," he said. "Natural gas is a bridge to nowhere"—or at least nowhere green elites want to go.

And so with the Obama administration content to be a noncombatant, the war on fracking has had to wage its fight at the state and local levels, in some states where fracking has already achieved a beachhead and shown its benefits to people's and state's bottom lines.

States such as Texas, Wyoming, and Louisiana may seem like lost causes for the anti-fracking left (although citizens' groups in the liberal university town of Denton, Texas, have recently mobilized to stop local frackers). But Pennsylvania has become an emerging battleground. In 2014, its attorney general filed criminal charges against ExxonMobil for an alleged waste-water spill by its subsidiary XTO Energy, back in 2010—the first criminal charges for activities related to fracking in the Marcellus Shale. This, in spite of the fact that XTO wasn't responsible for the spill of 57,000 gallons of waste water (which is about three swimming pools' worth) into a tributary of the Susquehanna; it was the work of a contractor. But XTO had already paid a $100,000 penalty and agreed to pay $20 million to clean it up. ExxonMobil has the deep pockets to fight back, but smaller companies and contractors won't if suing fracking operations becomes the new legal sport in Pennsylvania.

Anti-frackers also thought they had a shot at stopping the industry in Colorado. The state is one of the wellsprings of environmental activism, after all, with plenty of willing foot soldiers from campuses such as the University of Colorado at Boulder and the University of Denver. But Colorado also sits on one of the biggest shale fields in North America and is one of the top natural-gas states. In 2013, oil and gas contributed $30 billion to Colorado's economy, in addition to thousands of jobs.

A serious effort to launch an anti-fracking initiative, which would have banned drilling within 2,000 feet of homes and hospitals and given local community councils effective veto power over fracking efforts, ran aground early in 2014. Colorado Democrats realized it could endanger the reelections of Governor John Hickenlooper and Senator Mark Udall. Fracking is popular with Colorado voters, especially working-class voters. They convinced the multimillionaire congressman Jared Polis to set aside his petition drive for the bill just as Hickenlooper and Udall suddenly turned squishy on the fracking issue, to the fury of local environmentalists. (Udall lost; Hickenlooper was reelected.)

For a while, anti-frackers seemed to have more luck in Illinois, which was an important oil producer until its vertical wells dried up in the 1940s. Downstate counties such as Wayne and White have been in economic decline for decades. Fracking the rich, underlying New Albany Shale could revive their fortunes.

Starting in 2011, drillers began leasing more than 500,000 acres of land, with Woolsey Energy investing more than $100 million in setting up wells that could earn as much as 1.3 million dollars per well for landowners. In Clay County, every working well would produce $172,000 in mineral taxes for the state.

That's when anti-fracking activists began to get nervous. Groups such as Frack Free Illinois, Global Warming Solutions Group of Central Illinois, and Progressive Democrats of Greater Springfield put pressure on the state legislature and its then-governor, Pat Quinn, to intervene. In June 2013, Governor Quinn signed legislation allowing the state's department of natural resources to write stringent new rules on regulating fracking—rules that opponents hoped and supporters expected would signal the death of fracking in Illinois.

The proposed new rules required 28 separate certifications before a well could open, including a "cumulative impact statement" that would be wide open to public objections. Indeed, every permit was to be subject to extensive public hearings that would let any "adversely affected person" file an objection—and of course allow activist groups to flood the room.

And yet, when the final rules were unveiled in August 2014, activists were shocked to discover that some of them were far less stringent than—and even undercut—the rules Quinn had recommended. Industry groups were equally frustrated by rules they didn't like, and they fought back. So the department of natural resources went back to the drawing board to start again. But in November, Quinn lost his reelection bid. Fracking hadn't been a major issue in the campaign except in downstate counties, but the key political stakeholder in the anti-fracking campaign had been voted out of office. The environmentalist movement's final hope was to block publication of the new rules; if no one knew what the rules were, they couldn't drill. No luck. At the end of November, an Illinois judge gave the order that the rules were to be published. However stringent those rules may be, the road to fracking in Illinois is open at last.

For activist groups, this was a major defeat and one that will repeat itself if regulators are even minimally honest. When regulatory agencies actually investigate the dire charges made against the industry, most of the charges evaporate under scrutiny. Remaining health and safety matters, such as waste disposal, turn out to be manageable with simple oversight. In the end, this means that the fight to ban fracking outright is steadily turning into a losing battle.

And when politicians and courts decide to quit the field, what's left for the left? More protests, even civil disobedience. "We will resist this with our bodies, our hearts, and our minds," one southern Illinois organic farmer told the website Green Progress. "We will block this, we will chain ourselves to trucks." Or, as some choice lyrics from "Fracking Gasholes" by XOEarth put it: "2,000 big trucks per well/Dusty growling beasts from hell,/For all the critturs that love to live,/Block the roads, or bid farewell."

While the activists are lying in the road, fracking and its technologies are constantly evolving. Far from rejecting the environmentalists' demands for more safety and for meeting community standards, companies are constantly adjusting to make their work as clean as possible. Many now employ reusable water for the hydro-fracking process, for example, while cutting back their use of toxic chemicals. Technologies for water-free fracking are already here and will become increasingly widespread in areas where water resources are scarce. That will be another body blow to fracking's opponents, who like to claim it wastes water needed for human consumption or agriculture.

And we haven't even begun to explore the possibilities of natural gas. While fracking has yielded record levels of oil production in the United States, those reserves-in-rock are limited. American natural-gas reserves are not. According to a recent Colorado School of Mines study, they amount to 2.3 *quadrillion* cubic feet of technically recoverable natural gas in the United States, enough to fuel our energy needs for decades—and the constant technological innovations of the industry will make extracting those reserves increasingly cost-efficient.

Already, in 2013, we saw a 41 percent increase in natural-gas production over 2005 levels, more than 40 billion cubic feet a day. As the economy shifts to rely more on natural gas than on coal and petroleum, the positive change won't be limited to greenhouse-gas emissions. Natural gas will become a ubiquitous fuel source as it gets converted to alternative transportation fuels that have higher octane levels, and lower emissions, than gasoline does.

Beyond that, there are methane hydrates—deep deposits of crystalline natural gas, embedded in large parts of the Arctic permafrost and ocean bottoms. Even when shale oil and gas have eventually run out, technologies to extract methane hydrates will be able to supply almost limitless energy—according to the U.S. Geological Survey, more than all previous discovered oil and gas put together, even while wind and solar are still trying to figure out how to generate power efficiently.

Progressives who believe themselves to be on the side of science and the little guy at the same time are in fact defying both. This is a battle between the partisans of a discredited ideology from the past and those who see the fast-advancing future. As Peter Huber and Mark Mills point out in their book, *The Bottomless Well,* energy is the fuel of growth and of life itself. The environmentalists' target is greater than the future prosperity of America's least fortunate—it's their survival.

ARTHUR HERMAN is a senior fellow at the Hudson Institute. His latest books are *Freedom's Forge: How American Business Produced Victory in World War II* (Random House, 2012), and *The Cave and the Light: Plato versus Aristotle and the Struggle for the Soul of Western Civilization* (Random House, 2013).

Paul Solotaroff    **NO**

What's Killing the Babies of Vernal, Utah?

Every NIGHT, DONNA YOUNG GOES TO BED WITH HER PISTOL, a .45 Taurus Judge with laser attachment. Last fall, she says, someone stole onto her ranch to poison her livestock, or tried to; happily, her son found the d-CON wrapper and dumped all the feed from the troughs. Strangers phoned the house to wish her dead or run out of town on a rail. Local nurses and doctors went them one better, she says, warning pregnant women that Young's incompetence had killed babies and would surely kill theirs too, if given the chance.

"Before they started spreading their cheer about me, I usually had 18 to 25 clients a year, and a spotless reputation in the state," says Young, the primary midwife to service Vernal, Utah, a boom-and-bust town of 10,000 people in the heart of the fracked-gas gold rush of the Uintah Basin. A hundred and fifty miles of sparse blacktop east of Salt Lake City, Vernal has the feel of a slapdash suburb dropped randomly from outer space. Half of it is new and garishly built, the paint barely dry after a decade-long run of fresh-drilled wells and full employment. "Now, I'm down to four or five ladies, and don't know how I'll be able to feed my animals if things don't turn around quick."

Young, a fifty-something, heart-faced woman with a story-time lilt of a voice, cuts a curious figure for a pariah. She's the mother of six, a grandmother of 14 and an object of reverence among the women she's helped, many of whom she's guided through three and four home births with blissfully short labors and zero pain meds. And the sin for which she's been punished with death threats and attacks on her reputation? Two years ago, she stumbled onto the truth that an alarming number of babies were dying in Vernal—at least 10 in 2013 alone, what seemed to her a shockingly high infant mortality rate for such a small town. That summer, she raised her hand and put the obvious question to Joe Shaffer, director of the TriCounty Health Department: Why are so many of our babies dying?

In most places, detecting a grave risk to children would inspire people to name a street for you. But in Vernal, a town literally built by oil, raising questions about the safety of fracking will brand you a traitor and a target. "Me and my kids are still cautious: If someone kicked in my front door tonight, it'd take an hour for the sheriff to get here," says Young, whose house on 60 acres is well out of town and a quarter-mile clear of her closest neighbor. "The first person they'd meet is me on the staircase, pointing that .45 dead at 'em. And I know how to use these things—I can nail a coyote in the pasture from 100 yards."

Prodded by Young and the concerns she pushed along, which made their way through channels to state officials, TriCounty Health announced a study in 2014 to assess Young's concerns over the infant mortality rate. But Young, backed up by experts in Salt Lake City, believed the study was designed to fail. She says that any serious inquiry would have started with Suspect One: the extraordinary levels of wintertime pollution plaguing the Basin since the vast new undertaking to frack the region's shale filled the air with toxins. The county merely counted up infant deaths and brushed aside the facts about Vernal air pollution: ozone readings that rivaled the worst days of summer in New York, Los Angeles or Salt Lake City; particulate matter as bad as Mexico City; and ground air fraught with carcinogenic gases like benzene, rogue emissions from oil and gas drilling. Indeed, pollution was so bad in this rural bowl that it broke new ground in climate science. For decades, experts believed that life-threatening smog occurred only in or near big cities. But the Basin, which is bound on all four sides by mountains, is a perfectly formed bowl for winter inversions, in which 20-below weather clamps down on the valley and is sealed there by warmer air above it. During those spells, when the haze is visible and the air in one's lungs is a cold chisel, the sun's rays reflect off the snow on the ground and cook the volatile gases into ozone. The worst such period in the Basin's recent history was the winter of 2012–13, when nearly all the Uintah mothers whose babies died were pregnant.

Other key information was available to TriCounty, including multiple recent studies that link mothers' exposure to toxic air with fetal disasters of all kinds, including stillbirths, birth defects and developmental syndromes.

But four months after he announced the study, Shaffer retired as TriCounty's chief; six months later, the department's findings were released. The deaths were deemed "not statistically insignificant," Sam LeFevre, an epidemiologist with the Utah State Health Department who conducted the study for TriCounty, told an assembly of concerned Vernal citizens. When pressed on possible causes for the deaths, he suggested the health problems of mothers, citing smoking, diabetes and prenatal neglect among the Basin's residents. LeFevre made it clear he was sympathetic to the crowd's concerns. "I know what it's like to lose a pregnancy," he announced. "My wife's had eight, and only four live births."

Which raises a question you might ask in a state whose legislature is so rabid for oil and gas money that it set aside millions to sue the federal government for the right to drill near Moab and Desolation Canyon, some of the state's most sacrosanct places: How many dead infants does it take before you'll accept that there's a problem?

IN JANUARY 2001, DAYS AFTER taking office as the 43rd president of the United States, George W. Bush convened a closed-door task force to confront the country's addiction to foreign oil. Since the early 1970s, American motorists (and administrations) had ridden the loop-de-loop of peak demand: shortages, price spikes and the market manipulations of OPEC's billionaire princes. Two-thirds of the crude being refined here for gas arrived on overseas freighters, and the industry's bids for new offshore formations were blocked by an executive order from Bush's father. A bold plan was called for, including "environmentally sound production of energy for the future." Or so went the rhetoric in the announcement that heralded the group's formation. But Bush named Dick Cheney, the former CEO of Halliburton, to lead the effort—"Can't think of a better man to run it," he said—and any hope for a rational, climate-sparing program went up in a flare of hydrocarbons.

The vice president sat down with supplicants from the fossil-fuel sector and gold-star donors to his campaign. For months, he or his small staff met in secret with the likes of James Rouse, the then-vice president of Exxon Mobil Corp.; Enron's Kenneth Lay; Red Cavaney, the then-president of the American Petroleum Institute; and dozens of lobbyists and senior executives from the coal, mining, electric and nuclear sectors. What Cheney sent the president, four months later, was a policy essentially written by the barons themselves: a massive expansion of domestic drilling on federally owned lands; tens of billions of dollars in annual subsidies to Big Oil; and wholesale exemptions to oil-and-gas firms from environmental laws and oversight. In essence, Cheney's program turned the Department of the Interior into a boiler-room broker for Big Oil, and undercut the power of the Environmental Protection Agency.

Cheney's plan was such a transparent coup for Big Oil that it took four years, two elections and the Republican capture of both houses of Congress to make it to Bush's desk as legislation. Along the way, the bill gained a crucial addendum, known today as the "Halliburton loophole": a carte-blanche exemption from the Safe Drinking Water Act for an emergent technique called fracking. A form of extraction dating back to the Civil War, when miners used nitroglycerin to blow holes in oil-soaked caves (a subsequent version, in the 1960s, used subterranean nukes to fracture rock), fracking has since evolved into a brute[-force] but nimble method for blasting oil and gas deposits that couldn't be recovered by conventional derricks, at least not at a rate that made them profitable.

The process, perfected and marketed by Halliburton, shoots huge amounts of fluid at very high pressure down a mile or more of pipe to break the rock. That fluid, a trademarked secret called "slickwater" that has toxic solvents, is mixed with a million gallons of water, roughly a fifth of which come barreling back as wastewater. It's a desperately dirty job, marked by horrors of all kinds: blowouts of oil wells near houses and farms; badly managed gas wells flaring uncapped methane, one of the planet's most climate-wrecking pollutants.

Then there's pollution of the eight-wheeled sort: untold truck trips to service each fracking site. Per a recent report from Colorado, it takes 1,400 truck trips just to frack a well—and many hundreds more to haul the wastewater away and dump it into evaporation ponds. That's a lot of diesel soot per cubic foot of gas, all in the name of a "cleaner-burning" fuel, which is how the industry is labeling natural gas.

"Fracking moved the oil patch to people's backyards, significantly increasing the pollution they breathed in small towns," says Amy Mall, a senior policy analyst for the Natural Resources Defense Council. "Basically, it industrialized rural regions, and brought them many of the related health problems we were used to seeing in cities."

Mall, who had just moved to Colorado when the frack rigs arrived, en masse, in 2006, soon began hearing anguished reports from communities overwhelmed by dirt and fumes. At first, it was all direct-symptom stuff: bloody noses, coughs and rashes, migraine headaches and such. Eventually, though, worse news came from Garfield County, where gas drilling exploded, figuratively and otherwise, in the rural western slope of the state. Residents with cancers and neurological disorders; people passing out from exposure to chemical leaks; wells that blew out and would burn all day, while more than 100 million cubic feet of gas leaked into Divide Creek, which flows to the Colorado River. "It's the long-haul exposure that nails you—I watched people get progressively sicker," says filmmaker Debra Anderson, who shot a documentary in Garfield County that recorded the devastation of towns with names like Silt and Rifle; her film *Split Estate* won an Emmy and became essential viewing in Ohio, West Virginia and Pennsylvania, as the frackers moved east. "As soon as it aired, we were deluged with calls from communities," she says. "Same story, same symptoms, different town."

Workers found dead atop separator tanks from exposure to wastewater fumes. Cows birthing stillborn calves on ranches near well-pad clusters. Children with cancers—leukemia, lymphoma—in places with no known clusters. "For a while, all we had were anecdotal reports, which the industry bashed as 'bad science,'" says Miriam Rotkin-Ellman, a senior health scientist for the NRDC. "But in the past few years, there's been a torrent of studies finding worrisome air pollution stemming from oil and gas sites. The impacts of this pollution are *regional,* not just local, meaning it can make you really sick from miles away," and that the people most susceptible to its toxic effects are the ones at either end of the life spectrum: "fetuses and the elderly."

In some of these communities, leaders came forward to seek help and information from county officials. What came back, over and over, though, was ringing silence, as health-department representatives shrugged and hung up. "In Karnes County alone, we had two blowouts last week, one that covered everything in a coat of oil and methane, including people's homes and livestock," says Sharon Wilson, the state organizer in Texas for a national nonprofit called Earthworks, which helps small communities, like Karnes City in southeast Texas, fight back against billionaire drillers. In another disaster, a well leaked methane for days, but when Wilson called the Texas Commission on Environmental Quality, she was told that they wouldn't send an inspector because she didn't "live in the area." "I told him I was only calling because the residents there tried to, but couldn't get a response from him." (A spokeswoman for TCEQ told *Rolling Stone* that since "Ms. Wilson is not a resident [of Karnes County], she has limited ability to document nuisance conditions," adding that they'd previously conducted investigations in the area.) Karnes is a poor and sparsely inhabited place, but even inlying suburbs of Dallas—towns like Denton and Irving and Arlington—are quickly discovering how little recourse they have once the frackers come to town. The new governor, Gregg Abbot, signed a bill that quashed the rights of municipalities to ban fracking within their boundaries, after Denton's

townspeople voted thunderously to do so. That freed that town's drillers to go back about their business—digging wells across the street from preschools and hospitals, and snaking gas pipes around people's houses. "State governments have fallen down on protecting the public," says Sharon Buccino, a senior lawyer for the NRDC. "The upshot is that towns have lost control of their future. They no longer have a say in what happens there."

Except for the rare leaders who have said no to frackers—New York Gov. Andrew Cuomo, Vermont Gov. Peter Shumlin—Big Gas has been on a 10-year joyride unlike any in American annals. There are now more than 1 million active oil and gas wells in the country, and our oil companies posted profits of $600 billion during the Bush years. President Obama, who promised to cap and trade emissions while building out America's post-oil future, instead has presided over the breakneck expansion of fossil-fuel drilling. Under his watch, U.S. production has risen each year—up 35 percent for oil, 18 percent for gas—and enabled the country to barge past the Saudis as the world's lead producer of oil and gas. (He also broke his word to end tax cuts for oilmen; those subsidies are up nearly 50 percent since he took office.)

Whatever Cheney's doing now, he must look upon his handiwork and smile. OPEC has lost its whip hand over oil prices, SUVs are selling off the lot again, and Obama takes victory laps because we now produce more oil than we import. Glad tidings for all—except the people in more than 30 states who wake up to the thump of fracking rigs. To them, the message from Washington has been tacit but final: You folks are on your own out there.

IT WAS NEVER DONNA YOUNG'S plan to raise a racket about fracking. She grew up around coal mines and bears no brief against the grunts who work the rigs and the men who own them. "I've got one son commuting to North Dakota" to work a rig and "another who's done every job there is, from tearing down the rigs, putting them on flatbeds and driving 'em clear back from Kansas," she says. "I believe we can live with drilling—as long as the politicians make sure it's done responsibly."

But then, nothing in Young's life has gone to plan—not that she minds the left turns. The impulse to become a midwife at 39, then move back to Utah nine years later so she could help her ailing father run his ranch—it's all been improvised and guided by feel. She was born in Moab to a Mormon family, raised around horses and miners and men on old tractors who came home reeking of cow shit. Her father was a range rider for the Bureau of Land Management who bred and trained racehorses on the side. When he retired to Idaho, Young joined her folks there and opened a health-food store. A mother of two, she earned a degree in naturopathy, then found her true vocation, birthing babies. "I'd been working with lots of people, some cancer patients and chronically sick people, and here were these clients who had a clean slate—or would have, if their moms had ate healthy. I thought, 'Oh, this is what I'm put here to do. Bring 'em into the world with no drugs or toxins, then teach the moms to raise them that way.'"

She put together a method that was two parts nutrition to one part personal trainer. "From the git-go, my girls give up flour, milk, sugar, soda, caffeine and anything microwaved—and they know I'll urine-test them to check." They exercise for at least an hour each day and do floor work to bring the baby's head down to the proper position for birthing. "I don't have patients, I have athletes—and you should see the kids that come from them."

After 20 years and hundreds of births, Young has every reason to be proud. But in the fall of 2013, her client Caren Moon was pregnant with her third child and not doing well in the first trimester. She was cramping a lot and feeling weak; Young ordered bed rest and a natural progesterone cream to help with the bouts of mild bleeding. Moon was up on her feet again shortly, chasing after her toddlers, both birthed by Young. Then, the week before Thanksgiving, an early snowstorm led in a cold-air inversion. Moon felt ill again, took to bed, and lost the pregnancy while her house was filled with holiday guests. "It was right in that period of heavy ozone," Moon says. "I thought we'd taken all the precautions."

The Moons live on Bonanza Highway, a major conduit between Vernal and the oil fields due south. All day and into the night, massive trucks barreled by, farting CO_2 and diesel soot that hung over the yard like clouds of no-see-ums. Five minutes east, her friend Melissa Morgan was also struggling to keep her baby. "I got pregnant about the same time Caren did, and was sick with all the stuff that she had—bleeding, cramping, feeling bad when I went out," says Morgan. "There was a horrible, thick haze hanging around here for weeks. You could see it when you drove up the mountain and looked back at just this blanket of gray . . . yuck."

Morgan spent weeks on bed rest while women from her church cooked and looked after her kids. The baby, her fifth, somehow made it to term, but weighed nearly a third less than her previous four and was in and out of doctors' offices until she was eight months old. "It's a miracle she's here at all," says Morgan. "When I saw the placenta, it was small and deformed, like it had used up all its tissue to protect her."

I HEARD SOME VERSION OF THAT tale all over town. Avery Lawton, a radiant redhead, was pregnant that winter with her second child, but the fetus wasn't growing. It was so frail at 30 weeks that an obstetrician told her it could die during labor, and she should deliver at the hospital and not at home. Defying him, she went for a second, and third, opinion; her daughter, almost two now, was born with a rare and profound vision disorder, for which she wears Coke-bottle goggles.

In all the years Young has delivered babies, she says this was her first with a birth defect—and four more followed in 15 months. A girl with a shredded epiglottis, choking her when she tried to feed; a boy born tongue-tied and with a club-foot; a girl born tongue-tied and lip-tied as well, preventing her from latching onto her mother's breast. All required surgeries days after birth. Still others were born tiny or with mangled placentas—but at least they were alive and intact.

In May 2013, Young delivered a girl who was pink and fully formed; the child never took her first breath. She came out of her mother and collapsed in her arms; Young performed CPR, then raced her to the Ashley Regional Medical Center while the mother remained at home. She called 911 on the way, and a uniformed officer escorted her into the emergency room. Efforts to revive the child proved useless, however, and Young, who was heartsick and staggered by the loss, decided to join the mother at home. But a staffer, Young claims, wouldn't let her leave the building. She says he put Young and her daughter Holt, a 15-year-old who often accompanies her during the births, in a room. ("We did not prevent Ms. Young from leaving our hospital," a spokeswoman for ARMC said via e-mail. "Police onsite who were gathering information may have, but no one from our hospital was involved in that.") After an hour, Young says, she was let go at the insistence of the dead infant's father. She got home at 5 a.m. and wept and paced her bedroom well past sunup.

At 10 a.m. that day, a detective drove out and interrogated Young. She explained how a typical home birth happens and took him through the evening step by step. At the end, he concluded she'd done nothing wrong and declared the matter closed from his end. Devastated, she joined the bereaved parents at the graveside that week. There, at Rock Point Cemetery in Vernal, an acquaintance pulled her aside and whispered, "This isn't the only baby to die this year." She led Young to a pair of fresh-dug graves; two newborns had been laid to rest there since the first of the year. Young went home and combed through online obits: four other babies from Vernal or close by had died already that year. It was a shockingly big number for a small town.

Then she plotted the coordinates of the dead, and another bolt went through her. Three of the babies, including the one she'd just lost, were from moms who lived or worked near the intersection of 500 West and 500 South, a four-way stop sign that bottlenecks traffic and forces big-rig drivers to brake-start-brake, which drapes the block in shrouds of hydrocarbons. "Looking back, there were red flags," says Young. "Every time I'd visit for a checkup, I'd come back with a splitting headache and my eyes and nose running."

Five more babies would die that year, bringing the body count to at least 10 in Vernal; three more were lost in towns nearby. Young searched back to the start of the decade. In 2010, there were two, about average for a small town, then one in 2011 and four in 2012, including one whose mom worked at the senior facility on that smog-bound corner. And then the big jump in 2013, on the heels of a historic run in production that began a decade earlier. The Uintah Basin alone was home to more than 11,000 wells—that's an enormous concentration of soot and volatile organic compounds (VOCs) drifting into Vernal, then sitting there; in that inversion-filled winter, the VOC count was equivalent to 100 million cars' exhaust. Reached for comment about the region's pollution, Kathleen Sgamma, vice president of public affairs at the Western Energy Alliance, a trade association for the drillers, said, "We acknowledged that the emissions were our responsibility, [and] have worked with the state to reduce them." Asked about a link between those toxins and infant deaths, Sgamma said that "the epidemiologist showed there was not enough data to find the cause, and to make the jump you're making is not supported."

~~~~~~~~

By June 2013, Young had seen enough. Accompanied by Bo Hunter, her 23-year-old son, she paid a call on Joe Shaffer, the TriCounty health director. She didn't know these mothers or their medical histories—so had no idea what was killing their babies—and acknowledges that the cause may never be determined. But she was acutely fearful for her other clients' babies and wanted Shaffer's advice on keeping them safe. She and Hunter say she'd barely broached the subject of infant losses when Shaffer admitted he too had concerns about the air quality in Vernal and the effect it might have on area families, including his own. (Shaffer, who retired in the summer of 2014 and hasn't spoken publicly since he left, was reached by phone at his home but declined to comment.)

Frantic now, Young called a local advocacy group, who connected her with Dr. Brian Moench. Moench, an anesthesiologist in Salt Lake City who co-founded Utah Physicians for a Healthy Environment, is a cross between Bill Nye and Bill McKibben, a science-geek activist and erudite spokesman for a growing clean-air coalition. With

the roughly 350 doctors in Utah he's recruited to the cause, he and his colleagues gathered dozens of studies about pollution and its long- and short-term damage to the unborn. "What we know now," he says, "from several blue-ribbon studies, is that the chemicals Mom inhales in industrial zones are passed to her baby through the umbilical cord, exposing them to many complications. We also know these toxins like to live in fat cells—and the brain is the largest fat reservoir in a developing fetus." At Moench's urging, Young ordered her clients to stay in on bad air-quality days, and to equip their homes with high-end filters that trapped both soot and gases. Finally, in May 2014, LeFevre, the state health official, met with the TriCounty Health Department to present his proposed method to study the deaths. It would not, however, look at environmental factors; this was strictly about the statistical significance of the infant deaths. That might have been the end of it if not for Moench. He looped in a contact at *The Salt Lake Tribune,* who sent a writer down to cover the announcement. For the next two days, the *Tribune* ran page-one stories about Young's efforts to learn the truth about those deaths.

That's when some people in Vernal started to turn on Donna Young. The phone calls went on for months. Several times a week she'd pick up the phone to snarling curses and personal accusations that she was "trying to bust up the economy." Staffers at Ashley Regional Medical Center trashed her to clients, she says, and denounced her in online comments as a baby killer. (The ARMC spokeswoman denies this, adding that "if anyone employed by our facility said this, it was not on behalf of our hospital.") Ben Cluff, its CEO, threatened Young with legal action for "[communicating] inaccurate information regarding the number of infant deaths at our facility." When Young took Avery Lawton for an ultrasound there, both women recall that a staffer told Young that everyone was out to destroy her, "and it's political."

IT'S SAD BUT UNSURPRISING that Young would get push-back from a town that leans on oil as much as Vernal. Since crude was first pumped in this High Plains town shortly after World War II, its fortunes have tracked the price point of gas, riding its fluctuations up and down. Then along came the fracking boom, which extracted fossil fuels at rates undreamt of 10 years back, and Vernal was suddenly awash in real money. Virtually the whole west side is newly constructed, with big-box chain stores, midrange hotels and three brewpubs serving the roughnecks who rent the prefab townhomes. Oil money helped fund the new City Hall, as well as the 32-acre convention center, one of the largest such spreads in the West. There's the juice bar hawking T-shirts that say i heart drilling, the July 4th parade featuring girls on derrick floats and the yearly golf tourney called Petroleum Days.

So it's moot to expect much Green Party ferment from a place where boys quit high school in boom years to work the rigs at 16. But where are all the worried parents? "A huge number of my kids have breathing problems—it averages six or seven in every class," says Rodd Repsher, a health teacher at Uintah High who hails from Pennsylvania. "Come January, they're out sick for a week at a time. I never saw anything like it back home," says another teacher, who relocated from the Northeast.

I met the two teachers at a town-hall forum led by Moench and three of his colleagues from Salt Lake City. Though they'd papered the town with fliers about the forum—a primer on pollution and ways to protect your family from it—and invited the mayor, Sonya Nelson, and the three Uintah County commissioners, only 40 people showed up at the Vernal Junior High School auditorium. Several were Young's clients and their husbands and kids. Young was there, too, along with her daughter Holt. As a precaution, she'd brought a bodyguard.

In an easy-to-follow slide show about the air in the Basin and its calamitous level of pollution, Moench and his fellow doctors, two of them obstetricians, spent an hour and a half building a brick-by-brick indictment against the effect of those toxins on fetal neurons. "Think of them as bullets to developing brain cells," said Moench. "They either kill some of those cells, alter them or switch them off, blocking their connections to other cells." Citing a wave of new studies that link inhaled contaminants to everything from diabetes and obesity to ADD, he added that babies "are being born now pre-polluted. Lower IQs, less serotonin, less white-brain matter: We're literally changing who they are as human beings."

As Moench spoke, I heard grunts and impatient stirring from a plump man sitting behind me. He introduced himself to me as Bill Stringer, one of the three Uintah County commissioners. In the 10 years before he took office in 2014, Stringer ran the Vernal branch of the Bureau of Land Management. Under him, the outpost grew from a single-story affair to one of the busiest licensing offices in the country. Stringer and his staff approved nearly three times the number of permits per year as his predecessor did. They granted "every application put before them," says Stan Olmstead, an inspector for the BLM who quit in disgust under Stringer. "We couldn't do site inspections; anyone with integrity up and left." (Stringer tells *Rolling Stone* Olmstead has it wrong. He says his office performed the inspections required by law, and that Olmstead, an environmental inspector in the field, had no direct knowledge of permits granted or rejected by

the Vernal office. When pressed, however, Stringer could cite no example of a permit being denied to area drillers.) According to *The New York Times,* Stringer's office worked to quash a government study of the impact of drilling on Vernal's air. He fought, instead, for an industry-backed assay, which found "no unacceptable effects on human health." That was in 2009; months later, the Basin posted horrifically high readings of ozone and CO_2.

Asked what he'd thought of the doctors' presentation, Stringer dismissed it as "apples-to-oranges" science. "We have much more reliable research in town," he says, naming two environmental scientists at the local campus of Utah State University. When pressed for details about their findings, he turned to leave. Seth Lyman and Marc Mansfield, the scientists Stringer mentioned, agreed to talk about their ongoing study of air quality in the Basin. They concede that the region has an ozone problem, particularly near the gas fields in the low-elevation areas south of town, and agree that there have been established health risks associated with this contamination, such as low birth weights and an increase in asthma symptoms. However, they question its impact on stillbirths in Vernal, noting that in 2010 and 2011 there were many high-ozone days, without a significant jump in dead infants. "Ozone here is a long-term problem, and a lot of work has to be done," says Lyman. "But a lot of smart people here are working on solutions."

FORTIFIED BY those tidings, I drove out to inspect a massive evaporation pond 12 minutes west of town, accompanied by Moench and his associate Tim Wagner, the executive director of Utah Physicians for a Healthy Environment, who'd brought air-testing canisters to measure emissions. When water bolts back to the surface after fracking, it's laced with gases and salts and chemical waste, and it has to be trucked, in the hundreds of thousands of gallons, to disposal sites. There, the fluid sits and dissipates, the sediment sinking as the water thins—a process sometimes assisted by giant misters—until nothing is left but a bog-thick sludge, which is scooped up and trucked to landfills. If the pond dries slower than the company receives waste, they simply dig a new one beside it.

Then once *that* pond fills, they dig another, then another, and another, and so on. Seen from the air, these waste ponds resemble a kid's watercolor tray, though the water turns shades not seen in any paint tube: Imagine melanoma as a liquid. Generally, the ponds are set back hundreds of yards from the desert roads, but their stench wedges into your car's interior no matter how tightly it's sealed. On the several occasions I drove to Young's place, I was sickened by the fumes of a pit en route.

Across the country, there have been disastrous spills of wastewater into rivers and streams, and illegal dumping in an aquifer. Last winter, millions of gallons polluted Yellowstone River, dumped from leaky pipes in North Dakota. Untold gallons from evap ponds have fouled streams and springs in Pennsylvania; that state recorded 53 spills in 2014 alone, and fined one offender, Range Resources, more than $4 million. These aren't small run-offs that seep through soil and spit fire from some ranch hand's spigot. These are industrial crimes that can potentially taint the drinking water for millions of people downstream.

Stunningly, though, the feds gave the industry a pass when, this June, a five-year EPA study found no systemic contamination of drinking-water sources by slick-water fluids used in fracking. But in the next breath, it cited case after case where *precisely* that had happened, then said it couldn't gauge the frequency of such events because the industry hadn't furnished essential data: the quality of the water *before* they started fracking. The result: Activists and industry both claimed victory, and the EPA called for more study.

It was with a healthy dram of fear, then, that I took the red-dirt road to the La Point Recycle and Storage pond. We hiked up a half-mile path from our car, stepping over cow shit and shed deer antlers. We smelled the pond well before we reached the rise: a molten stench that stabbed the back of our noses and burned our eyes bloodshot on contact. A cyclone fence surrounded the pit, but the gate at the north end was unlocked and unmanned. (La Point declined to comment for this story.) Holding jackets over our mouths, we crept across the deck so that Moench could hook a particle counter to the fence. The air now was a shock wave of solvents that sent us scrambling for higher ground above the pit. Looking down from our perch on a sandy bluff, we saw the evap pond in its immensity: a green-black sheet so thick with sludge its surface didn't ripple in the breeze.

"The solvents you're smelling, they can travel for miles—and there were about 50 of these pits at the height of the boom," said Wagner.

I did a quick accounting in my head: a half-million gallons of waste from each of thousands of wells, either hauled to ponds like this or pumped to under-ground pits. Add to that more than 2,000 wells that have been granted but not drilled yet—nearly all of them approved by the Vernal field office. Where will all that poison go, and who will still be here to breathe and drink it?

A COUPLE OF WEEKS later, Young called me with horrible news: "Four of my five ladies lost their babies. Four miscarriages in just two weeks! How'm I s'posed to do this anymore?"

I asked her what she thought might have caused this spate of losses. "They all live in town and said their water tasted bad, so I went to their houses and took samples." She tested the water with a monitoring device used by drillers; most of the batches tested were positive for extreme toxicity from hydrogen sulfide, H_2S, one of the most deadly of the gases released by drilling. Exposure to it has killed a number of rig workers over the past few decades. In high enough concentration, just one breath is enough. In much smaller amounts, H_2S can cause miscarriages—and the amounts Young says she found were more than 7,000 times the EPA threshold for safety.

"I know I have to call somebody, but who?" Young says. "Who is there to trust in this town?"

PAUL SOLOTAROFF is a contributing editor to *Rolling Stone*. His latest book is *The Body Shop: Parties, Pills, and Pumping Iron—Or, My Life in the Age of Muscle* (Little, Brown, 2010).

EXPLORING THE ISSUE

Is the Fracking Industry Adequately Regulated for Public Safety?

Critical Thinking and Reflection

1. Do we need energy so badly that we should ignore risks to water supply and human health?
2. How will ample supplies of cheap natural gas affect development of renewable energy supplies such as wind and solar power?
3. Is it true that if greater oversight of an industry (such as the shale gas industry) costs a few more bucks, in the interest of public health, it's worth it?

Is There Common Ground?

Both the proponents and the opponents of unrestrained exploitation of shale gas and oil by fracking agree that it makes us independent of foreign suppliers, lowers the cost of energy, boosts the economy, and improves the lives of workers. They disagree sharply on whether the side effects of fracking, both on the environment and on human health, are worthy of concern. Even in Vernal, Utah, those who benefit from fracking do not want to hear about possible problems.

It is worth considering that the supply of shale gas and oil will not last forever. The public—and its health—will remain, as will concern over carbon emissions and the need for ample amounts of energy to run our civilization.

1. What must we do if we wish both to enjoy the benefits of fracking and to protect the public health?
2. Given that fracking has greatly increased the supply of gas and oil and reduced the price of energy, should we stop investing public money in developing alternative energy sources? If not, why not?

3. Is government regulation essential to protect public health? Visit the Public Health Service at http://www.usphs.gov/aboutus/mission.aspx to explore one agency's approach.

Additional Resources

Michelle Bamberger, Robert Oswald, and Sandra Steingraber, *The Real Cost of Fracking: How America's Shale Gas Boom Is Threatening Our Families, Pets, and Food* (Beacon Press, 2014).

Chris Faulkner, *The Fracking Truth: America's Energy Revolution: the Inside, Untold Story* (Platform Press, 2014).

Russell Gold, *The Boom: How Fracking Ignited the American Energy Revolution and Changed the World* (Simon & Schuster, 2014).

Andrew A. Rosenberg, Pallavi Phartiyal, Gretchen Goldman, and Lewis M. Branscomb, "Exposing Fracking to Sunlight," *Issues in Science and Technology* (Fall 2014).

Internet References . . .

Energy from Shale

http://www.energyfromshale.org/hydraulic-fracturing/shale-gas

Fracking at Pro Publica

http://www.propublica.org/series/fracking

National Oil Shale Association

http://oilshaleassoc.org/

Selected, Edited, and with Issue Framing Material by:
Thomas A. Easton, *Mount Ida College*

ISSUE

Is the Process for Decommissioning Nuclear Reactors Sound?

YES: **Marvin S. Fertel**, from "Testimony before the U.S. Senate Committee on Environment and Public Works, Hearing on 'Nuclear Reactor Decommissioning: Stakeholder Views,'" U.S. Senate (2014)

NO: **Geoffrey H. Fettus**, from "Testimony before the U.S. Senate Committee on Environment and Public Works, Hearing on "Nuclear Reactor Decommissioning: Stakeholder Views,'" U.S. Senate (2014)

Learning Outcomes
After reading this issue, you will be able to:
• Explain why nuclear power plants must be taken out of service and "decommissioned" after 40–60 years of service.   • Describe the decommissioning process.   • Explain how decommissioning is funded.   • Describe the obstacles that must be overcome before nuclear power can be more widely used.

ISSUE SUMMARY

YES: Marvin S. Fertel argues that existing procedures for decommissioning nuclear power plants are proven, appropriate, and adequate for protecting public health and the environment.

NO: Geoffrey H. Fettus argues that decommissioning nuclear power plants is a long-term process that requires long-term monitoring and regulation, currently not provided for in decommissioning procedures. In addition, current funding approaches leave a "plausible risk" that taxpayers could be left to bear large portions of the costs involved.

The technology of releasing for human use the energy that holds the atom together did not get off to an auspicious start. Its first significant application was military, and the deaths associated with the Hiroshima and Nagasaki explosions have ever since tainted the technology with negative associations. It did not help that for the ensuing half-century, millions of people grew up under the threat of nuclear Armageddon. But almost from the beginning, nuclear physicists and engineers wanted to put nuclear energy to more peaceful uses, largely in the form of power plants. Touted in the 1950s as an astoundingly cheap source of electricity, nuclear power soon proved to be more expensive than conventional sources, largely because safety concerns caused delays in the approval

process and prompted elaborate built-in precautions. Safety measures have worked well when needed—Three Mile Island, often cited as a horrific example of what can go wrong, released very little radioactive material to the environment. The Chernobyl disaster occurred when safety measures were ignored. In both cases, human error was more to blame than the technology itself. The related issue of nuclear waste has also raised fears and proved to add expense to the technology.

Nuclear waste is generated when uranium and plutonium atoms are split to make energy in nuclear power plants, when uranium and plutonium are purified to make nuclear weapons, and when radioactive isotopes useful in medical diagnosis and treatment are made and used. These wastes are radioactive, meaning that as they break down they emit radiation of several kinds. Those that break down fastest are most radioactive; they are said to have a short half-life (the time needed for half the material to break down). Uranium-238, the most common isotope of uranium, has a half-life of 4.5 billion years and is not very radioactive at all. Plutonium-239 (bomb material) has one of 24,000 years and is radioactive enough to be quite hazardous to humans.

According to the U.S. Department of Energy, high-level waste includes spent reactor fuel (52,000 tons) and waste from weapons production (91 million gallons). Transuranic waste includes clothing, equipment, and other materials contaminated with plutonium and other radioactive materials (11.3 million cubic feet, some of which has been buried in the Waste Isolation Pilot Plant salt cavern in New Mexico). Low- and mixed-level waste includes waste from hospitals and research labs, remnants of decommissioned nuclear plants, and air filters (472 million cubic feet). The high-level waste is the most hazardous and poses the most severe disposal problems. In general, experts say, such materials must be kept away from people and other living things, with no possibility of contaminating air, water (including ground water), or soil for ten half-lives. For a summary of the nuclear waste problem and the disposal controversy, see Michael E. Long, "Half Life: The Lethal Legacy of America's Nuclear Waste," *National Geographic* (July 2002).

The Nuclear Age began in the 1940s. As nuclear waste accumulated, there also developed a sense of urgency about finding a place to put it where it would not threaten humans or ecosystems for a quarter million years or more. In 1982, the Nuclear Waste Policy Act called for locating candidate disposal sites for high-level wastes and choosing one by 1998. Since no state chosen as a candidate site was happy, and many sites were for various reasons less than ideal, the schedule proved impossible to meet. In 1987, Congress attempted to settle the matter by designating Yucca Mountain, Nevada, as the one site to be intensively studied and developed. It was to be opened for use in 2010. However, it proved politically controversial, and in 2011 the Obama administration ended funding for work on the site.

Nuclear waste is scary stuff, and disposing of it safely is expensive. Building nuclear power plants is also expensive. It is thus no surprise that nuclear power has not been as widely adopted as its early proponents hoped. If we could somehow alleviate the factors of fear and expense, we might then be able to gain the benefits of the technology. Among those benefits are that nuclear power does not burn oil, coal, or any other fuel, does not emit air pollution and thus contribute to smog and haze, does not depend on foreign sources of fuel and thus weaken national independence, and does not emit carbon. Avoiding the use of fossil fuels is an important benefit; see Robert L. Hirsch, Roger H. Bezdek, and Robert M. Wendling, "Peaking Oil Production: Sooner Rather Than Later?" *Issues in Science and Technology* (Spring 2005). But avoiding carbon dioxide emissions may be more important at a time when society is concerned about global warming, and this is the benefit that prompted James Lovelock, creator of the Gaia Hypothesis and hero to environmentalists everywhere, to say, "If we had nuclear power we wouldn't be in this mess now, and whose fault was it? It was [the anti-nuclear environmentalists']." See his autobiography, *Homage to Gaia: The Life of an Independent Scientist* (Oxford University Press, 2001). Others have also seen this point, and the nuclear industry touts the idea of a "nuclear renaissance" (http://www.world-nuclear.org/info/current-and-future-generation /the-nuclear-renaissance/).

Iain Murray, "Nuclear Power? Yes, Please," *National Review* (June 16, 2008), argues that the world's experience with nuclear power has shown it to be both safe and reliable. Costs can be contained, and if one is concerned about global warming, the case for nuclear power is unassailable. Yet pursuing nuclear power for such reasons will not be easy. Stephen Ansolabehere et al., "The Future of Nuclear Power: An Interdisciplinary MIT Study" (MIT, 2003), note that in 2000 there were 352 nuclear power plants in the developed world as a whole, and a mere 15 in developing nations, and that even a very large increase in the number of nuclear power plants—to 1,000 to 1,500—will not stop all releases of carbon dioxide. In fact, if carbon emissions double by 2050 as expected, from 6,500 to 13,000 million metric tons per year, the 1,800 million metric tons not emitted because of nuclear power will seem relatively insignificant. Nevertheless, say John M. Deutch and Ernest J. Moniz, "The Nuclear Option," *Scientific American* (September 2006), such a cut in carbon emissions would be "significant."

Even though President Obama declared support for "a new generation of safe, clean nuclear power plants" in his January 27, 2010, State of the Union speech and the Department of Energy soon proposed massive loan guarantees for the industry (see Pam Russell and Pam Hunter, "Nuclear Resurgence Poised for Liftoff," *ENR: Engineering News-Record* [March 1, 2010]), the debate over the future of nuclear power is likely to remain vigorous for some time to come. One reason is that nuclear power poses its own problems. Alvin M. Weinberg, former director of the Oak Ridge National Laboratory, notes in "New Life for Nuclear Power," *Issues in Science and Technology* (Summer 2003), that to make a serious dent in carbon emissions would require perhaps four times as many reactors as suggested in the MIT study. The accompanying safety and security problems would be challenging. Are new reactor technologies needed? Richard K. Lester, "New Nukes," *Issues in Science and Technology* (Summer 2006), says that better centralized waste storage is what is needed, at least in the short term, despite the closing down of the Yucca Mountain site.

At the moment, high-level radioactive waste (spent fuel) generated by nuclear power plants is being stored on site, awaiting the permanent disposal sites long promised by government (and paid for by a tax on the industry). Currently under investigation is a disposal method known as "deep borehole disposal," which involves drilling deep holes in the Earth's crust, using technology very similar to that used for oil and gas drilling, and dropping canisters of waste into the depths; see Charles Q. Choi, "40 Percent of Hanford Nuclear Waste Would Fit in One 5-km Deep Borehole," *IEEE Spectrum* (April 20, 2015) (http://spectrum.ieee.org/energywise/energy/nuclear/40-percent-of-hanford-nuclear-waste-would-fit-in-one-5km-deep-borehole). Lacking this or some other method of safe disposal, we are left with constantly growing accumulations of nuclear waste. The problem will be made enormously greater if we increase the number of nuclear reactors as much as fighting global warming in that way would require.

And it's not just spent fuel. Every nuclear reactor has a limited life of 40–60 years before reactor components can no longer be trusted to operate as intended (for instance, prolonged exposure to radiation can weaken steel). After that it must be decommissioned. This means halting electricity generation, removing and disposing of high-level nuclear waste (such as spent fuel) and any portions of the plant that have become contaminated by radioactive material, disassembling the rest of the plant, and eventually returning the site to a condition that will permit its use for other purposes. The costs are covered by funds set aside over the years of the plant's operation by the operator. (See http://www.nrc.gov/reading-rm/doc-collections/fact-sheets/decommissioning.html.)

We have long known of the spent-fuel nuclear waste disposal problem. The wastes associated with decommissioning have come to greater attention in recent years largely because so many nuclear power plants have reached or will soon reach the end of their 40–60 year lifetime (despite extensions of their operating licenses). Concern over the environmental impacts of decommissioning has grown; see "The Decommissioning of Nuclear Reactors and Related Environmental Consequences," UNEP Global Environmental Alert Service (August 2011) (http://na.unep.net/geas/getuneppagewitharticleidscript.php?article_id=70). An answer may lie with deep borehole disposal, which may well be able to handle all the contaminated components of a nuclear power plant, though it would need more boreholes. But that disposal method is not yet available. For now, we are stuck with existing methods, and whether those methods are adequate for protecting public safety is being debated. In the YES selection, Marvin S. Fertel argues that existing procedures for decommissioning nuclear power plants are proven, appropriate, and adequate for protecting public health and the environment. In the NO selection, Geoffrey H. Fettus argues that decommissioning nuclear power plants is a long-term process that requires long-term monitoring and regulation, currently not provided for in decommissioning procedures. In addition, current funding approaches leave a "plausible risk" that taxpayers could be left to bear large portions of the costs involved.

YES

Marvin S. Fertel

Testimony before the U.S. Senate Committee on Environment and Public Works, Hearing on "Nuclear Reactor Decommissioning: Stakeholder Views"

. . .

NRC Decommissioning Process Is Sound, Promotes State Involvement

Decommissioning is the process by which nuclear power plants are retired from service. It primarily involves decontaminating the facility to reduce residual radioactivity, dismantling the structures, removing contaminated materials and components to appropriate disposal facilities, and releasing the property for other uses. Decommissioning begins after the power plant licensee permanently ceases operation of the facility.

Nuclear Regulatory Commission regulations and associated guidance detail the requirements and process for decommissioning to ensure the process is safe and secure and meets applicable requirements.

The closure of more than 70 test and power reactors since 1960—including 17 power reactor sites that are undergoing decommissioning—shows the strength and flexibility of the NRC's approach to the process. In addition to federal oversight, the NRC's decommissioning process facilitates participation by state and local authorities at several points along the way.

The decommissioning process as regulated and overseen today by the NRC is a safe and environmentally sound method for remediating nuclear power plant sites for other uses.

Overview of the Decommissioning Process

Decommissioning a nuclear plant involves removing the used nuclear fuel rods from the reactor, dismantling systems or components containing radioactive products (such as the reactor vessel) and dismantling contaminated materials from the facility. All radioactive materials generally have to be removed from the site and shipped to a waste-processing, storage or disposal facility.

Contaminated materials may be cleaned of contamination on site, cut off and removed (leaving most of the component intact in the facility) or removed and shipped to a waste-processing, storage or disposal facility. Each company decides how to decontaminate materials based on the amount of contamination, the ease with which it can be removed and the cost to remove the contamination.

It also includes removing used fuel from the reactor and, ultimately, placing the fuel into robust and shielded dry storage containers for storage at the site. The company that produced electricity at the facility remains accountable to the NRC until decommissioning has been completed and its federal license is terminated. However, without the demands of running a power plant and with the greatly decreased risk of a significant accident after fuel is removed from the reactor, staffing in areas such as operations, maintenance, engineering, emergency preparedness and security and other onsite resources can be substantially reduced at this time.

Ten reactors have completed decommissioning and 17 commercial reactor sites are in the decommissioning process, including the recently closed Kewaunee, Crystal River 3 and San Onofre 2 and 3 power stations. Of these 17, 10 are using or transitioning to the SAFSTOR option, four are using the DECON option, and two have not yet chosen a decommissioning option. Three Mile Island 2—site of the 1979 accident—is in post-defueling monitored storage.

Decommissioning Planning Occurs over Life of the Facility

Although the decommissioning process begins when the facility operator ceases electricity production, planning for decommissioning takes place over the life of the facility.

Testimony before the U.S. Senate Committee on Environment and Public Works, Hearing on "Nuclear Reactor Decommissioning: Stakeholder Views," U.S. Senate, May 2014.

For example, throughout the operation of a nuclear power plant, from licensing through decommissioning, the licensee must provide the NRC with the assurance that sufficient funding will be available for the decommissioning process. Further, five years before expiration of an operating license, the licensee must provide the NRC with both a preliminary decommissioning cost estimate and a program description for managing used reactor fuel at the site after electricity production is stopped.

Once the licensee permanently ceases operation, it must submit a certification of permanent cessation to the NRC within 30 days. At this point, the reactor can be defueled. In that process, trained reactor technicians remove nuclear fuel from the reactor vessel so that the facility is no longer able to produce electricity. Generally, this fuel is first placed in the used fuel storage pools on site to reduce its heat and radioactivity. After several years, this used fuel will be moved to container storage on site. After the reactor is defueled, the licensee must submit a certification of permanent fuel removal to the NRC. Once the NRC has docketed both certifications, the license no longer authorizes placement of fuel into the reactor.

Choosing a Decommissioning Option

Within two years of shutting down the facility, the company must submit a post-shutdown decommissioning activities report (PSDAR) to the NRC and the affected states. Licensees have three options for decommissioning the site: decontamination (DECON), safe storage (SAFSTOR) or entombment (ENTOMB). The report must include a description of the planned decommissioning option:

- *SAFSTOR (Safe Storage).* In the SAFSTOR process, a nuclear plant is kept intact and placed in protective storage for up to 60 years. During this time, the main components including the reactor vessel, fuel pools, turbine and other elements remain in place. All fuel is removed from the reactor vessel and placed in fuel pools on site. Maintenance and security operations continue and the operator maintains an NRC license. The NRC continues to inspect the site and maintains regulatory oversight of maintenance and security. This method of decommissioning uses time as a decontaminating agent by allowing the radioactive elements in components to decay to stable elements. For example, if a plant is allowed to sit idle for 30 years, the radioactivity from cobalt 60 will be reduced to 1/50th of its original level; after 50 years, the radioactivity will be about 1/1,000th of its original level. After radioactivity

has decayed to lower levels, the plant is dismantled in a process similar to the DECON option. Facilities using SAFSTOR include Dresden 1, Indian Point 1, LaCrosse and Peach Bottom 1.

- *DECON (Decontamination).* In DECON, all components and structures that have been exposed to radiation are cleaned or dismantled, packaged, and shipped to a low-level radioactive waste disposal site or stored temporarily on site. This work can take five years or more. Generally, used nuclear fuel rods in the fuel storage pool are placed in container storage at the site. When decontamination is completed, the used fuel will continue to be managed at that site under the NRC license and subject to agency oversight until it is shipped offsite for consolidated storage or permanent disposal.

- *ENTOMB.* This option involves encasing radioactive structures, systems and components in a long-lived substance, such as concrete. The encased plant would be appropriately maintained, and surveillance would continue until the radioactivity decays to a level that permits termination of the plant's license and unrestricted release of the property. To date, no company has requested this option.

The PSDAR report to the NRC also must include a schedule to complete decommissioning, a discussion of how site-specific decommissioning activities will adhere to previously issued environmental impact statements, and an estimate of expected costs. The NRC reviews the report and holds public meetings to discuss the company's decommissioning plans and the regulatory oversight process.

While this process is under way, the licensee may perform routine activities, such as maintenance and controlled disposal of small radioactive components. The licensee does not have access to the full amount of funds it has put aside for decommissioning until the site-specific cost estimate has been accepted by the NRC.

Ninety days after submittal of the PSDAR, the operator may begin major decommissioning activities. These include the permanent removal of large components—such as the reactor vessel, steam generators and other components that are comparably radioactive—as well as permanent changes to the containment structure. NRC's regulations dictate when and for what purposes decommissioning funds can be used.

The site must be decommissioned within 60 years of the plant ceasing operations. Licensees can choose to end SAFSTOR at any point during the 60-year period and transition to DECON. Alternatively, licensees can choose to begin DECON at the beginning of the 60-year period.

All sites must transition to DECON at some point so that decontamination can begin. Generally, sites must spend no longer than 50 years in SAFSTOR to allow 10 years for the DECON stage of decommissioning.

The SAFSTOR and DECON options allow licensees to choose the optimal time and method for decommissioning their particular site. The NRC maintains continual oversight of a nuclear energy facility until it is fully decommissioned.

What Happens During the DECON Phase?

In the DECON phase, the operator first decontaminates or removes contaminated equipment and materials. Used nuclear fuel rods and equipment account for more than 99 percent of the plant's radioactivity. Their removal lowers the level of radiation and thus reduces the potential exposure of workers during subsequent decommissioning operations.

Next, the plant operator addresses the small amount of radioactivity remaining in the facility, which must be reduced to harmless levels through a cleanup phase called decontamination. Workers remove surface radioactive material that has accumulated inside pipes and heat exchangers or on floors and walls that were not decontaminated during normal plant operations because of inaccessibility or operational considerations. Workers are aided in decontamination activities by the records that plants are required to keep during operation. Chemical, physical, electrical and ultrasonic processes are used to decontaminate equipment and surfaces. The removed radioactive material is packaged and transported or stored for disposal at a designated low-level radioactive waste management site.

Throughout the decommissioning process, regulatory oversight is provided by the NRC, Occupational Safety and Health Administration, Department of Transportation and U.S. Environmental Protection Agency. State agencies also have played a significant role in the decommissioning of certain sites.

Terminating the NRC License, Releasing the Site

As DECON nears completion, the licensee must submit a license termination plan to the NRC at least two years before the proposed license termination date. The NRC will make the plan available for public comment and schedule a public meeting near the facility to discuss its contents. Most plans envision releasing the site to the public for unrestricted use, meaning any residual radiation would be below NRC's limits of 25 millirem annual exposure.

The licensee's license termination plan must include:

- Site characterization.
- Identification of remaining site dismantlement activities.
- Plans for site remediation.
- Detailed plans for final radiation surveys for release of the site.
- A method for demonstrating compliance with the radiological criteria for license termination.
- Updated site-specific estimates of remaining decommissioning costs.
- A supplement to the environmental report that describes any new information or significant environmental changes associated with the owner's proposed termination activities.

The NRC uses its "Standard Review Plan for Evaluating Nuclear Power Reactor License Termination Plans" (NUREG-1700) to ensure the quality and uniformity of license termination plan reviews. The NRC also will notify and solicit comment from state and local governments in the vicinity of the site.

NRC approval of the license termination plan would be issued in the form of a license amendment, which triggers an opportunity to request an adjudicatory hearing. Once any concerns with the plan are addressed, the NRC will approve the plan.

Finally, if the NRC determines that all work has followed the approved license termination plan—and if the final radiation survey demonstrates that the facility and site are suitable for release—the agency will terminate the license.

Opportunities for State and Local Engagement

There are multiple opportunities for public involvement and state participation in the decommissioning process, including:

- The licensee's PSDAR report to the NRC is shared with affected states.
- After submittal of the PSDAR report, the NRC holds a public meeting in the vicinity of the facility. Affected states may also submit comments on the PSDAR.
- Licensees must notify the NRC in writing before performing any decommissioning activity inconsistent with PSDAR and copy any affected states.

- Another public meeting is scheduled when the NRC receives the license termination plan. At this time, affected states, local communities and tribes may submit comments on the plan.

In addition, when the NRC holds a meeting with the licensee, members of the public may observe the meeting (except when the discussion involves proprietary, sensitive, safeguards or classified information).

Funding Requirements for Decommissioning

The NRC's decommissioning funding regulations are the product of a decade-long deliberative rulemaking that resulted in a 1988 rule. Since then, the NRC has continued to develop its regulatory framework for decommissioning funding through subsequent rulemakings and the issuance and updating of guidance. As a result, reactor licensees must comply with the robust decommissioning funding framework to assure that adequate funds will be available when needed. Every company that operates a U.S. nuclear energy facility is required to accumulate the funds needed to decommission all portions of its facility that have been contaminated by radioactive material. Specifically, the NRC's regulatory structure provides decommissioning funding assurance through multiple layers of requirements and limitations, including:

- Establishing a minimum certification amount for decommissioning, which is based on technical studies and serves as a standard representing the minimum amount of decommissioning financial assurance that licensees must provide during plant life.
- Requiring adjustment of the minimum certification amount annually to account for inflation over time.
- Limiting funding assurance mechanisms to those considered appropriate by the NRC for assuring that decommissioning funding will be available when needed.
- Limiting the estimated future growth of decommissioning funds over time to a conservative rate of return over inflation, absent allowance of a different rate of return by a rate-setting authority.
- Requiring submittal of a report on the status of decommissioning funds compared to the minimum certification amount on a biennial basis.
- Providing for updating of funding levels, if necessary.

- Requiring a more precise preliminary decommissioning cost estimate at or about five years prior to plant shutdown.
- Requiring a site-specific cost estimate within two years of plant shutdown.
- Requiring an updated site-specific estimate of remaining decommissioning costs at least two years prior to license termination.
- Prohibiting use of decommissioning funds for any purpose other than decommissioning, both during and after plant shutdown.

The NRC's regulatory framework has been proven effective by the fact that every power reactor that has shut down, and has been or is currently being decommissioned, has been able to fund and safely perform required decommissioning activities. This has been the case even in situations in which the licensee did not operate the facility to the end of its license term.

Further, in 2013, the NRC found that commercial reactor operators have adequate funds for decommissioning their facilities and that the agency's formula for determining the minimum amount of required funding assurance yields sound results. NRC staff noted in a report, SECY-13-0105, that as of Dec. 31, 2012, licensees for 100 of the then-104 reactors provided the full amount of decommissioning funding assurance. The remaining four had "provided information to resolve their [decommissioning funding] shortfalls." Another agency paper, SECY-13-0066, said the NRC staff is satisfied with the adequacy of the funding formula used to determine the required level of decommissioning funding.

Conclusion

The nuclear energy industry has proven that it has the technology, resources and expertise to successfully decommission commercial nuclear reactors. The decommissioning process, as overseen by the NRC with input from state and local government, is a proven and appropriate method for ensuring that the decommissioning of nuclear energy facilities is accomplished in a safe, secure and environmentally friendly manner. The process also is flexible, allowing licensees to choose one of three decommissioning options—overseen by the regulator—over a 60-year period. The decommissioning process provides ample opportunities for interaction from states, local communities and tribes—allowing the public to attend meetings, provide comments and have access to plant-specific decommissioning information. Finally, the NRC ensures that adequate funds for decommissioning will be available when needed through a system that requires licensees to amass funds needed to decommission their facilities.

Decommissioning nuclear energy facilities—with independent oversight by the NRC and timely interaction with and state and local authorities—has been effectively managed and funded in a safe and environmentally sound manner under existing regulations.

MARVIN S. FERTEL is the president and chief executive officer of the Nuclear Energy Institute, an industry group that works on unified nuclear industry policy on regulatory, financial, technical, and legislative issues affecting the industry.

Geoffrey H. Fettus    **NO**

Testimony before the U.S. Senate Committee on Environment and Public Works, Hearing on "Nuclear Reactor Decommissioning: Stakeholder Views"

For the first three decades of the atomic age, federal and industry attention to nuclear matters was almost entirely directed at nuclear weapons production and commercial nuclear power generation. Disposal of spent nuclear fuel and the mounting radioactive by-products of nuclear weapons production, and the eventual decommissioning of commercial and defense facilities, were hardly on the radar screen.

It was not until the 1980s that serious interest, effort and money [were] devoted to the task of decommissioning and properly disposing of nuclear power plants themselves. The still ongoing spate of commercial nuclear reactor relicensing that commenced in the 1990s and has extended the life of most of our domestic reactor fleet from 40 to 60 years unfortunately relieved some of the pressure to address the adequacy of industry plans and federal requirements for decommissioning. Indeed, it was only a few years ago that NRDC believed this topic would most urgently need addressing prior to the year 2030, as that date marks the period when the U.S. reactors that have received twenty-year license extensions—probably most of them by then—will begin reaching the sixty-year mark and presumably be shut down and eventually decommissioned.

But with the gradual drumbeat of retiring reactors in the past few years for varied aging, safety and economic reasons prior to the end of their licenses—SONGS in Southern California, the Kewaunee reactor in Wisconsin, Vermont Yankee in Vermont, and Crystal River in Florida—it is now timely for this Committee to take up the matter of decommissioning and press ahead on addressing some significant safety and regulatory flaws. In any event, between 2014 and 2050, nearly all of the current fleet of U.S. power reactors is slated for retirement unless there is another round of twenty year extensions, a prospect NRDC views with considerable skepticism and concern for public safety.

Just a top line examination of decommissioning reveals a host of serious issues and challenges. And, unfortunately, we do not have consensus among the Nuclear Regulatory Commission (NRC), industry, states and the public on the relative adequacy and protectiveness of existing requirements. Only a few large commercial power reactors have been decommissioned over the past two decades in the United States, and therefore our experience with the process is comparatively limited.

Moreover, it is apparent certain challenges will present themselves in each instance of decommissioning. In 2012 the *New York Times* reported the owners of 20 of the nation's aging nuclear reactors, including some whose licenses expire soon, have not saved nearly enough money for prompt and proper dismantling. The *Times* noted that, if it turns out the reactors must close before expiration of their operating licenses, the owners intend to let them sit like radioactive industrial relics for 20 to 60 years or even longer while interest accrues in the reactors' decommissioning accounts. States such as New York and Vermont have at various times expressed concern over this prospect. Further, there can be disagreements over the extent of and safest treatment for the contamination left onsite; there are no firm plans for safely removing each plant; ultimate destinations and transport routes for dismantled debris [have] not been identified for each plant; and the health and environmental limits for release of sites and license termination, including the time window noted above, have been contested. And that's just a first cut at the list of decommissioning issues and challenges.

Nearly two decades ago, Dr. Martin J. Pasqualetti, a professor of geography in the School of Geographical Sciences and Urban Planning at Arizona State University in Tempe, Arizona, and one of the first analysts to grapple with decommissioning's challenges, wisely observed this about the NRC's basic definition of decommissioning—"to

Testimony before the U.S. Senate Committee on Environment and Public Works, Hearing on "Nuclear Reactor Decommissioning: Stakeholder Views," U.S. Senate, May 2014.

remove nuclear facilities safely from service and to reduce residual radioactivity to a level that permits release of the property for unrestricted use and termination of license—masks a huge and never-ending duty involving not only technical but social problems." We commend the Committee for holding this hearing and beginning a review of the adequacy of our federal decommissioning requirements. I will touch on what we feel are the two top line matters for this hearing—relaxing the rules on decommissioned reactors and the adequacy of funding.

The Decommissioning Process

In 2011 the NRC updated its planning process for decommissioning power reactors and nuclear material production and utilization facilities, and permits essentially three options. First, there is the decontamination (DECON) option, where all reactor and associated structures and components contaminated with radioactivity are either cleaned or removed and shipped to a licensed radioactive dump site, and the reactor location is returned to unrestricted use with all dispatch. The second option, we understand by far the most likely in most instances, is the safe storage (SAFSTOR) option, where the reactor is defueled but all associated parts of the facility are left in place for up to six decades for later decontamination. Finally, there is still an entombment (ENTOMB) option, where the facility is basically covered over and left forever, a final option we do not expect to see domestically. An extreme and challenging example of a version of the entombing option, at the contaminated Chernobyl Reactor in Ukraine, was recently well described in mixed media presentation by the *New York Times*. The ENTOMB option was available in the United States for some of the early, small reactors that did not operate at high power levels or for extended periods so as to develop much of a radioactive footprint.

The decommissioning process includes a Post Shutdown Decommissioning Activities Report (PSDAR), a listing of the tasks, schedule and estimated budget. The Final Status Survey Report (FSSR) is an inventory of the radioactively decontaminated pieces of the plant that require special handling. And the License Termination Plan (LTP) is the final document, and it presents the planned final state of the site and potential future uses (essentially, the extent of the cleanup and the manner in which any contamination will be left on site). The PSDAR, FSSR, and LTP are submitted by owners to the NRC and become publicly available. Detailed treatments of this process are found in the NRC's Decommissioning Planning, Final Rule.

The process described above presents a host of sometimes conflicting policy goals. Nearly twenty years ago Dr. Pasqualetti identified eight fundamental decommissioning policy considerations that could, in some instances, work in opposition to one another:

- Minimizing radiological hazards for workers (health and safety);
- Minimizing radiological hazards for the general public (health, safety and long term environmental impacts);
- Leaving a cleared and decontaminated site for future non-nuclear purposes (land use, health and safety);
- Ensuring that decommissioning costs are as low as reasonable and practicable (economic);
- Maximizing economic benefits of operations, including those to stockholders, by operating power plants as long as possible (economics);
- Securing sufficient decommissioning funding (economics, ethics); and
- Meeting legal requirements (law).

With the operating reactor experience of the last two decades, and especially the last two years, NRDC also suggests a clarification as to how one might consider maximizing economic benefit in light of the safety considerations attendant to reactor aging. Keeping an aging reactor operating for financial reasons not only raises safety concern[s] but the financial consideration of appropriate investment to ensure safe operations. In any event, we find those eight considerations a useful frame for considering current deficiencies in decommissioning power reactors.

Consideration # 1—The Rules No Longer Apply

Our primary concern with the decommissioning process is that both regulatory requirements and the agency's oversight regime are significantly scaled back when nuclear power reactors cease operation. Such waivers have been granted and are being sought even in the event that sizable quantities of spent nuclear fuel are left in pools for potentially decades.

The nuclear fuel cycle has a number of significant environmental and public safety impacts (not covered in this hearing). But chief among nuclear power's environmental impacts, in addition to severe nuclear accidents, is nuclear waste—specifically, the production of spent nuclear fuel. The nuclear fuel cycle produces a deadly and long-lasting byproduct: highly radioactive spent nuclear fuel. At high doses, radiation exposure will cause death. At lower doses, radiation still has serious health effects, including increased cancer risks and serious birth defects such as mental retardation, eye malformations, and small brain or head size.

And regarding these serious health consequences from exposure, spent nuclear fuel remains dangerous for millennia. The United States Court of Appeals for the D.C. Circuit described it thus: "radioactive waste and its harmful consequences persist for time spans seemingly beyond human comprehension. For example, iodine-129, one of the radionuclides expected to be buried at Yucca Mountain, has a half-life of seventeen million years." *Nuclear Energy Institute, Inc. et al., v. Environmental Protection Agency*, 373 F.3d 1251, 1258 (D.C.Cir. 2004), *citing*, Comm. on Technical Bases for Yucca Mountain Standards, Nat'l Research Council, *Technical Bases for Yucca Mountain Standards,* 18–19 (1995).

As NRDC has noted before this Committee and your colleagues in the Energy & Natural Resources Committee, there is no evidence that continued reliance on densely packed wet storage should be accepted as adequate in light of the health, safety and security risks that spent fuel pools pose. This is true regardless of the local seismicity, population density, or other environmental factors that might create concern with the current storage configuration. NRDC and our colleagues at the Union of Concerned Scientists and many others noted President Obama's Blue Ribbon Commission for America's Nuclear Future was negligent in not recommending Congress statutorily direct movement of spent fuel from wet pools to hardened dry casks as soon as practical, *i.e.*, as soon as spent fuel has cooled sufficiently to permit safe dry cask storage, generally about five to seven years following discharge from the reactor. We again urge Congress to act on this issue in comprehensive legislation or even in a stand-alone bill.

Illustrating the importance of this point, in a May 2, 2014 letter sent to NRC Chairman Allison Macfarlane, Senator Edward J. Markey (D-Mass.), this Committtee's Chairman Barbara Boxer (D-Calif.), and Senators Bernard Sanders (I-Vt.), Patrick Leahy (D-Vt.) and Kirsten Gillibrand (D-N.Y.) called on the NRC to halt the policy of issuing exemptions to emergency response regulations to decommissioning nuclear reactors which house decades-worth of spent nuclear fuel.

The Senators noted the exemptions for compliance with the emergency response regulations—such as those that require evacuation zones and siren systems to warn of problems—have been granted to all of the ten reactor licensees that have requested them in the past. Moreover, the Senators pointed out licensees of reactors that are or will soon begin the decommissioning process (including San Onofre in California and Vermont Yankee) have

already submitted a wide range of exemption requests from emergency response, security and other regulations to the NRC. Indeed, now Dominion's Kewaunee plant seeks the same set of waivers and this week a spokesman for the plant stated "[w]hat we are looking for is a waiver for requirements that really no longer are applicable."

While industry suggests the requirements are no longer applicable, at the same time under its ongoing review of the long-term environmental and safety impacts of spent nuclear fuel (the Waste Confidence Generic EIS currently under review), NRC suggests spent nuclear fuel can be stored safely for at least 60 years beyond the licensed life of a nuclear power plant, but bases its determination in significant measure on the assertion that emergency preparedness and security regulations remain in place during decommissioning.

Such is clearly not the case. Waivers from a protective regulatory regime, including relaxing the fifty mile Emergency Planning Zone, are inappropriate while spent nuclear fuel remains stored in densely packed pools. We concur with the Senators' and their letter cited above that accidents or attacks on spent fuel pools could trigger a spent fuel fire or explosive dispersal of radionuclides that would put neighboring populations at risk of experiencing harmful levels of exposure to radioactivity and potentially widespread economic damage from land contamination.

With those observations in mind, NRDC urges the Committee to write legislative language for a pilot project to address the total stranded spent fuel at closed reactor sites (currently 13 sites and soon to be more), where spent nuclear fuel would be stored in dry casks within one or more hardened buildings similar to the Ahaus facility in Germany. Potential volunteer sites that have in the past demonstrated "consent" to host spent nuclear fuel are operating commercial reactors. The utility of using existing commercial operating reactor sites rather than burdening new areas with spent nuclear fuel should be apparent: existing sites require far less new infrastructure, already have the capacity for fuel management and transportation and have the consent necessary for hosting nuclear facilities. And by keeping consolidated, interim-stored spent nuclear fuel under the guardianship of the nuclear industry that produced the waste in the first instance, Congress ensures careful progress continues with the repository program because all parties will know that it is necessary.

And while a diminished safety regime for spent fuel pools is a primary concern, there are other problematic manifestations of a relaxed regulatory scheme. For example, aging management measures adopted to support the 20 year renewal of reactor operating licenses apply during the period of extended reactor operation—but not during the potentially six decades of spent fuel pool storage that can ensue under the SAFSTOR option. Our colleague David Lochbaum at the Union of Concerned Scientists detailed many and more of these concerns late last year in the comments to the NRC on the Draft Waste Confidence Generic EIS.

Another example of a relaxed regulatory scheme concerns NRC's reliance on a volunteer, industry-run groundwater monitoring program. In the agency's ongoing "Waste Confidence" proceeding, NRC states "[l]icensees that have implemented a groundwater monitoring program consistent with the Nuclear Energy Institute Groundwater Protection Initiative are considered to have an adequate program for the purposes of the Decommissioning Planning Rule. Therefore, based on results from a one-time, voluntary, industry created initiative at currently operating plants, NRC apparently considers the voluntary groundwater monitoring program to be adequate over the entire 60-year short-term storage period at shutdown plants. NRC should rethink this policy and alter it with all dispatch. The industry's Groundwater Protection Initiative is a voluntary measure that is currently not being routinely inspected by the NRC at either operating or permanently shut down nuclear power plants. As such, crediting a non-mandatory, non-inspected program with detecting and correcting leaks during the 60-year storage period is simply not credible, and not supported by the industry's failure to prevent leaks of tritium to groundwater from its existing reactors.

Consideration #2 Is the Funding Adequate?

Four nuclear power reactors (Crystal River 3 in Florida, Kewaunee in Wisconsin, and San Onofre Units 2 and 3 in California) permanently shut down over the last two years and the owner of another reactor (Vermont Yankee in Vermont) announced it would permanently shut down in the fourth quarter of this year.

Decommissioning, a painstaking and complicated process that by any measure can take decades, carries with it cost projections from $400 million to $1 billion per reactor. The *Times* reported last year that Entergy Corporation is at least $90 million short of a projected $560 million cost of dismantling Vermont Yankee. But in a positive development, late last year Vermont's Governor Shumlin and Entergy, Vermont Yankee's operator, announced an agreement that, among other matters, sets a path for decommissioning Vermont Yankee as promptly as funds in the Nuclear Decommissioning Trust allow, rather than delaying decommissioning under SAFSTOR guidelines. Entergy VY also committed in the agreement to prepare a site assessment and cost study by the end of this year. . . .

In any event, NRDC has concerns that current decommissioning funding mechanisms will prove insufficient to fully decommission the power reactors due to come off line in the next several years. The United States Government Accountability Office (GAO) issued a report where its top line findings were:

- "NRC's formula may not reliably estimate adequate decommissioning costs. According to NRC, the formula was intended to estimate the "bulk" of the decommissioning funds needed, but the term "bulk" is undefined, making it unclear how NRC can determine if the formula is performing as intended. In addition, GAO compared NRC's formula estimates for 12 reactors with these reactors' more detailed site-specific cost estimates calculated for the same period. GAO found that for 5 of the 12 reactors, the NRC formula captured 57 to 76 percent of the costs reflected in each reactor's site-specific estimate; the other 7 captured 84 to 103 percent.

- The results of more than one-third of the fund balance reviews that NRC staff performed from April 2008 to October 2010 to verify that the amounts in the 2-year reports match year-end bank statements were not always clearly or consistently documented. As an example of inconsistent results, some reviewers provided general information, such as "no problem," while others provided more detail about both the balance in the year-end bank statement and the 2-year report. As of October 2011, NRC did not have written procedures describing the steps that staff should take for conducting these reviews, which likely contributed to NRC staff not always documenting the results of the reviews clearly or consistently.

- NRC has not reviewed licensees' compliance with the investment standards the agency has set for decommissioning trust funds. These standards specify, among other things, that fund investments may not be made in any reactor licensee or in a mutual fund in which 50 percent or more of the fund is invested in the nuclear power industry. As a result, NRC cannot confirm that licensees are avoiding conditions described in the standards that may impair fund growth. Without awareness of the nature of licensees' investments, NRC cannot determine whether it needs to take action to enforce the standards."

With our limited national experience in decommissioning power reactors, we view this as an evolving concern. We also note it is unclear to us whether NRC's Decommissioning Planning Rule has directly addressed persistent shortfalls in the decommissioning trust funds, especially in instances where there is subsurface and groundwater site contamination. When coupled with the notable and heretofore unacknowledged costs of remediating subsurface and groundwater contamination at numerous sites, it seems apparent the decommissioning trust funds could in some instances be exhausted long before full decommissioning has been accomplished. Adding to this uncertainty [about] funds for decommissioning is the fact that over 40 reactors operate in merchant power markets, where long-term financial assurances are not in place as had been the case for U.S. reactors already entering into decommissioning.

Put bluntly, a plausible risk exists that States and their taxpayers could be placed in a position where they may foot significant portions of the bill to decommission, decontaminate and restore the reactor sites and degraded resources, and accept blighted and unproductive areas in their midst for generations that have been granted waivers for essential security and environmental safeguards. Rather than leave this burden to the States, we urge the Commission to revise the Decommissioning Final Rule in accordance with the State of New York's 2010 comments, wherein NRC was urged to increase the strength and timeliness of the financial assurance monitoring regime so that decommissioning funds will not operate at shortfalls. Moreover, the Commission should adopt New York's wise suggestion that the formula by which decommissioning costs are estimated for each successive reactor should take into account "site-specific" factors such as the presence of contamination so that the ultimate costs will not be borne by States and their citizens.

GEOFFREY H. FETTUS is a senior attorney with the Natural Resources Defense Council, a national, nonprofit organization dedicated to protecting public health and the environment.

EXPLORING THE ISSUE

Is the Process for Decommissioning Nuclear Reactors Sound?

Critical Thinking and Reflection

1. Which is more dangerous? Nuclear power or global warming? (See *The Anatomy of a Silent Crisis*, Global Humanitarian Forum Geneva, 2009; http://www.ghf-ge.org/human-impact-report.pdf.)
2. Explain how nuclear power avoids the release of greenhouse gases.
3. Explain why it will be difficult to shift from fossil fuels to nuclear power rapidly.
4. How are nuclear wastes handled today?

Is There Common Ground?

Whether one approves of nuclear power or not, the fact is that we have over the last several decades built a fair number of nuclear power plants. Another fact is that some have already reached and many more are nearing the ends of their useful lives. They have to be decommissioned, and those parts that endanger public health and the environment by reason of their radioactivity must be handled safely. They can't just be bulldozed into the nearest river!

There are procedures—and options—for safe decommissioning. Are they adequate? And is the funding required to implement them adequate? These are the important questions at the moment.

1. Utilities set money aside for future decommissioning costs. If the total amount available when it is time for decommissioning is not enough, how can utilities gain more funds without raising electricity rates or passing the problem to taxpayers?
2. Decommissioning can take decades. Is there anything to be gained by taking even longer?
3. Is there anything to be gained by rushing the process?

Additional Resources

Decommissioning Fukushima (video) (http://www.amazon .com/The-Battle-to-Contain-Radioactivity/dp/B017OP84F6 /ref=sr_1_9?ie=UTF8&qid=1451331565&sr=8-9&keywords =nuclear+power+decommissioning).

M. Laraia, ed., *Nuclear Decommissioning: Planning, Execution and International Experience* (Woodhead, 2012).

Barry Pemberton, *Corporate Governance and the Nuclear Industry* (Routledge, 2015).

Internet References . . .

Greenpeace: Decommissioning Risks

http://www.greenpeace.org/usa/wp-content/ uploads/2015/07/Decommissioning-Risks.pdf?a1481f

Jon Samseth et al., *Closing and Decommissioning Nuclear Power Reactors*, UNEP Yearbook 2012.

http://www.unep.org/yearbook/2012/pdfs/UYB_2012 _CH_3.pdf

World Nuclear Association: Decommissioning Nuclear Facilities

http://www.world-nuclear.org/information-library /nuclear-fuel-cycle/nuclear-wastes/decommissioning -nuclear-facilities.aspx

Selected, Edited, and with Issue Framing Material by:
Thomas A. Easton, *Mount Ida College*

ISSUE

Should Genetically Modified Foods Be Labeled?

YES: Todd Daloz, from "Testimony before the U.S. House of Representatives Committee on Energy and Commerce, Subcommittee on Health, Hearing on 'A National Framework for the Review and Labeling of Biotechnology in Food,'" U.S. House of Representatives (2015)

NO: L. Val Giddings, from "Testimony before the U.S. House of Representatives Committee on Energy and Commerce, Subcommittee on Health, Hearing on 'A National Framework for the Review and Labeling of Biotechnology in Food,'" U.S. House of Representatives (2015)

Learning Outcomes

After reading this issue, you will be able to:

- Describe the potential benefits of applying genetic engineering to food crops.
- Describe the potential adverse effects of genetically modified foods.
- Explain why some people want genetically modified foods to be labeled as such.

ISSUE SUMMARY

YES: Todd Daloz argues that Vermont's legislation requiring labeling of genetically modified (GM) crops is amply justified by the public's need for factual information about the food they eat, and that federal preemption of state labeling laws, without providing a suitable substitute, is unreasonable.

NO: L. Val Giddings argues that there is no scientific doubt that GM crops are safe to eat, the federal government already has sufficient authority to regulate the sale and labeling of GM foods, and the push for labeling laws is a thinly disguised effort to ban GM foods in favor of less safe and more expensive alternatives, such as organic foods.

In the early 1970s, scientists first discovered that it was technically possible to move genes—biological material that determines a living organism's physical makeup—from one organism to another and thus (in principle) to give bacteria, plants, and animals new features and to correct genetic defects of the sort that cause many diseases, such as cystic fibrosis. Most researchers in molecular genetics were excited by the potentialities that suddenly seemed within their grasp. However, a few researchers—as well as many people outside the field—were disturbed by the idea; they thought that genetic mix-and-match games might spawn new diseases, weeds, and pests. Some people even argued that genetic engineering should be banned at the outset, before unforeseeable horrors were unleashed.

By 1989 the technology had developed tremendously: researchers could obtain patents for mice with artificially added genes ("transgenic" mice); firefly genes had been added to tobacco plants to make them glow (faintly) in the dark; and growth hormone produced by genetically engineered bacteria was being used to grow low-fat pork and increase milk production by cows. Critics argued that genetic engineering was unnatural and violated the rights of both plants and animals to their "species integrity"; that expensive, high-tech, tinkered animals gave the competitive advantage to big agricultural corporations and drove small farmers out of business; and that putting human genes into animals, plants, or bacteria was downright offensive. See Betsy Hanson and Dorothy Nelkin, "Public Responses to Genetic Engineering," *Society* (November/December 1989). Most of the initial attention aimed at genetic engineering focused first on its use to modify bacteria and other organisms to generate drugs such as insulin needed to fight human disease and second on its potential to modify human genes and attack hereditary diseases at their roots. See Eric B. Kmiec, "Gene Therapy," *American Scientist* (May–June 1999).

Pharmaceutical and agricultural applications of genetic engineering have been very successful, the latter largely because, as Robert Shapiro, CEO of Monsanto Corporation, said in 1998, it "represents a potentially sustainable solution to the issue of feeding people." In "Biotech's Plans to Sustain Agriculture," *Scientific American* (October 2009) interviewed several industry representatives, who see biotechnology—including genetic engineering—as essential to meeting future demand in a sustainable way. Between 1996 and 2014, the area planted with genetically engineered crops jumped from 1.7 million hectares to 181 million hectares, according to the International Service for the Acquisition of Agri-Biotech Applications, "ISAAA Brief 49-2014: Executive Summary: Global Status of Commercialized Biotech/GM Crops: 2014" (www.isaaa.org/resources/publications/briefs/49/default.asp). Many people are not reassured by such data. They see potential problems in nutrition, toxicity, allergies, and ecology. Brian Halweil, "The Emperor's New Crops," *World Watch* (July/August 1999), notes that although genetically engineered crops may have potential benefits, they may also have disastrous effects on natural ecosystems and—because high-tech agriculture is controlled by major corporations such as Monsanto—on less developed societies. He argues that "ecological" agriculture (using, e.g., organic fertilizers and natural enemies instead of pesticides) offers much more hope for the future. Similar arguments are made by those who demonstrate against genetically modified (GM) foods—sometimes by destroying research labs and test plots of trees, strawberries, and corn—and lobby for stringent labeling requirements or for outright bans on planting and importing these crops. See Claire Hope Cummings, "Risking Corn, Risking Culture," *World Watch* (November/December 2002). Many protestors argue against GM technology in terms of the precautionary principle; see "GMOs and Precaution in EU countries," *Outlook on Science Policy* (September 2005). Georgina Gustin, "Seeds of Change?" *Columbia Journalism Review* (January/February 2010), reviews press coverage of GM crops and notes that despite the numerous objections by environmental groups there are no data that indicate problems. Alessandro Nicolia, Alberto Manzo, Fabio Veronesi, and Danielle Rosellini, "An Overview of the Last 10 Years of Genetically Engineered Crop Safety Research," *Critical Reviews in Biotechnology* (online September 13, 2013), find no "significant hazards directly connected with the use of GM crops." Steven Novella, "No Health Risks from GMOs," *Skeptical Inquirer*

(July/August 2014), notes that "Not only is there extensive independent research and evidence for the safety of GMOs generally and of specific GMOs, but this evidence is greater than for any other food crop. [But f]or anti-GMO activists, apparently, no amount of evidence is sufficient." He concludes that GMO "fearmongering is largely based on misinformation, a misunderstanding of evolution and our place in the natural world, and vague fears of contamination. In reality, GMO safety testing is extensive and has not uncovered any safety concerns for current GMOs. There are other issues with GMOs that are worth discussing, but fears of adverse health effects are not legitimate." The U.S. Food and Drug Administration (FDA) concurs. Michael Landa, director of the FDA's Center for Food Safety and Applied Nutrition, told a House Energy and Commerce subcommittee hearing that GMOs are as safe as their conventional counterparts.

Many researchers see great hope in GM foods. In July 2000, the Royal Society of London, the U.S. National Academy of Sciences, the Indian Academy of Sciences, the Mexican Academy of Sciences, and the Third World Academy of Sciences issued a joint report titled "Transgenic Plants and World Agriculture" (http://www.nap.edu/catalog.php?record_id=9889). This report stresses that during the twenty-first century, both the population and the need for food are going to increase dramatically, especially in developing nations. According to the report, "Foods can be produced through the use of GM technology that are more nutritious, stable in storage, and in principle, health promoting. . . . New public sector efforts are required for creating transgenic crops that benefit poor farmers in developing nations and improve their access to food. . . . Concerted, organized efforts must be undertaken to investigate the potential environmental effects, both positive and negative, of GM technologies [compared to those] from conventional agricultural technologies. . . . Public Health regulatory systems need to be put in place in every country to identify and monitor any potential adverse human health effects." The United States National Research Council reports that the economic and environmental benefits of GM crops are clear; see Erik Stokstad, "Biotech Crops Good for Farmers and Environment, Academy Finds," *Science* (April 16, 2010), and Committee on the Impact of Biotechnology on Farm-Level Economics and Sustainability, *The Impact of Genetically Engineered Crops on Farm Sustainability in the United States* (National Academies Press, 2010) (http://www.nap.edu/catalog.php?record_id=12804). See also David Rotman, "Why We Will Need Genetically Modified Foods," *Technology Review* (December 17, 2013) (http://www.technologyreview.com/featuredstory/522596/why-we-will-need-genetically-modified-foods/).

The worries surrounding GM foods and the scientific evidence to support them are summarized by Kathryn Brown, in "Seeds of Concern," and Karen Hopkin, in "The Risks on the Table," both in *Scientific American* (April 2001). Jeffrey M. Smith, *Seeds of Deception: Exposing Industry and Government Lies about the Safety of the Genetically Engineered Foods You're Eating* (Chelsea Green, 2003), argues that the dangers of GM foods have been deliberately concealed. Henry I. Miller and Gregory Conko, in *The Frankenfood Myth: How Protest and Politics Threaten the Biotech Revolution* (Praeger, 2004), address at length the fallacy that GM foods are especially risky. Rod Addy and Elaine Watson, "Forget 'Frankenfood,' GM Crops Can Feed the World, Says FDF," *Food Manufacture* (December 2007), note that "EU trade commissioner Peter Mandelson said that the inability of European politicians to engage in a rational debate about GM was a source of constant frustration. They were also creating barriers to trade by banning GM crops that had repeatedly been pronounced safe by the European Food Safety Authority (EFSA)." Early in 2010, the EFSA reinforced this point; see "EFSA Rejects Study Claiming Toxicity of GMOs," *European Environment & Packaging Law Weekly* (February 24, 2010). According to Gemma Masip et al., "Paradoxical EU Agricultural Policies on Genetically Engineered Crops," *Trends in Plant Science* (available online April 25, 2013), EU attitudes toward GM crops obstruct policy goals; GM crops are essential to EU agricultural competitiveness. By 2014, a bill was before the European Parliament that would permit member states to ban GM crops even after regulators have judged them safe; see Tania Ravesandratana, "E.U. to Let Wary Members Ban Genetically Modified Crops," *Science* (December 12, 2014). The bill passed, much to the dismay of GM proponents, and many European countries are restricting the use of GMO crops.

Some people clearly think the safety of GMOs has not been tested. Others disagree. Jon Entine finds "2000+ Reasons Why GMOs Are Safe to Eat and Environmentally Sustainable," *Forbes* (October 14, 2013) (http://www.forbes.com/sites/jonentine/2013/10/14/2000-reasons-why-gmos-are-safe-to-eat-and-environmentally-sustainable/). **Keith Kloor, "GMO Opponents Are the Climate Skeptics of the Left,"** *Slate* **(September 26, 2012), charges that anti-GMO activists manipulate studies and the media in order to frighten the public; see also William Saletan, "Unhealthy Fixation,"** *Slate* **(July 15, 2015) (http://www.slate.com/articles/health_and_science/science/2015/07/are_gmos_safe_yes_the_case_against_them_is_full_of_fraud_lies_and_errors.html).** David Rotman, "Why We Will Need Genetically Modified Foods," *Technology Review* (December 17, 2013) (http://www.technologyreview.com/featuredstory/522596/why-we-will-need-genetically-modified-foods/), argues

that genetic engineering is an essential tool if we hope to feed nine billion people by 2050 (and more later) in the face of droughts, floods, heat waves, and plant diseases. However, Cary Funk and Lee Rainie, "Scientific Consensus on GMO Safety Stronger Than for Global Warming," Pew Research Center (January 29, 2015) (http://www.pewinternet.org/2015/01/29/public-and-scientists-views-on-science-and-society/), report that the general public is far more skeptical about the safety and benefits of GM crops than are scientists.

And there's the controversy over labeling. Many people argue that GM foods—even if they are judged to be safe—should be labeled so that people can choose to avoid them. See Robin Mather, "The Threats from Genetically Modified Foods," *Mother Earth News* (April–May 2012); Amy Harmon and Andrew Pollack, "Battle Brewing over Labeling of Genetically Modified Food," *New York Times* (May 24, 2012); and Molly Ball, "Want to Know If Your Food Is Genetically Modified?" *The Atlantic* (May 14, 2014) (http://www.theatlantic.com/politics/archive/2014/05/want-to-know-if-your-food-is-genetically-modified/370812/). Jane Black, "As Nature Made Them," *Prevention* (April 2012), adds a call for more independent (not sponsored by seed companies) research into GMO safety. Vermont was the first state to pass a law requiring that foods with GMO ingredients be labeled as such; effective July 1, 2016. The justifications include potential hazards, consumer choice, and even religion. Similar legislation has failed to make much headway in California and Illinois, among other states.

At the federal level, the House of Representatives has passed "the hotly contested Safe and Accurate Food Labeling Act of 2015, which bars states from issuing mandatory labeling laws for foods that contain genetically modified organisms, or GMOs. Instead, it would create a federal standard for the voluntary labeling of foods with GMO ingredients" (http://thehill.com/blogs/floor-action/house/248974-house-passes-gmo-labeling-reform-bill). The readings below were drawn from the debate over this legislation. In the YES selection, Todd Daloz argues that Vermont's legislation requiring labeling of GM crops is amply justified by the public's need for factual information about the food they eat, and that federal preemption of state labeling laws, without providing a suitable substitute, is unreasonable. In the NO selection, L. Val Giddings argues that there is no scientific doubt that GM crops are safe to eat, the federal government already has sufficient authority to regulate the sale and labeling of GM foods, and the push for labeling laws is a thinly disguised effort to ban GM foods in favor of less safe and more expensive alternatives, such as organic foods.

YES

Todd Daloz

Testimony before the U.S. House of Representatives Committee on Energy and Commerce, Subcommittee on Health, Hearing on "A National Framework for the Review and Labeling of Biotechnology in Food"

Summary

. . . [T]he State of Vermont has been deeply involved in the labeling of food produced with genetic engineering, passing a law requiring the labeling of such products a little over a year ago. Vermont's Attorney General, Bill Sorrell, is tasked with enforcing this law and has adopted the regulations that will implement the labeling requirement. I am here today to testify on behalf of Attorney General Sorrell about your draft legislation ("Discussion Draft") and to discuss Vermont's experience with labeling food produced with genetic engineering.

One of the primary roles of states in our federal system is to act, to paraphrase Justice Brandeis, as laboratories of democracy to develop "novel social and economic experiments without risk to the rest of the country." That is what Vermont has done in requiring the labeling of food produced with genetic engineering. Our primary concern with the draft legislation before you today is that it would prematurely end all state efforts to require labeling—before Vermont's labeling law even takes effect—without offering a substantive federal requirement in its place. We urge the Committee not to support a bill that preempts all state labeling requirements for genetically engineered foods. . . .

Vermont's Genetically Engineered Food Labeling Law

On May 8, 2014, after hearing testimony from more than one hundred individuals and reviewing literature on all sides of the issue over the course of two years, the Vermont Legislature enacted Act 120 to address concerns related to genetically engineered ("GE") foods. Act 120 came about in response to tremendous constituent concern over the lack of available information about the use of GE foods in grocery products in the absence of a federal standard for such labeling, and in the face of a threatened—now actual—constitutional challenge. Put simply, this first-in-the-nation labeling law requires manufacturers and retailers to label GE foods offered for retail sale in Vermont.

The Purpose of Act 120

At its core, Act 120 endeavors to provide consumers with accurate factual information on which they can base their purchasing decisions. In enacting this law, the Vermont Legislature expressly recognized a variety of principal reasons why consumers would want this information, and codified them at Vt. Stat. Ann. tit. 9, sec. 3041(1)–(4). As the Legislature found, consumers want to "make informed decisions regarding the potential health effects of the food they purchase and consume," and, if they choose, to "avoid potential health risks of food produced from genetic engineering."

Likewise, the Legislature recognized that consumers wish to "[i]nform the[ir] purchasing decisions . . . [based on] concern[s] about the potential environmental effects of food from genetic engineering." The Legislature found that the use of GE crops contributes to genetic homogeneity, loss of biodiversity, and increased vulnerability of crops to pests, diseases, and variable climate conditions. It also found that pollen drift from GE crops threatens to contaminate organic crops and impairs the marketability

Testimony before the U.S. House of Representatives Committee on Energy and Commerce, Subcommittee on Health, Hearing on "A National Framework for the Review and Labeling of Biotechnology in Food," U.S. House of Representatives, June 2015.

of those crops. In addition, the Legislature found that GE crops can adversely affect native plants through the transfer of unnatural DNA, thereby displacing natural wildlife. The Legislature concluded that a labeling requirement will allow Vermonters who are concerned about the environmental impact of GE foods to adjust their purchasing decisions accordingly. Finally, the Legislature understood that consumers desire "data from which they may make informed decisions for religious reasons."

In articulating these purposes, the Vermont Legislature relied on a wealth of testimony. Scientists, traditional and organic farmers, manufacturers, consumers, attorneys, regulators, and lobbyists alike provided hours of testimony on *both* sides of the issues: the benefits and risks of GE foods and whether consumers should (or should not) be informed whether a product was made with GE technology or derived from GE crops.

Significantly, the Legislature also heard evidence showing consumer confusion about the prominence of GE foods, including two national surveys showing that Americans are generally unaware that many of the products sold in supermarkets today have been genetically engineered. *See* Allison Kopicki, *Strong Support for Labeling Modified Foods,* New York Times (July 27, 2013) (fewer than half those polled knew that many foods sold at supermarkets had been genetically engineered); Thomson Reuters, *National Survey of Healthcare Consumers: Genetically Engineered Food* (Oct. 2010) (only 69.2% knew that food available in stores had been genetically engineered, and only 51.3% of those earning less than $25,000 per year had such knowledge). Motivated by the expressed need for this information, the Legislature developed the provisions of Act 120.

The Labeling Requirements of Act 120

The mechanics of Act 120 are relatively straight forward: manufacturers and retailers must label GE foods offered for retail sale in Vermont with the simple statement that the food is "Produced with Genetic Engineering." As a general matter, packaged food produced entirely or in part from genetic engineering must be labeled on the package by manufacturers as "produced with genetic engineering." In addition, such foods may be labeled as "partially produced with genetic engineering," or "may be produced with genetic engineering." In the case of unpackaged food, Act 120 requires retailers to post a "produced with genetic engineering" label on the retail store shelf or bin where the product is displayed for sale.

Act 120 exempts certain categories of food from its labeling requirements, including food "derived entirely from an animal which has not itself been produced with genetic engineering"; processing aids and enzymes produced with genetic engineering; alcoholic beverages; processed foods not packaged for retail and intended for immediate consumption; food served in restaurants; food containing only minimal amounts of GE material; and certain foods not "knowingly or intentionally" produced with genetic engineering.

Importantly, Act 120 does not require manufacturers to identify which ingredients were genetically engineered. Nor does it prohibit manufacturers from including additional information or disclaimers on their packaging about the difference (or lack thereof) between GE crops and their traditional counterparts. In fact, in enacting the law, the Legislature saw fit to provide significant flexibility for the Vermont Attorney General to develop regulations implementing Act 120.

Regulations Implementing Act 120

As provided in Act 120, the Vermont Attorney General formally adopted rules regulating the labeling of food produced with genetic engineering on April 17, 2015. *See* Vermont Consumer Protection Rule CP 121 (eff. July 1, 2016). The Rule, CP 121, further clarifies Act 120 by giving detailed definitions of key terms, specific requirements for the size and placement of the required disclosures, thorough descriptions of the various exemptions to the labeling requirements, and details on the enforcement of the law. In so doing, CP 121 draws on areas of existing federal and state law, including FDA and USDA regulations. At its heart, CP 121 ensures Vermont consumers have accurate information available to them at the point they decide to purchase a food item, while at the same time providing industry some flexibility in complying with the labeling law.

Prior to adopting the Rule, the Attorney General's Office provided significant opportunities for input from the public, generally, and from industry groups, in particular. Beyond general outreach, our office specifically contacted industry groups, including the Grocery Manufacturers Association, the Snack Food Association, the Vermont Retail & Grocers Association, the Vermont Specialty Food Association, and various organizations representing regional grocery store chains and national commodity producers. Through an on-line questionnaire, submitted questions and comments, multiple face-to-face meetings, and a series of informal public conversations, we heard from numerous Vermonters and people from all across the country and around the world about the importance of this law. Out of this robust process of public input—including the formal notice and comment rulemaking procedures required under the Vermont Administrative Procedures Act, and further discussions with industry groups—CP 121 was formed.

The Rule focuses on the requirements and process of labeling in a framework that provides industry with flexibility in compliance. In detailing the placement and prominence of the "Produced with Genetic Engineering" disclosure on packaged, processed foods, CP 121 requires that the disclosure be "easily found by consumers when viewing the outside of the [food's] package" and that the disclosure is "in any color that contrasts with the background of the package so as to be easily read by consumers." A manufacturer is "presumed to satisfy" the "easily found" requirement of the Rule if the disclosure is "located on the same panel as the Nutrition Facts Label or Ingredient List," but a manufacturer is not required to place the disclosure in any given location. Likewise, a manufacturer meets the "easily read" requirement if the disclosure is either "in a font size no smaller than the size of the words "Serving Size" on the Nutrition Facts label" or is "in a font size no smaller than the Ingredient list . . . and printed in bold type-face." So long as a consumer can easily find and read the disclosure, the purpose of Act 120 is met. These location and font-size standards give packaged, processed food manufacturers flexibility in providing the required disclosure in a manner that works with the constraints of their product's packaging.

In a similar vein, CP 121 provides a variety of means for manufacturers to document that their products fall outside the scope of labeling under Act 120. Manufacturers can rely on the sworn statement of the person who sold them the product, certifying that the food "(1) was made or grown from food or seed that has not been knowingly or intentionally produced with genetic engineering and (2) has been segregated from and has not been knowingly or intentionally commingled with food or seed that may have been produced with genetic engineering." Alternatively, food certified as "organic" by an organization "accredited to make such certifications under the USDA National Organic Program" is also free of the labeling requirements. Finally, the Attorney General is in the process of authorizing third-party organizations to verify that a manufacturer's product has not been produced with genetic engineering. Each of these various avenues provide differing benefits for manufacturers interested in complying with Act 120.

Finally, CP 121 expressly permits, subject to other applicable legal requirements, manufacturers to include other disclosures about the GE contents of their product on the product's label, enabling them to speak further on the subject of GE food, generally. The Rule specifically allows manufacturers to state that "the United States Food and Drug Administration does not consider food produced with genetic engineering to be materially different from other foods." There is nothing in the Rule, or Act 120, that limits the breadth and depth of these additional, optional disclosures, or their location and prominence on the product's package. Indeed, if a manufacturer so desired, it could dwarf Act 120's required disclosure with the manufacturer's views on the safety and importance of GE food to the national and global food system.

In sum, Act 120, together with CP 121, responds to a wide-spread constituent desire—held by a majority of Vermonters and other consumers around the country—for accurate factual information about the contents of food. But despite the broad demand for this purely factual disclosure, Act 120's labeling requirements were challenged almost immediately upon passage.

Overview of the Litigation Challenging Act 120

In June 2014, one month after Act 120 was enacted, a group of industry associations representing food manufacturers filed suit challenging the Act on various constitutional grounds. After Vermont moved to dismiss the Complaint, the industry associations filed for a preliminary injunction to prevent the State from enforcing the law, claiming they were likely to win their constitutional challenge and would be irreparably harmed if the law were to take effect.

On April 27, 2015, the District Court issued its decision denying the group's preliminary injunction motion in its entirety, finding they were not likely to prevail on their claims or could not establish irreparable harm. The Court also dismissed a significant portion of the group's Complaint, disallowing claims that Act 120 is preempted by federal law and violates the Commerce Clause of the United States Constitution.

Significantly, as to the group's First Amendment claims, the Court sided with Vermont on several important questions. In particular, the Court rejected the group's argument that Act 120 must face strict scrutiny. Instead, the Court adopted the Attorney General's position that the lowest level of scrutiny applies to the disclosure law, whereby the State need only show that the GE label is reasonably related to the State's interests. The Court found that the "safety of food products, the protection of the environment, and the accommodation of religious beliefs and practices are all quintessential governmental interests," as is the "desire to promote informed consumer decision-making."

Further, the Court agreed that the disclosure requirement was not a warning label, but rather mandates the disclosure of purely factual and noncontroversial information, precisely as the Legislature intended. Thus, the Court indicated Act 120 would survive the "rational basis" test. Indeed, the Court initially sustained the fundamental "heart and soul" of Act 120—the mandatory labeling of foods made with genetic engineering.

On May 6, 2015, the group of industry associations filed an appeal from the Court's denial of their preliminary injunction motion with the U.S. Court of Appeals for the Second Circuit.

Provisions of the Discussion Draft of H.R. 1599

The Discussion Draft presents a vision for the labeling of foods produced with GE that recognizes consumers' strong desire to have factual information about food available to them at the time of purchase; however, rather than ensuring the accuracy of this information—as other federal food labeling regulations do, and as Act 120 will do—the current draft fails to mandate the labeling of GE food, and immediately cuts short any state initiatives in labeling GE food while presenting only a vague future regulatory structure in its place.

The Discussion Draft suggests an encouraging concept: increased FDA and USDA involvement in the review of GE foods. Indeed, the notion of federal labeling to inform consumers of the presence of GE materials in their food is one the Vermont Attorney General strongly supports. That said, the Discussion Draft falls short in two particulars. First, any such labeling is discretionary, not mandatory, which fails to provide a reliable standard for consumers. Second, any elective labeling is permitted only when the Secretary of Health and Human Services determines that the GE variety of a food is "materially different" from its parent variety; and the definition provided for this operative term is overly strict and fails to recognize the information—apart from nutritional value or presence of allergens—that consumers desire when making a decision to purchase and consume food.

Most importantly, the Discussion Draft expressly preempts state labeling laws that require disclosure if a food was produced with GE. If enacted as drafted, H.R. 1599 would have two central, and in my view, negative effects. The first would be to immediately—upon enactment—cancel existing legislation like Vermont's Act 120. The second would be to provide only a[n] incomplete federal structure for the labeling of GE foods, and one that lacks any meaningful statutory standards and places much, if not all, of the responsibility for creating the structure in the hands of a federal agency.

In principle, delegation to an agency is a logical and appropriate legislative tool—indeed, the Vermont Legislature delegated the crafting of Act 120's regulations to the Attorney General. In the Discussion Draft, however, vital components to the National Standard for Labeling Genetically Engineered Food are absent (e.g. the identity or criteria for selecting "certifying agents," which are central in the development of a Genetically Engineered Food Plan), making the proposal a bare skeleton. This lack of guidance, coupled with the immediate preemption of existing state and voluntary labeling programs, highlight the central drawback of the proposed bill: rather than advancing a uniform national standard for mandatory GE food labeling, H.R. 1599 halts any efforts to label such foods and delays implementation of the proposed voluntary system until administrative regulations pass through the gauntlet of rulemaking. This would create a regulatory vacuum and would further delay consumers' access to accurate information about the food they are consuming.

In effect, passage of H.R. 1599, as presented in the Discussion Draft, would impose preemption without concurrent federal action.

The Federalism Values in Consumer Protection

States and the federal government share responsibility for protecting consumers. As noted above, what is most troubling about this proposed legislation is that it would prematurely end state efforts to require labeling—before Vermont's law even takes effect—and offers no substantive federal requirement in its place. Vermont does not oppose all federal regulation in this area or even all concepts in this proposed law. The FDA and Department of Agriculture have primary responsibility for regulating food safety, and those agencies must take any steps necessary to protect our food supply. At some point, a federal labeling requirement might appropriately supersede state-imposed labels. But if the federal government is not ready to require national labeling for foods produced with genetic engineering, Congress should not rush in to ban state efforts to provide this information to their citizens. And Congress certainly should not do so before state measures have even become effective.

Cutting off state efforts in this area is contrary to established principles of federalism. Vermont's labeling law is a direct response to strong public support in our state for mandatory labeling and consumers' right to know. It is no surprise that a state would take the first step in this area. One of "the most valuable aspects of our federalism" is that "the 50 States serve as laboratories for the development of new social, economic, and political ideas." Historically, many important reforms began as state initiatives, including women's right to vote, minimum-wage and child labor laws, and unemployment insurance. By preempting state labeling laws before any label even appears on a package of food, this proposed bill would permanently disable the States' ability to experiment and to provide useful lessons and models for national legislation.

State innovation continues to play an invaluable role in our federal system. State and local governments are more accessible and more responsive to new problems and concerns. We do not have to look back a hundred years to find examples of state initiatives that provide a model for later federal regulation:

- Vermont and other states pioneered consumer protections in credit reporting—a fact that is reflected in the Fair Credit Reporting Act's provisions leaving untouched certain preexisting state laws.
- Federal law will soon require disclosure of calorie and other nutritional information on chain-restaurant menus nationwide. The effort to get this important information to consumers began in New York, which as the *New York Times* explained, "became a kind of natural experiment when it began requiring chain restaurants to post calorie counts on menus in 2006." After a number of other states and cities adopted similar disclosure rules, the National Restaurant Association joined consumer groups in supporting a national rule.
- Another area in which federal regulation followed on successful state initiatives is transparency in the marketing of prescription drugs. The federal Physician Payment Sunshine Act, and its implementing rules, create "a national program that promote stransparency by publishing data on the financial relationships between the health care industry (applicable manufacturers and group purchasing organizations, or GPOs) and health care providers (physicians and teaching hospitals)." Many states, including Vermont, Minnesota, and Massachusetts, led the way in requiring transparency and disclosure of payments to doctors by pharmaceutical companies.

What these examples convey is the value and importance of state legislation. In each case, individual states took the first crack at a serious problem, and in so doing, provided experiences that other states and eventually the federal government could learn from and build on. Sometimes federal legislation reaches farther, to deal more

comprehensively with a problem. Sometimes a federal approach will be narrower, recognizing problems with earlier state approaches. Sometimes federal law preempts existing state laws, while in other areas federal law leaves room for complementary state regulation. Regardless, the pioneering state laws provided guideposts, models good and not-so-good, and useful information for voters and policymakers nationwide.

The proposed legislation on GE labeling would cut off this learning process before it even begins. No one benefits from such an approach, least of all the consumers who have pressed loudly and consistently for the right to know how their food is produced.

The Importance of Consumer Choice and Information

Vermonters overwhelmingly supported labeling of food produced with genetic engineering. A central purpose of Act 120 is to allow consumers to make "informed decisions." As the Vermont Legislature found, "[l]abeling gives consumers information they can use to make decisions about what products they would prefer to purchase."

Vermonters are not alone in their interest in having accurate information about their food. A recent national poll found that fully 66% of Americans support mandatory labeling of foods produced with genetic engineering. Both Democrats and Republicans expressed this strong support for labeling GE foods. One popular grocery chain has announced that it will require labeling of foods produced with genetic engineering by 2018.

Opponents of labeling have voiced no persuasive basis for keeping Americans in the dark on this important issue. Food manufacturers contend that foods produced with genetic engineering are safe and argue that GE technology benefits consumers and the environment. Yet they adamantly oppose letting consumers have this information to make their own decisions in the grocery aisle and at the dinner table. As the U.S. Supreme Court has recognized, consumers have a "keen" "interest in the free flow of commercial information." Labeling serves the interest of consumers and food manufacturers. It lets food manufacturers make their case for the benefits of GE technology directly to the American people. And it lets American consumers evaluate the evidence and make an *informed* choice.

Trusting people to make their own decisions is a fundamental American principle. Our current requirements for labeling food reflect and enforce this principle. A consumer can pick up a can of soup, read the label, and find out the ingredients, the amount of sodium and added sugar, the number of calories, and the amount of protein, fat, and carbohydrates. Consumers can readily see whether shrimp were harvested in southeast Asia, grapes grown in South America, or cherries produced in the United States. Food labels provide information needed to avoid nuts or gluten, favor high protein content or stay away from high-fructose corn syrup. Armed with that information—and trusting it to be accurate— parents decide what fruits and vegetables to feed their kids and people with food sensitivities make the choices they consider best for their own health. And some people ignore all the labels and buy what they like to eat, whether it's candy bars or avocados.

A common complaint from those who oppose labeling is that a label is necessarily the equivalent of a warning and that consumers will assume that foods produced with genetic engineering are bad. In fact, the short disclosure required by Vermont law—"produced with genetic engineering"—is not a warning label, and the regulations do not require it to be presented as such. All that is required is a straightforward, accurate disclosure of factual information, similar to labels that say "product of United States" or "product of Mexico," available to consumers at the point of purchase. Indeed, Congress has repeatedly directed that consumers be given information about the country of origin for meat, fish, and fresh produce. In upholding country-of-origin labeling for meat, the D.C. Circuit Court of Appeals observed that "[s]upporting members of Congress identified the statute's purpose as enabling customers to make informed choices based on characteristics of the products they wished to purchase."

The proposed bill would deprive American consumers of information they want to have when deciding what foods to eat and how to spend their money. The bill would preempt state efforts, including Vermont's, to require that this basic information be included on package labeling— but not replace those state laws with any mandatory federal label. Insisting that this information be kept from consumers is profoundly disrespectful of the American consumer's right and ability to make intelligent, informed choices. The Supreme Court has long rejected arguments that presume consumers are incapable of making rational decisions. To the contrary, the Court has recognized that in our "free enterprise economy," the public interest is best served when consumers' decisions are "intelligent and well informed."

Conclusion

The federal government plays a vital role in regulating the labeling of food, and doubtless there is an important role for Congress to play in shaping the national standards for labeling food produced with genetic engineering. But H.R. 1599 does not fulfill that role. It contravenes our federal system by regulating Vermont's ability to enact legislation demanded by its citizens, thwarting the very type of experiment necessary for the development of solid public policy. By preempting Vermont's law and any similar measures that citizens in the other forty-nine states may desire, the proposed law ignores the intellect of American consumers to act upon accurate factual information presented to them.

TODD DALOZ is the assistant attorney general of Vermont.

L. Val Giddings

 **NO**

Testimony before the U.S. House of Representatives Committee on Energy and Commerce, Subcommittee on Health, Hearing on "A National Framework for the Review and Labeling of Biotechnology in Food"

Introduction and Summary

. . . The Information Technology and Innovation Foundation (ITIF) is a non-partisan research and educational institute—a think tank—whose mission is to formulate and promote public policies to advance technological innovation and productivity internationally, in Washington, and in the states. Recognizing the vital role of technology in ensuring prosperity, ITIF focuses on innovation issues. Because of its importance in enabling agricultural innovation, we have long been involved in the conversations about agricultural biotechnology and how best to ensure its widely shared benefits to humans and the environment are not unduly burdened by ill-considered policies, especially those based on fear and misunderstanding. I very much appreciate the opportunity to comment on these issues here today.

My comments come in the context of HR 1599. While I agree strongly with the obvious and logical importance of pre-empting State level efforts to require labels for food containing "GMOs," I concur with former FDA Commissioner Dr. Margaret Hamburg, who stated last summer that FDA already has clear and sufficient authority over food labels, and that FDA's authority pre-empts State level action. As you have heard from other witnesses, the costs and negative impacts of a fifty state patchwork of inconsistent and incoherent standards would be significant. In view of the scientific consensus on, and unblemished safety record of bioengineered foods, together with clear Congressional supremacy, there is no conceivable justification for a state by state approach, much less for any mandatory labeling initiatives other than those that have already been in place at the federal level for decades.

It is worthwhile to focus on the reason for HR 1599. It has been put forward as a means of addressing campaigns to create exactly the sort of 50 state patchworks for which there is simply no justification. Legal mandates already require that consumers have all information relevant to health, safety, and nutrition, on federally approved labels. Numerous measures now in place (some already for years) provide consumers with abundant opportunities to choose to avoid foods derived from crops improved through biotechnology, should they wish to do so despite the abundant data and experience confirming their safety and environmental benefits. Yet a small group of professional campaigners has spent no small amount of money and effort to create the illusion of a demand for federal action that was, in fact, taken more than two decades ago. This entire issue, then, is merely a subterfuge through which ideologically-based anti-technology special interests are seeking to roll back and ultimately completely remove from the market GMO-based products.

On the issue of safety, though some will claim otherwise, the fact is that hundreds of billions of meals have been eaten by more than a hundred billion livestock animals, and billions of humans, in the two decades these foods have been on the market. There has been not a single solitary case of a negative health consequence as a result. It is a record of which the organic industry, for one, should be envious. The global scientific consensus on the safety of these foods and crops is remarkable in its breadth and depth.

The wisdom of FDA's 1992 policy statement is therefore clear. Just as scientific and professional bodies around the world have done, the FDA found that there is nothing

---

about the processes of bioengineering that necessarily changes the resulting foods in any way related to health, safety or nutrition. If such a change were to result, as in the case of cooking oils modified to be more heart healthy, or soybeans with improved nutrition thanks to the addition of a gene encoding protein from a tree nut, the resulting foods would already be required, under existing FDA policy, to carry a label that would inform consumers of such changes.

Some have claimed that consumers have a "right to know" if their food has been "genetically modified." Those making such claims overlook the fact that "genetic modification" is a process, not a thing. And as a geneticist, I can state categorically that every food any human has ever eaten has been "genetically modified" in the literal meaning of the term. Proponents of mandatory labels so misunderstand the facts as we find them in nature that they define "GM" as a process resulting in genetic changes in a manner not found in nature. This ignores that the processes used by genetic engineers are ones we learned about by finding them operating everywhere in nature. In fact, no process is more natural than genetic modification, and the scientists who use it to improve seeds do so using systems they bring from nature into the lab for the purpose.

Current FDA policy requires that any food that has been changed, by any means, so that its composition is different in any way related to health, safety, or nutrition, must inform consumers of such changes on the label. Furthermore, this must be done in a manner that is safe, informative, and not misleading. In short, the things proponents of mandatory labels claim they want, they already have. But of course, proponents of mandatory labeling do not want labeling to inform consumers, they want labeling to scare consumers and force food companies into not buying food inputs with "GMO" ingredients.

Authority to Set Labeling Standards—Congress or the States?

Article I, Section 8, Clause 3 of the Constitution, the "interstate commerce clause," clearly locates the authority "to regulate Commerce with foreign Nations, and among the several States, and with the Indian Tribes" among the powers reserved to Congress. Congress in turn has delegated to FDA, through the Federal Food Drug & Cosmetic Act, authority over food labels. And FDA has laid out national policy in this regard in a 1992 Guidance Document. In publishing this guidance, FDA has followed the strong international consensus.

As mentioned above, existing FDA regulations already require that any novel ingredient that may affect

the health, safety, or nutritional value of a food must be identified on the label. Existing federal law requires all food placed on the market to be safe, with criminal penalties for violators. Consumers have a right to labels that are accurate, informative, and not misleading.

Some claim that the processes used to produce bioengineered foods are fundamentally different from those used to develop other foods, and that insufficient studies have been done to allow us to be confident of their safety. Such allegations are false. Plant breeders and credible scientists around the world agree that the techniques used to produce transgenic plants, derived directly from natural phenomena, are but an extension of traditional plant breeding, and that the potential hazards are the same. The U.S. National Academy of Sciences explicitly rejected this claim in its very first publication in this area and has upheld this view in every subsequent study. The Government of Canada in its regulatory structure has specifically repudiated the assertion that plants improved through recombinant techniques are necessarily and intrinsically different than those produced through conventional breeding. The government of Australia has done likewise and the overwhelming majority of scientists around the world concur in this assessment.

Indeed, the advent of modern genomics has shown us that genes are shared and transferred widely not only among different species, but between genera, families, and even phyla and kingdoms. Recent discoveries have confirmed that gene exchange was the essential element in the survival of ferns when the explosive radiation of flowering plants radically changed their environment. This natural gene transfer is just like that used by modern genetic engineers to create plants improved through biotechnology. These natural processes of gene exchange are so widespread among plants, animals, and microbes on planet Earth that the single most common gene in humans is one that came from a virus; as did half of the other genes in our genomes; and humans share 98% of our genes with chimpanzees, 92% with mice, 44% with fruit flies, 26% with yeast, and 18% with dandelions. Those who claim crops improved through biotechnology are "unnatural" could not be more profoundly refuted than by what we find throughout nature.

Global Consensus on the Safety of Foods Derived from Crops Improved Through Biotechnology

Some claim there are unresolved safety concerns about GIFs [genetically improved foods], and that they have been insufficiently studied. These claims are false, robustly contradicted by the scientific literature, worldwide scientific opinion, and vast experience. Some have claimed that there is a dearth of independent research evaluating the safety of crops and foods produced through biotechnology, and that companies hide behind intellectual property claims to prevent such research from being done. These claims are false. The American Seed Trade Association has a policy in place to ensure research access to transgenic seeds, and Monsanto has made public a similar commitment. The academic scientists who made the 2009 complaint cited above, in fact, had the access they sought at the time they made the unfounded complaint.

In fact, there has been an abundance of independent research over the years, including a massive compilation underwritten by the EU involving more than 130 research projects, covering a period of more than 25 years, involving more than 500 independent research groups, concluding "that biotechnology, and in particular GMOs, are not per se more risky than e.g. conventional plant breeding technologies. . . ."

Some representative voices include the following:

"Indeed, the use of more precise technology and the greater regulatory scrutiny probably make them even safer than conventional plants and foods; and if there are unforeseen environmental effects—none have appeared as yet—these should be rapidly detected by our monitoring requirements. On the other hand, the benefits of these plants and products for human health and the environment become increasingly clear."

". . . because the technique is so sophisticated, in many ways it is probably safer for you to eat GM products—plants that have been generated through GM—than normal plant foods, if you have any sort of reaction to food, because you can snip out the proteins that cause the negative reaction to certain parts of the population."

"In contrast to adverse health effects that have been associated with some traditional food production methods, similar serious health effects have not been identified as a result of genetic engineering techniques used in food production. This may be because developers of bioengineered organisms perform extensive compositional analyses to determine that each phenotype is desirable and to ensure that unintended changes have not occurred in key components of food."

The Union of the German Academies of Science and Humanities found: ". . . in consuming food derived from GM

plants approved in the EU and in the USA, the risk is in no way higher than in the consumption of food from conventionally grown plants. On the contrary, in some cases food from GM plants appears to be superior in respect to health."

The Chief Scientific Advisor to the European Union stated, "If we look at evidence from [more than] 15 years of growing and consuming GMO foods globally, then there is no substantiated case of any adverse impact on human health, animal health or environmental health, so that's pretty robust evidence, and I would be confident in saying that there is no more risk in eating GMO food than eating conventionally farmed food."

"GMO products have been tested to a particularly high extent and are subjected to rigid legislation control."

"Food from GM Maize is more healthy than from conventionally grown maize . . . samples with the highest fumonisin concentrations are found in products labeled 'organic.'"

". . . The dangers of unintentional DNA mutation are much higher in the process of conventional plant breeding . . . than in the generation of GM plants. Furthermore, GM products are subject to rigid testing with livestock and rats before approval."

"Whereas for conventional varieties there is no legal requirement for allergy tests of their products, for GMO products, very strict allergy tests are mandatory . . . for this reason, the risk of GM plants causing allergies can be regarded as substantially lower than that of products from conventional breeding."

As for claims of "unexpected effects"—to date, there are none reported, and

"According to present scientific knowledge, it is most unlikely that the consumption of . . . transgenic DNA from approved GMO food harbors any recognizable health risk."

The most recent scientific publication in this crowded catalogue examined the effects on livestock of eating feed derived through biotech improved crops over the course of 29 years through more than a trillion meals. This unprecedented observational study not only failed to find any negative impacts, it found that over this period the average health of livestock animals improved.

Claims of the Anti-GMO Advocacy Groups

Despite the overwhelming consensus documented above, professional anti-technology campaigners claim that this consensus does not exist, and that its absence is demonstrated by "a petition signed by over three hundred scientists." This false assertion presents no new arguments or data, and ignores the staggering mass of studies already cited demonstrating the safety of these foods, and their unblemished safety record. Instead, it recycles the usual stable of discredited claims such as those of Séralini et al. It is worthwhile therefore to note that the group behind this press release is comprised of individuals with a long history of opposition to agricultural biotechnology that relies on ignoring or distorting reality. Indeed, the group is merely one element in a campaign that has propagated claims that the biology is unclear despite the fact that the science is far more settled on GM foods than it is on climate change. One observer has dismissed them with these words:

"A group of [300] scientists have signed a letter saying 'GMO is bad . . .' They did so in response to a roundup of more than 2,000 actual studies, almost all done over the last decade, that have failed to produce any evidence that GMO is anything other than plain old food, and some of the safest food we consume."

"Scientific consensus is not done by opinion poll, nor is it done by petition. . . . The scientific consensus is a consensus of data, born out by peer reviewed study and published work. Thus a meta-analysis of a topic is a perfect way of determining consensus. The consensus, by the way has stood for decades. GMO is not only as safe as any other food, it is provably so (most other food never having been tested) and in fact it is simply food, not magic."

The Australian Agricultural Biotechnology Council reaffirmed this judgment, and further showed that European agriculturalists are keen to adopt the technology, and increasingly dissatisfied with the innovation stifling and scientifically indefensible European regulatory regime. . . .

"The World Health Organization (WHO) has said that: 'No effects on human health have been shown as a result of the consumption of such foods by the general population in the countries where they have been approved'."

"The Agricultural Biotechnology Council (ABC) of Australia said the ENSSER's statement 'flies in the face of a consensus of an overwhelming majority of scientists.'"

"Every legitimate scientific organization that has examined the evidence has arrived at the conclusion that GM crops and the foods they produce pose no risk to human health or the environment beyond those posed by their conventional counterparts," added ABC Australia.

"Meanwhile, EU farming groups, including the NFU, NFU Cymru, NFU Scotland and the Ulster Farmers' Union (UFU), have added their name to a different letter, which voices 'deep concern' about the effects of GM policies and regulations in the EU."

"In an open letter sent to the European Commission on behalf of the French Association for Plant Biotechnology (AFBV) [and 13 other groups], they called for better for access to the best crops, including GM varieties, so that agriculture in Europe can be more sustainable and less reliant on imported products. The letter states that the lack of options for GM technology available to farmers in Europe can equate to significant loss of income and a missed opportunity."

Ignoring all this, professional anti-biotechnology campaigners persist in their claims that there are studies raising legitimate questions about the safety of GIFs. One frequently cited example is that of a long term feeding study in rats, conducted by a well-known organic advocate and biotech opponent from France, who dissembled about his financial conflicts of interest that lay behind his claims. Biotech opponents claim this study has been wrongly criticized, but the facts repudiate this claim. The alleged "attacks in the media" aimed at the Séralini "study" were the direct consequence of its remarkably poor design, execution, and analysis and the unprecedented media manipulations imposed on journalists prior to its release, in an attempt to compel favorable media coverage. The criticisms of the study and the way it was released were spontaneous and widespread among credible scientists and journalists. That is how peer review works. The criticisms were, in fact, more severe than is commonly seen, but this was entirely due to the extraordinary shortcomings in design, execution, and interpretation of the experiment, and the unprecedented departure from the norms of publication designed to produce slanted media coverage.

One consistent opponent of agricultural biotechnology has claimed that *"the French Food Safety Agency and the European Food Safety Authority have functionally agreed with Doctor Séralini."* This claim is flatly contradicted by the historical record. Regulatory bodies in Europe and around the world uniformly rejected the study, and have made strongly critical statements.

The European Food Safety Authority: "EFSA is presently unable to regard the authors' conclusions as scientifically sound." Six French National Academies of Science (Agriculture, Medicine, Pharmacology, Sciences, Technology, and Veterinary Medicine) condemned the study, stating "Given the numerous gaps in methods and interpretation, the data presented in this article cannot challenge previous studies which have concluded that NK603 corn is harmless from the health point of view, as are, more generally, genetically modified plants that have been authorized for consumption by animals and humans." They further dismissed the study as "a scientific non-event" that served only "to spread fear among the public that is not based on any firm conclusion." These findings were echoed by the French Higher Biotechnologies Council (HCB) and the National Agency for Food Safety (ANSES).

The German Federal Institute for Risk Assessment: (BfR): "The authors' main statements are not sufficiently corroborated by experimental evidence, due to deficiencies in the study design and in the presentation and interpretation of the study results."

The Australia New Zealand Food Safety Authority stated, "On the basis of the many scientific deficiencies identified in the study, FSANZ does not accept the conclusions made by the authors and has therefore found no justification to reconsider the safety of NK603 corn, originally approved in 2002." Canada's Health agency concluded, "The overwhelming body of scientific evidence continues to support the safety of NK603, genetically modified food and feed products in general, and glyphosate containing herbicides."

Indeed, the condemnation of the Séralini study from the international scientific and regulatory community was so deep, broad, and spontaneous, that even Marion Nestle, NYU Professor of Nutrition and food safety advocate long known for her skepticism of agricultural biotechnology, agreed, "It's a really bad study." One blogger distilled the consensus, and coined the "Séralini Rule": "If you favorably cite the 2012 Séralini rats fed on Roundup ready maize study, you just lost the argument."

In the end, the evidence of the study's inadequacies was so overwhelming that the journal in which it was published retracted it. . . . Séralini apologists have made numerous false and misleading claims about the retraction, but these have failed to persuade.

It must be noted that in citing the robustly discredited Séralini study opponents illustrate a pattern they have followed throughout their public representations. Repeatedly they cite one or another from a small handful of studies published by well-known campaigners against biotechnology. In so doing, they ignore the devastating criticisms they have received from the scientific community (peer review) as well as the vast body of accepted scientific literature contradicting their unsustainable claims.

This pattern of advocacy is deemed to be scientific misconduct under widely accepted standards.

Some have claimed that crops improved through biotechnology have resulted in an increase in the use of pesticides. This claim is, at least, mischievous, if not false, and depends on a number of intellectual gymnastics:

- It wrongly conflates "herbicides" with "pesticides" in a way that is flatly misleading. Pesticides are commonly understood to kill pests, usually insects. Herbicides are used to control weeds, which are certainly pestiferous, but agriculturalists use the different words for very good reasons;
- The argument is based on the misleading measurement "pounds on the ground" when that has long since been supplanted in the weed control literature by the "Environmental Impact Quotient" developed at Cornell University. The EIQ gives a vastly more accurate and useful way to evaluate comparative environmental impacts;
- The argument measures absolute application rates, instead of the far more logical rates per unit yield, which actually show a decline in herbicide usage;
- Such claims ignore the devastating critiques that have been leveled specifically . . . in at least 17 peer reviewed papers in the literature and several accessible blogposts;
- Such claims are, in fact, directly contradicted by USDA's interpretations of their own data.

In addition to these spurious claims that seem designed deliberately to mislead consumers about the environmental safety of foods derived from crops improved through biotechnology, we are routinely bombarded with a host of claims about alleged dangers to humans from their consumption. In an arena marked by the incredible, it is hard to find claims that are farther "out there," divorced from reality, than those that have been advanced by Dr. Stephanie Seneff, an engineering PhD who seems to have some difficulty identifying any evils that cannot be laid at the feet of glyphosate.

The facts tell quite a different story. One can hardly do better than to consult a summary of the data on the safety of glyphosate compiled by independent scientists at BioFortified last year, with a useful primer also available. Bottom line—glyphosate is less toxic than table salt, baking soda, chocolate, or caffeine. Yet some would have us believe it is responsible for nearly every ailment imaginable, and these claims find a ready echo chamber in a credulous and scientifically ill-trained press.

The claims made by Dr. Seneff are so outlandish they cannot be taken seriously. Let me draw your attention to a few relevant points. The paper in which the claims were made was published in an obscure, pay-for-play journal that is not even indexed in the standard catalogue of biomedical journals, PubMed, and not devoted to the topic of the paper. Moreover, no credible mechanism is presented which could conceivably explain the wide range of disparate claims of harm nor is the argument based on any demonstration of causality, but on dubious inferences of correlation.

At the end of the day, it is important to remember that unlike conventional or organic foods, bioengineered foods are routinely screened in the United States and other industrial nations (per regulations rooted in the OECD guidelines) to ensure they have no toxins or known allergens. The emergence of previously unknown, novel allergens is so vanishingly rare as not to constitute even a remotely legitimate concern. No such hazards have ever been reported from bioengineered foods in the scientific literature, nor any credible hypothesis through which such hazards might possibly arise.

The claim, therefore, that labeling is needed to inform consumers of potential hazards is not only unfounded, but the opposite of the truth: the only safety differential ever reported between bioengineered and other foods shows the bioengineered foods to be safer.

Motivations of the Anti-GMO Advocacy Groups

If protecting human health or the environment is not the objective for these anti-technology opponents, what is? To be clear, the real objective behind the campaign for legislation to mandate "GMO" labels being advanced in a number of legislatures is to falsely stigmatize foods derived from crops improved through biotechnology as a means of driving them from the market. Proponents of mandatory labels have on occasion been honest in acknowledging these objectives as the following quotes show:

Andrew Kimbrell, Executive Director of the "Center for Food Safety, has stated "We are going to force them to label this food. If we have it labeled, then we can organize people not to buy it."

Joseph Mercola, who makes a living selling unregulated, unlabeled supplements at mercola.com, has stated "Personally, I believe GM foods must be banned entirely, but labelling is the most efficient way to achieve this. Since 85% of the public will refuse to buy foods they know to be genetically modified, this will effectively eliminate them from the market just the way it was done in Europe."

Jeffrey Smith, self-publisher of some of the most imaginative anti-biotechnology claims, has said "By avoiding GMOs you contribute to the tipping point of consumer rejection, forcing them out of our food supply."

Professional campaigner Vandana Shiva said "With labeling it (GMOs) will become 0% . . . for you the label issues is vital, if you get labeling then GMOs are dead end."

And the Director of the Organic Consumers Association, Ronnie Cummins, said "The burning question for us all then becomes how—and how quickly—we can move healthy, organic products from a 4.2% market niche, to the dominant force in American food and farming? The first step is to change our labeling laws."

And most recently "mandatory labeling and bans, or GMO-free zones, should be seen as complementary, rather than contradictory."

It takes very little digging to uncover the motivations behind this organized push for mandatory labeling: it is a fear-based marketing campaign motivated by an attempt to expand the market share for organic foods. And this is because these advocates simply distrust technological innovation *per se*, preferring Americans, and the rest of the world, to live in an idyllic, simpler world they believe is closer to a "nature" that meant life spans were half or less what they are today, child mortality at 80 percent or more, and malnutrition and starvation widespread. The reality is that if these neo-Luddites are able to impose their vision of a world on us—a world without GMOs—it will be a world with higher food prices. Perhaps labeling advocates can afford to pay higher prices for organic foods at upscale stores like Whole Foods—which is and should be their right—but using state legislatures to force all Americans down this path (e.g., to spend much more than necessary for safe and wholesome food) is elitist at its core.

Consumers have a right not only to not be deceived and misled. They also have a right not to be forced to pay more for food so they have more money for health care, education and other needs. Compulsory labeling of "GMOs" would deprive them of these rights.

L. VAL GIDDINGS is a senior fellow with the Information Technology and Innovation Foundation, a nonpartisan think tank in Washington, DC.

EXPLORING THE ISSUE

Should Genetically Modified Foods Be Labeled?

Critical Thinking and Reflection

1. What is the greatest threat to human health posed by GM foods?
2. Should tests of genetically modified foods performed by industry scientists be trusted?
3. Should regulation of a new technology be based on demonstrated risks? On potential risks? On the nature of the press coverage?
4. Considering that non-GM foods are frequently contaminated by disease-causing bacteria, should there be a law to require food labels to say "May be contaminated by disease-causing bacteria"?

Is There Common Ground?

The participants in the debate over genetically modified foods agree that it is important to ensure a healthy, safe, and abundant food supply. They differ dramatically on whether genetically modified foods offer any reason to worry about their impact on human health.

1. It can be instructive to consider other threats to a healthy, safe, and abundant food supply. Among these threats are plant diseases known as rusts and blights. Read Rachel Ehrenberg, "Rust Never Sleeps," *Science News* (September 25, 2010), and discuss the global effects of a massive rust outbreak.
2. Another threat is the contamination of ordinary foods by disease-causing bacteria. Visit http://www .foodsafety.gov/ to see how serious this threat is. Discuss how this threat compares to that of GMOs.
3. Anti-GMO activists are charged with using demands for labeling laws as a step toward banning GMOs, or at least forcing them off the market. How would labeling laws accomplish that?

Additional Resources

Steven Druker, *Altered Genes, Twisted Truth: How the Venture to Genetically Engineer Our Food Has Subverted Science, Corrupted Government, and Systematically Deceived the Public* (Clear River Press, 2015).

Sheldon Krimsky and Jeremy Gruber, eds., *The GMO Deception: What You Need to Know about the Food, Corporations, and Government Agencies Putting Our Families and Our Environment at Risk* (Skyhorse Publishing, 2014).

Henry I. Miller and Gregory Conko, *The Frankenfood Myth: How Protest and Politics Threaten the Biotech Revolution* (Praeger, 2004).

National Research Council, Committee on the Impact of Biotechnology on Farm-Level Economics and Sustainability, *The Impact of Genetically Engineered Crops on Farm Sustainability in the United States* (National Academies Press, 2010) (http://www .nap.edu/catalog.php?record_id=12804).

Jeffrey M. Smith, *Seeds of Deception: Exposing Industry and Government Lies about the Safety of the Genetically Engineered Foods You're Eating* (Chelsea Green, 2003).

Internet References . . .

AgBioWorld, Arguments in Favor of Genetically Modified Crops

http://www.agbioworld.org/biotech-info/articles/biotech-art/in_favor.html

Center for Food Safety

http://www.centerforfoodsafety.org/

Information Technology and Innovation Foundation

https://itif.org/

Monsanto on GMOs

http://discover.monsanto.com/monsanto-gmo-foods

World Health Organization

http://www.who.int/foodsafety/biotech/en/

Unit 4

UNIT

SPACE

*M*any interesting controversies arise in connection with technologies that are so new that they may sound more like science fiction than fact. Some examples are technologies that allow the exploration of space, the detection (and perhaps prevention) of space-based threats, and the search for extraterrestrial intelligence. We have capabilities undreamed of in earlier ages, and they raise genuine, important questions about what it is to be a human being, the limits on human freedom in a technological age, the degree to which humans are helpless victims of fate, and the place of humanity in the broader universe. They also raise questions of how we should respond: Should we accept the new devices and abilities offered by scientists and engineers? Or should we reject them? Should we use them to make human life safer and more secure? Or should we remain, as in past ages, at the mercy of the heavens?

Selected, Edited, and with Issue Framing Material by:
Thomas A. Easton, *Mount Ida College*

ISSUE

Can We Stop an Asteroid or Comet Impact?

YES: Michael F. A'Hearn, from "Testimony before the U.S. House of Representatives Committee on Science, Space, and Technology, Hearing on 'Threats from Space: A Review of Private and International Efforts to Track and Mitigate Asteroids and Meteors, Part II,'" U.S. House of Representatives (2013)

NO: Clark R. Chapman, from "What Will Happen When the Next Asteroid Strikes?" *Astronomy Magazine* (2011)

Learning Outcomes

After reading this issue, you will be able to:

- Explain why asteroid and comet impacts are considered a risk to society.
- Explain what options are available to prevent asteroid and comet impacts or mitigate their effects.
- Explain the importance of advance planning to deal with potential disasters such as asteroid and comet impacts.

ISSUE SUMMARY

YES: Michael F. A'Hearn argues that even impacts by small (less than 140 meters in diameter) near-Earth-objects (NEOs) can be damaging and that present detection programs focus only on larger NEOs and will take many years to complete their inventory. The probability that even a small NEO will strike Earth in the near future is small, but the potential damage is so great that investing in identifying and tracking NEOs, and researching ways of preventing impact, is worthwhile.

NO: Clark R. Chapman argues that though the consequences of an asteroid or comet impact would be catastrophic, efforts to prevent the impact would be futile. It is far more appropriate to incorporate such impact disasters into more conventional disaster planning.

Thomas Jefferson once said that he would rather think scientists were crazy than believe that rocks could fall from the sky. Since then, we have recognized that rocks do indeed fall from the sky. Most are quite small and do no more than make pretty streaks across the sky as they burn up in the atmosphere; they are known as meteors. Some—known as meteorites—are large enough to reach the ground and even to do damage. Every once in a while, the news reports one that crashed through a car or house roof, as indeed one did in January 2007 in New Jersey. Very rarely, a meteorite is big enough to make a crater in the Earth's surface, much like the ones that mark the face of the Moon. An example is Meteor Crater in Arizona, almost

a mile across, created some 50,000 years ago by a meteorite 150 feet in diameter. (The Meteor Crater website, http://www.meteorcrater.com/, includes an animation of the impact.) A more impressive impact is the one that occurred 65 million years ago, when a comet or asteroid 10 kilometers (6 miles) in diameter struck near what is now Chicxulub, Mexico: The results included the extinction of the dinosaurs (as well as a great many other species). Chicxulub-scale events are very rare; a hundred million years may pass between them. Meteor Crater-scale events may occur every thousand years, releasing as much energy as a 100-megaton nuclear bomb and destroying an area the size of a city. And it has been calculated that a human being is more likely to die as the result of such an event than in an airplane crash (crashes are much more common but they don't kill as many people as a large impact would).

It is not just Hollywood sci-fi, *Deep Impact* and *Armageddon*. Some people think we really should be worried. We should be doing our best to identify meteoroids (as they are called before they become meteors or meteorites) in space, plot their trajectories, tell when they are coming our way, and even develop ways of deflecting them before they cause enormous losses of life and property. In 1984, Thomas Gehrels, a University of Arizona astronomer, initiated the Spacewatch project, which aimed to identify space rocks that cross Earth's orbit. In the early 1990s, NASA workshops considered the hazards of these rocks. NASA now funds the international Spaceguard Survey, which finds about 25 new near-Earth asteroids every month and has identified more than 600 asteroids over 1 kilometer (2/3 of a mile) in diameter; none seem likely to strike Earth in the next century. On the other hand, in February 2013 an asteroid the size of a skyscraper missed Earth by about 17,000 miles and a 10-ton meteor exploded over Chelyabinsk, Russia (the shock wave broke windows and caused numerous injuries; see Richard Stone, "Siberian Meteor Spurs Dash for Data, Calls for Safeguards," *Science*, March 8, 2013). There are many other large rocks in space, and eventual large impacts on Earth are very likely. According to NASA, there are some 4,700 asteroids more than 100 meters (330 feet) across, of which only 20–30 percent have actually been discovered so far. Greg Easterbrook, "The Sky Is Falling," *Atlantic* (June 2008), argues that human society faces so much risk from asteroid and comet impacts that Congress should place a much higher priority on detecting potential impactors and devising ways to stop them.

In the debate over the risks of near-Earth object (NEO) impacts on Earth, there are a few certainties: They have happened before, they will happen again, and they come in various sizes. As Mike Reynolds says, in "Earth Under Fire," *Astronomy* (August 2006), the question is not whether impacts will happen in the future. "It's just a matter of when and how big the object will be." Many past craters mark the Earth, even though many more have been erased by plate tectonics and erosion. Ivan Semeniuk, "Asteroid Impact," *Mercury* (November/December 2002), says, "If there is one question that best sums up the current state of thinking about the impact hazard, it is this: At what size do we need to act? In the shooting gallery that is our solar system, everyone agrees we are the target of both cannonballs and BBs. The hard part is deciding where to draw the line that separates them. For practical reasons, that line is now set at 1 kilometer. Not only are objects of this diameter a global threat (no matter where they hit, we're all affected to some degree), they are

also the easiest to spot." However, as Richard A. Kerr notes, "The Small Ones Can Kill You, Too," *Science* (September 19, 2003). Edward T. Lu, "Stop the Killer Rocks," *Scientific American* (December 2011), argues that "All civilizations that inhabit planetary systems must eventually deal with the asteroid threat, or they will go the way of the dinosaurs." Action is essential.

What if a "killer rock" does present a threat? In September 2002, NASA held a "Workshop on Scientific Requirements for Mitigation of Hazardous Comets and Asteroids," which concluded "that the prime impediment to further advances in this field is the lack of any assigned responsibility to any national or international organization to prepare for a disruptive collision and the absence of any authority to act in preparation for some future collision mitigation attempt" and urged that "NASA be assigned the responsibility to advance this field" and "a new and adequately funded program be instituted at NASA to create, through space missions and allied research, the specialized knowledge base needed to respond to a future threat of a collision from an asteroid or comet nucleus." The results of the workshop appeared as *Mitigation of Hazardous Impacts Due to Asteroids and Comets* (Cambridge University Press, 2004).

The Organization for Economic Cooperation and Development (OECD) Global Science Forum held a "Workshop on Near Earth Objects: Risks, Policies and Actions" in January 2003. It too concluded that more work is needed. In May 2005, the House Science Committee approved a bill to establish and fund a NASA program to detect and assess near-Earth asteroids and comets down to 100 meters in diameter. As Michael A'Hearn notes in his congressional testimony (see below) that became a Congressional mandate to find 90 percent of NEOs greater than 140 meters in diameter. See also David H. Levy, "Asteroid Alerts: A Risky Business," *Sky & Telescope* (April 2006). NASA's March 2007 "Near-Earth Object Survey and Deflection: Analysis of Alternatives, Report to Congress" argues that although progress is being made, much more would be possible if Congress increased funding.

Given political will and funding, what could be done if a threat were identified? Richard Stone, "Target Earth," *National Geographic* (August 2008), says that "Two facts are clear: Whether in 10 years or 500, a day of reckoning is inevitable. More heartening, for the first time ever we have the means to prevent a natural disaster of epic proportions." There have been numerous proposals, from launching nuclear missiles to pulverize approaching space rocks to sending astronauts (or robots) to install rocket engines and deflect the rocks onto safe paths (perhaps into the sun to forestall future hazards).

A December 2008 study by the U.S. Air Force found that we are woefully unprepared for a NEO impact; see David Shiga, "Asteroid Attack: Putting Earth's Defences to the Test," *New Scientist* (September 23, 2009). Not much has changed since Bill Cooke, "Killer Impact," *Astronomy* (December 2004), warned that for the foreseeable future, our only real hope will be evacuation of the target zone. All proposed methods of warding off disaster require a stronger space program than any nation now has. Lacking such a program, knowing that a major rock is on the way would surely be of little comfort. However, given sufficient notice—on the order of decades—a space program might be mobilized to deal with the threat. Led by ex-astronauts Ed Lu and Rusty Schweickart, the B612 Foundation (http://b612foundation.org/) hopes to address this problem with a privately funded survey satellite called Sentinel; see Robert Irion, "The Save-the-World Foundation," *Science* (August 23, 2013).

At the moment, Europe appears to be taking the lead in the effort to ward off disaster from the skies. In January 2012, the German space agency's (DLR) Institute of Planetary Research in Berlin held the kickoff meeting for Project NEOShield, an international effort to study how to prevent asteroid and comet impacts. See http://www.neoshield.net/en/index.htm.

In the YES selection, Michael F. A'Hearn argues that though the probability that a near-Earth-object (NEO) will strike Earth in the near future is small, the potential damage is so great that investing in identifying and tracking NEOs, and researching ways of preventing impact, is worthwhile. Since much time is likely to be needed to develop technology that can safely and reliably divert a threatening object, it is now time to discuss how to go about it. In the NO selection, planetary scientist Clark R. Chapman argues that though the consequences of an asteroid or comet impact would be catastrophic, efforts to prevent the impact would be futile. It is far more appropriate to incorporate such impact disasters into more conventional disaster planning.

YES ⤶

Michael F. A'Hearn

Testimony before the U.S. House of Representatives Committee on Science, Space, and Technology, Hearing on "Threats from Space: A Review of Private and International Efforts to Track and Mitigate Asteroids and Meteors, Part II"

Mr. Chairman and members of the Committee, thank you for the opportunity to appear today to discuss the potential threats of near-Earth objects (NEOs) in the context of the [National Research Council (NRC)] report on this topic that was issued in 2010. I was the chairman of the mitigation sub-panel for the NRC report, but today I am not representing the NRC, nor NASA, nor the University of Maryland.

The NRC Study: As mandated by Congress in the Consolidated Appropriations Act, 2008, NASA commissioned the NRC to study Surveys for Near-Earth Objects and Hazard Mitigation Strategies. The Steering Committee was chaired by Dr. Irwin Shapiro of Harvard University and the two sub-panels, one for Surveys and Characterization and one for Mitigation Strategies, were chaired by Dr. Faith Vilas, then Director of the MMT Observatory in Arizona, and by myself, respectively. The committee had a wide variety of expertise, ranging over the entire scope of the impact hazard problem. Several public hearings were held, with testimony from numerous experts, some of whom were advocates of specific projects while others were experts in impact prediction and risk communication, and yet others were policy experts.

The committee concluded that the money being expended at that time on NEO surveys was inadequate to meet the congressional mandate of finding 90% of potential impactors larger than 140 m on any reasonable time scale. The committee did not make a specific recommendation on the forward path, but described forward paths for surveys and discovery as a function of how much money Congress wished to appropriate to "buy insurance" against an impact. The amount of money to be appropriated

would directly affect the timeline. The committee also recommended initiating a search for potential impactors in the 50–140-m range. The committee noted that there are basically four approaches to mitigation—evacuation for the smallest impactors, slow push-pull techniques, such as the gravity tractor, for moderately sized impactors with long warning times, and then kinetic impactors and standoff nuclear explosions for successively larger impactors and/or shorter warning times. A research program to better understand these mitigation approaches was recommended. Actual mitigation experiments in space were suggested, provided sufficient funding was provided, and overall programs were described for three different levels of funding.

The committee's report, Defending Planet Earth—Near-Earth-Object Surveys and Hazard Mitigation Strategies, was released in 2010. The remainder of this testimony concerns the details of some of these recommendations, both as recommended by the NRC and including my personal perspectives on the issues.

Impactors <140 meters: At the time of the NRC report, results newly published at that time indicated that previous modeling of impacts, by scaling from nuclear explosions of known yield, were incorrect due to the rapid downward motion of an external impactor compared to a nuclear explosion, for which the source can be considered to be at a fixed altitude. These results, which are still neither refuted nor explicitly confirmed, show that substantial damage can be inflicted by objects that are even smaller than 50 meters in diameter. To be specific, the new calculations suggested that the Tunguska event, which in 1908 flattened every tree over roughly 2000 square km in Siberia, was due to a body in the range of 30–50 meters diameter. Based on our knowledge of the size distribution of NEOs that corresponds to an event that should occur roughly every century or two. For comparison, the best estimate of the Chelyabinsk meteor in February, which caused one building collapse and lots of broken windows with many people injured, is that it had a diameter of 15–20 meters, much smaller than any of the previous estimates of a hazardous size. The size of the Chelyabinsk meteor is better known than most since the trajectory has yielded a reliable velocity and the recovered samples can be used to infer the density of the body. Such an event should occur every several decades. Thus it is clear that objects much smaller than 140 meters are frequent and are capable of significant damage on Earth, although most of these impacts in the past went unnoticed because they occurred over the ocean or over very sparsely inhabited land areas. Detailed modeling of the effects of small impactors, say from Chelyabinsk-size to 140-m diameter, is a gap that should be filled, although most of the computer codes to tackle this problem accurately are under restricted access.

It is widely understood that small objects are much more abundant than large ones in nearly all the populations of the solar system, and specifically among the NEOs. Very roughly, a 14-m NEO is 1000 times more likely than a 140-m NEO. Thus the "next" significant impactor will most likely be closer in size to Chelyabinsk than to 140 meters. It therefore is important to plan for such an event, even if the hazard to life is small.

A key issue for the small impactors is that they are normally so faint prior to impact that we do not know how to detect them very far in advance. Many of them can only be discovered days to weeks before impact. Fortunately, this limitation coincides with the fact that the region of destruction by such an impactor is sufficiently small that evacuation (aka "duck and cover") is a realistic mitigation to minimize loss of life (but not property damage). . . .

Programs at Various Funding Levels: The NRC report noted that any program dealing with NEO hazards as policy, as opposed to programs dealing with NEOs as scientific targets, should be considered as a form of insurance. The hazard is different from other terrestrial hazards, however, in that the insurance can be used to prevent damage rather than paying for restoration after damage. The question should be thought of, therefore, as a question of how much insurance the nation should [buy]. The committee then described three different scenarios, depending on how much insurance was being bought, with rather arbitrary levels being chosen for the scenarios.

At a level of $10 million per year, the then operating survey programs could continue, as could a modest research program into issues related to the NEO hazard. This level would not meet the congressionally mandated

George E. Brown survey to detect 90% of potential impactors larger than 140 meters in diameter.

I note that current spending in NASA's NEO program has increased to roughly $20 million per year, allowing some new initiatives such as the ATLAS program, operations of the PanSTARRS system (currently only one telescope but soon to be two telescopes), and research grants into mitigation related topics. Spending for the Large Synoptic Survey Telescope [(LSST)] is not included in these totals – that telescope, if operated in NEO survey mode only, could meet the 140-meter goal relatively quickly.

At a level of $50 million per year, operation of a telescope such as LSST could be funded for NEO-optimized searches, although this assumes construction funding for astronomical research, e.g., from NSF. Alternatively, an in-flight mitigation mission might be feasible if conducted as a minor part of an international partnership.

At a level of $250 million per year for a decade, the advanced surveys to 140 meters could be completed, either from the ground or from space, and a unilateral mitigation experimental mission would be feasible.

None of the NRC's recommended funding levels addressed the question of impactors smaller than 140 meters. With current technology, late detection appears to be the only feasible approach. Limits for the Sentinel system are not readily available to me, nor are the actual limits of the ATLAS system so I cannot comment on their relative contributions. The NEO program office at JPL has funded an independent study to assess the capability of the ATLAS system.

One also needs to remember that, once the George E. Brown survey to 140 meters is complete (90%), the remaining unidentified impactors include both the smaller impactors and the long-period comets. Although the long-period comets very rarely impact Earth, cumulatively they are likely to lead to as many or more deaths as the much more frequent small events. They have been ignored up to this point because they have been such a small fraction of the total threat, but that situation will change dramatically. One has to decide whether to deal with the small, frequent events or with the rare, large events, or both, analogous to deciding whether to deal with frequent auto accidents or infrequent large airliner or ship accidents or both.

International Cooperation and Collaboration: International collaboration is very important in the entire effort to deal with the impact hazard, from discovery, through impact prediction, to mitigation. Unfortunately, despite considerable discussion at the individual scientist level and considerable discussion at the governmental level up to the United Nations, the U. S. is the only nation with a funded, active and effective survey/discovery program.

Canada has just launched (February 2013) and Germany will soon launch a small satellite designed to discover sub-populations of NEOs, but the U.S. is still the predominant nation in funding an active program for tracking NEOs, both through the JPL NEO Program Office and through funding the entire operation of the Minor Planet Center that is nominally sponsored by the International Astronomical Union.

It should be pointed out that the only terrestrial impactor ever predicted in advance was 2008 TC₃, an impactor much smaller (roughly 4 meters) than the Chelyabinsk meteor. This was discovered less than one day before impact, by R. Kowalski at the Catalina survey, based in Arizona. The impact was predicted only because the Catalina survey included a (NASA-funded) telescope in Australia in addition to the telescopes in Arizona, which allowed very rapid follow up data, and it was the combination of data from both telescopes that allowed the rapid prediction of the impact, including a prediction of the time and location of impact, both of which were extremely accurate. Thus an internationally distributed, and closely interactive, network of telescopes is critical for predicting small impactors. Fortunately, 2008 TC₃ was so small that it caused no damage on the Sahara Desert in northern Sudan where it entered Earth's atmosphere, although small pieces were subsequently recovered days later.

The area in which international collaboration is even more important is mitigation, due largely to the fact that incorrectly changing the orbit of a potential impactor could merely move the impact site from one country to another, with obvious international implications. Even the Chelyabinsk meteor was claimed by a fringe politician in Russia to be an American weapons test, but fortunately the Russian Academy of Sciences was in the forefront of public announcements, clearly declaring that this was a natural meteor. Unfortunately, there has been even less international discussion on this topic than on the survey /discovery/prediction topic, although there have been discussions within the UN's Action Team 14 of COPUOS [(UN Committee on the Peaceful Uses of Outer Space)]. This is an area in which international collaboration, not just discussion, must be established before action is needed.

Contributions of Basic Research to Detection, Characterization, and Mitigation: There is considerable overlap between basic scientific research on comets and asteroids, *i.e.*, on the bodies that include NEOs, and policy-based work on the issues of hazard prediction and mitigation. However, the focus is very different between the two areas and consequently there are significant activities that are not included in one focus or the other. It is for this reason that NEO hazard activities require a separately identified source of funding, associated with national policy, that is not taken out of the scientific programs.

The research activities related to surveys and discovering bodies are aimed at finding statistically significant samples to enable interpretation, and these were the precursors of the specific hazard surveys, which are aimed at discovering as close to all of the objects as is practical (widely being taken to be 90% of the estimated total population). The research surveys, coupled with the work of dynamical researchers studying the orbits of the bodies, are what led to the recognition of the scale of the hazard and many of the individuals involved in those surveys are also involved in the hazard-driven surveys.

Research activities are also directly related to mitigation, but clearly distinct from actual mitigation planning. One of the key issues in mitigation, and for that matter even in predicting the scale of the damage from an impact, is to understand the physical properties of the impactors. Research programs using remote sensing have shown unambiguously that there is a wide variety of physical characteristics among the NEOs, ranging from likely coherent bodies that are the source of iron meteorites through really porous cometary nuclei that are likely to have been the source of the dinosaur-killer K-T impact 65 million years ago. Remote sensing can study a large number of objects and they are sensitive primarily to surface properties of the objects, to their size, and in some cases to a crude measure of their shape and their density.

Important, detailed characteristics of the NEOs can only be learned from *in situ* studies and PI [(Principle Investigation)]-led, competitively selected missions, under NASA's Discovery and New Frontiers programs, provide the key mechanism to carry out these studies. Such missions can only be used to study a very few targets for budgetary reasons. A team led by Mike Belton and myself proposed the Deep Impact mission to the Discovery Program many years ago purely as a scientific mission, with only two sentences in the proposal about the possible peripheral benefits for NEO hazard mitigation. What the mission did for hazard mitigation was to demonstrate active targeting to impact on a small body, the nucleus of comet 9P/Tempel 1 (a technique needed for our science but also a technique needed for mitigation) and it also demonstrated the very porous nature of cometary nuclei (probably 10% of NEOs are inactive cometary nuclei). The observations of the ejecta were used both to determine the bulk density (much empty space inside!) and to estimate the momentum transfer efficiency of the impact as relatively low (roughly 2), a critical parameter for altering an NEO's orbit with a kinetic impactor. The mission also showed the challenges of attitude control in the last minute of approach to a cometary nucleus. These results have been presented to various groups directly concerned about mitigation, such as the Defense Threat Reduction Agency. The results of the subsequent flyby of comet Hartley 2 as part of the EPOXI mission showed the diversity among cometary nuclei and the heterogeneity from place to place on a single nucleus, both of which must be taken into account in mitigation.

The OSIRIS-REx mission, scheduled for launch in 2016, is a very different mission to a different type of NEO, the asteroid 1999 RQ_{36}. This mission will return a sample of the asteroid to Earth for detailed analysis, but while at the asteroid it will also produce, for example, a detailed map of the gravity. In addition to the material properties learned from the returned sample, gravitational mapping can be used to understand the internal structure of the asteroid, critical information for understanding how to mitigate by changing the orbit, whether by kinetic impact, or nuclear explosion, or even with a gravity tractor, which depends less on the physical structure but does depend on the bulk density and the shape.

These competitively chosen "research" missions are not sufficient to completely address mitigation, but they provide most of the necessary information on the range of physical properties one might encounter. Unfortunately, the NASA budget for planetary exploration has been such that NASA's Discovery program (competitively selected, PIled missions with a cost cap of $425M in the latest round), have been devastated compared to even a decade ago. The NRC's recent decadal survey of planetary science recommended that NASA's priorities should be first to maintain a cadre of good researchers, and then to maintain a regular cadence, averaging a new start every two years, for the smallest missions (the Discovery Program), then the New Frontiers program (similar to the Discovery Program but for missions twice as expensive), and finally flagship missions (center directed missions that have lately cost more than $2 billion). Although not every mission in Discovery and New Frontiers is relevant to hazard mitigation (the most recent selection in the Discovery program is a mission to Mars), restoring Discovery to the originally intended cadence of research missions would significantly help with the mitigation effort by ensuring the existence of other missions to comets and asteroids to provide information necessary for mitigation.

Ultimately, however, specific mitigation missions must be considered as discussed above under program levels. They should be funded over and above the research program and they could be either separately funded add-ons to scientific missions or stand-alone missions, or international collaborations, with the international collaboration a high priority. Note that once the range of physical properties is understood, it is still very difficult to determine the physical properties of an actually threatening NEO without sending a mission to it, a possibility with very early discoveries but not with late discoveries.

What Should Be Done in the Event of an Identified NEO Threat? After an NEO threat is identified, the initial steps are well defined. NASA is the lead agency for identifying threats and they have a reporting path through the U.S. government that covers all relevant federal agencies and the POTUS [(President of the United States)]. Reporting to other countries is also urgent and should be done through the U.N. in order to reach all governments. In addition, there should be direct communication with countries and international agencies that have relevant capabilities for mitigation. Immediately following the alert, it is crucial to share all available data publicly. This is routine for the positional observations of the NEO and for the resultant orbital computations through the Minor Planet Center and through JPL's NEO Program Office. Beyond this, however, it is crucial to share all available information on the physical characteristics of the NEO from whatever source and on the details of the impact prediction. In the case of 2008 TC_3, which presented no hazard, this information was communicated through the channels normally used worldwide by astronomers and information was made readily available to news media.

The next steps depend critically on the nature of the threat—how big the impact will be, how far in the future it will occur, and where it will occur. An all-out effort to determine the characteristics of the particular impactor is crucial—remote sensing being needed in any case and, if time permits, a mission to characterize the NEO should be initiated in order to optimize the mitigation. Short warning times, however, may preclude an advance characterization mission and in that case the range of expected properties must be used to design a fail-safe mitigation. Action paths are, to my limited knowledge, not yet in place domestically. For a small impactor, a plausible route is through FEMA. For a larger impactor, however, either the military or NASA might be the one to take charge. For truly large impactors, the lead country and agency should be coordinated among those countries that have the capability to execute any mitigation. This decision/action tree should be fleshed out and made publicly available long before any specific threat is identified.

MICHAEL F. A'HEARN is Professor Emeritus in the Astronomy Department, University of Maryland. His research for many years has emphasized the study of comets and asteroids.

Clark R. Chapman    **NO**

What Will Happen When the Next Asteroid Strikes?

On October 6, 2008, I was on my way to the Johns Hopkins Applied Physics Laboratory when I turned on the news in the car and could hardly believe my ears: An asteroid discovered late the previous night was predicted to strike Earth in just a few hours—at 2:46 UT on October 7, to be precise. Ground zero would be in Sudan's Nubian Desert, just south of the Egyptian border.

For 2 decades, astronomers had reported minute chances that an asteroid might strike in the distant future, and also about "close calls" as near-Earth asteroids (NEAs) sailed by our planet at distances comparable to that of the Moon. This, however, was the first confident prediction in history of an impending asteroid impact—and it would happen less than 20 hours after discovery.

Fortunately, the incoming rock wasn't dangerous, measuring just 10 to 13 feet (3 to 4 meters) across. But a larger asteroid would cause significant destruction; would we have enough warning?

Collecting Space Rocks

A congressional hearing in 1998 mandated that scientists discover and catalog 90 percent of NEAs larger than 0.6 mile (1 kilometer) wide within 10 years, thus finding them years or decades before one might strike. Immediately after the mandate, astronomers formed the Spaceguard Survey to do just that. (It is a bit behind schedule, having found about 83 percent of them by late 2010.) The hope is we find an NEA on a likely collision course with enough time to do something about it: for example, design and launch a spacecraft mission to tug on the object or run into it. This would nudge it onto a slightly different path, missing Earth.

The Catalina Sky Survey (CSS) telescopes on Mount Bigelow, north of Tucson, Arizona, are part of the Spaceguard Survey, and it was CSS's Richard Kowalski who first noted the moving spot of light October 6, 2008, which scientists later dubbed 2008 TC3. He immediately reported it to the Minor Planet Center in Cambridge, Massachusetts, which made a preliminary calculation of the asteroid's orbit. This time, there would be no decades of warning—just hours. Luckily, physicists had calculated that objects like 2008 TC3 would explode brilliantly, but harmlessly, high in the atmosphere. Thus, asteroids smaller than about 100 feet (30m) were nothing to fear, they said.

2008 TC3 exploded high in the atmosphere, but not exactly harmlessly. Thousands of stone fragments struck the desert beneath its flight path (an area perhaps 20 miles [32 km] long and a few miles across). About 600 pieces have been recovered so far. Ground zero was empty except for a small train station, which scientists named the meteorites after (Almahata Sitta means "Station 6" in Arabic).

A Range of Consequences

2008 TC3 was a small rock, so what about larger ones? When will the "Big One" hit? (And what defines the "Big One"?) Asteroids tend to travel at similar speeds—about 100 times faster than a jet airliner—so it is primarily their masses that determine their destructive potential when they strike Earth.

The monster object that struck 65 million years ago—eradicating most species of life, including dinosaurs, and paving the way for the emergence of mammals—was a "Big One." It was probably about 6 to 9 miles (10 to 15 km) wide. Its explosive force of a hundred million megatons of TNT disrupted the planet's ecosphere and caused the mass extinction. (Scientists call this collision the K-T boundary event because it represents the sharp change in fossils at the boundary between the Cretaceous [K] and Tertiary [T] periods.) Such an event could happen again this century, but the odds are exceedingly small; the Spaceguard Survey tells us that no NEA even close to that size will hit. Huge objects impact every hundred million years or so.

A large comet, however, could come from the outer solar system and reach Earth in a couple of years, and we could do nothing about it but fearfully await the demise of our species. But the chances of that happening are almost infinitesimally tiny—maybe one in 10 million during this century.

With modest tweaks to CSS observing protocols, or using modest-sized telescopes dedicated to searching for objects on their final plunge to Earth's surface, we could plausibly have advance warning—of tens of hours to weeks—for perhaps half of infalling asteroids larger than a few feet. The other half, coming from the Sun's direction, would still strike without warning.

Notifications of days to weeks provide no chance for a deflection mission. Even attempting to destroy the object as it approaches would risk converting a precisely known ground-zero location into an unpredictable, scattered-shotgun outcome. However, such warnings, just as those for hurricanes, could enable people to evacuate ground zero, potentially saving many lives. In the case of 2008 TC₃, the warning process didn't work perfectly; luckily, there was almost no one in the desert to warn.

The 2008 TC3 event was mostly good luck: It was the first successful prediction of an asteroid strike (and on such short notice), and the meteorites were recovered (which would have been much less likely if it fell in a swamp or jungle). Largely informal Internet communications enabled many astronomers—professionals and amateurs alike—to observe 2008 TC₃ before it entered Earth's shadow and struck. So, for the first time, we have rocks in our laboratories that we can compare directly with telescopic observations of their progenitor asteroid in space. But 20 hours is extremely short notice. The October 2008 collision showed that we still don't have enough protocols for warning and evacuation in place.

History Shows Collisions

The largest well-documented asteroid impact occurred in 1908. Near the Podkamennaya Tunguska River in Siberia, a multi-megaton atmospheric explosion caused much destruction. Scientists think a roughly 130-foot-wide (40m) asteroid exploded with an energy 30 million times less powerful than the K-T boundary impact. Luckily, the mosquito-infested taiga forest was only sparsely inhabited—the explosion knocked down and burned trees for many miles around. Had the Tunguska blast been over a densely populated region, the natural disaster would have rivaled the worst earthquakes of recent decades. There is a fair chance, maybe one in three or four, that another Tunguska-like impact will happen this century,

but it would likely occur over an ocean or a barren desert because a larger percentage of Earth's area is either one of these environments rather than a city.

Asteroids and comets are much more plentiful, but also less damaging, the smaller they are. Although a few K-T-boundary-sized NEAs exist, interplanetary space is voluminous. The chance that such a large cosmic body and Earth would arrive in the same place in our lifetime at the same time is tiny. 2008 TC₃-like impacts are much more likely (we think they occur roughly annually, but we can't see them all). There are hundreds of such NEAs for every Tunguska-sized object, and hundreds of millions for every K-T boundary impactor. And still smaller-sized objects are visible as meteor flashes on any clear, dark night due to countless tiny pebbles and an occasional larger rock burning up harmlessly in the night sky.

Target Earth

A cosmic body vastly more massive and energetic than Tunguska but 100 times less energetic than the K-T boundary event could have serious consequences. It might kill a billion people, destroy the infrastructure of our civilization, and return us to a dark age—but probably not render the human species extinct. Humanity has never experienced a cataclysm more devastating than the Black Plague of the 14th century, so it is difficult to predict the outcome of an impact by such a 1.2- to 1.9-mile-diameter (2 or 3 km) object. Fortunately, the damage would pale before the ecological collapse at the K-T boundary.

Such an impact will happen, although it's much more likely to be millions of years from now rather than during this century. These events have happened in the past, but probably not since human beings first evolved. With objects this size, it won't matter whether the incoming rock strikes the ocean or a desert—the environmental consequences will be enormous worldwide.

Let's play out the scenario. It would start with someone discovering a comet (the Spaceguard Survey has a complete census of large NEAs showing that no asteroid larger than 1.2 miles [2 km] will hit in this century). After a few nights of additional measurements, scientists would calculate a tentative orbit and soon after realize that Earth might be in its path. They would redouble their efforts to observe the comet. Let's say astronomers find that the comet is 1.5 miles (2.4 km) across—rather small as comets go but twice the size of Comet 103P/Hartley, recently visited by NASA's EPOXI mission. They could then calculate the exact date of impact. (Even when the chance of collision is tiny, scientists can determine what date the object would hit, as well as the location of a narrow path across

Earth where it would hit.) After weeks and months, the likelihood of an Earth impact would grow.

There might be talk of trying to deflect the comet with a spacecraft—unfortunately for us, that mission would be futile. We couldn't launch enough mass to crash into it. (Engineers have in mind a sphere of metal or rock several tons in mass.) A "gravity tractor" probably wouldn't work either—it moves small bodies large distances, or larger objects small distances. Just conceivably, a large nuclear blast might be energetic enough to boil off the surface on one side of the comet, forcing it to move slightly in reaction. But we couldn't build and launch such a mission in time to intersect the comet years in advance, which is the time needed for nuclear-blast deflection to work. And most comets move unpredictably because of their own outgassing, so it might just as likely nudge the comet toward Earth as away. If we break apart the comet nucleus, smaller pieces with unknown trajectories could pummel our planet.

The Aftermath

I'll leave it to science fiction to describe how individuals, nations, emergency planners, religions, and economic interests worldwide might respond to the ever-more-confident predictions of a cometary calamity as the months pass. But we can estimate what would happen, physically, when the comet struck.

First, we can calculate the immediate damage in the region where the object hits. Planetary scientist Jay Melosh of Purdue University in West Lafayette, Indiana, and his colleagues have a starting place for the calculation: They created a website application called "Impact: Earth" (www.purdue.edu/impactearth) where you can plug in values to simulate collision aftereffects. In our scenario, we have a comet 1.5 miles (2.4 km) in diameter, with a density of 1,000 kilograms per cubic meter (the density of ice). It strikes at 20 miles/second (32 km/s) into a rural area of sedimentary rock.

At 50 miles (80 km) from ground zero, the fireball of the exploding comet—which would appear 60 times bigger than the Sun—would immediately burn us and every flammable thing around us. Surrounding buildings would suffer major damage from the resulting earthquake—nearly as big as the Chilean one of February 2010—that would reach our charred remains about 16 seconds after impact. Some 4 minutes after impact, an enormous airblast with winds approaching 1,200 mph (1,900 km/h) would sweep away anything left standing.

If we were 300 miles (480 km) away from ground zero, we would likely survive, at least initially. Because

we know of the impending impact, we could hide in a well-constructed building to avoid burns from the fireball, protect ourselves from falling rocks, and endure the earthquake and airblast. Either the earthquake about 1.6 minutes after impact or the hurricane-force airblast arriving 24.4 minutes after the impact might badly damage ordinary wood-frame houses.

Our best option would be to evacuate far away from ground zero long before the comet approached Earth. But we still wouldn't be safe. What calculations such as "Impact: Earth" don't describe are the global environmental and infrastructure damage, which could disrupt civilization worldwide for months and years to come. For example, as the comet penetrates the atmosphere, chemical reactions would likely destroy Earth's protective ozone layer. Some scientists think there could be an enormous electromagnetic pulse (EMP) that might disable electrical grids around the world and render communications and electronic equipment (including Earth's orbiting satellites) nonfunctional. Unfortunately, we don't know much about the effect; scientists haven't seriously researched impact-induced EMPs.

In addition, Earth would undergo significant climate changes as Sun-blocking dust is launched into the atmosphere after impact. As dust circles the globe during the ensuing weeks, perhaps crossing the equator into the opposite hemisphere, temperatures would cool dramatically, threatening an agricultural growing season and hence the world's food supply.

With more than a year of warning, the international community could mitigate the worst effects before impact: prepare for unprecedented food shortages, the required medical effort, and the possible collapse of the world's economic infrastructure. Maybe humanity could weather the storm without letting fears of the terrible prognosis exacerbate tensions, which would magnify the unfolding tragedy. With foreknowledge, civilization might survive, depending on whether we can stay resilient as we face such a natural disaster.

Closer to Impact

Fortunately, the chance of a 1.5-mile-wide comet striking within the next few centuries is tiny. Instead of worrying about the highly improbable, let's focus on how we will face more 2008 TC_3-sized objects, and even bigger ones like a Tunguska. Civil defense and emergency managers are not yet sufficiently informed about asteroids, nor are communications channels established and tested to reliably warn people near ground zero in time to evacuate.

We must incorporate our future handling of these infrequent events into the "all hazards" methods that nations and localities use when facing the much more frequent floods, tornadoes, and avalanches. The National Research Council, the President's Office of Science and Technology, and NASA's Planetary Defense Task Force published reports about the NEA impact hazard in 2010.

Our country, along with the United Nations, is taking the first steps toward becoming more robustly prepared. . . .

CLARK R. CHAPMAN is a planetary scientist in the Department of Space Studies at the Southwest Research Institute in Boulder, Colorado.

EXPLORING THE ISSUE

Can We Stop An Asteroid or Comet Impact?

Critical Thinking and Reflection

1. Suppose that astronomers announce that an asteroid big enough to destroy the United States will strike Ohio in 10 years. What could we do about it?
2. Make that 25 years. What could we do about it?
3. Given the inevitability of an eventual asteroid impact, how important is it that we plan ahead? How much should we spend per year on preparations for warding off the impact or recovering afterward?

Is There Common Ground?

No one thinks that if an asteroid or comet struck the Earth, the consequences would be trivial. But because such impacts are rare events, many people are inclined to think they don't need to worry *now*, there is nothing that could be done to stop them, and besides, there are a great many other problems—from malaria to global hunger to climate change—that deserve funding more immediately. As the selections for this issue point out, however, it doesn't take huge amounts of funding to maintain a watch on the skies, inventory potential threats, and plan ahead. Our essayists even agree that for small NEO impacts, evacuation and disaster relief programs (e.g., FEMA) are most appropriate. They differ on what can usefully be done about larger impacts.

There are other potential disasters for which a precautionary approach is appropriate. Look up the following terms (begin with the listed URLs) and discuss how people are preparing for future problems.

1. Volcanoes (http://www.scientificamerican.com/article.cfm?id=volcano-monitoring-jindal)
2. Supervolcanoes (http://volcanoes.usgs.gov/volcanoes/yellowstone/yellowstone_sub_page_49.html)
3. Tsunamis (http://www.ess.washington.edu/tsunami/general/warning/warning.html)
4. Earthquakes (http://earthquake.usgs.gov/)

Additional Resources

Committee to Review Near-Earth-Object Surveys and Hazard Mitigation Strategies Space Studies Board, *Defending Planet Earth: Near-Earth Object Surveys and Hazard Mitigation Strategies* (National Academies Press, 2010).

Greg Easterbrook, "The Sky Is Falling," *Atlantic* (June 2008).

Edward T. Lu, "Stop the Killer Rocks," *Scientific American* (December 2011).

National Research Council, *Defending Planet Earth: Near-Earth Object Surveys and Hazard Mitigation Strategies* (National Academies Press, 2010; http://www.nap.edu/catalog.php?record_id=12842).

Richard Stone, "Target Earth," *National Geographic* (August 2008).

Internet References . . .

National Aeronautics and Space Administration

http://www.nasa.gov

Near Earth Object Program

http://neo.jpl.nasa.gov/index.html

NEOShield: Preparing to Protect the Planet

http://www.neoshield.net/en/index.htm

Meteor Explodes above Urals

http://www.youtube.com/watch?v=yWTanCmQAxk&noredirect=1

The Near Earth Object Dynamic Site (NEODyS)

http://newton.dm.unipi.it/neodys/

Selected, Edited, and with Issue Framing Material by:
Thomas A. Easton, *Mount Ida College*

ISSUE

Will the Search for Extraterrestrial Life Ever Succeed?

YES: Seth Shostak, from "Using Radio in the Search for Extraterrestrial Intelligence," U.S. House of Representatives (2014)

NO: Peter Schenkel, from "SETI Requires a Skeptical Reappraisal," *Skeptical Inquirer* (2006)

Learning Outcomes

After studying this issue, students will be able to:

- Explain why it ever seemed reasonable to use radio telescopes to search for extraterrestrial intelligence.
- Explain why some people think, despite the lack of success to date, that it remains worthwhile to search for extraterrestrial intelligence.
- Explain why some people think SETI is not a worthwhile endeavor.
- Discuss the likely consequences of successful SETI.

ISSUE SUMMARY

YES: Radio astronomer and Search for Extraterrestrial Intelligence (SETI) researcher Seth Shostak defends SETI and argues that if the assumptions behind the search are well grounded, "it is not hyperbole to suggest that scientists could very well discover extraterrestrial intelligence within two decades."

NO: Peter Schenkel argues that SETI's lack of success to date, coupled with the apparent uniqueness of Earth's history and suitability for life, suggests that intelligent life is probably rare in our galaxy and that the enthusiastic optimism of SETI proponents should be reined in.

In the 1960s and early 1970s, the business of listening to the radio whispers of the stars and hoping to pick up signals emanating from some alien civilization was still new. Few scientists held visions equal to those of Frank Drake, one of the pioneers of the SETI field. Drake and scientists like him use radio telescopes—large, dish-like radio receiver-antenna combinations—to scan radio frequencies (channels) for signal patterns that would indicate that the signal was transmitted by an intelligent being. In his early days, Drake worked with relatively small and weak telescopes out of listening posts that he had established in Green Bank, West Virginia, and Arecibo, Puerto Rico. See Carl Sagan and Frank Drake, "The Search for Extraterrestrial Intelligence," *Scientific American*

(May 1975), and Frank Drake and Dava Sobel, *Is Anyone Out There? The Scientific Search for Extraterrestrial Intelligence* (Delacorte Press, 1992).

There have been more than 50 searches for extraterrestrial (ET) radio signals since 1960. The earliest ones were very limited. Later searches have been more ambitious, using multiple telescopes and powerful computers to scan millions of radio frequencies per second. New technologies and techniques continue to make the search more efficient. See Monte Ross, "The New Search for E.T.," *IEEE Spectrum* (November 2006).

At the outset, many people thought—and many still think—that SETI has about as much scientific relevance as searches for the Loch Ness Monster, Bigfoot, and the Abominable Snowman. However, to SETI fans it seems inevitable that with so many stars in the sky, there must be other worlds with life upon them, and some of that life must be intelligent and have a suitable technology and the desire to search for alien life too.

Writing about SETI in the September–October 1991 issue of *The Humanist*, physicist Shawn Carlson compares visiting the National Shrine of the Immaculate Conception in Washington, D.C., to looking up at the stars and "wondering if, in all [the] vastness [of the starry sky], there is anybody out there looking in our direction . . . [A]re there planets like ours peopled with creatures like us staring into their skies and wondering about the possibilities of life on other worlds, perhaps even trying to contact it?" That is, SETI arouses in its devotees an almost religious sense of mystery and awe, a craving for contact with the *other*. Success would open up a universe of possibilities, add immensely to human knowledge, and perhaps even provide solutions to problems that our interstellar neighbors have already defeated.

SETI also arouses strong objections, partly because it challenges human uniqueness. Many scientists have objected that life-bearing worlds such as Earth must be exceedingly rare because the conditions that make them suitable for life as we know it—composition and temperature—are so narrowly defined. Others have objected that there is no reason whatsoever to expect that evolution would produce intelligence more than once or that, if it did, the species would be similar enough to humans to allow communication. Still others say that even if intelligent life is common, technology may not be so common, or technology may occupy such a brief period in the life of an intelligent species that there is virtually no chance that it would coincide with Earth scientists' current search. Whatever their reasons are, SETI detractors agree that listening for ET signals is futile. Ben Zuckerman, "Why SETI Will Fail," *Mercury* (September/October 2002), argues that the simple fact that we have not been visited by ETs indicates that there are probably very few ET civilizations, and SETI is therefore futile.

Are we in fact alone or first? Are the conditions that lead to life and intelligence rare? Are there aliens living in disguise among us? Or are we quarantined? Reservationed? Zooed? Or maybe there is nobody there at all—not even us! (Sure, that could be it—if we are just simulations in some cosmic computer.) In *Where Is Everybody? Fifty Solutions to the Fermi Paradox and the Problem of Extraterrestrial Life* (Copernicus Books, 2002), Stephen Webb describes Fermi and his paradox (if they're out there, why haven't we been visited?) in great detail and offers a variety of answers that have been suggested—most seriously, some a bit tongue-in-cheek—for why the search has not succeeded.

His own opinion is on the pessimistic side. The SETI community, however, remains convinced that their effort is worthwhile.

Astronomers have found a great many stars with planets, but so far they have not seen signs of life. Steve Nadis, "How Many Civilizations Lurk in the Cosmos?" *Astronomy* (April 2010), discusses how the latest data have improved estimates of how many ET civilizations might exist in the galaxy. Nadis quotes Frank Drake as saying that early estimates may have been much too low. There may be 10,000 such civilizations, and detecting even one may require that we examine 20 million stars. There is, however, an even larger obstacle to success. Paul Davies, *The Eerie Silence* (Houghton Mifflin Harcourt, 2010), notes that our efforts at detection are severely limited by the communications technologies we are familiar with, and ET civilizations may use those technologies for only a brief period in their history, moving on to others that we have not yet thought of and have no way to detect. We need new thinking, meaning that we must look for signals in neutrinos from space, embedded in the genes of viruses, and much more. See also Elizabeth Quill, "Can You Hear Me Now?" *Science News* (April 24, 2010). Unfortunately, our efforts at detection are also limited by funding difficulties here at home; M. Mitchell Waldrop, "SETI Is Dead, Long Live SETI," *Nature* (July 28, 2011), discusses the closure of the Allen Telescope Array at the Hat Creek Radio Observatory in California, ending a "big science" approach to SETI (however, private funding has kept the Array open for now; see Nicole Gugliucci, "SETI's Allen Telescope Array Is Back on Track!" *Discovery*, August 27, 2011; http://news.discovery.com/space/setistars-successful-funding-jodie-foster-110817.htm). Smaller projects, however, do continue. There is also more emphasis today on detecting life—not the presumably rarer *intelligent* life—on other worlds, using techniques ranging from Mars rovers seeking sedimentary rocks that bear the chemical signatures of life to spectroscopic analyses of the atmospheres of planets circling distant stars, looking for oxygen, methane, or even industrial pollutants; see Michael D. Lemonick, "The Hunt for Life Beyond Earth," *National Geographic* (July 2014); Bruce Dorminey, "A New Way to Search for Life in Space," *Astronomy* (June 2014); Timothy D. Brandt and David S. Spiegel, "Prospects for Detecting Oxygen, Water, and Chlorophyll on an Exo-Earth," *Proceedings of the National Academy of Sciences of the United States of America* (September 16, 2014); and Henry W. Lin, Gonzalo Gonzalez Abad, and Abraham Loeb, "Detecting Industrial Pollution in the Atmospheres of Earth-Like Exoplanets," http://arxiv.org/abs/1406.3025 (July 21, 2014).

What if SETI succeeds? Frank Drake noted in *Is Anyone Out There? The Scientific Search for Extraterrestrial Intelligence*) that positive results would have to be reported to everyone, at once, in order to prevent attempts to suppress or monopolize the discovery. Albert A. Harrison, "Confirmation of ETA: Initial Organizational Response," *Acta Astronautica* (August 2003), focuses on the need for a response to success, but he is skeptical that an effective response is possible; he says, "Foresight and advance preparation are among the steps that organizations may take to prepare for contact, but conservative values, skepticism towards SETI, and competing organizational priorities make serious preparation unlikely." Should our response include sending an answer back to the source of whatever radio signals we detect? H. Paul Schuch, "The Search for Extraterrestrial Intelligence," *Futurist* (May/June 2003), suggests that there may be dangers in such a move. These dangers are addressed by Ivan Almar and H. Paul Schuch in "The San Marino Scale: A New Analytical Tool for Assessing Transmission Risk," *Acta Astronautica* (January 2007); see also Ivan Almar, "SETI and Astrobiology: The Rio Scale and the London Scale," *Acta Astronautica* (November 2011), and Douglas A. Vakoch, "Responsibility, Capability, and Active SETI: Policy, Law, Ethics, and Communication with Extraterrestrial Intelligence," *Acta Astronautica* (February 2011). A few nonscientists have also begun to consider the implications of successful contact. See, for instance, Thomas Hoffman, "Exomissiology: The Launching of Exotheology," *Dialog: A Journal of Theology* (Winter 2004). David Brin, "The Dangers of First Contact," *Skeptic* (vol. 15, no. 3, 2010), argues that because the idea of free and open exchange of information is a historical anomaly here on Earth, any attempts to reply to a signal should not include our most valuable assets—our art, music, science, and other information. Instead, we should seek equal exchange, *quid pro quo*. He does not agree that those scientists are necessarily right who say that ETs must be highly advanced ethically and thus likely to treat us benignly. At the same time, he argues that we should not count on ET messages to solve our problems; it is better that we rely on ourselves.

Have the results of SETI to date been totally blank? Researchers have found nothing that justified any claim of success, but there have been a few "tantalizing signals." T, Joseph W. Lazio and Robert Naeye discuss them in "Hello? Are You Still There?" *Mercury* (May/June 2003).

In the YES selection, Seth Shostak defends SETI and argues that if the assumptions behind the search are reasonable, "it is not hyperbole to suggest that scientists could very well discover extraterrestrial intelligence within two decades." In the NO selection, Peter Schenkel, a retired political scientist, argues that SETI's lack of success to date, coupled with the apparent uniqueness of Earth's history and suitability for life, suggests that intelligent life is probably rare in our galaxy. It is time, he says, "to dampen excessive ET euphoria and to adopt a . . . stand, compatible with facts."

YES ↵

Seth Shostak

Using Radio in the Search for Extraterrestrial Intelligence

The question of whether we share the universe with other intelligent beings is of long standing. Written speculation on this subject stretches back to the classical Greeks, and it hardly seems unreasonable to suppose that even the earliest *Homo sapiens* gazed at the night sky and wondered if beings as clever as themselves dwelled in those vast and dark spaces.

What is different today is that we have both sufficient scientific knowledge and adequate communications technology to permit us to address this question in a meaningful way.

Finding extraterrestrial intelligence would calibrate humanity's place in the cosmos. It would also complete the so-called Copernican revolution. Beginning about 470 years ago, observation and scientific reasoning led to an accurate understanding of our place in the physical universe. The goal of SETI—the Search for Extraterrestrial Intelligence—is to learn our place in the intellectual universe. Are our cognitive abilities singular, or are they simply one instance among many?

Just as large sailing ships and the compass inaugurated the great age of terrestrial exploration at the end of the 15th century, so too does our modern technology—coupled to a far deeper understanding of the structure of the universe than we had even two decades ago—give us the possibility to discover sentient life elsewhere. SETI is exploration, and the consequences of exploration are often profoundly enlightening and ultimately of unanticipated utility. We know that our species is special, but is it unique? That is the question that SETI hopes to answer.

Why We Think that Life Exists Elsewhere

There is, as of now, no compelling evidence for biology beyond Earth. While the widely reported claims of fossilized microbes in a Martian meteorite generated great excitement in 1996, the opinion of most members of the astrobiology community today is that the claims are unconvincing.

Nonetheless these same astrobiologists, if asked if they think it likely that extraterrestrial life is both commonplace and discoverable, would nod their heads affirmatively.

They would do so largely because of what we've learned in the past two decades concerning the prevalence of life-friendly cosmic habitats. Until 1995, we knew of no planets around other stars, habitable or otherwise. And yes, there was speculation that such worlds might be common, but that sunny thought was *only* speculation.

In the last two decades, astronomers have uncovered one so-called exoplanet after another. The current tally is approximately two thousand, and many more are in the offing thanks to continued analysis of data from NASA's enormously successful Kepler space telescope.

Estimates are that at least 70 percent of all stars are accompanied by planets, and since the latter can occur in systems rather than as individuals (think of our own solar system), the number of planets in the Milky Way galaxy is of order one trillion. It bears mentioning that the Milky Way is only one of 150 billion galaxies visible to our telescopes—and each of these will have its own complement of planets. This is plentitude beyond easy comprehension.

The Kepler mission's principal science objective has been to determine what fraction of this planetary harvest consists of worlds that could support life. The usual metric for whether a planet is habitable or not is to ascertain whether liquid water could exist on its surface. Most worlds will either be too cold, too hot, or of a type (like Jupiter) that may have no solid surface and be swaddled in noxious gases. Recent analyses of Kepler data suggest that as many as one star in five will have a habitable, Earth-size planet in orbit around it. This number could be too large by perhaps a factor of two or three, but even so it implies that the Milky Way is home to 10 to 80 billion cousins of Earth.

There is, in other words, more than adequate cosmic real estate for extraterrestrial life, including intelligent life.

A further datum established by recent research is that the chemical building blocks of life—the various carbon compounds (such as amino acids) that make up all terrestrial organisms—are naturally formed and in great abundance throughout the cosmos. The requisites for biology are everywhere, and while that doesn't guarantee that life will be spawned on all the worlds whose physical conditions are similar to our own, it does encourage the thought that it occurs frequently.

If even only one in a thousand "earths" develop life, our home galaxy is still host to tens of millions of worlds encrusted by flora and fauna.

However, SETI is a class of experiments designed to find not just life, but technologically sophisticated life—beings whose level of intellect and development is at least equal to our own. So it is germane to ask, even assuming that there are many worlds with life, what fraction will eventually evolve a species with the cognitive talents of *Homo sapiens*? This is a question that's both controversial and difficult to answer.

As some evolutionary biologists (including most famously Ernst Mayr and Stephen Jay Gould) have pointed out, the road from early multicellular life forms (e.g., trilobites) to us is an uncertain one with many forks. For example, if the asteroid that wiped out the dinosaurs (and two-thirds of all other land-dwelling species) 65 million years ago had arrived in our neighborhood 15 minutes later, it could have missed the Earth. The stage might never have been cleared for the mammals to assert themselves and eventually produce us. This simple argument suggests that, while life could be commonplace, intelligence might be rare.

On the other hand, recent research has shown that many different species of animals have become considerably more clever in the last 50 million years. These include of course simians—but also dolphins, toothed whales, octopuses, and some birds. One plausible interpretation of these findings is that intelligence has so much survival value that—given a complex biota and enough time—it will eventually arise on any world.

We don't know what the truth is regarding the emergence of cognition. But finding another example of an intelligent species would tell us that *Homo sapiens* is not singular. The possibility of elucidating this evolutionary question is one of the most enticing motives for doing SETI experiments.

Finding Extraterrestrial Intelligence

Although encounters with intelligent aliens are a frequent staple of movies and television, the idea of establishing the existence of these putative beings by traveling to their home planets is one that will remain fiction for the foreseeable future. The planets that orbit the Sun may include other worlds with life (Mars, various moons of the planets Jupiter and Saturn). But they are surely devoid of any life that would be our cerebral equals. Intelligent beings—assuming they exist—are on planets (or possibly large moons) orbiting other stars. Those are presently unreachable: Even our best rockets would take 100 thousand years to traverse the distance to the nearest other stellar systems. The idea that extraterrestrials have come here (the so-called UFO phenomenon), while given credence by approximately one-third of the populace, is not considered well established by the majority of scientists.

However, the methods used by SETI to discover the existence of intelligence elsewhere don't require that either we or they pay a visit. All we need do is find a signal, come to us at the speed of light. The first modern SETI experiment was conducted in 1960, when astronomer Frank Drake used an 85-foot diameter antenna at the newly constructed National Radio Astronomy Observatory in West Virginia in an attempt to "eavesdrop" on signals either deliberately or accidentally transmitted by beings light-years away. Drake used a very simple receiver, and examined two nearby star systems.

By contrast, later SETI experiments have made use of far more sensitive equipment, and have greatly expanded the scope of the search. Project Phoenix—a survey by the SETI Institute of 1,000 star systems—used antennas that ranged from 140—1,000 feet in diameter with receivers that could look for weak signals in ten million radio channels simultaneously. Today's efforts by the Institute use a small grouping of 42 antennas known as the Allen Telescope Array, situated in the Cascade Mountains of northern California. The advantage of this instrument is that it can be used for a very high percentage of time for SETI experiments, unlike previous campaigns that relied on antennas that were shared with radio astronomers doing conventional research projects. This latter circumstance greatly constrained the number of possible searches.

The other large radio SETI group in the U.S. is at the University of California, Berkeley. Their long-running Project SERENDIP uses the very large (1,000-foot diameter) antenna at Arecibo, Puerto Rico in a commensal mode. By piggybacking on this antenna, the Berkeley group gets virtually continuous use of the antenna, but the price is that they have no control of where it is aimed. However, over the course of several years, this random scrutiny covers roughly one-third of the sky. The receiver can simultaneously monitor more than 100 million channels, and some of the Berkeley data are made available for processing by individuals on their home computers using the popular screen saver, SETI@home. Approximately ten million people have downloaded the screen saver.

At the moment, the only other full-time radio SETI experiment is being conducted by a small group at the Medicina Observatory of the University of Bologna, in Italy.

Radio SETI searches preceded efforts to look for brief laser light pulses, known as optical SETI, largely because the development of practical radio occurred more than a half-century before the invention of the laser. Nonetheless, radio remains a favored technique for establishing the existence of intelligence beyond Earth. The amount of energy required to send a bit of information from one star system to another using radio is less than other schemes, and therefore it seems plausible that, no matter what other communication technologies intelligent species might develop, radio will always have a function. As a simple analogy: the wheel is an ancient technology for us, yet we use it every day and undoubtedly always will.

Radio SETI experiments have not yet detected a signal that is unambiguously extraterrestrial. Some people, both in and out of the science community, have ascribed undue significance to this fact, claiming that it indicates that no one is out there. While this may be comforting to those who would prefer to think that our species is the only one with the wit to comprehend the cosmos, it is a thoroughly unwarranted conclusion. Despite a many-decades long history of effort, our scrutiny of star systems still remains tentative. The number of star systems carefully examined over a wide range of the radio dial is no more than a few thousand. In the Milky Way, there are hundreds of billions of star systems. Consequently, our reconnaissance is akin to exploring Africa for megafauna, but one that has so far been limited to a square city block of territory.

While no one knows how prevalent signal generating civilizations might be, the more conservative estimates suggest that—to find a transmission that would prove others are out there—requires surveillance of a million star systems or more. This could be done in the near future, given the relentlessly increasing power of digital electronics. It is not hyperbolic to suggest that scientists could very well discover extraterrestrial intelligence within two decades' time or less, given resources to conduct the search.

However, funding for SETI is perennially problematic. The most ambitious SETI program, the one planned by NASA in the 1980s and 1990s, had scarcely begun observations when Congress canceled funding in the Fall of 1993. Since then, SETI efforts in this country have either been privately funded, or been an incidental part of university research. As a telling metric of the limitations of this approach, note that the total number of scientists and engineers doing full-time SETI in this country is approximately one dozen, or comparable to the tally of employees at a car wash.

Progress and Evolution of Radio SETI

A rough and ready estimate suggests that today's radio SETI experiments are about 100 trillion times more effective—as judged by speed, sensitivity, and range of radio frequencies investigated—than Frank Drake's pioneering 1960 search. The rapid development of both analog and digital electronics has spinoffs that are accelerating the capabilities of SETI.

As example, in 1980 typical SETI efforts sported receivers able to monitor 10 thousand channels simultaneously. Today's experiments sport 10—100 million channels, causing a thousand-fold increase in search speed.

Speed is essential to success. As mentioned above, conservative estimates of the prevalence of broadcasting societies hint that—in order to find a signal from another species—our SETI experiments will need to "listen" in the direction of at least 1 million stellar systems. Cheaper digital technology, which can be read as greater compute power, immediately leads to receivers with more channels—which means that it takes less time to check out all the interesting frequencies for a given SETI target.

In the case of antenna arrays, cheaper computing can also speed observations by increasing the number of star systems looked at simultaneously. As example, the Allen Telescope Array currently has the ability to examine three such systems at once. But this could be increased to hundreds or even thousands with more computing power—bringing with it a concomitant augmentation of speed.

Current and Future Resources

As noted above, the level of radio SETI effort today is small, employing roughly a dozen full- time scientists and engineers. At the height of the NASA SETI program (1992), the annual budget for this activity was $10 million, or one-thousandth of the space agency's budget. This supported equipment development and observations for a two-pronged strategy—a low-sensitivity survey of the entire sky, and a high-sensitivity targeted search of the nearest thousand star systems. The number of scientists involved was five times greater than today.

The financial support for all radio SETI efforts in the United States now is approximately 20 percent of the earlier NASA program, and comes from either private donations or from research activities at the University of California. This is, frankly, a level inadequate for keeping this science alive. The cost of developing and maintaining the requisite equipment and software, as well as paying for the scientists and engineers who do the experiments, is—at minimum—$5 million annually. Without this level of funding, the U.S. SETI efforts are likely to be overtaken by Asian and European initiatives (such as the Square Kilometer Array) in the next decade. SETI is exploration. There's no way to guarantee that if only sufficient effort is made, success will inevitably follow. Like all exploration, we don't know what we'll find, and it's possible that we'll not find anything. But if we don't search, the chances are good that the discovery of intelligence elsewhere in the cosmos will be made by others. That discovery will rank among the most profound in the history of humankind. The first evidence that we share the universe with other intelligence will be viewed by our descendants as an inflection point in history, and a transformative event.

The Public's Interest

The idea of extraterrestrials resonates with the public in a way that little of the arcane research of modern science does. While much was made of the discovery of the Higgs boson in 2012, people who weren't schooled in advanced physics had a difficult time understanding just why this was important, and what justified the multi-billion dollar price tag of the collider used in its discovery.

The idea of life in space on the other hand is science that everyone grasps. Countless creatures from the skies infest both movies and television. In addition, the techniques of SETI—while complex in detail—are simple in principle. Carl Sagan's novel and movie, "Contact," enjoyed considerable popularity, and familiarized millions with the technique of using radio to search for extraterrestrials. Documentaries on SETI and the search for life in general can be found on cable television every week. Compare that with the frequency of programming on, say, organic chemistry.

In other words, SETI is an endeavor that everyone "gets." And that includes school kids. This makes the subject an ideal hook for interesting young people in science. They come for the aliens, but along the way they learn astronomy, biology, and planetary science. Even if SETI fails to find a signal for decades, it does great good by enticing youth to develop skills in science.

It's even possible that we are hard-wired to be interested in extraterrestrial life, in the same way that we are programmed to be interested in the behavior of predators. The latter has obvious survival value (and might explain why so many young people are intrigued by dinosaurs!) Our interest in "aliens" could simply derive from the survival value of learning about our peers. Extraterrestrials are the unknown tribe over the hill—potential competitors or mates, but in any case someone we would like to know more about.

There's no doubt that SETI occasionally provokes derision. It's easy to make fun of an effort whose goal is to find "space aliens." But this is to conflate science fiction with science. As our telescopes continue to peel back the film that has darkened our view of the cosmos since *Homo sapiens* first walked the savannahs, we are learning that the Earth is only one of 100,000 billion planets, spinning quietly in the vast tracts of space. It would be a cramped mind indeed that didn't wonder who might be out there.

SETH SHOSTAK is senior astronomer at the SETI Institute. He frequently presents the Institute's work in the media, through lectures, and via the Institute's weekly radio show, *Are We Alone?*

Peter Schenkel  **NO**

SETI Requires a Skeptical Reappraisal

The possible existence of extraterrestrial intelligence (ETI) has always stirred the imagination of man. Greek philosophers speculated about it. Giordano Bruno was burnt on the stake in Rome in 1600, mainly [for] positing the likelihood of other inhabited worlds in the universe. Kant and Laplace were also convinced of the multiplicity of worlds similar to ours. In the latter part of the nineteenth century Flammarion charmed vast circles with his books on the plurality of habitable worlds. But all these ideas were mainly philosophical considerations or pure speculations. It was only in the second half of the twentieth century that the Search for Extraterrestrial Intelligence (SETI) became a scientifically underpinned endeavor. Since the late 1950s distinguished scientists have conducted research, attempting to receive intelligent signals or messages from space via radio-telescopes. Hundreds of amateur astronomers, members of the SETI-League in dozens of countries, are scanning the sky, trying to detect evidence of intelligent life elsewhere in our galaxy. SETI pioneers, such as Frank Drake and Carl Sagan, held the stance that the Milky Way is teeming with a large number of advanced civilizations. However, the many search projects to date have not succeeded, and this daring prediction remains unverified. New scientific insights suggest the need for a more cautious approach and a revision of the overly optimistic considerations.

The standard argument for the existence of a multiplicity of intelligent life runs like this: There are about 200 to 300 billion stars in our galaxy and probably hundreds of millions, maybe even billions of planets in our galaxy. Many of these planets are likely to be located in the so-called "habitable zone" in relation [to] their star, enjoying Earth-favorable conditions for the evolution of life. The physical laws, known to us, apply also to the cosmos, and far-away stellar formations are composed of the same elements as our solar system. Therefore, it is assumed, many should possess water and a stable atmosphere, considered to be basic requisites for the development of life. Such planets must have experienced geological and biological processes similar to those on Earth, leading to the development of primitive life organisms. Then, in the course of time, following a similar course of Darwin's theory of natural selection, these evolved into more complex forms, some eventually developing cognitive capacities and—as in our case—higher intelligence.

In other words, it is maintained, our solar system, Earth, and its evolution are not exceptional cases, but something very common in our Milky Way galaxy. Consequently it must be populated by a huge number of extraterrestrial civilizations, many of them older and more advanced than ours.

Considering the enormous number of stars and planets, these seem like fair and legitimate assumptions. It indeed appears unlikely that intelligence should have evolved only on our planet. If many of these civilizations are scientifically and technologically superior to us, contact with them would give mankind a boost in many ways.

These optimistic views are based mainly on the famous Drake formula. . . . It considers the formation of stars in the galaxy, the fraction of stars with planetary systems, the number of planets ecologically suited for life, the fraction of these planets on which life and intelligent life evolves, and those reaching a communicative stage and the length of time of technical civilizations. On the basis of this formula it was estimated that a million advanced civilizations probably exist in the galaxy. The nearest one should be at a distance of about 200 to 300 light-years from Earth. German astronomer Sebastian von Hoerner estimated a number between ten thousand and ten million such civilizations.

But because of many new insights and results of research in a number of scientific fields, ranging from paleontology, geology, biology to astronomy, I believe this formula is incomplete and must be revised. The early optimistic estimates are no longer tenable. A more realistic and sober view is required.

I by no means intend to discredit SETI; the search for extraterrestrial intelligent life is a legitimate scientific endeavor. But it seems prudent to demystify this interesting subject, and to reformulate its claims on a new level, free of the romantic flair that adorns it.

Years ago, I readily admit, I myself was quite taken in by the allegations that intelligence is a very common phenomenon in the galaxy. In books, articles, and on radio and television I advocated the idea that our world, beset by problems, could learn a lot from a civilization more advanced than ours. But, in the meantime, I became convinced that a more skeptical attitude would do reality better justice. There are probably only a few such civilizations in the galaxy, if any at all. The following considerations buttress this rather pessimistic appraisal.

First of all, since project OZMA I in 1959 by Frank Drake, about a hundred radio-magnetic and other searches were conducted in the U.S. and in other countries, and a considerable part of our sky was scanned thoroughly and repeatedly, but it remained disappointingly silent. In forty-six years not a single artificial intelligent signal or message from outer space was received. Some specialists try to downplay this negative result, arguing that so far only a small part of the entire spectrum has been covered, and that more time and more sophisticated equipment is required for arriving at a definite conclusion. Technological and economic criteria may thwart the possibility of extraterrestrial civilizations beaming signals into space over long stretches of time, without knowing where to direct their signals. Or, they may use communication methods unknown to us. Another explanation is that advanced ETI may lack interest in contacting other intelligences, especially those less developed. The argument of the Russian rocket expert Konstantin Tsiolkovski is often quoted: "Absence of evidence is not evidence of absence."

But neither of these arguments, which attempt to explain why we have not received a single intelligent signal from space, is convincing. True, future search projects may strike pay dirt and register the reception of a signal of verified artificial origin. But as long as no such evidence is forthcoming, the possibility of achieving success must be considered remote. If a hundred searches were unsuccessful, it is fair to deduce that estimates of a million or many thousands ETI are unsustainable propositions. As long as no breakthrough occurs, the probability of contact with ETI is near to zero. The argument that advanced extraterrestrials may not be interested in contact with other intelligences is also—as I will show—highly implausible.

Second, as recent research results demonstrate, many more factors and conditions than those considered by the Drake formula need to be taken into account. The geologist Peter D. Ward and the astronomer Donald Brownlee present in their book *Rare Earth* a series of such aspects, which turn the optimistic estimates of ETI upside down.

According to their reasoning, the old assumption that our solar system and Earth are quite common phenomena in the galaxy needs profound revision. On the contrary, the new insights suggest, we are much more special than thought. The evolution of life forms and eventually of intelligent life on Earth was due to a large number of very special conditions and developments, many of a coincidental nature. I'll mention only some that seem particularly important: The age, size, and composition of our sun, the location of Earth and inclination of its axis to it, the existence of water, a stable oxygen-rich atmosphere and temperature over long periods of time—factors considered essential for the evolution of life—and the development of a carbon-based chemistry. Furthermore an active interior and the existence of plate tectonics form the majestic mountain ridges like the Alps, the Himalayas and the Andes, creating different ecological conditions, propitious for the proliferation of a great variety of species. Also the existence of the Moon, Jupiter, and Saturn (as shields for the bombardment of comets and meteorites during the early stages of Earth). Also the repeated climatic changes, long ice ages, and especially the numerous and quite fortuitous catastrophes, causing the extinction of many species, like the one 65 million years ago, which led to the disappearance of dinosaurs but opened the way for more diversified and complex life forms.

Though first primitive life forms on Earth, the prokaryotic bacteria, evolved relatively rapidly, only about 500 million years after the cooling off of Earth's crust and the end of the dense bombardment of meteorites and comets, they were the only life forms during the first two billion years of Earth's 4.6-billion-year history. Mammals—including apes and man—developed much later, only after the extinction of the dinosaurs 65 million years ago. The first human-like being, the Proconsul, emerged in the Miocene Period, just about 18 million years ago. The Australopithecus, our antecessor, dates only 5 to 6 million years. In other words, it took almost 4 billion years, or more than 96 percent of the age of Earth, for intelligence to evolve—an awfully long time, even on the cosmic clock.

In this regard we should note also the caveat of the distinguished biologist Ernst Mayr, who underscored the enormous complexity of human DNA and RNA and their functions for the production of proteins, the basic building blocks of life. He estimated that the likelihood that similar biological developments may have occurred elsewhere in the universe was nil.

The upshot of these considerations is the following: Because of the very special geological, biological, and other conditions which propitiated the evolution of life and intelligence on Earth, similar developments in our galaxy are probably very rare. Primitive life forms, Ward and Brownlee conclude, may exist on planets of other stellar systems, but intelligent life, as ours, is probably very rare, if it exists at all.

Third is the so-called "Fermi Paradox," another powerful reason suggesting a skeptical evaluation of the multiplicity of intelligence in the galaxy. Italian physicist Enrico Fermi posed the annoying question, "If so many highly developed ETIs are out there, as SETI specialists claim, why haven't they contacted us?" I already expressed great doubt about some of the explanations given [for] this paradox. Here I need to focus on two more. The first refers to the supposed lack of interest of advanced aliens to establish contact with other intelligent beings. This argument seems to me particularly untrustworthy. I refer to a Norwegian book, which explains why the Vikings undertook dangerous voyages to far-away coasts in precarious vessels. "One reason," it says, "is fame, another curiosity, and a third, gain!" If the Vikings, driven by the desire to discover the unknown, reached America a thousand years ago with a primitive technology, if we—furthermore—a still scientifically and technically young civilization, search for primitive life on other planets of the solar system and their moons, it is incredible that higher developed extraterrestrial intelligences would not be spurred by likewise interests and yearnings. One of the fundamental traits of intelligence is its unquenchable intellectual curiosity and urge to penetrate the unknown. Elder civilizations, our peers in every respect, must be imbued by the same daring and scrutinizing spirit, because if they are not, they could not have achieved their advanced standards.

A second argument often posited is that distances between stars are too great for interstellar travel. But this explanation also stands on shaky ground. Even our scientifically and technically adolescent civilization is exploring space and sending probes—the Voyager crafts—which someday may reach other stellar systems. We are still far from achieving velocities, near the velocity of light, necessary for interstellar travel. But some scientists predict that in 200 or 300 years, maybe even earlier, we are likely to master low "c" velocities, and once we reach them, our civilization will send manned exploratory expeditions to the nearest stars. Automatic unmanned craft may be the initial attempts. But I am convinced that nothing will impede the desire of man to see other worlds with his own eyes, to touch their soil and to perform research that unmanned probes would not be able to perform. Evidently, civilizations tens of thousands or millions of years in our advance will have reached near c velocities, and they will be able to explore a considerable part of the galaxy. Advanced ETI

civilizations would engage in such explorations not only out of scientific curiosity, but in their own interest, for instance for spreading out and finding new habitats for their growing population, or because of the need to abandon their planet due to hazards from their star, and also because with the help of other civilizations it may confront dangers, lurking in the universe, more successfully than alone. The Fermi Paradox should therefore put us on guard, and foster a sound skepticism. Lack of interest in meeting a civilization such as ours is the least plausible reason why we have not heard from ETI.

A little mental experiment illustrates this point. Carl Sagan held once that intelligent aliens would visit Earth at least once every thousand years. But such visits have not taken place. Even extending this period to a million years, we fare no better. Let us assume an extraterrestrial craft landed on Earth any time during the era of the dinosaurs, lasting about 140 million years. It is only logical to assume the aliens would have returned at reasonable intervals to study our world and these fascinating animals, but also to find out if any one of them evolved the capability of reasoning, higher math, and building a civilization. There would have been reason for much surmise. According to paleontologists, Drake stresses, the dinosaur sauronithoides was endowed with such a potential. It was a dinosaur resembling a bird of our size and weight and possessing a mass of brain well above average, and, Drake speculates, if it had survived for an additional ten or twenty million years, it might have evolved into the first intelligent being on Earth. But it didn't happen, because the dinosaurs went extinct due to a cosmic catastrophe. When *Homo australopithecus*, then *Homo faber* and *habilis*, and lastly *Homo sapiens* evolved, shouldn't that have provoked on the part of visiting extraterrestrials a high level of interest? But no such visits are recorded. Only a few mythological, undocumented and highly suspect accounts of alleged visiting aliens exist. It is fair to assume, if advanced aliens had visited Earth during the past 200 million or, at least, during the past 16 million years, they would have left some durable, indestructible and recognizable mark, probably on the moon. But nothing has been detected. The most likely explanation? No such visits took place! There are no advanced extraterrestrial civilizations anywhere in our vicinity. If they existed, they already would have responded to our world's television signals, reaching some 60 light-years into space—another reason invalidating the claim that our galaxy is teeming with intelligence.

Another argument supporting the skeptical point of view sustained here is the fact that none of the detected planets around other stars comes close to having conditions apt for creating and sustaining life. Since Michel

Mayor's Swiss group discovered the first planet outside our solar system around the star 51 Pegasi ten years ago, about 130 other planets have been identified within a distance of 200 light-years. Research results show that most are of gaseous composition, some many times the size of Jupiter, some very close to their stars, very hot and with extremely rapid orbital cycles. So far, not one presents conditions favorable for the development of even the most primitive forms of life, not to speak of more complex species. Again it may be argued that only a very tiny fraction of planets were surveyed and future research might strike upon a suitable candidate. This may well be, and I would certainly welcome it. But so far the evidence fails to nourish optimistic expectations. The conditions in our universe are not as favorable for the evolution of life as optimists like to think.

Even if water or fossils of microorganisms should be found underneath the surface of Mars, the importance of such a finding for the theory of a multiplicity of inhabited worlds would be insignificant. Some astronomers think that Titan, the famous moon of Saturn, may have an ocean, possibly of methane. Primitive life forms may exist in it, but this remains to be seen. Even if it does, the evolutionary path from such primitive forms to complex life as human beings is—as we have seen—a long one, studded with a unique sequence of chance and catastrophes.

I am not claiming that we are probably the only intelligent species in our galaxy. Nor do I suggest that SETI activities are a waste of time and money. Though, so far, they have failed to obtain evidence for the existence of ETI, they enrich man's knowledge about the cosmos in many ways. They helped develop sophisticated search techniques, and they contribute decisively to the perception of man's cosmic destiny. Carl Sagan and Frank Drake, the two most distinguished pioneers of SETI, did ground breaking work. That their efforts and those of other dedicated SETI experts on behalf of this great cause are tinged with a dash of too optimistic expectation is understandable and profoundly human.

However, in the interest of science and sound skepticism, I believe it is time to take the new findings and insights into account, to dampen excessive SETI euphoria and to adopt a more pragmatic and down-to-earth stand, compatible with facts. We should quietly admit that the early estimates—that there may be a million, a hundred thousand, or ten thousand advanced extraterrestrial civilizations in our galaxy—may no longer be tenable. There might not be a hundred, not even ten such civilizations. The optimistic estimates were fraught with too many imponderables and speculative appraisals. What is required is to make contact with a single extraterrestrial intelligence, obtaining irrefutable, thoroughly verified evidence, either via electromagnetic or optical waves or via physical contact, that we are not the only intelligent species in the cosmos. Maybe an alien spacecraft, attracted by our signals, will decide to visit us some day, as I surmised in my novel *Contact: Are We Ready for It?* I would be the first one to react to such a contact event with great delight and satisfaction. The knowledge that we are not alone in the vast realm of the cosmos, and that it will be possible to establish a fruitful dialogue with other, possibly more advanced intelligent beings would mark the biggest event in human history. It would open the door to fantastic perspectives.

But SETI activities so far do not justify this hope. They recommend a more realistic and sober view. Considering the negative search results, the creation of excessive expectations is only grist to the mill of the naysayers—for instance, members of Congress who question the scientific standing of SETI, imputing to it wishful thinking, and denying it financial support. This absolutely negative approach to SETI is certainly wrong, because contrary to the UFO hoax, SETI (as UCLA space scientist Mark Moldwin stressed in a recent issue of this magazine) is based on solid scientific premises and considerations. But exaggerated estimates fail to conform to realities, as they are seen today, tending to backfire and create disappointment and a turning away from this fascinating scientific endeavor. The dream of mankind to find brethren in space may yet be fulfilled. If it is not, man should not feel sorry for his uniqueness. Rather that circumstance should boost the gratitude for his existence and his sense of responsibility for making the most of it.

PETER SCHENKEL is a retired political scientist interested in the question of what contact with advanced aliens would mean to humanity.

EXPLORING THE ISSUE

Will the Search for Extraterrestrial Life Ever Succeed?

Critical Thinking and Reflection

1. Why do SETI fans think searching for extraterrestrial signals is worth the effort?
2. Why do SETI critics think the effort is wasted?
3. If SETI researchers ever detect extraterrestrial signals, should they reply? If so, what should they say?
4. Why aren't real-life extraterrestrials likely to be much like the ones on TV and in the movies?

Is There Common Ground?

In the debate over this issue, there seems to be little common ground. One side thinks it worth continuing SETI. The other side says, "Forget it." But there are related areas of research, such as the search by astronomers for planets circling other stars, which to many have the ultimate goal of finding life-bearing worlds.

1. What are "exoplanets" and why do astronomers search for them? (http://planetquest.jpl.nasa.gov/; www.superwasp.org/exoplanets.htm)
2. One recent exoplanet discovery was briefly dubbed the "Goldilocks planet." Look up the term and discuss why both the astronomers and the media were excited.
3. To many people, the "Fermi Paradox" is no paradox at all. It posits that we have not been visited by aliens, but what about UFOs, the Roswell incident, alien abductions, and so on?

Why don't SETI researchers take such things seriously?

Additional Resources

Ronald D. Ekers, *SETI 2020: A Roadmap for the Search for Extraterrestrial Intelligence* (SETI Press, SETI Institute, 2002).

Michael D. Lemonick, "The Hunt for Life Beyond Earth," *National Geographic* (July 2014).

Alan Penny, "SETI: Peering into the Future," *Astronomy & Geophysics* (February 2011).

H. Paul Shuch, *Searching for Extraterrestrial Intelligence: SETI Past, Present, and Future* (Springer, 2011).

Douglas A. Vakoch, "Responsibility, Capability, and Active SETI: Policy, Law, Ethics, and Communication with Extraterrestrial Intelligence," *Acta Astronautica* (February 2011).

Internet References . . .

SETI at Home

http://setiathome.ssl.berkeley.edu/

SETI Institute

http://www.seti.org

The Allen Telescope Array

http://www.seti.org/ata

The Exoplanet Data Explorer

http://exoplanets.org/

Selected, Edited, and with Issue Framing Material by:
Thomas A. Easton, *Mount Ida College*

ISSUE

Should the United States Continue Its Human Spaceflight Program?

YES: Committee on Human Spaceflight, from "Pathways to Exploration: Rationales and Approaches for a U.S. Program of Human Space Exploration," The National Academies Press (2014)

NO: Amitai Etzioni, from "Final Frontier vs. Fruitful Frontier: The Case for Increasing Ocean Exploration," *Issues in Science and Technology* (2014)

Learning Outcomes

After reading this issue, you will be able to:

- Explain the potential benefits of space exploration.
- Explain the potential benefits of ocean exploration.
- Argue both in favor of and against sending human beings on space missions.
- Explain how political and budgetary factors make it difficult to justify manned space exploration.

ISSUE SUMMARY

YES: The National Research Council's Committee on Human Spaceflight argues that the combination of the pragmatic benefits of and the human aspirations associated with human spaceflight are great enough to justify continuing the United States' human spaceflight program.

NO: Professor Amitai Etzioni argues that the Earth's oceans offer more potential discoveries, more resources for human use, and more contributions to national security and disaster preparedness than outer space. The exploration of space should be replaced by the exploration of the oceans, and the necessary budgetary resources should be taken from NASA.

The dream of conquering space has a long history. The Russian Konstantin Tsiolkovsky (1857–1935) and the American Robert H. Goddard (1882–1945), the pioneers of rocketry, dreamed of exploring other worlds, although neither lived long enough to see the first artificial satellite, the Soviet *Sputnik*, go up in 1957. That success sparked a race between America and the Soviet Union to be the first to achieve each step in the progression of space exploration. The next steps were to put dogs (the Soviet Laika was the first), monkeys, chimps, and finally human beings into orbit. Communications, weather, and spy satellites were designed and launched. And on July 20, 1969, the U.S. Apollo Program landed the first men on the moon.

There were a few more *Apollo* landings, but not many. The United States had achieved its main political goal of beating the Soviets to the moon and, in the minds of the government, demonstrating the United States' superiority. Thereafter, the United States was content to send automated spacecraft (computer-operated robots) off to observe Venus, Mars, and the rings of Saturn; to land on Mars and study its soil; and even to carry recordings of Earth's sights and sounds past the distant edge of the solar system, perhaps to be retrieved in the distant future by intelligent life from some other world. (Those recordings are attached to the *Voyager* spacecraft, launched in 1977; published as a combination of CD, CD-ROM, and book, *Murmurs of Earth: The Voyager Interstellar Record*

[Ballantine, 1978; available from Amazon]). Humans have not left near-Earth orbit for two decades, even though space technology has continued to develop. The results of this development include communications satellites, space shuttles, space stations, and independent robotic explorers such as the *Mariners* and *Vikings,* the Mars rovers *Spirit, Opportunity,* and *Curiosity*, and the polar lander *Phoenix*, which finally found water on Mars in July 2008.

Why has human space exploration gone no further to date? One reason is that robots are now extremely capable. Although some robot spacecraft have failed partially or completely, there have been many grand successes that have added enormously to humanity's knowledge of Earth and other planets. Another is money: Lifting robotic explorers into space is expensive, but lifting people into space—along with all the food, water, air, and other supplies necessary to keep them alive for the duration of a mission—is much more expensive. And there are many people in government and elsewhere who cry that there are many better ways to spend the money on Earth.

Still another reason for the reduction in human space travel seems to be the fear that astronauts will die in space. This point was emphasized by the explosion on takeoff of the space shuttle *Challenger* in January 1986, which killed seven astronauts and froze the entire shuttle program for over two and a half years. The point was reinforced by the breakup of *Columbia* on entry February 1, 2003. After the latter event, the public reaction included many calls for an end to such risky, expensive enterprises. See Jerry Grey, "Columbia—Aftermath of a Tragedy," *Aerospace America* (March 2003); John Byron, "Is Manned Space Flight Worth It?" *Proceedings* (of the U. S. Naval Institute) (March 2003) (and Richard H. Truly's response in the May issue); and "Manned or Unmanned into Space?" *USA Today* (February 26, 2003), among many others. Robert Zubrin, "How Much Is an Astronaut's Life Worth?" *Reason* (February 2012), argues that risk is an inescapable part of manned spaceflight and the refusal to accept risk has hamstrung the space program. "Human spaceflight vehicles . . . are daring ships of exploration that need to sail in harm's way if they are to accomplish a mission critical to the human future. The mission needs to come first."

In 2004 when President George W. Bush announced his plan to send humans to the Moon and Mars, beginning as soon as 2015, the reaction was immediate. James A. Van Allen asked "Is Human Spaceflight Obsolete?" in *Issues in Science and Technology* (Summer 2004). Andrew Lawler asked "How Much Space for Science?" in *Science* (January 30, 2004). Physicist and Nobel laureate

Steven Weinberg, "The Wrong Stuff," *New York Review of Books* (April 8, 2004), argued that nothing needs doing in space that cannot be done without human presence. Until we find something that does need humans on the scene, there is no particular reason to send humans—at great expense—into space.

John Derbyshire, "Space Is for Science," *National Review* (June 5, 2006), argues that the expense and hazards of putting humans in space do not justify the benefits when much cheaper automated spacecraft (robots) can make all necessary observations. Paul D. Spudis, "Who Should Explore Space? Astronaut Explorers Can Perform Science in Space that Robots Cannot," *Scientific American* (Special Edition, January 2008), argues that there is no substitute for human astronauts in installing and maintaining equipment and in conducting field exploration because humans provide skills that are unlikely to be automated in the foreseeable future. Francis Slakey, "Who Should Explore Space? Unmanned Spacecraft Are Exploring the Solar System More Cheaply and Effectively than Astronauts Are," *Scientific American* (Special Edition, January 2008), argues that NASA sends humans into space chiefly for public relations purposes. Unmanned probes are much cheaper and more effective than astronauts, and many scientific organizations have recommended that *space* science should instead be done through robotic and telescopic missions. See also Louis D. Friedman and G. Scott Hubbard, "Examining the Vision," *American Scientist* (July/August 2008).

The question of whether robots can do the job is particularly relevant because of the success of the Mars rovers, *Spirit, Opportunity,* and *Curiosity*. If robots continue to be successful, it seems likely that efforts to promote manned space travel will meet resistance. Funding for space exploration remains low largely because problems on Earth (environmental and other) seem to need money more urgently than space exploration projects do. The prospects for manned space expeditions to the moon, Mars, or other worlds seem very dim, although Paul D. Spudis, "Harvest the Moon," *Astronomy* (June 2003), argues that there are four good reasons for putting people at least on the Moon: "The first motivation to revisit the Moon is that its rocks hold the early history of our own planet and the solar system. Next, its unique environment and properties make it an ideal vantage point for observing the universe. The Moon is also a natural space station where we can learn how to live off-planet. And finally, it gives us an extraterrestrial filling station, with resources to use both locally and in near-Earth space." See also Paul D. Spudis, "The New Moon,"

Scientific American (December 2003). Nader Elhefnawy, "Beyond *Columbia*: Is There a Future for Humanity in Space?" *The Humanist* (September/October 2003), says that we cannot ignore the wealth of resources in space. Alex Ellery, "Humans versus Robots for Space Exploration and Development," *Space Policy* (May 2003), argues that "though robotics and artificial intelligence are becoming more sophisticated, they will not be able to deal with 'thinking-on-one's-feet' tasks that require generalisations from past experience. . . . there will be a critical role for humans in space for the foreseeable future." Carl Gethmann, "Manned Space Travel as a Cultural Mission," *Poiesis & Praxis* (December 2006), argues that costs should not be used to reject manned space travel as a pointless option. The dream and the effort are part of our culture, and we should pursue them as far as we can afford to. Arthur Woods, "The Space Option," *Leonardo* (vol. 41, no. 4, 2008), argues that space resources are the most realistic way to ensure future human survival and success.

Jeff Foust, "The Future of Human Spaceflight," *Technology Review* (January/February 2010), summarizes the report of the Augustine Commission (*Seeking a Human Spaceflight Program Worthy of a Great Nation*, October 2009, http://www.nasa.gov/pdf/396093main_HSF_Cmte_FinalReport .pdf) and argues that the ultimate goal of manned space exploration is to "chart a path for human expansion into the solar system." To support that goal will require extending the life of the International Space Station (ISS),

providing more funding for mission development, and encouraging the private sector to take over transportation to and from the ISS. At present, human spaceflight is not sustainable. Early in 2010, President Barack Obama announced plans to cancel existing plans for a new launch system that would replace the present Space Shuttle, shift support missions for the International Space Station to commercial spaceflight companies, and to start work on a new system that would be able to support missions to asteroids and even Mars; see Andrew Lawler, "Obama Backs New Launcher and Bigger NASA Budget," *Science* (January 1, 2010). In May 2012, the first commercial flight—the unmanned SpaceX Dragon—successfully reached the International Space Station; see "SpaceX Dragon Triumph: Only the Beginning," *CNN online* (May 25, 2012) (http://lightyears.blogs.cnn.com/2012/05/25 /spacex-orbital-mission-just-the-beginning/).

In the YES selection, the National Research Council's Committee on Human Spaceflight argues that the combination of the pragmatic benefits of and the human aspirations associated with human spaceflight are great enough to justify continuing the United States' human spaceflight program. In the NO selection, Professor Amitai Etzioni argues that the Earth's oceans offer more potential discoveries, more resources for human use, and more contributions to national security and disaster preparedness than outer space. The exploration of space should be replaced by the exploration of the oceans, and the necessary budgetary resources should be taken from NASA.

YES ↵

Committee on Human Spaceflight

Pathways to Exploration: Rationales and Approaches for a U.S. Program of Human Space Exploration

Summary

The United States has publicly funded its human space-flight program continuously for more than a halfcentury. Today, the United States is the major partner in a massive orbital facility, the International Space Station (ISS), that is a model for how U.S. leadership can engage nations through soft power and that is becoming the focal point for the first tentative steps in commercial cargo and crewed orbital spaceflights. Yet, a national consensus on the long-term future of human spaceflight beyond our commitment to the ISS remains elusive.

   The task for the Committee on Human Spaceflight originated in the National Aeronautics and Space Administration [NASA] Authorization Act of 2010, which required that the National Academies perform a human-spaceflight study that would review "the goals, core capabilities, and direction of human space flight." The explicit examination of rationales, along with the identification of enduring questions, set the task apart from numerous similar studies performed over the preceding several decades, as did the requirement that the committee bring broad public and stakeholder input into its considerations. The complex mix of historical achievement and uncertain future made the task faced by the committee extraordinarily challenging and multidimensional. Nevertheless, the committee has come to agree on a set of major conclusions and recommendations, which are summarized here.

Enduring Questions

Enduring questions are questions that serve as motivators of aspiration, scientific endeavors, debate, and critical thinking in the realm of human spaceflight. The questions endure in that any answers available today are at best provisional and will change as more exploration is done. Enduring questions provide motivations that are immune to external forces and policy shifts. They are intended not only to stand the test of time but also to continue to drive work forward in the face of technological, societal, and economic constraints. Enduring questions are clear and intrinsically connect to broadly shared human experience. . . . The committee asserts that the enduring questions motivating human spaceflight are these:

- How far from Earth can humans go?
- What can humans discover and achieve when we get there?

Rationales for Human Spaceflight and the Public Interest

All the arguments that the committee heard in support of human spaceflight have been used in various forms and combinations to justify the program for many years. In the committee's view, these rationales can be divided into two sets. Pragmatic rationales involve economic benefits, contributions to national security, contributions to national stature and international relations, inspiration for students and citizens to further their science and engineering education, and contributions to science. Aspirational rationales involve the eventual survival of the human species (through off-Earth settlement) and shared human destiny and the aspiration to explore. In reviewing the rationales, the committee concluded as follows:

- *Economic matters.* There is no widely accepted, robust quantitative methodology to support comparative assessments of the returns on investment in federal R&D programs in different economic sectors and fields of research. Nevertheless, it is clear that the NASA human spaceflight program, like other government R&D programs, has stimulated economic activity and has advanced development of new products and technologies that have had or may in the future generate significant economic impacts. It is impossible, however, to develop a reliable comparison of the returns on spaceflight versus other government R&D investment.

- *Security*. Space-based assets and programs are an important element of national security, but the direct contribution of human spaceflight in this realm has been and is likely to remain limited. An active U.S. human spaceflight program gives the United States a stronger voice in an international code of conduct for space, enhances U.S. soft power, and supports collaborations with other nations; thus, it contributes to our national interests, including security.

- *National stature and international relations*. Being a leader in human space exploration enhances international stature and national pride. Because the work is complex and expensive, it can benefit from international cooperative efforts. Such cooperation has important geopolitical benefits.

- *Education and inspiration*. The United States needs scientists and engineers and a public that has a strong understanding of science. The challenge and excitement of space missions can serve as an inspiration for students and citizens to engage with science and engineering although it is difficult to measure this. The path to becoming a scientist or engineer requires much more than the initial inspiration. Many who work in space fields, however, report the importance of such inspiration, although it is difficult to separate the contributions of human and robotic spaceflight.

- *Scientific discovery*. The relative benefits of robotic versus human efforts in space science are constantly shifting as a result of changes in technology, cost, and risk. The current capabilities of robotic planetary explorers, such as Curiosity and Cassini, are such that although they can go farther, go sooner, and be much less expensive than human missions to the same locations, they cannot match the flexibility of humans to function in complex environments, to improvise, and to respond quickly to new discoveries. Such constraints may change some day.

- *Human survival*. It is not possible to say whether human off-Earth settlements could eventually be developed that would outlive human presence on Earth and lengthen the survival of our species. That question can be answered only by pushing the human frontier in space.

- *Shared destiny and aspiration to explore*. The urge to explore and to reach challenging goals is a common human characteristic. Space is today a major physical frontier for such exploration and aspiration. Some say that it is human destiny to continue to explore space. While not all share this view, for those who do it is an important reason to engage in human spaceflight.

. . . The pragmatic rationales have never seemed adequate by themselves, perhaps because the benefits that they argue for are not unique to human spaceflight. Those that are—the aspirational rationales related to the human destiny to explore and the survival of the human species—are also the rationales most tied to the enduring questions. Whereas the committee concluded from its review and assessment that no single rationale alone seems to justify the costs and risks of pursuing human spaceflight, the aspirational rationales, when supplemented by the practical benefits associated with the pragmatic rationales, do, in the committee's judgment, argue for a continuation of our nation's human spaceflight program, provided that the pathways and decision rules recommended by the committee are adopted (see below).

The level of public interest in space exploration is modest relative to interest in other public-policy issues such as economic issues, education, and medical or scientific discoveries. Public opinion about space has been generally favorable over the past 50 years, but much of the public is inattentive to space exploration, and spending on space exploration does not have high priority for most of the public.

Horizon Goal

The technical analysis completed for this study shows clearly that for the foreseeable future the only feasible destinations for human exploration are the Moon, asteroids, Mars, and the moons of Mars. Among that small set of plausible goals for human space exploration,[1] the most distant and difficult is a landing by human beings on the surface of Mars; it would require overcoming unprecedented technical risk, fiscal risk, and programmatic challenges. Thus, the "horizon goal" for human space exploration is Mars. All long-range space programs, by all potential partners, for human space exploration converge on that goal.

Policy Challenges

A program of human space exploration beyond low Earth orbit (LEO) that satisfies the pathway principles defined below is not sustainable with a budget that increases only enough to keep pace with inflation. . . . The current program to develop launch vehicles and spacecraft for flight beyond LEO cannot provide the flight frequency required to maintain competence and safety, does not possess the "stepping-stone" architecture that allows the public to see the connection between the horizon goal and near-term accomplishments, and may discourage potential international partners.

Because policy goals do not lead to sustainable programs unless they also reflect or change programmatic, technical, and budgetary realities, the committee notes that those who are formulating policy goals will need to keep the following factors in mind:

- Any defensible calculation of tangible, quantifiable benefits—spinoff technologies, attraction of talent to scientific careers, scientific knowledge, and so on—is unlikely ever to demonstrate a positive economic return on the massive investments required by human spaceflight.
- The arguments that triggered the Apollo investments—national defense and prestige—seem to have especially limited public salience in today's post-Cold War America.
- Although the public is mostly positive about NASA and its spaceflight programs, increased spending on spaceflight has low priority for most Americans. However, although most Americans do not follow the issue closely, those who pay more attention are more supportive of space exploration.

International Collaboration

International collaboration has become an integral part of the space policy of essentially all nations that participate in space activities around the world. Most countries now rarely initiate and carry out substantial space projects without some foreign participation. The reasons for collaboration are multiple, but countries, including the United States, cooperate principally when they benefit from it.

It is evident that near-term U.S. goals for human exploration are not aligned with those of our traditional international partners. Although most major spacefaring nations and agencies are looking toward the Moon, specifically the lunar surface, U.S. plans are focused on redirection of an asteroid into a retrograde lunar orbit where astronauts would conduct operations with it. It is also evident that given the rapid development of China's capabilities in space, it is in the best interests of the United States to be open to its inclusion in future international partnerships. In particular, current federal law that prevents

NASA from participating in bilateral activities with the Chinese serves only to hinder U.S. ability to bring China into its sphere of international partnerships and substantially reduces the potential international capability that might be pooled to reach Mars. Also, given the scale of the endeavor of a mission to Mars, contributions by international partners would have to be of unprecedented magnitude to defray a significant portion of the cost. . . .

Recommendations for a Pathways Approach

NASA and its international and commercial partners have developed an infrastructure in LEO that is approaching maturity—that is, assembly of the ISS is essentially complete. The nation must now decide whether to embark on human space exploration beyond LEO in a sustained and sustainable fashion. Having considered past and current space policy, explored the international setting, articulated the enduring questions and rationales, and identified public and stakeholder opinions, the committee drew on all this information to ask a fundamental question: What type of human spaceflight program would be responsive to these factors? The committee argues that it is a program in which humans operate beyond LEO on a regular basis—a sustainable human exploration program beyond LEO.

A sustainable program of human deep-space exploration requires an ultimate horizon goal that provides a long-term focus that is less likely to be disrupted by major technological failures and accidents along the way or by the vagaries of the political process and the economic scene. There is a consensus in national space policy, international coordination groups, and the public imagination for Mars as a major goal for human space exploration. NASA can sustain a human space-exploration program that pursues the horizon goal of a surface landing on Mars with meaningful milestones and simultaneously reassert U.S. leadership in space while allowing ample opportunity for substantial international collaboration—but only if the program has elements that are built in a logical sequence and if it can fund a frequency of flights sufficiently high to ensure the maintenance of proficiency among ground personnel, mission controllers, and flight crews. In the pursuit of that goal, NASA needs to engage in the type of mission planning and related technology development that address mission requirements and integration and develop high-priority capabilities, such as entry, descent, and landing for Mars; radiation safety;

and advanced in-space propulsion and power. Progress in human exploration beyond LEO will be measured in decades with costs measured in hundreds of billions of dollars and significant risk to human life.

In addition, the committee has concluded that the best way to ensure a stable, sustainable human-spaceflight program that pursues the rationales and enduring questions that the committee has identified is to develop a program through the rigorous application of a set of pathway principles. The committee's highest-priority recommendation is as follows:

NASA should adopt the following pathway principles:

I. **Commit to designing, maintaining, and pursuing the execution of an exploration pathway beyond low Earth orbit toward a clear horizon goal that addresses the "enduring questions" for human spaceflight.**

II. **Engage international space agencies early in the design and development of the pathway on the basis of their ability and willingness to contribute.**

III. **Define steps on the pathway that foster sustainability and maintain progress on achieving the pathway's long-term goal of reaching the horizon destination.**

IV. **Seek continuously to engage new partners that can solve technical or programmatic impediments to progress.**

V. **Create a risk-mitigation plan to sustain the selected pathway when unforeseen technical or budgetary problems arise. Such a plan should include points at which decisions are made to move to a less ambitious pathway (referred to as an "off-ramp") or to stand down the program.**

VI. **Establish exploration pathway characteristics that maximize the overall scientific, cultural, economic, political, and inspirational benefits without sacrificing progress toward the long-term goal, namely,**
   a. **The horizon and intermediate destinations have profound scientific, cultural, economic, inspirational, or geopolitical benefits that justify public investment.**
   b. **The sequence of missions and destinations permits stakeholders, including taxpayers, to see progress and to develop confidence in NASA's ability to execute the pathway.**
   c. **The pathway is characterized by logical feed-forward of technical capabilities.**
   d. **The pathway minimizes the use of dead-end mission elements that do not contribute to later destinations on the pathway.**
   e. **The pathway is affordable without incurring unacceptable development risk.**
   f. **The pathway supports, in the context of available budget, an operational tempo that ensures retention of critical technical capability, proficiency of operators, and effective use of infrastructure.**

The pathway principles will need to be supported by a set of operational decision rules as NASA, the administration, and Congress face inevitable programmatic challenges along a selected pathway. The decision rules that the committee has developed provide operational guidance that can be applied when major technical, cost, and schedule issues arise as NASA progresses along a pathway. Because many decisions will have to be made before any program of record is approved and initiated, the decision rules have been designed to provide the framework for a sustainable program through the lifetime of the selected pathway. They are designed to allow a program to stay within the constraints that are accepted and developed when the pathway principles are applied. The committee recommends that,

Whereas the overall pathway scope and cost are defined by application of the pathway principles, once a program is on a pathway, technical, cost, or schedule problems that arise should be addressed by the administration, NASA, and Congress by applying the following decision rules:

A. **If the appropriated funding level and 5-year budget projection do not permit execution of a pathway within the established schedule, do not start down that pathway.**

B. **If a budget profile does not permit the chosen pathway, even if NASA is well along on it, take an "off-ramp."**

C. **If the U.S. human spaceflight program receives an unexpected increase in budget for human spaceflight, NASA, the administration, and Congress should not redefine the pathway in such a way that continued budget increases are required for the pathway's sustainable execution; rather, the increase in funds should be applied to rapid retirement of important technology risks or to an increase in operational tempo in pursuit of the pathway's previously defined technical and exploration goals.**

D. Given that limitations on funding will require difficult choices in the development of major new technologies and capabilities, give high priority to choices that solve important technological shortcomings, that reduce overall program cost, that allow an acceleration of the schedule, or that reduce developmental or operational risk.

E. If there are human spaceflight program elements, infrastructure, or organizations that are no longer contributing to progress along the pathway, the human spaceflight program should divest itself of them as soon as possible.

Recommendations for Implementing a Sustainable Program

The committee was not charged to recommend and has not recommended any particular pathway or set of destination targets. The recommended pathways approach combines a strategic framework with practical guidance that is designed to stabilize human space exploration and to encourage political and programmatic coherence over time.

If the United States is to have a human space-exploration program, it must be worthy of the considerable cost to the nation and great risk of life. The committee has found no single practical rationale that is uniquely compelling to justify such investment and risk. Rather, human space exploration must be undertaken for inspirational and aspirational reasons that appeal to a broad array of U.S. citizens and policy-makers and that identify and align the United States with technical achievement and sophistication while demonstrating its capability to lead or work within an international coalition for peaceful purposes. Given the expense of any human spaceflight program and the substantial risk to the crews involved, it is the committee's view that the only pathways that fit those criteria are ones that ultimately place humans on other worlds.

Although the committee's recommendation to adopt a pathways approach is made without prejudice as to which particular pathway might be followed, it was clear to the committee from its independent analysis of several pathways that a return to extended surface operations on the Moon would make substantial contributions to a strategy ultimately aimed at landing people on Mars and would probably provide a broad array of opportunities for international and commercial cooperation. No matter which pathway is selected, the successful implementation of any plan developed in concert with a pathways approach and decision rules will rest on several other conditions. In addition to its highest-priority recommendation of the pathways approach and decision rules, the committee offers the following priority-ordered recommendations as being the ones that are most critical to the development and implementation of a sustainable human space-exploration program.

NASA should

1. Commit to design, maintain, and pursue the extension of human presence beyond low Earth orbit (LEO). This step should include
   a. Committing NASA's human spaceflight asset base, both physical and human, to this effort.
   b. Redirecting human spaceflight resources as needed to include improving program-management efficiency (including establishing and managing to appropriate levels of risk), eliminating obsolete facilities, and consolidating remaining infrastructure where possible.

2. Maintain long-term focus on Mars as the horizon goal for human space exploration, addressing the enduring questions for human spaceflight: How far from Earth can humans go? What can humans do and achieve when we get there?

3. Establish and implement the pathways approach so as to maximize the overall scientific, cultural, economic, political, and inspirational benefits of individual milestones and to conduct meaningful work at each step along the pathway without sacrificing progress toward long-term goals.

4. Vigorously pursue opportunities for international and commercial collaboration in order to leverage financial resources and capabilities of other nations and commercial entities. International collaboration would be open to the inclusion of China and potentially other emerging space powers in addition to traditional international partners. Specifically, future collaborations in major new endeavors should seek to incorporate
   a. A level of overall cost-sharing that is appropriate to the true partnerships that will be necessary to pursue pathways beyond LEO.
   b. Shared decision-making with partners, including a detailed analysis, in concert

with international partners, of the implications for human exploration of continuing the International Space Station beyond 2024.

5. Engage in planning that includes mission requirements and a systems architecture that target funded high-priority technology development, most critically
   a. Entry, descent, and landing for Mars.
   b. Advanced in-space propulsion and power.
   c. Radiation safety.

In this report the committee has provided guidance on how a pathways approach might be successfully pursued and the likely costs of the pathways if things go well. However, the committee also concludes that if the resulting plan is not appropriately financed, it will not succeed. Nor can it succeed without a sustained commitment on the part of those who govern the nation—a commitment that does not change direction with succeeding electoral cycles. Those branches of government—executive and legislative—responsible for NASA's funding and guidance are therefore critical enablers of the nation's investment and achievements in human spaceflight, commissioning and financing plans and then ensuring that the leadership, personnel, governance, and resources are in place at NASA and in other federally funded laboratories and facilities to advance it.

Note

1 Although there is no strictly defined distinction between human spaceflight and human space exploration, the committee takes the latter to mean spaceflight beyond low Earth orbit, in which the goal is to have humans venture into the cosmos to discover new things.

THE COMMITTEE ON HUMAN SPACEFLIGHT of the Aeronautics and Space Engineering Board, Space Studies Board, Division on Engineering and Physical Sciences, of the National Research Council, was charged with assessing the goals, core capabilities, and direction of human spaceflight as directed by the National Aeronautics and Space Administration (NASA) Authorization Act of 2010.

Amitai Etzioni

Final Frontier vs. Fruitful Frontier: The Case for Increasing Ocean Exploration

Possible solutions to the world's energy, food, environmental, and other problems are far more likely to be found in nearby oceans than in distant space.

Every year, the federal budget process begins with a White House-issued budget request, which lays out spending priorities for federal programs. From this moment forward, President Obama and his successors should use this opportunity to correct a longstanding misalignment of federal research priorities: excessive spending on space exploration and neglect of ocean studies. The nation should begin transforming the National Oceanic and Atmospheric Administration (NOAA) into a greatly reconstructed, independent, and effective federal agency. In the present fiscal climate of zero-sum budgeting, the additional funding necessary for this agency should be taken from the National Aeronautics and Space Administration (NASA).

The basic reason is that deep space—NASA's favorite turf—is a distant, hostile, and barren place, the study of which yields few major discoveries and an abundance of overhyped claims. By contrast, the oceans are nearby, and their study is a potential source of discoveries that could prove helpful for addressing a wide range of national concerns from climate change to disease; for reducing energy, mineral, and potable water shortages; for strengthening industry, security, and defenses against natural disasters such as hurricanes and tsunamis; for increasing our knowledge about geological history; and much more. Nevertheless, the funding allocated for NASA in the Consolidated and Further Continuing Appropriations Act for FY 2013 was 3.5 times higher than that allocated for NOAA. Whatever can be said on behalf of a trip to Mars or recent aspirations to revisit the Moon, the same holds many times over for exploring the oceans; some illustrative examples follow. (I stand by my record: In *The Moondoggle*, published in 1964, I predicted that there was less to be gained in deep space than in near space—the sphere in which

communication, navigations, weather, and reconnaissance satellites orbit—and argued for unmanned exploration vehicles and for investment on our planet instead of the Moon.)

Climate

There is wide consensus in the international scientific community that the Earth is warming; that the net effects of this warming are highly negative; and that the main cause of this warming is human actions, among which carbon dioxide emissions play a key role. Hence, curbing these CO_2 emissions or mitigating their effects is a major way to avert climate change.

Space exploration advocates are quick to claim that space might solve such problems on Earth. In some ways, they are correct; NASA does make helpful contributions to climate science by way of its monitoring programs, which measure the atmospheric concentrations and emissions of greenhouse gases and a variety of other key variables on the Earth and in the atmosphere. However, there seem to be no viable solutions to climate change that involve space.

By contrast, it is already clear that the oceans offer a plethora of viable solutions to the Earth's most pressing troubles. For example, scientists have already demonstrated that the oceans serve as a "carbon sink." The oceans have absorbed almost one-third of anthropogenic CO_2 emitted since the advent of the industrial revolution and have the potential to continue absorbing a large share of the CO_2 released into the atmosphere. Researchers are exploring a variety of chemical, biological, and physical geoengineering projects to increase the ocean's capacity to absorb carbon. Additional federal funds should be allotted to determine the feasibility and safety of these projects and then to develop and implement any that are found acceptable.

Iron fertilization or "seeding" of the oceans is perhaps the most well-known of these projects. Just as CO_2 is used by plants during photosynthesis, CO_2 dissolved in the oceans is absorbed and similarly used by autotrophic algae and other phytoplankton. The process "traps" the carbon in the phytoplankton; when the organism dies, it sinks to the sea floor, sequestering the carbon in the biogenic "ooze" that covers large swaths of the seafloor. However, many areas of the ocean high in the nutrients and sunlight necessary for phytoplankton to thrive lack a mineral vital to the phytoplankton's survival: iron. Adding iron to the ocean has been shown to trigger phytoplankton blooms, and thus iron fertilization might increase the CO_2 that phytoplankton will absorb. Studies note that the location and species of phytoplankton are poorly understood variables that affect the efficiency with which iron fertilization leads to the sequestration of CO_2. In other words, the efficiency of iron fertilization could be improved with additional research. Proponents of exploring this option estimate that it could enable us to sequester CO_2 at a cost of between \$2 and \$30/ton—far less than the cost of scrubbing CO_2 directly from the air or from power plant smokestacks—\$1,000/ton and \$50-100/ton, respectively, according to one Stanford study.

Despite these promising findings, there are a number of challenges that prevent us from using the oceans as a major means of combating climate change. First, ocean "sinks" have already absorbed an enormous amount of CO_2. It is not known how much more the oceans can actually absorb, because ocean warming seems to be altering the absorptive capacity of the oceans in unpredictable ways. It is further largely unknown how the oceans interact with the nitrogen cycle and other relevant processes.

Second, the impact of CO_2 sequestration on marine ecosystems remains underexplored. The Joint Ocean Commission Initiative, which noted in a 2013 report that absorption of CO_2 is "acidifying" the oceans, recommended that "the administration and Congress should take actions to measure and assess the emerging threat of ocean acidification, better understand the complex dynamics causing and exacerbating it, work to determine its impact, and develop mechanisms to address the problem." The Department of Energy specifically calls for greater "understanding of ocean biogeochemistry" and of the likely impact of carbon injection on ocean acidification. Since the mid-18th century, the acidity of the surface of the ocean, measured by the water's concentration of hydrogen ions, has increased by 30% on average, with negative consequences for mollusks, other calcifying

organisms, and the ecosystems they support, according to the Blue Ribbon Panel on Ocean Acidification. Different ecosystems have also been found to exhibit different levels of pH variance, with certain areas such as the California coastline experiencing higher levels of pH variability than elsewhere. The cost worldwide of mollusk-production losses alone could reach \$100 billion if acidification is not countered, says Monica Contestabile, an environmental economist and editor of *Nature Climate Change*. Much remains to be learned about whether and how carbon sequestration methods like iron fertilization could contribute to ocean acidification; it is, however, clearly a crucial subject of study given the dangers of climate change.

Food

Ocean products, particularly fish, are a major source of food for major parts of the world. People now eat four times as much fish, on average, as they did in 1950. The world's catch of wild fish reached an all-time high of 86.4 million tons in 1996; although it has since declined, the world's wild marine catch remained 78.9 million tons in 2011. Fish and mollusks provide an "important source of protein for a billion of the poorest people on Earth, and about three billion people get 15 percent or more of their annual protein from the sea," says Matthew Huelsenbeck, a marine scientist affiliated with the ocean conservation organization Oceana. Fish can be of enormous value to malnourished people because of its high levels of micronutrients such as Vitamin A, Iron, Zinc, Calcium, and healthy fats.

However, many scientists have raised concerns about the ability of wild fish stocks to survive such exploitation. The Food and Agriculture Organization of the United Nations estimated that 28% of fish stocks were overexploited worldwide and a further 3% were depleted in 2008. Other sources estimate that 30% of global fisheries are overexploited or worse. There have been at least four severe documented fishery collapses—in which an entire region's population of a fish species is overfished to the point of being incapable of replenishing itself, leading to the species' virtual disappearance from the area—worldwide since 1960, a report from the International Risk Governance Council found. Moreover, many present methods of fishing cause severe environmental damage; for example, the *Economist* reported that bottom trawling causes up to 15,400 square miles of "dead zone" daily through hypoxia caused by stirring up phosphorus and other sediments.

There are several potential approaches to dealing with overfishing. One is aquaculture. Marine fish cultivated through aquaculture is reported to cost less than other animal proteins and does not consume limited freshwater sources. Furthermore, aquaculture has been a stable source of food from 1970 to 2006; that is, it consistently expanded and was very rarely subject to unexpected shocks. From 1992 to 2006 alone, aquaculture expanded from 21.2 to 66.8 million tons of product.

Although aquaculture is rapidly expanding—more than 60% from 2000 to 2008—and represented more than 40% of global fisheries production in 2006, a number of challenges require attention if aquaculture is to significantly improve worldwide supplies of food. First, scientists have yet to understand the impact of climate change on aquaculture and fishing. Ocean acidification is likely to damage entire ecosystems, and rising temperatures cause marine organisms to migrate away from their original territory or die off entirely. It is important to study the ways that these processes will likely play out and how their effects might be mitigated. Second, there are concerns that aquaculture may harm wild stocks of fish or the ecosystems in which they are raised through overcrowding, excess waste, or disease. This is particularly true where aquaculture is devoted to growing species alien to the region in which they are produced. Third, there are few industry standard operating practices (SOPs) for aquaculture; additional research is needed for developing these SOPs, including types and sources of feed for species cultivated through aquaculture. Finally, in order to produce a stable source of food, researchers must better understand how biodiversity plays a role in preventing the sudden collapse of fisheries and develop best practices for fishing, aquaculture, and reducing bycatch.

On the issue of food, NASA is atypically mum. It does not claim it will feed the world with whatever it finds or plans to grow on Mars, Jupiter, or any other place light years away. The oceans are likely to be of great help.

Energy

NASA and its supporters have long held that its work can help address the Earth's energy crises. One NASA project calls for developing low-energy nuclear reactors (LENRs) that use weak nuclear force to create energy, but even NASA admits that "we're still many years away" from large-scale commercial production. Another project envisioned orbiting space-based solar power (SBSP) that would transfer energy wirelessly to Earth. The idea was proposed in the 1960s by then-NASA scientist Peter Glaser and has since been revisited by NASA; from 1995 to 2000, NASA actively investigated the viability of SBSP. Today, the project is no longer actively funded by NASA, and SBSP remains commercially unviable due to the high cost of launching and maintaining satellites and the challenges of wirelessly transmitting energy to Earth.

Marine sources of renewable energy, by contrast, rely on technology that is generally advanced; these technologies deserve additional research to make them fully commercially viable. One possible ocean renewable energy source is wave energy conversion, which uses the up-and-down motion of waves to generate electrical energy. Potentially-useable global wave power is estimated to be two terawatts, the equivalent of about 200 large power stations or about 10% of the entire world's predicted energy demand for 2020 according to the *World Ocean Review*. In the United States alone, wave energy is estimated to be capable of supplying fully one-third of the country's energy needs.

A modern wave energy conversion device was made in the 1970s and was known as the Salter's Duck; it produced electricity at a whopping cost of almost $1/kWh. Since then, wave energy conversion has become vastly more commercially viable. A report from the Department of Energy in 2009 listed nine different designs in precommercial development or already installed as pilot projects around the world. As of 2013, as many as 180 companies are reported to be developing wave or tidal energy technologies; one device, the Anaconda, produces electricity at a cost of $0.24/kWh. The United States Department of Energy and the National Renewable Energy Laboratory jointly maintain a website that tracks the average cost/kWh of various energy sources; on average, ocean energy overall must cost about $0.23/kWh to be profitable. Some projects have been more successful; the prototype LIMPET wave energy conversion technology currently operating on the coast of Scotland produces wave energy at the price of $0.07/kWh. For comparison, the average consumer in the United States paid $0.12/kWh in 2011. Additional research could further reduce the costs.

Other options in earlier stages of development include using turbines to capture the energy of ocean currents. The technology is similar to that used by wind energy; water moving through a stationary turbine turns the blades, generating electricity. However, because water is so much denser than air, "for the same surface area, water moving 12 miles per hour exerts the same amount of force as a constant 110 mph wind," says the Bureau of Ocean Energy Management (BOEM), a division of the Department of the Interior. (Another estimate from a separate BOEM report holds that a 3.5 mph current "has the kinetic energy of winds in excess of [100 mph].") BOEM further estimates that total worldwide power potential from currents is five terawatts—about a quarter of predicted global energy demand for 2020—and that "capturing just 1/1,000th of the available energy from the Gulf Stream . . . would supply Florida with 35% of its electrical needs."

Although these technologies are promising, additional research is needed not only for further development but also to adapt them to regional differences. For instance, ocean wave conversion technology is suitable only in locations in which the waves are of the same sort for which existing technologies were developed and in locations where the waves also generate enough energy to make the endeavor profitable. One study shows that thermohaline circulation—ocean circulation driven by variations in temperature and salinity—varies from area to area, and climate change is likely to alter thermohaline circulation in the future in ways that could affect the use of energy generators that rely on ocean currents. Additional research would help scientists understand how to adapt energy technologies for use in specific environments and how to avoid the potential environmental consequences of their use.

Renewable energy resources are the ocean's particularly attractive energy product; they contribute much less than coal or natural gas to anthropogenic greenhouse gas emissions. However, it is worth noting that the oceans do hold vast reserves of untapped hydrocarbon fuels. Deep-sea drilling technologies remain immature; although it is possible to use oil rigs in waters of 8,000 to 9,000 feet, greater depths require the use of specially-designed drilling ships that still face significant challenges. Deep-water drilling that takes place in depths of more than 500 feet is the next big frontier for oil and natural-gas production, projected to expand offshore oil production by 18% by 2020. One should expect the development of new technologies that would enable drilling petroleum and natural gas at even greater depths than presently possible and under layers of salt and other barriers.

In addition to developing these technologies, entire other lines of research are needed to either mitigate the side effects of large-scale usage of these technologies or to guarantee that these effects are small. Although it has recently become possible to drill beneath Arctic ice, the technologies are largely untested. Environmentalists fear that ocean turbines could harm fish or marine mammals, and it is feared that wave conversion technologies would disturb ocean floor sediments, impede migration of ocean animals, prevent waves from clearing debris, or harm animals. Demand has pushed countries to develop

technologies to drill for oil beneath ice or in the deep sea without much regard for the safety or environmental concerns associated with oil spills. At present, there is no developed method for cleaning up oil spills in the Arctic, a serious problem that requires additional research if Arctic drilling is to commence on a larger scale.

More Ocean Potential

When large quantities of public funds are invested in a particular research and development project, particularly when the payoff is far from assured, it is common for those responsible for the project to draw attention to the additional benefits—"spinoffs"—generated by the project as a means of adding to its allure. This is particularly true if the project can be shown to improve human health. Thus, NASA has claimed that its space exploration "benefit[ted] pharmaceutical drug development" and assisted in developing a new type of sensor "that provides real-time image recognition capabilities," that it developed an optics technology in the 1970s that now is used to screen children for vision problems, and that a type of software developed for vibration analysis on the Space Shuttle is now used to "diagnose medical issues." Similarly, opportunities to identify the "components of the organisms that facilitate increased virulence in space" could in theory—NASA claims—be used on Earth to "pinpoint targets for antimicrobial therapeutics."

Ocean research, as modest as it is, has already yielded several medical "spinoffs." The discovery of one species of Japanese black sponge, which produces a substance that successfully blocks division of tumorous cells, led researchers to develop a late-stage breast cancer drug. An expedition near the Bahamas led to the discovery of a bacterium that produces substances that are in the process of being synthesized as antibiotics and anticancer compounds. In addition to the aforementioned cancer fighting compounds, chemicals that combat neuropathic pain, treat asthma and inflammation, and reduce skin irritation have been isolated from marine organisms. One Arctic Sea organism alone produced three antibiotics. Although none of the three ultimately proved pharmaceutically significant, current concerns that strains of bacteria are developing resistance to the "antibiotics of last resort" are a strong reason to increase funding for bioprospecting. Additionally, the blood cells of horseshoe crabs contain a chemical—which is found nowhere else in nature and so far has yet to be synthesized—that can detect bacterial contamination in pharmaceuticals and on the surfaces of surgical implants. Some research indicates that between

10 and 30 percent of horseshoe crabs that have been bled die, and that those that survive are less likely to mate. It would serve for research to indicate the ways these creatures can be better protected. Up to two-thirds of all marine life remains unidentified, with 226,000 eukaryotic species already identified and more than 2,000 species discovered every year, according to Ward Appeltans, a marine biologist at the Intergovernmental Oceanographic Commission of UNESCO.

Contrast these discoveries of new species in the oceans with the frequent claims that space exploration will lead to the discovery of extraterrestrial life. For example, in 2010 NASA announced that it had made discoveries on Mars "that [would] impact the search for evidence of extraterrestrial life" but ultimately admitted that they had "no definitive detection of Martian organics." The discovery that prompted the initial press release—that NASA had discovered a *possible* arsenic pathway in metabolism and that thus life was *theoretically* possible under conditions different than those on Earth—was then thoroughly rebutted by a panel of NASA-selected experts. The comparison with ocean science is especially stark when one considers that oceanographers have *already* discovered real organisms that rely on chemosynthesis—the process of making glucose from water and carbon dioxide by using the energy stored in chemical bonds of inorganic compounds—living near deep sea vents at the bottom of the oceans.

The same is true of the search for mineral resources. NASA talks about the potential for asteroid mining, but it will be far easier to find and recover minerals suspended in ocean waters or beneath the ocean floor. Indeed, resources beneath the ocean floor are already being commercially exploited, whereas there is not a near-term likelihood of commercial asteroid mining.

Another major justification cited by advocates for the pricey missions to Mars and beyond is that "we don't know" enough about the other planets and the universe in which we live. However, the same can be said of the deep oceans. Actually, we know much more about the Moon and even about Mars than we know about the oceans. Maps of the Moon are already strikingly accurate, and even amateur hobbyists have crafted highly detailed pictures of the Moon—minus the "dark side"—as one set of documents from University College London's archives seems to demonstrate. By 1967, maps and globes depicting the complete lunar surface were produced. By contrast, about 90% of the world's oceans had not yet been mapped as of 2005. Furthermore, for years scientists have been fascinated by noises originating at the bottom of the ocean, known creatively as "the Bloop" and "Julia," among others. And the world's largest known "waterfall" can be found

entirely underwater between Greenland and Iceland, where cold, dense Arctic water from the Greenland Sea drops more than 11,500 feet before reaching the seafloor of the Denmark Strait. Much remains poorly understood about these phenomena, their relevance to the surrounding ecosystem, and the ways in which climate change will affect their continued existence.

In short, there is much that humans have yet to understand about the depths of the oceans, further research into which could yield important insights about Earth's geological history and the evolution of humans and society. Addressing these questions surpasses the importance of another Mars rover or a space observatory designed to answer highly specific questions of importance mainly to a few dedicated astrophysicists, planetary scientists, and select colleagues.

Leave the People at Home

NASA has long favored human exploration, despite the fact that robots have become much more technologically advanced and that their (one-way) travel poses much lower costs and next to no risks compared to human missions. Still, the promotion of human missions continues; in December 2013, NASA announced that it would grow basil, turnips, and Arabidopsis on the Moon to "show that crop plants that ultimately will feed astronauts and moon colonists and all, are also able to grow on the moon." However, Martin Rees, a professor of cosmology and astrophysics at Cambridge University and a former president of the Royal Society, calls human spaceflight a "waste of money," pointing out that "the practical case [for human spaceflight] gets weaker and weaker with every advance in robotics and miniaturisation." Another observer notes that "it is in fact a universal principle of space science—a 'prime directive,' as it were—that anything a human being does up there could be done by unmanned machinery for one-thousandth the cost." The cost of sending humans to Mars is estimated at more than $150 billion. The preference for human missions persists nonetheless, primarily because NASA believes that human spaceflight is more impressive and will garner more public support and taxpayer dollars, despite the fact that most of NASA's scientific yield to date, Rees shows, has come from the Hubble Space Telescope, the Chandra X-Ray Observatory, the Kepler space observatory, space rovers, and other missions. NASA relentlessly hypes the bravery of the astronauts and the pioneering aspirations of all humanity despite a lack of evidence that these missions engender any more than a brief high for some.

Ocean exploration faces similar temptations. There have been some calls for "aquanauts," who would explore the ocean much as astronauts explore space, and for the prioritization of human exploration missions. However, relying largely on robots and remote-controlled submersibles seems much more economical, nearly as effective at investigating the oceans' biodiversity, chemistry, and seafloor topography, and endlessly safer than human agents. In short, it is no more reasonable to send aquanauts to explore the seafloor than it is to send astronauts to explore the surface of Mars.

Several space enthusiasts are seriously talking about creating human colonies on the Moon or, eventually, on Mars. In the 1970s, for example, NASA's Ames Research Center spent tax dollars to design several models of space colonies meant to hold 10,000 people each. Other advocates have suggested that it might be possible to "terra-form" the surface of Mars or other planets to resemble that of Earth by altering the atmospheric conditions, warming the planet, and activating a water cycle. Other space advocates envision using space elevators to ferry large numbers of people and supplies into space in the event of a catastrophic asteroid hitting the Earth. Ocean enthusiasts dream of underwater cities to deal with overpopulation and "natural or man-made disasters that render land-based human life impossible." The Seasteading Institute, Crescent Hydropolis Resorts, and the League of New Worlds have developed pilot projects to explore the prospect of housing people and scientists under the surface of the ocean. However, these projects are prohibitively expensive and "you can never sever [the surface-water connection] completely," says Dennis Chamberland, director of one of the groups. NOAA also invested funding in a habitat called Aquarius built in 1986 by the Navy, although it has since abandoned this project.

If anyone wants to use their private funds for such outlier projects, they surely should be free to proceed. However, for public funds, priorities must be set. Much greater emphasis must be placed on preventing global calamities rather than on developing improbable means of housing and saving a few hundred or thousand people by sending them far into space or deep beneath the waves.

Reimagining NOAA

These select illustrative examples should suffice to demonstrate the great promise of intensified ocean research, a heretofore unrealized promise. However, it is far from enough to inject additional funding, which can be taken from NASA if the total federal R&D budget cannot be increased, into ocean science. There must also be an agency with a mandate to envision and lead federal efforts to bolster ocean research and exploration the way that President Kennedy and NASA once led space research and "captured" the Moon.

For those who are interested in elaborate reports on the deficiencies of existing federal agencies' attempts to coordinate this research, the Joint Ocean Commission Initiative (JOCI)—the foremost ocean policy group in the United States and the product of the Pew Oceans Commission and the United States Commission on Ocean Policy—provides excellent overviews. These studies and others reflect the tug-of-war that exists among various interest groups and social values. Environmentalists and those concerned about global climate change, the destruction of ocean ecosystems, declines in biodiversity, overfishing, and oil spills clash with commercial groups and states more interested in extracting natural resources from the oceans, in harvesting fish, and utilizing the oceans for tourism. (One observer noted that only 1% of the 139.5 million square miles of the ocean is conserved through formal protections, whereas billons use the oceans "as a 'supermarket and a sewer.'") And although these reports illuminate some of the challenges that must be surmounted if the government is to institute a broad, well-funded set of ocean research goals, none of these groups have added significant funds to ocean research, nor have they taken steps to provide NASA-like agency to take the lead in federally-supported ocean science.

NOAA is the obvious candidate, but it has been hampered by a lack of central authority and by the existence of many disparate programs, each of which has its own small group of congressional supporters with parochial interests. The result is that NOAA has many supporters of its distinct little segments but too few supporters of its broad mission. Furthermore, Congress micromanages NOAA's budget, leaving too little flexibility for the agency to coordinate activities and act on its own priorities.

It is hard to imagine the difficulty of pulling these pieces together—let alone consolidating the bewildering number of projects—under the best of circumstances. Several administrators of NOAA have made significant strides in this regard and should be recognized for their work. However, Congress has saddled the agency with more than 100 ocean-related laws that require the agency to promote what are often narrow and competing interests. Moreover, NOAA is buried in the Department of Commerce, which itself is considered to be one of the weaker cabinet agencies. For this reason, some have suggested that it would be prudent to move NOAA into the Department of the Interior—which already includes the United States Geological Service, the Bureau of Ocean

Energy Management, the National Park Service, the U.S. Fish and Wildlife Service, and the Bureau of Safety and Environmental Enforcement—to give NOAA more of a backbone.

Moreover, NOAA is not the only federal agency that deals with the oceans. There are presently ocean-relevant programs in more than 20 federal agencies—including NASA. For instance, the ocean exploration program that investigates deep ocean currents by using satellite technology to measure minute differences in elevation on the surface of the ocean is currently controlled by NASA, and much basic ocean science research has historically been supported by the Navy, which lost much of its interest in the subject since the end of the Cold War. (The Navy does continue to fund some ocean research, but at levels much lower than earlier.) Many of these programs should be consolidated into a Department of Ocean Research and Exploration that would have the authority to do what NOAA has been prevented from doing: namely, direct a well-planned and coordinated ocean research program. Although the National Ocean Council's interagency coordinating structure is a step in the right direction, it would be much more effective to consolidate authority for managing ocean science research under a new independent agency or a reimagined and strengthened NOAA.

Setting priorities for research and exploration is always needed, but this is especially true in the present age of tight budgets. It is clear that oceans are a little-studied but very promising area for much enhanced exploration. By contrast, NASA's projects, especially those dedicated to further exploring deep space and to manned missions and stellar colonies, can readily be cut. More than moving a few billion dollars from the faraway planets to the nearby oceans is called for, however. The United States needs an agency that can spearhead a major drive to explore the oceans—an agency that has yet to be envisioned and created.

***

AMITAI ETZIONI is University Professor and professor of International Affairs and director of the Institute for Communitarian Policy Studies at George Washington University.

EXPLORING THE ISSUE

Should the United States Continue Its Human Spaceflight Program?

Critical Thinking and Reflection

1. Exploring space is a great idea—but what's in it for us?
2. In a space program dominated by robotic spacecraft and landers, what role remains for human beings?
3. How will the U.S. government respond if China puts an astronaut on the Moon?

Is There Common Ground?

Those who argue over the merits of manned space exploration tend to agree that space is worth exploring. They disagree on whether it is necessary to send people into space when robots are already very capable and likely to be much more capable in a few years.

1. Just how capable are robots today? (There is a great deal of material on this question.)
2. Look up "telepresence" (see Tom Simonite, "The New, More Awkward You," *Technology Review*, January/February 2011; http://www.technologyreview .com/computing/26941/?a=f). Does this technology offer a compromise on the question of using either robots or humans in space?
3. Would telepresence also benefit ocean exploration?

Additional Resources

Augustine Commission, *Seeking a Human Spaceflight Program Worthy of a Great Nation* (October 2009) (http://www.nasa.gov/pdf/396093main_HSF_Cmte _FinalReport.pdf).

Robert D. Ballard, "Why We Must Explore the Sea," *Smithsonian* (October 2014).

Mark Schrope, "Journey to the Bottom of the Sea," *Scientific American* (April 2014).

Robert Zubrin, "How Much Is an Astronaut's Life Worth?" *Reason* (February 2012).

Internet References . . .

Ocean Exploration Trust

> http://www.oceanexplorationtrust.org/

Ocean Explorer

> http://oceanexplorer.noaa.gov/backmatter
> /whatisexploration.html

Space.com

> http://www.space.com/11364-human-space
> -exploration-future-50-years-spaceflight.html

The Coalition to Save Manned Space Exploration

> http://www.savemannedspace.com/

Unit 5

UNIT

The Computer Revolution

*F*ans of computers have long been sure that the electronic wonders offer untold benefits to society. When the first personal computers appeared in the early 1970s, they immediately brought unheard-of capabilities to their users. Ever since, those capabilities have been increasing. Today children command more sheer computing power that major corporations did in the 1950s and 1960s. Computer users are in direct contact with their fellow users around the world. Information is instantly available and infinitely malleable.

Some observers wonder about the purported untold benefits of computers. Specifically, will such benefits be outweighed by threats to children (by free access to pornography and by online predators), civil order (by free access to sites that advocate racism and violence), traditional institutions (will books, for example, become an endangered species?), or to human pride (computers have already outplayed human champions at chess, checkers, and go)? If computers can outthink humans at games, how long will it be before they are as intelligent and even as conscious as we are? What happens to our jobs and careers then? Do we have to worry about cyber-war? And must all software be produced as proprietary product?

Selected, Edited, and with Issue Framing Material by:
Thomas A. Easton, *Mount Ida College*

ISSUE

Will Robots Take Your Job?

YES: Kevin Drum, from "Welcome, Robot Overlords. Please Don't Fire Us?" *Mother Jones* (2013)

NO: Peter Gorle and Andrew Clive, from "Positive Impact of Industrial Robots on Employment," Metra Martech (2011)

Learning Outcomes
After reading this issue, you will be able to:
• Explain what kinds of jobs are now and may soon be suitable for robots.
• Discuss the impact of robotics on their future job prospects.
• Apply their understanding of how robots will affect future jobs in a discussion of career choices.
• Discuss how, if robots indeed do cause widespread unemployment, the world's economies will have to change.

ISSUE SUMMARY

YES: Kevin Drum argues that we are about to make very rapid progress in artificial intelligence, and by about 2040, robots will be replacing people in a great many jobs. On the way to that "robot paradise," corporate managers and investors will expand their share of national wealth, at the expense of labor's share, even more than they have in recent years. That trend, however, depends on an ample supply of consumers—workers with enough money to buy the products the machines are making. It is thus already time to start rethinking how the nation ensures that its citizens have enough money to be consumers and keep the economy going.

NO: Peter Gorle and Andrew Clive argue that robots are not a threat to human employment. Historically, increases in the use of automation almost always increase both productivity and employment. Over the next few years, the use of robotics will generate 700,000–1,000,000 new jobs.

The idea that technology threatens jobs is not new. In the early 1800s, the "Luddites" were textile workers who destroyed new weaving machinery that could be operated by unskilled labor. The movement faded away with the end of the Napoleonic Wars, but its name has continued to be applied to those who oppose industrialization, automation, computerization, and even any new technology. See, for example, Steven E. Jones, *Against Technology: From the Luddites to Neo-Luddism* (CRC Press, 2006).

Not surprisingly, modern computer technology arouses many job-related fears, for computers seem to be growing ever more capable. When IBM's "Watson" won a dramatic victory in the game of *Jeopardy*, many wondered if we were finally seeing true artificial intelligence. Kirk L. Kroeker, "Weighing Watson's Impact," *Communications of the ACM* (July 2011), notes that despite many dismissive comments, Watson is an excellent demonstration of the power of machine learning. Future applications of the technology will soon play important roles in medicine (extracting information from vast numbers of medical books and journals), law, education, and the financial industry. Many of these applications do not require that a robot look and act like a human being, but researchers are working on that, too; see Alex Wright, "Robots Like Us," *Communications of the ACM* (May 2012); and Dennis Normile, "In Our Own Image," *Science* (October 10, 2014).

"Robocars"—cars that drive themselves, with no human hand at the wheel—have already been demonstrated and their capabilities are improving rapidly; see Sebastian Thrun, "Toward Robotic Cars," *Communications of the ACM* (April 2010), and Alex Wright, "Automotive Autonomy," *Communications of the ACM* (July 2011). Before they can be broadly used, there must be changes in legislation (can you be guilty of OUI if the car drives itself?) and insurance, among other things; see "The Future of the Self-Driving Automobile," *Trends E-Magazine* (December 2010), and John Markoff, "Collision in the Making Between Self-Driving Cars and How the World Works," *New York Times* (January 23, 2012). Given such changes, we can expect to see job losses among taxi drivers and truckers, among others.

Robots may also cost other people their jobs. Jason Borenstein, "Robots and the Changing Workforce," *AI & Society* (2011), notes that robotic workers are going to become ever more common, and though new job opportunities are bound to arise from this, many jobs will disappear and the human workforce will change in many ways—including necessary education and worker income. Judith Aquino, "Nine Jobs that Humans May Lose to Robots," *Business Insider* (March 22, 2011), says the endangered list includes drivers, but also pharmacists, lawyers and paralegals, astronauts, store clerks, soldiers, babysitters, rescuers, and sportswriters and other reporters. John Sepulvado asks "Could a Computer Write This Story?" (CNN, May 11, 2012) (http://edition.cnn.com/2012/05/11/tech/innovation/computer-assisted-writing/index.html). By 2014, robowriters from the company, Narrative Science (http://www.narrativescience.com/), were already being deployed; see Francie Diep, "Associated Press Will Use Robots to Write Articles," *Popular Science* (July 1, 2014) (http://www.popsci.com/article/technology/associated-press-will-use-robots-write-articles). Farhad Manjoo asks (and answers) "Will Robots Steal Your Job? If You're Highly Educated, You Should Still Be Afraid," *Slate* (September 26, 2011) (http://www.slate.com/articles/technology/robot_invasion/2011/09/will_robots_steal_your_job.html). "Robots to Take 500,000 Human Jobs . . . for Now," *The Fiscal Times* (December 29, 2011), notes that every industry, from agriculture to the military, will be affected. Martin Ford, "Google's Cloud Robotics Strategy—and How It Could Soon Threaten Jobs," *Huffington Post* (January 3, 2012), says that "nearly any type of work that is on some level routine in nature—regardless of the skill level or educational requirements—is likely to someday be impacted by [robotic] technologies. The only real question is how soon it will happen." This foreboding

thought is echoed by Dan Lyons, "Who Needs Humans?" *Newsweek* (July 25, 2011). David J. Lynch is more optimistic in "It's a Man vs. Machine Recovery," *Bloomberg Businessweek* (January 5, 2012), he notes that businesses are buying machines more than hiring people, but "there's nothing wrong with the labor market that resurgent demand wouldn't fix." There may also be a need to consider the ethics involved, for as more robots enter the workplace, they will bring with them changed expectations (robots are tireless, and they don't need health insurance, retirement plans, vacations, and even pay; will employers expect the same of humans?); this may even mean restricting the use of robots; see Jason Borenstein, "Computing Ethics: Work Life in the Robotic Age," *Communications of the ACM* (July 2010).

Not everyone agrees on the degree of the threat. In "Will Work for Machines" (August 2014), *Scientific American*'s editors note that it is actually hard to tell whether there is a threat at all, for there is a serious shortage of data. David Bourne, "My Boss the Robot," *Scientific American* (May 2013), sees a future in which humans and robots collaborate to get jobs done more rapidly and efficiently than either could do alone. See also John Bohannon, "Meet Your New Co-Worker," *Science* (October 10, 2014). David H. Autor, "Polanyi's Paradox and the Shape of Employment Growth," report prepared for the Federal Reserve Bank of Kansas City symposium on "Re-Evaluating Labor Market Dynamics" (August 21–13, 2014) (http://www.kansascityfed.org/publicat/sympos/2014/093014.pdf), concludes that most "commentators overstate the extent of machine substitution for human labor and ignore the strong complementarities." Neil Irwin, "Why the Robots Might Not Take Our Jobs After All: They Lack Common Sense," *New York Times* (August 22, 2014), thinks robots aren't going to replace humans any time soon, except in very limited ways. See also John Tamny, "Why Robots Will Be the Biggest Job Creators in World History," *Forbes* (March 1, 2015 @ 9 AM) (http://www.forbes.com/sites/johntamny/2015/03/01/why-robots-will-be-the-biggest-job-creators-in-history/).

How bad might it get? Stuart Elliott, in "Anticipating a Luddite Revival," *Issues in Science and Technology* (Spring 2014), compares the capabilities of computers as reflected in the literature with job skills as defined in the Department of Labor's O*NET system. He finds that computers are already close to being able to meet skills requirements of 75 percent of jobs. "Safe" jobs that demand more skills are in education, health care, science, engineering, and law, but even those may be matched within a few decades. "In principle," he says, "there is no problem with imagining a transformation in the labor market that substitutes technology for workers for 80 percent of current jobs and then expands in the remaining 20 percent to absorb the entire labor force. [But} We do not know how successful the nation can be in trying to prepare everyone in the labor force for jobs that require these higher skill levels. It is hard to imagine, for example, that most of the labor force will move into jobs in health care, education, science, engineering, and law. . . . At some point it will be too difficult for large numbers of displaced workers to move into jobs requiring capabilities that are difficult for most of them to carry out even if they have the time and resources for retraining. When that time comes, the nation will be forced to reconsider the role that paid employment plays in distributing economic goods and services and in providing a meaningful focus for many people's daily lives." Marcus Wohlsen, in "When Robots Take All the Work, What'll Be Left for Us to Do?" *Wired* (August 8, 2014) (http://www.wired.com/2014/08/when-robots-take-all-the-work-whatll-be-left-for-us-to-do/), says that "The scariest possibility of all is that [the loss of jobs means] that only then do we figure out what really makes us human is work." William H. Davidow and Michael S. Malone, "What Happens to Society When Robots Replace Workers?"

Harvard Business Review (December 10, 2014) (https://hbr .org/2014/12/what-happens-to-society-when-robots-replace -workers), reach a similar conclusion: "Ultimately, we need a new, individualized, *cultural*, approach to the meaning of work and the purpose of life."

In the YES selection, Kevin Drum argues that we are about to make very rapid progress in artificial intelligence, and by about 2040, robots will be replacing people in a great many jobs. On the way to that "robot paradise," corporate managers and investors will expand their share of national wealth, at the expense of labor's share, even more than they have in recent years. That trend, however, depends on an ample supply of consumers—workers with enough money to buy the products the machines are making. It is thus already time to start rethinking how the nation ensures that its citizens have enough money to be consumers and keep the economy going. In the NO selection, Peter Gorle and Andrew Clive argue that robots are not a threat to human employment. Historically, increases in the use of automation almost always increase both productivity and employment. Over the next few years, the use of robotics will generate 700,000 to 1,000,000 new jobs.

YES

Kevin Drum

Welcome, Robot Overlords.
Please Don't Fire Us?

This is a story about the future. Not the unhappy future, the one where climate change turns the planet into a cinder or we all die in a global nuclear war. This is the *happy* version. It's the one where computers keep getting smarter and smarter, and clever engineers keep building better and better robots. By 2040, computers the size of a softball are as smart as human beings. Smarter, in fact. Plus they're *computers*: They never get tired, they're never ill-tempered, they never make mistakes, and they have instant access to all of human knowledge.

The result is paradise. Global warming is a problem of the past because computers have figured out how to generate limitless amounts of green energy and intelligent robots have tirelessly built the infrastructure to deliver it to our homes. No one needs to work anymore. Robots can do everything humans can do, and they do it uncomplainingly, 24 hours a day. Some things remain scarce—beachfront property in Malibu, original Rembrandts—but thanks to super-efficient use of natural resources and massive recycling, scarcity of ordinary consumer goods is a thing of the past. Our days are spent however we please, perhaps in study, perhaps playing video games. It's up to us.

Maybe you think I'm pulling your leg here. Or being archly ironic. After all, this does have a bit of a rose-colored tint to it, doesn't it? Like something from *The Jetsons* or the cover of *Wired*. That would hardly be a surprising reaction. Computer scientists have been predicting the imminent rise of machine intelligence since at least 1956, when the Dartmouth Summer Research Project on Artificial Intelligence gave the field its name, and there are only so many times you can cry wolf. Today, a full seven decades after the birth of the computer, all we have are iPhones, Microsoft Word, and in-dash navigation. You could be excused for thinking that computers that truly match the human brain are a ridiculous pipe dream.

But they're not. It's true that we've made far slower progress toward real artificial intelligence than we once thought, but that's for a very simple and very human reason: Early computer scientists grossly underestimated the power of the human brain and the difficulty of emulating one. It turns out that this is a very, very hard problem, sort of like filling up Lake Michigan one drop at a time. In fact, not just *sort of* like. It's *exactly* like filling up Lake Michigan one drop at a time. If you want to understand the future of computing, it's essential to understand this.

What do we do over the next few decades as robots become steadily more capable and steadily begin taking away all our jobs?

Suppose it's 1940 and Lake Michigan has (somehow) been emptied. Your job is to fill it up using the following rule: To start off, you can add one fluid ounce of water to the lake bed. Eighteen months later, you can add two. In another 18 months, you can add four ounces. And so on. Obviously this is going to take a while.

By 1950, you have added around a gallon of water. But you keep soldiering on. By 1960, you have a bit more than 150 gallons. By 1970, you have 16,000 gallons, about as much as an average suburban swimming pool.

At this point it's been 30 years, and even though 16,000 gallons is a fair amount of water, it's nothing compared to the size of Lake Michigan. To the naked eye you've made no progress at all.

So let's skip all the way ahead to 2000. Still nothing. You have—maybe—a slight sheen on the lake floor. How about 2010? You have a few inches of water here and there. This is ridiculous. It's now been *70 years* and you still don't have enough water to float a goldfish. Surely this task is futile?

But wait. Just as you're about to give up, things suddenly change. By 2020, you have about 40 feet of water. And by 2025 you're done. After 70 years you had nothing. Fifteen years later, the job was finished.

If you have any kind of background in computers, you've already figured out that I didn't pick these numbers out of a hat. I started in 1940 because that's about when the first programmable computer was invented. I chose a doubling time of 18 months because of a cornerstone of computer history called Moore's Law, which famously estimates that computing power doubles approximately every 18 months. And I chose Lake Michigan because its size, in fluid ounces, is roughly the same as the computing power of the human brain measured in calculations per second.

In other words, just as it took us until 2025 to fill up Lake Michigan, the simple exponential curve of Moore's Law suggests it's going to take us until 2025 to build a computer with the processing power of the human brain. And it's going to happen the same way: For the first 70 years, it will seem as if nothing is happening, even though we're doubling our progress every 18 months. Then, in the final 15 years, seemingly out of nowhere, we'll finish the job.

True artificial intelligence really is around the corner, and it really will make life easier. But first we face vast economic upheaval.

And that's exactly where we are. We've moved from computers with a trillionth of the power of a human brain to computers with a billionth of the power. Then a millionth. And now a thousandth. Along the way, computers progressed from ballistics to accounting to word processing to speech recognition, and none of that really seemed like progress toward artificial intelligence. That's because even a thousandth of the power of a human brain is—let's be honest—a bit of a joke. Sure, it's a billion times more than the first computer had, but it's still not much more than the computing power of a hamster.

This is why, even with the IT industry barreling forward relentlessly, it has never seemed like we were making any real progress on the AI front. But there's another reason as well: Every time computers break some new barrier, we decide—or maybe just finally get it through our thick skulls—that we set the bar too low. At one point, for example, we thought that playing chess at a high level would be a mark of human-level intelligence. Then, in 1997, IBM's Deep Blue supercomputer beat world champion Garry Kasparov, and suddenly we decided that playing grandmaster-level chess didn't imply high intelligence after all.

So maybe translating human languages would be a fair test? Google Translate does a passable job of that these days. Recognizing human voices and responding appropriately? Siri mostly does that, and better systems are on the near horizon. Understanding the world well enough to win a round of *Jeopardy!* against human competition? A few years ago IBM's Watson supercomputer beat the two best human *Jeopardy!* champions of all time. Driving a car? Google has already logged more than 300,000 miles in its driverless cars, and in another decade they may be commercially available.

The truth is that all this represents more progress toward true AI than most of us realize. We've just been limited by the fact that computers still aren't quite muscular enough to finish the job. That's changing rapidly, though. Computing power is measured in calculations per second—a.k.a. floating-point operations per second, or "flops"—and the best estimates of the human brain suggest that our own processing power is about equivalent to 10 petaflops. ("Peta" comes after giga and tera.) That's a lot of flops, but last year an IBM Blue Gene/Q supercomputer at Lawrence Livermore National Laboratory was clocked at 16.3 petaflops.

Of course, raw speed isn't everything. Livermore's Blue Gene/Q fills a room, requires eight megawatts of power to run, and costs about $250 million. What's more, it achieves its speed not with a single superfast processor, but with 1.6 million ordinary processor cores running simultaneously. While that kind of massive parallel processing is ideally suited for nuclear-weapons testing, we don't know yet if it will be effective for producing AI.

But plenty of people are trying to figure it out. Earlier this year, the European Commission chose two big research endeavors to receive a half billion euros each, and one of them was the Human Brain Project led by Henry Markram, a neuroscientist at the Swiss Federal Institute of Technology in Lausanne. He uses another IBM supercomputer in a project aimed at modeling the entire human brain. Markram figures he can do this by 2020.

The Luddites weren't wrong. They were just 200 years too early.

That might be optimistic. At the same time, it also might turn out that we don't need to model a human brain in the first place. After all, when the Wright brothers built the first airplane, they didn't model it after a bird with flapping wings. Just as there's more than one way to fly, there's probably more than one way to think, too.

Google's driverless car, for example, doesn't navigate the road the way humans do. It uses four radars, a 64-beam laser range finder, a camera, GPS, and extremely detailed high-res maps. What's more, Google engineers drive along test routes to record data before they let the self-driving cars loose.

Is this disappointing? In a way, yes: Google *has* to do all this to make up for the fact that the car can't do what any human can do while also singing along to the radio, chugging a venti, and making a mental note to pick up the laundry. But that's a cramped view. Even when processing power and software get better, there's no reason to think that a driverless car should replicate the way humans drive. They will have access to far more information than we do, and unlike us they'll have the power to make use of it in real time. And they'll never get distracted when the phone rings.

True artificial intelligence will very likely be here within a couple of decades. By about 2040 our robot paradise awaits.

In other words, you should still be impressed. When we think of human cognition, we usually think about things like composing music or writing a novel. But a big part of the human brain is dedicated to more prosaic functions, like taking in a chaotic visual field and recognizing the thousands of separate objects it contains. We do that so automatically we hardly even think of it as intelligence. But it is, and the fact that Google's car can do it at all is a real breakthrough.

The exact pace of future progress remains uncertain. For example, some physicists think that Moore's Law may break down in the near future and constrain the growth of computing power. We also probably have to break lots of barriers in our knowledge of neuroscience before we can write the software that does all the things a human brain can do. We have to figure out how to make petaflop computers smaller and cheaper. And it's possible that the 10-petaflop estimate of human computing power is too low in the first place.

Nonetheless, in Lake Michigan terms, we finally have a few inches of water in the lake bed, and we can see it rising. All those milestones along the way—playing chess, translating web pages, winning at *Jeopardy!*, driving a car—aren't just stunts. They're precisely the kinds of things you'd expect as we struggle along with platforms that aren't quite powerful enough—yet. True artificial intelligence will very likely be here within a couple of decades. Making it small, cheap, and ubiquitous might take a decade more.

In other words, by about 2040 our robot paradise awaits.

AND NOW FOR THE BAIT and switch. I promised you this would be a happy story, and in the long run it is.

But first we have to get there. And at this point our tale takes a darker turn. What do we do over the next few decades as robots become steadily more capable and steadily begin taking away all our jobs? This is the kind of thing that futurologists write about frequently, but when I started looking for answers from mainstream economists, it turned out there wasn't much to choose from. The economics community just hasn't spent much time over the past couple of decades focusing on the effect that machine intelligence is likely to have on the labor market. Now is a particularly appropriate time to think about this question, because it was two centuries ago this year that 64 men were brought to trial in York, England. Their crime? They were skilled weavers who fought back against the rising tide of power looms they feared would put them out of work. The Luddites spent two years burning mills and destroying factory machinery, and the British government was not amused. Of the 64 men charged in 1813, 25 were transported to Australia and 17 were led to the gallows.

Since then, Luddite has become a derisive term for anyone afraid of new technology. After all, the weavers turned out to be wrong. Power looms put them out of work, but in the long run automation made the entire workforce more productive. Everyone still had jobs—just different ones. Some ran the new power looms, others found work no one could have imagined just a few decades before, in steel mills, automobile factories, and railroad lines. In the end, this produced wealth for everyone, because, after all, someone still had to make, run, and maintain the machines.

But that was then. During the Industrial Revolution, machines were limited to performing physical tasks. The Digital Revolution is different because computers can perform cognitive tasks too, and that means machines will eventually be able to run themselves. When that happens, they won't just put individuals out of work temporarily. Entire classes of workers will be out of work permanently.

In other words, the Luddites weren't wrong. They were just 200 years too early.

This isn't something that will happen overnight. It will happen slowly, as machines grow increasingly capable. We've already seen it in factories, where robots do work that used to be done by semiskilled assembly line workers. In a decade, driverless cars will start to put taxi hacks and truck drivers out of a job. And while it's easy to believe that some jobs can never be done by machines—do the elderly really want to be tended by robots?—that may not be true. Nearly 50 years ago, when MIT computer scientist Joseph Weizenbaum created a therapy simulation program named Eliza, he was astonished to discover just how addictive it was. Even though Eliza was almost laughably crude, it was endlessly patient and seemed interested in your problems. People *liked* talking to Eliza.

Robots will take over more and more jobs. As this happens, capital will become ever more powerful and labor will become ever more worthless.

And that was 50 years ago, using only a keyboard and an old Teletype terminal. Add a billion times more processing power and you start to get something much closer to real social interaction. Robotic pets are growing so popular that Sherry Turkle, an MIT professor who studies the way we interact with technology, is uneasy about it: "The idea of some kind of artificial companionship," she says, "is already becoming the new normal."

It's not hard to see why. Unlike humans, an intelligent machine does whatever you want it to do, for as long as you want it to. You want to gossip? It'll gossip. You want to complain for hours on end about how your children never call? No problem. And as the technology of robotics advances—the Pentagon has developed a fully functional robotic arm that can be controlled by a human mind—they'll be able to perform ordinary human physical tasks too. They'll clean the floor, do your nails, diagnose your ailments, and cook your food.

Increasingly, then, robots will take over more and more jobs. And guess who will own all these robots? People with money, of course. As this happens, capital will become ever more powerful and labor will become ever more worthless. Those without money—most of us—will live on whatever crumbs the owners of capital allow us.

This is a grim prediction. But it's not nearly as far-fetched as it sounds. Economist Paul Krugman recently remarked that our long-standing belief in skills and education as the keys to financial success may well be outdated. In a blog post titled "Rise of the Robots," he reviewed some recent economic data and predicted that we're entering an era where the prime cause of income inequality will be something else entirely: capital vs. labor.

Until a decade ago, the share of total national income going to workers was pretty stable at around 70 percent, while the share going to capital—mainly corporate profits and returns on financial investments—made up the other 30 percent. More recently, though, those shares have started to change. Slowly but steadily, labor's share of total national income has gone down, while the share going to capital owners has gone up. The most obvious effect of this is the skyrocketing wealth of the top 1 percent, due mostly to huge increases in capital gains and investment income.

In the economics literature, the increase in the share of income going to capital owners is known as capital-biased technological change. Let's take a layman's look at what that means.

The question we want to answer is simple: If CBTC is already happening—not a lot, but just a little bit—what trends would we expect to see? What are the signs of a computer-driven economy? First and most obviously, if automation were displacing labor, we'd expect to see a steady decline in the share of the population that's employed.

Second, we'd expect to see fewer job openings than in the past. Third, as more people compete for fewer jobs, we'd expect to see middle-class incomes flatten in a race to the bottom. Fourth, with consumption stagnant, we'd expect to see corporations stockpile more cash and, fearing weaker sales, invest less in new products and new factories. Fifth, as a result of all this, we'd expect to see labor's share of national income decline and capital's share rise.

These trends are the five horsemen of the robotic apocalypse, and guess what? We're already seeing them, and not just because of the crash of 2008. They started showing up in the statistics more than a decade ago. For a while, though, they were masked by the dot-com and housing bubbles, so when the financial crisis hit, years' worth of decline was compressed into 24 months. The trend lines dropped off the cliff.

How alarmed should we be by this? In one sense, a bit of circumspection is in order. The modern economy is complex, and most of these trends have multiple causes. The decline in the share of workers who are employed, for example, is partly caused by the aging of the population. What's more, the financial crisis has magnified many of these trends. Labor's share of income will probably recover a bit once the economy finally turns up.

Doctors should probably be worried as well. Remember Watson, the *Jeopardy!*-playing computer? In another decade, there's a good chance that Watson will be able to do this without any human help at all.

But in another sense, we should be *very* alarmed. It's one thing to suggest that robots are going to cause mass unemployment starting in 2030 or so. We'd have some time to come to grips with that. But the evidence suggests that—slowly, haltingly—it's happening already, and we're simply not prepared for it.

How exactly will this play out? Economist David Autor has suggested that the first jobs to go will be middle-skill jobs. Despite impressive advances, robots still don't have the dexterity to perform many common kinds of manual labor that are simple for humans—digging ditches, changing bedpans. Nor are they any good at jobs that require a lot of cognitive skill—teaching classes, writing magazine articles. But in the middle you have jobs that are both fairly routine and require no manual dexterity. So that may be where the hollowing out starts: with desk jobs in places like accounting or customer support.

That hasn't yet happened in earnest because AI is still in its infancy. But it's not hard to see which direction the wind is blowing. The US Postal Service, for example, used to employ humans to sort letters, but for some time now, that's been done largely by machines that can recognize human handwriting. Netflix does a better job picking movies you might like than a bored video-store clerk. Facial recognition software is improving rapidly, and *that's* a job so human there's an entire module in the human brain, the fusiform gyrus, solely dedicated to this task.

In fact, there's even a digital sports writer. It's true that a human being wrote this story—ask my mother if you're not sure—but in a decade or two I might be out of a job too. Doctors should probably be worried as well. Remember Watson, the *Jeopardy!*-playing computer? It's now being fed millions of pages of medical information so that it can help physicians do a better job of diagnosing diseases. In another decade, there's a good chance that Watson will be able to do this without any human help at all.

This is, admittedly, pretty speculative. Still, even if it's hard to find concrete examples of computers doing human work today, it's going to get easier before long.

Take driverless cars. My newspaper is delivered every day by a human being. But because humans are fallible, sometimes I don't get a paper, or I get the wrong one. This would be a terrific task for a driverless car in its early stages of development. There are no passengers to worry about. The route is fixed. Delivery is mostly done in the early morning, when traffic is light. And the car's abundance of mapping and GPS data would ensure that it always knows which house is which.

The next step might be passenger vehicles on fixed routes, like airport shuttles. Then long-haul trucks. Then buses and taxis. There are 2.5 million workers who drive trucks, buses, and taxis for a living, and there's a good chance that, one by one, all of them will be displaced by driverless vehicles within the next decade or two. What will they do when that happens? Machines will be putting everyone else with modest skill levels out of work too. There will be no place to go but the unemployment line.

WHAT CAN WE DO about this? First and foremost, we should be carefully watching those five economic trends linked to capital-biased technological change to see if they rebound when the economy picks up. If, instead, they continue their long, downward slide, it means we've already entered a new era.

Next, we'll need to let go of some familiar convictions. Left-leaning observers may continue to think that stagnating incomes can be improved with better education and equality of opportunity. Conservatives will continue to insist that people without jobs are lazy bums who shouldn't be coddled. They'll both be wrong.

Corporate executives should worry too. For a while, everything will seem great for them: Falling labor costs will produce heftier profits and bigger bonuses. But then it will all come crashing down. After all, robots might be able to *produce* goods and services, but they can't consume them. And eventually computers will become pretty good CEOs as well.

Solutions to this will remain elusive as long as we resist facing the real change in the way our economy works. When we finally do, we'll probably have only a few options open to us. The simplest, because it's relatively familiar, is to tax capital at high rates and use the money to support displaced workers. In other words, as The *Economist*'s Ryan Avent puts it, "redistribution, and a lot of it."

There's not much question that this could work, but would we be happy in a society that offers real work to a dwindling few and bread and circuses for the rest? Most likely, owners of capital would strongly resist higher taxes, as they always have, while workers would be unhappy with their enforced idleness. Still, the ancient Romans managed to get used to it—with slave labor playing the role of robots—and we might have to, as well.

Alternatively, economist Noah Smith suggests that we might have to fundamentally change the way we think about how we share economic growth. Right now, he points out, everyone is born with an endowment of labor by virtue of having a body and a brain that can be traded for income. But what to do when that endowment is worth a fraction of what it is today? Smith's suggestion: "Why not also an endowment of capital? What if, when each citizen turns 18, the government bought him or her a diversified portfolio of equity?"

In simple terms, if owners of capital are capturing an increasing fraction of national income, then that capital needs to be shared more widely if we want to maintain a middle-class society. Somehow—and I'm afraid a bit of vagueness is inevitable here—an increasing share of corporate equity will need to be divvied up among the entire population as workers are slowly but surely stripped of their human capital. Perhaps everyone will be guaranteed ownership of a few robots, or some share of robot production of goods and services.

But whatever the answer—and it might turn out to be something we can't even imagine right now—it's time to start thinking about our automated future in earnest. The history of mass economic displacement isn't encouraging—fascists in the '20s, Nazis in the '30s—and recent high levels of unemployment in Greece and Italy have already produced rioting in the streets and larger followings for right-wing populist parties. And that's after only a few years of misery.

So far, though, the topic has gotten surprisingly little attention among economists. At MIT, Autor has written about the elimination of middle-class jobs thanks to encroaching technology, and his colleagues, Erik Brynjolfsson and Andrew McAfee of MIT's Center for

Digital Business, got a lot of attention a couple of years ago for their e-book *Race Against the Machine*, probably the best short introduction to the subject of automation and jobs. (Though a little too optimistic about the future of humans, I think.) The fact that Paul Krugman is starting to think about this deeply is also good news.

But it's not enough. When the robot revolution finally starts to happen, it's going to happen fast, and it's going to turn our world upside down. It's easy to joke about our future robot overlords—R2-D2 or the Terminator?—but the challenge that machine intelligence presents really isn't science fiction anymore. Like Lake Michigan with an inch of water in it, it's happening around us right now even if it's hard to see. A robotic paradise of leisure and contemplation eventually awaits us, but we have a long and dimly lit tunnel to navigate before we get there.

Kevin Drum is a political blogger for *Mother Jones* magazine. He was a blogosphere pioneer when, after a stint in marketing, he went online as Calpundit in 2003. Prior to joining *Mother Jones*, he blogged at the *Washington Monthly's Political Animal*.

Peter Gorle and Andrew Clive  **NO**

Positive Impact of Industrial Robots on Employment

Introduction

Study Aim

The study analyses the impact of the use of robots in the industrialized production of goods on employment. The study covers years 2000 to 2016.

Project Scope

The sectors considered are:

1. The large automotive players as well as the component suppliers.
2. Electronics and its interface with specialist plastics [solar cells, photovoltaics etc or other advanced materials], particularly clean rooms [but not the very specialised microchip manufacturing application].
3. Food and beverage, [health, cleanliness and safety*]
4. Plastics [and Rubber] Industry as such, not only in combination with Electronics, Chemicals and Pharmaceuticals, . . .

Other than the automotive sector, the brief specified that **SMEs** (Small and Medium Enterprises) up to 250 employees were specified as the target where possible. By agreement, this has been given less emphasis in the project as there is little available information on the use of robots specifically by smaller companies.

Industrial Robots Are the Target

Global markets are covered by the economic background data. The study then focused on six key countries. Brazil, China, Germany, Japan, Republic of Korea and USA.

Method

The project is based largely on analyses of economic data on the six selected countries. This has been combined with the data on Robot use provided by IFR [International Federation of Robotics].

Conclusions were drawn by the Metra Martech team based on economic and industry knowledge. There are considerable gaps in the information available and the main quantifications show orders of magnitude rather than precise numbers. These conclusions have been tested on IFR members in the countries. The testing process involved a two stage set of questions which were responded to by eighteen of these experts. The first question set established the validity of the main assumptions made by Metra Martech; the second was a more detailed set of questions, sent by IFR to selected experts. . . .

The Economic Factors: And Their Effects on the Use of Robotics

Displacement and Re-Employment

Where automation displaces people in manufacturing it almost always increases output. In some cases it allows such an increase in production and related decrease in unit price that it creates a whole new market and generates the need for downstream jobs to get the product to the consumer. It releases employees for other, often new jobs outside manufacturing. Historically, this has always been the case.

An alternative view is that this displacement in the future will be more difficult to place, as service robotics may take over many of the new job opportunities in human tasks such as in banking, fast food chains, and retailing petrol forecourts.

What is likely is that the growth of the production, marketing, selling and maintaining of service robots will create the next wave of employment.

The USA has provided a good example, where the total number of people in employment has grown, driven by increase in population, increased participation by women and increased immigrant labour. The long downward trend in manufacturing as a proportion of total employment has been caused by failure to remain competitive in manufacturing as the industrialising countries have grown capacity. . . .

What is driving this trend to fewer employees in manufacturing is that manufacturers have steadily improved manufacturing productivity, largely by increasing the size of production units, automating tasks and sourcing components globally.

... [D]oubling use of robots in the past ten years in USA has not affected the trend. By contrast, Germany, which has proportionately many more robots, also doubled the number of robots and has achieved slightly higher growth with almost no reduction in manufacturing employment.

Pressure to increase productivity in the developed countries, has been precipitated by greatly increased competition from overseas manufacturers, and passing of high labour content production to the low labour cost areas.

Pressure to use robotics in the developing countries has been that, despite availability of low cost labour, consistency and accuracy required to compete with or meet the requirements of the developed markets, can sometimes only be achieved by robotics.

Five other economic factors have to be considered:

- Globalisation
- Increasing speed of technology development
- Age and skills profiles
- Wage levels
- Health and safety legislation levels

Globalisation of the Market

There has been very rapid growth of the very large developing markets of China and India.

These are low labour cost countries and while labour costs can be expected to level up around the world, these two countries are likely to be relatively low cost areas for at least 20 years. The markets are so large that they encourage the development of locally grown research and technology. This means the phase when China, for example, largely produced goods to western specifications is passing.

Two defences that the developed countries have to maintain their wealth creating production capacity [without putting up trade barriers] are:

1. To put more money into research and development. The success of the Frauenhofer Institutes in Germany, and the new 150bn Yen FIRST projects [Funding program for world leading Innovative R&D on Science and Technology] in Japan are examples of this.

2. To reduce dependence on high cost labour by introducing automation when it offers an economic alternative.

Increasing Speed of Technology Development

This is about the pace of technological development, and the opportunity which this provides for those who can introduce the new technologies. It results in the shortening of product life cycles. Shorter cycles call for more flexible robotics. The product sectors which are the target for this report are not all affected to the same degree by shortening life cycles. Length of production run is an allied factor. Increasing customisation of products, and the flexibility needed by smaller companies are likely to be met by the next generation of robots.

Age and Skills Profiles

The ageing populations in, for example China, Japan and Germany are often cited as an added reason for adoption of robotics. USA is also affected but to a lesser degree.

A very significant ageing is forecast, but if we consider the workforce, within the timescale of the survey, only Japan is significantly affected, with a projected 5% loss of people of employable age. The German situation will become critical in the following years, but is projected to be less than 2% loss in workforce because of ageing, between now and 2016. Our discussions with robotics experts identify specific problems with ageing workforce in the aerospace sector in USA, but this is outside the scope of the present study.

The existence of skills gaps is reported to be a problem, but this is more a question of education and training regimes than the effect of population ageing.

Several factors are involved in addition to age, the change in population as a whole, the change in people of [currently] employable age, the overall number of people employed and the success of skills training in the country. . . .

Skills Gaps

Even with increasing levels of technology training around the world, reports on the subject show that skills gaps are occurring. The recession has accelerated this. The idea of a jobless recovery [see extract below] favours investment in productivity rather than people. There is another factor connected to this which is the much greater computer and electronic interface skills of the up and coming generation. They also have higher expectations about the type of work they would like to do.

The problem is more of skills mismatch than over-all skills availability. This is a structural training problem rather than a consequence of the ageing population.

- jobs are changing
- educational attainment is lagging. . . .

Wage Costs and Availability of Low Cost Labour

One of the arguments against robots, contested by the suppliers, is that they are less flexible in operation and demand more up-front investment than the employment of low cost [often immigrant in the developed countries] labour.

The high labour cost sectors are more likely to use robots.

The differences between the countries are large too, although the interpretation of comparative data is often difficult. . . .

Low Cost Labour

China, and to some extent Brazil, have had access to low cost indigenous labour.

Japan and to a lesser extent Korea have restricted incoming workers.

USA and parts of Europe have until recently allowed this inflow, and both areas have used fewer robots pro-portionately as a partial result of this, with the exception of Germany. The table shows very large differences in immigration. . . .

Health, Safety [H&S] and Environment

The increasing attention to these factors adds impetus to the employment of robotics in hazardous environments, or those involving great monotony. In the developed countries, H&S is a steadily advancing area; in the devel-oping countries, progress is very sporadic.

According to the International Labor Organization (ILO), 270 million workers fall victim to occupational injuries and illnesses, leading to 2.3 million deaths annu-ally, showing that the problem is significant.

There is pressure from consumer groups to force manufacturers in developing countries to look after their workers to a standard approaching that achieved by the developed world manufacturers, but progress is slow.

However, no specific new initiatives have been iden-tified in the study so far, which would cause a *step change* in the current trend to gradual improvement of health and safety practices in the six countries being studied. . . .

Summary
Overall Rise in Employment

Overall paid employment has risen in most coun-tries. In the six considered here, only Japan has seen a decline.

This is driven by increasing participation of women, and increases in population, including immigration in some cases. It is also caused by the increasing demand for services, and the creation of completely new products and markets, often related to the application of electronics to communication.

The statistics mainly point to reduction in employment in manufacturing in the developed coun-tries, but this is often a small reduction. It coincides with an increase in output and an increase in robotics use except in the case of Japan.

The extra number that have gained employment in the years 2000 to 2008 is far greater than the small numbers losing their jobs in manufacturing.

The new jobs have been in:

1. distribution and services, some of the distribution jobs are the result of manufacturers outsourcing their distribution. In the past these jobs would have been classified as part of manufacturing.
2. and also in new manufacturing applications, particularly using technology advances to cre-ate new consumer products [mobile phones, computers, games etc].

In the industrialising countries, as could be expected, there has been a sharp rise in employment in manufacturing, as well as increase in output.

Productivity increases are not just caused by auto-mation and robotics, but it is one of three main factors, along with increased size of manufacturing plants and the globalisation of sourcing. *Note: while the IFR numbers provide a clear basis from which to work, it has not always been possible to separate robotics from automation in our analyses.*

Individual countries differ greatly, the impor-tance of manufacturing is only 11% of employment in USA . . . but 24% in Germany and as high as 27% in more recently industrialising countries such as the Republic of Korea.

The level of robotics use has almost always dou-bled, in all of the six countries [except Japan] in the eight years covered by the study. The proportion of the workforce that is unemployed has hardly changed in this period. . . .

Employment *Directly* Due to the Use of Robotics [World]

The robot industry itself generates on the order of 150,000 jobs worldwide, to which can be added the support staff and operators, another 150,000 people.

There are three other types of application where robotics create or preserve jobs. These are jobs which can only be done by robots.

I Where the product cannot be made to satisfactory precision, consistency and cost, without robotics.

II Where the conditions under which the current work is done are unsatisfactory [may be illegal in the developed countries], but where a robot will operate.

III Where [particularly] a developed country manufacturing unit with high labour costs is threatened by a unit in a low labour cost area.

Employment *Indirectly* Due to the Use of Robotics

A much larger source of employment, at least partly due to robotics, is the newly created downstream activity necessary to support manufacturing which can only be done by robots. We have been conservative in what we have chosen to include here. Some of the people we have spoken to, for example, would have liked us to have included large parts of the automotive sector sales and distribution employment. Our conclusion was that much of this infrastructure was in place before robots were widely used, and so not resulting from the use of robots.

The best example is the communication and leisure equipment business, from distribution to retailing. In the USA, this part of retailing is of the order of 1 million. In world terms this accounts for 3 to 5 million of jobs which would not exist if automation and robotics had not been developed to allow production of millions of electronic products, from phones to Playstations. . . .

Note that China now produces more cars than USA, but the number of robots used in vehicle manufacture in China is estimated at 28,000 compared with 77,000 in USA.

Robot density in a sector only provides a partial view of employment which is dependent on robotics. For example, use of robotics in the automotive sector does not cover all parts of the industry. However, large parts of the motor vehicle assembly sector would be lost to a country if it did not employ robotics. Probably not the components side, this is often highly automated but less likely to depend on robotics.

In the electronics sector some components could not be made without robotics, or could not be made at a cost which would sell, which would cause job losses not just in manufacture but downstream as well.

Potential for New Job Creation in the Years up to 2016

There are five main areas where new jobs may be created in the next five years by the use of robotics.

I. Continued development of new products based on the development of electronics and communication technology. One of the new areas identified, for example, is the manufacture of service robots. Another is the development and mass adoption of renewable energy technologies.
II. Expansion of existing economies and industries, notably automotive.
III. Greater use of robotics in the SME [small and medium enterprises] sectors, particularly in the developed countries, to protect or win back manufacture from the low cost countries, or to win back production which had been seen as hazardous, but which had been taken up by the developing countries.
IV. Greater use of robotics in the food sector [where current use is low] as processed meals develop, to meet more stringent hygiene conditions.
V. Expansion of the robotics sector itself, to cope with the growth in demand. We have assumed a 15% growth which adds 45,000 people.

Overall Effect

Direct employment due to robotics:

2 to 3 million jobs created in world manufacturing.

Considering the world population of industrial robots at just over 1 million, **that is 2 to 3 jobs per robot in use.**

Indirect employment downstream of this more than doubles this number.

For the future, 700,000 to 1 million new jobs to be created by robots in the next five years.

PETER GORLE is the managing director of Metra Martech, a firm specializing in industrial and economic analysis for governments and international organizations.

ANDREW CLIVE is a senior consultant with Metra Martech, a firm specializing in industrial and economic analysis for governments and international organizations.

EXPLORING THE ISSUE

Will Robots Take Your Job?

Critical Thinking and Reflection

1. What are "industrial" robots?
2. What kinds of jobs now held by humans may robots be able to do in the near future?
3. Why do robots threaten more than just industrial jobs?
4. In what ways might robots create jobs?
5. If robots take all the jobs, what will people do?

Is There Common Ground?

Computer technology (including robotics) is a rapidly growing field. Indeed, in the past whenever someone would say "Computers can't do X!" someone else would add "Yet!" They'd be right, too, for computers can now do a great many things their predecessors could not. Surely this applies to robotics as well, and robots have been expanding their presence in the workplace for decades. They will continue to do so, and Kevin Drum and Peter Gorle and Andrew Clive may well agree that there is a fine line between robots taking jobs and—in a faltering economy—robots keeping companies alive without hiring more humans. It is also worth stressing that the two selections reprinted here differ in their timelines. Kevin Drum says job loss will be severe before the middle of the twenty-first century. Peter Gorle and Andrew Clive say many (up to 1 million) jobs will be created in the next five years. If they had tried to project further into the future, perhaps they would have agreed with Kevin Drum.

1. Why have employers welcomed robots in the workplace?

2. What jobs seem to you to be out of reach for robots (so far!)?
3. Kevin Drum suggests that it is time to rethink our economy to achieve a more equitable distribution of national wealth. Where would you begin?

Additional Resources

Jason Borenstein, "Robots and the Changing Workforce," *AI & Society* (2011).

Erik Brynjolfsson and Andrew McAfee, *Race against the Machine* (Digital Frontier Press, 2011) (http://raceagainstthemachine.com/).

Kirk L. Kroeker, "Weighing Watson's Impact," *Communications of the ACM* (July 2011).

Aaron Smith and Janna Anderson, *AI, Robotics, and the Future of Jobs* (PEW Internet Research Project, August 2014) (http://www.pewinternet.org/2014/08/06/future-of-jobs/).

Alex Wright, "Automotive Autonomy," *Communications of the ACM* (July 2011).

Internet References . . .

MIT Computer Science and Artificial Intelligence Laboratory

http://www.csail.mit.edu/

Carnegie Mellon Robotics Institute

https://www.ri.cmu.edu/

Why Robots Will Be the Biggest Job Creators in World History

http://www.forbes.com/sites/johntamny/2015/03/01/why-robots-will-be-the-biggest-job-creators-in-history/

Selected, Edited, and with Issue Framing Material by:
Thomas A. Easton, *Mount Ida College*

ISSUE

Do We Need New Laws to Protect the Public against Cybercrime?

YES: Dean C. Garfield, from "Testimony before the U.S. House of Representatives Committee on Science, Space, and Technology, Subcommittee on Research and Technology, Hearing on 'The Expanding Cyber Threat,'" U.S. House of Representatives (2015)

NO: Cheri F. McGuire, from "Testimony before the U.S. House of Representatives Committee on Science, Space, and Technology, Subcommittee on Research and Technology, Hearing on 'The Expanding Cyber Threat,'" U.S. House of Representatives (2015)

Learning Outcomes

After reading this issue, you will be able to:

- Discuss the need for new legislation to aid in the fight against cybercrime.
- Explain how cybercriminals get into the computers of corporations, government agencies, and individuals to steal data.
- Explain how cyber-attackers can interfere with the computers of corporations, government agencies, and individuals even without stealing data.
- Describe the basic techniques of cybersecurity.

ISSUE SUMMARY

YES: Dean C. Garfield argues that technological defenses are essential in the fight against cybercrime and are in continuous development, but there is a need for new laws that improve "the government's ability to deter, investigate, and prosecute cybercrime."

NO: Cheri F. McGuire argues that government and industry must cooperate to fight cybercrime and emphasizes "strong technical capabilities [and] effective countermeasures."

Physicist Gregory Benford says he wrote the very first computer virus, way back in the late 1960s. It was not designed to do harm, just to test the idea of a program that could spread from computer to computer, but it was a virus. As computers became more sophisticated, so did viruses and other "malware." By the 1990s, there was much alarm about hackers (see Bruce Sterling, *The Hacker Crackdown: Law and Disorder on the Electronic Frontier*, Bantam, 1992; http://www.gutenberg.org/ebooks/101). With the advent of the Internet a little later, malware starred in credit card fraud, identity theft, and more. As the problem got worse, it gave rise to antivirus software and the computer security industry. Today cybercrime costs the United states a bit less than 1 percent of its gross domestic product (GDP) (see "Net Losses: Estimating the Global Cost of Cybercrime: Economic Impact of Cybercrime II," Center for Strategic and International Studies, June 2014; http://www.mcafee.com/us/resources/reports/rp-economic-impact-cybercrime2.pdf).

Come the twenty-first century, and while computer security and fraud remain of immense concern, people have begun to worry about cyberwar. In June 2010, the Stuxnet worm attacked Iranian nuclear facilities. It used stolen digital certificates to take over control software and interfere with the normal function of nuclear power plants, electrical distribution systems, and oil pipelines.

Early reports said the Stuxnet worm was so complex that it must have taken large teams of programmers, millions of dollars in funding, and many months of work to produce it. Iran insisted it had to be an Israeli-American cyber-attack, and on June 1, 2012, David E. Sanger reported in "Obama Order Sped Up Wave of Cyberattacks against Iran," *New York Times*, that interviews with European, U.S., and Israeli officials have revealed that in 2006, President George W. Bush initiated the development of the Stux-net worm under the code name Olympic Games. Samuel Greengard, "The New Face of War," *Communications of the ACM* (December 2010), considers this a sign of the way wars will be fought in the future. "The risk of cyber-warfare is growing, and many . . . warn that political leaders aren't entirely tuned into the severity of the threat." It must be taken seriously, for it is only a matter of time before cyber-war is real. Richard A. Clarke and Richard K. Knake, *Cyber War: The Next Threat to National Security and What to Do about It* (HarperCollins, 2010), stress that because society is now totally dependent on telecommunications networks, it is also vulnerable to widespread, long-lasting damage. James P. Farwell and Rafal Rohozinski, "Stuxnet and the Future of Cyber War," *Survival* (February/March 2011), note that cyberwar "offers great potential for striking at enemies with less risk than using traditional means." They also note that many cyberwar techniques are rooted in cybercrime (viruses, worms, DDOS attacks, bot-nets, iden-tity theft, hacking, fraud, and more).

Keren Elazari, "How to Survive Cyberwar," *Scientific American* (April 2015), stresses the importance of indi-viduals' behavior in defending against cybercrime and cyberwar by keeping software up-to-date, using secure Web browsers, and doing a better job of authenticating our identities (passwords, fingerprints, etc.). Indeed, few people today do not have antivirus and/or antimalware software on their computers. However, there is pressure to weaken such defenses of security in the name of security. The United States government has long sought extensions to digital communications and the Internet of traditional wiretapping laws that permitted law-enforcement agen-cies to listen in on the conversations of criminal suspects (see Declan McCullagh, "FBI: We Need Wiretap-Ready Web Sites—Now," *CNET News*, May 4, 2012; http://news .cnet.com/8301-1009_3-57428067-83/fbi-we-need-wiretap-ready -web-sites-now/). After September 11, 2001, the War on Ter-rorism began and every tool that promised to help identify terrorists before or catch them after they committed their dreadful acts was seen as desirable. However, when the Department of Defense's Defense Advanced Research Pro-jects Agency (DARPA) proposed a massive computer sys-tem capable of sifting through purchases, tax data, court records, Google searches, emails, and other information from government and commercial databases to seek suspi-cious patterns of behavior, many people objected that this amounted to a massive assault on privacy and was surely in violation of the Fourth Amendment to the United States Constitution (which established the right of private citizens to be secure against unreasonable searches and seizures; "unreasonable" has come to mean "without a search warrant" for physical searches of homes and offices and "without a court order" for interceptions of mail and wiretappings of phone conversations). This Total or Terrorism Information Awareness (TIA) program soon died, although many of its components continued under other names; see Shane Harris, "TIA Lives On," *National Journal* (February 25, 2006). See also Hina Shamsi and Alex Abdo, "Privacy and Surveillance Post-9/11," *Human Rights* (Winter 2011).

The use of encryption by terrorists, criminals, and ordinary citizens is also under threat on the grounds that encryption can hide signs of dangers to society. In 2015, the British government passed laws to forbid the use of unbreakable encryption (Tom Whitehead, "Internet Firms to Be Banned from Offering Unbreakable Encryp-tion under New Laws," *The Telegraph*, November 2, 2015; http://www.telegraph.co.uk/news/uknews/terrorism-in-the -uk/11970391/Internet-firms-to-be-banned-from-offering-out-of -reach-communications-under-new-laws.html). However, J. D. Tuccile, "Ban Encryption? It's an Impossible Idea Whose Time Will Never Come," *Reason* (November 24, 2015), argues that "The sight of blustering politicians' steadfast determination to erode civil liberties in every nook and corner of society that they *can* reach is unlikely to con-vince the public at large to surrender its digital money and encrypted communications."

Can cybercrime writ large be more like cyberwar? Matthew Goldstein, Nicole Perlroth, and David E. Sanger report in "Hackers' Attack Cracked 10 Financial Firms in Major Assault," *New York Times* (October 4, 2014), that the hackers responsible for breaching JPMorgan Chase and nine other major financial firms, affecting more than 80 million homes and businesses, "are thought to be oper-ating from Russia and appear to have at least loose con-nections with officials of the Russian government." There is now serious concern that a hacker attack could cause a major financial crisis. And with the involvement of for-eign governments, it could easily be regarded as an act of war. John Stone is sure that "Cyber War Will Take Place!" *Journal of Strategic Studies* (February 2013); if commercial attacks are acts of war, the war may already be under way. At the end of 2014, Sony Pictures was hacked, embarrass-ing documents were released, and threats were issued to keep the movie *The Interview* (about the assassination of North Korea's leader) from being released; the U.S. government accused North Korea of the hacking and called it an act of cyberwar; see, e.g., "Sony Hack: North Korea Threatens US as Row Deepens" (http://www.bbc.com/news/world-asia-30573040).

Peter Sommer and Ian Brown, "Reducing Systemic Cybersecurity Risk," OECD (Organization for Economic Co-operation and Development)/IFP (International Futures Programme) Project on "Future Global Shocks," 2011, conclude "that very few single cyber-related events have the capacity to cause a global shock. Governments nevertheless need to make detailed preparations to withstand and recover from a wide range of unwanted cyber events, both accidental and deliberate. There are significant and growing risks of localized misery and loss as a result of compromise of computer and telecommunications services." Simson L. Garfinkel, "The Cybersecurity Risk," *Communications of the ACM* (June 2012), argues that the reason why we have not already built more secure computer systems is that "it is more cost-effective to create systems without redundancy or resiliency." Gary McGraw, "Cyber War Is Inevitable (Unless We Build Security In)," *Journal of Strategic Studies* (February 2013), argues that this needs to change.

What is the best way to defend against cyber-criminals and their more extreme cousins, the cyber-warriors? R. Scott Kemp, "Cyberweapons: Bold Steps in a Digital Darkness?" *Bulletin of the Atomic Scientists* (June 7, 2012) (http://www.thebulletin.org/web-edition/op-eds/cyberweapons-bold-steps-digital-darkness), argues that "We are at a key

turning point . . . in which a nation must decide what role cyberweapons will play in its national defense. . . . [F]or the United States and other highly developed nations whose societies are critically and deeply reliant on computers, the safe approach is to direct cyber research at purely defensive applications." According to Richard Stone, "A Call to Cyber Arms," *Science* (March 1, 2013), the U.S. and other governments are putting a great deal of effort not only into devising ways to defend against cyber-espionage and cyber-attacks against industrial, defense, and commercial infrastructure, but also into ways to go on the offensive.

Most discussions of the topic focus on the role of technology in defending against cyber-attacks, and indeed on January 27, 2015, the United States House of Representatives Committee on Science, Space, and Technology, Subcommittee on Research and Technology, held a hearing on "The Expanding Cyber Threat." The YES selection is drawn from the testimony before this hearing of Dean C. Garfield, president and CEO of the Information Technology Industry Council. He argues that technological defenses are essential and are in continuous development, but there is a need for new laws that improve "the government's ability to deter, investigate, and prosecute cybercrime." The NO selection is drawn from the testimony of Cheri F. McGuire, vice-president for global government affairs and cybersecurity policy of the major cybersecurity company Symantec. She argues that government and industry must cooperate to fight cybercrime and emphasizes "strong technical capabilities [and] effective countermeasures."

YES ⤶

Dean C. Garfield

Testimony before the U.S. House of Representatives Committee on Science, Space, and Technology, Subcommittee on Research and Technology, Hearing on "The Expanding Cyber Threat"

ITI is the global voice of the leading technology companies from all corners of the information and communications technology (ICT) sector, including hardware, software, and services—the majority of whom are based here in the United States. Cybersecurity is critical to our members' success—the protection of our customers, our brands, and our intellectual property are essential components of our business and our ability to grow and innovate in the future. Consequently, ITI has been a leading voice in advocating effective approaches to cybersecurity.

In addition, as both producers and users of cybersecurity products and services, our members have extensive experience working with governments around the world on cybersecurity policy. That's important to keep in mind because when it comes to cybersecurity, our connectedness is through an Internet that is truly global and borderless. We acutely understand the impact of governments' policies on security innovation and the need for U.S. policies to be compatible with—and lead—global norms.

I will focus my testimony on four areas: (1) The cybersecurity challenges facing our society today; (2) how industry's response to cyber threats and challenges has evolved from the start and will continue to do so; (3) how our industry sees the future of cybersecurity; and (4) how the federal government can partner with industry, or assist our work, in protecting our assets from successful cyber-attacks.

The Cybersecurity Challenges Facing Us Today

As you have heard from the other panelists, the threats and challenges are certainly many, they continually evolve, and are becoming more sophisticated.

For example, a key challenge facing us now are advanced persistent threats (APT), which use multiple phases to break into a network, avoid detection, and harvest valuable information over the long term. APTs differ from traditional threats in that they are targeted, persistent, evasive and extremely advanced. Although there are many challenges in addition to APT, there is a common theme—our cyber adversaries are becoming more and more intelligent, creative, and resourceful. These challenges do not just face American industry, but industry globally, and they impact citizens and our use of the Internet and e-commerce.

But I want to stress that not all cybersecurity threats are, or should be, of equal concern. The risks to all companies, government agencies, or citizens are inherently different because threats do not impact all of us the same way—if at all.

The risk differs by entities, depending on industry, size, and assets. Banks face different risks than manufacturers, hospitals, railroads, or movie studios. Some industries are targeted for money, others for personal data, others for confidential business information, such as trade secrets, that can help a competitor bring a product to market faster or allow them to get the upper hand in business negotiations. The threat of an organized crime syndicate seeking credit card numbers is more pertinent to an online commerce company or bank than a steel manufacturer, for example. A global bank headquartered on Wall Street will likely be a bigger target than a corner bank in a small town. Individuals at home are much less likely than companies to be the target of an advanced persistent threat. The threat may not even be a sophisticated one at all. Unpreparedness or simple error can make a gateway for the worst havoc.

Testimony before the U.S. House of Representatives Committee on Science, Space, and Technology, Subcommittee on Research and Technology, Hearing on "The Expanding Cyber Threat," U.S. House of Representatives, January 2015.

When it comes to cybersecurity, one size does not fit all. The varying challenges underscore why the best approach is a system in which entities are empowered to manage their own cybersecurity risks. Each entity has a distinct risk, and needs to allocate their cybersecurity resources in their own unique way depending on what their "crown jewels" are, where they are kept, and who might want them. Our sector's innovation allows us to create products and services for all stakeholders to identify, manage, and mitigate their ever-changing risks.

ICT Industry Evolving Responses to Cyber Threats and Challenges

The ICT industry is improving cybersecurity in two distinct and important ways: via the products and services we make, and the cybersecurity risk management practices we employ and promote.

In the products and services realm, we are innovating technologies to counter and stop criminals that are increasingly able to penetrate companies' information technology (IT) systems. We are also making security easier to use and investing in managed security services. In terms of corporate cybersecurity risk management, ITI's members are major, multinational companies that have managed cybersecurity risks for decades.

Our products and services to improve security. ITI's member companies—and the global ICT industry generally—have innovated and invented security for decades. It is important to stress that the real advancements in security are not large and splashy, however. Like our bodies' immunity system, there are millions of small innovations that accumulate and come together piece-by-piece to make security more pervasive in our interconnected lives and economies. And these millions of innovations are driven by our companies, as well as thousands of new entrepreneurs and companies around the world, inventing in this space.

Like a collaborative network, the growing marketplace helps all of us deal with hackers, conduct remediation, and build skills. Enabling all of these inventions is our commitment to research and development (R&D). ITI companies invest incredible amounts in R&D. In fact, many ITI member firms have annual R&D budgets orders of magnitude greater than that of the Defense Advanced Research Project Agency (DARPA), which is renowned as our government's incubator for new technologies like networked computing. Given that DARPA's FY2014 R&D budget was $2.9 billion, our member companies are investing a staggering sum.

I am sure Members of the Committee are familiar with some of the more widely known security technologies that have evolved and captured the spotlight over the past few years. These included firewalls to protect the perimeter of your computer or network, anti-virus software to detect and remove computer viruses, and intrusion detection software (to figure out if a network had been breached), or intrusion prevention software (to try to predict and prevent being breached). These types of technologies evolved to meet changing threats and risks and continue to evolve.

Using sophisticated analytics to detect and react to anomalies. The technologies I mentioned above are just the tip of the innovation iceberg, and we are beyond the stage where firewall defenses are adequate. Each time we "up our game," hackers innovate in tandem to get around such defenses. Thus, the ICT industry has created and uses sophisticated data analytic software to monitor data, learn what is normal or aberrant, identify suspicious or anomalous activities, and react in real-time, such as by quarantining data before it can be exfiltrated. Companies also use data analytics to spot and tackle issues like fraud. And our innovations are certainly not only in products; we also innovate security services.

Making security the default norm, and easier to use. The reality is most security incidents involve some kind of human error: use of weak passwords, an employee clicking on spam and inadvertently downloading malware that hijacks a computer hard drive and exfiltrates valuable data, or inadequate network management that does not appropriately segment and section off data to those who truly need to access it.

Some of the most high profile cases over the past several months have shown how criminals are exploiting human weaknesses or mistakes made by users. One reason these mistakes happen is that security, particularly online, is difficult, complex, and time-consuming, and it is human nature to try to avoid things that are complex and take time.

To address this weak link, ICT companies are making it easier for the user to enable their own secure environments. This means we are creating products where security features such as encryption are turned on by default. Some smartphones now come with fingerprint readers in lieu of passwords to allow access. What used to be the realm of science fiction or blockbuster films are now in a phone that you can buy for a few hundred dollars.

Ensuring more experts are managing security. Our companies are also helping to make security the responsibility of experts who know how to handle it. This is happening as we migrate to managed technology services where an IT system is maintained by an outside vendor as a service-based contract, and security is built into the contracts. In the service-based world, the service provider and its cybersecurity experts remain part of that relationship and have the incentive to have a secure and resilient network. If, because of a security incident, a managed service provider's IT system is down and unable to serve customers, the provider will face financial consequences.

Our corporate cybersecurity risk management practices. ITI's members are major multinational companies that have understood and managed cybersecurity risks for decades. Our companies build risk management into their ongoing daily operations through legal and contractual agreements, cybersecurity operational controls, cybersecurity policies, procedures, and plans, adherence to global risk management standards, and many other common practices. Many operate 24-hour, 7-day-a-week network operations centers (NOCs) and participate in a host of entities that help them to understand and manage their risks, such as Sector Coordinating Councils (SCCs) and information sharing and analysis centers (ISACs). We are confident that many large, multinational companies are similar to ITI companies in these ways.

One very useful tool I want to highlight is the Framework for Critical Infrastructure Cybersecurity (Framework) released by the National Institute of Standards and Technology (NIST) in February 2014.

The Framework has great potential to help individual organizations manage their cyber risks, collectively strengthening our nation's cybersecurity. It represents an effective approach to cybersecurity because it leverages public-private partnerships, is based on risk management, and is voluntary. It references existing, globally recognized, voluntary, consensus-based standards, and best practices that are working effectively in industry now. It is technologically neutral, fostering innovation in the private sector and allowing industry to nimbly meet ever-changing cybersecurity challenges. And it nicely articulates how organizations should be factoring privacy considerations into their cybersecurity activities.

Importantly, the Framework is flexible, recognizing that different types of entities may use it for different purposes. Although it is aimed at critical infrastructure owners and operators, it can be useful to entities regardless of their size or relevance to U.S. national and economic security.

The process that went into developing this Framework has been a model for how the public and private sectors can work together to serve the national interest. In effect, the U.S. Government leveraged a tremendous amount of stakeholder input in an open, transparent, and collaborative manner, to create a major cybersecurity policy initiative. Government, industry, and other private stakeholders have a shared interest in improving cybersecurity, and the Framework moves us significantly toward that goal.

The Future of Cybersecurity and Our Top Concerns

We see the threat becoming greater and more persistent, and constantly changing. Our efforts will continue to evolve in tandem. We believe our efforts both in inventing security technologies and services, as well as in managing risks to the security of our networks, are effective approaches to cybersecurity.

But we should all be clear: there is no silver bullet to cybersecurity, and there never will be. For every new defense, there will be an adversary bent on breaching it. The beauty of technology and the Internet—that technologies and business models constantly evolve—means that targets, and attack methods, will constantly change too.

Our efforts aim to reduce the effectiveness of attack methods, and we invest in technology, processes, and education to eliminate human error as much as possible. Our goal is managing our risks and becoming resilient. And that is something we are doing very well. But this is a long journey that does not have an end.

Frankly speaking, a key concern of the ICT industry as we continue to constantly improve cybersecurity is that overbroad and inflexible policies will hamper our ability to innovate or prevent us from changing course when needed to meet dynamic threats. This isn't hyperbolic. The technology sector can point to scores of laws that were crafted in a different age that are incapable of keeping up with technology. That is not the course anyone should want when it comes to securing our connected world. In fact, the current, non-regulatory, non-prescriptive approach to cybersecurity policy in the United States that allows the most innovative minds in industry to lead and respond to the changing cyber threat is one that should not be altered.

How the Government Can Be Helpful

As policymakers, your interest in getting cybersecurity policy right is welcomed and encouraged. However, governments must resist thinking that just because there is an incident online that government must be the first responder. As I have outlined above, companies are making investments, and more and more executives are focused on solving the problems.

Working with all stakeholders, including governments, we are well-positioned to manage these risks. To complement and enable industry efforts, U.S. government efforts should focus on:

- **Supporting federal agencies' outreach on the Framework.** ITI strongly supports the Framework for Improving Critical Infrastructure Cybersecurity, and believes Congress should allow further time for it to enhance cybersecurity practices. Congress can help the Framework achieve its goals by ensuring NIST, the Department of Homeland Security, and other relevant departments have the funding they need to conduct ongoing and extensive outreach and awareness about the Framework.
- **Continuing government funding for cybersecurity research and development (R&D).** I noted earlier that our companies invest strongly in cybersecurity R&D. We will continue to do so. But federal investments will remain essential, because we count on the government to perform R&D that simply is not viable for the private sector. By necessity, companies' R&D efforts tend to be commercially focused. We need the government to fund early-stage, high-risk research that can create breakthrough technologies and new market segments. The government can also look out over a longer time horizon, helping to set our R&D long-term sights correctly. The Cybersecurity Enhancement Act of 2014, which became law late last year, is an important down payment on government-supported R&D. For example, we look forward to reviewing the cybersecurity R&D strategic plan that will enable federal agencies to have a more unified approach to cybersecurity and information technology R&D. We hope those efforts take a similar approach to the development of the Framework by including a robust public-private engagement.
- **Continuing government efforts to raise awareness.** Government should work to raise awareness among users of technology (individuals of all ages and businesses of all sizes) about their cybersecurity risks and empower all stakeholders to understand and act upon their roles and responsibilities. In any awareness-raising, governments should partner with the private sector, which has already invested substantially in such efforts. The Cybersecurity Enhancement Act of 2014 also made strides in this area. Cybersecurity competitions

and challenges for students, universities, veterans and other groups to recruit new cybersecurity talent, a cybersecurity scholarship for service program for individuals to help meet the needs of the federal government's cybersecurity mission, and the National Cybersecurity Awareness & Preparedness Program are also parts of a growing and effective education program. To meet a cyber threat that will always evolve, we need to encourage a strong workforce to bring their talents to secure our online world.

- **Passing legislation improving the government's ability to deter, investigate, and prosecute cybercrime.** While many private-sector entities are making substantive efforts to manage their risks and protect their networks, intellectual property, and businesses, criminals continually evolve their tactics and are becoming much more sophisticated. The breadth of criminal activity and number of bad actors make getting ahead of them and crafting responses to incidents difficult. Cyberspace, with its global connectivity, poses considerable challenges to those tasked with protecting it. While the tools might be different from those used by criminals offline, those who wield them are criminals nonetheless. Leveraging and strengthening these laws and enforcement capabilities of law enforcement agencies to combat cyber crime will help to increase cybersecurity.
- **Passing effective cyber threat information-sharing legislation.** Lawmakers should focus on legislation improving cybersecurity threat information sharing in a way that protects privacy and offers adequate legal liability protection for businesses.

As I noted earlier in my testimony, threats will continue to evolve, and so must our responses. Thus, there will be changing needs for education, awareness, R&D, and legislation. In order to effectively and nimbly stay ahead of the threats, Congress must approach these challenges by employing flexible, risk-based approaches that are technology-neutral and foster robust public-private collaboration.

Conclusion

Members of the subcommittee, ITI and our member companies are pleased you are examining the important issue of cybersecurity in the 21st Century. As I said at the opening of my testimony, while the challenges are many, we also have an opportunity to get it right. The ICT industry is constantly innovating and is committed to addressing those threats. We stand ready to provide you any additional input and assistance in our collaborative efforts to develop balanced policy approaches that help all of us to collectively improve cybersecurity risk management and resilience.

DEAN C. GARFIELD is president and CEO of the Information Technology Industry Council, a trade group dedicated to advocacy and policy.

Cheri F. McGuire    **NO**

Testimony before the U.S. House of Representatives Committee on Science, Space, and Technology, Subcommittee on Research and Technology, Hearing on "The Expanding Cyber Threat"

Symantec protects much of the world's information, and is a global leader in security, backup and availability solutions. We are the largest security software company in the world, with over 32 years of experience developing Internet security technology and helping consumers, businesses and governments secure and manage their information and identities. Our products and services protect people's information and their privacy across platforms—from the smallest mobile device, to the enterprise data center, to cloud-based systems. We have established some of the most comprehensive sources of Internet threat data in the world through our Global Intelligence Network, which is comprised of millions of attack sensors recording thousands of events per second, and we maintain 10 Security Response Centers around the globe. In addition, we process billions of e-mail messages and web requests across our 14 global data centers. All of these resources allow us to capture worldwide security data that give our analysts a unique view of the entire Internet threat landscape.

The cyber headlines of the past year have focused largely on massive data breaches, but that is just one corner of the cyber threat landscape. In my testimony today, I will discuss:

- Some common types of attacks;
- Methods attackers use to compromise systems;
- Partnering to fight cybercrime; and
- How individuals and organizations can protect themselves.

The Current Cyber Threat Landscape

Most of the recent headlines about cyber attacks have focused on data breaches across the spectrum of industries. Sadly, breaches have become an all too common

occurrence, impacting not only those breached but also creating geo-political challenges for governments around the world. The organizations that suffered significant breaches over the past year include a "who's who" of the business world: Target, Michael's, Home Depot, The New York Times, and Sony are just a sampling of recent victims.

The theft of personally identifiable information (PII) in this timeframe was unprecedented. According to our most recent Internet Security Threat Report (ISTR), over 550 million identities were exposed in 2013, and eight different breaches exposed 10 million identities or more. We expect that our final statistics from 2014 will be similarly alarming. Interestingly, the Online Trust Alliance just released a report that found that 90% of last year's breaches could have been prevented if businesses relooked at their cyber risk strategies and implemented basic cyber best practices.

While the focus on these public breaches and the identities put at risk is certainly warranted, it is important not to lose sight of the other types of cyber activity that are equally concerning and that can also have dangerous and broad consequences. There are a wide range of tools available to the cyber attacker, and the attacks we see today range from basic confidence schemes to massive denial of service attacks to sophisticated (and potentially destructive) intrusions into critical infrastructure systems. The economic impact can be immediate with the theft of money, or more long term and structural, such as through the theft of intellectual property. It can ruin a company or individual's reputation or finances, and it can impact citizens' trust in their government.

Attackers run the gamut and include highly organized criminal enterprises, individual cybercriminals, so-called "hacktivists," and state-sponsored groups. The motivations vary—the criminals generally are looking for

Testimony before the U.S. House of Representatives Committee on Science, Space, and Technology, Subcommittee on Research and Technology, Hearing on "The Expanding Cyber Threat," U.S. House of Representatives, January 2015.

some type of financial gain, the hacktivists are seeking to promote or advance some cause, and the state actors can be engaged in espionage (whether traditional spycraft or economic espionage) or infiltrating critical infrastructure systems. These lines, however, are not set in stone, as criminals and even state actors might pose as hacktivists, and criminals sometimes will offer their skills to the highest bidder. Attribution has always been difficult in the cyber landscape, and is further complicated by the ability of cyber actors to mask their motives and objectives through misdirection and obfuscation.

Common Types of Attacks

Distributed Denial of Service ("DDoS")

Distributed denial-of-service (DDoS) attacks attempt to deny service to legitimate users by overwhelming the target with activity. The most common method is to flood a server with network traffic from multiple sources (hence "distributed"). These attacks are often conducted through "botnets"—armies of compromised computers that are made up of victim machines that stretch across the globe and are controlled by "bot herders" or "bot masters." One recent study found that over 60% of traffic on the internet today is from bots.

DDoS attacks have grown larger year over year and in 2014 some attacks reached 400 Gigabits per second, a previously unimaginable volume of data. This is roughly equivalent to blasting a network every second with the data stored on more than 10 DVDs. In the past few years we have seen attacks go from the equivalent of a garden hose to a fire hose to the outflow pipes of the Hoover dam. Even the most prepared networks can buckle under that volume of data the first time it is directed at them, which is why even some of the country's biggest financial institutions initially suffered outages from recent DDoS attacks. In addition to increasing in volume, the attacks are getting more sophisticated and varying the methods used, which makes them harder to mitigate. In particular, in 2014 attackers used new techniques to amplify the strength of an attack which made it easier for even the "average" attack to reach levels of volume that were unthinkable just years before.

According to a survey by Neustar, 60% of companies were impacted by a DDoS attack in 2013 and 87 percent were hit more than once. The most affected sectors were the gaming, media, and software industries. The purpose of most attacks is to disrupt, not to destroy. Cybercriminals can rent DDoS attack services on the black market for as little as $5, allowing them to conduct a short, minutes-long DDoS attack against any chosen target. If successful, even such a short attack is enough to garner attention—or to distract an organization's security team, as another recent use of DDoS attacks has been to provide cover for other, more sophisticated attacks. Organized crime groups have been known to launch DDoS attacks against banks to divert the attention and resources of the bank's security team while the main attack is launched, which can include draining customer accounts or stealing credit card information.

Targeted Attacks

Targeted attacks are another tool in the cybercriminal's tool box. . . . Some attacks are directed at a company's servers and systems, where attackers search for unpatched vulnerabilities on websites or undefended connections to the internet. But most rely on social engineering—in the simplest of terms, trying to trick people into doing something that they would never do if fully aware of their actions. They can be targeted at almost any level, even at an entire sector of the economy or a group of similar organizations or companies. They also can target a particular company or a unit within the company (*e.g.*, research and development or finance) or even a specific person.

Most of the data breaches and other attacks that have been in the news were the result of a targeted attack, but the goal of the attacker can vary greatly. One constant is that after attackers select a target they will set out to gain access to the systems they want to compromise and once inside there are few limits on what they can do if the system is not well-protected. The malware used today is largely commoditized, and while we still see some that is custom-crafted, most of the attacks rely on attack kits that are sold on the cyber black market. But even these commodity attack kits are highly sophisticated and are designed to avoid detection—some even come with guarantees from the criminal seller that they will not be stopped by common security measures. This makes it all the more important—but also more challenging—to stay ahead of them.

Scams, Blackmail, and Other Cyber Theft

Like most crime, cyber attacks are often financially motivated, and some of the most common (and most successful) involve getting victims to pay out money, whether through trickery or direct threats. One early and widely successful attack of this type was known as "scareware." Scareware is a form of malware that will open a window on your device that claims your system is infected, and offer to "clean" it for a fee. Some forms of scareware open pop-ups claiming to be from major security companies (including Symantec), and if a user clicks in the window they are taken to a fake website that can look very much like that of the real company. Of course, in most cases the only infection on your computer is the scareware itself. Victims are lucky if they only lose the $20 or $30 "cost" for the fake software, but most are out much more as they typically provide credit card information to pay the scammer in the mistaken belief they are purchasing legitimate security software. Not only did they authorize a payment to the scammer, but they also provided financial information that could then be sold on the criminal underground. And by allowing the scammer to install the supposed cleaning software on their device, they give the criminal the ability to install additional malware and potentially steal more financial information or turn their system into a zombie soldier in a botnet.

First widely seen in 2007, scareware began to diminish in 2011 after users became alerted to the scams and they became much less effective. Nevertheless, criminals have made millions from this type of scam.

Once scareware began to be less effective, criminals turned to "ransomware," and it has grown significantly since 2012. Ransomware is another type of deception where the malware locks the victim's device and displays a screen that purports to be from a law enforcement entity local to the user. The lock screen states that there is illegal content on the computer—everything from pirated movies to child pornography—and instructs the victim to pay a "fine" for their "crime." The criminals claim that the victim's device will be unlocked once the "fine" is paid, but in reality the device frequently remains locked. Should your device become infected, it is important to disconnect it quickly from the Internet and any other computers or devices. This will help prevent the theft of additional personal information from your computer as well as keep the infection from spreading further and stop your computer from being used as part of a botnet. Both of these types of attacks can be removed from your computer and we offer instructions and free tools on our Norton.com website to assist victims in doing so. Unfortunately, some of the more sophisticated variants can require some expertise to remediate.

Unfortunately, criminals have moved beyond even ransomware and are now using a more insidious and harmful form of malware known as "ransomcrypt." While scareware and ransomware are more classic confidence schemes, ransomcrypt is straight-up blackmail: pay a ransom or your computer will be erased. And unlike scareware and ransomware, there is often no easy way to get rid of it—the criminals use high-grade encryption technology to scramble the victim's computer, and only they have the key to unlock it. Unless the system is backed up, the victim

faces the difficult choice of paying the criminals or losing all the data, and there have been reports of even police departments paying to regain control of their systems.

This is not meant to suggest that the criminals are unstoppable; in fact, in June 2014 we were part of a team that helped take down Cryptolocker. Symantec assisted the FBI and several other international law enforcement agencies to mount a major operation during which authorities seized a large portion of the infrastructure that had been used by the cybercriminals. As a result of Symantec's research into the threat, we were able to provide technical insights into their operation and impact. Since June, the Cryptolocker infection rate has dropped to near zero. But other forms are still out there, and the fight goes on.

Threats to Critical Infrastructure

Critical infrastructure such as the power grid, water system, and mass transit are also at risk. As more of these devices become connected and are controlled remotely, attackers have more opportunities to try to exploit them. In June 2014, we notified and provided detailed Indicators of Compromise (IoC) to more than 40 national computer security incident response teams around the world about a new threat we named *DragonFly*. This was an ongoing cyber espionage campaign against a range of targets, mainly in the energy sector, which gave attackers control over computers that they could have used to damage or destroy critical machinery and disrupt energy supplies in affected countries. Among the targets of *Dragonfly* were energy grid operators, electricity generation firms, petroleum pipeline operators, and industrial equipment providers—the majority of which were located in the U.S., Spain, France, Italy, Germany, Turkey, and Poland. Quick and detailed notification was critical in mitigating the threat.

This was not the first campaign targeted at the energy sector. In 2012, cyber attackers mounted a campaign against Saudi Arabia's national oil firm Saudi Aramco, which destroyed approximately 30,000 computers and took its network off line for days. The infected computers were rendered unusable and displayed the image of a burning American flag. Though operations were not impacted, there was speculation in the press that oil production was the ultimate target. Shortly after the Saudi Aramco attack, a Qatari producer of liquefied natural gas, RasGas, suffered a similar attack which damaged its networks and took down its website. Other sectors have seen attacks too. In the manufacturing sector, the German Government recently disclosed that a cyber attack on a steel plant resulted in the failure of multiple components and, according to one report, "massive physical damage."

In the U.S. we have yet to see major destructive attacks on critical infrastructure. However, there have been widespread reports that foreign actors have sought to gain a foothold on the networks of U.S. critical infrastructure providers. And we have seen the actual compromise of one water treatment facility in South Houston, Texas, though the attacker did not alter any controls or settings and claimed to be trying to bring attention to the vulnerabilities that exist in critical infrastructure. This particular facility was not following security best practices and was still using default passwords that were widely known. There are undoubtedly many other critical systems that are similarly exposed.

Methods Attackers Use to Compromise Systems—Inside the Attacker's Tool Kit

All of the attacks outlined above started with a common factor—a compromised device. From this one computer, attackers often are able to move within a system until they achieve their ultimate goal. But the threshold question is how do they get that foothold—how do they make that initial compromise that allows them to infiltrate a system?

We frequently hear about the sophistication of various attackers and about "Advance Persistent Threats" or "APTs," but the discussion of cyber attacks—and of cyber defense—often ignores the psychology of the exploit. Most attacks rely on social engineering—in the simplest of terms, trying to trick people into doing something that they would never do if fully cognizant of their actions. For this reason, we often say that the most successful attacks are as much psychology as they are technology.

Spear phishing, or customized, targeted emails containing malware, is the most common form of attack. Attackers harvest publicly available information and use it to craft an email designed to dupe a specific victim or group of victims. The goal is to get victims to open a document or click on a link to a website that will then try to infect their computers. While good security will stop most of these attacks—which often seek to exploit older, known vulnerabilities—many organizations and individuals do not have up-to-date security or properly patched operating systems. And many of these attacks are extremely well-crafted; in the case of one major attack, the spear phishing email was so convincing that even though the victim's system automatically routed it to junk mail, he retrieved it and opened it—and exposed his company to a major breach.

Social media is an increasingly valuable tool for cyber criminals in two different ways. First, it is particularly effective in direct attacks, as people tend to trust links and postings that appear to come from a friend's social media feed and rarely stop to wonder if that feed may have been compromised or spoofed. Thus, attackers target social media accounts and then use them to "like" or otherwise promote a posting that contains a malicious link. But social media is also widely used to conduct reconnaissance for spear phishing or other highly targeted attacks as it often provides just the kind of personal details that a skilled attacker can use to get a victim to let his or her guard down. The old cliché is true when it comes to cyber attacks: we have to be right 100% of the time while the attacker only has to get it right once.

Beginning in 2012, we saw the rapid growth of a new type of targeted web-based attack, known as a "watering hole" attack. Like the lion in the wild who stalks a watering hole for unsuspecting prey, cybercriminals have become adept at lying in wait on legitimate websites and using them to try to infect visitors' computers. They do so by compromising legitimate websites that their victims are likely to visit and modifying them so that they will surreptitiously try to deliver malware to every visitor. For example, one attacker targeted mobile application developers by compromising a site that was popular with them. In another case, we saw employees from 500 different companies in the same industry visit one compromised site in just 24 hours, each running the risk of infection. Cybercriminals gained control of these websites through many of the same tactics described above—spear phishing and other social engineering attacks on the site managers, developers, or owners. Many of these websites were compromised through known attack vectors, meaning that good security practices could have prevented them from being compromised.

Attackers will also periodically remove malware from an infected site to avoid regular security scans that might otherwise detect the compromise. At Symantec, we constantly scan websites for vulnerabilities and our Norton Safe Web will alert customers if they are trying to connect to a site that has vulnerabilities or might try to infect their computer with malware.

Partnering to Fight Cybercrime

To assist in combating cyber threats, Symantec participates in various industry organizations and public-private partnerships with all levels of governments in the U.S. and abroad.

We share high-level cybercrime and cyber threat trends and information on a voluntary basis through a number of different fora to help protect our customers and their networks. Effective sharing of actionable information among the public and private sectors on cyber threats, vulnerabilities, and incidents is an essential component of improving cybersecurity and combatting cybercrime. In 2014, together with Palo Alto Networks, Fortinet, and McAfee we co-founded the Cyber Threat Alliance (CTA), a group of cybersecurity providers, to share threat information to improve defenses against advanced cyber adversaries. The CTA adheres to strict guidelines that protect privacy and anonymize data, while at the same time pooling a broad array of resources to fight cybercriminals.

Symantec also has a formal partnership program whereby we work with government entities around the globe to help raise awareness, mitigate threats, share cyber threat information, assist in policy development and help with training and awareness. Partnership agreements include the EUROPOL's European Cybercrime Centre (EC3), the Korean National Police Agency, AMERIPOL and the Organization of American States (OAS), among others.

Symantec also partners with a number of non-profit organizations, including the Society for the Policing of Cyberspace (POLCYB), the National Cyber-Forensics and Training Alliance (NCFTA) and InfraGard. All three organizations are excellent examples of how private industry and law enforcement can yield real world success in the areas of training, criminal investigations and threat information sharing. Through POLCYB, Symantec provides training to law enforcement around the globe. Our partnership with the NCFTA includes more than 80 other industry partners—from financial services and telecommunications to manufacturing and others—working with federal and international partners to provide real-time cyber threat intelligence to an actionable level for law enforcement to neutralize those threats.

Law enforcement and the private sector—working together—have made significant progress in recent years. Not too long ago, numerous technological, cultural and organizational barriers prevented federal agencies from coordinating with each other or with industry on the investigation and prosecution of international cybercriminals. Those barriers have largely come down, and today we see that kind of cross-agency and public-private coordination on a regular basis.

Symantec's operation to bring down the ZeroAccess botnet, one of the largest botnets in history, estimated at 1.9 million infected devices, is a good example of how effective coordination between industry and law enforcement can yield results. A key feature of the ZeroAccess botnet was that it communicates widely across all infected computers rather than from a few command and control servers out to all those infected. This "peer to peer" architecture gives the botnet a high degree of availability and redundancy since it is not possible simply to disable a few servers and bring down the botnet. Early in 2013, Symantec's engineers identified a weakness that offered a difficult, but not impossible, way to shut down the botnet. Once we began to sinkhole ZeroAccess, over half a million bots were quickly detached, and later that year Microsoft filed a civil suit against the operators of the ZeroAccess botnet. These actions appear to have put an end to the botnet and the bot masters have halted their activity. They even included the words "White Flag" in the code of one of the last updates sent to infected computers.

Another significant win came in June of last year, when the FBI and a number of international law enforcement agencies mounted a major operation against financial fraud botnet Gameover Zeus and ransomware network Cryptolocker. We worked with the FBI and a broad industry coalition during this operation, and authorities seized a large proportion of the infrastructure used by the cybercriminals behind both threats. Gameover Zeus was the largest financial fraud botnet in operation last year and is often described as one of the most technically sophisticated variants of the ubiquitous Zeus malware.

A final example is the operation that helped to bring down the Bamital botnet, a major takedown that occurred in early 2013. This effort was the culmination of a multi-year investigation conducted by a public-private partnership including Symantec, Microsoft, and law enforcement. The Bamital botnet had taken over millions of computers for criminal activities such as identity theft and advertising-related fraud, and threatened the $12.7 billion online advertising industry. This successful takedown demonstrates what can be done when private industry and law enforcement join forces to go after cybercriminal networks.

It is also important to remember the toll that cybercrime takes on its victims. Part of our effort to stop cybercrime *writ large* is to focus on individual victims. In April of last year, we partnered with the National White Collar Crime Center (NWC3) to develop an online assistance program that helps cybercrime victims better understand the investigation process and help prevent future attacks. We also make tools available to the public to assist them if their computers are part of a botnet. In addition to our Norton Security software, we do offer some free tools online that allow victims of ransomware and botnets to remove this malware from their systems (http://www.symantec.com/security_response/removaltools.jsp).

How Individuals and Organizations Can Protect Themselves

The starting point for any organization is a plan that includes both proactive security measures and reactive steps to take in the event of an attack. Strong security is layered security, and must go beyond the basics such as good computer hygiene and antivirus software. It includes comprehensive protection that includes intrusion protection, reputation-based security, behavioral-based blocking, data encryption, and data loss prevention tools. Organizations should also back up their systems regularly so that they are protected from an attack that could destroy their data. There is no such thing as 100% security, but a layered defense approach to security can significantly reduce risk and a well-thought out and regularly exercised plan can mitigate any damage that might occur.

In addition, the NIST Cyber Security Framework, developed by industry and government in 2014 and in which Symantec was an active contributor, provides a solid structure for risk management. It lays out five core cybersecurity functions (Identify, Protect, Detect, Respond and Recover) that all organizations can use to plan for managing cyber events, as well as useful references to international standards.

Good security still starts with the basics. Though criminals' tactics are constantly evolving, basic cyber hygiene is still the simplest and most cost-effective first step. Strong passwords remain the foundation of good security—on home and work devices, email, social media accounts, or whatever you use to communicate or any sites or device you log into. And these passwords must be different, because using a single password means that a breach of one account exposes all of your accounts. Using a second authentication factor (whether a smart card, biometrics, or a token with a changing numeric password) significantly increases the security of a login.

Patch management of operating systems and other software applications is also critical. Individuals and organizations should not delay installing patches, because the same patch that closes a vulnerability on one computer can be a roadmap for a criminal to exploit that vulnerability and compromise any unpatched computers. The reality is that a large percentage of computers around the world do not get patched regularly, and cyber criminals count on this. While so-called "zero days"—previously unknown critical vulnerabilities for which there is not yet a patch—get the most press, it is older, un-patched vulnerabilities that cause most systems to get compromised.

But poor or insufficiently deployed security can also lead to a breach, and a modern security suite that is being fully utilized is also essential. While most people still commonly refer to security software as "anti-virus," good security needs to be much more than that. In the past, the same piece of malware would be delivered to thousands or even millions of computers. Today, cyber-criminals can take the same malware and create unlimited unique variants that can slip past basic anti-virus software. If all your security software does is check for signatures (or digital fingerprints) of known malware, you are by definition not protected against even moderately sophisticated attacks.

Modern security software does much more than look for known malware; it monitors your computer, watching for unusual internet traffic, activity, or system processes that could be indicative of malicious activity. At Symantec we also use what we call Insight and SONAR, which are reputation-based and heuristic security technologies. Insight is a reputation-based technology that uses our Global Intelligence Network to put files in context, using their age, frequency, location and more to expose emerging threats that might otherwise be missed. If a computer is trying to execute a file that we have never seen anywhere in the world and that comes from an unknown source, there is a high probability that it is malicious—and Insight will block it.

Conclusion

Citizens are increasingly aware of the cyber risk and the need to take precautions to secure their data and protect their privacy. It is important that Americans know of the risk but also understand that there are things they can do to protect themselves. Every time someone patches their computer, changes a password, or utilizes a modern security suite, he or she is making it more difficult for cybercriminals to operate. Like any other crime, cybercrime will never be completely eliminated, but it can be fought. For example, the criminals did not stop using the scareware described above because they wanted to—they quit when it stopped working, and it stopped working when the targets no longer allowed themselves to be victimized.

At all levels, both government and industry recognize the imperative for cooperation to fight cybercrime. No single company or government can "go it alone" in the current threat landscape. The threats are too complex and the stakes are too high. Ultimately, stopping cyber attacks and the criminal networks behind them requires strong technical capabilities, effective countermeasures, industry collaboration and law enforcement coopera-tion to be successful. At Symantec, we are committed to improving online security across the globe, and will con-tinue to work collaboratively with international industry and government partners on ways to do so.

CHERI F. McGUIRE is vice-president for global government affairs and cybersecurity policy at Symantec, a major cyber-security company.

EXPLORING THE ISSUE

Do We Need New Laws to Protect the Public against Cybercrime?

Critical Thinking and Reflection

1. Is there a difference between "cyberwar" and "cybercrime"?
2. Is all the worry about cybercrime just hype?
3. With conventional crime, it is possible to locate and arrest criminals. Why is it difficult to find cybercriminals?
4. Given that cybercrime often (and cyberwar always) originates beyond a nation's borders, is it likely that new laws would deter or prosecute those responsible?

Is There Common Ground?

Dean C. Garfield and Cheri F. McGuire agree that technology must play a role in keeping intruders out of computer networks and limiting the damage they can do if they do get in. No one wants criminal hackers to be able to steal private information—usernames and passwords, in particular—so they can steal from bank accounts, use credit cards, steal identity, and even destroy financial institutions and the economy, disrupt electricity generation, shut down factories, shut down the Internet, or perhaps just mess with a city's traffic lights to cause traffic jams (among other things). Keeping them out is what cybersecurity is all about.

1. How do you protect your own computer? (passwords, firewalls, encryption, etc.)
2. Visit your campus IT department and ask how it protects the campus network from intruders.
3. Do you think similar measures would work against a cyberwar or cyber-terrorist attack?
4. Is knowing that you should NOT click links in mystery emails a technological defense? Or is it something else?

5. Many people use a single password for all the sites that demand one. Do you? How many passwords do you use? How strong are they?

Additional Resources

Jonathan Clough, *Principles of Cybercrime* (Cambridge University Press, 2010).

Scott E. Donaldson, Stanley G. Siegel, Chris K. Williams, and Abdul Aslam, *Enterprise Cybersecurity: How to Build a Successful Cyberdefense Program against Advanced Threats* (Apress, 2015).

R. Scott Kemp, "Cyberweapons: Bold Steps in a Digital Darkness?" *Bulletin of the Atomic Scientists* (June 7, 2012) (http://www.thebulletin.org/web-edition/op-eds/cyberweapons-bold-steps-digital-darkness).

Thomas J. Mowbray, *Cybersecurity: Managing Systems, Conducting Testing, and Investigating Intrusions* (Wiley, 2013).

P. W. Singer and Allan Friedman, *Cybersecurity and Cyberwar: What Everyone Needs to Know* (Oxford University Press, 2014).

Internet References . . .

Department of Homeland Security, Cybersecurity

http://www.dhs.gov/topic/cybersecurity

Federal Bureau of Investigation, Cybercrime Page

http://www.fbi.gov/about-us/investigate/cyber

Interpol, Cybercrime

http://www.interpol.int/Crime-areas /Cybercrime/Cybercrime

United States Department of Defense, Cybersecurity Initiative

http://dodcio.defense.gov/Portals/0/Documents /Cyber/The%20Comprehensive%20National %20Cybersecurity%20Initiative%20%28CNCI%29.pdf

Selected, Edited, and with Issue Framing Material by:
Thomas A. Easton, *Mount Ida College*

ISSUE

Does the Public Have a Stake in How Drones Are Used?

YES: Amie Stepanovich, from "Testimony before the U.S. Senate Judiciary Committee, Hearing on 'The Future of Drones in America: Law Enforcement and Privacy Considerations,'" U.S. Senate (2013)

NO: U.S. Department of Homeland Security, Office of Inspector General, from "CBP's Use of Unmanned Aircraft Systems in the Nation's Border Security," U.S. Department of Homeland Security, Office of Inspector General (2012)

Learning Outcomes
After reading this issue, you will be able to: • Explain what unmanned aerial systems or drones are.   • Explain how they can be used to support the missions of various public agencies, including law enforcement.   • Explain how their use may impinge on citizens' right to privacy.   • Explain why domestic drone use is likely or unlikely to increase.

ISSUE SUMMARY

YES: Amie Stepanovich argues that the increased use of unmanned aerial systems (or "drones") to conduct surveillance in the United States must be accompanied by increased privacy protections. The current state of the law is insufficient to address the drone surveillance threat to the interests of the general public, who clearly have a stake (are stakeholders) in the issue.

NO: The U.S. Department of Homeland Security, Office of Inspector General, argues that planning is inadequate for the use of resources devoted to serving the purposes of the U.S. Customs and Border Protection (CBP) unmanned aircraft systems program, to provide reconnaissance, surveillance, targeting, and acquisition capabilities to serve the needs of stakeholders. The list of stakeholders does not include the general public, and privacy concerns are not mentioned.

Remote-controlled drones, more properly known as "unmanned aerial vehicles" or UAVs, first appeared on the modern battlefield over a decade ago. Today, according to Paul Scharre, "Why Unmanned," *Joint Force Quarterly* (2nd quarter 2011), there are thousands, and they include both UAVs and UGVs (unmanned ground vehicles, robotic bomb diffusers, and cargo carriers). They were initially used for reconnaissance, taking pictures of distant locations. Later they were armed and used for combat. Since they were not autonomous robots, there was never any risk that they would turn on their masters. Indeed, the risk to the masters is reduced because it is drones, not human soldiers, who go into harm's way.

As Scharre notes, the capabilities of the computers that control these machines are constantly improving and "more capable systems will be possible in the future." The result may be human-robot combat teams that are far more efficacious than humans alone. And as the cost of the necessary hardware and software continues to fall, the same technology will appear in the hands of adversaries, from nation states to terrorists. As a result, the military is motivated to continue developing better and better drones.

Yet it is not the military applications of drones that raise concerns in civilian circles. Many agencies find them appealing; see Nick Paumgarten, "Here's Looking at You," *New Yorker* (May 14, 2012). Law enforcement agencies find them appealing for tracking criminals, and the Obama administration has indicated that under very special circumstances armed drones could be used against terrorists (see Michael Isikoff, "Justice Department Memo Reveals Legal Case for Drone Strikes on Americans," NBC News, http://openchannel.nbcnews.com/_news/2013/02/04/16843014 -justice-department-memo-reveals-legal-case-for-drone-strikes -on-americans?lite). Emergency management folks want them for surveying the extent and severity of floods and fires and even for carrying supplies and cell phones to people in trouble. Amazon is reportedly planning to use them for package delivery (Alistair Blair, "Amazon Testing Delivery by Drone, CEO Bezos Says," *USA Today*, December 2, 2013). Researchers want to use them for environmental surveys. Environmental activists want to use them to look for offenses against environmental laws. And the Federal Aviation Administration is developing regulations to govern the use of drones in domestic airspace; see Paul Rosenzweig, et al., "Drones in U.S. Airspace: Principles for Governance," Heritage Foundation Backgrounder (September 20, 2012). Since there may be more than 10,000 drones in the air by 2020, such regulations will be essential. There is also a need to make their control signals hard to disrupt; see Kyle Wesson and Todd Humphreys, "Hacking Drones," *Scientific American* (November 2013).

Not surprisingly, many people see drones as both intrusive and threatening. Yet the numbers are perhaps less than overwhelming. A 2012 survey found that 44 percent support police use of drones; only 36 percent were opposed, while only a third were concerned about privacy; see Steve Watson, "Almost Half of All Americans Support Domestic Surveillance Drones," Infowars.com (September 28, 2012) (http://www.infowars.com/almost-half-of -all-americans-support-domestic-surveillance-drones/). Privacy advocates see their abilities to follow individuals, monitor political demonstrations, pick faces out of a crowd (the necessary software is under development), hover outside a window or over a backyard, and more—whether when operated by public agencies or by private interests (such as jealous spouses and private detectives)—as especially alarming. See "The Spies Above Your Backyard," *Scientific American* (April 2013). Tyler Wall and Torin Mona-

han, "Surveillance and Violence from Afar: The Politics of Drones and Liminal Security-Scapes," *Theoretical Criminology* (August 2011), find the use of drones dehumanizes people into targets for remote monitoring and destruction and removes reasons to refrain from action.

In "The Predator Comes Home: A Primer on Domestic Drones, Their Huge Business Opportunities, and Their Deep Political, Moral, and Legal Challenges," Brookings Institution, March 8, 2013 (http://www.brookings.edu /research/papers/2013/03/08-drones-singer), Peter W. Singer, director of the Center for 21st Century Security and Intelligence at the Brookings Institution, argues that the potential benefits of unmanned aerial systems (drones) are huge. And "While many are surprised by the existing use of robotics, the pace of change won't stop. We may have thousands now, but as one three-star U.S. Air Force general noted . . . very soon it will be 'tens of thousands' . . . of tomorrow's robots, with far different capabilities." Aerial robots will gain in intelligence and autonomy and the number of potential users will expand tremendously. The number of drones in the air may reach "tens of billions." There will therefore be a huge need for federal and state action to regulate the use of unmanned aerial systems, but much of the regulatory responsibility is likely to be borne by the courts.

The Association for Unmanned Vehicle Systems International (AUVSI), a manufacturers' organization, is lobbying intensely for laws that will permit drones to operate much more freely in U.S. airspace. In testimony before the Senate Judiciary Committee March 20, 2013, Michael Toscano, President and CEO of AUVSI, said that "The industry is at the forefront of a technology that will not only benefit society, but the U.S. economy as well. Earlier this month, my organization released a study, which found the unmanned aircraft industry is poised to help create 70,000 new jobs and $13.6 billion in economic impact in the first three years following the integration of unmanned aircraft into the national airspace." To the industry's dismay, a great many people find the prospect of drones being used within the United States an alarming prospect, perhaps because of their origins in war. Cities and states are passing laws against their use even as the industry lobbies Congress to promote their use. See Alec MacGillis, "Don't Fear the Reaper," *New Republic* (March 11, 2013). The Aviation Committee of the International Association of Chiefs of Police has formulated "Recommended Guidelines for the Use of Unmanned Aircraft" (http://www.theiacp.org/portals/0/pdfs/IACP_UAGuidelines.pdf) that include recognition of privacy and civil rights concerns and discourage the use of armed drones. The AUVSI has a Code of Conduct (http://www.auvsi.org/conduct) that calls for respect for individual privacy, rights, and concerns, but the code contains no penalties for those who ignore its requirements. Indeed its purpose seems to instill "confidence in our systems."

Will remotely controlled drones give way to autonomous robots? Will they be armed, and will they be tasked with deciding when and whom to kill? This has long been a theme in science fiction (see Fred Saberhagen's Berserker stories [e.g., http://www.amazon.com/Berserker-Saberhagens -Fred-Saberhagen-ebook/dp/B00A4Q4FLK/ref=sr_1_1?s =books&ie=UTF8&qid=1392907070&sr=1-1&keywords =saberhagen+berserker] and David R. Bunch's Moderan stories [http://www.amazon.com/Moderan-David-R-Bunch/dp /B002TJT4LG]), but it is no longer just science fiction. In December 2012, the Department of Defense issued a Directive calling for "the development and use of autonomous and semi-autonomous functions in weapons systems, including manned and unmanned platforms" (http://www.dtic.mil/whs/directives/corres/pdf/300009p .pdf). Mark Gubrud, "US Killer Robot Policy: Full Speed Ahead," *Bulletin of the Atomic Scientists* (September 20, 2013), the new "policy in effect overrides longstanding resistance within the military . . . and signals to developers and vendors that the Pentagon is serious about autonomous weapons." Resistance to the policy has been developing rapidly (see Charli Carpenter, "Beware the Killer Robots," *Foreign Affairs,* July 3, 2013, and Richard Stone, "Scientists Campaign Against Killer Robots," *Science*, December 2013). In May 2014, the 117 state parties to the Convention on Certain Conventional Weapons (CCW; it currently bans or regulates the use of land mines, blinding lasers, and other weapons) will meet in Geneva, Switzerland, to discuss banning killer robots; see Mia Gandenberger, "CCW Adopts Mandate to Discuss Killer Robots," Reaching Critical Will (November 15, 2013) (http://www.reachingcriticalwill.org/news/ latest-news/8583-ccw-adopts-mandate-to-discuss-killer-robots).

So far, the drones are not true robots; that is, they do not make their own decisions. Nevertheless, some people still find them worrisome. In the YES selection, Amie Stepanovich argues that the increased use of unmanned aerial systems (or "drones") to conduct surveillance in the United States must be accompanied by increased privacy protections. The current state of the law is insufficient to address the drone surveillance threat to the interests of the general public, who clearly have a stake (are stakeholders) in the issue. In the NO selection, the U.S. Department of Homeland Security, Office of Inspector General (OIG), argues that inadequate resources are devoted to serving the purposes of the U.S. Customs and Border Protection (CBP) unmanned aircraft systems program, to provide reconnaissance, surveillance, targeting, and acquisition capabilities to serve the needs of stakeholders. The OIG does not say "public be damned," but the list of stakeholders does not include the general public, and privacy concerns are not mentioned.

YES ↵

Amie Stepanovich

Testimony before the U.S. Senate Judiciary Committee, Hearing on "The Future of Drones in America: Law Enforcement and Privacy Considerations"

EPIC is a non-partisan research organization, established in 1994, to focus public attention on emerging privacy and civil liberties issues. We work with a distinguished panel of advisors in the fields of law, technology, and public policy. We have a particular interest in the protection of individual privacy rights against government surveillance. In the last several years, EPIC has taken a particular interest in the unique privacy problems associated with aerial drones.

The Federal Aviation Administration ("FAA") has been directed to fully integrate drones into the National Airspace by 2015. In 2012 EPIC petitioned the FAA, as it considers new regulations to permit the widespread deployment of drones, to also develop new privacy safeguards. The FAA heeded our warning, and is now considering privacy policies for drone operators. However, more must be done to protect the privacy of individuals in the United States.

We appreciate the Committee's interest in domestic drone use and its substantial impact on the privacy of individuals in the United States. In my statement today, I will describe the unique threats to privacy posed by drone surveillance, the problems with current legal safeguards, and the need for Congress to act.

I. Aerial Drones Pose a Unique Threat to Privacy

A drone is an aerial vehicle designed to fly without a human pilot on board. Drones can either be remotely controlled or autonomous. Drones can be weaponized and deployed for military purposes. Drones can also be equipped with sophisticated surveillance technology that makes it possible to spy on individuals on the ground. In a report on drones published by EPIC in 2005, we observed, "the use of [drones] gives the federal government a new capability to monitor citizens clandestinely, while the effectiveness of the . . . surveillance planes in border patrol operations has not been proved." Today, drones greatly increase the capacity for law enforcement to collect personal information on individuals.

We recognize that there are many positive applications for drones within the United States. With little to no risk to individual privacy, drones may be used to combat forest fires, conduct search and rescue operations, survey emergency situations, and monitor hurricanes and other weather phenomena. In Dallas, a drone used by a hobbyist photographer was able to pinpoint an instance of gross environmental abuse at a nearby factory. In Alabama, drones were recently used to assist in monitoring a hostage situation involving a young boy abducted off of the school bus.

However, when drones are used to obtain evidence in a criminal proceeding, intrude upon a reasonable expectation of privacy, or gather personal data about identifiable individuals, rules are necessary to ensure that fundamental standards for fairness, privacy, and accountability are preserved.

The technology in use today is far more sophisticated than most people understand. Cameras used to outfit drones are among the highest definition cameras available. The Argus camera, featured on the PBS Nova documentary on drones, has a resolution of 1.8 gigapixels and is capable of observing objects as small as six inches in detail from a height of 17,000 feet. On some drones, sensors can track up to 65 different targets across a distance of 65 square miles. Drones may also carry infrared cameras, heat sensors, GPS, sensors that detect movement, and automated license plate readers.

Recent records received by EPIC under the Freedom of Information Act demonstrate that the Bureau of Customs and Border Protection procured drones outfitted with technology for electronic signals interception and human

From U.S. Senate, March 20, 2013.

identification. Following receipt of these documents, EPIC and a broad coalition of privacy and civil liberties organizations petitioned the CBP to suspend the domestic drone program, pending the establishment of privacy safeguards.

Much of this surveillance technology could, in theory, be deployed on manned vehicles. However, drones present a unique threat to privacy. Drones are designed to maintain a constant, persistent eye on the public to a degree that former methods of surveillance were unable to achieve. Drones are cheaper to buy, maintain, and operate than helicopters, or other forms of aerial surveillance. Drone manufacturers have recently announced new designs that would allow drones to operate for more than 48 consecutive hours, and other technology could extend the flight time of future drones into spans of weeks and months. Also, "by virtue of their design, size, and how high they can fly, [drones] can operate undetected in urban and rural environments."

Drones are currently being developed that will carry facial recognition technology, able to remotely identify individuals in parks, schools, and at political gatherings. The ability to link facial recognition capabilities on drones operated by the Department of Homeland Security ("DHS") to the Federal Bureau of Investigation's Next Generation Identification database or DHS' IDENT database, two of the largest collections of biometric data in the world, further exacerbates the privacy risks.

Law enforcement offices across the country have expressed interest in the purchase and use of drone technology to assist with law enforcement operations. Records released in 2012 by the Federal Aviation Administration show that over 220 public entities have already received approval to operate drones over the United States, including Police departments from Texas, Kansas, Washington, and other states. The Florida Police Chiefs Association expressed a desire to use drones to conduct general crowd surveillance at public events. News reports demonstrate that other police departments are not only interested in invasive surveillance equipment, but have also voiced interest in outfitting drones with non-lethal weapons.

II. Current Privacy Safeguards Are Inadequate

The Supreme Court has not yet considered the limits of drone surveillance under the Fourth Amendment, though the Court held twenty years ago that law enforcement may conduct manned aerial surveillance operations from as low as 400 feet without a warrant. In addition, no federal statute currently provides adequate safeguards to protect privacy against increased drone use in the United States.

Accordingly, there are substantial legal and constitutional issues involved in the deployment of aerial drones by law enforcement and state and federal agencies that need to be addressed. Technologist and security expert Bruce Schneier observed earlier this year at an event hosted by EPIC on Drones and Domestic Surveillance, "today's expensive and rare is tomorrow's commonplace." As drone technology becomes cheaper and more common, the threat to privacy will become more substantial. High-rise buildings, security fences, or even the walls of a building are not barriers to increasingly common drone technology.

The Supreme Court is aware of the growing risks to privacy resulting from new surveillance technology but has yet to address the specific problems associated with drone surveillance. In *United States v. Jones*, a case that addressed whether the police could use a GPS device to track the movement of a criminal suspect without a warrant, the Court found that the installation and deployment of the device was an unlawful search and seizure. Justice Sotomayor in a concurrence pointed to broader problems associated with new forms of persistent surveillance. And Justice Alito, in a separate concurrence joined by three other Justices, wrote, "in circumstances involving dramatic technological change, the best solution to privacy concerns may be legislative."

Regarding the invasive use of drones by commercial operators, current law does not anticipate the use of mobile devices that can hover outside a bedroom window or follow a person down a street. Legal standards should be established to protect people from a violation of reasonable expectations of privacy, including surveillance in public spaces. In considering legislation to address law enforcement use of drones, it would be appropriate also to establish privacy standards for the commercial use of drones.

III. Congress Should Establish Safeguards Related to the Use of Drones

As the Chairman has indicated, the privacy and security concerns arising from the use of drones needs to be addressed. In order to mitigate the risk of increased use of drones in our domestic skies, Congress must pass targeted legislation, based on principles of transparency and accountability.

State and local governments have considered a wide array of laws and regulations to prevent abuses associated with drone technology. A current survey demonstrates that over 30 states have proposed legislation to protect against unregulated drone surveillance of individuals. Most of these bills mandate a warrant requirement for the collection of information by drones operated by law enforcement officials. Other bills require reporting requirements for drone operators. A bill in Georgia restricts law enforcement use of drones strictly to felony investigations, and a bill circulating in Oregon would require state approval for all drones, including federal drones, that would fly over the state's airspace.

Even as states consider these various measures, it would be appropriate for Congress to establish privacy standards for the operation of drones in the United States. First, Congress should require all drone operators, both public and commercial, to submit, prior to receipt of a drone license, a detailed report on the drones' intended use. This report should describe, the specific geographic area where the drone will be deployed, the mission that the drone is expected to fulfill, and the surveillance equipment with which the drone will be outfitted. Each of these reports should be made publicly available at a publicly accessible web site. A private right of action and, in certain instances, federal prosecution authority should be included to ensure that drone operators comply with the terms of these statements.

In order to prevent abuses associated with the use of this technology, a strict warrant requirement needs to be implemented for all drone surveillance conduct by law enforcement. A warrant requirement would establish a presumption that evidence obtained by means of an aerial search should require judicial approval. Statutory exceptions could be created for exigency in order to address drone use in emergency situations or when necessary to protect human life. In addition, mandatory public reporting requirements, similar to those required by the Wiretap Act, would increase the transparency and accountability of law enforcement drone operations.

Ongoing surveillance of individuals by aerial drones operating in domestic airspace should be prohibited. The invasiveness of drone technology represents a privacy risk to individuals as they pursue their daily activities. A drone, with the capability of staying aloft for hours or days at a time, could monitor a person's entire life as they go from home to work to school to the store and back. Even if law enforcement is not able to immediately discern exactly what a person says or does or buys at a particular location, simply tracking an individual's public movements in a systematic fashion for extended periods of time can create a vivid description of their private life. Broad, unregulated drone surveillance would have a chilling effect on the speech and expression rights of individuals in the United States. Drones should not be used as robotic patrol officers for law enforcement.

Finally, drone surveillance technology may allow the collection of information and images that would otherwise be inaccessible to prying eyes, such as activities within the home. Congress should prohibit drone operators from conducting surveillance of individuals that infringes on property rights. A federal "Peeping Tom" statute, recognizing the enhanced capabilities of aerial drones, would provide baseline privacy protection for individuals within the home. Additional provisions should prevent against any use of drones to collect information that would not otherwise be retrievable without a physical trespass.

Additional drone legislation should include:

- Use Limitations—Prohibitions on general surveillance that limit law enforcement drone surveillance to specific, enumerated circumstances, such as in the case of criminal surveillance subject to a warrant, a geographically-confined emergency, or for reasonable non-law enforcement use where privacy will not be substantially affected;
- Data Retention Limitations—Restrictions on retaining or sharing surveillance data collected by drones, with emphasis on personally identifiable information;
- Transparency and Public Accountability—A requirement for all federal agencies that choose to operate drones to promulgate privacy regulations, subject to the notice and comment provisions of the Administrative Procedure Act. In addition, the law should provide for third party audits and oversight for law enforcement drone operations.

These three principles would further help protect the privacy interests of individuals against both government and commercial drone operators.

IV. Conclusion

The increased use of drones to conduct surveillance in the United States must be accompanied by increased privacy protections. The current state of the law is insufficient to address the drone surveillance threat. EPIC supports legislation aimed at strengthening safeguards related to the use of drones as surveillance tools and allowing for redress for drone operators who fail to comply with the mandated standards of protection. We also support compliance with the Administrative Procedure Act for the deployment of drone technology and limitations for federal agencies and other organizations that initially obtain a drone for one purpose and then wish to expand that purpose.

AMIE STEPANOVICH is the director of the Domestic Surveillance Project at the Electronic Privacy Information Center (EPIC).

Department of Homeland Security
Office of Inspector General

CBP's Use of Unmanned Aircraft Systems in the Nation's Border Security

Executive Summary

We conducted a review of U.S. Customs and Border Protection (CBP) actions to establish its unmanned aircraft systems program. The purpose of the program is to provide reconnaissance, surveillance, targeting, and acquisition capabilities across all CBP areas of responsibility. Our objective was to determine whether CBP has established an adequate operation plan to define, prioritize, and execute its unmanned aircraft mission.

CBP had not adequately planned resources needed to support its current unmanned aircraft inventory. Although CBP developed plans to use the unmanned aircraft's capabilities in its Office of Air and Marine mission, its Concept of Operations planning document did not adequately address processes (1) to ensure that required operational equipment, such as ground control stations and ground support equipment, is provided for each launch and recovery site; (2) for stakeholders to submit unmanned aircraft mission requests; (3) to determine how mission requests are prioritized; and (4) to obtain reimbursement for missions flown on stakeholders' behalf. This approach places CBP at risk of having invested substantial resources in a program that underutilizes resources and limits its ability to achieve Office of Air and Marine mission goals.

CBP needs to improve planning of its unmanned aircraft system program to address its level of operation, program funding, and resource requirements, along with stakeholder needs. We made four recommendations that will aid CBP in maximizing the use of unmanned aircraft. CBP management concurred with all four recommendations.

Background

The mission of the Office of Air and Marine (OAM) is to protect the American people and the Nation's critical infrastructure through the coordinated use of integrated air and marine forces. Air and marine forces are used to detect, interdict, and prevent acts of terrorism and the unlawful movement of people, illegal drugs, and other contraband toward or across U.S. borders. The unmanned aircraft system (UAS) provides command, control, communication, intelligence, surveillance, and reconnaissance capability to complement crewed aircraft and watercraft, and ground interdiction agents. A UAS is composed of a long-endurance, medium-altitude remotely piloted aircraft, ground control station, ground data terminal, data and voice communications, and other ground support equipment required to operate and maintain the system. UASs provide reconnaissance, surveillance, targeting, and acquisition (RSTA) capabilities across all CBP areas of responsibility.

CBP began UAS operations in fiscal year (FY) 2004 with a pilot study conducted by the Office of Border Patrol to determine the feasibility of using UASs in the southwest border region. The pilot study proved the UAS was successful in providing RSTA and actionable intelligence to Border Patrol ground agents. In addition, the study concluded that UASs provided unique law enforcement capabilities, such as the ability to carry a variety of sensors and payloads and to remain airborne for extended periods without the limitations imposed by requiring onboard pilots. CBP has since expanded UAS operations to the Caribbean, gulf, and northern border regions.

CBP reported that, subsequent to the FY 2004 pilot, Congress appropriated approximately $240.6 million to establish a UAS program within CBP. CBP also reported that it has expended $152.3 million to purchase nine aircraft and related equipment. CBP had seven operational aircraft during our review. CBP received two additional aircraft in late 2011. CBP was awaiting delivery of a tenth aircraft purchased with FY 2011 funds. Each aircraft system costs approximately $18 million. In June 2011, CBP had 23 pilots who were capable of launching and recovering unmanned aircraft. UAS missions are launched and recovered from National Air Security

From United States Department of Homeland Security, Office of Inspector General, 2012.

Operation Centers (NASOCs) in Sierra Vista, Arizona; Corpus Christi, Texas; Cocoa Beach, Florida; and Grand Forks, North Dakota. An unmanned aircraft mission crew generally consists of a Command Duty Officer, Pilot-in-Command, Sensor Operator, and one or more contract technicians. . . .

Results of Review

CBP Needs to Improve Planning of Its UAS Program to Maximize Operations

CBP had not adequately planned for resources needed to support the current unmanned aircraft inventory. Although CBP developed plans to utilize the unmanned aircraft's capabilities in its OAM mission, its Concept of Operations planning document did not adequately address processes (1) to ensure that required operational equipment, such as ground control stations and ground support equipment, is available for each launch and recovery site; (2) for stakeholders to submit unmanned aircraft mission requests; (3) to determine how mission requests are prioritized; and (4) to obtain reimbursement for missions flown on stakeholders' behalf. This approach places CBP at risk of having invested substantial resources in a program that underutilizes resources and limits its ability to achieve OAM mission goals.

Resource Planning

CBP has not ensured that adequate resources are available to effectively operate its unmanned aircraft. CBP's Strategic Plan requires the agency to develop and implement a planning framework to incorporate investment, resource, and program management processes to ensure that CBP can acquire and effectively manage its resources. The plan requires CBP to accomplish its high-priority missions and objectives in a way that maximizes return on investment. CBP procured unmanned aircraft before implementing adequate plans to do the following:

- Achieve the desired level of operation;
- Acquire sufficient funding to provide necessary operations, maintenance, and equipment; and
- Coordinate and support stakeholder needs.

UAS Level of Operation

CBP has not achieved its scheduled nor desired levels of flight hours of its unmanned aircraft. The Office of Inspector General (OIG) estimates that, based on the contract performance specifications, seven UASs should support

10,662 flight hours per year to meet the mission availability threshold (minimum capability) and 13,328 flight hours to meet the mission availability objective (desired capability). However, resource shortfalls of qualified staff and equipment coupled with restrictions imposed by the Federal Aviation Administration, weather, host airfields, and others have resulted in CBP scheduling just 7,336 flight hours for its seven unmanned aircraft and limited actual flight hours to 3,909 hours. This usage represents 37 percent of the unmanned aircraft's mission availability threshold and 29 percent of its mission availability objective. Despite the current underutilization of unmanned aircraft, CBP received two additional aircraft in late 2011 and was awaiting delivery of a tenth aircraft in 2012. . . .

Funding of Operations and Maintenance

CBP reported that, since the UAS program's inception, Congress has appropriated a total of $12.6 million for operations and maintenance. The operations and maintenance funding category includes training, satellite links, facility rental, and contractor support. CBP also reported that from FY 2006 through FY 2011, it expended $55.3 million for operations and maintenance, but has not made a specific operations and maintenance budget request for the UAS program. This has resulted in a budget shortfall. According to CBP, it was required to transfer approximately $25 million from other programs in FY 2010 to address operations and maintenance funding shortfalls. As a result of CBP's insufficient funding approach, future UAS missions may have to be curtailed.

Funding of Equipment

CBP has not adequately planned to fund unmanned aircraft-related equipment. The procurement funding category includes aircraft and related equipment, such as ground control stations, ground support equipment, cameras, and navigation systems. This approach has resulted in insufficient equipment to perform UAS missions. For example:

- Corpus Christi NASOC received a maritime version of the Predator aircraft, which was placed in service in February 2011, but Corpus Christi did not receive a compatible ground control station. As a result, the Corpus Christi NASOC was not initially able to use the system's SeaVue maritime radar capability. However, Cocoa Beach NASOC transferred its backup ground control station to Corpus Christi to facilitate mission operations. A compatible ground control station is expected to be delivered in May 2012. This transfer was required because Corpus Christi was not designed for launch and recovery operations.

- On at least three occasions, NASOC Grand Forks could not conduct flight operations because maintenance could not be performed due to lack of ground support equipment. One aircraft was down for 4 days in January 2011 due to lack of wing-jacks and 3 days in February due to lack of go-jacks and fuselage stands. Another aircraft was down for 2 days in February 2011 due to lack of go-jacks and fuselage stands. Ground support equipment must be transferred from one NASOC to another because each NASOC does not have its own equipment.

- CBP does not have an adequate number of ground control stations to ensure safe operations. CBP's *MQ-9 Supplement to the Aviation Operations Handbook* requires a permanent ground control station and a mobile ground control station for the safe operation of unmanned aircraft. The handbook requires NASOC directors to submit written requests for relief from any provision of the handbook to the Executive Director of Test, Training, Safety, and Standards. At the time of our fieldwork, three of four NASOCs were operating without the required mobile backup ground control stations. However, only one of four NASOCs was granted a waiver to operate without this equipment.

Stakeholder Needs

CBP's planning has not adequately addressed coordination and support of stakeholders. Although CBP identified stakeholders and has flown missions on their behalf, it has not implemented a formal process for stakeholders to submit mission requests and has not implemented a formal procedure to determine how mission requests are prioritized. It also does not have agreements with exterior stakeholders for reimbursement of mission costs.

An OAM manager and stakeholders we interviewed said that CBP had flown missions to support the following stakeholders:

- Department of Homeland Security (DHS) agencies, including Office of Border Patrol, United States Secret Service, Federal Emergency Management Agency (FEMA), and Immigration and Customs Enforcement (ICE);
- Bureau of Land Management;
- Federal Bureau of Investigation;
- Department of Defense;
- Texas Rangers;
- United States Forest Service; and

- National Oceanic and Atmospheric Administration (NOAA).

Also, OAM management and stakeholders we interviewed discussed the following examples of missions performed by the UAS program:

- Provided NOAA with videos of dams, bridges, levees, and riverbeds where flooding occurred or was threatened;
- Provided FEMA with video/radar images of flooding;
- Provided surveillance over a suspected smuggler's tunnel, which yielded information that, according to an ICE representative, would have required many cars and agents to obtain;
- Provided radar mapping, or overlying radar images taken a few days apart, to show changes in location of flooding, allowing the National Guard to deploy high-water vehicles and sandbags to where they were most needed;
- At the request of the State Department, participated in discussions with another country on the use of unmanned aircraft;
- Participated in joint efforts with the U.S. Army to leverage capabilities of unmanned aircraft and test new technology; and
- Participated in efforts to establish a quarterly forum to share lessons learned with the Air Force and other government agencies.

Stakeholders we interviewed from NOAA, ICE, FEMA, and the Army National Guard were generally satisfied with support provided by the UAS program. However, they were unaware of a formal process to request UAS support and of how CBP prioritizes missions. CBP included a process to satisfy requests for UAS support in its *Concept of Operations for CBP's Predator B Unmanned Aircraft System, FY 2010 Report to Congress*, but this process was not implemented. Instead, tasking decisions are usually made by the Director of Air Operations at the NASOC with responsibility for the area of the stakeholder surveillance requirement. Missions are requested by various means, including from headquarters, Border Patrol agents, local law enforcement agencies, and other Federal agencies. We interviewed four stakeholders, three of whom recommended a standardized process to request UAS missions. A standardized process would provide transparency and ensure that requests are processed in a timely, predictable manner. This process would allow stakeholders to better plan their operations to meet mission needs.

The Robert T. Stafford Disaster Relief and Emergency Assistance Act, as amended, provides a system by which a

Presidential disaster declaration of an emergency triggers financial assistance through FEMA. CBP seeks reimbursement for services provided to FEMA under this Act since Federal agencies may be reimbursed for expenditures from the Act's appropriations. However, CBP does not have agreements to obtain reimbursement for missions flown on behalf of other stakeholders. When appropriate and authorized by law, obtaining reimbursement for such missions would provide additional funding needed for staff, operations and maintenance, and essential equipment.

Recommendations

We recommend that the Assistant Commissioner, Office of Air and Marine:

Recommendation #1:
Analyze requirements and develop plans to achieve the UAS mission availability objective and acquire funding to provide necessary operations, maintenance, and equipment.

Recommendation #2:
Develop and implement procedures to coordinate and support stakeholders' mission requests.

Recommendation #3:
Establish interagency agreements with external stakeholders for reimbursement of expenses incurred fulfilling mission requests where authorized by law.

Recommendation #4:
Postpone additional UAS purchases until recommendation #1 has been implemented.
. . . the actual funding is subject to changing Department and Agency criteria.

U.S. DEPARTMENT OF HOMELAND SECURITY, OFFICE OF INSPECTOR GENERAL, serves as an independent and objective inspection, audit, and investigative body to provide independent oversight and promote excellence, integrity, and accountability within DHS programs and operations.

EXPLORING THE ISSUE

Does the Public Have a Stake in How Drones Are Used?

Critical Thinking and Reflection

1. What concerns over the use of drone technology will be most affected as the technology becomes cheaper and more available?
2. What is a stakeholder? What does the term mean in this context?
3. Why do many people not trust government agencies to be responsible in their use of surveillance technologies?
4. Is protecting national security more important than protecting individual liberties?

Is There Common Ground?

Most law enforcement and emergency management agencies seem to be aware that the public has a strong interest in their use of technologies that may impinge on privacy and civil liberties. They therefore go to some lengths to assure the public that they will be responsible in their use of such technologies. As noted in the Introduction to this issue, the Aviation Committee of the International Association of Chiefs of Police has formulated "Recommended Guidelines for the Use of Unmanned Aircraft" that include recognition of privacy and civil rights concerns and discourage the use of armed drones. Yet even though the public agrees that these technologies have useful roles to play, it remains concerned.

1. Has government ever abused its surveillance powers? (Recent news has extensively covered surveillance of phone and Internet messages by the National Security Agency or NSA.)
2. "Quis custodiet ipsos custodies" is an old Latin saying. What does it mean, and what is its relevance to this issue?

Additional Resources

Ben Alusten, "The Terminator Scenario," *Popular Science* (January 2011).

Mark Gubrud, "US Killer Robot Policy: Full Speed Ahead," *Bulletin of the Atomic Scientists* (September 20, 2013).

Peter W. Singer, "The Predator Comes Home: A Primer on Domestic Drones, Their Huge Business Opportunities, and Their Deep Political, Moral, and Legal Challenges," Brookings Institution (March 8, 2013) (http://www.brookings.edu/research /papers/2013/03/08-drones-singer).

"Review of the 2012 US Policy on Autonomy in Weapons Systems," Human Rights Watch (April 15, 2013) (http://www.hrw.org/news/2013/04/15 /review-2012-us-policy-autonomy-weapons-systems).

Internet References . . .

Living under Drones

http://www.livingunderdrones.org/

Rise of the Drones

http://www.pbs.org/wgbh/nova/military /rise-of-the-drones.html

Shadowview Foundation

http://www.shadowview.org/?gclid=CLelqdX _2rwCFS7xOgoduWQATw

Unit 6

UNIT

Ethics

*S*ociety's standards of right and wrong have been hammered out over millennia of trial, error, and (sometimes violent) debate. Accordingly, when science and technology offer society new choices to make and new things to do, debates are renewed over whether or not these choices and actions are ethically acceptable. Today there is vigorous debate over such topics as the use of animals in research, genetic engineering of insects for disease control, and gene-editing of human embryos.

Selected, Edited, and with Issue Framing Material by:
Thomas A. Easton, *Mount Ida College*

ISSUE

Is "Animal Rights" Just Another Excuse for Terrorism?

YES: John J. Miller, from "In the Name of the Animals: America Faces a New Kind of Terrorism," *National Review* (2006)

NO: Steven Best, from "Dispatches from a Police State: Animal Rights in the Crosshairs of State Repression," *International Journal of Inclusive Democracy* (2007)

Learning Outcomes
After studying this issue, students will be able to:
• Explain why animals are used in research.
• Explain why alternatives to the use of animals in research are sought.
• Describe the difference between "animal welfare" and "animal rights."
• Explain why society chooses to restrain extreme protests.

ISSUE SUMMARY

YES: Journalist John J. Miller argues that animal rights extremists have adopted terrorist tactics in their effort to stop the use of animals in scientific research. Because of the benefits of such research, if the terrorists win, everyone loses.

NO: Professor Steven Best argues that the new Animal Enterprise Protection Act is excessively broad and vague, imposes disproportionate penalties, endangers free speech, and detracts from prosecution of real terrorism. The animal liberation movement, on the other hand, is both a necessary effort to emancipate animals from human exploitation, and part of a larger resistance movement opposed to exploitation and hierarchies of any and all kinds.

Modern biologists and physicians know a great deal about how the human body works. Some of that knowledge has been gained by studying human cadavers and tissue samples acquired during surgery and through "experiments of nature." Some knowledge of human biology has also been gained from experiments on humans, such as when patients agree to let their surgeons and doctors try experimental treatments.

The key word here is *agree*. Today it is widely accepted that people have the right to consent or not to consent to whatever is done to them in the name of research or treatment. In fact, society has determined that research done on humans without their free and informed consent is a form of scientific misconduct. However, this standard does not apply to animals, experimentation on which has produced the most knowledge of the human body.

Although animals have been used in research for at least the last 2000 years, during most of that time, physicians who thought they had a workable treatment for some illness commonly tried it on their patients before they had any idea whether or not it worked or was even safe. Many patients, of course, died during these untested treatments. In the mid-nineteenth century, the French physiologist Claude Bernard argued that it was sensible to try such treatments first on animals to avoid some human suffering and death. No one then questioned whether or not human lives were more valuable than animal lives. In the twentieth century, Elizabeth Baldwin, in "The Case for Animal Research in Psychology," *Journal of Social Issues* (vol. 49, no. 1, 1993), argued that animals are of immense value in medical, veterinary, and psychological research, and they do not have the same moral rights as humans. Our obligation, she maintains, is to treat them humanely.

Today geneticists generally study fruit flies, roundworms, and zebra fish. Physiologists study mammals, mostly mice and rats but also rabbits, cats, dogs, pigs, sheep, goats, monkeys, and chimpanzees. Experimental animals are often kept in confined quarters, cut open, infected with disease organisms, fed unhealthy diets, and injected with assorted chemicals. Sometimes the animals suffer. Sometimes the animals die. And sometimes they are healed, albeit often of disease or injuries induced by the researchers in the first place.

Not surprisingly, some observers have reacted with extreme sympathy and have called for better treatment of animals used in research. This "animal welfare" movement has, in turn, spawned the more extreme "animal rights" movement, which asserts that animals—especially mammals—have rights as important and as deserving of regard as those of humans. Thus, to kill an animal, whether for research, food, or fur, is the moral equivalent of murder. See Steven M. Wise and Jane Golmoodall, *Rattling the Cage: Toward Legal Rights for Animals* (Perseus, 2000), and Roger Scruton and Andrew Tayler, "Do Animals Have Rights?" *The Ecologist* (March 2001).

As the idea that people must give informed consent to what is done to them in the name of research gained currency, along with the related idea that whatever is done should aim to benefit them, some people have tried to extend these ideas to animals. They say that just as scientists cannot do whatever they wish to humans, they cannot do whatever they wish to animals. Harriet Rivo, "Toward a More Peaceable Kingdom," *Technology Review* (April 1992) says that the animal rights movement "challenges the ideology of science itself . . . forcing experimenters to recognize that they are not necessarily carrying out an independent exercise in the pursuit of truth—that their enterprise, in its intellectual as well as its social and financial dimensions, is circumscribed and defined by the culture of which it is an integral part."

Among books that are pertinent to this issue are F. Barbara Orlans, *In the Name of Science: Issues in Responsible Animal Experimentation* (Oxford University Press, 1993); Rod Strand and Patti Strand, *The Hijacking of the Humane Movement* (Doral, 1993); Deborah Blum, *The Monkey Wars* (Oxford University Press, 1994); Tom Regan, *Empty Cages: Facing the Challenge of Animal Rights* (Rowman and Littlefield, 2005); and Paul Waldau, *Animal Rights: What*

Everyone Needs to Know (Oxford University Press, 2011). Adrian R. Morrison provides a guide to responsible animal use in "Ethical Principles Guiding the Use of Animals in Research," *American Biology Teacher* (February 2003). Barry Yeoman, "Can We Trust Research Done with Lab Mice?" *Discover* (July 2003), notes that the conditions in which animals are kept can make a huge difference in their behavior and in their responses to experimental treatments.

The same research that leads to treatments for human illness also enhances the treatment tools of veterinarians. Thus Damon Linker, in "Rights for Rodents," *Commentary* (April 2001), can say, "Can anyone really doubt that, were the misanthropic agenda of the animal-rights movement actually to succeed, the result would be an increase in man's inhumanity, to man and animal alike? In the end, fostering our age-old 'prejudice' in favor of human dignity may be the best thing we can do for animals, not to mention for ourselves." An editorial in *Lancet*, "Animal Research Is a Source of Human Compassion, Not Shame" (September 4, 2004), insists that the use of animals in biomedical research is both an essentially humanistic endeavor and necessary. University of Pittsburgh assistant professor of anesthesiology and radiology Stuart Derbyshire writes in "Vivisection: Put Human Welfare First," *Spiked-Online* (June1, 2004), that the use of animals in research is justified by the search for knowledge, not just the search for medical treatments, and reflects a moral choice to put humans first. Josie Appleton, "Speciesism: A Beastly Concept: Why It Is Morally Right to Use Animals to Our Ends," *Spiked-Online* (February 23, 2006), contends that the development of human civilization has been marked by increasing separation from animals. Humans come first, and it is entirely moral to use animals for own ends. Torturing animals is wrong, but mostly because it reflects badly upon the torturer. Wesley J. Smith, *A Rat Is a Pig Is a Dog Is a Boy: The Human Cost of the Animal Rights Movement* (Encounter, 2010), defends the stance that human interests must come before those of animals; granting rights to animals is an attack on human dignity.

Animal-rights extremists defend the opposing view vigorously, even going so far as to firebomb researchers' homes and cars; see Greg Miller, "Scientists Targeted in California Firebombings," *Science* (August 8, 2008). John Hadley, "Animal Rights Extremism and the Terrorism Question," *Journal of Social Philosophy* (Fall 2009), questions whether such extremist actions really fall under the "terrorism" label, but most people seems to have no trouble using the label. P. Michael Conn and James V. Parker of the Oregon National Primate Research Center describe in *The Animal Research War* (Palgrave Macmillan, 2008) how animals are used and protected in research and the benefits of their use, while also detailing the movement of terrorist tactics from the United Kingdom to the United States. In their view, "It is extremely important that an informed public know what is really going on and how it impacts on the future of health care and medical advances."

Yet the idea that animals have rights too continues to gain ground. Steven M. Wise finds in *Drawing the Line: Science and the Case for Animal Rights* (Perseus, 2002) that there is a spectrum of mental capacities for different species, which supports the argument for rights. Niall Shanks, in "Animal Rights in the Light of Animal Cognition," *Social Alternatives* (Summer 2003), considers the moral/philosophical justifications for animal rights and stresses the question of consciousness. Jim Motavalli, in "Rights from Wrongs," *E Magazine* (March/April 2003), describes with approval the movement toward giving animals legal rights (though not necessarily human rights). Jeffrey Stinson, "Activists Pursue Basic Legal Rights for Great Apes," *USA Today* (July 15, 2008), describes current efforts to grant such rights to the great apes. Paul Starobin, "Animal Rights on the March," *National Journal* (May 22, 2010), notes that the animal rights movement is shifting toward legislative efforts to meet their goals. In India, the use of live animals in most research has been banned; see Linah Baliga, "Govt Bans Use of Live Animals for Education, Research," *Times of India* (April 17, 2012).

The animal welfare movement has led to important reforms in the treatment of animals, to the development of several alternatives to using animals in research, and to a considerable reduction in the number of animals used in research. See, for example, Robert A. Coleman, "Human Tissue in the Evaluation of Safety and Efficacy of New Medicines: A Viable Alternative to Animal Models?" *ISRN Pharmaceutics* (special section) (2011); Alan Dove, "The Search for Animal Alternatives," *Drug Discovery & Development* (May 2010); and Manfred Liebsch, et al.,

"Alternatives to Animal Testing: Current Status and Future Perspectives," *Archives of Toxicology* (August 2011). There is also a scientific Journal, ALTEX: Alternatives to Animal Experimentation (http://altweb.jhsph.edu/altex/index.html). However, it has also led to hysterical objections to in-class animal dissections, terrorist attacks on laboratories, the destruction of research records, and the theft of research materials (including animals).

The Animal Enterprise Protection Act (AEPA) was designed to prevent attacks on laboratories and researchers, and since its passage, such attacks indeed have diminished. Yet critics do object that it may have a chilling effect on legitimate protest; see Michael Hill, "United States v. Fullmer and the Animal Enterprise Terrorism Act: 'True Threats' to Advocacy," *Case Western Reserve Law Review* (Spring 2011), and Dara Lovitz, *Muzzling a Movement: The Effects of Anti-Terrorism Law, Money, and Politics on Animal Activism* (Lantern Books, 2010). One lawsuit was dismissed in March 2013 for failure to show that such "chilling" actually existed; see Rose Bouboushian, "Terror Fears of Animal Rights Group Tossed," *Courthouse News* (March 21, 2013).

In the YES selection, Journalist John J. Miller argues that animal rights extremists have adopted terrorist tactics in their effort to stop the use of animals in scientific research. Because of the benefits of such research, if the terrorists win, everyone loses. In the NO selection, Professor Steven Best argues that new laws against animal rights "terrorism" represent the efforts of animal exploitation industries that seek immunity from criticism. The new Animal Enterprise Protection Act is excessively broad and vague, imposes disproportionate penalties, endangers free speech, and detracts from prosecution of real terrorism. The animal liberation movement, on the other hand, is both a necessary effort to emancipate animals from human exploitation and part of a larger resistance movement opposed to exploitation and hierarchies of any and all kinds.

YES ⬅

John J. Miller

In the Name of the Animals: America Faces a New Kind of Terrorism

Six days after the World Trade Center was destroyed, the New York Stock Exchange rang its opening bell and traders sang "God Bless America" from the floor: They wanted to send a loud-and-clear message to the world that al-Qaeda could not shut down the U.S. economy. Even though the Dow suffered its biggest one-day point-loss in history, the mere fact that buying and selling could resume so quickly marked an inspiring day for capitalism and against terrorism.

On September 7, 2005, however, terrorists struck again, and the NYSE still hasn't recovered. This time, they didn't target a couple of skyscrapers near the exchange, but rather a company called Life Sciences Research (LSR). It had recently qualified for a NYSE listing and its senior management had gathered on Wall Street to celebrate the occasion. Just a few minutes before the first trades were set to occur, NYSE president Catherine Kinney informed her guests that their listing would be postponed. It was immediately obvious to everyone from LSR what had happened: "A handful of animal extremists had succeeded where Osama bin Laden had failed," Mark Bibi, the company's general counsel, would say in congressional testimony the next month.

LSR is better known by the name of its operating subsidiary, Huntingdon Life Sciences (HLS), which is in the business of testing products on animals to assess their safety and comply with government regulations. Most people probably don't like to think about what goes on in these labs—vivisections of monkeys, for instance—but they also appreciate the importance of research whose ultimate goal is the protection and enhancement of human health. About 95 percent of all lab animals are rats and mice, but for animal-rights extremists who believe that "a rat is a pig is a dog is a boy" (as Ingrid Newkirk of People for the Ethical Treatment of Animals once said), the whole endeavor is deeply immoral. And some of them have decided that because the traditional practices of honest persuasion and civil disobedience haven't changed

many hearts or minds, they must now adopt a different strategy—something they euphemistically call "direct action." These are efforts to intimidate and harass animal researchers and everyone who comes into contact with them. In recent years, hardcore activists have embraced property destruction and physical assaults. "This is the number-one domestic terrorist threat in America," says Sen. James Inhofe, an Oklahoma Republican. Keeping LSR off the Big Board probably represents their greatest achievement yet.

Red in Tooth and Claw

The animal-rights movement may be wrongheaded, but there's no denying that most of its members are motivated by genuine compassion for animals and a sincere commitment to preventing cruelty. There's also no denying that violence in their name has become a significant problem. Just as the pro-life movement is haunted by the murderers of abortion doctors, the environmental and animal-rights movements are cursed by their own packs of fierce radicals. A year ago, the FBI said that 35 of its offices were conducting more than 150 investigations into "animal rights/ecoterrorist activities." The number of illegal incidents involving these activities has risen sharply, from 220 in the 1980s and 1990s to 363 in just the last five years, according to a recent report by the Foundation for Biomedical Research, an association of businesses and universities that conduct animal research. (By contrast, abortion-clinic violence appears to be subsiding.)

"Other groups don't come close in terms of the financial damage they've done," says John Lewis, an FBI agent who until recently coordinated federal efforts against domestic terrorism. Not even militants in the mold of Timothy McVeigh, the man behind the Oklahoma City bombing in 1995? "We have an acute interest in all of these groups, but when the rubber meets the road, the eco- and animal-rights terrorists lately have been way out in front."

Lewis estimates that they've caused around $100 million in damage, mostly property destruction affecting businesses, much of it from arson. This fall, eleven defendants will face trial in Oregon for causing an estimated $20 million in damage in five states.

Although animal-rights terrorism is fundamentally barbaric, its execution has assumed increasingly sophisticated forms. The campaign against Huntingdon Life Sciences began in the United Kingdom seven years ago with the formation of a group called Stop Huntingdon Animal Cruelty, or SHAC. Soon after, SHAC recruited members in the United States to focus on an HLS facility in New Jersey, using methods that were deployed to great effect in the U.K. A federal trial earlier this year—perhaps the most important trial ever held involving animal-rights extremism—put the group's methods on full display.

Many of SHAC's efforts targeted HLS directly. An electronic attack in 2002, for instance, caused the HLS server to overload. But other confrontations involved HLS employees away from work: cars vandalized in driveways, rocks tossed through the windows of homes, and graffiti messages such as "PUPPY KILLER" spray-painted on houses. Descriptions of these incidents were dutifully posted on SHAC's own website, often with an unnerving sense of glee. After a tire-slashing visit to the home of one HLS employee, for example, the SHACtivists seemed pleased that "his wife is reportedly on the brink of a nervous breakdown and divorce." These messages were meant to generate publicity, build a sense of momentum, and serve as models for activists spread across the country. In Britain, one top HLS employee was attacked by a group of hooded men wielding ax handles. "It's only a matter of time before it happens in the United States," warns Frankie Trull, head of the Foundation for Biomedical Research. "Everything they do over there eventually comes over here."

Intimidating employees in their private lives places pressure on HLS itself. But SHAC's harassment didn't stop with HLS employees. They also engaged in "tertiary targeting"—i.e., taking aim at companies with ties to HLS, plus their workers. Dozens of firms decided that doing business with HLS simply wasn't worth it. Deloitte & Touche, which had audited the HLS books, ended its relationship. Lawn gardeners quit. Even a security company that provided services to HLS succumbed to the abuse.

SHAC's methods certainly can be menacing, as transcripts from the trial make clear. One of SHAC's main targets was Marsh, a company that sold insurance to HLS. There was a smoke-bomb attack at an office in Seattle, forcing the evacuation of a high-rise building. In San Antonio, SHAC members glued the locks to a Marsh office and plastered the windows and doors of the building with pictures of a mutilated dog. Once they even stormed inside, screaming threats: "You have the blood of death on your hands! . . . We know where you live! You cannot sleep at night! We will find you!"

And they made good on these threats. Marsh employees were repeatedly harassed at home. There were late-night phone calls: "Are you scared? Do you think the puppies should be scared?" Other calls were more menacing: "We know where you live. You shouldn't sleep at night. You shouldn't rest until the puppies rest." Marion Harlos, who was managing director for Marsh in San Antonio, said that people went through her mail, ordered magazine subscriptions in her name, and rang her doorbell and dashed off in a kind of never-ending Devil's Night. Sometimes protesters would gather in front of her house, banging drums and hollering into megaphones. "They proceeded to parade the neighborhood, shout my name, that of my children," she said. "I was petrified. I was petrified for my children." The kids were kept indoors: "We did not know what was going to take place. Would someone be in the front yard? Would someone be in the back yard? Would someone come up and talk to them? Would someone try and take them?" To make a bad situation even worse, a neighbor threatened to sue Harlos, claiming that the ongoing presence of protesters was hurting property values. Harlos eventually moved.

Sally Dillenback, a Marsh employee in Dallas, had a similarly harrowing experience. A SHAC website published private information, some of it probably obtained by going through her trash: her home address, her car's license-plate number, and even her auto-insurance policy number. Most unsettling, however, was the information about her children: their names, the names of their schools and teachers, and descriptions of their after-school activities. "I felt that my family might be threatened with that kind of information being posted," she testified. The activists certainly didn't leave her alone; they plastered pictures on the side of her house, her mailbox, and her sidewalk. A SHAC website described the strategy: "Let the stickers serve to remind Marsh employees and their neighbors that their homes are paid for in the blood, the blood of innocent animals." On other occasions, animal-rights radicals held protests outside her home with drums and bullhorns. They followed her to church. The scariest moment may have been when Dillenback read an e-mail: "It asked how I would feel if they cut open my son . . . and filled him with poison the way that they, Huntingdon, [were] doing to animals." Her husband bought a semi-automatic shotgun, even though Mrs. Dillenback doesn't like guns: "He was wanting to protect the family."

Pundits in Black Ski Masks

Marsh employees were by no means the only tertiary victims of abuse. Two bombs went off at a California office of Chiron, a biotech company. Nobody was hurt, but the second explosion was delayed—a tactic sometimes used by terrorists to kill first responders. Workers at GlaxoSmithKline, a pharmaceutical company, also had their windows smashed and mail stolen. In one case, SHAC posted information about the spouse of a GSK employee who was undergoing treatment for alcoholism. Another employee was summoned to the Baltimore morgue to identify a dead relative—but when she arrived, she learned the call was a hoax.

Sometimes, the connections between SHAC targets and HLS were so tenuous as to be almost nonexistent. Elaine Perna, a housewife who is married to an executive who retired from the Bank of New York—another company with ties to HLS—confronted SHAC when protesters appeared on her porch. "When I opened the door, they were yelling at me through the bullhorn. One spat at my face through the screen and yelled obscenities at me, about me, about my husband." A defense lawyer's attempt to minimize the incident—"All Ms. Gazzola did was she screamed through the bullhorn, didn't she?"—irritated Perna: "They were yelling at me through a bullhorn, they were calling me effing this and my husband effing that and spitting in my face through a screen. Now, if you think that 'that's all,' you know, you can call it 'that's all.' But to me, it wasn't 'that's all.'" The mayhem didn't stop until the police arrived.

On March 2, a jury convicted six members of SHAC (at press time, sentencing had not yet occurred). This is an important victory, but animal-rights extremism isn't going away—groups such as Hugs for Puppies and Win Animal Rights are now on the scene, continuing their perverse crusade. They certainly don't lack for true believers. In Senate testimony last fall, Jerry Vlasak of the North American Animal Liberation Press Office announced that violence against HLS was "extensional self-defense" in behalf of "non-human animals." Recently, a mysterious full-page advertisement appeared in the *New York Times* and the *Wall Street Journal*. It featured the image of a man in a black ski mask, alongside the words "I Control Wall Street" and a short account of the NYSE fiasco. "Nobody knows who paid for it," says Trull. One theory proposes that a group of institutional investors are responsible; another claims that it's a backhanded attempt by animal-rights activists to raise anxieties even further. HLS still isn't listed.

Several members of Congress have tried to address this species of domestic terrorism by proposing legislation that would toughen the Animal Enterprise Protection Act, a law that was passed before the advent of "tertiary targeting." At the recent trial, prosecutors secured convictions against SHAC only because they were able to rely on anti-stalking laws. "They had to scour the federal code, looking for violations," says Brent McIntosh, a deputy assistant attorney general at the Department of Justice. "This is an enormous, surreptitious, and interstate conspiracy. We need to strengthen laws against it." Bills to do so have been introduced in both the House and the Senate, but a crowded legislative calendar probably means they won't be debated until a new Congress convenes next year.

The stakes are high. "Five years from now, we don't want to count up another $100 million in losses," says the FBI's Lewis. That's true, although the real costs of animal-rights terrorism aren't really quantifiable: They come in the form of medical discoveries that are delayed or never made, products that aren't approved, and careers that aren't started. Whatever the real price tag, one thing is certain: Each time an animal-rights terrorist wins, people lose.

JOHN J. MILLER is *National Review's* national political reporter. His latest book is *A Gift of Freedom: How the John M. Olin Foundation Changed America* (Encounter Books, 2005).

Steven Best

 **NO**

Dispatches from a Police State: Animal Rights in the Crosshairs of State Repression

Welcome to the post-constitutional America, where defense of animal rights and the earth is a terrorist crime.

In the wake of 9/11, and in the midst [of] the neoliberal attack on social democracies, efforts to grab dwindling resources, and crush dissent of any kind, the US has entered a neo-McCarthyist period rooted in witch-hunts and political persecution. The terms and players have changed, but the situation is much the same as the 1950s: the terrorist threat has replaced the communist threat, Attorney General Alfred [sic] Gonzalez dons the garb of Sen. Joseph McCarthy, and the Congressional Meetings on Eco-Terrorism stand in for the House Un-American Activities Committee. The Red Scare of communism has morphed into the *Green Scare* of ecoterrorism, where the bad guy today is not a commie but an animal, environmental, or peace activist. In a nightmare replay of the 1950s, activists of all kinds today are surveilled, hassled, threatened, jailed, and stripped of their rights. As before, the state conjures up dangerous enemies in our midst and instills fear in the public, so that people willingly forfeit liberties for an alleged security that demands secrecy, non-accountability, and centralized power. . . .

The bogus "war on terror" has served as a highly-effective propaganda and bullying device to ram through Congress and the courts a pro-corporate, anti-environmental, authoritarian agenda. Using vague, catch-all phrases such as "enemy combatants" and "domestic terrorists," the Bush administration has rounded up and tortured thousands of non-citizens (detaining them indefinitely in military tribunals without right to a fair trial) and surveilled, harassed, and imprisoned citizens who dare to challenge the government or corporate system it protects and represents.

"The Animal Enterprise Protection Act"

While dissent in general has become ever-more criminalized in the dark days of the Bush Reich, animal rights activists especially have been caught in the crosshairs of

state repression, targeted by "anti-terrorist" legislation that subverts First Amendment rights to protect the blood money of corporate exploiters. This is because the animal rights/liberation movement is not only one of the most dramatic forms of resistance alive today (such as [is] evident in the dramatic raids, rescues, sabotage, and arson attacks of the Animal Liberation Front, a global movement), but also is an economic threat to postindustrial capital which is heavily rooted in science and research, and therefore dependent upon (it believes) animal experimentation.

In 1992, a decade before the passage of the USA PATRIOT Act, animal exploitation groups such as the National Association for Biomedical Research successfully lobbied Congress to pass a federal law called the Animal Enterprise Protection Act (AEPA). This legislation created the new crime of "animal enterprise terrorism," and laid out hefty sentences and fines for any infringement. The law applies to anyone who "intentionally damages or causes the loss of any property" of an "animal enterprise" (research facilities, pet stores, breeders, zoos, rodeos, circuses, furriers, animal shelters, and the like), or who causes an *economic loss* of any kind. The AEPA defines an "animal rights or ecological terrorist organization" as "two or more persons organized for the purpose of supporting any politically motivated activity intended to obstruct or deter any person from participating in any activity involving animals or an activity involving natural resources." The act criminalizes actions that obstruct "any lawful activity involving the use of natural resources with an economic value."

Like the category of "domestic terrorism" that is a keystone in the USA PATRIOT Act attack on civil liberties, the frightening thing about the AEPA is its strategic vagueness that subsumes any and every form of protest and demonstration against exploitative industries to a criminal act, specifically, to a *terrorist* act. Thus, the actions of two or more people can be labeled terrorist if they leaflet a circus, protest an experimental lab, block a road to protect a forest, do a tree-sit, or block the doors of a fur store. Since, under the purview of the AEPA, any action that interferes with the profits and operations of animal and environmental industries, even boycotts and whistle-blowing could be criminalized and denounced as terrorism. On the sweeping interpretations of such legislation, Martin Luther King, Mahatma Gandhi, and Cesar Chavez would today be vilified and imprisoned as terrorists, since the intent of their principled boycott campaigns was precisely to cause "economic damage" to unethical businesses. And since the AETA, like the legal system in general, classifies animals as "property," their "theft" (read: *liberation*) is unequivocally defined as a terrorist offense.

There already are laws against sabotage and property destruction, so isn't the AEPA just a redundant piece of legislation? No—not once [one] understands its hidden agenda which strikes at the heart of the Bill of Rights. The real purpose of the AEPA is to protect animal and earth exploitation industries from protest and criticism, not property destruction and "terrorism." The AEPA redefines vandalism as ecoterrorism, petty lawbreakers as societal menaces, protestors and demonstrators as domestic terrorists, and threats to their blood money as threats to national security. Powerful economic and lobbying forces, they seek immunity from criticism, to intimidate anyone contemplating protest against them, and to dispatch their opponents to prison.

Free Speech on Trial: The SHAC 7

Hovering over activists' heads like the sword of Damocles for over a decade, the AEPA dropped in March, 2006, with the persecution and conviction of seven members of a direct action group dedicated to closing down the world's largest animal-testing company, Huntingdon Life Sciences (HLS). Exercising their First Amendment rights, activists from the Stop Huntingdon Animal Cruelty (SHAC) campaign ran a completely legal and highly effective campaign against HLS, driving them to the brink of bankruptcy. Since 1999, SHAC activists in the UK and US have waged an aggressive direct action campaign against HLS, notorious for extreme animal abuse (torturing and killing 500 animals a day) and manipulated research data. SHAC roared onto the historical stage by combining a shrewd knowledge of the law, no nonsense direct action tactics, and a singular focus on one corporation that represents the evils of the entire vivisection industry. From email and phone blockades to raucous home demonstrations, SHACtivists have attacked HLS and pressured over 100 companies to abandon financial ties to the vivisection firm. By 2001, the SHAC movement drove down HLS

stock values from $15/share to less than $1/share. Smelling profit emanating from animal bloodshed, investment banking firm Stephens Inc. stepped in to save HLS from bankruptcy. But, as happened to so many companies before them, eventually Stephens too could not withstand the intense political heat and so fled the SHAC kitchen. Today, as HLS struggles for solvency, SHAC predicts its imminent demise.

Growing increasingly powerful through high-pressure tactics that take the fight to HLS and their supporters rather than to corrupt legislatures, the SHAC movement poses a clear and present danger to animal exploitation industries and the state that serves them. Staggered and driven into the ropes, it was certain that SHAC's opponents would fight back. Throwing futile jabs here and there, the vivisection industry and the state recently teamed up to mount a major counterattack.

Alarmed indeed by the new form of animal rights militancy, HLS and the biomedical research lobby commanded special sessions with Congress to ban SHAC campaigns. On May 26, 2004, a police dragnet rounded up seven prominent animal rights activists in New Jersey, New York, Washington, and California. Hordes of agents from the FBI, Secret Service, and other law agencies stormed into the activists' homes at the crack of dawn, guns drawn and helicopters hovering above. Handcuffing those struggling for a better world, the state claimed another victory in its phony "war against terror." Using the AEPA, HLS successfully prosecuted the "SHAC 7," who currently are serving prison sentences up to six years.

After the SHAC 7 conviction, David Martosko, the noxious research director of the Center for Consumer Freedom and a fierce opponent of animal rights, joyously declared: "This is just the starting gun." Indeed, corporations and legislators continue to press for even stronger laws against animal rights and environmental activism, as the Bush administration encloses the nation within a vast web of surveillance and a militarized garrison.

In September 2006, the US senate unanimously passed a new version of the AEPA (S3990), significantly renamed the "Animal Enterprise *Terrorism* Act" (AETA). To prevent critical discussion, the Senate fast-tracked the bill without hearings or debate, and just before adjourning for the election recess. In November 2006, the House approved the bill (HR 4239), and President Bush obligingly signed it into law. Beyond the portentous change in name, the new and improved version extends the range of legal prosecution of activists, updates the law to cover Internet campaigns, and enforces stiffer penalties for "terrorist" actions. Created to stop the effectiveness of the SHAC-style tactics that biomedical companies had habitually complained about to Congress, the AETA makes it a criminal offense to interfere not only with so-called "animal enterprises" directly, but also with third-party organizations such as insurance companies, law firms, and investment houses that do business with them.

Thus, the Senate version of the bill expands the law to include "any property of a person or entity having a connection to, relationship with, or transactions with an animal enterprise." The chain of relations, like the application of the law, extends possibly to the point of infinity. As journalist Will Potter notes, "The clause broadens the scope of legislation that is already overly broad." This problem is compounded further with additional vague concepts such as criminalize actions that create "reasonable fear" in the targets of protest, making actions like peaceful home demonstrations likely candidates for "ecoterrorism."

As the Equal Justice Alliance aptly summarizes the main problems with the AETA:

- "It is excessively broad and vague.
- It imposes disproportionately harsh penalties.
- It effectively brands animal advocates as 'terrorists' and denies them equal protection.
- It effectively brands civil disobedience as 'terrorism' and imposes severe penalties.
- It has a chilling effect on all forms of protest by endangering free speech and assembly.
- It interferes with investigation of animal enterprises that violate federal laws.
- It detracts from prosecution of real terrorism against the American people."

ACLU Betrayal

A sole voice of dissent in Congress, Representative Dennis Kucinich (D-Ohio) stated that the bill compromises civil rights and threatens to "chill" free speech. Virtually alone in examining the issue from the perspective of the victims rather than victimizers, Kucinich said: "Just as we need to protect people's right to conduct their work without fear of assault, so too this Congress has yet to address some fundamental ethical principles with respect to animals. How should animals be treated humanely? This is a debate that hasn't come here."

One of the most unfortunate aspects of the passing of this bill was the failure of the American Civil Liberties Union to challenge it. The ACLU did indeed write a letter to Congress about the passing of the AETA, to caution against conflating illegal and legal protest, but the organization failed to challenge the real terrorism perpetuated by animal and earth exploitation industries, and ultimately consented to their worldview and validity.

In an October 30, 2006, letter to Chairman of the House Judiciary Committee F. James Sensenbrenner and Ranking Member John Conyers, the ACLU writes that it "does not oppose this bill, but believes that these minor changes are necessary to make the bill less likely to chill or threaten freedom of speech." Beyond proposed semantic clarifications, the ACLU mainly warns against broadening the law to include legal activities such as boycotts: "Legitimate expressive activity may result in economic damage. . . . Care must therefore be taken in penalizing economic damage to avoid infringing upon legitimate activity."

Thus, unlike dozens of animal protection groups who adamantly reject the AETA *en toto*, the ACLU "does not oppose the bill." In agreement with corporate interests, the ACLU assures the government it "does not condone violence or threats." It thereby dodges the complex question of the legitimacy of sabotage against exploitative industries. The ACLU uncritically accepts (1) the corporate–state definition of "violence" as intentional harm to *property*, (2) the legal definition of animals as "property," and (3) the use of the T-word to demonize animal liberationists rather than animal exploiters. Ultimately, the ACLU sides with the government against activists involved in illegal forms of liberation or sabotage, a problematic alliance in times of global ecocide. The ACLU thereby defends *the property rights* of industries to torture and slaughter billions of animals over the *moral rights* of animals to bodily integrity and a life free from exploitation and gratuitous violence.

The ACLU failed to ask the tough questions journalist Will Potter raised during his May 23, 2006 testimony before the House Committee holding a hearing on the AETA, and to follow Potter in identifying key inconsistencies in bill. Does the ACLU really think that their proposed modifications would be adequate to guarantee that the AETA doesn't trample on legal rights to protest? Are they completely ignorant and indifferent to the fact that the AEPA was just used to send the SHAC 7 to jail for the crime of protesting fraudulent research and heinous killing? And just where was the ACLU during the SHAC 7 trial, one of the most significant First Amendment cases in recent history? Why does the ACLU only recognize violations of the Constitution against human rights advocates? Do they think that animal rights activists are not citizens? Do they not recognize that tyrannical measures used against animal advocates today will be used against all citizens tomorrow? How can the world's premier civil rights institution [be] blatantly speciesist and bigoted toward animals? *Why will they come to the defense of the Ku Klux Klan but not the SHAC 7?* The ACLU's silence in the face of persecution of animal rights activists unfortunately is typical of most civil rights organizations that are too bigoted and myopic to grasp the implications of state repression of animal rights activists for human rights activists and all forms of dissent.

Animal Liberation as a New Social Movement

Corporate exploiters and Congress have taken the US down a perilous slippery slope, where it becomes difficult to distinguish between illegal and legal forms of dissent, between civil disobedience and terrorism, between PETA and Al Qaeda, and between liberating chickens from a factory farm and flying passenger planes into skyscrapers. The state protects the corporate exploiters who pull their purse strings and stuff their pockets with favors and cash.

The right to free speech ends as soon as you begin to exercise it. As the politics of nature—the struggle for liberation of animals and the earth—is the most dynamic fight today, one that poses a serious threat to corporate interests, animal and earth liberationists are under ferocious attack. The growing effectiveness of direct action anti-vivisection struggles will inevitably bring a reactionary and retaliatory response by the corporate–state complex to crack down on democratic political freedoms to protest, as well as new Draconian laws that represent a concerted effort by power brokers to crush the movement for animal liberation.

In the "home of the brave, land of the free," activists are followed by federal agents; their phone conversations and computer activity [are] monitored, their homes are raided, they are forced to testify before grand juries and pressured to "name names," they are targets of federal round ups, they are jailed for exercising constitutionally protected rights and liberties. Saboteurs receive stiffer prison sentences than rapists, bank robbers, and murderers. There has never been freedom of speech or action in the US, but in the post-9/11 climate, where the USA PATRIOT Act is the law of the land, not the Constitution and Bill of Rights, activists are demonized as terrorists—not just the Animal Liberation Front (ALF), Earth Liberation Front (ELF), and SHAC, but also completely legal and peaceful groups like Food Not Bombs and vegan outreach organizations.

The massive police resources of the US state are being used far more to thwart domestic dissent than to improve homeland insecurity. While Big Brother is obsessed with the email, conversations, and meetings of people who know a thing or two about the duties of citizenship, the airlines, railways, subways, city centers, and nuclear power plants remain completely vulnerable to an attack, which, according to the elites, is imminent.

The contemporary animal liberation movement is an *extension of the new social movements,* and as such issues "post-materialist" demands that are not about higher wages but the end to hierarchy and violence, and a new relation with the natural world.

Second, it is a *postindustrial movement,* operating within a global postindustrial society where the primary aspects of the economy no longer center on processing of physical materials as much as information, knowledge, science, and research. Transnational corporations such as Monsanto, pharmaceutical industries such as GlaxoSmith-Kline, AstraZeneca, Novartis, and Pfizer, and drug testing corporations such as Huntingdon Life Sciences show the importance of science and research for the postindustrial economy, and thus the relevance of the animal liberation movement.

This movement also is an *anti-globalization* movement in that the corporations it attacks often are transnational and global in scope, part of what I call the Global Vivisection Complex (GVC). The GVC is comprised of pharmaceutical industries, biotechnology industries, medical research industries, universities, and testing laboratories, all using animal experimentation to test and market their drugs. As animals are the gas and oil for these corporate science machines, the animal liberation movement has disrupted corporate supply chains, thwarted laboratory procedures, liberated captive slaves, and attacked the legitimacy of biomedical research as an effective scientific paradigm.

Fourth, the animal liberation movement is an *abolitionist movement,* seeking empty cages not bigger cages, demanding rights not "humane treatment" of the slaves, opposing the greatest institution of domination and slavery ever created—the empire of human supremacy over millions of species and billions of animal slaves.

To an important degree, the historical and socioeconomic context for the emergence of the animal advocacy movement (in all its diverse tendencies and aspects) is the industrialization of animal exploitation and killing. This is dramatically evident with the growth of slaughterhouses at the turn of the 20th century, the emergence and globalization of factory farming after World War II, and the subsequent growth of research capital and animal experimentation. To this, one would have to add expanding human population numbers, the social construction of carnivorous appetites, and the rise of fast food industries which demand the exploitation and massacre of ever-growing numbers of animals, now in the tens of billions on a global scale. Along with other horrors and modes of animal exploitation, the industrialization, mechanization, and globalization of animal exploitation called into being an increasingly broad, growing, and powerful animal liberation movement.

Animal liberation builds on the great abolitionist struggle of past centuries and is the abolitionist movement of our day. Animal liberationists are waging war against the oldest and last form of slavery to be formally abolished—the exploitation of nonhuman animals. Just as the modern economy of Europe, the British colonies in America, and the United States after the Revolutionary War were once entirely dependent on the trafficking in human slaves, so now the current global economy would crash if all animal slaves were freed from every lab, cage and other mode of exploitation. Animal liberation is in fact the anti-slavery movement of the present age and its moral and economic ramifications are as world-shaking, possible more so, than the abolition of the human slavery movement (which of course itself still exists in some sectors of the world in the form of sweatshops, child sex slavery, forced female prostitution, and the like).

The animal liberation movement is a profound threat to the corporate–state complex and hierarchical society in two ways.

First, it is a serious economic threat, as the planetary capitalist system thrives off animal exploitation with the meat/dairy and biomedical research industries. In the UK, for instance, where the animal rights movement has been particularly effective, drug-makers are the third most important contributor to the economy after power generation and oil industries. The animal rights movement has emerged as a powerful anti-capitalist and anti-(corporate) globalization force in its ability to monkeywrench the planetary vivisection machine and challenge transnational corporations such as HLS, GlaxoSmithKline, and Novartis.

Second, the animal rights movement is a potent ideological and psychological threat. The fight for animal liberation demands radical transformations in the habits, practices, values, and mindset of all human beings as it also entails a fundamental restructuring of social institutions and economic systems predicated on exploitative practices. The philosophy of animal liberation assaults the identities and worldviews that portray humans as conquering Lords and Masters of nature, and it requires entirely new ways of relating to animals and the earth. Animal liberation is a direct attack on the power human beings—whether in premodern or modern, non-Western or Western societies—have claimed over animals, since at least the dawn of agricultural society ten thousand years ago.

Total Liberation

As the dynamics that brought about global warming, rainforest destruction, species extinction, and poisoning of communities are not reducible to any single factor or cause—be it agricultural society, the rise of states, anthropocentrism, speciesism, patriarchy, racism, colonialism, industrialism, technocracy, or capitalism—all radical groups and orientations that can effectively challenge the ideologies and institutions implicated in domination and ecological destruction have a relevant role to play in the global social-environmental struggle. While standpoints such as deep ecology, social ecology, ecofeminism, animal liberation, Black liberation, and the Earth Liberation Front are all important, none can accomplish systemic social transformation by itself. Working together, however, through a diversity of critiques and tactics that mobilize different communities, a flank of militant groups and positions can drive a battering ram into the structures of power and domination and open the door to a new future.

Although there is diversity in unity, there must also be unity in diversity. Solidarity can emerge in recognition of the fact that all forms of oppression are directly or indirectly related to the values, institutions, and *system* of global capitalism and related hierarchical structures. To be unified and effective, however, anti-capitalist and anti-imperialist alliances require mutual sharing, respectful learning, and psychological growth, such that, for instance, black liberationists, ecofeminists, and animal liberationists can help one another overcome racism, sexism, and speciesism.

The larger context for current dynamics in the animal liberation movement involves the emergence of the neoliberal project (as a response to the opening of the markets that was made necessary by the continuous expansion of transnational corporations in the post-war period) which was crucial in the elites' effort to destroy socialism and social democracy of any kind, to privatize all social structures, to gain total control of all resource markets and dwindling resources, and to snuff out all resistance. The animal rights/liberation movement has come under such intense fire because it has emerged as a threat to operations and profits of postindustrial capital (heavily rooted in research and therefore animal experimentation) and as a significant form of resistance. The transnational elite want the fire crushed before its example of resistance becomes a conflagration.

Conversely, the animal liberation movement is most effective not only as a single-issue focus to emancipate animals from human exploitation, but to join a larger resistance movement opposed to exploitation and hierarchies of any and all kinds. Clearly, SHAC and the ALF alone are not going to bring down transnational capitalism, pressuring HLS and raiding fur farms and laboratories will not themselves ignite revolutionary change, and are more rear-guard, defensive actions. The project to emancipate animals, in other words, is integrally related to the struggle to emancipate humans and the battle for a viable natural world. To the extent that the animal liberation movement grasps the big picture that links animal and human oppression struggles as one, and seeks to uncover the roots of hierarchy including that of humans over nature, they can be viewed as a profound new liberation movement that has a crucial place in the planetary struggles against injustice, oppression, exploitation, war, violence, capitalist neo-liberalism, and the destruction of the natural world and biodiversity.

Yet, given the profound relation between the human domination of animals and the crisis—social, ethical, and environmental—in the human world and its relation to the natural world, the animal liberation movement is in a unique position to articulate the importance of new relations between human and human, human and animal, and human and nature.

New social movements and Greens have failed to realize their radical potential. They have abandoned their original demands for radical social change and become integrated into capitalist structures that have eliminated "existing socialist countries" as well as social democracies within the present neoliberal globalization which has become dominant. A new revolutionary force must therefore emerge, one that will build on the achievements of classical democratic, libertarian socialist, and anarchist traditions; incorporate radical green, feminist, and indigenous struggles; synthesize animal, Earth, and human liberation standpoints; and build a global social-ecological revolution capable of abolishing transnational capitalism so that just and ecological societies can be constructed in its place.

Notes

For Feinstein's pathetic capitulation to the Green Scare and her sordid alliance with neo-McCarthyite Senator James "Global Warming Is a Myth" Inhofe (R-Okla.), see her press release. . . .

The text of the "Animal Enterprise Protection Act of 1992" is available online.

In states such as Oregon and California, related legislation has already passed which declares it a felony terrorist offense to enter any animal facility with a camera or video recorder "with the intent to defame the facility or facility's owner." See Steven Best, "It's War: The Escalating Battle Between Activists and the Corporate-State Complex," in *Terrorists or Freedom Fighters? Reflections on the Liberation of Animals* (Lantern Books, 2004), pp. 300–339 (eds. Steven Best and Anthony J. Nocella II).

For a more detailed analysis of the SHAC struggle in the context of political economy, see Steven Best and Richard Kahn, "Trial By Fire: The SHAC 7, Globalization, and the Future of Democracy," *Animal Liberation Philosophy and Policy Journal,* Volume II, Issue 2, 2004 . . .

On the SHAC 7 trial, see Steven Best and Richard Kahn, "Trial By Fire: The SHAC7, Globalization, and the Future of Democracy."

For the text of S3880, the final bill that passed in both houses, see . . .

Will Potter, "Analysis of Animal Enterprise Terrorism Act."

"Why Oppose AETA."

. . . Kucinich also challenged the AETA as being redundant and created a "specific classification" to repress legitimate dissent.

The ACLU letter to Congress is available at . . .

For a list of animal advocacy groups opposed to the AETA, see . . .

For Potter's testimony before the House Committee on the Judiciary Subcommittee on Crime, Terrorism, and Homeland Security see . . .

STEVEN BEST is an associate professor of philosophy at the University of Texas, El Paso. His most recent book (coauthored with Anthony J. Nocella) is *Igniting a Revolution: Voices in Defense of the Earth* (AK Press, 2006). According to his website (www.drstevebest.org/), "He has come under fire for his uncompromising advocacy of 'total liberation' (humans, animals, and the earth) and has been banned from the UK for the power of his thoughts."

EXPLORING THE ISSUE

Is "Animal Rights" Just Another Excuse for Terrorism?

Critical Thinking and Reflection

1. What is the difference between the "animal rights" and the "animal welfare" movements?
2. Why must drugs be tested for safety and efficacy?
3. Should extreme forms of protest be restrained for the good of society?
4. Do all animals (including cockroaches, for instance) have rights? If not, where do we draw the line?

Is There Common Ground?

Both the animal welfare and animal rights movements are rooted in awareness of past abuses of animals. Unfortunately, animal abuse is not just in the past. It shows up far too often in the daily news.

1. Check your local paper (or favorite news site) for stories on animal abuse. They may involve puppy mills, farms, dog tracks, dog or cock fighting, and more. Discuss what is being done about these cases, and by whom (animal welfare or animal rights groups).
2. Do some animals seem more deserving of "rights" than others? Does intelligence matter? Or, how closely are they related to us? (There have been proposals to grant great apes legal rights very similar to human rights; in Spain, in 2008, such rights were actually granted; see www .time.com/time/world/article/0,8599,1824206,00.html.)

3. How is animal welfare protected in your state? (See www.animallaw.com/.)

Additional Resources

P. Michael Conn and James V. Parker, *The Animal Research War* (Palgrave Macmillan, 2008).

John Hadley, "Animal Rights Extremism and the Terrorism Question," *Journal of Social Philosophy* (Fall 2009).

Manfred Liebsch, et al., "Alternatives to Animal Testing: Current Status and Future Perspectives," *Archives of Toxicology* (August 2011).

Tom Regan, *Empty Cages: Facing the Challenge of Animal Rights* (Rowman and Littlefield, 2005).

Internet References . . .

Americans for Medical Progress

Americans for Medical Progress (AMP) nurtures public understanding of and support for the humane, necessary and valuable use of animals in medicine.

www.amprogress.org/animal-research

Center for Alternatives to Animal Testing

The Johns Hopkins Center for Alternatives to Animal Testing (CAAT) promotes humane science by supporting the creation, development, validation, and use of alternatives to animals in research, product safety testing, and education.

http://caat.jhsph.edu/

Selected, Edited, and with Issue Framing Material by:
Thomas A. Easton, *Mount Ida College*

ISSUE

Should Genetically Engineered Mosquitoes Be Released into the Environment to Fight Disease?

YES: Hadyn Parry, from "Testimony before the U.S. House of Representatives Committee on Science, Space, and Technology, Hearing on 'Science of Zika: The DNA of an Epidemic,'" U.S. House of Representatives (2016)

NO: Eric Hoffman, from "Genetically Engineered Mosquitoes in the U.S.," *Friends of the Earth* (2012)

Learning Outcomes

After reading this issue, you will be able to:

- Describe the threat posed by mosquito-borne diseases such as malaria and dengue.
- Assess whether reducing mosquito populations is likely to reduce disease transmission.
- Explain in what ways the release of genetically engineered mosquitoes might threaten the environment.
- Compare the benefits and costs of using pesticides to control mosquitoes to those of using genetic engineering.

ISSUE SUMMARY

YES: Hadyn Parry argues that genetically engineered mosquitoes hold the potential to reduce mosquito populations and control the spread of diseases such as Zika and dengue.

NO: Eric Hoffman, a biotechnology campaigner with Friends of the Earth, argues that a great deal of research remains to be done to prove the safety to both the environment and public health of releasing genetically engineered mosquitoes. In addition, medical ethics require that participants in a medical trial must be able to opt out at any time, which means that a single resident of a release area must be able to call a halt to the release program.

Mosquitoes spread a number of diseases among humans. One of the most well-known such diseases is malaria, caused by a protozoan parasite that is injected into human hosts when an infected mosquito takes a blood meal; it kills some half a million people per year, mostly children in Africa. Growing in awareness is dengue fever, caused by a virus that produces fever, severe muscle and bone pain, and even death. It is native to tropical regions, where it causes some 390 million infections per year, but as climate warms it is already spreading into temperate zones, including the southern United States. Another tropical virus that is spreading into temperate areas is chikungunya; symptoms include fever and joint pain. Since there are no vaccines or drugs for the disease, the U.S. Centers for Disease Control say the best way to avoid it is to avoid being bitten by mosquitoes (http://www.cdc.gov/media/DPK/2014/dpk-chikungunya.html). The Zika virus came to public attention in Brazil in 2015; it too is spread by mosquitoes and it is related to the dengue virus; among its effects, it appears to be responsible for a great increase in the incidence of microcephaly in newborns; public health authorities in several countries are recommending that women delay child-bearing (http://www.cdc.gov/zika/). Among other mosquito-borne diseases are West Nile virus and yellow fever. Only yellow fever has a preventative vaccine at present.

One might think that such diseases could be prevented by using insecticides to kill mosquitoes, and indeed this has been tried for many years. Unfortunately, insecticides kill non-target insects, including beneficial ones, as well, and they can be toxic to humans and other animals. And natural selection ensures that mosquito populations become resistant to insecticides, so the chemical approach never works for long.

Researchers have therefore long sought new and more effective methods of controlling mosquito populations. One technique, first developed in the 1950s to control the screwworm fly, which lays its eggs in open sores on the hides of cattle and can kill cattle within 10 days, depends on a peculiarity of the insect's life cycle: the females mate just once. Researchers found that if they raised large numbers of screwworms in the lab, exposed them to radiation to sterilize the males, and released them, many or most females would mate with a sterile male and then fail to reproduce. The technique successfully eliminated the screwworm as a problem, both in North America and in Africa; see "War Is Won against Screwworm," *United Nations Chronicle* (June 1992).

It has also been applied to other insects such as the Mediterranean fruit fly and mosquito, though with less dramatic success because the females mate more than once. There is great potential for use of the technique against agricultural pests; see V. A. Dyck, J. Hendrichs, and A. S. Robinson (eds.), *Sterile Insect Technique: Principles and Practice in Area-Wide Integrated Pest Management* (Springer 2005), and Marc J. B. Vreysen and Alan S. Robinson, "Ionising Radiation and Area-Wide Management of Insect Pests to Promote Sustainable Agriculture: A Review," *Agronomy for Sustainable Development* (January 2011). In the public-health realm, the target is mosquitoes and great effort is going into making the technique more effective; see e.g. Jeremie R. L. Gilles, et al., "Towards Mosquito Sterile Insect Technique Programmes: Exploring Genetic, Molecular, Mechanical, and Behavioural Methods of Sex Separation in Mosquitoes," *Acta Tropica* (April 2014 Supplement), and Mark Q. Benedict and Alan S. Robinson, "The First Releases of Transgenic Mosquitoes: An Argument for the Sterile Insect Technique," *Trends in Parasitology* (August 2003).

One international collaboration, Eliminate Dengue (http://www.eliminatedengue.com/program), is working intensively on using a bacterial symbiote, *Wohlbachia,* which

research shows can reduce the ability of mosquitoes to pass on dengue, chikungunya, malaria, and yellow fever. They propose to release *Wohlbachia*-infected mosquitoes in disease-prone areas and have already done so on a trial basis in Australia, Vietnam, Indonesia, Brazil, and Columbia to see how well the technique can reduce dengue outbreaks. See Kostas Bourtzis, et al., "Harnessing Mosquito-*Wohlbachia* Symbiosis for Vector and Disease Control," *Acta Tropica* (April 2014). However, there is reason to expect that even if it works well, success may be relatively short-lived; see James J. Bull and Michael Turelli, "*Wohlbachia* versus Dengue: Evolutionary Forecasts," *Evolution, Medicine, and Public Health* (online September 2013).

As techniques for modifying an organism's genome (genetic engineering) have advanced, researchers have endeavored to change the mosquito itself. In one approach, genes are modified to make males sterile (instead of exposing them to radiation). In a second approach, new genes are introduced to make offspring die before they can mature and transmit disease; here the goal is to impair reproduction of mosquitoes in an area so that their numbers and disease transmission both decline. In a third approach, the genes affect the sex ratio of offspring so that almost all offspring are male; this too reduces reproduction and disease transmission. In a fourth approach, genes that can make the mosquito less able to host disease organisms and then pass them on are introduced; the idea is that as engineered mosquitoes are released and breed with wild mosquitoes, the genes will spread throughout the wild population. All of these methods are currently under active development. See Paolo Gabrieli, Andrea Smidler, and Flaminia Catteruchia, "Engineering the Control of Mosquito-Borne Infectious Diseases," *Genome Biology* (November 2014) (http://www.genomebiology.com/2014/15/11/535). Adrienne LaFrance, "Genetically Modified Mosquitoes: What Could Possibly Go Wrong?" *Atlantic* (April 26, 2016), recognizes the need to control mosquito populations and notes that many objections to genetic engineering are rooted in misinformation. Nevertheless, she says, fear of disease is likely to mean genetically engineered mosquitoes will be released into the environment.

So far most modified mosquitoes have been tested only in laboratory cages. However, the British company Oxitec has released genetically engineered male mosquitoes whose offspring die. Oxitec's intent is to reduce transmission of the dengue and Zika viruses, but so far testing has focused on determining how well the Oxitec mosquitoes mate with wild females and then how much the mosquito population declines. They have reported success in the Cayman Islands in the Caribbean (2009) and in Brazil (2013). They are now planning a test release in Key West,

Florida, with the FDA's Center for Veterinary Medicine currently reviewing the application. Activists are trying hard to prevent approval; see Food and Water Watch's call for the FDA to say no at "Advocates Urge FDA to Halt Risky GMO Mosquito Release" (http://www.foodandwaterwatch.org /pressreleases/advocates-urge-fda-to-halt-risky-gmo-mosquito -release/). There is also an anti-"mutant bug" petition at https:// www.change.org/p/say-no-to-genetically-modified-mosquitoes -release-in-the-florida-keys).

In the YES selection, Oxitec CEO Hadyn Parry argues that genetically engineered mosquitoes hold the potential to reduce mosquito populations and control the spread of diseases such as dengue and Zika. In the NO selection, Eric Hoffman, a biotechnology campaigner with Friends of the Earth, argues that a great deal of research remains to be done to prove the safety to both the environment and public health of releasing genetically engineered mosquitoes. In addition, medical ethics require that participants in a medical trial must be able to opt out at any time, which means that a single resident of a release area must be able to call a halt to the release program.

YES ⤸

Hadyn Parry on the right.

Hadyn Parry

Testimony before the U.S. House of Representatives Committee on Science, Space, and Technology, Hearing on "Science of Zika: The DNA of an Epidemic"

Oxitec Limited has pioneered the use of bioengineering to provide a solution for controlling the mosquito *Aedes aegypti* that spreads Zika virus. Oxitec developed its product OX513A, a self-limiting strain of *Aedes aegypti* in 2002 and since that date has conducted rigorous indoor and then outdoor evaluation and development. OX513A, therefore, has 14 years of data to support efficacy, environment and safety aspects. In all efficacy trials to date, Oxitec has demonstrated a reduction in the target *Aedes aegypti* population by over 90% in about six months. Over recent years, Oxitec has placed considerable focus and investment on its ability to scale up, supply and distribute its insects and OX513A should now be considered a fully operational solution, enabled to be deployed.

OX513A received a preliminary Finding of No Significant Impact (FONSI) from the Food and Drug Administration (FDA) in 2016 following an Investigational New Animal Drug (INAD) filing that was initiated in 2011. The public comment period ended on May 13, 2016 and a final opinion from the FDA is awaited before Oxitec has the regulatory approval to carry out a small trial in the Florida Keys as part of its application. We are hopeful that, in light of the public health need, FDA will act quickly to finalize its finding.

OX513A has national biosafety approval from the National Biosafety Technical Commission (CTNBio) for use in Brazil (April 2014) and Oxitec has been informed that we will shortly receive special registration from ANVISA, an agency within the Ministry of Health, to enable availability in Brazil.

OX513A has a specific recommendation from the World Health Organization (WHO) Vector Control Advisory Group for pilot deployment under operational conditions. WHO rarely recommends a specific product, but

took this step as part of its emergency response and preparedness for the Zika virus.

Oxitec's Bioengineering Technology and Status

Aedes aegypti

While the current urgent threat is the Zika virus, the real target is the mosquito that carries the disease. Despite the present and widespread use of insecticides, over the last 50 years, there has been a sharp increase in both incidence and number of diseases spread by *Aedes aegypti* across the world. Before 1970, only nine countries had experienced severe dengue epidemics. The disease is now endemic in more than 100 countries in the WHO regions of Africa, the Americas, the Eastern Mediterranean, South-East Asia and the Western Pacific. WHO reported an estimate of over 390 million dengue infections per year. Chikungunya came into the Caribbean in December 2013 and within one year, there were over one million cases across the Central America and Caribbean region.

By focusing on the mosquito, rather than the disease, Oxitec has accumulated years of development, well ahead of the Zika threat emerging. It also should be noted that it is unlikely that Zika will be the last disease transmitted by *Aedes aegypti*. It is clear that new tools are needed [to] control this vector to guard against not only the current threat but also known threats such as dengue and Yellow Fever along with future, unidentified threats.

Aedes aegypti is the prime vector for Zika virus as well as for dengue, chikungunya and Yellow Fever. Understanding and then controlling the vector is key to controlling the spread of Zika or any other current or future virus transmitted by the mosquito. This mosquito species originated from

Africa and has been spread around the world by human activities. This distribution has occurred via the transport of eggs, which are highly durable and easily carried in freight. Unlike many mosquito species which are adapted to the rural environment, this mosquito has adapted to be pre-dominantly an urban one. It bites humans by preference and lives in and around the home and other areas where people congregate. Its larvae and pupae develop in still water pools such as unused containers, birdbaths and blocked gutters. This mosquito can breed in as little as a bottle cap of water.

It is notoriously difficult to control with conventional insecticides not only because it has developed resistance to the most common insecticides but mainly because containers create multiple breeding sites in the urban setting that are often on private property and inaccessible to mosquito control staff. There are just too many dispersed inaccessible breeding sites that need to be continuously treated for this mosquito to be controlled through application of chemical insecticides.

Oxitec has used some key features of this mosquitoes' biology to design our solution. First, only females bite. Males cannot bite and, therefore, males represent no threat to humans.

Second, males are extremely effective at finding females. They tune in to the sound of the female wing beat to locate the female in order to mate. Once the female has mated successfully, she does not need to mate again and she will engage in a cycle of biting humans (to acquire blood), laying eggs, then biting again and will continue on this cycle. A single female can lay up to 500 eggs in her lifetime, which develop from egg to larvae to pupae to adult in a little over one month.

Third, it is important to note that neither male nor female mosquitoes have a significant spontaneous flight range. An adult mosquito will only fly up to about 200 yards in its lifetime.

Oxitec's Approach

To control *Aedes aegypti*, Oxitec uses the mosquito against itself. We release males (that cannot bite) that mate with wild females. The offspring inherit self limiting genes and die before becoming functional adults, thereby reducing the wild population. A male is biologically tuned to seek out females for mating purposes. The wild females cannot distinguish between an Oxitec OX513A male and a wild one, meaning that, provided sufficient Oxitec males are released across an urban area for a period of time, the population will rapidly decrease. In trials in several countries, we have shown that the population of *Aedes aegypti* may be reduced by over 90% in around six months. Moreover, as this species

cannot fly far, the effect of the control can be highly specific to the area of release. Specifically, we can treat broad urban areas by releasing in a pattern to cover a town or city, and we can modify the release rate to concentrate more on areas of higher mosquito population. Or we can even specifically target "hotspots." Once controlled, low level releases can be continued in areas of likely re-infestation to sustain the control over the longer term. Unlike chemical insecticides, the OX513A mosquito affects **only** the *Aedes aegypti* species, and has no measurable impact on other mosquito populations, or the overall insect population of the treated region.

Oxitec's Technology

There are two key elements to the Oxitec bioengineering approach.

a) **A self-limiting gene.** Each released OX513A insect carries two alleles of the self-limiting gene meaning that each of its offspring inherits one copy. That single copy prevents the offspring from developing to become a functioning adult, so the offspring of a mating between an OX513A mosquito and a wild one die in early development. Oxitec uses the term self-limiting; meaning offspring will die before becoming functional adult[s]. Therefore, these mosquitoes do not reproduce.

b) **A fluorescent biological marker.** In addition to inheriting the self limiting gene, all of the offspring inherit a fluorescent marker. This gene allows us to identify all the larvae. When viewed under a filter, the larvae show a distinct red color and pattern. This color provides an unparalleled system for monitoring and tracing the Oxitec mosquito.

While the self-limiting gene is the mechanism to reduce the population of *Aedes aegypti* and, hence reduce the threat of transmission of Zika, the marker allows the program to be precise, efficient and cost-effective. Throughout a program, Oxitec collects eggs from the area of release and determines the proportion of the larvae that have an OX513A parent. More or fewer adult males then can be released in each area. The release rate is tailored to specific requirements and, as a result, overall control of the whole *Aedes aegypti* population is achieved as swiftly as possible.

Programs, Results to Date and Status

An Oxitec program consists of the release of male mosquitoes from predetermined release points in a town or city each week. Global Positioning System (GPS) release points are programmed into a release plan. Male OX513A mosquitoes are released from each GPS point from a moving van. The males then disperse and seek females. Eggs and larvae are collected each week from simple ovitraps (that are commonly used by most mosquito control teams) not only to show the level of *Aedes aegypti* population but also, using the marker, to adjust the release plan for the following weeks. The overall number of males used, the frequency of release and the number of release points are all determined at the commencement of the program and refined as it continues; the marker allowing for an unprecedented level of control and precision.

Oxitec has demonstrated over **90%** reduction in the *Aedes aegypti* population in about six months in all efficacy trials. . . . Following first releases, the population starts to decline rapidly after about three months. As the population declines, releases continue but fewer OX513A males are used as they are not needed at the same level as when the wild population was higher. Even when the wet season starts, the wild *Aedes aegypti* do not recover in the release area with a continuing low level release. By contrast, the untreated area shows a reasonably consistent level of infestation throughout the year with a sharp seasonal rise in the wet season.

Oxitec has placed a major focus on operational preparedness. Oxitec has established permanent production units already in UK and Brazil and we are currently scaling up in Piracicaba, Brazil to a level to supply enough mosquitoes in the next phase to protect up to 1.5 million people. The supply chain can also use features of the mosquito biology to provide efficient logistics and quality control. Eggs can be produced at a central location for an entire country or region, from which they can be stored and distributed as required. More locally, a production hub can receive eggs, rear to pupae, separate males from females and produce the males for release.

Safety and Environment

Safety to environment and humans are key aspects of our approach. In stark contrast to insecticides (which will affect a broad array of insect life and respective food chains), Oxitec releases only affect the target mosquito so it is a species-specific approach. *Aedes aegypti* only mate and produce viable offspring with *Aedes aegypti*. Further, this species is an invasive or non-native one in all countries outside of Africa. From a historical perspective, it is a recent invader to the U.S. as well as an urban dweller so native ecosystems have not developed key dependencies. As a food source, it forms a very small part of the diet of other animals. For example, in the Florida Keys

Aedes aegypti forms less than 1% of the biomass of all mosquitoes.

But perhaps the most important environmental aspect of OX513A is that neither the released adults nor their offspring remain in the environment. Again, it is a self-limiting approach whereby the released males will die after a few days as will their offspring.

Over the last 14 years, Oxitec has conducted a broad array of studies on human safety and the environment and these studies have been used to inform regulatory decision making and these are publically available through the relevant country's regulatory mechanisms. Following the review of this data, the FDA's Center for Veterinary Medicine, working with experts from the Centers for Disease Control and Prevention (CDC) and the Environmental Protection Agency (EPA), has reached a preliminary Finding of No Significant Impact (FONSI). This finding corroborates that of the National Biosafety Technical Commission (CTNBio) in Brazil where OX513A has been approved for releases throughout the country.

Comparison to Other Forms of Vector Control

The main forms of vector control used today throughout the world are a combination of monitoring, good practice (through the prevention or removal of breeding sites though regular inspections and eliminating sources of standing water) and use of insecticides. While insecticides have been the mainstay of vector control products, insecticide resistance and the urban anthropophilic nature of *Aedes aegypti* mean that insecticides are not effective in controlling population of *Aedes aegypti* across an urban environment.

In addition to insecticides, there are a number of new innovations proposed that range from Oxitec's OX513A with proven efficacy along with over a decade of data, to those still in the research phase or suggested for future research. Perhaps the clearest way to differentiate these new innovations is based on

a) whether the released insects are designed to spread and persist in the environment, or not; and
b) field trial evidence and operational preparedness.

Spreading and Persisting Approaches (Population Replacement)

One school of thought relies on the concept of replacing the population of *Aedes aegypti* with a different, modified version. This could be achieved through genetic engineering or through other means. Using genetic engineering, genes may be introduced through the mosquito population (gene drive) with the intent of replacing the existing population in a biased or driven way that is less harmful. There are different early stage gene drive research programs investigating this approach.

Another approach is to try to achieve the same outcome (population replacement) by infecting the mosquito population with a bacterium. Wolbachia is an intracellular bacterium that is not naturally present in *Aedes aegypti* but, once infected with a specific wolbachia strain (wMel), investigators report a reduction in the viral load in the mosquito in laboratory experiments. To date, outdoor trials have concentrated on replacement of the wild *Aedes aegypti* population with the wolbachia (wMel) infected strain. Efficacy trials to examine the disease impact have not yet taken place.

Regardless of how these prototypes are developed, one needs to both replace the existing mosquito population with the modified version but also ensure that the new modified version is significantly less of a threat over the long term than the wild *Aedes aegypti* that it replaces. Both males and females will need to be released in order to allow the modified mosquito to replace the wild version. If the mechanism of action results in a reduction in virus rather than a complete block, then releasing biting females when virus is endemic may actually assist virus spread.

In practice, population replacement is more complex and a potentially riskier strategy than that of use of Oxitec's technology, since population replacement results in a new population of mosquitoes modified either by genetic means or through infection with a bacterium. It is therefore essential to consider the long-term impact of the evolving mosquito combined with the bacteria and combined with virus. A particular focus for products that are designed to spread and persist in the environment is the potential long-term effects as by their nature there is no obvious ability to contain the spread or engage a product recall if this is required. Stewardship will also be a key issue.

Non-Spreading and Non-Persisting (Population Reduction)

Population reduction approaches rest on using products that do not persist or spread in the environment. The product is used for as long as it is required and no longer. Some may argue that long-term control means ongoing releases but in effect we already have ongoing (but inadequate) vector control with chemical products. The ability

to suppress populations of disease-carrying mosquitoes without ongoing consequences is a key advantage of these approaches.

Oxitec is a leading proponent of this approach with OX513A. Both the released males and their offspring die, meaning that there is no spreading in the environment and no persistency.

There is also significant precedent in this approach in agriculture through the Sterile Insect Technique (SIT) that was developed using radiation in the 1950's and 1960's. The use of radiation devices can impose limitation on deployment and the damaging nature of the radiation can weaken the mating fitness of the insects. Mosquitoes have been a key target for radiation driven SIT but have enjoyed mixed success over many years. *Aedes aegypti* radiation based programmes have been suggested as a response to Zika but no field trials have yet taken place so the applicability of radiation-based SIT to *Aedes aegypti* is not yet tested or proven.

Field Trial Evidence and Operational Preparedness

A key consideration is that Oxitec commenced its development in 2002. At that time Oxitec's core focus was *Aedes aegypti* due to the unmet need to control this vector with respect to dengue. Even since 2002 the geographic spread of dengue and the number of cases has risen alarmingly. To this has been added the Chikungunya epidemic and now Zika. But this singular focus on the vector has meant that Oxitec's OX513A has accumulated an extensive body of efficacy and other supporting data, especially since first outdoor trials in 2009. Ironically as a genetically engineered organism it has undergone arguably a far higher standard of regulatory and independent scrutiny than non GE approaches.

Also, development has focused on operational practice, namely the development of methodologies, quality control and standards that have arisen as part of the maturation of the program. This level of data and operational use preparation sets OX513A apart from other approaches that are much earlier in the research and development cycle.

Regulatory Status with a Focus on the United States

The regulatory environment for all new approaches should be predictable, consistent and rigorous. The innovation that is needed in the area of vector control is stifled when regulatory delays occur. When serious diseases are involved, these delays can have life-altering consequences.

Oxitec's involvement in the United States began in 2009–10 when the Florida Keys experienced local transmission of dengue. The Florida Keys Mosquito Control District (FKMCD) determined that they needed new tools in order to protect their citizens from the mosquito that is the main disease vector: *Aedes aegypti*.

FKMCD sought the opportunity to evaluate Oxitec's technology, and it was agreed to conduct a small scale efficacy trial in a defined area in the Florida Keys to test our technology for the control of *Aedes aegypti*. Oxitec initially applied to USDA-Veterinary Services for permission to conduct the trial. In 2011, USDA-VS determined that it did not have regulatory authority over the Oxitec mosquitoes as it could envisage no risks to animal health from its use. Therefore, in the absence of another regulator, the FDA-CVM assumed regulatory responsibility by regulating OX513A under the new animal drug provisions of the Federal Food, Drug, and Cosmetic Act (FD&C Act). As set forth in FDA Guidance on Genetically Engineered Animals (referred to as "Guidance 187"), the agency regulates genetically engineered animals under its new animal drug authorities on the basis that the recombinant DNA construct introduced into the genome of the animal is intended to affect the "structure or function" of the animal and, thereby, meets the "drug" definition under the Act. As a result, genetically engineered animals are subject to mandatory pre-market approval by FDA.

In late 2011, Oxitec opened an investigational new animal drug (INAD) file with the FDA-CVM for a small scale efficacy trial in the Florida Keys, building on the promising efficacy results from Brazil and Cayman. While the recombinant DNA introduced into Oxitec mosquitoes is regulated by FDA as a new animal drug, bacteria, such as wolbachia, that are introduced into mosquitoes as a form of vector control are regulated by the Environmental Protection Agency (EPA) as pesticides. The impact of this distinction in regulatory jurisdiction is substantial as there are significant procedural differences between FDA's and EPA's approval pathways. The FDA regulatory process for new animal drug approval is rigorous and multi-faceted. Companies seeking FDA approval generally must provide considerable and comprehensive data and information to establish safety and effectiveness, perform an in-depth assessment of environmental impacts, develop drug labeling for FDA approval, and otherwise comply with several pre- and post-market regulatory requirements. In order to assess environmental impacts, FDA-CVM brought together regulators from EPA and CDC as well as other experts for this evaluation—this took a considerable time to form

the review team (6–9 months) as the agencies negotiated a memorandum of understanding to govern the interagency consultation. Meanwhile, Oxitec, as the regulated company, was prevented from moving forward with the efficacy trial in the Florida Keys.

FDA-CVM operates a modular dossier submission structure and Oxitec provided the first module in Dec 2013 and the last in Feb 2016, which was the final version of the sponsor-authored draft environmental assessment (EA) prepared in accordance with NEPA requirements and originally submitted to FDA in 2014. No items are outstanding from the FDA-CVM review for the efficacy trial and Oxitec has received letters of adequate response from FDA CVM on modules submitted. Following this lengthy and time-consuming pre trial process, FDA published on March 14th 2016 the draft Environmental Assessment (EA) for public comment along with a preliminary finding of no significant impact (FONSI) on human or environmental health. The public comment period was initially set for 30 days and the period was further extended for an additional 30 days at the request of non-governmental groups such as the Center for Food Safety. The public comment period finally closed on May 13th 2016, following the submission of over 2500 public comments. FDA-CVM is now required to review these comments for substantiveness and will prepare a final EA. Thereafter, Oxitec should be able to move forward with the efficacy trial in Florida. Given the urgency of moving forward, we hope that FDA will make the review of these comments one of its highest priorities and finalize their assessment quickly.

In the Keys, both the FKMCD and Oxitec have proceeded with a policy of transparency. The positive for this is that it allows for public information to accrue over a period of time. Interestingly, since 2013, there have been a number of public surveys that—despite the absence of recurring disease transmission in the Keys—show a consistent level of strong support for the approach. A recent study by Purdue University reports 78% support respondents for the use of GE mosquitoes as part of the battle against Zika.

There will always be a divergence of opinion for any new intervention and there are those who are against the trial. The Florida Keys Mosquito Control Board has now agreed to hold a referendum in Monroe County to ascertain local opinion on the trial being carried out. This is likely to occur in August 2016.

In Brazil the first trial with the Oxitec mosquito, OX513A, was conducted in 2010 in Juazerio, Bahia, NE Brazil. This was followed by additional trials. These trials demonstrated no adverse effects resulting from the release of the Oxitec mosquitoes. Moreover, the trials generated sufficient data to submit a commercial application to the Brazilian National Biosafety Technical Commission (CTNBio) in July 2013. In April 2014, CTNBio approved Oxitec's application for use of the Oxitec mosquitoes throughout Brazil.

Oxitec has been informed that we will shortly receive special registration from ANVISA, the Health Agency within the Ministry of Health, to enable widespread availability in Brazil. Oxitec should therefore be able to bring OX513A into use throughout the country to support the fight against Zika.

In Brazil, both dengue and Chikungunya are endemic and Zika has come into the public consciousness with alarm from 2015. Public support for the Oxitec approach has been at a high level—up to 96% support in Piracicaba; the first operational project. The Brazilian press has been almost uniformly supportive and indeed have given OX513A their own name describing it as *Aedes aegypti do Bem* or 'the friendly mosquito'.

Whilst at the time of writing there is no known local transmission of Zika on the United States mainland, local transmission is expected by many experts. However, there is already significant transmission in Puerto Rico and the first microcephaly case.

Considering it has already taken over 3 years due to a lack of clarity of the regulatory process for the analysis of a small scale efficacy trial we urge FDA to do the following:

a) expedite the final review of this dossier;
b) consider using its enforcement discretion to allow for rapid review of future environmental assessments, given the low risk profile of this product; and
c) given the current Zika crisis, grant emergency use or other expeditious regulatory solutions for the widespread approval of this promising vector control tool.

In conclusion, this technology has a very real potential of assisting in preventing and mitigating the Zika public health crisis. Here in the US and globally, I hope that we can work with the Congress and the Administration to expedite the approval and adoption of this promising technology. Our hope is that communities will have meaningful access to this technology in a timely manner as part of an integrated vector control approach.

HADYN PARRY is the Chief Executive Officer of Oxitec, Ltd.

Eric Hoffman

 **NO**

Genetically Engineered
Mosquitoes in the U.S.

Introduction

The UK biotechnology company Oxitec has developed a genetically engineered mosquito in an attempt to reduce mosquito populations and in turn limit the spread of disease such as dengue fever. This mosquito, *Aedes aegypti* (OX513A), has been engineered to survive only in the presence of tetracycline—a common antibiotic used in agriculture production and often found in sewage.

The GE mosquitoes are bred in a lab until adulthood, after which the males are released into the wild. In theory, the males will mate and then die off while their tetracycline-dependent gene passes onto their offspring. The offspring die early on in life—in the late larvae or pupae stage—and the mosquito population in a given area will theoretically be suppressed. These GE mosquitoes are not in fact sterile as some news reports claim but are engineered to pass on an "autocidal" gene that kills their offspring.

Oxitec has been moving ahead with field releases of its genetically engineered mosquitoes. The first-ever field releases of GE mosquitoes took place between 2009 and 2010 in the Cayman Islands, a British Overseas Territory, when three million mosquitoes were released. Malaysia was the second country to host Oxitec's experiments at the end of 2010 and six thousand more GE mosquitoes were released there. Between February and June 2011 more than 33,000 GE mosquitoes were then released in Brazil. According to Oxitec, results from the Cayman trials showed a reduction in *Aedes aegypti* populations of 80 percent.

Despite misleading reports published by the journal *Nature* on its website that "the controlled release of male mosquitoes genetically *engineered to be sterile has successfully wiped out dengue fever in a town of around 3,000 people, in Grand Cayman,*" (emphasis added) the mosquitoes are in fact not sterile and Oxitec never successfully eradicated dengue fever from any population. Dengue is not endemic in the Cayman Islands (only occasional cases occur in travelers). The company has only shown its technology

can reduce mosquito populations in the immediate term in controlled settings. Oxitec has not proven such population reductions lead to disease eradication.

Genetically Engineered Mosquitoes: Coming to the U.S.

Recent reports have revealed Oxitec's plan to release its GE mosquitoes in the Florida Keys. According to Michael Doyle, director of the Florida Keys Mosquito Control District, Oxitec intended to release 5,000 to 10,000 GE mosquitoes over a two week period and release them into an undisclosed 36-square-acre block area as early as January 2012—likely near the Key West Cemetery. Since then, the trial has been delayed . . . due to the regulatory challenges around the release of GE mosquitoes. The trial is expected to last about two months. The mosquitoes will be dusted with a fluorescent powder for identification purposes and then trapped to see how far they are flying. If the mosquito population declines, the trial will be considered a success.

While attempts to limit the spread of disease are laudable, there are many regulatory, environmental and ethical challenges facing the release of GE mosquitoes in the U.S. and there are even more unanswered questions.

Regulatory Gaps

Despite the fact that the Florida Keys Mosquito Control District and Oxitec are planning their trial as early as spring 2012 it is unclear which federal agency would regulate the field release of GE mosquitoes.

Originally, Oxitec and the Florida government agencies assumed the U.S. Department of Agriculture would regulate GE mosquitoes as it has other GE insects such as the first-ever release of a GE insect, a fluorescent pink bollworm. But in October 2011 the USDA issued a statement concluding Oxitec's mosquito was outside its jurisdiction since it supposedly didn't pose a threat to animal health.

In the statement, the USDA suggested that Oxitec reach out to other federal agencies—such as the Fish and Wildlife Service, the Centers for Disease Control and the Food & Drug Administration. It is unclear which agency will claim authority, if any, but the FDA could play a major role in any decision since it has authority over genetically engineered animals (such as a GE salmon currently being considered for human consumption), which it regulates through laws written for new animal drugs. In this instance, the engineered genes would be considered the animal drug.

Oversight by the FDA is important because release of GM mosquitoes is a medical experiment that could have effects on human health. But as a 2004 report by the Pew Initiative on Food and Biotechnology points out, if the FDA does regulate the release of GE mosquitoes it may not "have the expertise to assess the full range of environmental effects that could arise from the release of [GE] insects, including, for example, risks to plants, an expertise housed in other agencies like [USDA's Animal and Plant Health Inspection Service] or the Department of the Interior." Any agency that does have final regulatory authority over the field release of GE mosquitoes should be required to consult other relevant agencies and public stakeholders before making any final decision on whether GE mosquitoes should be released into the environment. The FDA's track record on consulting other agencies as it considers approval for GE salmon is less than encouraging.

Additionally, the U.S. is not a Party to the Cartagena Protocol on Biosafety to the Convention on Biological Diversity which governs international regulation, including transboundary movement, of genetically engineered organisms. Since the mosquito eggs will be shipped from the United Kingdom to the U.S. it is unknown how the Cartagena Protocol will apply to the field release of GE mosquitoes. Oxitec will be required to provide environmental assessments to the U.S. government *before* the shipment of the mosquito eggs—as mandated by the Protocol. But it is unclear which U.S. authority, if any, will publish, review and consult on this assessment.

Environmental Risks

The behavior of these mosquitoes and the risks they pose to human health and the environment are hard to predict, leaving the public with more questions than answers.

The most immediate environmental risk a decline in *Aedes aegypti* could have is that such a decline could leave an ecological niche to be filled by other, possibly more harmful pests. For example the Asian Tiger mosquito, *Aedes albopictus,* is considered one of the most invasive species in the world and carries many diseases including dengue fever and the West Nile virus. While the Asian Tiger mosquito has not yet been found in Key West, it could spread to the island if other mosquito populations decline as it has spread across many parts of the U.S. This could mean the spread of more disease and increased use of pesticides. A 2009 study in Gabon found that the Asian Tiger mosquito, in that instance, was more likely to spread dengue fever and the chikungunya virus than *Aedes aegypti*. The impacts from other, potentially more dangerous insects taking over the ecological niche left by *Aedes aegypti* have yet to be properly studied in the Florida Keys.

Ethical Concerns

The release of GE mosquitoes as an attempt to curb the spread of disease should be considered a medical trial and must follow the strict laws and guidelines in place to protect human subjects in medical trials. Central to ethics on human subject trials is the idea of free and informed consent.

According to paragraph 24 of the World Medical Association's Declaration of Helsinki—Ethical Principles for Medical Research Involving Human Subjects, the cornerstone of human research ethics:

> *In medical research involving competent human subjects, each potential subject must be **adequately informed of the aims, methods, sources of funding, any possible conflicts of interest, institutional affiliations of the researcher, the anticipated benefits and potential risks of the study and the discomfort it may entail, and any other relevant aspects of the study.** The potential subject must be informed of the **right to refuse to participate in the study or to withdraw consent to participate at any time without reprisal.** Special attention should be given to the specific information needs of individual potential subjects as well as to the methods used to deliver the information. After ensuring that the potential subject has understood the information, the physician or another appropriately qualified individual must then seek the potential subject's **freely-given informed consent, preferably in writing.** If the consent cannot be expressed in writing, the non-written consent must be formally documented and witnessed (emphasis added).*

Unfortunately, Oxitec has already shown a disregard of the importance of free and informed consent. The first releases of GE mosquitoes took place in the Cayman

Islands—first a small-scale trial in 2009 followed by the release of three million GE mosquitoes in 2010. According to Genewatch UK, the Cayman experiments were not revealed to the public until one month after the initial release and "no public consultation was undertaken on potential risks and informed consent was not sought from local people."

Equally troubling is that the Cayman Islands—a territory of the United Kingdom—does not have any biosafety laws and is not covered by either the Cartagena Protocol on Biosafety or the Aarhus Convention on Access to Information, Public Participation in Decision-making and Access to Justice in Environmental Matters, despite the UK being a Party to these treaties. These conventions would have required publication of and consultation on an environmental risk assessment prior to the release of GE mosquitoes. Instead, the only regulatory requirements were a local permit from the Cayman Islands Agriculture Department and a notification that GE mosquito eggs were shipped internationally. Neither of these documents appears to have been published.

In fact, the lack of public consultation for the Cayman experiments has been strongly criticized by one of Oxitec's powerful collaborators, the Gates Foundation. Anthony James, the lead investigator on the Gates team, said that he would "never" release genetically engineered mosquitoes the way Oxitec did in Grand Cayman.

Despite public concern over the unannounced Cayman field trials, Oxitec again released GE mosquitoes in Malaysia in 2010. According to an open letter sent to the Malaysian government from civil society organizations around the world, the public was only made aware of a field release trial of GE mosquitoes by a press release dated January 25, 2011—more than one month after the trial began on December 21, 2010. This is despite press reports as late as January 4, 2011 in the Malaysian press claiming the trials had been postponed. "It therefore appears," the letter stated, "that neither the local communities nor the Malaysian public at large knew that these trials had occurred." A larger trial, scheduled for an inhabited area, has not yet taken place.

Such a track record does not bode well for the Florida Keys community that will be the center of the first field release of GE mosquitoes in the United States. Community members must be informed throughout the process through a number of mechanisms—including the establishment of local institutional review boards and ethics committees and hosting of community meetings and public forums—and community members must have a right to leave the field trial area or demand the halt of the experiment entirely if they so decide.

Are Genetically Engineered Mosquitoes a Real Solution?

Misleading claims that Oxitec's mosquitoes are sterile make it appear as if the company's technology is a foolproof way to bring an end to mosquito-borne diseases. Unfortunately, its system has many problems that raise serious questions about the viability of GE insects as a way to limit the spread of disease.

As discussed, Oxitec's technology does not make its mosquitoes sterile; rather, they are engineered to be dependent on tetracycline and die in its absence. In fact, 3 to 4 percent of Oxitec's mosquitoes survived into adulthood in the lab in the absence of tetracycline despite supposedly carrying the lethal gene. If in the presence of the common antibiotic tetracycline, an Oxitec document showed, survival rates could be as high as 15 percent.

Since tetracycline is commonly found in sewage, and *Aedes aegypti* have been found to breed in sewage treatment plants, septic tanks, and cesspits in the Florida Keys, the possibility and risk that Oxitec's mosquitoes could survive in the environment must be studied before any release takes place. As Dr. John Mumford at Imperial College London, a leader and proponent in the field of genetically engineered insects, has said, "it would also be prudent in a risk analysis to seek evidence of the levels of tetracycline in the environment that would be likely to be encountered by released mosquitoes and their offspring. . . . If there are points of high tetracycline concentration then the risk analysis would need to consider a risk management measure that would deal effectively with it."

Additionally, Oxitec claims it only plans to release male GE mosquitoes into the environment since it's the female mosquito that bites humans and therefore spreads diseases such as dengue fever. But its process of sorting males and females is also not guaranteed. The sorting is conducted by hand and could result in up to 0.5 percent of the released insects being female. This would raise new human health concerns as people could be bit by GE mosquitoes. It could also hamper efforts to limit the spread of dengue fever.

Mosquitoes reproduce continually and Oxitec readily admits it will need to continually release GE mosquitoes in a given area in order to keep populations low. In fact, Oxitec does not expect its technology to lead to population collapses; rather, it states it is only able to decrease existing mosquito populations by approximately 80 percent. This claim is based on unpublished results from the Cayman Islands. In reality it remains unknown whether population suppression using this approach would be effective in the long term or over larger areas. Continual releases would need to occur every month or every few weeks, with upwards of a million mosquitoes per release. This is why Oxitec has suggested that 100 million to a billion GE mosquitoes should be stockpiled for each project.

This is problematic for a number of reasons. First, any environmental assessment of a full-scale field release of GE mosquitoes cannot simply look at the risks from one release; rather, the impacts of releasing millions of mosquitoes on a continual basis must be fully assessed.

Second, this system locks communities and nations into a permanent scheme of repeated ongoing payments to Oxitec once releases begin since Oxitec's mosquitoes are patented. The company stands to make significant profits if countries and communities must make continuous payments to it. These payments would presumably continue endlessly unless the community wanted the release of GE mosquitoes to stop in which case disease prevalence could rise when conventional mosquito populations rebound. The company has yet to provide data on what would happen to mosquito populations or prevalence of disease if releases were halted.

Concern also exists around the possibility of the dengue virus to evolve and become more virulent in response to the introduction of GE mosquitoes. The fact is that the virulence and spread of disease combined with mosquito population levels and behavior involve incredibly complex systems and [are] difficult to predict in advance. Significantly more research is needed on these and other potentially unintended consequences of the introduction GE mosquitoes.

Researchers do not know much about the correlation between population levels of *Aedes aegypti* and dengue fever infection in humans. According to a 2002 article in *Science*, the density of *Aedes aegypti* populations is at best weakly correlated with human infection rates. This is due to the fact that mosquitoes "persist and effectively transmit dengue virus even at very low population densities because they preferentially and frequently bite humans." Additionally, any introduction of GE mosquitoes that does not eradicate a population could lead to increased survivability of the dengue virus and increased risk of human infection.

In a 2003 review of research conducted in the 1970s by Dr. Phil Lounibos and colleagues, then at the International Centre of Insect Physiology and Ecology, in which sterile *Aedes aegypti* were released in Kenya, it was found that sterility levels needed to be very high in order to reduce the number of adult *aegypti* mosquitoes. In this study, introducing sterility levels of 60–70 percent of the mosquito population was not enough to actually reduce adult *Aedes aegypti* numbers. The dynamics between the wild and introduced strains, as well as the fitness of the introduced mosquitoes must be rigorously tested. For these reasons, the study concludes, "changes in human behavior might accomplish

reductions in vector-human contact more simply than genetic-control interventions." In other words changes in human practices, such as installing screens over windows or using bug spray may be a simpler and more direct route to reducing people's contact with *Aedes aegypti* and therefore dengue fever.

Alternatives

Genetically engineered mosquitoes are not the only tool available to try and limit the spread of dengue fever and other diseases. Community-based programs that educate communities about dengue prevention and low-cost ways to prevent mosquitoes from breeding are one way disease rates can be brought down. Community-based dengue prevention programs have been found to be successful across the world. For example, a 2005 study in Vietnam found that targeted biological control and community involvement was successful in eliminating *Aedes aegypti* in 32 of the 37 communities studied and as a result, no dengue cases have been reported since 2002. As the World Health Organization has stated, "community is the key to dengue prevention." What worked in Vietnam might not work in the Florida Keys and while community-based programs are not the only answer they do show that sometimes solutions can be low-cost, low-risk social innovations rather than expensive, patented technologies.

Bed nets may be a relatively cheap and effective way to prevent the spread of dengue fever. Preliminary results from a trial in Haiti found that insecticide-treated bed nets led to an immediate drop in dengue-carrying mosquito populations, despite the fact that these mosquitoes bite during the day. Treating other household materials with insecticides, such as window curtains and water jar-covers, was successful in significantly reducing *Aedes aegypti* numbers in a study conducted in Venezuela.

Recent research has even found that infecting mosquitoes with an engineered strain of the common bacteria, *Wolbachia pipientis*, completely prevents the dengue virus from growing in mosquitoes. Field trials in a remote part of Australia found that after releasing 300,000 infected adult mosquitoes, nearly all the wild mosquitoes tested were infected with the bacteria ten weeks later.

While there is currently no vaccine or cure for dengue fever, a dengue vaccine may become a reality in the next few years. According to the Health Ministry in Malaysia, a dengue vaccine is currently in its last trial phase and is expected to be released by 2014 or 2015. Sanofi Pasteur, the vaccines division of pharmaceutical giant Sanofi-aventis Group, has partnered with the International Vaccine Institute and the World Health Organization, among others, to develop its own dengue vaccine. The company is also in the final stage of testing its vaccine and is conducting clinical studies around the world. Clinical trials for vaccines, unlike the potential field release of GE mosquitoes in the U.S., must undergo years of testing to ensure the vaccine works and is safe.

While such experiments may carry their own unique risks (human health risks due to exposure to insecticides, mosquitoes growing a resistance to those insecticides, and unknown risks from the Wolbachia bacteria) they illustrate that there exists innovative ways to tackle dengue fever that do not involve expensive and risky genetic engineering technologies. In the end there will likely be no single "silver bullet" in fighting dengue fever since insect populations and the spread of disease are part of a much more complex ecosystem that will require numerous approaches in which communities are not just consulted but are integral actors.

Conclusion

Despite Oxitec's claims, questions still remain as to whether GE mosquitoes are safe for the environment, safe for people or are even effective in fighting the spread of dengue fever. While the goal of limiting the spread of disease is laudable, too many questions remain to allow the release of genetically engineered mosquitoes in the U.S.

The federal government and the state of Florida must be open and transparent throughout any deliberations on whether or not to allow Oxitec to release GE mosquitoes in Key West or anywhere in Florida. Our government must require the company to obtain the free and informed consent of the Florida community before any trial is allowed to move forward and mechanisms should be made available to halt the experiment if the community demands. Oxitec must not be allowed to repeat its mistakes in the Cayman Islands and Malaysia where it released mosquitoes without public knowledge or consent.

Comprehensive and independent analyses of the risks GE mosquitoes may pose to the environment and human health must be conducted and released to the public with ample time for review before any trial begins. These assessments must look at:

- The ecological risks of released GE mosquitoes including the risk of disrupting food chains or providing a new ecological niche more dangerous insects to take the place of *Aedes aegypti*;

- The risks of releasing biting females, including possible increased risk of allergic reactions if people are bitten;
- The risks associated with mosquitoes surviving into adulthood if tetracycline is present in the surrounding environment;
- The risk from the unintentional release of GE mosquitoes into the environment due to a natural disaster, wear-and-tear or human error;
- Potential adverse impacts the release of GE mosquitoes may have on the ability of dengue fever to evolve and become more virulent or the likelihood of the released mosquitoes leading to increases in disease transmission;
- The full range of impacts from releasing millions of mosquitoes on a regular basis;
- The consequences of ending a GE mosquito program would have for mosquito populations and disease, as well as the economic impacts on countries and communities that are indefinitely dependent on Oxitec for GE mosquito eggs to fight dengue fever; and
- Alternatives to using GE mosquitoes as a way to limit the spread of dengue fever such as bed nets, community-based prevention programs and other biological tools that do not depend on expensive and risky genetic engineering technologies.

Additionally, Oxitec must be legally liable in case something goes wrong with the field release of its GE mosquitoes. If its actions harm the environmental or public health, Oxitec must be legally responsible for the damages and must compensate the communities. It must also be required to repair the damage it caused to the greatest extent possible.

Until such studies have been independently completed and made available to the public, it is premature to allow the release of GE mosquitoes in the U.S. or elsewhere. The burden of proof rests with Oxitec to show the public its mosquitoes are safe. Until that burden of proof is met GE mosquitoes must remain inside the lab.

ERIC HOFFMAN was a biotechnology policy campaigner, Friends of the Earth U.S., when he wrote his selection. He is now a graduate student in the University of Maryland's School of Public Policy.

EXPLORING THE ISSUE

Should Genetically Engineered Mosquitoes Be Released into the Environment to Fight Disease?

Critical Thinking and Reflection

1. The *Aedes aegypti* mosquito that spreads the dengue virus is an invasive species, originally from Africa. It is thus not a native or natural part of American and Asian ecosystems. Does this make the effect of removing it from such ecosystems of less concern?
2. Imagine an area that has no history of dengue fever but that does have an ample population of *Aedes aegypti* mosquitoes. Does the arrival of a traveler infected with the dengue virus pose a problem?
3. Researchers are working on a vaccine against the dengue virus, and they are making progress. Instead of releasing genetically engineered mosquitoes, should we wait for the vaccine?
4. At the end of 2015, reports of microcephaly in newborns, possibly due to a virus (Zika) carried by *Aedes aegypti* mosquitoes, made the news (e.g., https://www.washingtonpost.com/news/to-your-health/wp/2015/12/23 /brazil-declares-emergency-after-2400-babies-are-born-with-brain-damage-possibly-due-to-mosquito-borne -virus/). Presumably this disease too could be controlled by releasing Oxitec's genetically engineered mosquitoes. If so, does this strengthen the case for releases?

Is There Common Ground?

Both sides in this issue agree that mosquito-borne diseases such as dengue and malaria are a threat to human health, traditional methods of mosquito control (including pesticides) still have a role to play, and even that genetically engineered mosquitoes may be a useful additional tool. They differ in how much to worry about possible risks to the environment and public health, with FOE calling for a great deal more research into potential safety issues.

1. Part of the reason for demanding more safety research seems to be that genetically engineered mosquitoes are being viewed as the equivalent of a drug that, if given to human beings, might have undesirable effects. Is it really appropriate to view genetically engineered mosquitoes in this way? Why or why not?
2. It is probably impossible, by any method, to eliminate a mosquito population or species totally. Yet it is possible to reduce a population. An important question is how much to reduce. When we are talking about disease transmission by mosquitoes,

that depends on how many cases of disease we—as a community or society—are willing to accept. How do we answer *that* question?
3. One of the objections of Friends of the Earth to genetically engineered mosquitoes is that they are patented and their use locks a community into a future of continuing payments to the patent owner. How does this differ from the use of insecticides, vaccines, or drugs that successfully treat a disease?

Additional Resources

J. Marshall Clark and Jeffrey Bloomquist, *Advances in Human Vector Control* (ACS Symposium Series) (American Chemical Society, 2010).

V. A. Dyck, J. Hendrichs, and A. S. Robinson (eds.), *Sterile Insect Technique: Principles and Practice in Area-Wide Integrated Pest Management* (Springer, 2005).

Andrew Spielman and Michael D'Antonio, *Mosquito: The Story of Man's Deadliest Foe* (Hachette, 2002).

Internet References . . .

Eliminate Dengue

http://www.eliminatedengue.com/program

Friends of the Earth

http://www.foe.org/

World Health Organization Fact Sheets for Malaria, Dengue, Chikungunya, West Nile, Yellow Fever

http://www.who.int/mediacentre/factsheets/fs094/en/

http://www.who.int/mediacentre/factsheets/fs117/en/

http://www.who.int/mediacentre/factsheets/fs327/en/

http://www.who.int/mediacentre/factsheets/fs354/en/

http://www.who.int/mediacentre/factsheets/fs100/en/

Selected, Edited, and with Issue Framing Material by:
Thomas A. Easton, *Mount Ida College*

ISSUE

Is Gene-Editing of Human Embryos Coming Soon?

YES: Antonio Regalado, from "Engineering the Perfect Baby," *MIT Technology Review* (2015)

NO: Elizabeth McNally, from "Testimony before the U.S. House of Representatives Committee on Science, Space, and Technology, Subcommittee on Research and Technology, Hearing on 'The Science and Ethics of Genetically Engineered Human DNA,'" U.S. House of Representatives (2015)

Learning Outcomes

After reading this issue, you will be able to:

- Explain what genetic engineering is.
- Explain how CRISPR technology makes genetic engineering easier.
- Describe the potential benefits of gene-editing of human embryos.
- Discuss the ethical dilemmas posed by this technology.

ISSUE SUMMARY

YES: Antonio Regalado describes recent progress in using the new CRISPR technology to edit the genes of mammalian cells, including embryos. He argues that although many people involved in the research are cautious, what was until recently only a theoretical possibility is now a very real possibility. We are very close to being able to engineer the genes of human embryos (for a variety of reasons) and most people have no idea of what is coming.

NO: Elizabeth McNally agrees that the technology is developing rapidly and has much to offer but is more reserved in her evaluation. She argues that it is necessary to regulate the technology and its uses, including limiting or prohibiting uses where changes would be passed to the next generation. However, "the justified use of this approach is certainly conceivable and may one day be appropriate."

In the early 1970s, scientists first discovered that it was technically possible to move genes—biological material that determines a living organism's physical makeup—from one organism to another and thus (in principle) to give bacteria, plants, and animals new features and to correct genetic defects of the sort that cause many diseases, such as cystic fibrosis. Most researchers in molecular genetics were excited by the potentialities that suddenly seemed within their grasp. However, a few researchers—as well as many people outside the field—were disturbed by the idea. Among other things, they feared that we were on the verge of an era when people would be so modified that they were no longer human. Some critics were also suspicious of the researchers' motives. Andrew Kimbrell, *The Human Body Shop: The Engineering and Marketing of Life* (HarperSanFrancisco, 1993), thought the development of genetic engineering was so marked by scandal, ambition, and moral blindness that society should be deeply suspicious of its purported benefits.

Since then the idea that human beings will one day be enhanced has grown. The idea now encompasses genetic changes to cure or prevent disease and modify height, muscle strength, and cognitive capabilities, the use of chemicals to improve performance in sports, and even the incorporation in the human body of electronic and robotic elements to add senses and enhance memory, thinking abilities, strength, and a great deal more. In fact, the idea has become a movement known as transhumanism that "promotes an interdisciplinary approach to understanding and evaluating the opportunities for enhancing the human condition and the human organism opened up by the advancement of technology." The goal is to eliminate aging, disease, and suffering. The transhumanist vision extends to "post-humanism," when what human beings become will make present-day humans look like chimpanzees by comparison. It even includes the possibility of uploading human minds into computers, although A. N. Poddyakov, "Can We Copy the Mind? Disputing with Transhumanism," *Cultural-Historical Psychology* (2013), thinks copying the mind unlikely to be possible. On the other hand, Jessica Roy, "The Rapture of the Nerds," *Time* (April 19, 2014), describes a "new religion" that proposes to transmit mind-copies into space in hope that benevolent aliens will someday copy them back into bodies.

Some people find this vision frightening. Francis Fukuyama, "Transhumanism," *Foreign Policy* (September/October 2004), has called transhumanism "the world's most dangerous idea." Critics find changing human form and capability objectionable because they believe the result is in some sense unnatural. They believe that making some people more capable will exacerbate social distinctions and put those who can afford the changes in the position of old-fashioned aristocracies. Life will be even more unfair than it is today. Tom Koch, "Enhancing Who? Enhancing What? Ethics, Bioethics, and Transhumanism," *Journal of Medicine & Philosophy* (December 2010), finds transhumanism "a new riff on the old eugenics tune," and the result must be destructive.

It's not just a matter of changing our genes. Josh Fischman, "A Better Life with Bionics," *National Geographic* (January 2010), describes current work in developing prostheses controlled by nerve signals from nerves that have been surgically rerouted to communicate more effectively with the artificial limb's circuitry, a clear example of "improvement" of the human being. He also discusses electronic cochlear implants and artificial retinas. An accompanying editorial comment says that "Bionics is technology at its most ingenious and humane." Among the most recent developments in this line is an electronic implant that can give the paralyzed robotic arms; see Ian Sample, "Brain Implant Allows Paralysed Woman to Control a Robot with Her Thoughts," *The Guardian* (May 16, 2012) (http://www.guardian.co.uk/science/2012/may/16/brain-implant-paralysed-woman-robot-thoughts).

Among those who favor such changes in the human condition, few come through more strongly than James Hughes, executive director of the Institute for Ethics and Emerging Technologies (http://ieet.org/). He has argued vigorously that enhancement technologies such as genetic engineering offer "such good that the risks are dwarfed" and finds "faith in the potential unlimited improvability of human nature and expansion of human powers far more satisfying than a resignation to our current limits." See his "Embracing Change with All Four Arms: A Post-Humanist Defense of Genetic Engineering," *Eubios: Journal of Asian and International Bioethics* (June 1996). David Gelles, "Immortality 2.0," *The Futurist* (January–February 2009), concludes that "skepticism of transhumanism is, arguably, natural. At the deepest level, living forever interferes with everything we understand about the world. . . . But such concerns may not matter anymore." The change is already under way, and we may be underestimating how far it will go. See also Jonathan Weiner, *Long for This World: The Strange Science of Immortality* (Ecco, 2010). However, A. Rajczi, "One Danger of Biomedical Enhancements," *Bioethics* (July 2008), cautions that "By spending too much time, energy, and resources on enhancements, we could set back our pursuit of our deepest goals such as living happily and leading ethical lives." On the other hand, human enhancement will have a serious impact on what we mean by diversity and inclusion; see Enno Park, "Ethical Issues in Cyborg Technology: Diversity and Inclusion," *NanoEthics* (December 2014).

One way in which the change is already upon us appears in the realm of sports. Steven Kotler, "Juicing 3.0," *Popular Science* (August 2008), notes that the use by athletes of many enhancement techniques—reaction time stimulants, hormones that affect muscle growth and strength, gene replacement, and even mechanical replacements for missing limbs—are going to become commonplace in the next few years. It may be necessary to accept enhancements as a legitimate part of athletics and other realms of endeavor. See Ivo Van Hilvoorde and Laurens Landeweerd, "Enhancing Disabilities: Transhumanism under the Veil of Inclusion?" *Disability & Rehabilitation* (December 2010), and Brendan Burkett, Mike McNamee, and Wolfgand Potthast, "Shifting Boundaries in Sports Technology and Disability: Equal Rights or Unfair Advantage in the Case of Oscar Pistorius?" *Disability & Society* (August 2011).

Engineering genetic changes is further off, but perhaps not that far off. Early in 2015, a team of sixteen researchers at Sun Yat-Sen University in Guangzhou, China, led by Junjiu Huang reported success in modifying genes in human embryos (deliberately chosen as nonviable) (see Puping Liang et al., "CRISPR/Cas9-Mediated Gene Editing in Human Tripronuclear Zygotes," *Protein & Cell*, May 2015). Even before this paper was published, the grapevine was provoking extreme concern. There were calls for a moratorium or even a ban on research in this area. Other reactions recognized the good that this technology could accomplish but worried about side effects and abuses. George Church, of Harvard Medical School, quipped "What is the scenario that we're actually worried about? That it won't work well enough? Or that it will work too well?" (See Gretchen Vogel, "Embryo Engineering Alarm," *Science*, March 20, 2015.)

Once the Chinese paper appeared, it was clear that the gene-editing did not work perfectly. Genes were not always inserted where the researchers wished them to go. There was thus the possibility of serious side effects. Yet the alarm did not diminish. Scientists divided on whether research should be allowed to go forward (Jocelyn Kaiser and Dennis Normile, "Embryo Engineering Study Splits Scientific Community," *Science*, May 1, 2015), with some calling for a moratorium. Within a month, David Baltimore et al., "A Prudent Path Forward for Genomic Engineering and Germline Gene Modification," *Science* (April 1, 2015), called for extensive discussion involving all interested parties. In the short term, they recommended that any actual attempts to apply the technology in a clinical setting be strongly discouraged; that forums be established where experts can discuss the ethical, social, and legal implications; that transparent research be encouraged and supported to properly inform those expert discussions; and that the discussions should be global. At about the same time, the United States Office of Science and Technology Policy announced that "The White House fully supports a robust review of the ethical issues associated with using gene-editing technology to alter the human germline. The Administration believes that altering the human germline for clinical purposes is a line that should not be crossed at this time" (John P. Holdren, "A Note on Genome Editing"; https://www.whitehouse.gov/blog/2015/05/26/note-genome-editing). Some people are calling for an outright ban on the technology; see Steve Connor, "Gene-Editing Embryos Should Be Banned to Prevent 'Genetically-Enhanced Children,'" *The Independent*, September 18, 2015; http://www.independent.co.uk/news/science/geneediting-embryos-should-be-banned-to-prevent-geneticallyenhanced-children-scientists-warn-10507860.html. On the other hand, Henry I. Miller and Drew L. Kershen, "Give Genetic Engineering Some Breathing Room," *Issues in Science and Technology* (Winter 2015), argue that genetic engineering in general is already heavily overregulated, largely because regulators are driven more by fear than by any sense of actual risk; we need better, more risk-based alternatives.

Antonio Regalado, "Everything You Need to Know About CRISPR Gene Editing's Monster Year," *Technology Review* (December 1, 2015) (http://www.technologyreview.com/news/543941/everything-you-need-to-know-about-crispr-gene-editings-monster-year/), points out that the technology is advancing very rapidly and the first home genetic engineering kit is already on the market. In December 2015, the National Academies of Science held an "International Summit on Human Gene Editing" (see Joel Achenbach, "Scientists Debate the Ethics of an Unnerving Gene-Editing Technique," *Washington Post*, December 1, 2015; https://www.washingtonpost.com/news/speaking-of-science/wp/2015/12/01/historic-summit-on-gene-editing-and-designer-babies-convenes-in-washington/). Some initial reports had an alarmist tone, but the intent was more measured (to address "issues such as the current state of the science and available technologies; the rationale[s] for and potential benefits and risks inherent in conducting such research and in potential applications; existing [as well as potentially needed] regulatory principles, standards, or guidance for such research and potential applications; ethical concerns; legal considerations; and ways to engage critical stakeholders"; see http://www.nationalacademies.org/gene-editing/gene_167925). At least some of those who suffer from inherited disorders, however, are eager to be able to keep from passing the disorders to their children; see Antonio Ragalado, "Patients Favor Changing the Genes of the Next Generation with CRISPR," *Technology Review* (December 2, 2015) (http://www.technologyreview.com/news/544141/patients-favor-changing-the-genes-of-the-next-generation-with-crispr/?utm_campaign=newsletters&utm_source=newsletter-daily-all&utm_medium=email&utm_content=20151203). However, one outcome of the December summit is a statement by the gathered gene-editing experts that patients will have to wait: "it would be 'irresponsible' to attempt to create gene-modified babies until the safety of the idea can be established, and until there is broad social consensus on whether such a step is desirable." See Antonio Regalado, "Scientists on Gene-Edited Babies: It's 'Irresponsible' for Now," *Technology Review* (December 3. 2015) (http://www.technologyreview.com/news/544161/scientists-on-gene-edited-babies-its-irresponsible-for-now/?utm_campaign=newsletters&utm_source=newsletter-daily-all&utm_medium=email&utm_content=20151204). See also "On Human Gene Editing: International Summit Statement" (December 3, 2015) (http://www8.nationalacademies.org/onpinews/newsitem.aspx?RecordID=12032015a&et_rid=49213837&et_cid=146252) and John Travis, "Germline Editing Dominates DNA Summit," *Science* (December 11, 2015).

In the YES selection, writing *before* the Chinese paper appeared, Antonio Regalado describes recent progress in using the new CRISPR technology to edit the genes of mammalian cells, including embryos. He argues that although many people involved in the research are cautious, what was until recently only a theoretical possibility is now a very real possibility. We are very close to being able to engineer the genes of human embryos (for a variety of reasons) and most people have no idea of what is coming. In the NO selection, Elizabeth McNally agrees that the technology is developing rapidly and has much to offer but is more reserved in her evaluation. She argues that it is necessary to regulate the technology and its uses, including limiting or prohibiting uses where changes would be passed to the next generation. However, "the justified use of this approach is certainly conceivable and may one day be appropriate."

YES

Antonio Regalado

Engineering the Perfect Baby

Why It Matters

New gene-editing techniques make it possible to precisely modify human DNA.

If anyone had devised a way to create a genetically engineered baby, I figured George Church would know about it.

At his labyrinthine laboratory on the Harvard Medical School campus, you can find researchers giving *E. coli* a novel genetic code never seen in nature. Around another bend, others are carrying out a plan to use DNA engineering to resurrect the woolly mammoth. His lab, Church likes to say, is the center of a new technological genesis—one in which man rebuilds creation to suit himself.

When I visited the lab last June, Church proposed that I speak to a young postdoctoral scientist named Luhan Yang. A Harvard recruit from Beijing, she'd been a key player in developing a powerful new technology for editing DNA, called CRISPR-Cas9. With Church, Yang had founded a small biotechnology company to engineer the genomes of pigs and cattle, sliding in beneficial genes and editing away bad ones.

As I listened to Yang, I waited for a chance to ask my real questions: Can any of this be done to human beings? Can we improve the human gene pool? The position of much of mainstream science has been that such meddling would be unsafe, irresponsible, and even impossible. But Yang didn't hesitate. Yes, of course, she said. In fact, the Harvard laboratory had a project under way to determine how it could be achieved. She flipped open her laptop to a PowerPoint slide titled "Germline Editing Meeting."

Here it was: a technical proposal to alter human heredity. "Germ line" is biologists' jargon for the egg and sperm, which combine to form an embryo. By editing the DNA of these cells or the embryo itself, it could be possible to correct disease genes and pass those genetic fixes on to future generations. Such a technology could be used to rid families of scourges like cystic fibrosis. It might also be possible to install genes that offer lifelong protection against infection, Alzheimer's, and, Yang told me, maybe the effects of aging. Such history-making medical advances could be as important to this century as vaccines were to the last.

That's the promise. The fear is that germ-line engineering is a path toward a dystopia of superpeople and designer babies for those who can afford it. Want a child with blue eyes and blond hair? Why not design a highly intelligent group of people who could be tomorrow's leaders and scientists?

Just three years after its initial development, CRISPR technology is already widely used by biologists as a kind of search-and-replace tool to alter DNA, even down to the level of a single letter. It's so precise that it's expected to turn into a promising new approach for gene therapy in people with devastating illnesses. The idea is that physicians could directly correct a faulty gene, say, in the blood cells of a patient with sickle-cell anemia. But that kind of gene therapy wouldn't affect germ cells, and the changes in the DNA wouldn't get passed to future generations.

In contrast, the genetic changes created by germ-line engineering would be passed on, and that's what has made the idea seem so objectionable. So far, caution and ethical concerns have had the upper hand. A dozen countries, not including the United States, have banned germ-line engineering, and scientific societies have unanimously concluded that it would be too risky to do. The European Union's convention on human rights and biomedicine says tampering with the gene pool would be a crime against "human dignity" and human rights.

But all these declarations were made before it was actually feasible to precisely engineer the germ line. Now, with CRISPR, it is possible.

The experiment Yang described, though not simple, would go like this: The researchers hoped to obtain, from a hospital in New York, the ovaries of a woman undergoing surgery for ovarian cancer caused by a mutation in a gene called *BRCA1*. Working with another Harvard laboratory, that of antiaging specialist David Sinclair, they would extract immature egg cells that could be coaxed to grow and divide in the laboratory. Yang would use CRISPR in these cells to correct the DNA of the *BRCA1* gene. They would try to create a viable egg without the genetic error that caused the woman's cancer.

Yang would later tell me that she dropped out of the project not long after we spoke. Yet it remained difficult to know if the experiment she described was occurring, canceled, or awaiting publication. Sinclair said that a collaboration between the two labs was ongoing, but then, like several other scientists whom I'd asked about germ-line engineering, he stopped replying to my e-mails.

Regardless of the fate of that particular experiment, human germ-line engineering has become a burgeoning research concept. At least three other centers in the United States are working on it, as are scientists in China, in the U.K., and at a biotechnology company called OvaScience, based in Cambridge, Massachusetts, that boasts some of the world's leading fertility doctors on its advisory board. . . .

The objective of these groups is to demonstrate that it's possible to produce children free of specific genes involved in inherited disease. If it's possible to correct the DNA in a woman's egg, or a man's sperm, those cells could be used in an in vitro fertilization (IVF) clinic to produce an embryo and then a child. It might also be possible to directly edit the DNA of an early-stage IVF embryo using CRISPR. Several people interviewed by *MIT Technology Review* said that such experiments had already been carried out in China and that results describing edited embryos were pending publication. These people, including two high-ranking specialists, didn't wish to comment publicly because the papers are under review.

All this means that germ-line engineering is much further along than anyone imagined. "What you are talking about is a major issue for all humanity," says Merle Berger, one of the founders of Boston IVF, a network of fertility clinics that is among the largest in the world and helps more than a thousand women get pregnant each year. "It would be the biggest thing that ever happened in our field." Berger predicts that repairing genes involved in serious inherited diseases will win wide public acceptance but says the idea of using the technology beyond that would cause a public uproar because "everyone would want the perfect child": people might pick and choose eye color and eventually intelligence. "These are things we talk about all the time," he says. "But we have never had the opportunity to do it."

Editing Embryos

How easy would it be to edit a human embryo using CRISPR? Very easy, experts say. "Any scientist with molecular biology skills and knowledge of how to work with [embryos] is going to be able to do this," says Jennifer Doudna, a biologist at the University of California,

Berkeley, who in 2012 co-discovered how to use CRISPR to edit genes.

To find out how it could be done, I visited the lab of Guoping Feng, a biologist at MIT's McGovern Institute for Brain Research, where a colony of marmoset monkeys is being established with the aim of using CRISPR to create accurate models of human brain diseases. To create the models, Feng will edit the DNA of embryos and then transfer them into female marmosets to produce live monkeys. One gene Feng hopes to alter in the animals is *SHANK3*. The gene is involved in how neurons communicate; when it's damaged in children, it is known to cause autism.

Feng said that before CRISPR, it was not possible to introduce precise changes into a primate's DNA. With CRISPR, the technique should be relatively straightforward. The CRISPR system includes a gene-snipping enzyme and a guide molecule that can be programmed to target unique combinations of the DNA letters, A, G, C, and T; get these ingredients into a cell and they will cut and modify the genome at the targeted sites.

But CRISPR is not perfect—and it would be a very haphazard way to edit human embryos, as Feng's efforts to create gene-edited marmosets show. To employ the CRISPR system in the monkeys, his students simply inject the chemicals into a fertilized egg, which is known as a zygote—the stage just before it starts dividing.

Feng said the efficiency with which CRISPR can delete or disable a gene in a zygote is about 40 percent, whereas making specific edits, or swapping DNA letters, works less frequently—more like 20 percent of the time. Like a person, a monkey has two copies of most genes, one from each parent. Sometimes both copies get edited, but sometimes just one does, or neither. Only about half the embryos will lead to live births, and of those that do, many could contain a mixture of cells with edited DNA and without. If you add up the odds, you find you'd need to edit 20 embryos to get a live monkey with the version you want.

That's not an insurmountable problem for Feng, since the MIT breeding colony will give him access to many monkey eggs and he'll be able to generate many embryos. However, it would present obvious problems in humans. Putting the ingredients of CRISPR into a human embryo would be scientifically trivial. But it wouldn't be practical for much just yet. This is one reason that many scientists view such an experiment (whether or not it has really occurred in China) with scorn, seeing it more as a provocative bid to grab attention than as real science. Rudolf Jaenisch, an MIT biologist who works across the street from Feng and who in the 1970s created the first gene-modified mice, calls attempts to edit human embryos "totally premature." He says he hopes these papers will be rejected and not published. "It's just a sensational thing that will stir things up," says Jaenisch. "We know it's possible, but is it of practical use? I kind of doubt it."

For his part, Feng told me he approves of the idea of germ-line engineering. Isn't the goal of medicine to reduce suffering? Considering the state of the technology, however, he thinks actual gene-edited humans are "10 to 20 years away." Among other problems, CRISPR can introduce off-target effects or change bits of the genome far from where scientists had intended. Any human embryo altered with CRISPR today would carry the risk that its genome had been changed in unexpected ways. But, Feng said, such problems may eventually be ironed out, and edited people will be born. "To me, it's possible in the long run to dramatically improve health, lower costs. It's a kind of prevention," he said. "It's hard to predict the future, but correcting disease risks is definitely a possibility and should be supported. I think it will be a reality."

Editing Eggs

Elsewhere in the Boston area, scientists are exploring a different approach to engineering the germ line, one that is technically more demanding but probably more powerful. This strategy combines CRISPR with unfolding discoveries related to stem cells. Scientists at several centers, including Church's, think they will soon be able to use stem cells to produce eggs and sperm in the laboratory. Unlike embryos, stem cells can be grown and multiplied. Thus they could offer a vastly improved way to create edited offspring with CRISPR. The recipe goes like this: First, edit the genes of the stem cells. Second, turn them into an egg or sperm. Third, produce an offspring.

Some investors got an early view of the technique on December 17, at the Benjamin Hotel in Manhattan, during commercial presentations by OvaScience. The company, which was founded four years ago, aims to commercialize the scientific work of David Sinclair, who is based at Harvard, and Jonathan Tilly, an expert on egg stem cells and the chairman of the biology department at Northeastern University. It made the presentations as part of a successful effort to raise $132 million in new capital during January.

During the meeting, Sinclair, a velvet-voiced Australian whom *Time* last year named one of the "100 Most Influential People in the World," took the podium and provided Wall Street with a peek at what he called "truly world-changing" developments. People would look back at this moment in time and recognize it as a new chapter in "how humans control their bodies," he said,

because it would let parents determine "when and how they have children and how healthy those children are actually going to be."

The company has not perfected its stem-cell technology—it has not reported that the eggs it grows in the lab are viable—but Sinclair predicted that functional eggs were "a when, and not an if." Once the technology works, he said, infertile women will be able to produce hundreds of eggs, and maybe hundreds of embryos. Using DNA sequencing to analyze their genes, they could pick among them for the healthiest ones.

Genetically improved children may also be possible. Sinclair told the investors that he was trying to alter the DNA of these egg stem cells using gene editing, work he later told me he was doing with Church's lab. "We think the new technologies with genome editing will allow it to be used on individuals who aren't just interested in using IVF to have children but have healthier children as well, if there is a genetic disease in their family," Sinclair told the investors. He gave the example of Huntington's disease, caused by a gene that will trigger a fatal brain condition even in someone who inherits only one copy. Sinclair said gene editing could be used to remove the lethal gene defect from an egg cell. His goal, and that of OvaScience, is to "correct those mutations before we generate your child," he said. "It's still experimental, but there is no reason to expect it won't be possible in coming years."

Sinclair spoke to me briefly on the phone while he was navigating in a cab across a snowed-in Boston, but later he referred my questions to OvaScience. When I contacted OvaScience, Cara Mayfield, a spokeswoman, said its executives could not comment because of their travel schedules but confirmed that the company was working on treating inherited disorders with gene editing. What was surprising to me was that OvaScience's research in "crossing the germ line," as critics of human engineering sometimes put it, has generated scarcely any notice. In December of 2013, OvaScience even announced it was putting $1.5 million into a joint venture with a synthetic biology company called Intrexon, whose R&D objectives include gene-editing eggs to "prevent the propagation" of human disease "in future generations."

When I reached Tilly at Northeastern, he laughed when I told him what I was calling about. "It's going to be a hot-button issue," he said. Tilly also said his lab was trying to edit egg stem cells with CRISPR "right now" to rid them of an inherited genetic disease that he didn't want to name. Tilly emphasized that there are "two pieces of the puzzle"—one being stem cells and the other gene editing. The ability to create large numbers of egg stem cells is critical, because only with sizable quantities can genetic changes be stably introduced using CRISPR, characterized using DNA sequencing, and carefully studied to check for mistakes before producing an egg.

Tilly predicted that the whole end-to-end technology—cells to stem cells, stem cells to sperm or egg and then to offspring—would end up being worked out first in animals, such as cattle, either by his lab or by companies such as eGenesis, the spinoff from the Church lab working on livestock. But he isn't sure what the next step should be with edited human eggs. You wouldn't want to fertilize one "willy nilly," he said. You'd be making a potential human being. And doing that would raise questions he's not sure he can answer. He told me, "'Can you do it?' is one thing. If you can, then the most important questions come up. 'Would you do it? Why would you want to do it? What is the purpose?' As scientists we want to know if it's feasible, but then we get into the bigger questions, and it's not a science question—it's a society question."

Improving Humans

If germ-line engineering becomes part of medical practice, it could lead to transformative changes in human well-being, with consequences to people's life span, identity, and economic output. But it would create ethical dilemmas and social challenges. What if these improvements were available only to the richest societies, or the richest people? An in vitro fertility procedure costs about $20,000 in the United States. Add genetic testing and egg donation or a surrogate mother, and the price soars toward $100,000.

Others believe the idea is dubious because it's not medically necessary. Hank Greely, a lawyer and ethicist at Stanford University, says proponents "can't really say what it is good for." The problem, says Greely, is that it's already possible to test the DNA of IVF embryos and pick healthy ones, a process that adds about $4,000 to the cost of a fertility procedure. A man with Huntington's, for instance, could have his sperm used to fertilize a dozen of his partner's eggs. Half those embryos would not have the Huntington's gene, and those could be used to begin a pregnancy.

Indeed, some people are adamant that germ-line engineering is being pushed ahead with "false arguments." That is the view of Edward Lanphier, CEO of Sangamo Biosciences, a California biotechnology company that is using another gene-editing technique, called zinc fingers nucleases, to try to treat HIV in adults by altering their blood cells. "We've looked at [germ-line engineering] for a disease rationale, and there is none," he says. "You can do it. But there really isn't a medical reason. People say,

well, we don't want children born with this, or born with that—but it's a completely false argument and a slippery slope toward much more unacceptable uses."

Critics cite a host of fears. Children would be the subject of experiments. Parents would be influenced by genetic advertising from IVF clinics. Germ-line engineering would encourage the spread of allegedly superior traits. And it would affect people not yet born, without their being able to agree to it. The American Medical Association, for instance, holds that germ-line engineering shouldn't be done "at this time" because it "affects the welfare of future generations" and could cause "unpredictable and irreversible results." But like a lot of official statements that forbid changing the genome, the AMA's, which was last updated in 1996, predates today's technology. "A lot of people just agreed to these statements," says Greely. "It wasn't hard to renounce something that you couldn't do." . . .

Others predict that hard-to-oppose medical uses will be identified. A couple with several genetic diseases at once might not be able to find a suitable embryo. Treating infertility is another possibility. Some men don't produce any sperm, a condition called azoospermia. One cause is a genetic defect in which a region of about one million to six million DNA letters is missing from the Y chromosome. It might be possible to take a skin cell from such a man, turn it into a stem cell, repair the DNA, and then make sperm, says Werner Neuhausser, a young Austrian doctor who splits his time between the Boston IVF fertility-clinic network and Harvard's Stem Cell Institute. "That will change medicine forever, right? You could cure infertility, that is for sure," he says.

I spoke with Church several times by telephone over the last few months, and he told me what's driving everything is the "incredible specificity" of CRISPR. Although not all the details have been worked out, he thinks the technology could replace DNA letters essentially without side effects. He says this is what makes it "tempting to use." Church says his laboratory is focused mostly on experiments in engineering animals. He added that his lab would not make or edit human embryos, calling such a step "not our style."

What is Church's style is human enhancement. And he's been making a broad case that CRISPR can do more than eliminate disease genes. It can lead to augmentation. At meetings, some involving groups of "transhumanists" interested in next steps for human evolution, Church likes to show a slide on which he lists naturally occurring variants of around 10 genes that, when people are born with them, confer extraordinary qualities or resistance to disease. One makes your bones so hard they'll break a surgical drill. Another drastically cuts the risk of heart attacks. And a variant of the gene for the amyloid precursor protein, or APP, was found by Icelandic researchers to protect against Alzheimer's. People with it never get dementia and remain sharp into old age.

Church thinks CRISPR could be used to provide people with favorable versions of genes, making DNA edits that would act as vaccines against some of the most common diseases we face today. Although he told me anything "edgy" should be done only to adults who can consent, it's obvious to him that the earlier such interventions occur, the better.

Church tends to dodge questions about genetically modified babies. The idea of improving the human species has always had "enormously bad press," he wrote in the introduction to *Regenesis,* his 2012 book on synthetic biology, whose cover was a painting by Eustache Le Sueur of a bearded God creating the world. But that's ultimately what he's suggesting: enhancements in the form of protective genes. "An argument will be made that the ultimate prevention is that the earlier you go, the better the prevention," he told an audience at MIT's Media Lab last spring. "I do think it's the ultimate preventive, *if* we get to the point where it's very inexpensive, extremely safe, and very predictable." Church, who has a less cautious side, proceeded to tell the audience that he thought changing genes "is going to get to the point where it's like you are doing the equivalent of cosmetic surgery."

Some thinkers have concluded that we should not pass up the chance to make improvements to our species. "The human genome is not perfect," says John Harris, a bioethicist at Manchester University, in the U.K. "It's ethically imperative to positively support this technology." By some measures, U.S. public opinion is not particularly negative toward the idea. A Pew Research survey carried out last August found that 46 percent of adults approved of genetic modification of babies to reduce the risk of serious diseases.

The same survey found that 83 percent said genetic modification to make a baby smarter would be "taking medical advances too far." But other observers say higher IQ is exactly what we should be considering. Nick Bostrom, an Oxford philosopher best known for his 2014 book *Superintelligence,* which raised alarms about the risks of artificial intelligence in computers, has also looked at whether humans could use reproductive technology to improve human intellect. Although the ways in which genes affect intelligence aren't well understood and there are far too many relevant genes to permit easy engineering, such realities don't dim speculation on the possibility of high-tech eugenics.

What if everyone could be a little bit smarter? Or a few people could be a lot smarter? Even a small number of "super-enhanced" individuals, Bostrom wrote in a 2013 paper, could change the world through their creativity and discoveries, and through innovations that everyone else would use. In his view, genetic enhancement is an important long-range issue like climate change or financial planning by nations, "since human problem-solving ability is a factor in every challenge we face."

To some scientists, the explosive advance of genetics and biotech means germ-line engineering is inevitable. Of course, safety questions would be paramount. Before there's a genetically edited baby saying "Mama," there would have to be tests in rats, rabbits, and probably monkeys, to make sure they are normal. But ultimately, if the benefits seem to outweigh the risks, medicine would take the chance. "It was the same with IVF when it first happened," says Neuhausser. "We never really knew if that baby was going to be healthy at 40 or 50 years. But someone had to take the plunge."

Wine Country

In January, on Saturday the 24th, around 20 scientists, ethicists, and legal experts traveled to Napa Valley, California, for a retreat among the vineyards at the Carneros Inn. They had been convened by Doudna, the Berkeley scientist who co-discovered the CRISPR system a little over two years ago. She had become aware that scientists might be thinking of crossing the germ line, and she was concerned. Now she wanted to know: could they be stopped?

"We as scientists have come to appreciate that CRISPR is incredibly powerful. But that swings both ways. We need to make sure that it's applied carefully," Doudna told me. "The issue is especially human germ-line editing and the appreciation that this is now a capability in everyone's hands."

At the meeting, along with ethicists like Greely, was Paul Berg, a Stanford biochemist and Nobel Prize winner known for having organized the Asilomar Conference, a historic 1975 forum at which biologists reached an agreement on how to safely proceed with recombinant DNA, the newly discovered method of splicing DNA into bacteria.

Should there be an Asilomar for germ-line engineering? Doudna thinks so, but the prospects for consensus seem dim. Biotechnology research is now global, involving hundreds of thousands of people. There's no single authority that speaks for science, and no easy way to put the genie back in the bottle. Doudna told me she hoped that if American scientists agreed to a moratorium on human germ-line engineering, it might influence researchers elsewhere in the world to cease their work.

Doudna said she felt that a self-imposed pause should apply not only to making gene-edited babies but also to using CRISPR to alter human embryos, eggs, or sperm—as researchers at Harvard, Northeastern, and OvaScience are doing. "I don't feel that those experiments are appropriate to do right now in human cells that could turn into a person," she told me. "I feel that the research that needs to be done right now is to understand safety, efficacy, and delivery. And I think those experiments can be done in nonhuman systems. I would like to see a lot more work done before it's done for germ-line editing. I would favor a very cautious approach."

Not everyone agrees that germ-line engineering is such a big worry, or that experiments should be padlocked. Greely notes that in the United States, there are piles of regulations to keep lab science from morphing into a genetically modified baby anytime soon. "I would not want to use safety as an excuse for a non-safety-based ban," says Greely, who says he pushed back against talk of a moratorium. But he also says he agreed to sign Doudna's letter, which now reflects the consensus of the group. "Although I don't view this as a crisis moment, I think it's probably about time for us to have this discussion," he says.

(After this article was published online in March, Doudna's editorial appeared in *Science*. Along with Greely, Berg, and 15 others, she called for a global moratorium on any effort to use CRISPR to generate gene-edited children until researchers could determine "what clinical applications, if any, might in the future be deemed permissible." The group, however, endorsed basic research, including applying CRISPR to embryos. The final list of signatories included Church, although he did not attend the Napa meeting.)

As news has spread of germ-line experiments, some biotechnology companies now working on CRISPR have realized that they will have to take a stand. Nessan Bermingham is CEO of Intellia Therapeutics, a Boston startup that raised $15 million last year to develop CRISPR into gene therapy treatments for adults or children. He says germ-line engineering "is not on our commercial radar," and he suggests that his company could use its patents to prevent anyone from commercializing it.

"The technology is in its infancy," he says. "It is not appropriate for people to even be contemplating germ-line applications."

Bermingham told me he never imagined he'd have to be taking a position on genetically modified babies so soon. Modifying human heredity has always been a theoretical possibility. Suddenly it's a real one. But wasn't the point always to understand and control our own biology—to become masters over the processes that created us?

Doudna says she is also thinking about these issues. "It cuts to the core of who we are as people, and it makes you ask if humans should be exercising that kind of power," she told me. "There are moral and ethical issues, but one of the profound questions is just the appreciation that if germ-line editing is conducted in humans, that is changing human evolution." One reason she feels the research should slow down is to give scientists a chance to spend more time explaining what their next steps could be.

"Most of the public," she says, "does not appreciate what is coming."

ANTONIO REGALADO is senior editor for biomedicine for *MIT Technology Review*.

Elizabeth McNally

Testimony before the U.S. House of Representatives Committee on Science, Space, and Technology, Subcommittee on Research and Technology, Hearing on "The Science and Ethics of Genetically Engineered Human DNA"

Introduction

On behalf of Northwestern University, I would like to thank Chairwoman Comstock and Ranking Member Lipinski for inviting me here today to speak at this hearing on Genetically Engineered Human DNA. I would like to also thank the Subcommittee for convening this hearing.

I am the Elizabeth J. Ward Professor of Genetic Medicine, and I direct the Center for Genetic Medicine at Northwestern. I am a cardiologist who specializes in providing care for patients and families with inherited forms of heart disease. I established one of the first Cardiovascular Genetics Clinics in the United States. Over the last decade, we have seen a dramatic increase in available genetic testing, and we now routinely provide genetic diagnosis, risk assessment, and risk reduction of genetic diseases that affect the heart. Many of the inherited diseases that we diagnose and manage are also those that affect muscle. The same gene mutations that cause heart muscle to weaken may elicit the same effect on skeletal muscle, causing those who carry the mutations to develop heart failure, life threatening irregular heart rhythms and muscle weakness. Genetic diagnosis is not restricted to heart and muscle disorders as nearly every area of medicine is influenced by genetic diagnosis.

Genetic Diseases

Diseases like Cystic Fibrosis, Duchenne Muscular Dystrophy, and Sickle Cell are those that are caused by mutations in single genes. It has been possible for some time to genetically diagnose these disorders. There is considerable

effort directed at devising targeted therapies to correct the underlying genetic defects responsible for causing disorders like these, and herein I will discuss the potential application of gene editing techniques for the treatment of genetic diseases.

The first draft human genome sequence was completed just 15 years ago. Now, with advances in DNA sequencing technology it is now possible to sequence an individual human genome in a matter of days. Moreover, human genome sequencing can be completed at comparatively low cost, less than the cost of an MRI, and can be analyzed with high accuracy. It is becoming routine to pinpoint single gene mutations responsible for devastating disorders, including those diseases that affect children. With this explosion in genetic analysis, the number of genetic disorders is increasing. The National Institutes of Health (NIH) Office of Rare Diseases identifies nearly 7000 rare diseases,[1] and many of these are genetic in origin, often arising from single mutations. The ORD estimates that nearly 30 million Americans are affected by rare diseases. More than half of rare diseases affect children.[2]

Gene Editing

Concomitant with advances in genetic diagnoses, there are parallel leaps in genome editing. The concept of genome editing is not new. Genome editing has been technically possible since the first reports of inserting genetic material in fertilized eggs of mice, reported by three independent groups in 1981.[3-5] It was around this very same time that the first successes in human in vitro fertilization were reported.[6] In the more than three decades since genetic

Testimony before the U.S. House of Representatives Committee on Science, Space, and Technology, Subcommittee on Research and Technology, Hearing on "The Science and Ethics of Genetically Engineered Human DNA," U.S. House of Representatives, June 2015.

editing became possible, there has been scientific and technological progress that has improved the proficiency and fidelity of genome editing. Early success in genomic editing relied on random insertion of new DNA sequences into fertilized eggs, stem cells, and cell lines. Random insertion allows new genes to be expressed but does not correct genetic defects. Homologous recombination refers to the process by which sequences can be exchanged between a vector that carries new sequences of insert and the genome to be edited. For most organisms, especially humans, homologous recombination is a remarkably inefficient process. However in other organisms, homologous recombination occurs at much higher rate. Understanding the precise means by which organisms can alter genetic structures has allowed researchers to isolate the machinery that edits genomes. In the last decade, there have been several key discoveries made to improve the ability to precisely change specific sequences. The precision of gene editing remains at the center of these discussions. Precise gene editing refers to producing the desired genetic change, and importantly doing so with high efficiency and with few off target effects.

The most recent advance capitalizes on the tools used by bacteria to ward off viral infection. This newest technology, referred to as CRISPR/Cas9, isolates the sequences and enzymes used by bacteria, and then applies these methods into complex cell types like those in mice, rats and humans.[7] First described in 2012, CRISPR/Cas9 is changing the path and pace of scientific discovery. Research depends on model systems, and model systems include cultured cells, as well as organisms like mice, yeast, flies, worms and other species. Genetically tractable systems are preferred, and mice remain a standard for the field of human biology. Cell models of disease are also highly useful since experiments can be completed with comparative ease and speed. The timeline of discovery is tied tightly to the model system of choice. The importance of CRISPR/Cas9 cannot be overstated. CRISPR/Cas9 offers a precision heretofore unseen. Cells and animals can be manipulated to more precisely to facilitate the ability to ask and answer critically important scientific questions.

Gene Editing in Stem Cells

Alongside these advances in genome editing, it is worthwhile to consider gains in stem cell biology. The application of genome editing goes hand in hand with stem cell biology, and because of this co-evolution of gene editing and stem cell biology, there is significant potential clinical application. The ethics, merits, and implications of human embryonic stem cell biology have been debated and will not be reiterated here. For the purposes of this testimony, it should be acknowledged that some human stem cell lines retain the ability to contribute to human germ cells. In contributing to human germ cells, there is the possibility to transmit stem cell-derived genetic material into new generations. Therefore, genome editing in certain stem cells, in principle, may have the ability to alter human germ lines. However, many stem cells only theoretically have the capacity to contribute to human germ lines. In practice, human stem cells are used in many experiment with no intent or possibility of contributing to human germ lines. Induced pluripotent human stem cells can be made from blood, skin and other mature somatic human cells. Induced pluripotent stem cells, in theory, could contribute to human germ lines but are not used for this purpose. In many laboratories, the true stem cell capacity of such stem lines is never evaluated, even in mice, as the germ line potential is irrelevant to the research.

Embryonic and induced pluripotent stem cells are an obvious venue in which to test and evaluate genome editing techniques. The value of stem cells lines is that we can study how mutations act in many different cell types. Cells can be induced to form beating heart-like cells in a dish. How a disease-causing mutation affects beating and function can now be readily understood in cell culture. Introducing new mutations into stem cells generates highly valuable models for human disease. These models are then used to identify and test new therapies. The human population is not placed at risk by these experiments in cells. It seems fair to state that the human population would actually be harmed by not doing these experiments since this research offers a potent opportunity to improve human health. This is not an opportunity that should be missed. Having genome-edited cell lines allows more rapid scientific advance and reduces the need for certain types of animal experimentation. At the same time, correcting defective genes in stem cells allows investigators to determine whether genomic correction is possible. In principle, a corrected stem cell could prove useful in cell transplant experiments to treat some diseases.

Gene editing is not restricted to pluripotent stem cells. Stem cells of the bone marrow, muscle, skin and other organs and tissues can be isolated and edited. In this case, editing and correction could be accompanied by transplant into a host human in order to treat disease. With this method, it would be possible to cure Sickle Cell Anemia or Duchenne Muscular Dystrophy. At present, the methods CRISPR/Cas9 require optimization in order for this to be reality. But the advances of CRISPR/Cas9 bring this approach into discussion. In mice, CRISPR/Cas9-mediated correction in fertilized oocytes corrected the defect of

Duchenne Muscular Dystrophy.[8] The method, while imperfect, was associated with remarkably high correction.

Germ Line Gene Editing

Recently a group of distinguished scientists called for a moratorium on gene editing in human fertilized oocytes fearing the potential of germ line gene editing and, ultimately, human eugenics.[9] These discussions were enhanced and prompted by the recent report of Liang et al. described efforts using CRISPR/Cas9 gene editing in fertilized human zygotes.[10] To limit concerns regarding human eugenics, the authors used tripronuclear zygotes that are genetically limited from progressing through development into humans. Notably, the authors concluded that CRISPR/Cas9, while an improvement over previous gene editing technologies, still has limited efficiency and importantly has serious off-target effects. The major off-target effect is the introduction of unintended mutations at sites throughout the genome at an unacceptably high rate for clinical purposes. Whether CRISPR/Cas9's efficiency and off-target effects differ across cell types is not well known at present. However, these same issues are present in all cell types subjected to gene editing to date. With knowledge of the enzymes, sequences and structures of the CRISPR/Cas9 system, optimization is an active area of research in academic, government and private industry laboratories in the United States and throughout the world.

Regulating Gene Editing

A regulatory framework for gene editing should encompass several key points:

1) Permit research to optimize and improve CRISPR/Cas9 and related technology.
2) Permit in vitro, cell-based gene editing technologies, including those in embryonic and induced pluripotent stem cells, respecting regulations currently protecting human embryonic stem cell lines.
3) Permit in vitro, cell-based gene editing with the intent to re-introduce into humans as a therapeutic measure for somatic cells. For example, this would apply to gene edited bone marrow derived stem cells. The treatment of a human with a gene edited cells would fall under the existing regulatory framework.
4) Permit the generation of gene-edited animals for the purposes of scientific research.
5) Limit or prohibit gene editing under circumstances where human transmission of gene-edited germ lines would occur.

Why Consider Germ Line Gene Editing?

With current technology, it is difficult to envision any justifiable use of gene editing in fertilized human zygotes where the resultant edited genome would be transmitted to future generations. Yet, we should consider the scenario of pre-implantation genetic diagnosis (PGD). PGD is pursued by families to avoid transmitting genetic diseases. Most commonly PGD is only pursued related to genetic diseases associated with significant early onset morbidity and mortality. With more widespread use of genetic diagnosis, as a clinician, I am asked about options to avoid passing deleterious genetic mutations to the next generation.

PGD involves in vitro fertilization coupled with genetic testing. In PGD, in vitro fertilization is used to create a fertilized oocyte that undergoes several rounds of cell division to become an embryo.[11] A single cell is removed from the embryo and tested genetically to identify those embryos that do not carry a specific genetic mutation. PGD allow parents to implant only those embryos free of the mutation in question. PGD is limited by the number of available embryos. PGD is typically not covered by insurance, and yet some families make this choice. These may be families who are already struggling with caring for one disabled child who cannot care for a second disabled child. These may be families where the parent is significantly afflicted with a genetic disease, and the parent wishes not to have his or her child burdened with the same diagnosis. PGD is a personal option and one that is made by solely by parents and families. PGD is not new and has been an available option for the last decade. A relatively small number of families choose this option and the choice to do so is often limited by technology, cost, religious and personal preference. PGD relies on nature to provide embryos free of a specific genetic mutation. Genetic altering of human embryos has occurred in the form of adding mitochondria from an external source, which introduces new mitochondrial DNA. In principle, it is possible that the efficiency of genome editing will improve so that preimplantation genetic correction could accompany PGD. With this process, gene editing to correct and eliminate a genetic disease could become reality. While the temptation may be to ban or limit this possibility, we should do so only with caution.

In my many years of working with patients and families with genetic disease, I can report that many parents of children with genetic disease express significant concern and responsibility for having passed on mutations to their children. A parent's desire to protect children is undeniable. As a society and as a nation, we embrace and endorse the importance of protecting children. It may be tempting, and perhaps easiest, to ban all gene editing where germ line transmission could occur. Yet, the justified use of this approach is certainly conceivable and may one day be appropriate.

References

1. https://rarediseases.info.nih.gov/about-ordr/pages/31/frequently-asked-questions. Date accessed June 9, 2014.

2. http://globalgenes.org/rare-diseases-facts-statistics/. Date accessed June 9, 2015.

3. Gordon J, Ruddle F (1981) Integration and stable germ line transmission of genes injected into mouse pronuclei. *Science* **214** (4526): PMID 6272397.

4. Costantini F, Lacy E (1981) Introduction of a rabbit β-globin gene into the mouse germ line. *Nature* **294** (5836): 92–4. PMID 6945481.

5. Brinster R, Chen HY, Trumbauer M, Senear AW, Warren R, Palmiter RD (1981) Somatic expression of herpes thymidine kinase in mice following injection of a fusion gene into eggs. *Cell* **27** (1 pt 2): 223–231. PMID 6276022.

6. http://www.nytimes.com/2014/03/04/health/a-powerful-new-way-to-edit-dna.html?_r=0. Date accessed June 9, 2015.

7. Wang J, Sauer MV (2006) In vitro fertilization: a review of three decades of clinical innovation and technical advancement. *Ther Clin Risk Management* **2** (4): 355–364. PMID: 18360648, PMCID: PMC1936357.

8. Long C, McAnally JR, Shelton JM, Mireault AA, Bassel-Duby R, Olson EN (2014) Prevention of muscular dystrophy in mice by CRISPR/Cas9 mediated editing of germline DNA. *Science* **345** (6201) 1184–1188. PMID: 25123483, PMCID: PMC4398027.

9. Baltimore D, Berg P, Botchan M, Carroll D, Charo RA, Church G, Corn JE, Daley GQ, Doudna JA, Fenner M, Greely HT, Jinek M, Martin GS, Penhoet E, Puck J, Sternberg SH, Weissman JS, Yamamoto KR (2015) Biotechnology. A prudent path forward for genomic engineering and germline gene modification. *Science* **348** (6230): 36–8. PMID: 25791083, PMCID: PMC4394183.

10. Liang P, Xu Y, Zhang X, Ding C, Huang R, Zhang Z, Lv J, Xie X, Chen Y, Li Y, Sun Y, Bai Y, Songyang Z, Ma W, Zhou C, Huang J (2015) CRISPR/Cas9-mediated gene editing in human tripronuclear zygotes. *Protein Cell* **6** (5): 363–72. PMID: 25894090, PMCID: PMC4417674.

11. Braude P, Pickering S, Flinter F, Ogilvie CM. (2002) Preimplantation genetic diagnosis. *Nat Rev Genet* **3** (12): 941–53. PMID: 12459724.

ELIZABETH MCNALLY is director of Northwestern University Feinberg School of Medicine's Center for Genetic Medicine and Elizabeth J. Ward Professor of Genetic Medicine and Professor in Medicine—Cardiology and Biochemistry and Molecular Genetics.

EXPLORING THE ISSUE

Is Gene-Editing of Human Embryos Coming Soon?

Critical Thinking and Reflection

1. Relatively few people object to gene-editing human embryos to correct obvious errors such as genetic diseases. Many more people object to efforts to increase intelligence, reaction speed, or longevity. Almost everyone would object to efforts to decrease intelligence or change skin color. Where do *you* draw the line?
2. *Decrease* intelligence? A government might think such a change would create a more docile populace. What other traits might a government like to standardize?
3. How cautious should we be about making gene-editing available to the general public?
4. One concern is that gene-editing technology could divide society as the children of the rich come to be more intelligent, healthier, and longer lived. Should we be concerned about providing equal access to gene-editing for all parents, even those who cannot afford it? How could we do that?

Is There Common Ground?

"Common ground" is clear in this case, for both essayists agree that gene-editing is developing rapidly and even if current versions have problems, new versions may not. The major disagreements seem to be over just how soon gene-editing will be available as a treatment of choice, and over how carefully it will have to be regulated. That said, many of those who object to "improving" human beings by genetics or technology seem to draw rather arbitrary lines to distinguish between enhancements they find acceptable and those they do not.

1. Is the line between internal and external improvements? Or between new and old? Consider eyeglasses versus artificial electronic retinas (currently being developed) versus pre-birth repair of genes for poor vision. Wheelchairs versus implanted circuitry to restore control of muscles (under development) versus pre-birth repair of genes that affect nerves and muscles.
2. Does it make a difference when we consider giving people new organs (prehensile tails?) or abilities? Would such changes make us "no longer human"?
3. Many technological (but not yet genetic) improvements of the human body are already readily accepted. Does the list of acceptable improvements expand as time goes on and technology progresses?

Additional Resources

Josh Fischman, "A Better Life with Bionics," *National Geographic* (January 2010).

Andrew Kimbrell, *The Human Body Shop: The Engineering and Marketing of Life* (HarperSanFrancisco, 1993).

Noel Merino, *Genetic Engineering* (Greenhaven Press, 2013).

Michael J. Sandel, *The Case against Perfection: Ethics in the Age of Genetic Engineering* (Belknap Press, 2009).

Julian Savalescu and Nick Bostrom, *Human Enhancement* (Oxford University Press, 2009).

Internet References . . .

Addgene Genome Engineering Guide

https://www.addgene.org/genome-engineering/

Humanity+

http://humanityplus.org/

Singularity Hub: Gene Editing Is Now Cheap and Easy . . .

http://singularityhub.com/2015/09/08/gene-editing
-is-now-cheap-and-easy-and-no-one-is-prepared
-for-the-consequences/